SIXTH EDITION

Political Science
AN INTRODUCTION

Michael G. Roskin

Lycoming College

Robert L. Cord

Northeastern University

James A. Medeiros

Walter S. Jones

Long Island University

Prentice-Hall International, Inc.

Photo credits. *Page 1:* Saw Lwin/United Nations; *pages 3, 41, 57, 71, 73, 91, 106, 114, 135, 145, 151, 195, 197, 253, 274, 275, 352, 358, 375, 377:* Michael Roskin; *page 10:* Library of Congress; *page 26:* United Air Lines; *page 44:* National Geographic Society, courtesy U.S. Capitol Historical Society; *page 61:* UPI/Bettmann; *page 72:* Charles Gatewood; *page 78:* AP/Wide World Photos; *pages 81, 92:* Laima Druskis; *page 98:* Thomas Kienzle, AP/Wide World Photos; *page 123:* AP/Wide World Photos; *page 134:* Joel Librizzi/Berkshire Eagle, AP/Wide World Photos; *page 143:* Irene Springer; *page 165:* AP/Wide World Photos; *page 171:* Eddie Adams, AP/Wide World Photos; *page 173:* UPI/Bettmann; *page 184:* Melissa Brown; *page 192:* Catholics for Free Choice; *page 203:* Stan Wakefield; *page 223:* Peter W. Main/The Christian Science Monitor; *page 227:* Laima Druskis; *page 237:* Wilfredo Lee, AP/Wide World Photos; *page 243:* Washington DC Convention and Visitors Assoc.; *page 245:* British Information Service; *page 263:* Doug Mills, AP/Wide World Photos; *page 264:* British Department of the Environment; *page 283:* UPI/Larry Rubenstein, Bettmann; *page 312:* AP/Wide World Photos; *page 371:* UPI/Bettmann; *page 296:* Michael Evans/The White House Photo Office; *page 303:* Eddie McCrossan/U.S. Air Force; *page 322:* J. Scott Applewhite, AP/Wide World Photos; *page 344:* John Duricka, AP/Wide World Photos; *page 348:* Irene Springer; *page 361:* Sadayuki Mikiami, AP/Wide World Photos; *page 388:* United Nations.

Editorial director: Charlyce Jones Owen
Editor-in-chief: Nancy Roberts
Acquisitions editor: Michael Bickerstaff
Editorial assistant: Anita Castro
Director of production and manufacturing: Barbara Kittle
Managing editor: Ann Marie McCarthy/Fran Russello
Editorial production/supervision
   and interior design: Joseph Barron/P. M. Gordon Associates, Inc.
Manufacturing manager: Nick Sklitsis
Prepress and manufacturing buyer: Bob Anderson
Cover design: Bruce Kenselaar
Cover photos: Adam Woolfit/Corbis Media
Photo research: Sherry Cohen
Copy editor: Bill Stavru

This book was set in 10/12 New Baskerville by ElectraGraphics, Inc. and was printed and bound by RR Donnelley & Sons Company. The cover was printed by the Lehigh Press, Inc.

Printed in the United States of America
10   9   8   7   6   5   4   3   2   1

ISBN 0-13-606674-7

Prentice-Hall International (UK) Limited, *London*
Prentice-Hall of Australia Pty. Limited, *Sydney*
Prentice-Hall Canada, Inc., *Toronto*
Prentice-Hall Hispanoamericana, S.A., *Mexico*
Prentice-Hall of India Private Limited, *New Delhi*
Prentice-Hall of Japan, Inc., *Tokyo*
Prentice-Hall of Southeast Asia Pte. Ltd., *Singapore*
Editora Prentice-Hall do Brasil, Ltda., *Rio de Janeiro*
Prentice-Hall, *Upper Saddle River, New Jersey*

Contents

PART TWO: POLITICAL ATTITUDES

6   *Political Ideologies*   *98*

7   *Political Culture*   *123*

11   *Political Parties and Party Systems*   203

12   *Voting*   223

PART FOUR: THE INSTITUTIONS OF POLITICS

PART FIVE: WHAT POLITICAL SYSTEMS DO

Preface

It is indeed gratifying to see a book one has worked on reach a sixth edition; it means one is doing something right. It also means that the editors at Prentice Hall recognize that the original approach in the first edition of 1974 was sound and should not be greatly altered. The success of the book owes something to the fact that it is neither a United States government text nor a comparative politics text. Instead, it draws from both United States and comparative examples to introduce the whole field of political science to new students.

The sixth edition continues with an eclectic approach that avoids selling any single theory, conceptual framework, or paradigm as the key to political science. Attempts to impose a methodological grand design are both unwarranted by the nature of the discipline and unconducive to the broadening of students' intellectual horizons. Instructors with a wide variety of viewpoints should have no trouble using this text. Above all, the sixth edition still views politics as exciting and tries to communicate that feeling to young people approaching the discipline for the first time.

Instructors familiar with earlier editions will see few major changes in the sixth edition. Events over the last few years have prompted the inclusion or expansion of discussions of statism (in Chapter 2), communitarianism (in Chapter 6), television-induced apathy (in Chapter 9), budget-balancing and entitlements (in Chapter 18), and national interest, peacekeeping, and U.S. foreign policy (in Chapter 20). With careful coordination between author, editor, and printer, we were able to include a discussion of the results of the 1996 U.S. presidential election. The overall structure of the text stays the same.

Several people reviewed this and earlier editions, and I sincerely heeded most of their comments. For this edition, I wish to thank Larry Elowitz, Georgia College; Daniel O'Connell, Palm Beach Community College; and Henry Pierson French, Jr., SUNY-Monroe Community College.

Are further structural changes needed in the book, or have I got it about right? Your input on this matter—or indeed on anything else related to the text or supplementary materials—would be highly valued. You may contact me directly at Lycoming College, Williamsport, Pennsylvania 17701.

Michael G. Roskin

· 1 ·

A Science of Politics?

Antigovernment protesters pour through the streets of a capital city, chanting slogans against the current leadership. They have had enough of depressed living standards and lack of political and civil rights. Even many ruling-party members, aware that the system is hugely corrupt and inefficient, have come out in favor of the government's resignation. The top leaders, fearful of chaos and total collapse, desperately offer policies that would have been unthinkable just a few years earlier. Although they had celebrated themselves as the benevolent saviors of their country, after a while, few citizens supported them. Without a political leg to stand on, they glumly contemplate their overthrow.

On another continent, members of a radical underground group meet in a

1

small apartment to plan a terrorist bombing. They are frustrated and impatient with what they perceive as the deprivation of their national rights. Everyone else has a country, so why shouldn't they? The government they hate refuses to grant them any recognition; it even defines them as enemies of the state. Peaceful political protest is met with truncheons and arrests, so the militants decide to make their case more forcefully. They pack a car full of explosives and park it near a bus stop; a timer sets it off, killing passersby. The terrorists think they have made an important point and are proud of their work.

Meanwhile, an American president is backpedaling on a question of policy. He was elected with a simple slogan that seemed to put him strongly on one side of a current issue. Once in office, however, he realizes how complicated the issue really is and how difficult it is to work his will on Congress, the bureaucracy, and interest groups. So the president tones down his policy, expresses his willingness to compromise, and tries to make himself look like a moderate on the issue. Critics say he is becoming indecisive and wishy-washy. Ironically, that was exactly what the president had said about the man he had defeated. Being president, he reflects silently, is a lot harder than he had thought.

What do a popular upheaval in one country, a terrorist bombing in another, and an American president's change in policy have in common? All are examples of politics. They involve groups of people with conflicting interests competing for government power. The protesters, fed up with a corrupt and inept government, replace it with a better one. The terrorists, seeing no point in trying to reason with a government that represses their aims, turn to violence in the hope of overthrowing that government. The American president, buffeted by conflicting pressures on all sides, is undergoing some painful rethinking before making a midcourse correction in his policy.

Political science is the study of these struggles and competitions for government power. In particular, it focuses on two interrelated questions: (1) Why and how do leaders make the decisions they do? (2) Why do citizens obey most of these decisions but sometimes disobey others? Let us consider the second question first.

The Three Faces of Legitimacy

The preceding three examples, which could be culled from almost any month's news accounts, illustrate some of the enduring and basic problems of politics. They underlie the great question posed by political philosophers for centuries: Why do people obey, or why do they *not* obey the decisions of their leaders? (A *political philosopher* is more likely to ask why people *should* or *should not* obey these decisions. A *political scientist* is more likely to ask why they *do* or *do not* obey.) The protesters, the terrorists, and the American president are all facing these questions in different ways. The three examples illustrate the related concepts of *legitimacy, sovereignty,* and *authority.*

LEGITIMACY

The protesters in the first example obviously no longer obey the corrupt regime. It has lost its *legitimacy*. Legitimacy is one of the most important concepts in political science. Originally it meant that the rightful king or queen was on the throne by reason of "legitimate" birth. Since the Middle Ages, the term *legitimacy* has broadened to mean not only the "legal right to govern" but also the *"psychological right to govern."* Legitimacy now refers to an attitude in people's minds that the government's rule is rightful. Therefore, even if we do not particularly like our government, we generally obey it. Most of us don't look forward to paying income tax, but most of us do it, and do it honestly, because we feel the government has a legitimate right to tax us.

Trouble begins for any government when that feeling of legitimacy erodes. People feel less obliged to pay their taxes and obey the law. Disobeying the law is no longer considered dirty or dishonest because the government itself is perceived as dirty and dishonest. Eventually, massive civil disobedience can break out. As the former shah of Iran, ex-President Marcos of the Philippines, and the late President Ceausescu of Romania discovered, once their regimes' legitimacy had disappeared,

The Berlin Wall crumbled in 1989 because the East German regime had totally lost legitimacy. Citizens no longer respected or obeyed it. Now only a few remnants of the wall remain, as West Germany has swallowed East Germany.

no amount of coercion could get people to obey. Indeed, attempts to apply force to control the disobedient crowds only made matters worse.

Legitimacy rests on consent, "the Consent of the Governed," as the Declaration of Independence puts it. Without consent, governments must rely on coercion. Accordingly, one way to determine the legitimacy of a given government is to see how many police are employed by the state. Where there are relatively few police, as in Sweden and Norway, it is a sign that legitimacy is high. Where there are many police, as in Franco's Spain or Ceausescu's Romania, it is a sign that legitimacy is low. In these last two countries, the presence of special riot police indicated that the regime needed coercion.

How does a government achieve legitimacy? First, by existing a long time. Long-established governments are generally well respected by their citizens. The fact that the Constitution is two centuries old confers a great deal of legitimacy on the U.S. government. New governments, on the other hand, have shaky legitimacy; many of their citizens are not quite sure whether or not to respect them.

Second, a government can also gain legitimacy for governing well. Ensuring economic growth and high employment, providing protection from foreign invasion or domestic disturbance, and dispensing equal justice to all help governments to develop legitimacy. The government of West Germany, founded in 1949 after defeat in World War II, had little legitimacy at first, but level-headed political leadership with sound economic policies, providing rapid growth and jobs for all, gradually earned the Bonn government a good deal of legitimacy. On the other hand, the German Weimar Republic that followed World War I faced a series of economic and political catastrophes that severely undermined its legitimacy and paved the way for Hitler's rise to power.

Third, the structure of government can also contribute to its legitimacy. If people feel they are fairly represented and have a say in the selection of their officials, they are more likely to obey. This is the most elemental reason for legislatures elected directly by the people. It's not that elected legislatures necessarily do a good job—often they are a shambles—but the people *feel* they are represented. Legislatures filled by appointment or by rigged elections, as Mexico discovered, do not contribute much to legitimacy.

Finally, governments try to shore up their legitimacy by the manipulation of national symbols. The national flag, historic monuments, patriotic parades, and ringing speeches are aimed at convincing people the government is legitimate and should be obeyed. When the other elements of legitimacy have fallen away, however, the manipulation of national symbols may appear to be a hollow joke. A gigantic statue of ex-dictator Marcos of the Philippines became an object of ridicule and a symbol of what was wrong with his regime. Symbols by themselves don't create legitimacy.

SOVEREIGNTY

In our second example, the terrorist bombers dispute not only the regime's legitimacy but also the legitimacy of the country itself. They want to destroy the *sover-*

eignty of the country they hate and replace it with another sovereign state. Legitimacy concerns the right of a given government to rule; sovereignty concerns the right of a given country to exist. For the terrorists, no change in regime will make them happy; they want not a new government but a new country.

Sovereignty, another word from the Middle Ages (from the Old French "to rule over"), originally meant the power of a monarch to rule over his or her kingdom. Later the term broadened to mean national control over the country's territory, boss of one's own turf. Nations are very jealous of their sovereignty, and governments take great care to safeguard it. They maintain armies to deter foreign invasion, they control their borders with passports and visas, and they hunt down terrorists.

Disputes over sovereignty are among the nastiest the world faces. The violence associated with them ripples out to many other countries. Most Palestinians would like Israel to disappear and be replaced with a new sovereign entity, Palestine. The Israelis, of course, are not about to give up their sovereignty, so they fight back tenaciously.

In Northern Ireland, too, there is a question of sovereignty. Among the Catholic minority, the Irish Republican Army turned to murder and bombings to pry Ulster away from British rule or sovereignty. The IRA wished to unite Northern Ireland with the Republic of Ireland in the south. Among the Protestant majority, equally determined Loyalists vowed they would never let that happen. The result: a low-level civil war in which 3,200 people were killed.

In former Yugoslavia, Serbs living in Croatia and Bosnia refused to accept declarations of independence by these two lands. The Serbs remembered how in World War II their relatives had been butchered by local Fascists. The Serbs refused to live under Croatian or Bosnian sovereignty, so they carved out wide areas of Croatia and Bosnia for their own Serbian sovereign entities and massacred thousands of Croats and Bosnians in the way. Interestingly, for centuries, when sovereignty was in the hands of either the Turkish or Austrian empire, these people—who are basically the same and speak the same language—got along. It was when sovereignty was up for grabs that they began to murder each other.

Obviously, sovereignty and legitimacy are connected. A king or queen might establish sovereignty by the sword, but the heirs to the throne will lose sovereignty unless they can make their rule appear to be legitimate. With a decline of legitimacy may also come a decline of sovereignty. Lebanon illustrates how a question of regime legitimacy can turn into a question of national sovereignty. Lebanon was ruled for decades by Christians, even though they were a minority. In the eyes of many Lebanese Muslims, the Lebanese government in Beirut lacked legitimacy because it listened mostly to Christian demands and tended to ignore Muslims. In 1975, civil strife broke out as a dozen politico-religious militias battled to assume a leading role. Syria occupied eastern Lebanon in 1976, and Israel occupied southern Lebanon in 1982. Essentially Lebanon had lost its sovereignty. It could neither control its own territory nor repel foreign invaders. Countries with weak legitimacy may lose sovereignty and be easy pickings for expansionist neighbors. On the other hand, the more diplomatic recognition a country can obtain from other nations, the more sovereignty and legitimacy it can maintain.

AUTHORITY

In our third example the American president, leader of a country with a high degree of legitimacy and sovereignty, is not automatically able to make his authority felt. *Authority* is the ability of a given leader to win obedience. Legitimacy is respect for a government, sovereignty is respect for a country, and authority is respect for an individual leader. Some political scientists distinguish authority from influence, manipulation, persuasion, and force.[1] Only authority (unlike influence, manipulation, persuasion, and force) relies on the obligation of the people to obey their leader by virtue of the legitimate power of his or her office. A private obeys a captain; a motorist obeys a state trooper; a student obeys a professor. But not all people obey authority. Some privates are insubordinate, some motorists are speeders, and some students neglect the assigned reading. Still, most people obey what they perceive as legitimate authority most of the time.

Some authority comes with the office, but it must also be cultivated. Like legitimacy, authority involves a psychological connection among people. An American president gets an awful lot of authority just because he is the president. Gerald Ford was respected and obeyed even though he was not elected either as president or vice-president. (Minority leader of the House of Representatives, he became vice-president when Spiro T. Agnew resigned and president when Richard Nixon resigned.) But his elected predecessor, Richard Nixon, had some problems. Implicated in Watergate scandal of 1972, Nixon suffered an "erosion of executive authority" so acute that he could not effectively govern, even if he were to be acquitted in possible impeachment proceedings before the Senate.[2] So he resigned in 1974 just before a House panel could vote on his impeachment. A president cannot rule by decree but must obtain the willing consent of Congress, the courts, the civil service, and important interest groups. When Nixon lost this consent, he was finished. His rule appeared to be increasingly without rightfulness.

How much obedience to authority derives from fear of punishment? Privates can be shot, motorists jailed, and students flunked. But this begs the question: What gives authorities the control over others so they will carry out orders to punish? The captain needs a command structure, the state trooper needs a criminal justice structure, and the college professor needs a disciplinary structure that will go along with orders or requests to punish. Without these structures to back them up, authority figures have little power. If a captain gets mad at a private and orders the soldier taken out and shot, chances are he or she would not be obeyed. The guards would say, "That's an illegal order and you have no authority to give it." If, on the other hand, the private is convicted by court-martial of desertion in the face of the enemy, he or she may indeed be taken out and shot by the same guards, who are now obeying duly constituted authority.

Just occupying an office may not be sufficient to command authority. The authority figure must also cultivate respect. A cowardly captain, a crooked police officer, or an indecisive professor may obtain only grudging compliance. Effective authority requires firm, fair, and wise leadership. Any taint of corruption undermines authority.

Notice that legitimacy, sovereignty, and authority are all related.[3] Where you find one, you find the others. Where one erodes, so usually do the others. What would have happened if Richard Nixon had tried to stay in office by blocking investigations of the Watergate scandal? Then the entire U.S. government might have started to seem illegitimate. His authority problem could have turned into a legitimacy problem. In 1958, Lebanese President Camille Chamoun, a Christian, tried to alter the constitution of his country to stay in power an additional term. As a result, a Muslim insurrection broke out and the legitimacy of Lebanon's government was severely damaged. Later, as previously stated, the problem grew so severe as to wreck Lebanon's sovereignty. A collapse of authority led to a collapse of legitimacy, which led to a collapse of sovereignty. President Nixon did his country a real service by resigning early.

If you think about it a minute, legitimacy, sovereignty, and authority are variations on the first term, *legitimacy*. If a government's rule is legitimate, it has legitimacy. If a country's existence is legitimate, it has sovereignty. If a leader's rule is legitimate, he or she has authority. All three terms can be grouped under the heading *political power.*

Political Power

Some people don't like the concept of political power. It smacks of coercion, inequality, occasionally of brutality. Sometimes you hear speakers denounce "power politics." Implicit in this statement is the notion of governance without power, of a happy band of brothers and sisters regulating themselves on the basis of love and sharing. Communities formed on such a basis do not last; or if they do last, they transform themselves into conventional structures of leaders and the led buttressed by obedience patterns that look suspiciously like nasty old power. Power—defined as one person getting another to do something—seems to be built into the human condition. But why? Why do some people hold political power over others? No one has come up with a definitive explanation of political power. Biological, psychological, cultural, rational, and irrational explanations have all been put forward to answer these questions.

BIOLOGICAL

Aristotle said it first and perhaps best: "Man is by nature a political animal."[4] He meant that humans live naturally in herds, like dolphins or deer. They biologically need each other for sustenance and survival. It is also natural that they array themselves into ranks of leaders and led, like all herd animals. Taking a cue from Aristotle, a modern biological explanation would say that forming a political system and obeying its leaders is innate human behavior, passed on to future generations with one's genes.[5] The advantage of this theory is its simplicity.

But it raises a number of questions. If we grant that humankind is naturally political, how do we explain the instances when political groups fall apart and people disobey authority? Perhaps we could improve the theory by modifying it: Humans are imperfectly political (or social) animals. Most of the time people form groups and obey authority, but sometimes, under certain circumstances, they don't. This begs the question of which circumstances promote or do not promote the formation of political groups.

PSYCHOLOGICAL

Psychological explanations of politics and obedience are closely allied with biological theories. Both posit innate needs in the formation of political groups. The psychologists have refined their views with empirical research. One is the famous Milgram study in which unwitting subjects were instructed by a professor to administer progressively larger electric shocks to a victim.[6] The "victim," strapped in a chair, was actually an actor who only pretended to suffer. Most of the subjects were willing to administer potentially lethal doses of electricity simply because the "professor"—an authority figure in a white lab smock—told them to do so. Most of the subjects didn't like hurting the victim, but they rationalized that they were just following orders and that any harm done to the victim was really the professor's responsibility. They surrendered their independence of thought and action because an authority figure told them to do so. The Milgram study has been replicated and confirmed in other settings.

Psychological studies also show that most people are naturally conformist. Most members of a group see things a certain way. Psychologist Irving Janis found many of the great mistakes of U.S. foreign and defense policy were made in a climate of "groupthink," a situation in which a leadership group tells itself that all is well and that the present policy is working.[7] Groups tend to ignore nonconformist troublemakers who tell them, for instance, that the Japanese will attack Pearl Harbor in 1941 or that the Bay of Pigs landing of Cuban exiles in 1961 will fail. "We know what we're doing," the group seems to say; "don't bother us with doubts."

Obedience to authority and groupthink suggest that humans have deep-seated needs—possibly innate—to fit into groups and go along with their norms. Perhaps this is what makes human society possible. But it also makes possible horrors such as the Nazi Holocaust and fiascoes such as the Iran arms deal. One of the fascinating questions is why some individuals can disobey authority and go against group conformity to decry acts that are obviously illegal, immoral, or just plain stupid.

CULTURAL

How much of human behavior is learned as opposed to biologically inherited? Social scientists have debated this question for decades without coming to a definitive answer. In the middle part of the twentieth century, however, the *cultural theorists*—

those who believe behavior is learned—have dominated the debate. Anthropologists especially, in exploring foreign and primitive societies, concluded that all differences in behavior were learned. If some societies are cooperative and peaceful, it is because their children have been raised that way. Political communities are formed and hold together on the basis of cultural values transmitted by parents, schools, churches, and the mass media.[8] Political science developed an interesting subfield called *political culture,* and researchers in this field often found that a country's political culture was formed by many long-term factors: child rearing, land tenure, economic development, religion, and so forth.[9]

The cultural school maintains that trouble comes when the political system gets out of touch with the cultural system, as when the shah of Iran attempted to modernize an Islamic society that did not like Western values and lifestyles. The Iranians threw the shah out and celebrated the return of a medieval-style religious leader, the Ayatollah Khomeini, who was much more in touch with their values. Cultural theories can also be applied to U.S. politics. Ronald Reagan won the presidency twice by articulating the values of religion, family, and self-reliance which are so deeply ingrained into American culture.

The cultural approach to political life contains an optimistic streak. If all human behavior is learned, bad behavior can be unlearned and society improved. Educating young people to be tolerant, cooperative, and just will gradually change a society's culture for the better.

Although most thinkers agree that culture contributes a lot to political behavior, the theory has some difficulties. First, where does culture come from? Is it a product of the class structure, as Marxists claim? Or is it a result of psychological interactions between parents and children, as Freudian psychologists argue? Or is it the current repository of the country's past, as historians think? Second, if all behavior is cultural, various political systems should be as different from each other as their cultures. But especially in the realm of politics, we see similar political attitudes and patterns in lands with very different cultures.

RATIONAL

Another school of thought approaches politics as largely the application of human rationality; that is, people know what they want most of the time, and they have good reasons for doing what they do. Classic political theorists, such as Hobbes and Locke, held that humans form "civil society" because their powers of reason tell them that it is much better than anarchy. In the "state of nature" you can trust no one; anyone might take your life or your property. Precisely this Hobbesian situation happened in Somalia in the early 1990s. Accordingly, to safeguard both life and property, people form governments to protect themselves. If those governments become abusive, the people have the right to dissolve them and start anew. This Lockean notion greatly influenced the U.S. Founding Fathers.[10]

The biological, psychological, and cultural schools just described all downplay human reason. People are either born or conditioned to do certain things, and individuals seldom think rationally. But how can we then explain those cases

JOHN HANCOCK'S DEFIANCE.

The Declaration of Independence, here being signed in large
bold letters by John Hancock, embodied a rational view of
politics.

in which people break away from group conformity and argue independently?
How can we explain a change of mind? "Well, I was for Jones until he came out with
his terrible economic policy, so now I'm voting for Smith."[11] People make judgments like that all the time, based at least in part on their ability to reason. A new
school of political science, "rational choice theory," based on the human ability to
choose what best suits them, has recently achieved great popularity.[12]

Further, a political system based on the presumption of human reason stands
a lot better chance of governing justly and humanely. If leaders believe that people
obey out of biological inheritance or cultural conditioning, they will think they can
get away with all manner of corruption and misrule. If, on the other hand, they believe people are rational, rulers will respect the public's ability to discern wrongdoing. Accordingly, even if people are not completely rational, it is good that rulers
fear their possible rationality and their ability to protest misrule.

IRRATIONAL

Late in the nineteenth century a group of thinkers founded a new school of
thought, called irrationalism, to explain political behavior. Taking the psychological view that people are basically emotional, dominated by myths and stereotypes,
some argue that politics is really the manipulation of symbols. A crowd is like a wild
beast that can be whipped up by a charismatic leader to do his or her bidding.

What people regard as rational is really just myth; all you have to do is keep feeding them myths and you will control them.

The first practitioner of this school was Mussolini, founder of fascism in Italy. He was followed by Hitler in Germany and Perón in Argentina. According to some, Stalin also used the techniques of the irrationalists in developing his hold on the Soviet people. He had himself turned into a demigod that most Russians willingly worshipped. Both Hitler's friends and enemies portrayed him as a genius at understanding and manipulating the innermost fears and feelings of the Germans.[13]

There may be a good deal of truth to the irrational view of human political behavior, but it has catastrophic consequences. The leaders who use irrationalist techniques start believing their own propaganda and eventually lead their nations to devastating war, economic ruin, or permanent slavery. Some detect irrationalism even in the most advanced societies, where much of so-called "reality" is filtered through myths.[14]

POWER AS A COMPOSITE

We can see elements of truth in all these explanations of political power. At different times in different situations, any one of them seems to explain power. The drafters of both the U.S. Declaration of Independence and the Constitution were deeply imbued with the rationalism of their age. Following the philosophers then popular, they framed their arguments as if human political activity were as logical as Newtonian physics. One contemporary historian referred to the Constitution as "the crown jewel of the enlightenment," the culmination of an age of reason.[15]

But how truly rational were they? By the late eighteenth century the thirteen American colonies had grown culturally separate from Britain. People thought of themselves as Americans rather than as English colonists. They increasingly read American newspapers and communicated among themselves rather than with Britain.[16] Perhaps the separation was more cultural than rational.

Nor can we forget the psychological and irrational factors. Samuel Adams was a gifted firebrand, Thomas Jefferson a powerful writer, and George Washington a charismatic general. Did Tom Paine's pamphlet *Common Sense* press rational or psychological buttons in his readers? It's hard to tell. And that is the point of this example. The American break with Britain and the founding of a new order is a complex mixture of all these factors. The same complex mixture of factors goes into any political system you can mention. To be sure, at times one factor seems more important than others, but we cannot exactly determine the weight to give any one factor. And notice how the various factors blend into one another. The biological factors lead to the psychological, which in turn lead to the cultural, the rational, and the irrational. A seamless web, difficult to untangle, is formed.

One common mistake about political power is to view it as a finite, measurable quantity. Power is a connection between people, the ability of one person to get another to do his or her bidding. Political power does not come in jars or megawatts. Revolutionaries in some lands speak of "seizing power," as if power were kept in the national treasury and they could sneak in and grab it at night. Afghan

Communists "seized power" in 1978, but they were a small minority of the Afghan population. Most Afghanis hated them and refused to cooperate with them. Some revolutionaries think that they automatically get legitimacy and authority when they "seize power"; they do not. Power is earned, not seized.

Is power identical to politics? Some power-mad people (including more than a few politicians) see the two as the same, but this is an oversimplification. We might see politics as a combination of goals or policies and the power necessary to achieve them. Power, in this view, is a prime *ingredient* of politics. It would be difficult to imagine a political system without political power. Even a religious figure who ruled on the basis of love would be exercising power over followers. It might be "nice power," but it would still be power. Power, then, is a sort of *enabling device* to carry out or implement policies and decisions. You can have praiseworthy goals, but unless you have the power to implement them, they remain wishful thoughts.

Others see the essence of politics as a *struggle for power,* a sort of gigantic game in which power is the goal. What, for example, are elections all about? The getting of power. There is a danger here, however. If power becomes the goal of politics, devoid of other purposes, it becomes cynical, brutal, and even self-destructive. The Hitler regime destroyed itself in the worship of power. Obsessed with retaining presidential power, President Nixon ruined his own administration. As nineteenth-century British historian and philosopher Lord Acton put it, "Power tends to corrupt; absolute power corrupts absolutely."

Is Politics a Science?

If we cannot pinpoint which factors contribute what weight to politics, how can politics possibly be called a science? Part of the problem here is the definition of *science*. The original meaning of *science,* from the French, is simply "knowledge." Later, the natural sciences, such as physics and chemistry, which rely on precise measurement and mathematical calculation, took over the term. Now most people think of science as precise and factual, supported by experiments and data. Some political scientists (as we will consider later) have in fact attempted to become like natural scientists; they collect quantified data and manipulate them statistically to validate hypotheses. The quantifiers have made some good contributions, but usually they focus on small questions of detail rather than on large questions of meaning. This is because they generally have to stick to areas that can be quantified—public opinion, election returns, and congressional voting. (And sometimes these data are open to different interpretations.)

But large areas of politics are not quantifiable. This moves us back to one of the questions we asked near the beginning of the chapter: How and why do leaders make the decisions they do? Many decisions are made in secret, even in democracies. We don't know exactly how decisions are made in the White House in Washington, the Elysée Palace in Paris, or the Kremlin in Moscow. When a member of

Congress votes on an issue, can we be certain why he or she voted that way? Was it for constituents' desires, the good of the nation, or the campaign contributions of interest groups? What did the Supreme Court have in mind when it ruled that laying off schoolteachers based on race is unconstitutional but hiring them based on race is not?[17] Try putting that into a computer in a quantifiable way. A lot of politics—especially dealing with how and why decisions are made—is just too complex to be quantified.

Does that mean that politics can never be like a natural science? Part of it can be—the areas in which we can get valid numbers—but much of it cannot be. Still, we can accumulate unquantified data. We can find persistent patterns in the way governments attempt to shore up their legitimacy, the way candidates strive for election, and the way alliances form and fall apart. After a while, one notices that nothing is happening for the first time, that there are precedents for just about every type of political activity. Gradually, one begins to generalize. When the generalizations become firmer, we may call them theories. In a few cases, the theories become so firmly established that we may even call them "laws." In this way, the study of politics accumulates knowledge—and "knowledge" is the original meaning of *science*. Some universities have departments of "politics" or of "government" in order to get away from the nagging question, Is politics a science? The answer to that question is up to you.

THE STRUGGLE TO SEE CLEARLY

In one way, political science does resemble a natural science: Its researchers, if they are professional, attempt to study things as they are, not as they wish them to be. This is more difficult in the study of politics than in the study of stars and molecules, although even in these areas scientists sometimes have strongly partisan views. Political scientists are deeply immersed in politics, and most of them have viewpoints on current issues. It is very easy to let these views contaminate the analysis of politics. Indeed, precisely because a given question interests us enough to study it indicates that we bring a certain passion with us. Can you imagine setting to work on a study of a topic you cared absolutely nothing about? Behind each choice of topic is usually a little fire of interest in the mind of the researcher. Accordingly, our subject comes to us contaminated from its very birth. A little bias is therefore to be expected. There is a certain point, however, at which too much bias renders the study useless; it becomes a partisan outcry rather than a scholarly search for the truth. How can you tell when this happens? It's difficult, but the traditional hallmarks of scholarship give us some guidance. A scholarly work should be *reasoned, balanced,* and supported with *evidence.*

Reasoned.   You must spell out your reasoning, and it should make sense. If you perspective is colored by an underlying assumption, such as one of those discussed previously, you should say so. You might say, "For the purpose of this study, we assume that people are rational" or "This is a study of the psychology of voters in a small town." It is understood that your basic assumptions influence what you study and how you study it, but you can minimize the bias by honestly stating your assumptions. Early in the twentieth century the German sociologist Max Weber, who contributed so much to all the social sciences, held that any of your findings that come out in support of your own political views must be discarded as biased.[18] A lot of research would never be undertaken if the researcher did not have some ax to grind. Nevertheless, Weber's point is well taken: Beware of structuring the study so that it comes out to support a given view. The axiom of computer specialists applies to political science: "Garbage in, garbage out."

Balanced.   You can also minimize bias by acknowledging that there are other ways of looking at your topic. In all fairness, you should mention the various approaches to your topic and what they have found. Instructors are impressed that you are familiar with the literature in a given area. They are even more impressed when you can then criticize the various studies and explain why you think they are incomplete or faulty: "The Jones study of voters found them largely apathetic, but this was an election of local officials, so apathy might be expected." By putting several approaches and studies side by side and stating what you think of them and why, you present a much more objective and convincing case. Do not totally commit yourself to a particular viewpoint or theory but admit that your view is one among several.

Evidence.   All scholarly studies require evidence, ranging from the quantified evidence of the natural sciences to the qualitative evidence of the humanities. Political science utilizes both types of evidence. Ideally, any statement open to interpretation or controversy should be supported with some evidence. Common knowledge does not have to be supported; you need not cite the U.S. Constitution to "prove" the president is inaugurated the January after the election. But if you say presidents have gained more and more power over the decades, you need to have some evidence. At a minimum, you would cite leading scholars who have amassed evidence to demonstrate this point. The evidence you use should be open to inspection and scrutiny. You cannot say, "I have classified information that proves this point, but it cannot be revealed." This is one of the problems faced by the political analysts employed by the U.S. State and Defense Departments. Anyone reading a study must be able to review your evidence and judge if it is valid.

WHAT GOOD IS POLITICAL SCIENCE?

Some students think political science is just opinions; they write exams or turn in papers that ignore all or some of the preceding points. Yes, we all have political views, but if we let them dominate our study we get invalid results. A professional political scientist pushes his or her personal views well to one side while engaged in study and research. A first-rate thinker is able to come up with results that actually refute his or her previously held opinion. When that happens, we have real intellectual growth, an exciting experience that should be your aim. Something else comes with such an experience: You start to conclude that you shouldn't have been so partisan in the first place. You may start to back away from the strong views you had earlier. You start to take political views, even your own, with a grain of salt. Accordingly, political science is not necessarily training to become a practicing politician. Political science is training in the calm, dispassionate analysis of politics, whereas the practice of politics often requires fixed, popular, and simplified opinions.

Political science can contribute to good government, mainly by warning those in office that all is not well, "speaking truth to power," as the Quakers say. Sometimes this advice is useful to working politicians. Public opinion polls, for example, showed a slow erosion of government legitimacy in the United States from the mid-1960s to the early 1980s.[19] The precise cause could be debated: Was it Vietnam, Watergate, or inflation? Or some combination of all three? Candidates for office, knowing public opinion, could tailor their campaigns and policies to try to counteract this potentially dangerous decline. Ronald Reagan, with his sunny disposition and upbeat views, utilized this discontent to his advantage.

For decades, American political scientists warned about the weaknesses of U.S. political parties, saying they were too decentralized and uncontrolled. Political parties in the United States cannot even define what they stand for or who can be regarded as a member. In 1989, David Duke, a former leader of the Ku Klux Klan with ties to Nazis, won a seat as a Republican in the Louisiana state legislature. The Republican National Committee tried to distance itself from Duke, but he continued to call himself a Republican and there was no legal way to stop him from doing so. Parties in the United States simply do not have that kind of control over the use of their names. As far back as 1950, the American Political Science Association had warned that weak parties bring negative consequences.[20]

In foreign affairs, political scientists warned for years of the weak basis of the shah's regime in Iran.[21] Unfortunately, such warnings were unheeded. Washington's policy was to support the shah; only two months before the end of his reign did the U.S. Embassy in Tehran start reporting accurately how unstable the nation had become.[22] This is an example of the contamination of political analysis by politics. The U.S. government would have had a more effective policy if it had listened to the political scientists and ignored its own embassy.

Changing Political Science

The discipline of political science does not stand still. Especially in the United States, it has passed through at least three distinct styles or approaches: the traditional, behavioral, and postbehavioral. It is impossible to say which is best, and all exist today, albeit sometimes uneasily with one another. To call the first "traditional" is a bit unfair—it was so named by the behavioralists—for it encompasses a wide range of approaches, ranging from the philosophical and ethical to the institutional and power-oriented.

Most of the Greek, medieval, and Renaissance political thinkers took a normative approach to the study of government and politics. They sought to discover the "ought" or "should" and were often rather casual about the "is," the real-world situation. Informed by religious, legal, or philosophical values, they tried to ascertain which system of government would bring humankind closest to the good life, often as defined by the prevailing wisdom of that time. Although sometimes dismissed by behavioral thinkers as hopelessly speculative, the ideas of Aristotle, Hobbes, Locke, Rousseau, and many others still provide tremendous insights, which, ironically, are often confirmed by the latest "scientific" research.

With Machiavelli emerged another approach, the focus on power. Although often depreciated by American political thinkers, who sometimes shied away from "power" as inherently dirty, the approach took root in Europe and contributed to the elite analyses of Mosca, Pareto, and Michels. Americans became acquainted with the power approach through the writings of the refugee German scholar of international relations Hans J. Morgenthau, who emphasized that "all politics is a struggle for power."[23]

American thinkers meanwhile focused heavily on institutions, the formal structures of government. In this they were showing the influence of law on the development of political science in the United States. Woodrow Wilson, for example, was a lawyer (albeit unsuccessful) before he became a political scientist; Wilson, too, concentrated on perfecting the institutions of government. Constitutions were a favorite subject for political scientists of this period, for they often assumed that the structure of the government on paper was pretty much how it worked in practice.

The rise of the Soviet, Italian, and German dictatorships and the horrors of World War II shook many political scientists in their belief in institutions. The constitution of Germany's ill-fated Weimar Republic (1919–1933) on paper looked fine; it had been drafted by experts. How it worked in practice was something else, for Germans of that time did not have the necessary experience with or commitment to democracy. Likewise, the Stalin constitution of 1936 made the Soviet Union look like a perfect democracy, but obviously it didn't work that way.

Growing out of this era was an effort to discover how politics really worked, not how it was supposed to work. Postwar American political scientists here followed in the tradition of the early nineteenth-century French philosopher Auguste Comte, who developed the doctrine of *positivism*, the application of natural science methods to the study of society. Comtean positivism was an optimistic philosophy, holding that as we accumulate valid data by means of scientific observation—without speculation or intuition—we will perfect a science of society and with it improve society. Psychologists were perhaps the most deeply imbued with this approach (and still are); many took the name "behavioralists" for their concentration on actual human behavior as opposed to thoughts or feelings.

Behaviorally inclined political scientists in the 1950s borrowed the psychologists' approach and accumulated statistics from elections, public opinion surveys, votes in legislatures, and anything else they could hang a number on. Behavioralists made some remarkable contributions to political science, shooting down some long-held but unexamined assumptions and giving political theory an empirical basis from which to work. Behavioral studies were especially good in examining the "social bases" of politics, the attitudes and values of average citizens, which go a long way in making the system work the way it does.[24]

THE POSTBEHAVIORAL SYNTHESIS

During the 1960s, the behavioral school established itself and won over much of the field. In the late 1960s, however, behavioralism came under heavy attack, and not just by rear-guard traditionalists. Many younger political scientists, some of them influenced by the radicalism of the anti–Vietnam war movement, complained that the behavioral approach was static, conservative, loaded with its practitioners' values, and irrelevant to the urgent tasks at hand. Far from being "scientific" and "value-free," behavioralists often defined the current situation in the United States as the norm and anything different as deviant. Easton's political system, discussed subsequently, is actually an idealized model of U.S. politics. Almond and Verba found that Americans embody all the good, "participant" virtues of the civic culture. By examining only what exists at a given moment, behavioralists neglect the possibility of change; their studies may be time-bound. Behavioralists have an unstated preference for the status quo; they like to examine settled, established systems, for that is where their methodological tools work best. They have a hard time grasping social upheaval and revolution because their systems theories teach them that all systems maintain balance or "equilibrium" and never break down. This is one reason many political scientists were caught by surprise at the collapse of the Soviet Union; "systems" aren't supposed to collapse.

Perhaps the most damaging criticism, though, was that the behavioralists focused on relatively minor topics and steered clear of the big questions of politics. Behavioralists can tell us, for example, what percentage of Detroit blue-collar Catholics vote Democratic, but they can't tell us much about what this means in terms of the quality of Detroit's governance or the kinds of decisions elected officials will make. There is no necessary connection between how citizens vote and what comes out of government. In short, the critics charged, behavioral studies were often irrelevant.

By 1969, even David Easton had to admit that there was something to the criticism of what had earlier been called the "behavioral revolution." He called the new movement the "postbehavioral revolution." The postbehavioral approach can be seen, to a certain extent, as a synthesis of traditional and behavioral approaches.[25] Postbehavioralists recognize that facts and values are tied together; they are willing to use both the qualitative data of the traditionalists and the quantitative data of the behavioralists. They are willing to look at history and institutions as well as current public opinion. It would be premature to say the postbehavioralists have won, for if you inquire around your political science department you are apt to find traditional, behavioral, and postbehavioral viewpoints among the professors—or even within the same professor.

The Importance of Theory

Why bother with theories at all, wonder many students new to political science. Why not just accumulate a lot of facts and let the facts structure themselves into a coherent whole? But just gathering facts without a guiding principle leads only to large collections of meaningless facts. To be sure, theories can grow too abstract and depart from the real world, but without at least some theoretical perspective, we don't even know what questions to ask. Even if you say you have no theories, you probably have some unspoken ones. Just the kind of questions you ask and which questions you ask first are the beginning of theories.

Take, for example, the structure of this book. We have adopted the view—which has been widespread in political science for decades—that the proper beginning of political analysis is the society. That is, we tacitly assume that politics grows out of society. You start with people's attitudes and opinions and see how they influence government. The subtitle of one widely read and highly influential book by a leading sociologist was *The Social Bases of Politics*.[26] The implied message: You start with society and see how that influences politics.

But doesn't that stack the deck? If you assume that society is the basis of political analysis and that attitudes and opinions are the important facts, you will gather a great deal of material on attitudes and opinions and relatively little material on the history, structure, and policies of government. Everything else will appear secondary to citizens' attitudes and opinions. And indeed, political science went through a period in which it was essentially sociology, and many political scientists did survey research. This was part of the behavioral tide (discussed previously) that surged into political science; survey research was seen as the only way to be "scientific" because through such research public opinion data were quantified.

Textbooks tended to offer a "percolation up" model of politics. The first major bloc of most studies was concerned with the society; how political views were distributed, how interest groups were formed, who supported political parties, and how people voted. That was the basis, the bottom part of the pyramid. The second major bloc was usually the institutions of government. They were assumed to be a reflection of the underlying social base. Legislatures and executives reacted to public opinion, interest groups, and political parties. The study of politics looked like Figure 1.1 below.

But just using the term *social base* assumes that society is the underlying element in the study of politics. Could it not be the other way around? To use a cof-

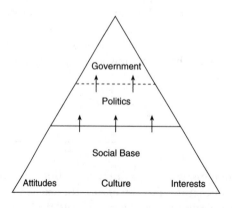

FIGURE 1.1 Pyramid with social base and political superstructure. Flow is from bottom to top.

fee-making metaphor, instead of "percolating up," could politics "drip down"? If there were a book entitled *The Political Basis of Society,* such a book would posit society as largely the result of political decisions made over the decades.[27] In that case, our model would look like Figure 1.2.

How can you prove which model is more nearly correct? It is possible (and very likely) that the flow is going both ways simultaneously and that both models are nearly correct. Why, then, emphasize one model over the other? There is no good reason; it is simply the current fashion in political study. Perhaps the society-based studies began as a reaction against the emphasis on institutions that dominated political science before World War II.

As has been noted, political science doesn't stand still. By the 1970s a certain reaction against the dominant behavioralism had begun. Political scientists began to voice discontent with the social-bases approach, arguing that politics is not simply a reflection of people's attitudes and that in many cases attitudes are the *result* of government policy. One text by a leading political scientist deliberately discussed institutions primarily and attitudes secondarily—and only in regard to political participation. He thereby indicated that the political culture approach was no longer so interesting.[28] Another political scientist, who had earlier been committed to the political culture approach, came to the conclusion that the modern democratic state is not simply the reflection of its society but, in fact, is quite autonomous from society and often guides society.[29] The trouble with this newer approach is that it stacks the deck in favor of institutions, perhaps a needed corrective to the emphasis on attitudes.

In this text we are going to continue putting attitudes before institutions, simply because we have to begin somewhere. We are suggesting, however, that the social base of politics are, in some measure, a reflection of political structures and decisions. Political attitudes are not simply givens; they are in large degree human reactions to the political structures one confronts through life. But how are political institutions created? By people who carry with the certain attitudes in forming political structures.

Notice how a seemingly minor matter—the order in which topics are presented—is itself a theoretical problem. Much as you might try to ignore the theo-

FIGURE 1.2 Pyramid with political institutions forming the social base. Flow is from top to bottom.

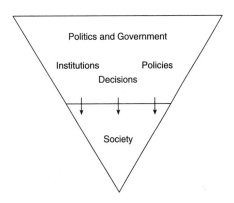

retical questions, you can't escape them entirely. A book that puts attitudes first is at least suggesting, if not stating outright, a theory that attitudes are basic. A book that puts institutions first is suggesting a theory that they are basic. The ordering of topics has been a subtle bias in political science for a long time. It is time for us to make it a topic for open discussion and debate.

Simplifying Reality

A model is a simplified picture of reality that social scientists develop to order data, to theorize, and to predict. We have already considered some of the models currently used in political science, and we will encounter others. By its very nature, a model must simplify reality. A model that is as complex as the real world would be of no help in understanding the real world, but in simplifying reality models run the risk of oversimplifying. The real problem is the finite capacity of the human mind. We cannot factor in all the information available at once; we must select which points are important and ignore the rest. But when we do this, we may drain the blood out of the study of politics and overlook many key points. Accordingly, as we encounter models of politics—and perhaps as we devise our own—pause a moment to ask if the model departs too much from reality. If it does, discard or alter the model. If there is conflict between the theoretical model and reality, always let reality be your guide.

POLITICAL SYSTEMS

Let us consider a prominent example, the "political systems" model, which has contributed to our understanding of politics by simplifying reality and has, in some cases, departed from reality.[30] The idea of looking at complex entities as systems originated in biology. Living entities are complex and highly integrated. The heart, lungs, blood, digestive tract, and brain perform their functions in such a way as to keep the animal alive. Take away one organ and the animal dies. Damage one organ and the other components of the system alter the way they work in an effort to compensate and keep the animal alive. The crux of systems thinking is this: You can't change just one component. A change in one component will also change all the others.

In the political systems model, the politics of a given country, many argued, worked the same way as a biological system. According to the Easton model (Fig. 1.3), citizens' demands, "inputs," are felt by the government decision makers, who process them into authoritative decisions and actions, "outputs." These outputs make an impact on the social, economic, and political environment that the citizens may or may not like. The citizens express their demands anew—this is the crucial "feedback" link of the system, which may modify the earlier decision. Precisely what goes on in the "conversion process" was left opaque, a "black box."

In some cases, the political systems approach describes reality well. A weak economy in the United States increasingly worried citizens. A presidential candi-

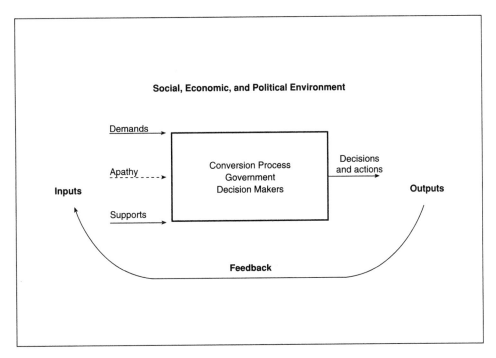

FIGURE 1.3   A Model of the Political System

Adapted from David Easton, *A Systems Analysis of Political Life* (Chicago: University of Chicago Press, 1965), p. 32.

date, Bill Clinton, vowed to speed economic growth and create more jobs. As president, Clinton attempted to couple such programs with tax increases, and the feedback was negative. In another example, during the Vietnam war, feedback on the military draft was very negative. The Nixon administration defused much youthful anger by ending the draft in 1971 and changing to an all-volunteer army. In yet another example, the socialist economics of French President François Mitterrand produced inflation and unemployment. The French people, especially the business community, complained loudly, and Mitterrand altered his policy away from socialism and back to capitalism. The new policy was reinforced when Mitterrand won reelection in 1988. The feedback loop was alive and well in France.

THE TROUBLE WITH SYSTEMS

But in other cases, the systems model falls flat.[31] Would Hitler's Germany or Stalin's Russia really fit the systems model? How much attention do dictatorships pay to citizens' demands? To be sure, there is always some citizen input and feedback. Hitler's generals tried to assassinate him—a type of feedback. Workers in Communist systems made an impact on government policy by not working hard. They expected more consumer goods, and by not exerting themselves they communicated this desire to the regime. Sooner or later the regime had to respond. In the USSR such a response came from the Gorbachev regime. All over the Soviet bloc, workers used to chuckle: "They pretend to pay us and we pretend to work."

How could the systems model explain the Vietnam war? Did the citizens of the United States demand that the administration send half a million troops to fight there? No, precisely the opposite: Lyndon Johnson ran for election in 1964 on an antiwar platform and won resoundingly. We could utilize the systems model to show how citizens' discontent with the war contributed to Johnson's declining popularity and his decision not to seek reelection in 1968. The feedback loop did go into effect and work, but only long after the decision to send troops to Vietnam had been made. By the same token, how could the systems model explain the Watergate scandal? Did U.S. citizens demand that members of President Nixon's staff order the Democratic headquarters bugged? No, but once details started leaking out in 1973 about the cover-up, the feedback loop went into effect, putting pressure on the House of Representatives to form an impeachment panel.

Plainly, there are some problems with the systems model, and they seem to be in the "black box" of the conversion process. A lot of things are happening in the mechanism of government that are not initiated by and have little to do with the wishes of citizens. Johnson was responding to the demands of a few generals and close advisers to send U.S. troops to Vietnam.[32] He was not happy about this because it was a betrayal of his election promise. But by early 1965, he could no longer ignore the demands of his advisers, which weighed more heavily in his thinking than the public's wishes.

Let us modify the systems model to better reflect reality. By diagramming it as in Figure 1.4, we logically change nothing. We have the same feedback loop: out-

FIGURE 1.4   A Modified Model of the Political System

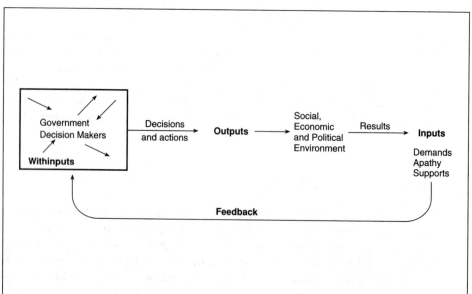

puts turning into inputs. But by putting the "conversion process" of government first, we suggested that it—rather than the citizenry—originates most decisions. The public reacts only later.

Next we add something that Easton himself later suggested. Inside the "black box" a lot more is happening than simply the processing of outside demands. Pressures from the various parts of government—government talking mostly to itself and short-circuiting the feedback loop—are what Easton called "withinputs."[33] These two alterations, of course, make our model more complicated, but this also reflects the complicated nature of reality.

We still do not have the perfect model to explain and predict political actions. We never will. Do the citizens decide and the leaders react? Or do the leaders decide and the people react? With the systems model, we have an example of how we must continually remake our ideas on politics to fit an ever-changing reality. Politics is slippery; it isn't easily confined to our mental constructs. By acknowledging this, we open our minds to the richness, complexity, and drama of political life.

Suggested Readings

ALMOND, GABRIEL A. *A Discipline Divided: Schools and Sects in Political Science.* Newbury Park, CA: Sage, 1989. A top comparativist, a founder of the political culture approach, worries about the sharp divisions and lack of communication within the discipline.

BAER, MICHAEL A., MALCOLM E. JEWELL, and LEE SIGLEMAN, eds. *Political Science in America: Oral Histories of a Discipline.* Lexington, KY: University Press of Kentucky, 1991. Important and interesting memories of some of the profession's guiding lights.

BOULDING, KENNETH E. *Three Faces of Power.* Newbury Park, CA: Sage, 1989. Trained as an economist, Boulding has become one of the greats of social science by exploring basic questions with clarity and wit.

DAHL, ROBERT A. *Modern Political Analysis,* 4th ed. Englewood Cliffs, NJ: Prentice Hall, 1984. An excellent introduction by a noted Yale scholar to the several theories and approaches to the discipline.

FINIFTER, ADA W., ed. *Political Science: The State of the Discipline.* II. Washington, DC: American Political Science Association, 1992. Some of the biggest names in the field give brief reviews of recent findings in their specialties. A good way to update oneself.

JOHNSON, NEVIL. *The Limits of Political Science.* New York: Oxford University Press, 1989.

What exactly are we to study, politics as practiced in the real world or political science as studied by academics?

KAGAN, JEROME. *Galen's Prophecy: Temperament and Human Nature.* New York: Basic Books, 1994. A Harvard psychologist emphasizes the biological as opposed to the cultural bases of behavior.

LASSWELL, HAROLD. *Politics: Who Gets What, When, How.* New York: McGraw-Hill, 1936. A classic statement, albeit heavy on unsupportable psychoanalytic insight, of the way politics works.

MINOGUE, KENNETH. *Politics: A Very Short Introduction.* New York: Oxford University Press, 1995. Classical political analysis is alive, well, and readable!

MORGENTHAU, HANS J. *Scientific Man vs. Power Politics.* Chicago: University of Chicago Press, 1946. Defines the limit of scientific approaches in the face of power realities.

ROSS, DOROTHY. *The Origins of American Social Science.* New York: Cambridge University Press, 1991. A history of how the social sciences and the biases of their practitioners influenced American thought.

WRONG, DENNIS H. *The Problem of Order: What Unites and Divides Society.* New York: Free Press, 1994. Taking cues from Hobbes and Freud, he argues that "culture" poorly explains order in human society.

Notes

1. David Easton, "The Perception of Authority and Political Change," in *Authority*, ed. Carl J. Friedrich (Cambridge, MA: Harvard University Press, 1958), pp. 178–81.

2. The quotation is from the memoirs of a close witness to the process, National Security Adviser and Secretary of State Henry A. Kissinger, *Years of Upheaval* (Boston: Little, Brown, 182), II, p. 123.

3. The great German sociologist Max Weber connected authority closely with legitimacy. In fact, he distinguished between three types of political authority based on the type of legitimacy that supports them: (1) the traditional, where legitimacy is inherited, as in kingdoms; (2) the rational, where legitimacy derives from effective government; and (3) the charismatic, where legitimacy comes from a leader. See Max Weber, *The Theory of Social and Economic Organization* (New York: Free Press, 1947), pp. 324–26.

4. Aristotle's words were *zoon politikon*, which can be translated as either "political animal" or "social animal," for the Greeks did not distinguish between polity and society. They lived in city-states in which the social system was the same as the political system. Richard McKeon, ed., *The Basic Works of Aristotle* (New York: Random House, 1941), p. 1129.

5. For a modern exposition of the biological view, see Edward O. Wilson, *Sociobiology: The New Synthesis* (Cambridge, MA: Harvard University Press, 1975).

6. Stanley Milgram, *Obedience to Authority: An Experimental View* (New York: Harper & Row, 1974).

7. Irving L. Janis, *Victims of Groupthink: A Psychological Study of Foreign-Policy Decisions and Fiascoes* (Boston: Houghton Mifflin, 1972).

8. The classic political culture study is by Gabriel A. Almond and Sidney Verba, *The Civic Culture: Political Attitudes and Democracy in Five Nations* (Princeton, NJ: Princeton University Press, 1965).

9. For a model study of political culture, one that tries to explain the poverty of southern Italy, see Edward Banfield, *The Moral Basis of a Backward Society* (New York: Free Press, 1958). Banfield later applied this "culture of poverty" approach to explain America's urban poverty in Edward Banfield, *The Unheavenly City Revisited* (Boston: Little, Brown, 1974).

10. For a view that the Founding Fathers engaged in the rational pursuit of liberty, see Robert H. Webking, *The American Revolution and the Politics of Liberty* (Baton Rouge: Louisiana State University Press, 1988).

11. A leading scholar of elections finds that Americans have reasoned opinions and cast their ballots rationally. See Samuel L. Popkin, *The Reasoning Voter: Communication and Persuasion in Presidential Campaigns* (Chicago: University of Chicago Press, 1991).

12. For a critical discussion of this approach, see Donald P. Green and Ian Shapiro, *Pathologies of Rational Choice Theory: A Critique of Applications in Political Science* (New Haven, CT: Yale University Press, 1994).

13. A German psychiatrist offers an explanation of Hitler's hold on the German people. See Erich Fromm, *Escape from Freedom* (New York: Holt, Rinehart & Winston, 1941).

14. See John Girling, *Myths and Politics in Western Societies: Evaluating the Crisis of Modernity in the United States, Germany, and Great Britain* (New Brunswick, NJ: Transaction, 1993).

15. Henry Steele Commager, *The Empire of Reason: How Europe Imagined and America Realized the Enlightenment* (Garden City, NY: Doubleday, 1977).

16. Richard L. Merritt, "Nation-Building in America: The Colonial Years," in *Nation-Building*, eds. Karl W. Deutsch and William J. Foltz (New York: Atherton Books, 1963).

17. *Wygant v. Jackson Board of Education* (1986).

18. Max Weber, "Science as a Vocation," in *From Max Weber: Essays in Sociology*, eds. Hans H. Gerth and C. Wright Mills (New York: Oxford University Press, 1946).

19. Arthur Miller, "Is Confidence Rebounding?" *Public Opinion*, June and July 1983, pp. 16–20.

20. Committee on Political Parties, American Political Science Association, "Toward a More Responsible Two-Party System," *American Political Science Review* 44 (September 1950 supplement).

21. Marvin Zonis, *The Political Elite of Iran* (Princeton, NJ: Princeton University Press, 1971); James Bill, *The Politics of Iran* (Columbus, OH: Merrill, 172); Richard Cottam, *Nationalism in Iran* (Pittsburgh: University of Pittsburgh Press, 1979).

22. Barry Rubin, *Paved with Good Intentions; The American Experience and Iran* (New York: Penguin, 1981), Chaps. 7 and 8.

23. Hans J. Morgenthau and Kenneth W.

Thompson, *Politics Among Nations: The Struggle for Power and Peace,* 6th ed. (New York: Knopf, 1985), p. 31.

24. An excellent behavioral capstone to the 1950s is Seymour Martin Lipset, *Political Man: The Social Bases of Politics* (New York: Doubleday, 1960). Lipset brought out an expanded and updated edition two decades later (Baltimore: Johns Hopkins University Press, 1981). A more recent summation of behavioral findings is Steven A. Peterson, *Political Behavior: Patterns in Everyday Life* (Newbury Park, CA: Sage, 1990).

25. For a useful comparison of the three approaches, see Ronald H. Chilcote, *Theories of Comparative Politics: The Search for a Paradigm* (Boulder, CO: Westview Press, 1981), pp. 56–58.

26. Lipset, *Political Man.*

27. For one recent study that has done this, see James G. March and Johan P. Olsen, *Rediscovering Institutions: The Organizational Basis of Politics* (New York: Free Press, 1989).

28. Joseph LaPalombara, *Politics Within Nations* (Englewood Cliffs, NJ: Prentice Hall, 1974).

29. Eric A. Nordlinger, *On the Autonomy of the Democratic State* (Cambridge, MA: Harvard University Press, 1981). Nordlinger's earlier work was a study of English political attitudes. See Eric A. Nordlinger, *The Working-Class Tories* (Berkeley: University of California Press, 1967).

30. The leading thinker on political systems has been David Easton, *A Systems Analysis of Political Life* (New York: Wiley, 1965). Gabriel Almond has accepted and refined a systems view of politics in Gabriel A. Almond and James S. Coleman, *Politics of Developing Areas* (Princeton, NJ: Princeton University Press, 1960), Chap. 1; and Gabriel A. Almond and G. Bingham Powell, Jr., *Comparative Politics: System, Process, and Policy,* 2nd ed. (Boston: Little, Brown, 1978).

31. For criticism of the political systems approach, see Chilcote, *Theories of Comparative Politics,* Chap. 5.

32. For a condensed account of decision making on the Vietnam war that utilizes numerous Defense Department documents, see Neil Sheehan et al., *The Pentagon Papers* (New York: Bantam Books, 1971).

33. David Easton, *A Framework for Political Analysis* (Englewood Cliffs, NJ: Prentice Hall, 1965), p. 114.

· 2 ·

Nations, States, and Governments

Which came first, states or nations? A nation is a population with a certain sense of itself, a cohesiveness, a commonality of attitudes and ideals, and often (but not always) a common language. A state is a government structure, usually sovereign and powerful enough to enforce its writ. (Notice that here we use *state* in its original sense; the fifty U.S. states are not states in this sense of the word.) Many people would argue that nations must have developed before states. States, after all, are rather artificial creations; they come and go and change form through the centuries. Surely nations must be the underlying element: Groups of people with kindred feelings must antedate government structures.

Historical research tends to refute this commonsense view. In most cases, it was states—government structures—that created their nations around them.[1] The Zulus of South Africa, for example, are not a tribe but an artificially created nation, one put together from many clans and tribes less than two centuries ago by a powerful and brutal warrior, Shaka. Present-day people think of themselves as Zulus only because Shaka united them by conquest, forced them to speak his language, and made them great warriors.

France often comes to mind as a "natural" nation, a neat hexagon with a common history, language, and culture. But present-day France consists of several regions with very different languages and histories that were united—mostly by the sword—over the course of centuries. Paris inculcated a sense of Frenchness by means of education, language, and centralized administration. The French nation is an artificial creation developed by the French state for its own convenience.

For many countries, the process of creation is not yet complete. The Spanish state coincides imperfectly with the Spanish nation. The kings of Toledo and Madrid tried to copy the French methods of centralization, but these Castilians were never able to impose a uniform sense of Spanishness on Catalans, Basques, Galicians, Andalucians, Navarese, and others. Regionalism bedevils Spanish politics to this day. In another example, India scarcely existed as a concept before the British conquered the Indian subcontinent and turned it into the Raj. The English language, the railroad, and the telegraph stitched India together. It, too, is plagued by breakaway ethnic movements such as the independence movement of the Sikhs in the Punjab.

The most artificial nation of all could well be the United States—put together through deliberate design by a group of men meeting in Philadelphia from thirteen different colonies. While assimilating tens of millions of immigrants with different languages and cultures, the United States developed a sense of nationhood over the years based largely on the ideals articulated in its founding documents. Nations do not fall from heaven; they are created by human craftsmanship of varying degrees of quality.

The Notion of Nation

What are we to call this entity that dominates our lives, structures our politics, and calls forth our patriotism? Many terms are used, sometimes interchangeably. The terms have somewhat different meanings, though. Let's see if we can separate them.

The common colloquial expression is *country*, as in "Have you ever visited another country?" *Country*, of course, can also mean a rural or farming area, and centuries ago the two meanings were one. When people spoke of their "country" (French *pays*, Spanish *país*, Italian *paese*, German *Land*) they meant their native locality, perhaps not much bigger than a large U.S. county, where people shared the same traditions and dialect. Later the term broadened to mean a big, sovereign political entity, a nation.

The term *nation* has also been around for centuries, but not necessarily in its present sense. Far back in history, human groups called themselves nations, but originally this meant something like a big tribe, such as the "nation of Israel" or "Sioux nation." The Latin root of *nation* means "birth," so the word connoted the group you were born into and had some blood linkage with. The term *ethnic group,* from the Greek *ethnos,* "nation," in turn is from the Greek for custom, *ethos,* indicating people with shared customs.

In the seventeenth century, the definition of nation changed to mean these large, powerful political entities that currently govern us. State power was merged with the notion of a people with much in common (history, culture, language) occupying a territory. This was the *nation-state,* a combination of people (nation) and government structure (state).[2] It is usually just called *nation.* As stated earlier, states often preceded and created their nations.

The rise of the modern nation changed the face of the globe. Citizens—an old Roman concept that originated with the Latin for "city" and that revived with the idea of nation-states—transferred their ultimate loyalties from kings, churches, and localities to this new entity, the nation.[3] Starting with the French Revolution in 1789 came a new force called *nationalism*—a people's heightened sense of cultural, historical, and territorial identity and sometimes greatness. This new force quickly spread over Europe and then over the globe, unleashing the desire for peoples to govern themselves as independent nations. Vast empires, such as those of Austria-Hungary and Britain, fell apart as subject peoples demanded their independence. As a result, many new countries were created, especially in Eastern Europe, the Americas, Asia, and Africa.[4] Today there are some 180 entities calling themselves nations.

THE ELEMENTS OF NATIONHOOD

Nations are commonly said to have several defining characteristics, such as territory, population, independence, and government. By each point, however, we could place a little question mark, for the characteristics are sometimes strong and clear and sometimes weak or absent.

Territory.   In general, every nation occupies a specific geographical area. It's hard to have a nation without territory. But what about peoples without territory who carry the idea of their "nation" around with them in their heads? Jews lost their territorial nation to Greek and Roman conquest some two millennia ago but, because many of them had a firm ideal of their peoplehood, were able to establish the modern state of Israel in 1948. Ironically, the people they displaced, the Palestinian Arabs, now also have a rather firm ideal of their peoplehood and strive to establish their own state. Should we count dispersed peoples, such as Jews or Palestinians, as a "nation"? Perhaps they are a potential nation, a people waiting or struggling to establish themselves on a territory.

And what occurs when territorial claims overlap? Wars often result. As stated

earlier, most states and nations are rather artificial things; few have natural boundaries. Germany has fought France over Alsace; the United States has fought Mexico over Texas; and Argentina still claims what it calls the Malvinas Islands from
Britain, which calls them the Falklands. Which claim is rightful? What criteria do
you use to decide?

History is often a poor guide, for there was almost always someone else there
first. Israelis and Arabs quarrel endlessly about this. (If you go back far enough,
neither of them was there first.) Language and ethnicity may also be poor guides
in deciding which territory belongs to which state. The peoples of the earth, unfortunately, are not neatly arrayed into nations; rather there is a lot of spillover into
neighboring states. Most Alsatians, for example, are or were originally German in
language, culture, and family names. Most, however, also speak perfect French and
think of themselves as French. To whom, then, does Alsace rightfully belong, to
Germany or to France?

Population.   Every nation has people within its borders. Ideally, it should be a
population with a sense of cohesion, of being a distinct nationality. Having a common language is a real help but is often not the case. For example, there has long
been conflict between French-speaking and Flemish-speaking Belgians. Still,
enough of both language groups "feel" Belgian to hold the country together. States
with populations diverse in language, culture, or identification are called *multina-
tional states.* Only half of the Soviet population was Russian; many other Soviet nationalities did not like being ruled by Moscow and broke away, producing fifteen
countries where there used to be one.

What if part of a nation's population doesn't want to belong to that particular nation? Some Basques in Spain would like to form an independent nation;
some Quebecois in Canada and Sikhs in India would like to do the same. Of
course, if a substantial portion of the population is unwilling, chances are the nation will fall apart. Many Slovaks resented being governed by Czechs, and in 1993
set up a separate Slovakia. Slovenes and Croats resented being governed by Serbs,
and in 1991 they declared their independence from Yugoslavia. Just because people are under the *control* of a particular state does not necessarily mean the state is
firmly established; it may be ready to explode.

Independence.   The nation should also be independent, meaning that it governs itself as a "sovereign" entity (see the previous discussion). Colonies, such as Algeria under the French, become nations only when they get formal independence,
as Algeria did in 1962. Subdivisions of a nation, such as Quebec or Nevada, are also
not considered nations since they lack sovereignty. Many Quebeckers, of course,
mean to change this situation.

There are some problems with the concept of independence, too. When a
large, powerful country dominates a smaller, weaker country, is the latter fully independent and sovereign? Soviet tanks crushed anti-Communist movements in
Eastern Europe and set up obedient puppet governments—which is why these
countries were known as Soviet "satellites." Were they truly independent? For that
matter, doesn't the United States supervise things in its own backyard, in the
Caribbean and Central America? Is Haiti, for example, truly sovereign and inde-

pendent? By definition, all nations are sovereign and independent, but some are more sovereign and independent than others.

Bolstering sovereign independence is "diplomatic recognition" by other countries, especially by the major powers. Recognition is an official announcement by one country that it is prepared to have dealings with another country. This statement may be followed by exchanges of ambassadors and the setting up of embassies. If most of the important nations recognize a new country, it automatically confers a certain legitimacy on it. If no one recognizes the country, its claim to exist is dubious. South Africa created nominally independent puppet states out of some of its "black homelands," but no one else recognized them; they were seen by the world as fake little republics unworthy of notice.

Government.   A nation must obviously have some organizing force over its population. The absence of such organization is anarchy, and it probably means that the territory will soon split apart or be conquered and absorbed by other nations. No government, no nation. Somalia is a recent example of the horrors of anarchy.

Government, however, can in certain circumstances exist independently of the nation. Underground governments or "governments-in-exile" struggle to expel occupiers or puppet governments. The Continental Congress was a protogovernment that preceded, conceived of, and fought for an independent United States. In 1940, General Charles de Gaulle declared a "Free French" government in London to expel the Germans, and many major powers recognized it as the government of France. With the liberation of Paris in 1944, it turned into a government with territory, population, and independence.

The existence of a legal government does not necessarily mean it is an effective government that controls its territory and population (discussed later). Where weak, governments may have trouble even staying alive in the face of domestic and foreign opposition. Colombia, for example, has difficulty controlling the drug bosses who make millions from cocaine and run private armies that defy the Colombian state.

Older political theorists, influenced by legal abstractions, tended to take these characteristics of nations as givens. Wherever there was a nation, they reasoned, it must automatically have territory, population, independence, government, and sometimes other qualities. Modern political scientists tend to discard purely legalistic notions and search for the empirical reality. Theoretically country X is a nation, but does it really have a cohesive population and an effective independent government that allows it to control its territory? Nations are not necessarily perfected, finished products. Many—perhaps all—are continually building and rebuilding themselves.

THE CRISES OF NATION BUILDING

Some social scientists argue that the process of constructing nations—if the process is to be successful—requires that countries go through the same five stages in approximately the same sequence.[5] Each opportunity for further growth represents a "crisis" in the life of the nation, which the state structure must resolve with greater or lesser success.

Identity. The "identity crisis" is the first hurdle in building a nation. People who previously identified with a tribe, region, or other subnational group must come to think of themselves as first and foremost citizens of the nation. This does not happen easily, quickly, or automatically. The American Civil War was fought over this point. France and Britain still contain regional groups that don't think of themselves as French or British but rather as Breton and Corsican (in France) or Scottish, Welsh, and Irish (in Britain). Swiss, except when traveling abroad, will identify themselves as members of a canton (Bern, Geneva, Basel). Yugoslavia never established a national identity for its Serbs, Croats, Slovenes, Bosnians, Macedonians, and others. In this, Yugoslavia resembles many Third World countries, which have not yet solved their identity crisis. In Africa, people still think of themselves as members of a tribe rather than as Ugandans or Nigerians.

Legitimacy. Nor does legitimacy fall from heaven. As discussed in Chapter 1, a government must cultivate the respect and willing obedience of its citizens, the widespread feeling among the people that the regime's rule is rightful. Regimes with legitimacy problems are prone to overthrow (often by military coup, as in Latin America and Africa) or revolution (as in Iran and Burma). Ultimately, as in the case of Yugoslavia, no legitimacy means no nation.

Penetration. Related to both identity and legitimacy, the "crisis of penetration" means that the nation must get substantially all the population, even in outlying or culturally distinct regions, to obey the government's writ. One quick check of penetration: Do all areas pay taxes? If not, there is a penetration problem. Typically, the regime establishes its rule first in the capital, then slowly extends its rule over the country, often encountering resistance that requires military strength to overcome. Lack of penetration means that a government can have a law on its books—against cocaine trafficking, for example—but much of the country, including some officials, disregard the law.

Participation. As people become more aware that they are being governed, they demand to have a say in their governance. This feeling typically starts with the educated, better-off, and prominent people. The knights and wealthy burghers in effect tell the king or queen, "If you want taxes and military service from us, we demand a say in policy." The monarch, usually desperate for taxes, sets up a representative body to gain their compliance, such as the Parliament in England or Riksdag in Sweden. At first only the elite of society are thus represented, but gradually, the desire for participation reaches all sectors of society—the common men and women—and they demand the right to vote. At a minimum, people need to *feel* they can participate in order for nationhood to evolve.

Regimes are often fearful of the consequences of expanding voting rights. Women got the right to vote in the United States only with the Nineteenth Amendment in 1920; Swiss women, only in 1971. The danger is that unrepresented people will oppose the government, and regime legitimacy will erode. Eventually, the regime usually decides that expanding participation is better than breeding revolution. Said one British parliamentarian in the nineteenth century, "We count ballots rather than crack skulls." The white minority regime of South Africa was slow to realize this basic point.

The best way to solve the participation crisis is through slow and incremental steps, as Britain succeeded in doing in the nineteenth century. A series of Reform Acts in Britain expanded the electoral franchise one step at a time, gradually giving more people the right to vote. This allowed both institutions and people time to adjust. Voting was meaningful and participation genuine. When suffrage is suddenly thrust on an unprepared people, however, the result is seldom democracy. On paper, Spain got universal male suffrage in 1874, well ahead of Britain, but in practice election results were controlled by local bosses and the interior ministry. Voting in much of the Third World—where largely uneducated people got the franchise all at once—is often problematic because local political bosses or tribal leaders tell people how to vote.

Distribution.   In a sense, the "crisis of distribution" is never permanently resolved. It concerns the classic question of "who gets what?"[6] Once the broad masses of citizens are participating in elections, it usually occurs to them that the economic rewards of the nation are unfairly apportioned, and they want to change the distribution of the nation's income in their favor. Much of the working class throws its votes to the party that promises higher wages, increased educational opportunities, and more welfare benefits. This is how the Labor parties of Britain and Norway and the Social Democratic parties of Germany and Sweden grew until they won power and established extensive welfare states funded by taxes that fall more heavily on the rich. To a lesser degree, the American working class gave much of its vote to the Democrats under Franklin D. Roosevelt and Lyndon Johnson in order to carry out a similar redistribution of national income.

The distribution question is never settled, however, because the poorer sectors of society always want more welfare, whereas the better-off, represented by the more conservative parties, argue that the welfare state has gotten out of hand, that taxes are too high and benefits too generous. When conservatives win elections—as Margaret Thatcher did in Britain in 1979 and Ronald Reagan did in the United States in 1980—they try to cut welfare programs. This raises a hue and cry from some voters who fear their benefits will be cut, and they try to preserve the benefits of the welfare state. In advanced, industrialized democracies most elections are, to some degree, centered around the distribution of wealth.

Few nations have had the luxury of being able to deal with these crises one at a time and with sufficient pauses in between each crisis. These circumstances would allow a country's institutions—its parties, parliament, executive departments, and so on—to become stronger each time they surmount a new crisis. But what if all five crises hit at the same time? This has especially been the situation in the Third World. Newly independent countries, many of them with serious identity and legitimacy problems, are expected to implement complex laws, to give all citizens the right to vote, and to provide rising and equitable living standards. It's too much for their weak institutions to bear all at once, and they collapse into revolution or military rule. The first item to go is usually participation, hence the many Third World dictatorships.[7] Unfortunately, the Third World does not have the luxury of spreading out its crises in this world of rapid change.

THE ROLE OF WAR

One of the unfortunate aspects of nation building is the role of warfare in the growth of states. We must recognize that most European nations were established and consolidated by conquest. Heresies, rebellions, and breakaway movements were put down with great bloodshed. In many lands, this is still happening.

For any ruler, state survival is the top priority. Monarchs and presidents alike will do whatever they must to avoid foreign conquest or internal dismemberment. They become ruthless when either threatens them. In the interest of survival they build their military power to counter any combination of threats, and this means that they must also enlarge and modernize their political systems.[8]

First, they must constantly increase taxes to provide for armies and equipment. Peter the Great of Russia ordered his officials "to collect money, as much as possible, for money is the artery of war." The French monarchs instituted the mercantilist economic system, with its protected industries, to raise revenues for defense. As mentioned previously, it was to raise money that kings and queens began sharing power with parliaments. The power to tax is the preeminent power of legislatures. James I and Charles I precipitated the English Civil War when they tried to bypass Parliament by decreeing their own taxes in order to pay for their wars in Europe. After winning the Civil War the Parliamentarians beheaded Charles I in 1649 and laid the groundwork for establishing the eventual predominance of the House of Commons.

The need for a larger and better military establishment forced monarchs to improve greatly the organization and administration of their kingdoms. They needed to raise both taxes and manpower. Prior to gunpowder and cannon in the fifteenth century, feudal lords in their castles could defy monarchs. However, because kings could afford more cannons, they were able to crack castle walls and assert their control over lords. This power was a blow to the feudal state and a boost to the absolutism of monarchs. But failure to modernize one's administration and army could lead to loss of power. The map of Europe became much simpler as small states succumbed to military conquest and were absorbed by larger states. War was the great engine of modernization and consolidation.

When French revolutionaries in 1792 faced an invading army of professional soldiers, they mobilized the entire population, "the nation in arms," and beat the invaders. Harnessing this new nationalism and using the new idea of drafting all young males, Napoleon built the largest army in Europe and proceeded to conquer the entire continent. To resist Napoleon's legions, other European lands turned to nationalism and conscription as well.

By either the power or example of its arms, European nations spread their organization, technology, and nationalism into what we call the Third World. In Asia, Africa, and the Middle East, one country after another fell to the conquering Europeans and soon adopted their ways. Those who were not conquered, the Turks and the Japanese, modernized sufficiently to stave off the Europeans. Warfare gave countries little choice: modernize or die.

Reflecting for a moment on U.S. history, we may ask which contributed more to modernization: the modest welfare measures of Roosevelt's New Deal or the gigantic industrial and manpower mobilization of World War II? Indeed, many welfare measures flowed as a result of the war. The G. I. Bill educated millions of ex-soldiers who never would have gone to college without it. The National Defense Education Act of 1958, triggered by the launch of the Soviet Sputnik the year before, pumped millions of dollars into U.S. higher education. One of the largest federal "welfare" programs is the new Department of Veterans Affairs, a department that even conservatives voted for.

We do not propose that war is a wonderful thing and should be promoted as an accelerator of modernization. War is ghastly, but it has the side effect of speeding up modernization. Much as we may dislike war, we must recognize that it plays a major role in the foundation and growth of the powers of government.

Government: What It Is and What It Does

All but the most primitive societies have had well-defined government structures. Humankind seems to need a way of organizing and making rules for communities, and various theories have been offered to explain this tendency. Psychologist Erich Fromm argued that people fear social isolation and the responsibilities of independence and form larger groups (whether national, religious, or ideological) to escape from the tensions and demands of individual freedom and autonomy.[9] On the other hand, political theorists such as John Locke have viewed governments as devices to protect the rights and property of the people. "The great and chief end," wrote Locke in *Two Treatises of Civil Government,* "of men uniting . . . under government, is the preservation of their property [and so, their natural rights]."[10] To Locke, government represented an agreement between the rulers and the ruled, who would support those in power as long as the government served in their interests.

A society without a government might be like a baseball game without umpires. The players would argue forever about whether the pitch was a ball or a strike or whether the runner was safe or out. Each contest would turn into a raucous brawl. Government performs the same tasks as the umpires: It sets down the basic ground rules that everyone must abide by.

In part, a government is able to enforce its rules (or laws) because it controls the supreme penalty of death and has a monopoly on the legal use of force. Yet to stay in power, a government must enjoy the support of its people. One way of maintaining legitimacy is to fulfill successfully the goals of nationhood.

COMMON GOALS OF GOVERNMENT

The task of government is to provide for the lives, stability, and economic and social well-being of all its citizens. (This does not necessarily mean that government
directly runs or supervises the economy or society.) These are the ultimate goals of
most nations in the modern world.

To this end, a nation must preserve itself as a state and ensure its national survival, so that the world community recognizes that nation's autonomy and the in-
tegrity of its boundaries, in a word, its sovereignty. Recognition by other nations depends in part on a country's stability. A politically stable nation has an established
system providing for the orderly transfer of power from one party or leader to another. It preserves domestic peace by maintaining law and order and by protecting
property. A government can also enlist popular support by promoting a good standard of living for all of its citizens; people who are receiving what they believe to
be their due are more likely to see the regime as legitimate. Promoting the general
welfare can include attempts to eliminate poverty, maximization of educational opportunities for all members of society, and technological advances.

How can government best advance the economic and social well-being of its
citizens? States face two questions, both economic: How much of the economy
should the state own or supervise? How much of the nation's wealth should be re-
distributed to help the poorer sectors of society? The answers produce four general
approaches to promoting the general welfare: laissez-faire, statism, socialism, and
the welfare state. These array themselves into a fourfold table, much beloved of political scientists:

HIGH

Statist (France, Brazil)	Socialist (Soviet Union, Cuba)
Laissez-faire (United States, Switzerland)	Welfare State (Sweden, Denmark)

State Ownership (vertical axis label)

LOW   HIGH

Welfare Benefits

A laissez-faire (from the French for "let it be") system owns little or no industry and redistributes relatively little in the form of welfare programs. As we shall
explore in Chapter 6 on ideologies, these countries are the followers of Adam
Smith, who argued that any government interference in the economy slows growth
and ultimately decreases prosperity. Thomas Jefferson summed up this approach
with his famous dictum, "That government is best that governs least." The theory

here is that people will prosper or fail on the basis of their abilities and drive and that government has no right to intervene in this natural process.

A welfare state owns little or no industry but does redistribute wealth to aid the less well-off. Sometimes also known as "social democracies," the welfare states of northwest Europe offer "cradle-to-grave" benefits in the form of health insurance, child care and nourishment, job training, and retirement funds. To pay for this, they charge the world's highest taxes—in Sweden and Denmark, for example, more than 50 percent of the country's gross domestic product (GDP). Industry, though, is almost strictly private and oriented to capitalist moneymaking.

Statism is an old system that predates laissez-faire. A statist system is one in which the state (meaning the national government) is the number-one capitalist, owning and running much major industry. It is little interested, however, in providing welfare benefits. Statism began when the French kings founded a powerful, centralized state that supervised industry for the sake of French wealth and power. Sometimes called by its French name *étatisme,* it typically includes state ownership of railroads, steel mills, banks, oil, and other big enterprises. Small and medium business is left in private hands. Statism caught on in much of Europe, but especially found a home in Latin America; Brazil and Mexico are good examples. The bureaucratic supervision of Japan's economy has led some to call it statist, even though there is no government ownership. Many developing countries have followed statist models with the arguments that only the government has the money, ideas, and talent to start up new industries. The economic results suggest state-owned firms are inefficient because they are run by bureaucrats and face no competition; often they operate at a loss and have to be subsidized by the national treasury. Statist systems such as Argentina and Chile grew more prosperous after they privatized their state-owned firms.

A socialist system practices both state ownership and extensive welfare benefits. Exemplified by the former Soviet Union, government owns most of the means of production, claiming it runs the economy in the interests of the society as a whole. However, the collapse of Communist regimes (which called themselves "socialist"; we called them "Communist") throughout Europe indicates those governments ran things poorly. Today, only China, Vietnam, North Korea, and Cuba remain as (negative) examples of socialism, and their systems seem ripe for change.

In actual practice, governments tend to combine elements of the above four systems. Even the basically laissez-faire United States has some government supervision of the economy and welfare measures. Even Communist China and Vietnam have private, capitalistic sectors of their economy. The questions are never settled, and countries often change their combinations. In our day, we have seen a massive shift away from state-owned industry in the ex-Soviet Union, France, and Latin America. Extensive welfare states like Sweden have felt the pinch of too-generous benefits and too-high taxes.

THE STATE AS AGENT OF MODERNIZATION

A basic American attitude is that government—known in other countries as "the state"—be kept small. In much of the rest of the world, however, state power is accepted as natural and good. In France, for example, a strong state was started by Louis XI in the fifteenth century, expanded under Louis XIII and Cardinal Richelieu in the seventeenth century, implanted itself into French consciousness, and later spread through most of Europe. It was taken for granted that the state should supervise the economy and education, collect taxes, build highways and canals, and field standing armies. An intellectual elite, trained in special schools, ran the country.

These attitudes lasted well into our century and are still present. Defeated by Germany in 1870–1871, the French elite used the state as an agent of modernization. The government in Paris tried to build a unified and cohesive population, to turn "peasants into Frenchmen."[11] A centralized school system stamped out local dialects, broke stagnant rural traditions, and recruited the best talent for universities. State-owned industries turned France into a major industrial power. Beaten by Germany again in World War II, the French elite again used state power to modernize France.

Did it work? France did modernize greatly, but was this the fastest or most efficient way to do so? Britain and the United States historically advanced farther with minimal government supervision; the competitive spirit of the free-market economy did the job faster and cheaper. (The comparison, of course, is not quite fair; Britain and the United States didn't face a powerful, expansionist Germany on their borders. If they had, the role of government probably would have been much bigger.)

Another example of state-led modernization is Japan. With the Meiji Restoration of 1868, Tokyo assigned various branches of industry to samurai clans, provided funds, and told them to copy the best of the West. In one generation, Japan went from the bamboo age to the steel age under the slogan "Rich nation, strong army!" After World War II, the Ministry of International Trade and Industry (MITI) supervised Japan's economic leap by aiming bank loans to growth industries, keeping out foreign products, and penetrating the world market with Japanese products. Before we say government supervision of the economy doesn't work, we had better explain why it worked in Japan. (The Japanese, of course, have an entirely different and more cooperative culture. An American MITI might not work in our economic and attitudinal context.)

Does—or should—the state serve as an agent of modernization? Should government attempt to supervise the economy by providing plans, suggestions, industry-wide cooperation, and loans? The traditional American answer is "No, it'll just mess things up." Looking more closely, though, we notice that the federal government has repeatedly goaded American society forward by acquiring gigantic territories, letting settlers homestead them, and giving railroads rights of way. Earlier in our century, the Tennessee Valley Authority brought electricity and flood control to a backward part of America. Faced with murderous competition in computers, the U.S. government, under conservative Ronald Reagan, set up a consortium of private firms to plan and build the next generation of computers before our friends across the Pacific could. America, too, has used the state as an agent of modernization, and the Clinton administration urged us to do more of it under the heading "industrial policy." One of the great questions of modern politics is how much state intervention do we want?

CLASSIFYING GOVERNMENTS

We could arrange all of the world's governments into a typology according to whether they follow the laissez-faire model, the socialist model, or the welfare state model. Of course, any model represents only an ideal situation and not its application in the real world. But models are very useful to social scientists in classifying and comparing different political systems, and they aid in the understanding of a nation's political culture and development. But categorizing according to the economic strategies of governments is only one of many schemes for understanding governments. The earliest and most famous system of classification was developed by the Greek philosopher Aristotle in the fourth century B.C.

Aristotle's Six Types of Government.   Aristotle distinguished among three benevolent kinds of government—where the ruling authority acts only according to legal guidelines, ruling in the interests of the entire society—and three corrupt counterparts—where government acts only in its own selfish interests (Table 2.1).

A monarchy is a benevolent dictatorship. Government power is vested in a person of preeminent virtue and wisdom. The ideal monarch rules on behalf of all and will not benefit any one person or group at the expense of another. But monarchy can degenerate into tyranny, the corrupt form, under which the monarch exercises all power for the benefit of himself or herself and his or her allies and ignores the good of the people.

Aristocracy is rule by the most virtuous, intelligent, and morally enlightened in the state. But this benevolent rule by an elite class can decay into oligarchy, the corrupt form. Instead of governing in the best interests of the society, the oligarchs only wish to defend their privileged positions.

Aristotle saw a polity (or constitutional democracy) as the most practical form of government because of the limitations of humankind. All citizens have a voice in the selection of leaders and the framing of the laws, but at the same time, formal constitutional procedures protect minority rights. In Aristotle's classification, democracy (the rule of the many) was a corruption of the polity and the worst form of government. Deluded into thinking that one person is as good as another, the masses in a democracy blindly follow the lead of corrupt and selfish demagogues and plunder the property of the hardworking and the capable.

The Autonomy of Subsystems.   Aristotle's classification system was used by scholars for nearly twenty-five centuries, but it is no longer satisfactory. Modern political scientists have had to create new models in order to understand a rapidly

TABLE 2.1   Aristotle's System for Classifying Governments

Who Governs	Legitimate Forms: Rule in the Interest of All	Corrupt Forms: Rule in the Interest of Selves
One	Monarchy	Tyranny
A few	Aristocracy	Oligarchy
Many	Polity	Democracy

changing world. One more recent approach identified the extent of *subsystem autonomy or pluralism* as a key feature that distinguishes one type of government from another.[12]

Every modern society contains many institutions and organizations that can be thought of as subsystems of society. Religious denominations, colleges, labor unions, industrial corporations, civic associations, political parties, and the mass media are all subsystems of a modern industrial society such as the United States or Great Britain. We can classify governments according to how much autonomy they allow these subsystems. In a pluralistic system, churches, unions, and colleges are largely free to run their own internal affairs and even try to influence government.

Totalitarian governments, such as Nazi Germany and the Soviet Union, permit little or no subsystem autonomy. As Carl J. Friedrich and Zbigniew Brzezinski pointed out, such societies have official and dogmatic ideologies to which all social institutions must adhere.[13] Thus, in the late 1930s, German churches had to reflect Nazi racial theories by trying to prove that Jesus Christ was a blond-haired, blue-eyed Aryan instead of a dark-haired, dark-eyed Jew.

Democratic or constitutional governments, on the other hand, give a high degree of independence to subsystems. Although limits are established for the conduct of any private association, a constitutional state will allow us as much autonomy as is consistent with the general well-being of the society. Thus, labor unions can strike without fear of government reprisal in the United States, except when the nation's security is affected. No subsystem has absolute freedom, but most are allowed to run their own affairs unless they threaten the public interest.

Centralization of Political Power Within the State. Governments differ not only in the degree of initiative they allow all subsystems but also in the way political power is distributed among its different levels. Nations can be classified as unitary states or federal states, depending on the way they distribute government authority.

Great Britain, France, Italy, Israel, and the vast majority of the world's 180-odd nations are unitary states. A single national or central government exercises supreme power over all areas of society and can override the decisions of local governments. Thus, the ministries in London and Paris can order Lincolnshire or Bordeaux to impose laws or programs in their localities. Such actions are unlikely in the world's twenty or so federal states. In federal nations such as the United States, Germany, Australia, and Canada, power is divided between the national government and the state or provincial governments. Usually, the national government controls foreign affairs, military defense, and currency, whereas local authorities handle education, welfare, and policing.

Modern Government: Making Public Policy

All modern governments are involved in the complex business of making public policy. Public policies, the authoritative actions (not proposals or debates) of government officials and agencies, are created to meet perceived national needs. Policies include legislation, judicial edicts, executive decrees, and administrative decisions. Policies are implemented through programs, which are specific measures aimed at influencing the direction of government activity and public life. Government adopts policies and programs consistent with the broad goals of the nation.[14] Since resources are always limited, a priority of values must be established. For example, is it more important for the United States to send a person to the moon or to rebuild our cities? Should we use public funds to clean up polluted rivers or to put additional police officers on our streets? Decision makers must face this kind of choice in formulating public policy.

The determination of national priorities involves complex decision making, which is a crucial part of the political process. In societies such as the United States, many groups lobby for policies that suit their own economic or ideological interests. The automobile industry works for increased spending for highways, and "right-to-life" groups pressure legislators into a strong stand against legalized abortions. Ultimately, the legislature and the executive must decide in the name of the people which policies the nation will pursue. If they bankroll the space program rather than public housing, they have in effect made a statement of national priorities. In this sense, the creation of public policies usually involves a public choice among competing values and needs. During the Johnson administration, the president faced a choice between spending government funds on "guns" (for the Vietnam war) or "butter" (the Great Society social program). Costs of the war had escalated so rapidly that he could no longer finance both "guns" and "butter," as he had previously hoped; "guns" received priority.

When public policies involve a choice, they are often controversial and must be defended as being in the "public interest." In theory, the public interest is defined as the benefit of everyone as opposed to one specific group of people. But in practice, this term is impossible to define and usually ends up being loosely invoked in public policy debates by all sides in an attempt to gain support for rather one-sided interpretations.

PUBLIC POLICIES: MATERIAL AND SYMBOLIC

Modern governments adopt and pursue many kinds of public policies to protect what they define as the public interest. These policies can range from extensive preparations for national defense to efforts to end racial, ethnic, and sexual discrimination in public and private agencies. All policies, however, fall into two major categories: those that are material in nature and those that are symbolic.

Material public policy decisions require the expenditure of public funds—a scarce national resource in every country. Government funds are finite. The national budget can be seen as a pie that must be divided among many hungry guests: There is only a limited amount to be distributed.

Once a national policy has been decided and a concrete legislative program has been enacted, machinery must be created to see that resources are properly distributed. For example, if Congress adopts a measure to defray hospital costs for the indigent, a government agency must determine who is eligible for such benefits. For a policy to be effective, adequate resources (both money and personnel) must be allocated to deal with the problem. If they are not, the program may disappoint the intended beneficiaries and accomplish little.

Unlike material policies, symbolic public policies usually do not involve much money or personnel and often are not a part of the legislative process. By symbolic or nonmaterial public policies is meant those acts of government that create sentimental attachments (patriotism, loyalty, deference, or national pride) or that confer social status on key segments of society. The proclamation of a new public holiday, such as for slain black civil rights leader Martin Luther King, Jr., is a symbolic policy.

As Murray Edelman pointed out in *The Symbolic Uses of Politics*, symbolic policies can be more important than actual government performance and results, for what people think often matters more than what the government really does.[15] Therefore, all governments are careful to support and foster outward symbols of national unity. Institutional symbols are created and popularized to give people something they can identify with. Thus, when Americans think of the United States, they may get an image of the Statue of Liberty, "Old Glory," or the Liberty Bell. Occasionally, such symbols can become a source of controversy: In Canada a bitter debate over a proposal for a new national flag contributed to the defeat of the Conservative party in 1963. (The maple leaf won, and is now accepted by most

Polish symbol. Three giant steel crosses at the Gdansk shipyard mark the spot where 45 workers were gunned down as they demonstrated against the regime in December 1970. This powerful symbol helped launch the Solidarity movement and bring down the Communist regime in 1989.

Canadians.) South Africa adopted a totally different flag with the advent of a black government in 1994.

Moral symbols are often invoked by public officials to build a climate supportive of the institutions in which they serve. Thus, in America, most candidates for public office like to be photographed in church, regardless of their true religious feelings, because religious worship has become a powerful moral symbol linked with national pride and stability. Few high public officials are seen smoking cigarettes in public or relaxing with a glass of scotch, and for many years it was taboo for elected officers to obtain a divorce. (Conservative Ronald Reagan, ironically, was the first divorced person to win the presidency.) Symbolic issues can become politically divisive, as in the question of prayer in public schools.

Symbols can even lead to war. When Croatia declared its independence from Yugoslavia in 1991, it restored the use of medieval Croatian currency, uniforms, and coat of arms. These old symbols made many Croats feel good, but they alarmed the Serbian minority of Croatia, for they were exactly the names and symbols used by the Croatian fascist regime of World War II, a regime that murdered some 350,000 Serbs. As a result, the Serbs of Croatia broke away with their mini-republic of Krajina, which the Croats finally retook in 1995. If the Croatian regime had been more sensitive with its symbols in 1991, it might have avoided much tragedy. Symbols can be dynamite.

Suggested Readings

BEBLER, ANTON, and JIM SEROKA, eds. *Contemporary Political Systems: Classifications and Typologies.* Boulder, CO: Lynne Rienner, 1990. Contributors from several countries offer an unusual cross-cultural attempt at the many ways to classify political systems.

BRASS, PAUL. *Ethnicity and Nationalism: Theory and Comparison.* Newbury Park, CA: Sage, 1992. The relationship between belonging to an ethnic group and how this may turn into nationalism, with several interesting case studies.

CAPORASO, JAMES A., ed. *The Elusive State: International and Comparative Perspectives.* Newbury Park, CA: Sage, 1989. The concept of "state," long disparaged by political science, here enjoys a sophisticated reappraisal by top thinkers.

CERNY, PHILIP. *The Changing Architecture of Politics: Structure, Agency, and the Future of the State.* Newbury Park, CA: Sage, 1990. Argues that the state structure is the basis of the political system and is changing profoundly in our day.

GOTTLIEB, GIDON. *Nation Against State: A New Approach to Ethnic Conflicts and the Decline of Sovereignty.* New York: Council on Foreign Relations, 1993. Beset by internal ethnic conflict, many states have seen their sovereignty wither away.

HANF, THEODOR. *Coexistence in Wartime Lebanon: Decline of a State and Rise of a Nation.* London: Centre for Lebanese Studies/I. B. Tauris, 1993. From the sufferings of a destroyed Lebanon may be emerging, at last, a sense of Lebanese nationhood.

KOHN, HANS. *Nationalism: Its Meaning and History.* New York: Crowell-Collier and Macmillan, 1955. A thorough examination of the historical development of the modern nation-state.

LIPSET, SEYMOUR MARTIN. *Revolution and Counterrevolution: Change and Persistence in Social Structures,* rev. ed. Rutgers, NJ: Transaction, 1988. A series of brilliant essays on how countries modernize, especially on the impact of values and religious beliefs.

SMITH, ANTHONY D. *National Identity.* Reno, NV: University of Nevada Press, 1993. Where does loyalty to a nation come from, and why is it crucial to modernization?

SO, ALVIN Y. *Social Change and Development: Modernization, Dependency, and World-System Theories.* Thousand Oaks, CA: Sage, 1990. A brilliant synthesis of why Third World countries develop or fail to develop.

VON BEYME, KLAUS. *America as a Model: The Impact of American Democracy in the World.* New York:

St. Martin's, 1987. A review of the history of the U.S. system as a pattern copied by others and some conjectures on the future of this system.

Notes

1. For studies of the multifaceted process of building nations in Western Europe, see Charles Tilly, ed., *The Formation of National States in Western Europe* (Princeton, NJ: Princeton University Press, 1975).

2. The most correct label for an autonomously governed territory is *nation-state,* but for purposes of simplicity, we will use the term *nation* throughout this text. The standard history of the rise of the modern nation is Hans Kohn, *Nationalism: Its Meaning and History* (New York: Crowell-Collier and Macmillan, 1955). Also useful are Karl Deutsch, *Nationalism and Social Communication: An Inquiry into the Foundations of Nationality* (New York: Wiley, 1953); Louis Snyder, *The Meaning of Nationalism* (New Brunswick, NJ: Rutgers University Press, 1954); and Seymour Martin Lipset, *The First New Nation: The United States in Historical and Comparative Perspective* (Garden City, NY: Doubleday, 1967).

3. Kohn, *Nationalism,* p. 9.

4. For treatments of non-Western nationalism and newly independent states, see Rupert Emerson, *From Empire to Nation: The Rise to Self-Assertion of Asian and African Peoples* (Cambridge, MA: Harvard University Press, 1960); David E. Apter, *The Politics of Modernization* (Chicago: University of Chicago Press, 1965); Fred R. von der Mehden, *Politics of the Developing Nations* (Englewood Cliffs, NJ: Prentice Hall, 1964); Gabriel A. Almond and James S. Coleman, *Politics of the Developing Areas* (Princeton, NJ: Princeton University Press, 1960); and John H. Kautsky, *Political Change in Underdeveloped Countries* (New York: Wiley, 1962).

5. The concept of crises in nation building was developed by Leonard Binder et al., *Crises and Sequences in Political Development* (Princeton, NJ: Princeton University Press, 1971). For historical case studies, see Raymond Grew, ed., *Crises of Political Development in Europe and the United States* (Princeton, NJ: Princeton University Press, 1978).

6. Formulated by the great American political scientist Harold Lasswell, *Politics: Who Gets What, When, How* (New York: Meridian Books, 1958).

7. For a pessimistic look at how difficult the problem is in the developing lands, see Joel S. Migdal, *Strong Societies and Weak States: State-Society Relations and State Capabilities in the Third World* (Princeton, NJ: Princeton University Press, 1988).

8. See Bruce D. Porter, *War and the Rise of the State: The Military Foundations of Modern Politics* (New York: Free Press, 1994), and Geoffrey Parker, *The Military Revolution: Military Innovation and the Rise of the West, 1500–1800,* 2nd ed. (New York: Cambridge University Press, 1996).

9. Erich Fromm, *Escape from Freedom* (New York: Holt, Rinehart & Winston, 1941).

10. John Locke, *Two Treatises of Civil Government* (London: J. M. Dent & Sons, 1924), p. 180. See also Ian Harris, *The Mind of John Locke: A Study of Political Theory in Its Intellectual Setting* (New York: Cambridge University Press, 1994).

11. The phrase is Eugen Weber's in his study of nation building under the Third French Republic, *Peasants into Frenchmen: The Modernization of Rural France, 1870–1914* (Stanford, CA: Stanford University Press, 1976).

12. Robert A. Dahl, *Modern Political Analysis,* 4th ed. (Englewood Cliffs, NJ: Prentice Hall, 1984), pp. 40–41. See also Gabriel A. Almond and G. Bingham Powell, Jr., *Comparative Policies: System, Process, and Policy.* 2nd ed. (Boston: Little, Brown, 1978), pp. 72–76.

13. Carl J. Friedrich and Zbigniew Brzezinski, *Totalitarian Dictatorship and Autocracy* (Cambridge, MA: Harvard University Press, 1965), p. 9.

14. At least in theory; Theodore Lowi, however, argues that the policies and programs of government, in practice, more often than not have little to do with any long-term visions of national goals. Instead, they tend to be rather shortsighted and stopgap measures. See Lowi's *The End of Liberalism: The Second Republic of the United States,* 2nd ed. (New York: Norton, 1979).

15. Murray Edelman, *The Symbolic Uses of Politics* (Urbana: University of Illinois Press, 1964), Chap. 1; and Murray Edelman, *Politics as Symbolic Action* (Chicago: Markham, 1971).

· 3 ·

Individuals and Constitutions

The problem of establishing and limiting power exists in every political system. Government and the people both must have certain powers and rights, but their activities must also be limited to keep them from encroaching on the rights of others. The choices involved in determining a fair balance between government powers and civil liberties, between the welfare of the majority and the rights of the minority, are not easy ones. For example, if air traffic controllers want higher wages, do they have the right to strike and inconvenience thousands of people until the federal government offers them a satisfactory raise? If Congress votes "legislative vetoes" into bills as a way to supervise the executive branch, does the Supreme Court have the right to declare them unconstitutional? If religious parents believe that children should pray in public schools, does this view conflict with the separation of church and state?

These questions raise problems of rights and political power, and some of these problems are admittedly more difficult than others. Most of us would probably agree that a Supreme Court decision is law even if Congress doesn't like it. We will probably disagree, though, on the right of air traffic controllers to strike. It can be argued that the controllers should not be denied the right to ask for higher wages simply because they perform a public service. Yet a case can also be made that no one, including overworked air traffic controllers, has the right to deny the people such an important element of public safety. The question of whether children should pray in public school is also difficult. Which prayers would suit all religions? What about children who do not wish to pray at all?

How does society determine how to limit political power and how to balance, in the most equitable fashion, the needs of the majority with the rights of individuals and minorities? Whereas decisions about who is right and who is wrong in specific cases such as those mentioned must always be made by the decision makers in office at a particular time, it is evident that governments need some guidelines in determining where this balance should fall. These guidelines are provided by traditions, by statutes, and by national constitutions, which lay down the basic ground rules for governing society.[1]

Constitutions in the Modern World

In common usage, we think of a constitution as a written document that sets forth the fundamental rules by which a society is governed. Political scientists, though, define the word more broadly: A constitution is that set of rules and customs, either written or unwritten, legally established or extralegal, by which a government conducts its affairs.[2] By this definition, all nations have constitutions since each nation operates according to some set of rules. Britain has no written constitution, but custom, law, precedent, and tradition are so strong that the British government considers itself bound by practices that have developed over the centuries. Thus, Britain is governed by a constitution.[3]

In the modern world, nearly every nation has a written constitution, which establishes the forms, institutions, and limits of government and sets guidelines for balancing minority and majority interests. The Constitution of the United States is very short. It is limited to seven articles, most of which have to do with establishing the powers of each branch of government, and twenty-six amendments. In contrast, most of the nations that have won independence since World War II have adopted constitutions of remarkable detail.[4] The post-war Japanese constitution, which was drafted by the U.S. military government after World War II, contains no less than forty separate articles outlining the rights and duties of the people alone.

Among the individual rights enumerated are the rights to productive employment, a decent standard of living, and social welfare benefits—a sharp contrast to the general values of "justice, domestic tranquillity, common defense, general welfare, and liberty" outlined in the American Preamble. Article I of the German constitution (the Basic Law) also enumerates a long list of rights. These include not only fundamental rights, such as legal and political freedoms, but also a number of social and economic safeguards, including state supervision of the educational system and public control of the economy.

If an established nation such as Britain is able to get by with no written constitution per se, and if another, such as the United States, manages to function with a very general constitution, why has almost every recently established nation (with the exception of Israel) found it necessary to commit itself to not only a written constitution but a very detailed constitution at that?

THE HIGHEST LAW OF THE LAND

Most modern nations adopt written constitutions for the same reason that the ancient Mesopotamian lawgiver Hammurabi codified the laws of Babylon: to establish a supreme law of the land. Constitutions state the fundamental laws of society and are not meant to be easily revised. They stand as a yardstick by which any activities of the government or the people are to be measured.[5] A legislature can pass a law one year and repeat it the next, but basic constitutional provisions cannot be amended so easily.[6] In Sweden, constitutional amendments must be passed by two successive legislatures, with a general election in between. In the United States, amending the Constitution is even more difficult. The most common procedure is to secure the approval of two-thirds of both the Senate and the House of Representatives, then obtain ratification by three-fourths of the state legislatures. The fact that our Constitution has been amended only sixteen times since the adoption of the Bill of Rights in 1791 illustrates how difficult the amendment procedure is. The Equal Rights Amendment failed to pass in 1983, for example, because fewer than three-fourths of the state legislatures voted to ratify it.

The General Nature of Constitutional Law.   Since constitutions, no matter how detailed, cannot provide specifically for every legal or administrative problem that may arise, they must be fairly general in nature. The United States Constitution says that "Congress shall make no law respecting an establishment of religion, or prohibiting the free exercise thereof" in Amendment I of the Bill of Rights. This is a very general statement. The way it will be interpreted in a specific case (such as the question of prayer in school or perhaps a satanic cult that believes that animal sacrifice or illegal drugs are necessary for the practice of their religion) must depend on the decision makers in power at the time the case arises.

Constitutional law must be interpreted to be applied to specific incidents. Who is given the immense authority to decide what the general wording of a constitution means? In some thirty nations, including the United States, this responsibility belongs to the highest national court. The procedure by which the court rules on the constitutionality of a government act and declares null and void those acts it considers unconstitutional is known as judicial review.[7] The power of judicial review is a controversial one. Many critics have accused the Supreme Court (most notably when Earl Warren was chief justice from 1953 to 1969) of imposing a personal philosophy as the law of the land. To a large extent, a constitution is indeed what its interpreters say it is, but the possibility of too subjective an interpretation seems to be a necessary risk taken by any nation that has one.[8]

The courts do not always interpret a constitution in a consistent fashion. In the United States, the Warren Court best exemplified the type of judicial philosophy generally known as "judicial activism." This does not necessarily mean "liberal." It refers to a judge's willingness to strike down certain laws and practices in order to guarantee citizens' rights. The opposite is that of "judicial restraint"—a generalization that describes a Supreme Court that sees its job not as legislating but as following the lead of Congress. Justices Oliver Wendell Holmes and Felix Frankfurter, who counseled the Court on judicial restraint, were regarded by many as great liberals.

Likewise, Germany's Federal Constitutional Court is no stranger to controversy. Modeled after the U.S. Supreme Court—except that it has sixteen justices—the German court is mandated to make sure all laws conform to the Basic Law. In 1975, the German court found that a law permitting abortions conflicted with the strong right-to-life provisions of the Basic Law—which had been put in to repudiate the horrors of the Nazi era—and declared abortion unconstitutional. In 1979, the Federal Constitutional Court found there was nothing unconstitutional about "worker codetermination"—that is, employees having nearly the same rights as owners and managers in determining the long-term future of businesses.

Few nations give their highest court the power to rule on the constitutionality of laws. In nations that do not have a clearly established procedure of judicial review, this responsibility is often given to the legislature. In Great Britain, Parliament itself makes the final determination of what is constitutional.

Constitutions and Constitutional Government. The meaning of a constitution depends largely on the way in which it is interpreted. Indeed, two separate nations could conceivably adopt the same constitution (with a few variations in wording or language) but have entirely different forms of government and allow their citizens very different rights. What is written in the constitution does not necessarily occur in practice. The Constitution of the Soviet Union set a framework for that nation's government—a federal system with a bicameral legislature, with executive and administrative powers given to the cabinetlike Council of Ministers—and accorded to its citizens a long list of democratic rights.[9] Yet in actuality, the government was controlled by the Communist party, with little authority given to the states or to the legislature, and rights were totally dependent on the interpretation of the leaders in power.

The governments of Canada, Great Britain, and the United States are constitutional governments; the government of the Soviet Union was not, although former party chief Mikhail Gorbachev may have been trying to make it more constitutional. Constitutionalism refers to the degree to which the power of government is limited and individual rights are respected. In a constitutionally governed nation (whether it has a written constitution or not), government is limited by internal institutions in such a way that the fundamental rights of citizens—such as freedom of speech, the right to practice one's religion, and freedom from arbitrary imprisonment—are safeguarded from violation by either government or hostile minorities. In contrast, an authoritarian government is not limited by the guidelines of the constitution. In this government, the individual citizen and minority groups are assured no protection against arbitrary acts of government, in spite of what the constitution may say.

THE PURPOSE OF A CONSTITUTION

If many nations seem to pay no heed to what is written in their constitutions, why do some nations bother to write a constitution at all? Constitutions fulfill a variety of roles: They provide the symbolic function of putting in writing a statement of national ideals, they formalize the structure of government, and they attempt to justify the government's right to govern.

A Statement of National Ideals.   According to the Preamble of the U.S. Constitution, our nation is dedicated to six goals: to form a more perfect union, to establish justice, to ensure domestic tranquillity, to provide for the common defense, to promote the general welfare, and to secure the blessings of liberty. The Soviet constitution proclaimed the Soviet Union to be a "developed socialist society" dedicated to building a classless utopia. The constitution of the Federal Republic of Germany, seeking to divest the nation of any traces of Nazi rule, states its determination to "serve the peace of the world" and expressly proclaims that no group of people can be stripped of their German citizenship—a reaction to Hitler's Nuremburg Laws, which declared hundreds of thousands of citizens to be non-citizens.

Preambles and lists of rights are symbolic statements: They indicate the values, ideas, and goals that seem to best express the spirit of the national political culture. But the value statements in preambles are by nature very general and have no legal force. How are they interpreted? What does the U.S. Constitution mean by a "more perfect union," for example? There is considerable disagreement over this question; in fact, debate over the meaning of this term led to the Civil War a century ago. What does the Constitution mean by "establishing justice"? What is justice, and is it the same for all citizens? If American blacks have been denied equal rights for two centuries, does this mean that it is just for them to be given an advantage now in admission to colleges, in hiring practices, or in securing low-rent housing? Or, again, what does the Preamble mean by "promoting general welfare"? The questions of what the general welfare is and how it is to be balanced against the rights of the individual or of a minority group are almost certain to produce different answers from everyone. Are children who wish to pray formally in school setting a precedent disruptive to the general welfare? Do laws allowing private citizens to purchase handguns like the "Saturday-night special," which are not accurate enough to have any legitimate use for hunting or target practice, harm the general welfare, even though the Bill of Rights seems to give citizens the right to bear arms?

Although constitutions provide a statement of national ideals, the interpretation of these goals and values necessitates an active choice by the decision makers of government.

Formalizes the Structure of Government.   In addition to acting as a symbolic statement of national values, a constitution is also a blueprint. It is a written description of who does what in government, defining the authority and limiting the powers of each branch and providing for regularized channels through which conflict may be resolved. Articles I through III of the U.S. Constitution outline the duties of Congress, the president, and the judiciary. Congress may collect taxes and customs duties but is prohibited from taxing exports. The president is named commander in chief of the armed forces but must have the "advice and consent" of the Senate to conclude treaties. In a system in which there is separation of powers, the constitution divides authority and responsibilities among the various branches of government; it also limits the power of each branch. No other constitution uses "checks and balances" like the American one in an elaborate attempt to limit power; most, in fact, specify the unification of power.

A constitution also outlines the division of power between central and regional governments in a federal state. In a federal system of government, powers and responsibilities are divided between one national government and several regional or state governments. Germany and Australia, like the United States, are federal states. Their constitutions give their central governments control over certain areas of responsibility, such as foreign policy, foreign commerce, and coinage. Thus, the *Land* of Bavaria in the Federal Republic of Germany may not sign a treaty with Austria; neither may the state of Texas mint its own currency. Whereas certain powers are delegated to the central government, the constitution leaves others to the states. In the U.S. Constitution, this division is a general one; any powers not accorded to the central government are reserved for the states and for the people. Thus, the states traditionally control education, police protection, health and welfare services, and local commerce. Of course, this division of power has become less clear-cut, especially in recent years, as the federal government has taken on a greater share of financing the operations of education, health, welfare, housing, and scores of other services. But in spite of federal control of many of the purse strings, the states still retain predominant control of these powers.

Establishes the Legitimacy of Government.   A third role of a constitution is to give a government the stamp of legitimacy. Although this function is undeniably symbolic, its practical utility cannot be denied. Many nations in the world community will not even recognize a new state until it has adopted a written constitution; it is a sign of permanence and responsibility.

Most constitutions were written shortly after revolutionary upheavals, and their purpose was to help establish the new regime's right to rule. The Articles of Confederation and subsequently the Constitution symbolized American independence by replacing British authority with tangible evidence of a new government.

The French constitution of 1791 (which never went into effect) tried to replace the divine right of Louis XVI with the sovereign right of the people. And the first Soviet constitution of 1918 established a "dictatorship of the people" to replace tsarist rule. Constitutions proclaim the values of a new regime while also establishing in writing a permanent outline for the organization of government. As a symbolic statement of intentions with a practical outline of structure, a constitution helps to set the stamp of legitimacy on a new regime. This is the primary reason why almost every nation, and especially new nations established since World War II, have adopted constitutions almost as soon as they have gained independence.

Of course, a written constitution is not absolutely necessary for a legitimate, stable regime. Neither Great Britain nor Israel has found it necessary to commit all their fundamental precepts and laws to writing in one document. Britain's constitution consists of many documents, such as the Magna Carta, the Petition of Rights, and the Bill of Rights; judicial decisions, which have established precedents of common law; major acts of Parliament; and customs and traditions that have grown over the centuries. Israel's constitution is also an accumulated body of documents and precedents, some of which date back to biblical times.

Even in nations that have written constitutions, there are countless traditions, customs, and laws that are also a part of the constitutional order. For instance, no mention is made of political parties anywhere in the U.S. Constitution. Yet our party system is an established part of the American political process; indeed, a change in the party system would very likely change the entire American political structure.[10] Judicial precedents and government traditions, too, make up the fundamental laws of society. Thus, the body of constitutional law encompasses a wide variety of documents and traditions in all nations, whether they have "written" or "unwritten" constitutions.

The Adaptability of the Constitution

THE UNITED STATES CONSTITUTION

In 1789, when the American Constitution was adopted, the world was far different from what it is today. The United States was primarily agrarian, needing little in the way of technological services. The communications network was limited to little-read newspapers and pamphlets, and mostly to word of mouth. There were no skyscrapers, automobiles, pollution, or internet systems. How can a constitution that was written to fill the needs of such a primitive world be adapted to the highly industrialized, urbanized, crime-ridden society of modern America? A look at the way in which the Constitution has adapted in two major areas of change—the "right to bear arms" in a violent society and the growth of "big government" in the twentieth century—might give some insight into the flexibility of this document.

The Right to Bear Arms.   In 1789, the United States was a sparsely settled frontier nation where people often literally had to fight for their lives. Guns were necessary to the settlers' survival, and the Constitution reflected this requirement. Amendment II of the Bill of Rights (adopted in 1791) guarantees the right of the citizens to "keep and bear arms."

Today the United States is no longer sparsely settled: It is highly urbanized. Guns are no longer necessary to the average citizen's survival; instead, they add fuel to the fire in an already tense and violent society. In recent decades we have witnessed the assassinations of President John F. Kennedy, Dr. Martin Luther King, Jr., and Senator Robert F. Kennedy. President Ronald Reagan and Alabama Governor George Wallace were seriously wounded by would-be assassins. Armed robbery and killings by drug dealers have reached alarming proportions. As a result, many concerned citizens argue that the age of the frontier has long since passed and that it is time to restrict drastically the sale of lethal weapons. Yet opponents of gun-control legislation argue that the Constitution ensures the right of every citizen to purchase and own firearms. Hunters, shopkeepers who find themselves constant victims of armed robberies, and those who may feel their persons or property are in danger but cannot secure full-time protection from the police all argue that their constitutional right to pursue a hobby or to protect their very lives will be jeopardized by gun-control legislation.

The "right to bear arms" case illustrates that a two-century-old constitution— at least in its traditional interpretation—may not provide the right answer for all of the needs of modern society.[11] If gun controls are necessary to limit violence in America (and there is by no means consensus on the issue), can the Constitution be interpreted to allow such legislation to be passed? The Constitution is written in very general terms; it lends itself to the interpretations dictated by the times. Amendment II reads, "A well regulated Militia, being necessary to the security of a free State, the right of the people to keep and bear Arms, shall not be infringed." Does this mean that the citizens can own guns privately or that they can own guns for the purpose of maintaining a militia, what we now call the National Guard? Due in large part to handguns, the U.S. murder rate is four to five times higher than European murder rates and three times higher than the Canadian rate.

The Constitution has other clauses that make it flexible enough to keep up with changing times. The so-called elastic clause gives Congress the power to enact all legislation necessary and proper to carry out its enumerated powers. Under this clause, too, the Constitution might be interpreted to mean that Congress can impose restrictions on the people's right to bear arms. So the general nature of the eighteenth-century Constitution does allow it to adapt to an age of violence even when it gives citizens the right to bear arms. How has the Constitution adapted to the more general shift from the sharp division between federal and state powers envisioned by the Founding Fathers to the highly centralized "big government" of the late twentieth century?

The Shift in the Federal Balance of Power.   The role of the central government has grown markedly in relation to the powers of the state governments since the era of the New Deal in the 1930s. This shift in balance stems partly from the changing needs caused by the Great Depression, which left around 12 million people out of work. They needed assistance in finding housing and in feeding their families, and the states could not afford to provide all of these services. In response, the federal government took on a broader range of education, welfare, health, and housing services than ever before, and this responsibility has grown since then. With the recent fiscal crises, which have hit all areas of American society from the cities to the farms, and with the great increase in the need for funds for environmental cleanup and the war on drugs and an endless list of other services, the role of the central government has continued to expand.

The writers of the American Constitution never envisioned that the federal government would someday take on the tasks of feeding welfare clients, licensing communications networks, financing chemical and atomic research, or building highways. They assumed that the basic balance of power between state and central governments would remain relatively stable, and that this balance would be quite even (or weighted more heavily toward the states). How has the document they wrote been able to adapt to the centralized system of modern American federalism?

As it has been able to adapt to the growing undesirability of making the right to own firearms a basic right, so, too, the Constitution has been able to adapt to the increased role of the central government. Whereas the powers of the federal government have expanded into areas that the Founding Fathers couldn't possibly have foreseen, the writers of the Constitution did have the foresight to realize that the nation would experience many changes and would develop many needs which they couldn't specifically provide for in the document. So the Constitution was written in a deliberately flexible form, and the result is that it can still be interpreted to fit the needs of modern society and government. Feeding welfare clients and financing scientific research can both be seen as promoting the general welfare (atomic and scientific research also helps to provide for the common defense), and licensing communications networks falls under the powers granted to the Congress to lay and collect taxes and to regulate commerce.

THE ADAPTABILITY OF CONSTITUTIONS: CAN THEY ENSURE RIGHTS?

The case of the right to bear arms illustrates that a constitution written for one age may not always provide the best solutions for another age. If this is the case, and if constitutions must constantly be reinterpreted to keep up with the times, how can they ensure the rights of citizens?

Civil Liberties and Civil Rights.   In the 1930s, Joseph Stalin imprisoned some 20 million Soviet citizens in labor camps. Another 15 million or so were killed for resisting his agricultural collectivization program. At about the same time, Heinrich Himmler, at Adolf Hitler's behest, began organizing scientifically designed concentration camps, which would systematically exterminate thousands of lives every hour of the day. And halfway around the world, the Japanese armies of Hideki Tojo were raping and pillaging their way through China. After the war, the Chinese Communists under Mao killed countless millions of their countrymen.

In reaction to the outrages of World War II, the world community took steps to try to prevent any future tragedies of such great magnitude. In 1948, the General Assembly of the United Nations adopted the Universal Declaration on Human Rights to guarantee basic rights to all the citizens of the world. As a symbolic statement of world opinion (with no real power of sanction), the Universal Declaration establishes fundamental precepts and ideals which most nations are reluctant to violate. Of course, if a nation does choose to violate the "universal rights" named in the declaration, there is little anyone can do, short of war, to stop them. The Universal Declaration's value is symbolic.

The Universal Declaration, patterned on the French Declaration of the Rights of Man and Citizen, and on the American Declaration of Independence and the Bill of Rights, affirms the basic civil and human rights thought by most Western political thinkers to be fundamental. It declares that all people have certain rights that government may not arbitrarily take away.[12] These include the rights to life, free assembly, freedom of expression, freedom of movement, freedom of religion, and freedom to participate in the political process by voting or holding office. In addition to the list of civil and political rights, the Universal Declaration provides for many of the economic and cultural needs of citizens of every land. It specifies that the rights to work and to receive equal pay for equal work; the right to an education; the right to marry, raise a family, and provide that family with a decent standard of living; and the right to live according to one's culture are the heritage of every citizen. The Universal Declaration is not the only international list of fundamental rights and liberties: the Organization of American States and the Council of Europe have also published similar documents.

The overwhelming sentiment of the civilized world favors equal rights for all. Yet in spite the lofty declarations that have been published, the fact is that rights and liberties are difficult to define, and all nations restrict civil liberties in some way. The problem of minority groups is almost universally applicable as a case in point.

Minority Groups and Civil Liberties. Of the more than 180 nations that make up the world community, few are homogeneous. Most have citizens with a variety of racial, ethnic, religious, cultural, or linguistic backgrounds, and as a result, nearly every nation has at least one minority group whose civil or cultural liberties are compromised to some extent. Haitians living in Florida or Chicanos living in New Mexico are at a disadvantage unless they speak a language foreign to their culture.[13] Indians and Pakistanis in Great Britain must conform to a way of life far different from what they are accustomed to. It is the minority group that must adjust itself to the ways of the majority.

The Universal Declaration states that minorities have the right to preserve their cultural uniqueness. But to make a statement such as this and to carry it through are two different things. Most difficult is defining exactly who or what a minority group is (Can black militants speak for African-Americans? Can the radical Jewish Defense League speak for American Jews?) and what its rights should be in a state controlled by a dominant group with different interests. It was easy to condemn South Africa because its discrimination against blacks was open and blatant.

But nations that grant all citizens a theoretical equality before the law may discriminate against minorities in other, more subtle ways. If German-speaking South Tyrolians are forced to use the Italian language, is their cultural heritage being stifled? Should Spanish Basques be permitted to set up their own school systems to teach their children about their heritage? If so, should African-Americans be permitted to do the same, with state funding? What of Spanish-speaking Puerto Ricans in New York, or Mexican-Americans in the Southwest, or Italian-Americans? Assimilation of minority groups involves a compromise of traditions and culture and, therefore, sometimes one of equal rights. But is also true that a state that does not assimilate its minorities stands little chance of remaining stable. Thus, despite the Universal Declaration's denunciation of discrimination against minorities, some discrimination is inevitable in every society.

In 1942, for example, some 120,000 Japanese-Americans on the West Coast were interned under the infamous Executive Order 9066. Robbed of their homes, businesses, and liberty without due process of law, they were sent to ramshackle, dusty camps surrounded by barbed wire and guard towers—in some ways similar to Nazi concentration camps. Not one case of disloyalty was ever demonstrated against a Japanese-American; they were victims of racism and wartime hysteria.[14] German- and Italian-Americans suffered no such suspicions or punishment. Even Secretary of War Henry L. Stimson, who signed the order, feared it "would make a tremendous hole in our Constitution." It did, but not until 1983 did a federal court overturn the legality of internment.[15] The incident shows that even a well-established democracy can throw its civil liberties out the window in a moment of exaggerated and groundless panic. The 442nd Regimental Combat Team, recruited from Japanese-Americans, covered itself with glory and was the most decorated U.S. unit of World War II.

Freedom of Expression in the United States

"Congress shall make no law . . . abridging the freedom of speech, or of the press; or the right of the people peaceably to assemble, and to petition the government for a redress of grievances." So says Amendment I of the U.S. Bill of Rights. We think of freedom of expression as one of the hallmarks of any nation calling itself democratic. Citizens who think the president or prime minister is ruining a nation's economy have every right to say so to whomever they wish. And a surrealist antigovernment film should draw no interference or investigation from any agencies of government.

But although freedom of expression seems at first glance to be a straight-forward guarantee, it is not that simple. Does freedom of speech give a campus bigot the right to incite hatred of African-American students? Does a newspaper have a right to publish information that might damage the security of the nation? Whereas we may all believe in the right of free expression, most of us would agree that this does not mean that anyone can say or write whatever one wants, whenever one wants, regardless of the consequences. In the example used by Justice Oliver Wendell Holmes, nobody should be permitted to yell "Fire!" in a crowded theater unless there really is a fire. Free speech does not necessarily include the right to spread dangerous or malicious falsehoods. Likewise, free speech does not include the right to call police to advise them that there is a bomb in city hall when there is not.

According to Justice Holmes, freedom of expression must also be restricted in cases in which statements or publications present a "clear and present danger" of bringing about "substantive evils," which Congress has a right to prevent. The Supreme Court in its 1925 *Gitlow* v. *New York* decisions also upheld the conviction of a radical who had called for the violent overthrow of the government on the grounds that his words had represented a "bad tendency," which could "corrupt morals, incite crime, and disturb the public peace."

The questions of what presents a "clear and present danger" and what is a "substantive evil" are, of course, open to very subjective interpretation. Many people today would see no danger in publicly advocating the violent overthrow of the government. And so the interpretation of the meaning of the constitutional guarantee of freedom of expression has varied considerably over the years since the Bill of Rights was adopted.[16]

Controversies relating to free speech are never-ending. In 1994, in another First Amendment case, the Supreme Court struck down the ordinance of a posh suburb prohibiting homeowners from posting political signs on their property. Recently, some have argued that free speech has gone too far, especially if it deals in racism and pornography or throttles others' speech in the name of "political correctness."[17]

A HISTORY OF FREEDOM OF EXPRESSION

Free Speech and Sedition.   Sedition is defined in the common law as any criticism of the government or government officials designed to produce discontent or rebellion among the populace. The charge of sedition has been used by the American government to suppress some forms of radical expression during several periods of our history since the adoption of the Bill of Rights.

Congress enacted the first Sedition Act in 1798, after the infamous XYZ affair. The law was aimed at the "Jacobins," as American defenders of the French Revolution were called, at a time when the United States was in an undeclared naval war with France. The Sedition Act was supposed to expire the day that President John Adams left office (a curious coincidence, which indicates that its raison d´être may have also had something to do with the election contest). The act aroused controversy, but it lapsed without any test of constitutionality in the Supreme Court. The next Sedition Act went into effect during the Civil War, when President Lincoln acted under the war powers vested in his office to suppress Northern opponents of the Union effort. The president's action was brought to the Supreme Court, which declined to judge on the legality of his actions. Whereas the action went untested, all "political prisoners" were pardoned at the end of the war. It was not until the twentieth century that another sedition act was passed in an attempt to tighten national security during World War I.

Twentieth-Century Sedition Acts.   It was the Espionage Act of 1917 that gave rise to Justice Holmes's "clear and present danger" doctrine. At a time when socialists and pacifists were urging people to protest U.S. involvement in World War I by refusing to serve in the army and to disrupt the war effort in other ways, this act prohibited any attempts to interfere with the military recruitment policies of the U.S. government. The Espionage Act resulted in several court cases in 1919. In one case, the Supreme Court upheld the law on the grounds that free speech could be restricted if it created a "clear and present danger" to national security.[18] And so several hundred people, including Socialist party leader Eugene Debs, were imprisoned under the act, but most were pardoned as soon as the war ended.

More recent sedition acts have been directed primarily against Communists. The Smith Act of 1940, the most comprehensive sedition act ever passed by Congress, made it a crime to advocate the violent overthrow of the government, to distribute literature urging such an overthrow, or to knowingly join any organization or group that advocated such actions. The Smith Act aroused much controversy but was not put to a constitutional test until 1951, when the Supreme Court upheld the convictions of the leaders of the American Communist party even though they had not been charged with any overt acts of force against the government. "It is the existence of the conspiracy which constitutes the danger," ruled Chief Justice Vinson, "not the presence or absence of overt action." Since then, there have been other court rulings on the constitutionality of the Smith Act, and they have fluctuated. In *Yates* v. *the United States* in 1957, the Warren Court reversed the conviction of the American Communist party leaders on the grounds that there was no overt action, only abstract advocacy of rebellion.[19] Four years later, in *Scales* v. *the United States*, the Court upheld the section of the Smith Act that makes membership in the Communist party illegal—but this ruling also specified that it is active membership, involving the direct intent to bring about the violent overthrow of the government, that is criminal. The Court was careful to point out that membership per se was not made illegal by the Smith Act.

Probably the most stringent legislation ever enacted in our history to counter the threat of Communist subversion was passed during the McCarthy era after World War II. The McCarran Act of 1950 (the Internal Security Act) barred Communists from working for the federal government or in defense-related industries, established a Subversive Activities Control Board (SACB) to enforce the act, and required organizations declared by the SACB to be Communist-influenced to register with the attorney general. The McCarran Act aroused a great deal of controversy. Its critics charged that the law not only encroached on the rights of free speech and free assembly but also violated the self-incrimination clause of the Fifth Amendment. Although the Internal Security Act in its entirety has never been declared unconstitutional, every action by the SACB demanding specific organizational or individual registration with the attorney general's office has been declared unconstitutional. Finally, with the realization on all sides that the SACB was accomplishing nothing, it was abolished in 1973.

The history of legislative action against sedition in the United States indicates that the guarantees of the First Amendment have been interpreted to mean different things at different periods, varying according to both the general aura of na-

Bizarre but legal, this peace vigil, in Lafayette Park across from the
White House since 1981, urges people to turn from war to God. In a
democracy, even slightly eccentric demonstrations are tolerated.

tional security and the president, Congress, and Supreme Court in power at the
time. The Supreme Court recognizes the danger of subversion, and it acknowl-
edges that government must have some powers to restrict the freedoms of expression and assembly for the preservation of society as a whole. But its interpretation
of what is subversive has fluctuated. Whereas recent decisions have leaned toward
the free exercise of liberties wherever possible, many of the decisions of earlier periods have been more protective of the state's security. It is almost impossible to
find a balance between the state's need to safeguard its own security and the exercise of free expression and free assembly. And so the courts have never been able
to produce a definitive statement on the extent to which government may restrict
freedom of speech.

Government by Constitution: Does It Guarantee Anything?

In the quick look we have taken at constitutions, two observations are striking.
First, almost every nation in the world has adopted a written constitution. Second,
in spite of the almost universal use of written constitutions, the documents must depend to a very great extent on the interpretation given them by whoever is in
power. After the Soviet Union adopted its 1936 constitution, which enumerated a

long list of democratic rights for its citizens, Stalin proceeded to strip those rights. And even in the United States, it is strikingly apparent that the freedoms of speech and free assembly have meant very different things at different times in our history, depending on the president, the Congress, the courts, the climate of American public attitude, and the general air of national security (or lack of it) which reign at the moment.

The primary purpose of constitutions is not to provide inflexible guarantees of human rights. Indeed, there is sound reasoning behind the argument that a citizen's wartime rights should be different from his or her peacetime liberties, for during periods of war the national security may be threatened and may require extra measures of protection. Nor is the primary purpose of constitutions to outline a structure for the organization of the government. The government of the Soviet Union could hardly be recognized from its description in that nation's constitution; and the federal system of the United States is a far cry from that envisioned by the writers of the Constitution.

Whereas in some countries, such as the United States, the constitution is the supreme law of the land, in almost all societies, written constitutions are more appropriately viewed as expressions of intention and ideals; they are embodiments of the highest goals of a people. A developing nation often feels that it must impose restrictions on its citizens' right to publish criticism of government, even though its constitution gives them the right of freedom of the press. The United States may have placed restrictions on free speech during World War I, but this action reflected the prevailing opinion that there was a need for tightened national security rather than an all-out abandonment of the ideal of free expression. Because the needs of a nation vary so sharply between periods of war and peace and of depression and prosperity, the function of a constitution must be symbolically rather than literally binding. And as a symbolic statement, its utility seems unquestionably to be borne out by its popularity. It is an accepted (if not quite universal) document of a nation's legitimacy in the modern world. Its ultimate test is what is practiced, not what is written.

Suggested Readings

ACKERMAN, BRUCE. *We the People. Vol. 1: Foundations.* Cambridge, MA: Harvard University Press, 1992. A Yale professor of law and political science argues that U.S. constitutional democracy is quite different from the European types.

BAILYN, BERNARD, ed. *The Debate on the Constitution: Federalist and Antifederalist Speeches, Articles, and Letters During the Struggle Over Ratification.* New York: Library of America, 1993. Massive study of how difficult and close it was to get the U.S. Constitution accepted.

BURNS, JAMES MACGREGOR, and STEWART BURNS. *A People's Charter: The Pursuit of Rights in America.* New York: Knopf, 1992. A noted scholar

and his son explore the incomplete nature of U.S. political and civil rights.

FREEDEN, MICHAEL. *Rights.* Minneapolis: University of Minnesota Press, 1991. Explores how what we call rights actually become rights.

GIGLIO, ERNEST. *Rights, Liberties and Public Policy.* Brookfield, VT: Avebury, 1995. An interesting comparison of British and U.S. civil rights and their political ramifications.

GRAHAM, HUGH DAVIS. *The Civil Rights Era: Origins and Development of National Policy, 1960-1972.* New York: Oxford University Press, 1990. The long and difficult struggle to implement equal rights for African-Americans and women.

Levy, Leonard W. *Seasoned Judgments: The American Constitution, Rights, and History.* New Brunswick, NJ: Transaction, 1994. A top scholar demonstrates "original intent" of Framers is ambiguous and insufficient for applying the Constitution.

Lewis, Anthony. *Make No Law: The Sullivan Case and the First Amendment.* New York: Random House, 1991. The famous 1960 libel case that changed and broadened freedom of speech.

Murphy, Paul L. *The Shaping of the First Amendment, 1791 to the Present.* New York: Oxford University Press, 1991. An excellent overview of the six rights guaranteed by the First Amendment.

Smolla, Rodney A. *Free Speech in an Open Society.* New York: Knopf, 1992. A noted First Amendment specialist explores and worries about some recent controversies and cases.

Tribe, Laurence A., and Michael C. Dorf. *On Reading the Constitution.* Cambridge, MA: Harvard University Press, 1991. A review and critique of various ways to interpret the Constitution.

Walker, Samuel. *In Defense of American Liberties: A History of The ACLU.* New York: Oxford University Press, 1991. The difficult but largely successful path of the American Civil Liberties Union since its founding in 1920.

Notes

1. See Charles H. McIlwain, *Constitutionalism Ancient and Modern* (Ithaca, NY: Cornell University Press, 1940); William G. Andrews, *Constitutions and Constitutionalism* (Princeton, NJ: Van Nostrand, 1961); and Herbert J. Spiro, *Government by Constitution* (New York: Random House, 1959).

2. See Francis D. Wormuth. *The Origins of Modern Constitutionalism* (New York: Harper & Brothers, 1949), p. 3.

3. See the famous work of Walter Bagehot, *The English Constitution* (New York: Oxford University Press, 1936).

4. The best compilation is Robert L. Maddex, *Constitutions of the World* (Washington, DC: CQ Books, 1995).

5. K. C. Wheare, *Modern Constitutions,* 2nd ed. (New York: Oxford University Press, 1966), Chap. 6.

6. Britain is a notable exception. Parliamentary procedures can be changed by a simple legislative majority and the monarch's approval. The fact that they never have been changed without prolonged debate can be used to argue the point that truly constitutional rules need not be committed to writing. See Spiro, *Government by Constitution,* p. 390.

7. Actually, the U.S. Constitution does not specifically give the Supreme Court the authority to rule acts of Congress unconstitutional. The precedent was set in 1803, when the Supreme Court under Chief Justice John Marshall declared a section of the 1789 Judiciary Act to be unconstitutional in the case of *Marbury v. Madison.* Thomas Jefferson, Andrew Jackson, and Abraham Lincoln all expressed the view that the Supreme Court was not the sole or final arbiter of constitutionality. However, it has been commonly recognized as such since the Civil War. See David Deener, "Judicial Review in Modern Constitutional Systems," *American Political Science Review* 46 (December 1952), 1079-99; also see William H. Riker, *Democracy in the United States* (New York: Macmillan, 1965).

8. See Leonard W. Levy, *Original Intent and the Framers' Constitution* (New York: Macmillan, 1988).

9. See Robert Sharlet, *The New Soviet Constitution of 1977: Analysis and Text* (Brunswick, OH: King's Court Communications, 1978).

10. See the discussion in Seymour Martin Lipset, *The First New Nation: The United States in Historical and Comparative Perspective* (Garden City, NY: Doubleday, 1967), Chap. 9.

11. See Robert J. Spitzer, *The Politics of Gun Control* (Chatham, NJ: Chatham House, 1995).

12. For an exploration of human rights, see Jack Donnelly and Rhoda E. Howard, eds., *International Handbook of Human Rights* (Westport, CT: Greenwood, 1987).

13. On the question of an official U.S. language, see Bill Piatt, *Only English? Law and Language Policy in the United States* (Albuquerque: University of New Mexico Press, 1990).

14. Peter Irons, *Justice at War* (New York: Oxford University Press, 1983).

15. See Peter Irons, ed., *Justice Delayed: The Record of the Japanese American Internment Cases* (Middletown, CT: Wesleyan University Press, 1989).

16. For accounts of the Supreme Court and First Amendment rights, see Robert L. Cord, *Protest, Dissent and the Supreme Court* (Cambridge, MA: Winthrop, 1971).

17. See Stanley Fish, *There's No Such Thing as*

Free Speech: And It's a Good Thing, Too (New York: Oxford University Press, 1993), Catharine A. MacKinnon, *Only Words* (Cambridge, MA: Harvard University Press, 1993), and Cass R. Sunstein, *Democracy and the Problem of Free Speech* (New York: Free Press, 1993).

18.   For an application of the "clear and present danger" rule to the case of some World War I anarchists, see Richard Polenberg, *Fighting* *Faiths: The Abrams Case, the Supreme Court, and Free Speech* (New York: Penguin, 1988).

19.   For accounts of the Warren Court and the First Amendment, see Milton R. Konvitz, *Expanding Liberties* (New York: Viking Press, 1966); and Philip B. Kurland, *Politics, the Constitution and the Warren Court* (Chicago: University of Chicago Press, 1970).

· 4 ·

Democracy, Totalitarianism, and Authoritarianism

In 1949, after many years of reflection on totalitarianism, George Orwell startled the public with his publication of *1984,* a thinly disguised portrayal of life in the Soviet Union in particular and in totalitarian societies in general. In this nightmare, individuals have no rights, only obligations. The government may spy on them, arrest them, and interrogate at will; television cameras monitor the streets, scan public places, and peer into homes. The purpose of this unrelenting surveillance is to make sure that everyone is under the state's control—even in private thoughts. The media are controlled carefully, and the people are told only what the government wants them to know. Every citizen needs the state's permission to marry, to bear children, and to change jobs or places of residence. Citizens are creatures of the state.

Perhaps the most extreme opposite we can find in the annals of history is the traditional image of life in Athens during the fifth century B.C. Here, all adult male citizens had the right to attend the General Assembly, which met ten times a year. Regardless of his wealth or social standing, each man's vote carried the same weight. The Assembly enacted all laws, elected the state's officers, and could compel the state's leaders to appear before it to justify their actions. Decisions of the Assembly were reached by a simple majority vote. In general, the individual had a role in the decision-making processes of state and was thereby accorded an important, if intangible, sense of dignity and human worth.

George Orwell's picture of totalitarianism and the Athenian ideal of democracy are at opposite ends of the spectrum of governmental power, and in between are many variations. Table 4.1 shows the principal gradations from perfect democracy to perfect totalitarianism and lists some characteristics typical of each of the systems. The table follows the custom in countries adhering to the Western political tradition (such as the United States) of classifying nations generally as either "democratic" or "nondemocratic"—the democratic nations having governments with limited powers, and the nondemocratic ones having governments with more or less unlimited power over citizens.

As with all attempts at generalization, the effort to list general characteristics for government systems in Table 4.1 cannot be wholly successful. There is no "average" democratic state or "average" nondemocratic state. Even Athens's democracy fell far short of being a perfect democracy, for most of the population—women, resident aliens, and slaves—were excluded from participation in the political process, and effective control actually belonged to an elite. The various characteristics listed for each government system may vary in different nations. For example, the Soviet Union claimed to offer a broad voting franchise to its adult citizens and reported that 99 percent of eligible voters turned out for elections. However, Soviet voters had little choice on the ballot, and therefore the franchise had limited value. Similarly, whereas the democracies claim to protect civil liberties carefully, some persons would argue that these liberties are accorded unevenly—in high degree to middle-class whites and grudgingly or not at all to impoverished nonwhites.

Modern Democracy

Within the entire vocabulary of political science, there is probably no single word that has been given more meanings than *democracy*. At the present time, the word has a rather magical connotation and a somewhat tranquilizing effect. Any citizenry which is persuaded that its own government system is a democratic one is likely to accept the political power exercised by that system. Hence the Soviet

TABLE 4.1 The Spectrum of Government Power

	Democratic Government			Nondemocratic Government		
Perfect Democracy (Power in Hands of the People)	Democracy (USA, Great Britain, France)	Limited Democracy (Mexico, Egypt, Yugoslavia)	Authoritarianism (Syria, Iraq, Burma)	Totalitarianism (Communist China, Fascist Italy, Nazi Germany)	Perfect Totalitarianism (All Power Held by Government)
Nonpartisan politics	Two-party or multiparty politics	Dominant-party politics	Single-party or no-party politics	Single-party politics	Single-party politics
Full individual participation in government	Popular elections with universal franchise	Popular elections with limited slate	Self-determined or party-determined leadership	Self-determined or party-determined leadership	Absence of voting franchise
Virtually unlimited individual liberties	Carefully protected individual liberties	Limited individual liberties	Elections without choices	Voting franchise varies in scope, limited to approval of party candidates	Absence of individual liberties
Absolute social and economic equality	Vertical mobility with progress toward social and economic equality	Approximate freedom of the press	Irregular tolerance of individual liberties	Absence of constitutionalism	Government control of press
Free access to administrative office	Detailed constitutional restraints on government	Some social and economic equality	Little or no constitutional restraint on government	Extremely narrow political liberties	Enforced economic and social stratification
Absolute freedom of the press	Freedom of the press	Limited constitutional restraint on government	Intermittent martial law	Social structure determined by state	Total economic control by government
	Broad access to public office	Some access to public office	Direct military influence on government	Substantial economic control by government	Thought control and obliteration of individual conscience
	Unrestricted formation of political groups	Formation of some political groups	Government determination of economic system and structure	Government control of mass media	
			Government control of press		

63

Union used to claim it was the most democratic system in the world, the government of mainland China still calls itself the "People's Republic," and governments the world over advertise their democratic attributes. However, the word *democracy* (from the Greek *dēmokratía; dēmos* = "people" and *kratía* = "government") was not always held in such esteem and carried an unfavorable meaning until the nineteenth century. The Athenian example of direct democracy was for many years interpreted to mean unrestrained mob rule, for a "true" democracy had to be a system in which all citizens who so desired met periodically to elect state officials and personally enact laws. This kind of government has been extremely rare throughout history (the few examples are Athens's General Assembly, the New England town meeting, and the Swiss *Landsgemeinde*) because the classic model of democracy is extremely difficult to execute. Although it may have been possible to have everyone's direct participation in a small town where the citizens were well known to one another and matters to be voted on were comparatively simple, it is far different to attempt direct democracy in a nation such as the United States, which has over 260 million people and which must deal with extremely complex issues. A government that had to submit each issue requiring a decision to so many voters would be too unwieldy to function efficiently in a modern technological society. Therefore, *representative* democracy has evolved as the only workable alternative.

REPRESENTATIVE DEMOCRACY

In the modern world, democracy is no longer the direct determination of all government policy by the people. Instead the people play a more general role. Democracy today is "a political system which supplies regular constitutional opportunities for changing the governing officials, and a social mechanism which permits the largest possible part of the population to influence major decisions by choosing among contenders for political office."[1] "Constitutional" means that the government is a limited one. Restrictions on the legal exercise of power apply not only to the people, who must usually wait for election time to change their leadership, but also to the government, which can wield its authority only in specific ways. Representative democracy has several essential ingredients.

Popular Support of Government.   Popular support is the crucial test of modern democratic government, for in a democracy the policymakers' legitimacy usually depends on the support they receive in the form of a majority or a plurality of votes cast. The preservation of such support for the leaders by their followers is a key underpinning of democracy, for in a democratic state no one has an inherent right to occupy a position of political power: He or she must be constitutionally elected by fellow citizens. To prevent legitimacy from becoming identified with only certain individuals, democratic systems provide for elections either at regular intervals (as in the United States) or at certain maximum time spans (as in Britain). Most systems permit reelection, although the Twenty-second Amendment to the Constitution limits each president to two full terms.

The institutions of democratic government also hold lesser officials accountable for their actions and provide for their dismissal if their leadership is found to be wanting. Senators, representatives, local justices of the peace, prime ministers, and presidents who perform their roles to most voters' satisfaction will usually be returned to office; if they fail to do what the majority of the voters want, they are not likely to be reelected. Thus, reelection is the people's means both of expressing support and of controlling the general direction of government policy.[2]

Political Competition. The people's right to reject unsatisfactory officials at the polls is bolstered when a choice of policies (usually represented by competing political parties) is offered on the ballot. In the United States, for example, the leadership of the Democratic party has stood, generally, for social programs to correct economic and social problems (e.g., Social Security, unemployment insurance, Medicare, and job training programs) and has—until recently—deemphasized a balanced budget. The leaders of the Republican party, on the other hand, have been more inclined to let the forces of the marketplace determine economic direction, and have—at least until Ronald Reagan—stressed fiscal responsibility. Whereas the lines between the two parties are usually not very clear-cut, in most elections there are discernible differences in both philosophy and approach between the two parties, which may aid in voter selection. But the party system is not the sole means (and often it is not the most important means) by which the people choose alternatives. In addition, in some systems, voters may choose among individual candidates, regardless of party backing. One representative or prime minister may be personally identified with an issue such as peace, the economy, or clean government. For example, Bill Clinton's election in 1992 drew people from both parties worried about unemployment, and in 1992 Britons from both major parties reelected John Major as prime minister because they couldn't quite trust the leadership of the other party.

Alternation in Power. In a democracy, the reins of power will occasionally alternate, both in terms of actual officeholders and in terms of prevailing ideals. The party that was in the majority then becomes a minority. A vivid illustration was the change in the presidency from Herbert Hoover to Franklin Roosevelt in 1933, from an almost complete laissez-faire ("hands off") economic approach toward government to the more controlled policies of the New Deal. The Republican party, which had been in the majority, had to assume a minority role. In a democratic system it is assumed that such changes will be accepted by those who identify themselves with the current minority party and that their opposition will be respectful, civil, legal, and tolerant. The British aptly label their out-parties as "the Loyal Opposition," which remains ready to take the reins of government by lawful means but which meanwhile engages vigorously in the political process in anticipation of the next election. These political tolerances are crucial to the maintenance of a stable democracy and for peaceful successions of power.

Can a system in which the ruling party stays in power seemingly forever really be democratic? Such parties like to claim that they are so popular that they are voted in every time. This is unlikely. More likely is that the ruling parties rig elections by disrupting the opposition and miscounting ballots. Mexico, whose Institutional Revolutionary Party (PRI) has ruled since the 1920s, looked less and less democratic as the decades went by. In 1988, the Mexican computers counting the vote "broke down"; when they were "fixed," PRI won. By occasionally allowing elections in which other parties made good showings recently, PRI showed a more democratic attitude. The real democratic test, however, will be when PRI allows itself to be voted out of office, as did India's Congress Party in 1989.

Popular Representation.   In representative democracies, the voters elect representatives to act as legislators and, as such, to voice and protect their general interest. Each legislator usually acts for a given district or group of people. The question of just how he or she should act has concerned political theorists for centuries. Some theorists claim that a system is not democratic unless legislators treat elections as a mandate to carry out constituents' wishes. In this case, the legislators inform constituents about the alternatives in forthcoming decisions, let them decide what course of action they prefer, and then vote in accordance with their preferences. Other theorists disagree, on the grounds that the constituents don't always have an opinion on issues, and claim that a representative must act as a trustee, carrying out the wishes of constituents when feasible but acting for what he or she feels are the best interests of the community as a whole. Joseph Schumpeter puts the argument against the mandate theory as follows: "Our chief problems about the classical (democratic) theory centered in the proposition that 'the people' hold a definite and rational opinion about every individual question and that they give effect to this opinion—in a democracy—by choosing 'representatives' who will see to it that the opinion is carried out."[3]

Of course, the people as a whole do not hold definite opinions on each subject. If they were asked to vote on every question of truck tonnage restrictions, parliamentary rules of order, or the staff organization of the Weather Bureau, few would bother voting. Representative democracy, therefore, does not mean that the representative must become a cipher for constituents; rather, it means that the people as a body must be able to control the *general* direction of government policy. For example, if the people have made the general policy decision that equal economic opportunity belongs to everyone, they will leave the administrative details of achieving this goal to their legislators. It is this partnership between the people and the lawmakers that is the essence of modern democracy. E. E. Schattschneider summarizes the case succinctly:

> The beginning of wisdom in democratic theory is to distinguish between the things that the people can do and the things the people cannot do. The worst possible disservice that can be done to the democratic cause is to attribute to the people a mystical, magical omnipotence which takes no cognizance of what very large numbers of people cannot do by the sheer weight of numbers. At this point the common definition of democracy has invited us to make fools of ourselves.[4]

Majority Rule.   In any government decision involving important policy-making, there is rarely complete agreement. Usually one group of citizens will favor an issue and another group will be against it. If the government is to be the instrument of the popular will, but there is disagreement on issues, how shall the popular will be determined? The simple answer is that the majority should decide: In any controversy, the policy that has the support of the greatest number of citizens should generally become the policy of government. This is the procedure that was used in the democracies of ancient Greece. However, our more modern and practical concept of democracy is "majority rule with minority rights."

A look at any political controversy reveals that as a fact of political and social life, political minorities do exist. Their members can be seen picketing outside Parliament in London, protesting in the streets of Paris, or making their presence known in most other major capitals. And the influence of these minorities on government is very important. It is safe to say that every view that is now widely held was once a minority view. Virtually everything that is now public policy—except for laws prohibiting crimes such as murder—became public policy as a result of conflict between majority and minority groups. Furthermore, just as it is true that a minority view may grow to be almost universally accepted over a period of time, so, to, a majority decision may eventually prove to be unwise, unworkable, or unwanted. Just as minorities may be right, so, too, may majorities be wrong.

Modern liberal democratic tradition tends to place limits on the concept of majority rule. It should not, for example, be used to oppress minorities, and minority rights should be overruled only within certain accepted standards. If minorities are oppressed by it, the will of the majority then becomes the "tyranny of the majority," which is just as foreboding as executive tyranny. In representative democracies, the burden is on the majority to persuade minorities rather than to coerce them, and the right of all citizens to dissent is protected. If the majority in power does *not* act in accordance with democratic practice, citizens may refuse to accept as legitimate the decisions of the governing party, since, in their judgment, it is not governing legitimately.

Ideally, in a democracy there should be a high level of social integration so that society will be tolerant of the differences among its members and so that political conflict will be interest-oriented—that is, directed to issues and policies— rather than based on differences of color, race, religion, nationality, or gender. In large industrialized states and in nations now striving to modernize, where society consists of groups having very different political interests, the prospects for democracy may depend in large measure on the ability of social organizations to resolve conflicts. If members of different groups do not have adequate contact with one another to realize the pettiness of their prejudices, their intolerances, and other differences and to thereby develop a sense of community, the fundamental conflicts of society may be irreconcilable by democratic and peaceful methods. The result is likely to be a tyranny of more powerful groups over less powerful ones, even though democratic institutions may exist, and members of the dominant groups may feel quite sure that they are practicing democracy. The smugness of majorities finally angered African-Americans, Roman Catholics in Northern Ireland, and Lebanese Shiites, all short-changed minorities.

Right of Dissent and Disobedience.   If government exists to serve the people, the people must have the right to resist the commands of government if those commands no longer serve the public will. This right was invoked in 1776 by Thomas

Jefferson in the Declaration of Independence, and Henry Thoreau made probably the most profound American defense of civil disobedience when he declared, "All men recognize the right of revolution; that is, the right to refuse allegiance to, and to resist, the government, when its tyranny or its inefficiency are great and unendurable."[5] But the most celebrated advocate of civil disobedience was the Indian philosopher Mahatma Gandhi. Gandhi considered his method of resistance to be "civil" because it was legal; that is, whereas it was disobedience, it did not exceed the general legal structure of the state and did not breach moral codes by doing personal harm to others through violence.

Whereas for the most part Thoreau and Gandhi looked on civil disobedience as an individual act of conscience, others have sought to organize it and mobilize it. The most prominent American organizer was Reverend Martin Luther King, Jr., whose nonviolent resistance campaigns of the 1960s in the name of civil rights brought him into controversy. The many sit-ins and marches which he planned, directed, and often led kept him face to face with the law for nearly a decade, and he and other members of his Southern Christian Leadership Conference were often imprisoned. The long-range consequence of their actions, however, was a minor revolution in judicial decisions concerning peaceful protest.

Political Equality. In a democracy, at least in theory, everyone is equally able to participate in government and to compete freely for public office. Critics of democracy point out that the reality is often different. They say it takes a great deal of money—and often specific racial and religious ties—to be able to enter public life, and so large numbers of people are barred from seeking public office. A less cynical observer will note, though, that our democratic system of government allows for a change in this situation. Opportunities to serve in public office, at least at the lower levels, are gradually broadening, and minority groups are becoming more adept at political organization.

But there is a second side to political equality, and that is responsibility. If, in a democratic political system, individuals have equal opportunity to express their talents and to achieve personal advancement, each individual is also honor-bound to resist the temptation to exploit society to achieve such personal advancement. In other words, democracy demands individual self-restraint. For example, a person who holds public office should not use that office for individual profit or for preferential treatment of a small group. Although citizens in a democracy are cynically (and perhaps rightly) prepared to assume that politicians are in politics for their own benefit, or that many selected officials are "on the take," they are still appalled by revelations of corruption in government and approve public censure of officials who misuse public funds or use their office for private gain.

A case in point is the public's reaction to the involvement of White House aides and presidential advisers in the 1972 attempts to place electronic surveillance equipment inside the Democratic National Headquarters in the Watergate. Some commentators, however, pointed to the success of the grand jury investigation, the House panel's vote to impeach, and President Nixon's resignation in 1974 as examples of the effectiveness of the built-in checks and balances in our political system. When both individual self-restraint and some form of checks and balances are lacking, the government may have to impose restraints. A familiar example of government-imposed restraint is antitrust legislation. Monopolistic business practices may provide an opportunity for a few businesspersons to become wealthy, but a business having a monopoly on a product is able to exploit its advantage by charging its customers high prices. Since the businesspersons, anxious to make the largest profits they can, may not regulate their own practices adequately, the government may introduce legislation to regulate their activities.

Popular Consultation.   Most government leaders realize that to govern effectively they must know what the people want and must be responsive to these needs and demands. Are citizens disturbed—and, if so, *how* disturbed—about foreign policy, taxes, unemployment, the cost of living? Intelligent leaders realize that they must not get too far ahead of—nor fall too far behind—public opinion. Therefore, a range of techniques has evolved to test opinion. Public opinion polls are taken on specific issues. The media, by thoughtful probing, can create a dialogue between the people and their leaders. At press conferences and news interviews with elected officials, reporters will ask those questions that they believe the people want answered. Editorials and letters to the editor are also indicators of citizens' moods and feelings.

In recent years, several critics have noted that U.S. officials often rely heavily on the opinions of small segments of their constituencies because they are well organized and highly vocal. On the issue of gun control, for example, polls have consistently shown the public at large to be in favor of stronger regulation of firearms. But the National Rifle Association, a tightly knit and outspoken lobbying organization, has usually managed to block efforts to strengthen legislation in this area.

Free Press.   Dictatorships cannot tolerate free and critical mass media; democracies cannot do without them. One of the clearest ways to determine the degree of democracy in a country is to see how free its press is. The press provides citizens with facts, raises public awareness, and keeps rulers responsive to mass demands. Without a free and critical press, rulers can disguise wrongdoing and corruption and lull the population into passive support. As China permitted a "democracy movement" in the late 1980s, the Chinese media became freer, more honest, and more critical. As part of the crushing of this movement in 1989, outspoken journalists were fired or arrested.

Some Americans argue that the U.S. media go too far, that they take an automatic adversarial stance that undermines government authority and weakens the nation. In some cases this may be true, but in a democracy there is no mechanism to decide what "too far" is. The checks on reckless reporting are competing journals and channels that can criticize and refute unfair commentary. Then citizens, with no government supervision, can decide for themselves if charges are accurate. Only half in jest has the U.S. press been called "the fourth branch of government."

Totalitarian Government

With the fall of Communist regimes in Eastern Europe and the former Soviet Union, totalitarianism is becoming an endangered species, perhaps on the brink of extinction. Totalitarianism's emphasis on total control, brainwashing, and worship of the state and its leaders has proven mistaken and inefficient. Few people are now attracted to such political models. Now, only North Korea and Cuba remain as pristine examples of totalitarianism, while China, Vietnam, and Yemen have shown signs of loosening up and changing. Earlier in the twentieth century, though, with the regimes of Stalin, Mussolini, and Hitler, it looked like totalitarianism was riding high and might even be the wave of the future. Now it is more likely that it will prove to be a disease of the twentieth century. In any case, most of our examples are historical, not current.

WHAT IS TOTALITARIANISM?

The twentieth-century phenomenon of totalitarianism is far removed from the autocracies of the past. Whereas rulers such as Peter the Great and Louis XIV were powerful despots, the scope and extent of their power and authority were severely limited by the relatively primitive means of communication and transportation and by the weaponry of the time. Until the twentieth century, communications were so slow and often so difficult that it was impossible for the most autocratic rulers to control effectively or completely all the territory in their domain. They could demand and receive outward submission to their rule and acknowledgment of their authority, but even Louis XIV—who perhaps came closest to the figure of a modern dictator—did not try to control everything in France. Average citizens retained control of their private lives. In contrast, totalitarian states of the twentieth century attempted to remold and transform the people under their control and to regulate every aspect of human life and activity.

Totalitarianism, then, is a unique development dating only from the post-World War I period and made possible by modern technology. It is essentially a system of government in which one party holds all political, economic, military, and judicial power. This party attempts to restructure society, to determine the values of society, and to interfere in the personal lives of individual citizens in such a way as to control their preferences, to monitor their movements, and to restrain their freedoms. Where autocratic rulers were largely indifferent to their subjects' wishes, the totalitarian state insists on mass participation in activities and makes a deliberate effort to generate enthusiasm for the success of the system. With modern electronic devices, the state is able to control communications and private activities and thereby regulate political life and thought; through electronic data control it is able to coordinate and centralize the utilization of resources and thereby regulate economic life.

Carl J. Friedrich and Zbigniew Brzezinski identified six basic features com-

Dictator's fantasy: The "People's Palace" in Bucharest, huge, outrageously expensive, and unfinished, was to be the personal palace of Romanian dictator Nicolae Ceausescu, who was deposed and shot in late 1989. With no checks or controls, dictators can launch insane projects.

mon to all totalitarian states.[6] Four of them would have been impossible to achieve in preindustrial societies and are central to the system.

An All-Encompassing Ideology.   Totalitarian ideology is an official body of doctrine that applies to all areas of human life. It includes theories of history, economics, and future political and social development and provides the philosophical framework according to which decisions are made. The ideology portrays the world in terms of black and white, with very little gray in between. Thus, a citizen is judged to be either for the state or against it. And the ideology usually points toward a perfect society, which humankind will attain at some distant point in the future (such as Marx's prediction that the classless society would lead to an eventual withering away of the state). All citizens must give tacit adherence to the official ideology, and they usually devote time to its study. Courses on Marxist-Leninist thought were required in the schools of all Communist states.

A Single Party.   Only one party may exist legally, and that party is usually led by one man who is so strongly identified with the doctrine and with the destiny of the state that he establishes a cult of personality while dictator. Throughout its history, fascist Italy was ruled by Mussolini; Hitler ruled Nazi Germany; Mao Zedong ruled the People's Republic of China; and Stalin ruled the Soviet Union.

Entrance into the party is controlled (official membership is usually less than 10 percent of the population) and is considered an honor. Certain privileges accompany membership, and in return the members give their dedication and support to the party. Hierarchically organized and oligarchically controlled, the party is either superior to or tied in with the formal institutions of government. The party leader wields considerable power in the government, and party functionaries hold important posts in the bureaucracy. The party's cadres are responsible for imposing at least outward conformity at all levels of society. Some are responsible for their streets or towns, some for their assembly lines at factories, and still others for their fellow students.

Organized Terror.   A secret police apparatus, using both physical and psychological methods, is an essential prop of totalitarian regimes to ensure mass allegiance to the party ideology. The Nazi Gestapo, the Soviet NKVD under Stalin, and Mussolini's OVRA were immune from judicial restraints. Constitutional guarantees either did not exist or were ignored in these societies, thus making possible secret arrests, holding people in jail without bringing charges, and torture. The secret police system may be directed not only against specific individuals but against whole classes of people as well. Depending on the particular society, these "enemies of the people" may be Jews, landlords, capitalists, socialists, or clergy. The threat of the "knock at the door" serves two purposes: It terrorizes large segments of the population into acquiescence, and it convinces the more gullible citizens that a conspiracy against the security of the state does, in fact, exist. The mass extermination of entire groups of people under Hitler and Stalin demonstrates the state's enormous power and the individual's corresponding helplessness. Systematic terror rarely enforces loyalty to the regime, however, and the Soviets long ago abandoned the more extreme tactics of Stalin's era. The purges and mass executions were replaced by more subtle forms of control and intimidation, such as loss of job or exile to a remote city.

Monopoly of Communications.   The primary function of the mass media in totalitarian states is to indoctrinate the people with the official ideology. Enlightenment and entertainment are subordinated to the needs of the state.

Monopoly of Weapons.   Governments of totalitarian nations have a complete monopoly on weapons, thus effectively discouraging armed resistance.

Before the breakup of the Soviet Union, long lines waited to file past Lenin's tomb in Red Square.

Now, hardly anyone waits in line to see Lenin, whose ideas and system became irrelevant with the collapse of communism.

Controlled Economy.   Rigid, centralized control is imposed on the economy of every totalitarian state. This control serves a twofold purpose. First, it helps make the state powerful, for all natural resources can be allocated to heavy industry, to the production of weapons, or to other requirements of the state. Second, a centralized economy serves as an instrument of political management. For example, people can be forcibly moved wherever they are needed, and incentive programs can be initiated to stimulate productivity. The needs or wants of the consumer are unimportant. This is demonstrated by comparing the technological development of two differently controlled national economies: The Soviet Union was the first to send men to outer space, for example, but the United States always had superior consumer products.

IMAGE AND REALITY OF TOTAL CONTROL

Just as there is no perfect democracy, so also is there no perfect totalitarian dictatorship. Often outsiders are overly influenced by the image of total control projected by these states. Visitors to fascist Italy were impressed by the seeming law, order, cleanliness, and purposefulness of what they thought was one-man rule. We know now that many Italians disliked Mussolini, that his organizations and economic plans were mostly for show, and that he wasn't even in firm command of the country. In 1943, as the British and Americans overran the southern part of Italy, Mussolini's own generals—who had been disobeying and lying to him for years— overthrew him in a coup. Then the king of Italy—yes, Italy was technically a kingdom until 1946—fired Mussolini as prime minister. Now what kind of total control is that?

Since Stalin's death, every Soviet party chief denounced the bureaucracy, the deadening hand of routine, and the economic irregularities that impeded Soviet growth. But neither Khrushchev, Brezhnev, nor Gorbachev fixed the problem.

Much of Soviet economic life ran by means of under-the-table deals and influence that defied centralized planning. Soviet workers stole everything from radios to locomotives and often showed up to work drunk or not at all. Where was the total control? The pages of *Pravda* and *Izvestia* thundered against these problems, but the government seemed unable to do anything about them.

We should bear in mind that the model of totalitarianism presented earlier is just that—a model—and it never precisely matched reality. The model describes an *attempt* to impose total control, not the achievement of it. Starting in late 1989, as one Communist country after another cast off its system, we beheld how weak the model was. In ideology, most citizens, even former party members, detested communism. The single ruling parties collapsed and handed power over to non-Communists. Organized terror lost its punch. The official mass media, widely ignored for years, was simply discarded in favor of a free press. The controlled economies were turned, with much pain, into market economies. We now realize that these Communist regimes had never exercised total control. In addition, we must be aware that there is more than one type of totalitarianism.

Right-wing Totalitarianism. Right-wing totalitarianism, as exemplified in Italian Fascism and German National Socialism, developed in industrialized nations that were plagued by economic depression, social upheaval, and political confusion and weakness, and in which democratic roots and traditions were shallow and weak. Germany in the late 1920s and early 1930s was in turmoil. The nation was saddled with an enormous reparations debt following World War I; unemployment was widespread; labor disputes were frequent and violent; and a runaway inflation had wiped out the savings of the lower-middle and middle classes—the shopkeepers, the petty bureaucrats, and the skilled workers. In his rise to power, Hitler promised to discipline the labor unions, to restore order, to renounce the humiliating Versailles Treaty, and to protect private property from the Communist menace to the east. His program appealed to industrialists, militarists, and middle-class people, who typically constitute the backbone of a fascist state's support.[7]

Right-wing totalitarianism does not seek to revolutionize society completely; rather it aims to strengthen the existing social order and to glorify the state. It attempts to get rid of those elements of society or those institutions that are believed to prevent the state from achieving greatness, as Hitler strove to annihilate Jews and Gypsies. Economic policies are also directed toward national glory; they usually control economic development and production through cartels and national trade associations. These organizations normally permit private ownership.

Authoritarianism

The terms *authoritarianism* and *totalitarianism* are often confused, but the two words have different meanings. Authoritarianism is a system of government in which power is exercised by a small group with minimum popular input. The group may be a family, in which case the authoritarian regime is an absolute monarchy. It may be a social class, as in a monarchy ruled by a king or queen with the assistance of the nobility or in an elitist technocracy where power is held by top bureaucrats. Or the group may be a strong political party, whose principal concern is to forge domestic solidarity at a time of national need. This type of one-party system is typical of the developing nations of Africa and most of Asia. Typically, however, it is the army that brings authoritarian rule in the wake of a military coup.

Authoritarian governments generally do not attempt to control every aspect of human activity. Many economic, social, religious, cultural, and familial matters are left up to individuals. Most of the six points of totalitarianism discussed earlier are diluted or absent. Authoritarian regimes, for example, rarely have a firm ideology to sell.

This is not to say that authoritarian regimes promote individual freedoms. Authoritarians view society as a hierarchical organization with a specific chain of command under the leadership of one ruler or group. Command, obedience, and order are higher values than freedom, consent, and involvement. Therefore, the citizen is expected to obey laws and pay taxes that he or she has no voice in establishing. Whereas elements of democracy may exist in an authoritarian state, they have little real function. The national legislature, for example, is usually little more than a "rubber stamp" to approve the ruling element's proposals. The theory and practice of an authoritarian ruler were expressed by Louis XIV when he declared, "I am the state."

Spain under Franco (1939–1975) was "traditional authoritarian" rather than totalitarian, as the *caudillo* (leader) sought political passivity and obedience rather than enthusiastic participation and mobilization. Franco and his supporters had no single ideology to promote, and the economy and press were pluralistic within limited bounds.[8] Jeane J. Kirkpatrick, a political scientist and President Reagan's ambassador to the United Nations, argued that there is a clear difference between authoritarian and totalitarian regimes. The former (such as Argentina, Chile, Brazil) can reform, but once a totalitarian system (such as communism) takes over, the system cannot reform itself.[9] Argentina, Chile, and Brazil did return to democracy in the 1980s.[10] Kirkpatrick's thesis was to some extent borne out in the fact that the Communist regimes of the Soviet bloc never did reform themselves; they collapsed while trying reform. In contrast, China illustrated the nature of totalitarian regimes by bloodily crushing its democracy movement in 1989.

AUTHORITARIANISM AND THE DEVELOPING NATIONS

Perhaps the most significant political movement since the end of World War II has been the breaking up of former colonial empires into independent nations. For the most part, the ideological struggle for national independence in these states followed the general philosophical argument of the American Declaration of Independence and the French Declaration of the Rights of Man and Citizen. Yet once national independence was won, democracy did not last long. A political culture in which self-rule and self-determination were never integral values may not adapt well to political democracy. Then, too, democracy in the Western tradition is characterized by an individualism that is in large part the result of a capitalist market system that stresses competition. The developing societies have preindustrial, traditional peasant economies in which family and tribal cooperation have traditionally been far more important than individual competition and self-enrichment. In many of these societies, in which the levels of education and income are low, the majority of the people are absorbed in the struggle to survive. The leadership often feels that political and economic survival and growth are dependent on strong leaders who can act according to what they perceive is really needed rather than according to what is immediately popular.

Rejecting both Western-style democracy and Communist totalitarianism, many of the developing countries tried a third alternative—that of single-party dominance. Zimbabwe started with a two-party system in 1980 but found that the parties encouraged tribal animosities and guerrilla terror. The leader of the largest party, Robert Mugabe, cracked down harshly with soldiers of his dominant tribe and created a single-party system, arguing that this was the only way to build unity and a socialist economy. Often the results are terrible. Government officials devise wasteful, unrealistic projects, stifle individual initiative by regulations and taxes, and crush critical viewpoints. In this way have such countries as Tanzania and Burma impoverished themselves, ending up with neither democracy nor economic growth.

The Democratization of Authoritarian Regimes

Since 1974, dozens of countries have abandoned authoritarian or totalitarian systems in favor of democratic systems.[11] Now, over half of the world's nations are at least approximately democratic. The expansion of democracy from the previous two dozen countries—mostly in Western Europe and North America—where it had earlier taken root became a major scholarly topic.[12] An excellent new quarterly appeared in 1989, *Journal of Democracy*, devoted to explaining and encouraging the spread of democracy.

There seem to be two types of regimes contributing to the trend toward more democracy: authoritarian regimes that enjoyed strong economic growth and collapsed Communist regimes whose economic growth lagged. The fast-growth authoritarian systems—such as Chile, South Korea, and Taiwan—were politically authoritarian but developed a market economy largely in private hands.[13] It was as if the dictator said, "I'll take care of politics; you just work on your various businesses." The pro-business regimes set macroeconomic policy (sound currency, low inflation, sufficient capital for loans) and held down demands from labor unions but otherwise left market forces alone. After a time, the growing economy starts transforming the whole society in the direction of democracy. As Peter Berger observed, "When market economies are successful over a period of time, pressure for democratization inevitably ensues."[14]

Why does this favorable sequence develop? First, economic growth creates a large middle class, one of the bases for democracy. Middle classes are inherently democratic. They have a stake in the system; they may wish to modify it but not overthrow it. Second, and related to the size of the middle class, education levels have risen. Most people are high school graduates, and many are college graduates. They are no longer ignorant and do not fall for demagogues or extremist ideas. Third, and related to both the previous two points, people increasingly recognize their interests and wish to express them. They have business, professional, regional, and religious points of view that they want considered. They can spot cruel, corrupt, or inefficient governments and do not like being treated like small children. Finally, the market itself teaches citizens about self-reliance, pluralism, tolerance, and not expecting too much, all attitudes that help sustain a democracy. Gradually, the regime eases up, permitting a critical press, the formation of political parties, and finally free elections. Even Mexico may be making this transition.[15]

How about the other trend that has led to newly democratic systems, the collapse of Communist regimes? Here, too, the economy has a great deal to do with the process, but in a negative sense. It was poor economic performance and slow growth, especially in comparison with the West and with the rapid-growth countries, that persuaded relatively liberal Communists, such as Mikhail Gorbachev, to attempt to reform the system. They knew they were falling behind, especially in crucial high-tech areas, and thought they could energize the system by bringing elements of the free market into an otherwise socialist economy. But communism, like other brands of totalitarianism, doesn't tolerate reform. By attempting to control everything, as in the six points outlined earlier by Friedrich and Brzezinski, they have created a brittle system that can break but not bend. Once they started admitting that the system needs to be fixed, they are admitting that they were wrong. The ideology was wrong; single-party control was wrong; the centralized economy was wrong; and so on. The attempt at reform turns into a system collapse so sudden and complete that observers, including the foremost scholars, are taken completely off guard.

Here contemporary political science deserves to be taken to task. It failed to provide early warning of the greatest political change of the late twentieth century. Some economists charted the slowing of the Soviet economy since the 1970s and concluded that at a certain point something drastic would happen;[16] and a few historians of conservative bent sensed that the Soviet system couldn't go on as before.[17] But very few political scientists heeded the warning signs. One suspects that the main culprit leading to this error was "systems theory," discussed in Chapter 1. Political scientists have tended to reify systems, to see them not as theories and suggestions but as reality. Systems thinking depicts political systems as stable, durable, and self-correcting feedback loops that never break down. At a minimum, systems theory must be enlarged to include the possibility of system collapse; perhaps the theory should be abandoned altogether. It never adequately explained totalitarian systems.

Will the countries that emerged from the wreckage of communism be able to establish lasting democracies? There are both good and bad signs. Most people in Eastern Europe and the ex-Soviet Union are in a middle economic condition; that is, they are neither rich nor poor. But neither are they middle class in the sense of having some property and a stake in the system. Education levels are good, but

Boris Yeltsin toughed out the 1991 coup attempt and emerged stronger than ever. Yeltsin represented sweeping change in favor of democracy and a market economy, which old-guard Russian Communists hated.

their education has not included tolerance, pluralism, and avoidance of extremism. Market systems are strange and rather frightening to them, and indeed the transition from a controlled to a market economy inflicts terrible hardships. Democracy, as we have seen, is a rather complex system and depends on a set of attitudes that grow best under certain conditions, namely, that of a market economy with a large, educated middle class. Perhaps the greatest task of democracy in our day is to foster the transformation of collapsed totalitarian societies into democracies. If they don't make the transition, the world's democracies may have to face new and even uglier forms of totalitarianism and authoritarianism.

Suggested Readings

AUNG SAN SUU KYI. *Freedom from Fear: And Other Writings.* New York: Viking Press, 1991. A plea for democracy from Nobel Peace Prize winner and opposition leader imprisoned by Burma's military government.

BEETHAM, DAVID, ed. *Defining and Measuring Democracy.* Thousand Oaks, CA: Sage, 1994. Methodologically sophisticated attempts to

pin down exactly what constitutes democracy and who has more of it.

BULLOCK, ALAN. *Hitler and Stalin: Parallel Lives.* New York: Knopf, 1992. A noted historian argues that the two great dictators had similar personalities.

CHIROT, DANIEL. *Modern Tyrants: The Power and Prevalence of Evil in Our Age.* New York: Free

Press, 1994. Totalitarian dictatorships are not a thing of the past but could easily return, warns this noted historian of the Balkans.

DIAMOND, LARRY, JUAN J. LINZ, and SEYMOUR MARTIN LIPSET, eds. *Politics in Developing Countries: Comparing Experiences with Democracy*, 2nd ed. Boulder, CO: Lynne Rienner, 1995. Strategies for promoting democracy in the Third World.

DIPALMA, GIUSEPPE. *To Craft Democracies: An Essay on Democratic Transitions.* Berkeley: University of California Press, 1991. The complex factors of how a country moves toward democracy condition the type and success of its democracy.

HUNTINGTON, SAMUEL P. *The Third Wave: Democratization in the Late Twentieth Century.* Oklahoma City: University of Oklahoma Press, 1991. A top empirical theorist examines why democracy is now growing in much of the world.

KIRKPATRICK, JEANE J. *The Withering Away of the Totalitarian State . . . and Other Surprises.* Lanham, MD: University Press of America, 1991. Controversial theorist of totalitarianism explains why it failed in the Communist countries.

LIPSET, SEYMOUR MARTIN, ed. *The Encyclopedia of Democracy*, four vols. Washington, DC: Congressional Quarterly, 1995. Excellent reference source, covering the historical as well as contemporary situation of democracy.

PIEKALKIEWICZ, JAROSLAW, and ALFRED WAYNE PENN. *Politics of Ideocracy.* Albany, NY: State University of New York Press, 1995. The crux of totalitarianism is the militant application of an exclusive ideology.

PRZEWORSKI, ADAM. *Sustainable Democracy.* New York: Cambridge University Press, 1995. Will the new democracies make it? A group report of 21 scholars weighs their chances.

RUESCHEMEYER, DIETRICH, EVELYNE HUBER STEPHENS, and JOHN STEPHENS. *Capitalist Development and Democracy.* Chicago: University of Chicago Press, 1992. Argues that economic growth creates working and middle classes, the bases of democracy.

VANHANEN, TATU. *The Process of Democratization: A Comparative Study of 147 States, 1980–88.* Bristol, PA: Crane Russak, 1992. Major study of statistical and empirical data on the factors that bring about democracy.

Notes

1. Seymour M. Lipset, *Political Man* (Garden City, NY: Doubleday, 1960), p. 27. This definition parallels and is drawn from the definition of democracy given in Joseph Schumpeter, *Capitalism, Socialism, and Democracy*, 3rd ed. (New York: Harper & Row, 1950).

2. The most important statement of this position, and of the logical consequences that follow from it, is in Anthony Downs, *An Economic Theory of Democracy* (New York: Harper & Row, 1957).

3. Schumpeter, *Capitalism, Socialism, and Democracy*, p. 269.

4. E. E. Schattschneider, *The Semisovereign People: A Realist's View of Democracy in America* (New York: Holt, Rinehart & Winston, 1960), p. 139.

5. Henry David Thoreau, *Civil Disobedience* (Brookline, MA: Godine, 1971).

6. Carl J. Friedrich and Zbigniew Brzezinski, *Totalitarian Dictatorship and Autocracy* (Cambridge, MA: Harvard University Press, 1965). Another important study in this area is Hannah Arendt's *The Origins of Totalitarianism* (New York: Harcourt Brace Jovanovich, 1951).

7. Arendt, *Origins of Totalitarianism.*

8. Juan J. Linz, "An Authoritarian Regime: Spain," in E. Allardt and Y. Littunen, eds., *Cleav-*

ages, Ideologies and Party Systems (Helsinki: Academic Bookstore, 1964).

9. Jeane J. Kirkpatrick, *Dictatorships and Double Standards: Rationalism and Reason in Politics* (New York: Simon & Schuster, 1982).

10. For an interesting collection of studies on how countries go from authoritarianism to democracy, see James M. Malloy and Mitchell A. Seligson, eds., *Authoritarians and Democrats: Regime Transition in Latin America* (Pittsburgh: University of Pittsburgh Press, 1987).

11. Samuel P. Huntington, "How Countries Democratize," *Political Science Quarterly* 106 (Winter, 1991–92), 579.

12. The leading scholars in this area were Larry Diamond, Juan Linz, and Seymour Martin Lipset, who wrote and edited such works as *Politics in Developing Countries: Comparing Experiences with Democracy*, 2nd ed. (Boulder, CO: Lynne Rienner, 1995). These three thinkers were also the guiding lights of the new *Journal of Democracy.*

13. For democratization in Chile, see Jeffrey M. Puryear, *Thinking Politics: Intellectuals and Democracy in Chile* (Baltimore, MD: Johns Hopkins University Press, 1994). For Taiwan, see Jaushieh Joseph Wu, *Taiwan's Democratization:*

Forces Behind the New Momentum (New York: Oxford University Press, 1995). For East Asian democratization in broader perspective, see Edward Friedman, ed., *The Politics of Democratization: Generalizing East Asia Experiences* (Boulder, CO: Westview Press, 1994).

14. Peter L. Berger, "The Uncertain Triumph of Democratic Capitalism," *Journal of Democracy* 3 (July 1992), 3.

15. See Miguel Angel Centeno, *Democracy Within Reason: Technocratic Revolution in Mexico* (College Park, PA: Pennsylvania State University Press, 1994).

16. See, for example, Marshall I. Goldman, *USSR in Crisis: The Failure of an Economic System* (New York: Norton, 1983).

17. Historian Richard Pipes of Harvard advised the Reagan administration to pursue a hard-line anti-Soviet policy that would force the Soviet systems to collapse. See his *Survival Is Not Enough: Soviet Realities and America's Future* (New York: Simon & Schuster, 1984). See also "Z" [Martin E. Malia], "To the Stalin Mausoleum," *Daedalus* 119 (Winter 1990), 1.

• 5 •

Democracy in Practice: Pluralist and Elitist Views

Among the many nations that claim democracy as the basis for government, is there one in which "the people" actually make decisions? Do the people really rule in the People's Republic of China? Do the citizens of the United States decide whether to build a road, raise taxes, or improve relations with Vietnam?

In theory, the American people do make these decisions—indirectly, through elected representatives. Few besides Ross Perot would maintain that in a country as large and complex as the United States a democracy should or could be run in the classical sense of mass participation in every political decision. This might have been possible in ancient Greece, but some theorists argue that classical democracy has never been possible—and never will be. Italian political scientist Gaetano Mosca, for example, argued that government always falls into the hands of a few.

> In all societies—from societies that are very undeveloped and have largely attained the dawnings of civilization, down to the most advanced and powerful societies—two classes of people appear—a class that rules and a class that is ruled. The first class, always the less numerous, performs all of the political functions, monopolizes power, and enjoys the advantages that power brings, whereas the second, the more numerous class, is directed and controlled by the first, in a manner that is now more or less legal, now more or less arbitrary and violent.[1]

Even those political scientists who question Mosca's generalization to "all societies" feel that participatory democracy is not possible in large modern societies. Government is too big and the issues too complex for every citizen to have a voice in decisions. In the words of Robert Dahl, "The key political, economic, and social decisions . . . are made by tiny minorities. . . . It is difficult—nay, impossible—to see how it could be otherwise in large political systems."[2]

Given the impracticality—even the impossibility—of classical, participatory democracy in modern societies, and given the variety of governments "by the few" that claim to be democratic, the problem is to find answers to two questions: How can we determine whether or not a government is democratic? And who actually governs in a democracy?

In Chapter 4, democracy was defined as a political system that provides opportunities for changing public officials and parties through competitive voting, along with tolerance for minorities and divergent viewpoints. But who actually governs in a democracy? Are the wishes and desires of the majority reflected in the decisions of elected officials? In the United States, do the people govern, or is this country, too, a government "by the few"? In an attempt to answer these questions, this chapter examines two theories of democracy—elitism and pluralism.

Two Theories: Elitism and Pluralism

ELITISM

Because this country's political culture is predominantly democratic, the concept of elitism is offensive to many Americans. We associate the term with the feudal aristocracies of medieval Europe, the warlords of China and Japan, and the political and military dictatorships of modern times (Hitler's and Stalin's inner circles). But an elite is not necessarily hereditary, tyrannical, or self-seeking.

Broadly defined, an elite is a small group of people who rule in the sense of directly initiating (or vetoing) decisions about "who gets what, when, and how." For example, in a hospital doctors constitute an elite. They decide who gets what treatment, when, and how. No one is born a doctor; their elite status derives from expertise that is available to anyone who can complete the medical training. Nor are doctors "tyrannical"; they do not deprive people of their freedom to move about or to eat certain foods out of caprice or out of desire for power.

A political elite may, like the medical profession, be open to anyone who seeks a position in government and is capable of filling that position, or it may be closed to all but those who were born to the "right" family or those with large sums of money or those of a certain religion. It may be responsive to the needs and desires of the many, or it may be aloof and self-seeking. A political elite may be temporary (lasting for a single administration or until a specific problem is solved) or long-lasting. It may hold a monopoly over power within a society, or it may share power with other, competing elites.

One prominent elite theorist was Robert Michels, a turn-of-the-century German Social Democrat, a believer in equality and democracy. Looking at his own party, though, Michels came to the conclusion that no matter what its democratic intent, the Social Democratic party was stratifying into clear classes of leaders and led and internally was not very democratic at all. Michels reasoned as follows: To accomplish its political goals, the Social Democrats had to be well organized; they were engaged in political combat with powerful conservative forces. Organization means leaders. Once these leaders were in the party's top positions, they tended to see their role as permanent, to lock themselves into power. Most of the rank-and-file party members agreed with this position, obeyed the leaders, and did not attempt to replace them. The leadership then became an oligarchy, rule by the few. Michels went so far as to call this tendency the "Iron Law of Oligarchy": No matter how democratic they start out, human organizations become oligarchic.[3]

Michels, despairing of democracy, moved to Mussolini's Italy to embrace fascism. Should Michels have been so pessimistic about democracy? Later studies suggest that his "Iron Law of Oligarchy" is an exaggeration. In a detailed study of Norway's parties, Henry Valen and Daniel Katz found that the relationship of leaders and led was a two-way street, with party leaders paying attention to members' demands. "The political process within the party structure is of the character of rubber rather than of iron," they concluded.[4] Accordingly, a "Rubber Law of Oligarchy" might be a more accurate term.

Some societies are clearly elitist in nature and are designed to be that way. France, for example, has long been governed by brilliant, highly trained graduates of elite colleges known as the *grandes écoles* (Great Schools), who then enter an administrative elite known as the Grand Corps.[5] With dispassionate reason this elite administers France, improves its education and culture, builds its economy, and enhances its stature in the world. Advice or input from pluralistic interest groups is to be ignored as "unobjective." The French administrative elite says in effect, "We know what's good for France, and we're smarter than anyone else." Their record of achievements is mixed, but most French people accept their right to rule. Americans, with a strong tradition of pluralism, would reject them as arrogant and undemocratic. What feels right in France would feel profoundly wrong in the United States. Much of Europe shares this elitist mentality with France; few share the U.S. emphasis on pluralism.

Elite theorists are divided over the question of what kind of elite or elites govern America. Some—for example, C. Wright Mills—take a "power elite" position.[6] According to this view, America is ruled by a relatively closed, upper-class elite that responds to public pressure only when its position is threatened. This group holds a power monopoly in America because it controls essential resources—including wealth, education, executive and legal experience, and "connections" (with political, military, business, and educational leaders). Membership in the ruling elite depends on socioeconomic status, not on elections or expertise. The elite is stable over time and through changing issues.

This view holds that America's power elite does admit new members—partly to rejuvenate its own ranks, partly to prevent potential leaders from building "counterelites." Once admitted, however, new members tend to become conservative. A common interest in preserving the system and their position in it holds the elite together. When members differ over specific issues, they accommodate one another rather than disturb the existing power structure. The elite does take the "masses" into account, but only when it chooses to do so. Elections are largely symbolic; a candidate can seldom be elected to public office without elite support (specifically, money and connections). In short, the people must choose between two candidates who basically share a common orientation and background; thus, they have little chance of making a dramatic change in public policy. A number of advocates of elite theory argue that in the United States and other Western democracies the elite actually protects the basic democratic values of individual liberty, due process of law, limited government, and free enterprise. Research shows that members of the elite are more tolerant than the average person, who is typically ill informed, intolerant, and antidemocratic.[7] The elitist position thus suggests that government by the elite, which seems inimical to the nature of democracy, is actually the means by which we preserve the basic tenets of our system.

PLURALISM

A second school of political scientists, the pluralists, contends that America is governed not by a single elite but by a number or plurality of specialized, competing groups.[8] Membership in these influential groups varies with the times and with the issues. Business lobbyists and union leaders, for example, may unite to support high tariffs on foreign goods but oppose one another on the issue of wage controls, neither taking an active role in the controversy over school busing. Competition among several groups prevents any one person or group from gaining control of the political system. Pluralists maintain that political decisions are the result of bargaining and competition among groups. The government, according to this view, plays the role of arbitrator, making sure that groups with differing interests adhere to the "rules of the game."

Robert Dahl, among others, believes that this pluralist system is essentially democratic, in the sense that individuals and minorities *can* influence decision makers through elections and interest groups. No public official can afford to ignore his or her electorate. If a group of people with a stake in a particular decision organize and speak out, and if their viewpoint is considered legitimate by the majority of the electorate, their representatives will respond.[9] In the American political system, Dahl writes, "all active and legitimate groups in the population can make themselves heard at some crucial stage in the process of decision."[10] Thus, pluralists suggest that America is governed by a plurality of groups that check one another in open competition.

Pluralism also contains a *normative* element, a "should" or an "ought." Pluralists argue not only that America works on the basis of the relatively free interplay of groups but also that this is a good thing, the way politics ought to be. Pluralism is seen as the basis for democracy, and countries that reject pluralism have trouble instituting democracy. American thinkers have freely advised Africans, Russians, Chinese, and others to institutionalize pluralism because it will foster economic growth, democracy, and freedom. Some countries, however, reject the advice out of fear that American-style pluralism will lead to infighting and chaos in societies that lack the basic consensus of the United States. As political scientist Aristide Zolberg put it, "One man's pluralism is another man's fragmentation."[11] What works for us might not work for them, for pluralism means that groups agree to play by the rules, not to push their claims too far and not to resort to violence. If groups cannot do this, urging them to practice pluralism might lead to new Bosnias.

Who Rules America?

Neither elitists nor pluralists accept the traditional image of America as a populist democracy governed by the common people. Both recognize that policy decisions are made by a small number of people who tend to be wealthier, better educated, and "better connected" than the average American. However, elitists and pluralists differ sharply over the question of elite solidarity and the meaning of public participation in elections and interest groups. Elitists hold that "those at the top" work together and that elections and interest groups are largely symbolic; pluralists contend that those in power are highly competitive and that elections and interest groups give the common people access to the system.

THE ELITE VIEW

America's Founding Fathers, according to elitists, were "bond holders, investors, merchants, real-estate owners, and planters"—not average citizens.[12] To these men, the primary function of government was to protect individuals from political tyranny (a king) and mass movements. They designed the Constitution to limit government and thus preserve economic individualism.

Between the Revolution and the Civil War, the government was dominated by three different elites. In 1800 Thomas Jefferson, a Virginia planter, unseated the mercantile aristocracy and its Federalist party; in 1828 Andrew Jackson, a western nouveau riche, replaced the Jeffersonians. But basic policy changed only slightly when Jefferson and Jackson each took office. This peaceful transfer, say elitists, is evidence that the elite considered stability more important than political ideology.

Only once in American history did elite consensus break down—in the years leading up to the Civil War. Both northern and southern elites saw the West as the key to power. This rivalry, not ideological differences, led to war. When the South was defeated, control of the economy and, indirectly, of government passed to the rising class of industrial capitalists, who ruled unchecked for the next fifty to sixty years.

Pluralists often cite the New Deal as evidence that the people do influence the government. Elitists disagree. Roosevelt himself was a member of the upper class. He saw that the "rugged individualism" of the early capitalists had failed in the Great Depression and realized that the elite would have to become more public-minded if it was to maintain its position. The New Deal was based on a growing sense of noblesse oblige, and his new attitude led directly to America's involvement in international affairs as the guardian of democracy and indirectly to the growth of the military.

The Power Elite.   Since World War II, the military has been industry's biggest consumer, and industry government's biggest supporter. "Political insiders," "corporate chieftains," and "professional warlords" rule America, according to C. Wright Mills.[13] The three form interlocking circles, he argued. The politicians, who get massive financial support from corporations, vote vast amounts for defense; the defense establishment in turn spends great sums with the corporations, which fund the politicians, and so on. The whole thing was leading to war, Mills predicted.[14] President Eisenhower, on leaving office in 1961, warned of a "military-industrial complex" that exercised "unwarranted influence" on U.S. life. Elite theorists, many of whom have a leftist bent, see this influence as continuing.[15]

A quick reading of *Who's Who in America,* elitists argue, shows that a relatively small group of men dominate executive positions in government, finance, industry, and education. These men move back and forth, working now in government, now in business. Elitists feel this overlap in personnel disproves the pluralist concept of independent, competing elites. Although formally separated, American business and American government are run by the same people.

The effect of personnel overlap is most obvious in the government's regulatory agencies, which often become covert lobbies for the interests they are supposed to regulate. Logically, the president appoints executives who have experience in the field. Most of these appointees consider their position in government temporary and are reluctant to make decisions that might jeopardize future jobs in the private sector. Because of budget limitations, regulatory agencies sometimes depend on private research for information. For example, a decision about whether to permit an oil company to drill offshore may depend on that company's study of the ocean floor. In addition, agency officials and industry lobbyists spend a good deal of time together. Familiarity—not necessarily corruption—gradually causes them to think alike.

To these arguments, elitists add the fact that most government officials are better-off and well educated—for several reasons. Only people who can afford to abandon their careers temporarily for a campaign or to take relatively low-paying government jobs are able to seek public office, appointed or elected. Moreover, a person who does not have executive experience and connections may fail as an administrator. C. Wright Mills wrote, "To be celebrated, to be wealthy, to have power, requires access to major institutions, for the institutional positions men occupy determine in large part their chances to have and to hold valued experience."[16]

Elite theorists suggest that the executives of the country's biggest corporations have as much or more to say about "who gets what, when, and how" than do government officials. Despite antitrust laws, a few dozen giant corporations dominate the economy. Like the government, they have the power to levy taxes (by raising prices), to affect the quality of life (with products and wages), and to change the environment (with chemical wastes, strip mining, smokestacks). Corporations influence legislators with campaign donations, with personal favors such as the loan of an airplane, and through their power to close a plant that constituents depend on for jobs.

In recent years, regulation of corporations has been complicated by the growth of holding companies (whose only "product" is stock certificates) and institutional investors (banks, mutual funds, and insurance companies) who have taken over the role once played by such men as Henry Ford. If the government suspects foul play, it prosecutes General Motors or the Dreyfus Fund, not individuals; corporate officials are not held accountable for their decisions. In addition, a single person may be on the board of directors of several companies. Antitrust laws are, according to some theorists, ineffective against these interlocking directorates.

Pluralists argue that the people—groups of people—*can* influence and regulate government and corporation policy. If a president or mayor appoints corrupt officials to regulatory agencies, the people can vote against that official. They can refuse to buy unsafe automobiles or they can give time and money to citizen's lobbies. Elitists do not feel that public pressure—through elections or interest groups—influences those in power.

Elections.   For elections to be a truly effective democratic institution, say elite theorists Thomas Dye and L. Harmon Zeigler, they would have to meet four conditions:

1. Competing candidates would offer clear policy alternatives.

2. Voters would be concerned with policy questions.

3. Majority preference on these questions would be ascertained in election results.

4. Elected officials would be bound by the positions they assumed during the campaign.[17]

Only rarely, these authors conclude, do the two major parties offer voters a true choice of "policy alternatives"—partly because Republicans and Democrats agree on goals, if not on methods, and partly because both recognize that voters do not respond to ideological debate. Despite party loyalties, few Americans can identify their own political position (liberal, middle of the road, conservative), and few see clear differences between the two major parties. Apparently voters choose candidates on the basis of their personalities and presentation, not for their policies. In 1964, for example, Lyndon Johnson strongly opposed Barry Goldwater's hawkish stand on Vietnam. Polls indicated, however, that 52 percent of those who favored a stronger stand—even if it meant invading North Vietnam—voted not for Goldwater but for Johnson.

Since so many eligible voters fail to exercise their franchise, no president in modern times has won the votes of a majority of the American people. In fact, in 1968 and 1980 a majority of eligible voters either stayed away from the polls or voted for a third-party candidate. In 1988, only 50 percent of the eligible population voted. The elections of 1992 were considered an improvement; all of 54 percent of those eligible voted. The winners of elections thus do not represent majority opinion.

But even if a majority of voters were to express their opinion on the issues at the polls, there is no guarantee that elected officials would abide by their campaign platforms. Once elected, President Johnson followed a policy in Vietnam that came close to Goldwater's platform. President Nixon took steps toward a wide-ranging détente with the USSR and reopened relations with the People's Republic of China even though he had campaigned domestically for years as a staunch anti-Communist. In 1932, Franklin D. Roosevelt campaigned as a fiscal conservative, but once in office he instituted the most liberal reforms of the century. In 1980, Ronald Reagan campaigned against federal budget deficits, but in office he produced the biggest budget deficits in U.S. history. President Bush campaigned on "no new taxes," but in office he raised them. President Clinton campaigned on "ending welfare as we know it," but in office fought to preserve the system. What goes in (voting) and what comes out (policy) are not necessarily connected.

For these reasons, elitists consider elections to be a mere "symbolic exercise" designed to give the people the feeling that they participate. According to Murray Edelman, elections allow the people to express "quiet resentments and doubts about particular political acts [and] reaffirm belief in the fundamental rationality and democratic nature of the system."[18]

Interest Groups.   Elite theorists note with accuracy that labor unions, professional associations, mass political movements, PTAs, and so on tend to become oligarchic. Few people have time to work actively in interest groups: Control falls into the hands of the active few. As long as these leaders act within broad limits of propriety, the inactive majority accepts their authority as spokespersons. Gradually the leaders begin to personify the group; rank-and-file opinions are considered "unofficial." For example, in the early 1960s, AFL–CIO officials backed Johnson's civil rights legislation, although the rank and file generally preferred *not* to compete with black workers. Like government and corporation officials, interest group leaders develop a vested interest in maintaining the system and their position in it. In a sense, they join the elite.

THE PLURALIST VIEW

The pluralist view of America is basically an extension of Madisonian democracy. Like other early American political thinkers, James Madison believed that power corrupts—that public officials tend to become tyrannical if left unchecked. "Ambition must be made to counteract ambition," he wrote.[19] The constitutional system of separated legislative, executive, and judicial functions he and others designed was intended to check the power of individuals and the interests they represented.

Madison also believed that class conflict was inevitable and potentially disruptive: "Those who hold and those who are without property have ever formed distinct interests in society."[20] At any time, the unpropertied majority might rise up, threatening the propertied minority. In a rather sophisticated argument, Madison suggested that the way to protect minorities (such as the wealthy Founding Fathers) was to extend the vote to the entire population. The diversity of the American population, he reasoned, would prevent majority tyranny.

> Extend the sphere, and you take in a greater variety of parties and interests; you make it less probable that a majority of the whole will have a common motive to invade the rights of other citizens; or if such a common motive exists, it will be more difficult for all who feel it to discover their own strength, and to act in unison with each other.[21]

In *A Preface to Democratic Theory,* pluralist Robert Dahl maintains that America *does* operate on a checks and balances system, although not exactly the one Madison foresaw. The writers of the Constitution assumed that the House would become the instrument of the people—a hotbed of radical, populist thinking—and that the president would check Congress with a veto. In practice today, according to Dahl, these roles are reversed: "It is the president who is the policymaker, the creator of legislation, and the self-appointed spokesman for the national majority, whereas the power of Congress is more and more that of a veto—a veto exercised, as often as not, on behalf of groups whose privileges are threatened by presidential policy."[22]

To carry out their policies, presidents depend heavily on their party's organization. Madison did not foresee the role political parties would play in the American political system.

How do pluralists rebut the evidence that a power elite rules America? They reject, first, the notion of elite consensus.

Decentralized Power.   Pluralists feel that there is abundant evidence of disagreement and competition among powerful individuals and groups, both in government and in the private sector. Congress sometimes rejects presidential nominations for high office and legislative proposals. The government, under congressional mandate, simultaneously subsidizes tobacco growing and warns against cigarette smoking. The federal government guaranteed loans to save Chrysler but did not put quotas or increase tariffs on Japanese cars. The gigantic U.S. oil industry is understandably pro-Arab, but Israel is the largest recipient of U.S. foreign aid. If government, industry, and military leaders were working together, as elite theorists suggest, these disagreements and inconsistencies would not occur.

What about personnel overlap? Pluralists argue that C. Wright Mills and other elitists overemphasize the influence of many positions in government and business, confusing potential and actual power. The fact that people are chairpersons or department secretaries or generals does not necessarily mean that they control their local school boards, interfere with plans for state highways, or influence foreign policy. They may not be interested in anything but their business, or their company or agency may be organized in a way that limits their influence. For example, in most cases, members of a board of directors limit participation in a company to selecting managers. These managers, not the directors, form company policy. Pluralists feel that Mills and others have failed to demonstrate that people in high positions actually command government policy.

In addition, elitists are criticized for having failed to show evidence of a significant level of interaction among individuals in key positions. Does America's elite meet regularly to decide how to proceed on new issues? Does the automobile industry consult with the president of IBM before announcing that it will not be able to meet a deadline for antipollution devices? Pluralists see little proof of continuing accommodation and cooperation among members of the elite.

In a study of New Haven, Connecticut, Dahl found that the upper class tended to be aloof toward politics and community affairs. Decisions were the result of bargaining among interested groups. Some business leaders supported the mayor's efforts in urban renewal, primarily because they had a stake in the inner city. They did not become involved in education (most of their children attended private or suburban schools) or in local party politics. Power in American communities, Dahl concluded, is highly decentralized.[23]

Electoral Accountability.   Pluralists categorically reject the idea that elections are merely a "symbolic exercise." All elected officials must go to the voters periodically, and this need eventually influences both their policy decisions and their personal conduct in office. "Elected officials," wrote Dahl, "keep the real or imagined preferences of constituents constantly in mind in deciding what policies to adopt or reject."[24]

How do officials judge what their constituents want? They read their mail, the newspapers, and the polls.[25] They meet with businesspersons who are bidding for a contract, backing a job training program or a new arts center, or contributing to their campaign fund. They also meet with senior citizens, black activists, and mothers demanding day-care centers—if these people are insistent. Their exposure to public opinion is thus biased in favor of those with a stake in a particular decision and those who express their views publicly. The so-called silent majority does not directly influence decisions, but active interest groups do. The people an elected official has either helped or offended are the people most likely to vote; he or she cannot afford to ignore them.

However, the silent majority does influence officials indirectly. If officials do not successfully reconcile competing or conflicting activists within their jurisdiction, they are likely to create new interest groups that oppose them. Elected officials must keep both the active and the potentially active constantly in mind in what political scientist Carl J. Friedrich called the "rule of anticipated reactions."[26] Even though the public is quiet for the moment, officials try to avoid decisions that will make people angry. In this way, even quiet people have an input.

Why are so many Americans apathetic? Nonvoting, according to pluralists, is primarily an expression of "passive consent," not just disillusionment with the political system. Although minority groups have been discouraged or prevented from voting, most nonvoters are simply more concerned about their homes, families, and jobs than about politics. It is only when these elements are threatened (e.g., by unemployment) that the politically passive form interest groups and vote; otherwise they often leave decisions to the experts. Elections thus tend to be a combination of interested minority will and tacit majority consent. Voters and nonvoters influence political decision makers, even though they do not control them directly.

But do interested voters have a choice in elections? Pluralists reject the idea that the elite consensus within and between the two major parties goes so deep as to deny conflict over issues. Both parties comprise people from different locales with different interests. The divisions within the Democratic party, which includes southern conservatives and northern liberals, are legendary. Because parties lack even internal consensus, party power is decentralized to state and local organizations. Party politics is a process of endless bargaining among interested minorities.

Interest Groups. Pluralists see interest groups as the key to American democracy. A single person may not be able to make his or her views heard, but organized groups can, in one of two ways. First, they can help candidates who are sympathetic to their cause by providing workers, special skills, equipment, money, and publicity. A printers' union may donate handbills and posters; a PTA may invite a candidate to address its meeting; an ethnic group may raise money with a street fair. The degree of positive support a group can offer depends on its membership and resources and on whether it finds a sympathetic elected official. If it does not, the second way it can influence decision makers is by threatening the stability of their district. The ability to influence public opinion extends power to the powerless—to average citizens. To restore stability and public confidence, an official must respond to organized pressure, whatever its source.

Similarly, interest groups can influence corporate policy by pressuring elected officials to intervene on their behalf or by generating adverse publicity. Civil rights groups pressured the government to insist on integration in construction companies working on federal contracts; environmentalists, galvanized by the Three Mile Island accident, forced the nuclear power industry to adhere to stricter standards; women's rights organizations forced businesses to change their policies toward women.

Pluralists thus argue that organized minorities and social movements play an integral role in the American system. As Dahl wrote, "The making of governmental decisions is not a majestic march of great majorities united on certain matters of basic policy. It is the steady appeasement of relatively small groups."[27]

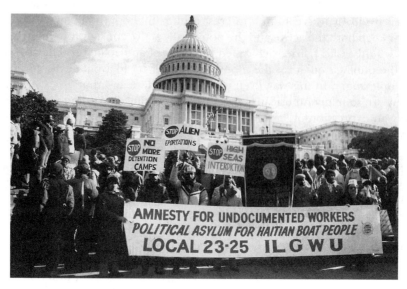

Interest groups such as these trade unionists are a key element in the pluralistic makeup of this country.

Crosscutting Cleavages.   If society is made up of many groups, some of them seriously opposed to one another, why doesn't it fall apart in violence and civil war? How can a pluralistic society, one that permits the free interplay of many groups, hold together? Political scientists have advanced an explanation based on the probability that individuals belong to or identify with more than one group, that they have "overlapping membership." This in turn produces what political scientists call "crosscutting cleavages": People belonging to more than one group must moderate their views and cooperate with other groups because they sometimes line up on the same side politically.[28]

The classic case of crosscutting cleavages is Switzerland. Some Swiss speak German, others French, and the two groups do not like each other. But some Swiss are also Catholic, whereas others are Protestant, and this religious cleavage cuts across the linguistic cleavage, giving four combinations: French-speaking Catholics, French-speaking Protestants, German-speaking Catholics, and German-speaking Protestants. French-speaking Catholics, for example, may not like German speakers, but they also recognize that German-speaking Catholics are their coreligionists and to a certain extent their allies in the face of Protestantism. Accordingly, francophone Catholics modify their dislike of German speakers because some of them are religious allies. Thus, crosscutting cleavages help hold Switzerland together.

Where cleavages do not cut across each other but instead reinforce each other, the country's unity is threatened. An example is Yugoslavia, where all Croats are Roman Catholic and all Serbs are Orthodox. Yugoslavia might have held together much better if half the Croats were Orthodox and half the Serbs Catholic. Unfortunately, Yugoslavia had no crosscutting cleavages.

We can see crosscutting cleavages in the United States and note their beneficial effects. Fundamentalist Protestants historically have not liked Catholics, but they find they line up on the same side on the abortion issue. They have learned to cooperate and have greatly moderated their dislikes. By the same token, white factory workers, who are often prejudiced against African-Americans, found they had to modify their views when the only national politician speaking to their needs was the Reverend Jesse Jackson. In this case, the working-class line cut across the color line.

Plural Elites: A Synthesis

As the student may have judged, there are elements of truth in both the elite and the pluralist pictures of politics. A more accurate picture would combine the two views. A first step is to recognize that elites are plural; that is, rarely does a society have a single, fused elite, as C. Wright Mills proposed. In a complex, modern society, one can discern business elites, bureaucratic elites, military elites, agricultural elites, labor elites, and so on. They cooperate or conflict, depending on circum-

The Reverend Jesse Jackson got a warm response from white workers out on strike, an example of "crosscutting cleavages." Such alliances, across lines of race and religion, moderate conflict and help make pluralist democracy possible.

stances, much as pluralists have argued. But this interaction is not the whole group in question interacting with other whole groups; it is small, elite representatives of one group interacting with small, elite representatives of other groups.

The pure elitist views society as a single pyramid, with a tiny elite at the top. The pure pluralist views society as a collection of billiard balls colliding with each other and with government to produce policy. Both views are overdrawn. A synthesis that more accurately reflects reality might be a series of small pyramids, each capped by an elite, or a collection of small planets with a large mountain at each north pole also topped by an elite. There is interaction of many units, as the pluralists would have it, but there is also stratification of leaders and followers, as elitist thinkers would have it. (See Fig. 5.1.)

Political scientists have tried to define this situation in various terms. Robert Dahl called it a "polyarchy," the rule of the leaders of several groups who have reached stable understandings with each other.[29] Arend Lijphart called it "consociational democracy," a means by which divided societies can prevent violence among groups.[30] The image of democracy offered by these authors goes beyond the one-person, one-vote definition of democracy. There may, of course, be universal suffrage, but in divided societies this can be a prescription for intergroup conflict and even civil war. What matters in such societies is that the elites of each important group have struck a bargain to play by the rules of a constitutional game and to restrain their followers from violence.

Lijphart's example of where this has worked successfully is the Netherlands, where there are serious differences among Catholics, Calvinists, and secular people. Why hasn't Holland fallen apart? Because the elites of these blocs have reached an "elite accommodation" or balance among each other. Such an accommodation is not automatically or necessarily the case. Elites must do two things: keep their people in line and reach bargains with the elites of other groups. When they do not, the results can be terrible to behold: Consider Lebanon.

For centuries Lebanon has been deeply divided along religious lines among Maronite Christians, the Greek Orthodox, Greek Catholics, Sunni Muslims, Shiite

FIGURE 5.1   Elite, Pluralist, and Polyarchy Models

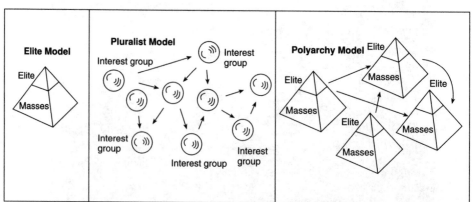

Muslims, the Druse, and others. In 1943, leaders of the two largest groups, the Maronite Christians and the Sunni Muslims, reached an unwritten agreement known as the National Pact, requiring that the president of Lebanon be a Maronite, the prime minister a Sunni, the speaker of parliament a Shiite, the deputy prime minister Greek Orthodox, and the defense minister a Druse.[31] For some thirty years the National Pact, a model of polyarchy or consociation, worked well, and Lebanon became an island of stability and prosperity in the Middle East; but this lasted only as long as elites were able to keep their people in line and accommodate other elites.

The delicate balance began to tip when Muslims demanded a bigger say. Muslims had been assigned minority status under the out-of-date 1932 census; Christians deliberately avoided a newer census, but most observers agreed the Muslims had become a majority. In 1958 the Muslims sided with the pan-Arab aspirations of Egyptian President Nasser, and serious fighting erupted, quelled in part by U.S. Marines. In 1975 Lebanon fell apart as the Muslims joined with radical Palestinians in full-scale civil war. Each religious group in Lebanon had its private army and sometimes massacred civilians. Only after many years of this horror did Lebanon begin to put itself back together.

The Lebanese case is graphic. When there was accommodation among elites, the system worked. When elite consensus broke down, so did the system. During the period of the National Pact, members of the various groups did not slowly learn to love each other and temper their differences; the differences were too great. But they did live in peace for as long as their plural elites were able to strike a bargain. The elite bargain did not erase conflict, but it did serve to *manage* conflict.

To what extent are other countries examples of "conflict management" by elites? The United States can be seen in this fashion, with its interplay of business, labor, ethnic, regional, and other elites, each delivering enough to keep their people in line, each cooperating to varying degrees with other elites. When elite consensus broke down, the United States, too, experienced a bloody civil war.

The "plural elites" model—or polyarchy or consociation—attempts to synthesize the partial views of the elitist and pluralist models. It explains some facets of political life, but not all. As with all models in political science, it must be taken as tentative and suggestive rather than as definitive.

Suggested Readings

ALBERTONI, ETTORE. *Mosca and the Theory of Elitism.* New York: Blackwell, 1987. An Italian historian examines the growth of Mosca's thought in the context of Italian politics.

BACHRACH, PETER. *The Theory of Democratic Elitism.* Boston: Little, Brown, 1967. A critique of pluralism and a discussion of the need for equal opportunity.

BENTLEY, ARTHUR F. *The Process of Government.*

San Antonio, TX: Principia Press. 1949. Originally published in 1908, Bentley's views on the importance of groups in politics, radical at the time, laid the groundwork for pluralist thinking.

DAHL, ROBERT A. *Polyarchy: Participation and Opposition.* New Haven, CT: Yale University Press, 1971. Dahl's theory of plural elites.

DOGAN, MATTEI, ed. *Comparing Pluralist Democra-*

cies; Strains on Legitimacy. Boulder, CO: Westview Press, 1988. A worried view by noted comparativists that group demands on democratic governments is eroding their bases of support.

DOMHOFF, G. WILLIAM. *The Power Elite and the State: How Policy Is Made in America.* Hawthorne, NY: Aldine de Gruyter, 1990. A more sophisticated and data-supported exploration of the U.S. elite than Mills's classic.

DYE, THOMAS R. *Who's Running America? The Reagan Years,* 4th ed. Englewood Cliffs, NJ: Prentice Hall, 1986. Latest edition of a readable and forceful elite argument.

EDELMAN, MURRAY. *The Symbolic Uses of Power.* Urbana: University of Illinois Press, 1964. A study of the power, operation, and use and abuse of symbols in politics.

ELDERSVELD, SAMUEL, J., LARS STRÖMBERG, and WIM DERKSEN. *Local Elites in Western Democracies: A Comparative Analysis of Urban Political Leaders in the U.S., Sweden, and the Netherlands.* Boulder, CO: Westview Press, 1995. Unusual

crossnational look at local elites, their powers, and their attitudes.

LIJPHART, AREND. *Democracy in Plural Societies: A Comparative Exploration.* New Haven, CT: Yale University Press, 1977. Develops the concept of "consociational democracy," akin to Dahl's "polyarchy."

PUTNAM, ROBERT D. *The Comparative Study of Political Elites.* Englewood Cliffs, NJ: Prentice Hall, 1976. Methodologically sophisticated synthesis of elite theory and data.

SCHWARTZ, MICHAEL, ed. *The Structure of Power in America: The Corporate Elite as a Ruling Class.* New York: Holmes & Meier, 1987. Millsian views of the United States as dominated by interlocking directorates and more subtle forms of capitalist hegemony.

SISK, TIMOTHY D. *Democratization in South Africa: The Elusive Social Contract.* Princeton, NJ: Princeton University Press, 1994. Emphasizes opposing elites were forced to negotiate a basis for South Africa's new democracy.

Notes

1. Gaetano Mosca, *The Ruling Class* (New York: McGraw Hill, 1939), p. 50.

2. Robert A. Dahl, "Power, Pluralism, and Democracy: A Modest Proposal" (paper delivered at the 1964 annual meeting of the American Political Science Association), p. 3.

3. Robert Michels, *Political Parties: A Sociological Study of the Oligarchic Tendency of Modern Democracy* (Glencoe, IL: Free Press, 1958).

4. Henry Valen and Daniel Katz, *Political Parties in Norway: A Community Study* (Oslo: Universitetsforlaget, 1967), p. 98.

5. The best exploration of France's Grand Corps is Ezra N. Suleiman, *Elites in French Society: The Politics of Survival* (Princeton, NJ: Princeton University Press, 1978).

6. C. Wright Mills, *The Power Elite* (New York: Oxford University Press, 1956).

7. An important early study that uncovered the greater liberalism of elites is Samuel Stauffer, *Communism, Conformity, and Civil Liberties* (Garden City, NY: Doubleday, 1955). A recent and more detailed confirmation of this thesis is Herbert McClosky and Alida Brill, *Dimensions of Tolerance. What Americans Believe About Civil Liberties* (New York: Russell Sage, 1983).

8. Note that pluralists do not believe America is a populist democracy, ruled by the people.

For this reason, pluralists are sometimes called "plural-elitists." See Robert Dahl, *A Preface to Democratic Theory* (Chicago: University of Chicago Press, 1956).

9. Organization is a key point here. Pluralists do not argue that private individuals can influence decision makers but that interest groups can.

10. Dahl, *Preface to Democratic Theory,* p. 137. Dahl suggests that to be effective, a group must be *both* active and legitimate. Blacks before the 1960s had a legitimate claim to a role in politics, but they were not active; Communists have long been organized and active, but the majority of the electorate does not consider their viewpoint legitimate.

11. Aristide Zolberg made the comment in his review of a book that urged pluralism for the developing countries. The book was Lucian W. Pye and Sidney Verba, eds., *Political Culture and Political Development* (Princeton, NJ: Princeton University Press, 1965). Zolberg's review appeared in the *American Political Science Review* 60 (March 1966), 121.

12. See Charles Beard, *An Economic Interpretation of the Constitution* (New York: Free Press, 1935); and Forrest McDonald, *We the People: The Economic Origins of the Constitution* (Chicago: University of Chicago Press, 1958).

13. Mills's *Power Elite* is the classic statement of this position.

14. C. Wright Mills, *The Causes of World War III* (New York: Ballantine, 1958).

15. See, for example, the critical analysis of Michael Parenti, *Democracy for the Few,* 5th ed. (New York: St. Martin's, 1987).

16. Mills, *Power Elite*, pp. 10–11.

17. Thomas R. Dye and L. Harmon Zeigler, *The Irony of Democracy: An Uncommon Introduction to American Politics,* 7th ed. (Monterey, CA: Brooks/Cole, 1986); this text forms the basis for this section.

18. Murray Edleman, *The Symbolic Uses of Power* (Urbana, IL: University of Illinois Press, 1964), p. 17.

19. *The Federalist,* No. 51.

20. *The Federalist,* No. 10.

21. Ibid. The writers of the Constitution, for example, might have stipulated that only landowners could vote; small farmers might then have banded together to force their will on large landowners. (In fact, this occurred in states that instituted property qualifications for the vote.) With everyone—that is, every white male—voting, clerks, merchants, shopkeepers, and so on would check the small farmers.

22. Dahl, *Preface to Democratic Theory,* p. 142.

23. Robert A. Dahl, *Who Governs?* (New Haven, CT: Yale University Press, 1961). This study is discussed further in the next section.

24. Ibid., p. 164.

25. A study of the factors that influence congressional voters showed that it is the officials' perception of their constituency's opinion rather than the constituency's actual attitude that influences their position. See Warren E. Miller and Donald E. Stokes, "Constituency Influence in Congress," *American Political Science Review* 57 (March 1963), 45–56.

26. Carl J. Friedrich, *Constitutional Government and Politics* (New York: Harper, 1937), pp. 16–18.

27. Dahl, *Preface to Democratic Theory,* p. 140.

28. The effects of crosscutting affiliations were first recognized early in the twentieth century by German sociologist Georg Simmel, *Conflict and the Web of Group Affiliations* (Glencoe, IL: Free Press, 1956). The concept was revived by American political scientist David Truman, *The Governmental Process* (New York: Knopf, 1951), especially Chap. 6.

29. Robert A. Dahl, *Polyarchy: Participation and Opposition* (New Haven, CT: Yale University Press, 1971).

30. Arend Lijphart, *Democracy in Plural Societies: A Comparative Exploration* (New Haven, CT: Yale University Press, 1977).

31. For an excellent discussion of Lebanon's problem, see Samir Khalaf, *Lebanon's Predicament* (New York: Columbia University Press, 1987).

· 6 ·

Political Ideologies

The Republican takeover of Capitol Hill in the 1994 elections reminded us that political ideology is still very much alive in the United States. These Republicans were distinctly ideological, prescribing what they called conservatism to solve problems ranging from the economy and inner cities to energy and the environment.[1] Probably few of them knew it, but they were actually classic *liberals*, harkening back to Adam Smith's two-century-old admonition to get government out of the economy. Their ideas on individual initiative, a deregulated economy, and the self-correcting power of the marketplace were pure Adam Smith.

The people that the Republicans put on the defensive, the so-called liberals, also had a history of which they were probably unaware. Although they accepted the name of liberalism, associated with Adam Smith, they actually applied a greatly changed brand of liberalism dating from the late nineteenth century. The point here is that Americans, who usually like to think of themselves as pragmatic rather than ideological, are heirs to centuries of ideological thought and are indeed subscribing (if unwittingly) to one or another doctrine that was penned generations ago.

What Is Ideology?

An ideology begins with the belief that things can be better than they are; it is basically a plan to improve society. As Anthony Downs put it, ideology is "a verbal image of the good society, and of the chief means of constructing such a society."[2] Followers of a given ideology argue that if their plan is followed, things will be much better than they are at present. Political ideologies, then, are not the same as political science; that is, they are not calm, rational attempts to understand political systems. They are, rather, commitments to *change* political systems. (The one exception here might be classical conservatism, which aims at keeping the system from changing too much.) People caught up in a political ideology are apt to make poor political scientists, for they often confuse the "should" or "ought" of ideology with the "is" of political science.

The eighteenth-century French philosopher Antoine Destutt de Tracy coined the term *ideology* to describe what he called the new "science of ideas." Most ideologies can be traced back in time (Fig. 6.1). Classical liberalism can be traced back to the seventeenth-century English philosopher John Locke, who emphasized individual rights, property, and reason.[3] Communism can be traced back to the late eighteenth-century German philosopher G. W. F. Hegel, who emphasized that all facets of a society—art, music, architecture, statecraft, law, and so on—hang together as a package, the expression of an underlying cause.

However, philosophers' ideas are often simplified, popularized, and changed beyond recognition. Ideologists want plans for action, not abstract ideas. Marx, for example, "stood Hegel on his head" to make economics the great underlying cause for everything else in society. Lenin later stood Marx on *his* head to make his ideas apply to a backward country where Marx doubted they should. Mao Zedong then applied Lenin's ideas to an even more backward country, where they didn't fit at all. Hegel and Marx must have been spinning in their graves. But ideologists are not concerned with fidelity to the original ideas; they want change.

As the ideas become more applied and less abstract, the ideology becomes an important cement, holding together movements, parties, or revolutionary groups. To fight well and endure sacrifices, people need ideological motivation. They need something to believe in. Americans have sometimes been unable to grasp this point. With their emphasis on moderation and pragmatism—"if it works, use it"— they fail to understand the energizing effect of ideology in the world today. "Our" Vietnamese, the South Vietnamese, were physically no different from the Vietcong

FIGURE 6.1   How Political Ideologies Relate to Each Other: Key Thinkers and Dates of Emergence

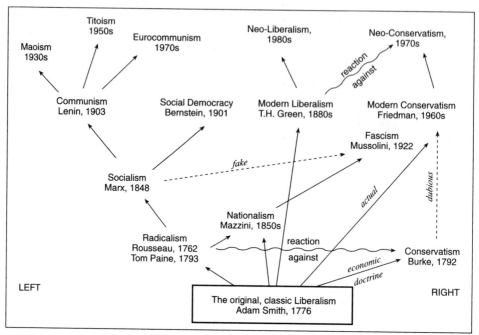

and North Vietnamese, and they were better armed. But in the crunch, the Vietnamese who had a doctrine to believe in—a mixture of Marx, Lenin, and Mao with heavy doses of nationalism and anticolonialism—won against the Vietnamese who didn't have much to believe in. By the same token, Americans were amazed at the fall of the shah and his replacement by fanatic politico-religious revolutionaries. We shouldn't have been so surprised; we should rather have looked more closely at whether the shah had a plausible ideological package to sell his people. We tend to forget that more than two centuries ago Americans were quite ideological, too, and—imbued with a passion for freedom and self-rule, via the pens of John Locke and Thomas Paine—beat a larger and better equipped army of Englishmen and Hessians who had no good reason to fight. Have we forgotten the power of ideas?

A large part of ideologies is their economic component. Most ideologies have quite a bit to say about economics, for it is economics that is to provide the basis for social improvement. This was as true of the conservatism of Ronald Reagan as it was of the communism of Mao Zedong: Both placed heavy emphasis on economics.

Ideologies can be classified—with some oversimplification—on a left-to-right spectrum. This system dates back to the meeting of the French National Assembly in 1789. To allow delegates of similar views to caucus and to keep apart strong partisans who might fight with their fists as well as with words, members were seated as follows in a semicircular chamber: Conservatives (who favored continuation of the monarchy) were on the speaker's right; radicals (who favored sweeping away the old system altogether in favor of a republic of freedom and equality) were seated to his left; and moderates (who wanted some change) were seated in the center. We have been calling their ideological descendants the left, the right, and the center ever since, even though the content of their views has changed quite a bit. The left now favors equality, welfare programs, and sometimes government intervention in the economy. The right stresses individual initiative and private economic activity. Centrists try to synthesize and moderate the views of both. People a little to one side or the other are said to be center-left or center-right. Sweden's political parties form a rather neat left-to-right spectrum: a small Communist party; a large Social Democratic party; and medium-sized Center (formerly Farmers'), Liberal, and Conservative parties.

An ideology is a plan. How do ideologies work in practice? They never work precisely the way their advocates claim. Some are hideous failures. All ideologies contain a certain amount of wishful thinking that frequently collapses in the face of reality. Ideologies imagine a perfect world; reality is highly imperfect. The classic liberalism of Adam Smith did contribute to the nineteenth century's economic growth, but it also led to great inequalities of wealth and recurring depressions; it had to be modified into modern liberalism. Communism led to a series of more or less brutal tyrannies, economic failures, and its own collapse in Europe. The millennial hopes of nationalist liberation movements have been repeatedly disappointed as soon as the revolutionaries have come to power. All ideologies, when measured against their actual performance, are to greater or lesser degrees defective. They should be taken with a grain of salt.

The Major Ideologies

CLASSIC LIBERALISM

According to the late Frederick Watkins of Yale, 1776 could be called "the Year One of the Age of Ideology," and not just for the American Revolution. In that same year the Scottish economist Adam Smith published *The Wealth of Nations,* thereby founding classic laissez-faire economics.[4] The true wealth of nations, Smith argued, is not in the amount of gold and silver they amass but in the amount of goods and services their people produce. Smith was refuting an earlier notion, called *mercantilism,* that the bullion in a nation's treasury determined whether it was a rich country. Spain had followed this view in its looting of the New World but actually grew poorer. The French, too, since at least the time of Louis XIV in the previous century, had followed mercantilist policies by means of government supervision of the economy with plans, grants of monopoly, subsidies, tariffs, and other restraints on trade.

Smith reasoned that that was not the way to produce maximum economic growth. Government interference always retards growth. If you give one firm a monopoly to manufacture something, you banish competition and with it efforts to produce new products at better prices: The economy stagnates. If you protect domestic industry by means of tariffs that effectively lock out foreign competition, you take away any incentive the domestic producer might have to make better or cheaper products. By getting the government out of the economy, by letting the economy alone (*laissez-faire* in French), you will actually have the best system.

But what about the chaos that will come with free competition unsupervised by government? Not to worry, said Smith; the market itself will regulate the economy. Efficient producers will prosper and the inefficient will go under. The public will get the best products for the lowest prices. Supply and demand determine prices better than any government official can. In the free marketplace, an "unseen hand" regulates and self-corrects the economy. If people want more of a given item, manufacturers increase production, new manufacturers enter the field, foreign producers bring in their wares, or there is a combination of all three. The unseen hand—actually, the rational calculations of myriad individuals all pursuing their self-interest—guides the economic adjustments needed.

This ideology acquired the name *liberalism* from the Latin word for "free," *liber:* Society should be free as possible from government interference. As aptly summarized by Thomas Jefferson, "That government is best that governs least." Americans took to classic liberalism like a duck takes to water. It seemed perfectly suited to the needs of a vigorous, freedom-loving population with plenty of room to expand. The noneconomic elements also suited Americans. Just as the government shouldn't supervise the economy, so also should it not supervise religion, the press, or free speech.

But, you say, what you're calling liberalism here is actually what everybody today calls conservatism. True. In the late nineteenth century liberalism changed and split into modern liberalism and what we now call conservatism, which we will discuss now. To keep our terminology straight, we should call the original ideas of Adam Smith "classic liberalism" to distinguish it from the modern variety.

CLASSIC CONSERVATISM

By the same token, we should call the ideas of Edmund Burke, published in the late eighteenth century, "classic conservatism," for his conservatism diverges in many ways from modern conservatism. Burke, who came from Ireland but was a member of Parliament representing Bristol, England, knew Adam Smith and agreed that a free market was the best economic system. Burke also opposed sending troops to crush the rebellious American colonists; after all, they were only trying to regain the ancient freedoms of Englishmen, said Burke. So far, Burke sounds like a liberal.

But what Burke strongly objected to was the way liberal ideas were being applied in France by revolutionists. There, liberalism turned into radicalism, influenced by philosopher Jean-Jacques Rousseau and, fresh from the U.S. revolution, Thomas Paine. As is often the case, an ideology devised in one place became warped when applied to different circumstances. To apply liberalism in America was easy; once the English and their Tory sympathizers cleared out, it fell into place without resistance. But in France, a large aristocratic class and a state-supported

Roman Catholic church had a lot to lose. The revolutionaries tried to solve the problem with the guillotine; they swept away all established institutions.

This, warned Burke, was a terrible mistake. Liberals place too much confidence in human reason. People are only partly rational; they also have wildly irrational passions. To contain them, society over the years has evolved traditions, institutions, and standards of morality, such as the monarchy and an established church. Sweep these aside, said Burke, and man's irrational impulses will lead to chaos, which in turn will end in tyranny far worse than that which the revolutionaries overthrew. Burke, in his 1792 *Reflexions on the Revolution in France,* actually predicted that France would fall under the rule of a military dictator. In 1799, Napoleon took over.

Institutions and traditions that currently exist can't be all bad, Burke reasoned, for they are the products of hundreds of years of trial and error. People have become used to them. The best should be preserved or "conserved" (hence the name "conservatism"). Never mind if they aren't perfect; they work. This is not to say that things should never change. Of course they should change, wrote Burke, but only gradually, giving people time to adjust. Burke was no "stand-patter," a point some current conservatives fail to grasp. "A state without the means of some change is without the means of its conservation," wrote Burke.[5]

Burke was an important thinker for several reasons. He helped discover the *irrational* in human behavior. He saw that institutions are like living things; they grow and adapt over time. And most important, he saw that revolutions tend to end badly, for society cannot be instantly remade according to the dictates of human reason. Although Burke's ideas have been called an *anti-ideology*—for they aimed to shoot down the radicalism that was then engulfing France—they have considerable staying power. Burke's emphasis on religion, traditions, and morality strikes a responsive chord in many a modern conservative's heart. His doubts about applying reason to solve social problems were echoed by Jeane Kirkpatrick, President Reagan's UN ambassador and a political scientist. She found that leftists are always imaging that things can be much better than they are when in point of fact violent upheaval always makes things worse.[6] In these ways, classic conservatism is still alive in modern thought.

MODERN LIBERALISM

What happened to the original, classic liberalism of Adam Smith? By the late nineteenth century it had become apparent that the free market was not as self-regulating as Smith had thought. Competition was not perfect. Manufacturers tended to rig the market—a point that Smith himself had warned about. There was a drift to bigness and fewness: monopoly. The system seemed to produce a large underclass of the terribly poor. Class positions to a certain extent were inherited: children of better-off families got a good education and the right connections to speed them on their way. Worst of all, there were recurring economic depressions in which the poor and the working class suffered greatly. In short, the laissez-faire society had some negative aspects.

The Englishman Thomas Hill Green rethought liberalism in the 1880s. The goal of liberalism, reasoned Green, was a free society. But what happens when economic developments take away that very freedom? The classic liberals placed great store in contracts (agreements between consenting parties with no government supervision): If you don't like the deal, don't take it. But what if the bargaining power of the two parties is greatly unequal, as between a rich employer and a poor person desperate for a job? Does the latter really have a free choice in accepting or rejecting a job with very low wages? Classic liberalism said let it be; wages will find their own level. But what if the wage is below starvation level? Here Green said it was time for government to step in. In such a case it would not be a question of government infringing on freedoms but of government protecting them. Instead of the purely negative "freedom from," there had to be a certain amount of the positive "freedom to." Green called this *positive freedom*. Government was to step in to guarantee the freedom to live at an adequate level.

Classic liberalism had expelled government from the marketplace; modern liberalism brought it back in, this time to protect people from a sometimes unfair economic system. Modern liberals championed wage and hour laws, the right to form unions, unemployment and health insurance, and improved educational opportunity for all. To do this, they were willing to place heavier taxes on the rich than on the working class. This is the liberalism we speak of in the twentieth-century United States, the liberalism of Woodrow Wilson and Franklin D. Roosevelt. One strand of the old liberalism remains in the new, however: the emphasis on freedom of speech and press.

MODERN CONSERVATISM

What happened to the other branch of liberalism, the people who stayed true to Adam Smith's original doctrine of minimal government? They are very much around, only we call them conservatives. (In Europe, "liberal" parties are generally pretty conservative by American standards; that is, they favor free-market solutions. Such is the orientation of Italian, Swedish, and German liberals.) American conservatives got a big boost from Milton Friedman, the Nobel Prize–winning economist. Friedman argued forcefully that the free market is still the best route, that the original doctrine of Adam Smith was right, that wherever government intervenes it messes things up.[7] Margaret Thatcher in Britain and Ronald Reagan in the United States attempted to apply this revival of classic liberalism in the 1980s. Results were mixed. Inflation came down, but unemployment went up, and budgets— long a conservative touchstone—went wildly into deficit. Both Britain and the United States experienced serious recessions. Government regulations were rolled back, but, especially in the United States, this raised cries that the government was giving away natural resources and relaxing environmental standards to make rich people richer. As is the case with all ideologies, what's supposed to work in theory doesn't always work in practice.

Modern conservatism also borrows from Edmund Burke a concern for tradition, especially in religion. American conservatives have been eager to get prayer into public schools, to outlaw abortion, and to obtain tax relief for parents who send their children to church schools. Modern conservatives are also traditional concerning women's and homosexual rights: They oppose them. Modern conservatism is thus a blend of the economic ideas of Adam Smith and the traditionalist ideas of Edmund Burke.

MARXIST SOCIALISM

Although liberalism (classic variety) dominated the nineteenth century, a strand of critical opinion arose in reaction to the obvious excesses of the capitalist system. Unlike T. H. Green, some critics didn't believe that a few reforms would suffice; they wanted the overthrow of the capitalist system. They were the socialists, and their leading thinker was a German living in London, Karl Marx.

There had been earlier socialist theories, going as far back as the French Revolution, but they tended to be mostly sentimental, concerned with the plight of the poor, rather than rigorously thought out. Rigorous thought is what Marx attempted to provide in the middle of the last century. Trained in Hegelian ideas and with a doctorate in philosophy, Marx produced an exceedingly complex ideology consisting of at least three interrelated elements: a theory of economics, a theory of social class, and a theory of history.

Economics.   In economics, Marx concentrated on the "surplus value"—what we would call profit. Workers produce things but get paid only a fraction of the value of what they produce. The capitalist owners skim off the rest, the surplus value. Not only is this unfair, argued Marx (who paid scant attention to the fact that capitalists pay overhead, risk their money, and often work quite hard themselves), but it also leads to recurring economic depressions. The workers, paid only for a fraction of what they produce, cannot go out on the market and buy all the products. The capitalist system pumps out an abundance of goods onto the market, but the bulk of the population—what Marx called the *proletariat* (industrial working class)—can't afford to buy them. The result is repeated overproduction, which, when products can't be sold, leads to depressions. Eventually, argued Marx, there will be a depression so big it will doom the capitalist system.

Social Class.   Perhaps the major element in Marx is social class. Every society divides into two classes: a small class of those who own the means of production and a large class of those who work for the small class. Society is run according to the dictates of the upper class, which sets up the laws, arts, and styles needed to maintain itself in power. Notice how many laws concern property rights, said Marx. That is not surprising, for the *bourgeoisie* (the capitalists) are obsessed with hanging on to their property, which, according to Marx, is nothing but skimmed-off surplus value anyway. If the country goes to war, said Marx, it is not because of the wishes of the common people but because the ruling bourgeoisie needs a war for economic gain. The proletariat, in fact, has no country; proletarians are international, all suffering under the heel of the capitalists.

Karl Marx glares down at the citizens of Tashkent, Uzbekistan, now an independent ex-Soviet republic. The communists built such statues—more of Lenin than of Marx—all over the Soviet Union.

History.   Now, putting together his economic theory and his social-class theory, Marx had an explanation for historical change. When the underlying economic basis of society gets out of kilter with the structure the dominant class has established (its laws, institutions, ways of doing business, and so on), the system collapses. This, said Marx, is what happened in the French Revolution. The ruling class before the revolution was the feudal nobility. Their system was from the middle ages, based on hereditary ownership of great estates worked by serfs, on laws stressing the inheritance of these estates and the titles that went with them, and on chivalry and honor. All were part and parcel of a feudal society. But the economic basis changed. Ownership of land and feudal values grew increasingly anachronistic with the rise of manufacturing. A new class came to the fore, the urban capitalists, or bourgeoisie. Their way of life and economy were quite different from those of the old feudal nobility. By the late eighteenth century, France had an economy based on manufacturing but was still dominated by feudal aristocrats with their minds in the past. The system was out of kilter: The economic basis had moved ahead, but the social class superstructure had stayed behind. In 1789, the superstructure came down with a crash, and the bourgeoisie took over with its new capitalist and liberal values of a free market, individual gain, and legal (but not material) equality.

The capitalists did a good job, Marx had to admit. They industrialized and modernized much of the globe. They put out new products and inventions that would have amazed people of the previous century. But they too are doomed, Marx wrote, because the faster they transform the economy, the more it gets out of step with the capitalist superstructure, just as the previous feudal society was left behind by the economy. This leads us back to Marx's theory of surplus value and recurring economic depressions. Eventually, reasoned Marx, the economy will be so far disjointed from the bourgeois setup that it too will come crashing down. What will come next?

Here Marx put his books aside and became a prophet. The next stage, he predicted, will be socialism. The proletariat will overthrow the bourgeoisie and establish a just, productive society *without* class distinctions. At a certain stage (and here Marx got awfully vague), this socialist society will reach a level of perfection in which there won't need to be police, money, or even government. Goods will be in such plenty that people will be able to just take what they need. There won't be private property, so there will be no need for police. Since government is simply an instrument of class domination, with the abolition of distinct classes there won't need to be government; it will "wither away." The name of this utopia is *communism*, the stage beyond socialism.

Marx himself was more of a theorist than an organizer, but during the late nineteenth century his ideas—or popularizations of them—caught on in the new socialist parties and labor movements of most of Europe, especially in that "mother of socialist parties," the German Social Democratic party (SPD), and in its daughter, the Russian Social Democratic Labor party. Marx was to socialism what Adam Smith was to liberalism: the original, the founder. But Marxian socialism also split, as we shall see. Marx might have trouble recognizing his offspring today.

SOCIAL DEMOCRACY

At the turn of the century the German Social Democrats, espousing a sort of Marxist theory, had become the biggest party in Germany. Marx hadn't thought much of conventional parties and labor unions; bourgeois governments would simply crush them, he believed. At most, they could be training grounds for more serious revolutionary action. But the German Social Democrats started having success. Their members got elected to the Reichstag and local offices; their unions started winning higher wages and better working conditions. Some began to think that the working class could accomplish its aims without revolution. Why use bullets when there are ballots?

Eduard Bernstein developed this viewpoint. In his *Evolutionary Socialism* (1901), he pointed out the very real gains the working class was making and concluded that Marx had been wrong about the necessity for collapse of the system and revolution. Reforms that won concrete benefits for the working class could also lead to socialism, he argued. In revising Marxism, Bernstein earned the name *revisionist*, originally a pejorative hurled at him by orthodox Marxists. Although the SPD as a whole was not won over, by the time of the ill-fated Weimar Republic in Germany (1919–1933), the Social Democrats had greatly toned down their militancy and worked together with Liberals and Catholics to try to save the faltering democracy. Persecuted by the Nazis, the Social Democrats revived after World War II. In 1959 they dropped Marxism altogether, as did virtually all social democratic parties. As social democrats in many countries moderated their positions, they found themselves getting elected more and more; voters no longer worried about them fomenting revolution.

Another important turnaround came in France with the election of a socialist government under François Mitterrand in 1981. It nationalized many industries and banks, increased wages, and hired more public sector employees. Naively, it paid no attention to where the money was going to come from. The French economy turned inflationary, unemployment climbed, and the currency dropped. Fortunately, Mitterrand saw the impending chaos and backed away from socialism. Most French Socialists had to admit that the state couldn't run the economy and that the free-enterprise market system was best. The French Socialists turned themselves from a leftist party to a centrist party. French intellectuals, who are influential around the world, for the first time in history embraced capitalism as a pretty good system. Along similar lines, in 1979 the Spanish Socialists (PSOE) dropped "Marxist" from party descriptions, and in 1982 they won national elections by a landslide and took over the government. Everywhere the social democrats had succeeded in transforming themselves into center-left parties.

What, then, do social democrats stand for?[8] They have abandoned their plans to nationalize industry. Sweden, for example, has only about 12 percent of its industry nationalized, and much of that was done a long time ago by conservatives to keep firms from going under and creating unemployment. Said the late Olof Palme, Sweden's Social Democratic prime minister, "If industry's primary purpose is to expand its production, to succeed in new markets, to provide good jobs for their employees, they need have no fears. Swedish industry has never expanded so rapidly as during these years of Social Democratic rule." Instead of nationalization of industry, social democrats have used *welfare* measures to improve living conditions: unemployment insurance, national medical plans, generous pensions, and subsidized food and housing. Social democracies have become welfare states: *welfarism* would be a more accurate term than *socialism*.

There's one catch—there's always at least one catch—and that is that welfare states are terribly expensive. To pay for these welfare measures, taxes climb. In Denmark and Sweden, taxes consume a majority of the gross domestic product (Table 6.1). One of every two kronas a Dane or Swede earns goes to the government. This is exactly the kind of thing conservative economist Milton Friedman warned about. With those kinds of taxes, soon you are not free to choose how you live. Social democrats and modern liberals have in some places grown close to one another, although they come from very different backgrounds. In Britain, moderate members of the Labour party split off and joined with the Liberal party. In the United States, what is called liberalism is tinged with social democratic ideas on the welfare state. It might be fair to say that the left wing of our Democratic party resembles ideologically the moderate wings of European social democratic parties.

TABLE 6.1 Taxes as a Percentage of GDP, 1994

Sweden	53
Netherlands	48
France	45
Germany	40
Britain	35
Canada	32
Japan	30
Australia	30
United States	30

Source: Organization for Cooperation and Development.

COMMUNISM

While the social democrats were undergoing their evolution into moderate reformists and welfarists, another, smaller wing of the original socialists stayed with Marx. These became the Communists. The key figure in this transformation was a Russian intellectual, Vladimir I. Lenin. He made several changes in Marxism to make it fit the situation Russia was in early in this century. The resultant combination, Marxism-Leninism, is another name for communism.

Imperialism. Marxism caught on early and deeply among Russian intellectuals in the last century. Many of them hated the tsarist system and found in Marxism a theory they could use to overthrow that system. Ironically, Marx meant his theory to apply in the most *advanced* capitalist countries, not in backward Russia, where capitalism was just beginning. But as noted before, ideologies often become warped when transplanted from their country of origin. Lenin, mostly in exile in Zurich, Switzerland, faced the problem of how to make Marxism fit backward Russia. To do so, he came up with a theory of economic imperialism, one borrowed from German Communist Rosa Luxemburg and English economist J. A. Hobson. These thinkers had all wondered why the proletarian revolutions Marx had foreseen had not broken out in the advanced industrialized lands. They concluded that capitalism had succeeded in transforming itself, expanding overseas into colonies to exploit their raw materials, cheap labor, and new markets. Capitalism had won a temporary new lease on life by turning into imperialism. The domestic market couldn't absorb what the capitalist system was producing, so it found overseas markets. Making enormous profits from its colonies, the mother imperialist country could also pay off its working class a bit to render it reformist rather than revolutionary.

While imperialism was expanding, Lenin noted, it was growing unevenly. Some countries, such as Britain and Germany, were highly developed, but where capitalism was just starting, as in Spain and Russia, it was weak. The latter sort of countries were exploited as a whole by the international capitalist system. It was in them that revolutionary fever burned brightest; they were imperialism's "weakest link." Accordingly, a revolution could break out in a backward country, reasoned Lenin, and then spread into advanced countries. The imperialist countries were highly dependent on their empires; once cut off from exploiting them, the imperialists would fall.[9] Further, Lenin thought he had an explanation for World War I: It was the collision of imperialist powers in an effort to dominate the globe economically.

Lenin, in effect, shifted the Marxian focus from the situation *within* capitalist countries to the situation *among* countries. The focus went from Marx's proletariat rising up against the bourgeoisie to exploited nations rising up against imperialist powers. Marx would probably not have approved of such a shift.

Organization.   But Lenin's real contribution lay in his attention to *organization*. With the tsarist secret police always on their trail, Lenin argued, the Russian socialist party could not be like other parties—large, open, and trying to win votes. Instead, it had to be small, secretive, made up of professional revolutionaries, and tightly organized under central command. In 1903 the Russian Social Democratic Labor party split over this issue. Lenin had enough of his supprters at their party's Brussels meeting to win the votes of thirty-three of the fifty-one delegates present. Lenin called his faction *bolshevik* (Russian for "majority"), whereas the losers, who advocated a more moderate line and a more open party, took the name *menshevik* ("minority"). In 1918 the Bolsheviks changed the party name to Communist.

In the chaos of 1917, Lenin's attention to organization paid off. Russia was terribly weakened by the war. In March 1917, a group of moderates had seized power from the tsar, but they were unable to govern the country. In November the Bolsheviks, shrewdly manipulating councils (*soviets* in Russian) that had sprung up in the leading cities, seized control from the moderates. After consolidating power in a desperate civil war, Lenin called on all true socialists around the world to join in a new international movement under Moscow's direct control. It was called the Communist International, or Comintern. Almost all socialist parties in the world split; their left wings went into the Comintern and became Communist parties in 1920–1921.

The resultant social democratic and Communist parties were more or less natural enemies ever since. Whereas the democratic socialist parties went on to cooperate with their fellow citizens, trying to promote welfare measures, the Communists denounced them as traitors and sellouts and followed Moscow's orders. Electorally, an interesting thing happened: Where socialist parties were big, Communist parties were small, and vice versa. They were sometimes bitter rivals.

How much Marxism-Leninism did the rulers of the Soviet Union really believe? They constantly used Marxist rhetoric, but many observers argued they were actually indifferent or even cynical about ideology and just used it as window dressing.[10] The Soviets never defined their society as Communist—that was yet to come; it was what they were working on. It is we in the West who called these countries "Communist." In 1961, party chief Nikita Khrushchev was rash enough to promise "communism in our generation," indicating that utopia would be reached by

1980.[11] Needless to say, they never made it, and in late 1991 the entire system collapsed.

Maoism and Titoism.   In the 1930s Mao Zedong concluded that the Chinese Communist Party (CCP) had to be based on poor peasants and guerrilla warfare. This was a break with Stalin's leadership, and after decades of fighting the CCP took over mainland China in 1949. Mao pursued a radical course that included a failed attempt at overnight industrialization (the Great Leap Forward in 1958), the destruction of bureaucratic authority (the Proletarian Cultural Revolution in 1966), and even border fighting with the Soviet Union in 1969. After Mao's death in 1976, calmer heads moved China away from Mao's extremism, which had severely damaged China's economic progress. Still, a few revolutionary groups hearken to Maoist extremism: Pol Pot's murderous Khmer Rouge and Peru's Shining Path. Maoism might be defined as a form of ultraradical communism.

Yugoslav party chief Josip Tito went the other way, developing a more moderate and liberal form of communism. Even though Tito's partisans fought the Germans in Stalin's name, Stalin felt he didn't fully control Tito, and in 1948 had Yugoslavia kicked out of the Communist camp. During the 1950s, the Yugoslav Communists radically reformed their system, basing it on decentralization, debureaucratization, and worker self-management. Trying to find a middle ground between a market and a controlled economy, Yugoslavia suffered severe economic problems in the 1980s. This might have served as a warning to Communist rulers who wanted to experiment with "middle ways" between capitalism and socialism. The combination is unstable. It tends to veer more and more to a market system but is repeatedly blocked from moving too far by party conservatives, who fear that communism is being abandoned. The bizarre combination of a partly free and partly controlled economy produces terrible economic distortions. The unstable Yugoslav system worked only because Tito ran it; when he died in 1980, Yugoslavia started coming apart until by the early 1990s it was a bloodbath.

NATIONALISM

So far, the ideologies we have discussed have been fairly complicated, especially the Marxist strand. But the real winner among ideologies—and the one that's still dominant today—is extremely simple: It is nationalism, the exaggerated belief in the greatness and unity of one's country.[12] Often there's little thought involved in nationalism, just "We won't be ruled by others!" But it has triumphed over all other ideologies and indeed has infected all the others, so that in the United States classic liberalism is combined with American nationalism, and in Russia, communism became intertwined with Russian nationalism.

It was not always so. Indeed, the very idea of a nation is fairly new. Go back far enough in history and you will find people unable to imagine themselves belonging to a "nation." Some scholars trace the beginning of nationalism back to the monarchs and princes who broke away from Rome in the sixteenth century. Henry VIII of England, Gustav Vasa of Sweden, and the Protestant princes of North Germany shattered the medieval image of a Europe united, at least nominally, under the pope. The wars of religion deepened the split and enabled ambitious monarchs to amass more power, centralizing authority in their kingdoms and bypassing the nobles. The movement was called *absolutism.* Absolute monarchs began to stress the unity and greatness of their kingdoms.

Still, nationalism didn't appear as a mass movement until the French Revolution. It let nationalism out of the bottle, and no one has been able to get it back in. The French Revolution, because it was based on the "people," heightened French feelings about themselves as a special, leading people destined to free the rest of Europe. When conservatives tried to invade France in 1792, the "nation in arms" stopped them at Valmy; enthusiastic volunteers beat professional soldiers. The stirring "Marseillaise," France's national anthem, appeared that same year. With Napoleon, French nationalism first conquered and then infected the rest of Europe. Whereas Napoleon's legions were ostensibly spreading the radical liberalism of the French Revolution, in actuality they were spreading nationalism. The conquered nations of Europe quickly grew to hate the arrogant French occupiers. Spaniards, Germans, and Russians soon became nationalistic themselves as they struggled to expel the French. Basic to nationalism is resentment of foreign domination, be it by British redcoats, Napoleon's legions, or European colonialists. Nationalism awoke in Europe in the nineteenth century and by the twentieth century had spread to Europe's colonies throughout the world. It is in the Third World that nationalism is now most intense.

By the midnineteenth century, thinkers all over Europe—and especially in Germany and Italy—were defining the nation as the ultimate human value. In some cases, they actually began to worship the nation, seeing in it the source of all things good. Italian writer Giuseppe Mazzini espoused freedom not for individuals—that was mere liberalism—but for nations instead. To be personally free was nothing; one achieved true freedom by subordinating oneself to the nation. Education, for example, had to inculcate a sense of nationalism that blotted out individualism, argued Mazzini.[13]

Nationalism generally arises when a population, invariably led by intellectuals, perceives an enemy or "other" to despise and struggle against. In the twentieth century, this has often been a colonial power such as Britain, France, or the Netherlands, against whom, respectively, Indians, Algerians, and Indonesians could rally in their fight for independence. At bottom, nationalism is the feeling that it is terribly wrong to be ruled by others. Thus Bosnian Serbs do not consent to be ruled by Bosnian Muslims, Palestinians on the West Bank do not consent to be ruled by Israelis, and Chechens do not consent to be ruled by Russians. Countries such as China and Iran (or more precisely certain leadership groups within them), feeling they have been repressed and controlled by outside powers, may lash out with highly nationalistic military and diplomatic policies. Even some Canadians, fearful of U.S. economic and cultural dominance, turn nationalistic.

A major problem with nationalism is that it is largely without content; that is, it has little to say about the great issues that face society: problems of unemployment, economic growth, and improvement of the human condition. Instead, nationalism suggests that if you keep cheering for your nation long and hard enough, other problems will sort themselves out. More than any of the previous ideologies, nationalism depends on emotional appeals. The feeling of belonging to a nation seems to cut to the psychological center of most of us. What other human organization would we fight and kill for?

Regional Nationalism. In recent decades the world has seen the rise of another kind of nationalism: regional nationalism. In a sense, it is the antithesis of the old nationalism, for it aims at breaking up existing nations into what its proponents argue are the true nations. Militant Québécois want to separate from Canada, Basques from Spain, Corsicans from France, Ossetians from Georgia, and Scots from the rest of the United Kingdom. The murderous fighting in the former Yugoslavia is a horrifying example of regional nationalism.

FASCISM

The big problem with nationalism is that in at least two cases it grew into fascism—in Italy and Germany. Fascism may be defined as an extreme form of nationalism with a small element of fake socialism added. One quick test of whether a movement is fascist: Do its members wear uniforms? Before World War I, Italian journalist Benito Mussolini was a fire-breathing socialist revolutionary. Military service changed him into an ardent nationalist. Italy was on the winning side in World War I but had suffered greatly and was full of discontented people after the war. Maximalist socialists seemed to be threatening revolution. In those chaotic times, Mussolini gathered around him a strange collection of people in black shirts who dreamed of getting rid of democracy and political parties and imposing stern central authority and discipline.[14] These Fascists—a word taken from the ancient Roman symbol of authority, a bundle of sticks bound around an ax (the *fasces*)—most of all hated disorder and wanted strong leadership to end it.

In 1922 they got their chance. Amid growing disorder, the king of Italy handed power to Mussolini. By 1924 Mussolini had turned Italy into a one-party state with himself as *Duce* (leader). Instead of nationalizing the economy the way the socialists might have, the Fascists supervised it by having their men in the right places. Italy looked impressive: There was little crime, much monumental construction, and stable prices, and as they used to say, "The trains ran on time." Behind the scenes, however, fascism was a mess, with hidden unemployment, poor economic performance, and corruption.

With the collapse of the world economy in 1929, however, Italian fascism looked impressive. Some thought it was the wave of the future. Adolf Hitler in Germany copied many of the trappings of fascism—the uniforms, the flare for spectacle, the hatred of democracy, the one-party state, the single dictator—but added a racist element. For Hitler, it wasn't just Germans as a nation that were rising up against the punitive and unfair Versailles Treaty and chaos of the Weimar Republic; it was Germans as a distinct and superior race. Hitler didn't invent German racism, which went back generations. Hitler adroitly utilized these widespread racist feelings. The racist line held that a special branch of the white race, the

Aryans, were the bearers of all civilization. A subbranch, the Nordics, were even better. The Germans, naturally, were all supposed to be Nordics. (Actually, Germans, like most Europeans, are of highly mixed stock, including Celts, Romans, several German tribes, Slavs, and even Jews.) Hitler argued that the superior Nordics were being subjugated to sinister, non-German forces. Judaism, communism, capitalism, even Roman Catholicism were all mixed up in a conspiracy to keep Germans down.

Like Mussolini, Hitler came to power legally; he was named chancellor (prime minister) in 1933 in a situation of turmoil and, like Mussolini, within two years had perfected a dictatorship. Although a free election was never held, probably a majority of Germans did support Hitler. With Nazis "coordinating" the economy, unemployment lessened, production increased, and a kind of prosperity appeared. Many working people felt they were getting a good deal with the jobs, vacations, and welfare the regime provided. After all, the Nazis' full name was the National Socialist German Workers Party; it sounded like a type of socialism, and indeed it had a pseudosocialist element. Hitler's true aim, however, was war, and his economic policies were designed to build a powerful military machine.

At a minimum, Hitler wanted Germany to dominate Europe completely, and for a brief time he nearly achieved his goal. He especially wanted the Slavic lands of Eastern Europe as a colony for Germans—*Lebensraum* (living space), he called it. Jews and many Slavic peoples were simply exterminated. Nazi death camps killed some 6 million Jews and a similar number of Christians who were in the way. Was Hitler mad? It's hard to say. Many of his views were widely held among Germans.

Work makes you free, proclaims the sign over the gate at the notorious concentration camp of Auschwitz. The Nazis' aim was to make prisoners think they were headed for work rather than for the gas chambers.

Hitler did not build and maintain the elaborate Nazi structure by himself; he had millions of enthusiastic helpers. Rather than insanity, Hitler and the Nazis demonstrate the danger of nationalism run amok.

The word *fascist* has been overused and misused. Some leftists hurl it at everything they don't like. Spanish dictator Francisco Franco, for example, was long considered a fascist, but on closer examination he was actually a "traditional authoritarian," for he tried to minimize mass political involvement rather than stir it up the way Mussolini and Hitler did. Brazilian President Getulio Vargas decreed a fascist-sounding "New State" in 1937, but he was merely borrowing some fascist rhetoric at a time when the movement was having its heyday in Europe. The Ku Klux Klan in the United States is sometimes called fascist, and its members do indeed wear uniforms. The Klan's populist racism is similar to the Nazis', but with one important difference: The Klan strongly opposes the power of the national government, whereas the Nazis and Fascists worshiped it.

Is fascism dead? In our day neofascists have raised their heads, for example, the anti-immigrant National Front parties in Britain and France, neo-Nazis in Germany, the Italian Social Movement, one branch of *Pamyat* (Memory) in Russia, and various fundamentalist–racist groups in the western United States. The possibility of fascism catching on in Russia should not be discounted; all the ingredients—despair, confusion, unemployment, extreme nationalism, the longing for a strong hand—are present.

Ideology in Our Day

THE COLLAPSE OF COMMUNISM

By the 1980s, communism the world over was showing signs of ideological exhaustion. Exceedingly few people in China, Eastern Europe, and even the Soviet Union believed in it any longer.[15] In the non-Communist world, leftists deserted Marxism in droves. Several West European Communist parties embraced "Euro-communism," a greatly watered-down ideology that renounced dictatorship and nationalization of industry. Capitalism was supposed to have collapsed or at least be in serious difficulty. Instead, it was thriving in the United States, Western Europe, and the rapidly industrializing countries on the rim of the Pacific. Soviet leaders were embarrassed to see their country's living standards, never high to begin with, fall further behind. They tried to reform the system, but the overly rigid system proved unreformable; instead, it collapsed.

Many Communist party leaders admitted that their economies were too rigid and centralized and that the cure lay in cutting back state controls and letting free enterprise take on a bigger role. Reform-minded Soviet President Mikhail Gorbachev (1985–1991) offered a three-pronged approach to revitalizing Soviet communism: *glasnost* (openness, or publicizing problems), *perestroika* (economic restructuring), and *demokratizatzia* (democratization). Applied haltingly and half-heartedly, the reforms actually heightened discontent, for now Soviets could speak openly about poor economic conditions and the discontents of non-Russian nationalities. Starting in Eastern Europe in 1989, things went much further, and non-Communist parties took over power as Communist regimes collapsed amid mass discontent. In effect, Communists admitted they had been wrong.

With that admission, things began to unravel swiftly in the Soviet Union. A partially free parliament was elected and began debating massive change. Non-Communist parties and movements began taking shape. Gorbachev still couldn't make up his mind how far and fast reforms should go, and the economy, barely reformed, turned wildly inflationary. Alarmed by the decay, some of Gorbachev's hand-picked assistants attempted a coup in August 1991. The bumbling attempt failed, partly because the Soviet armed forces split and partly because Boris Yeltsin, the elected head of the Russian part of the Soviet Union, stood firm. By the end of the year the Soviet Union had ceased to exist, the Communist party was largely out of power, and Yeltsin was taking an independent Russia in the direction of capitalism and democracy.

The speed and sweep of the change surprised nearly everyone. It showed, among other things, that the Soviet Union was not nearly as strong as we had thought, that communism is an inherently defective system, and that few Soviets had believed in it as a serious ideology. The danger now is, what do they have to believe in? Many observers fear that Western concepts of pluralism, tolerance, and democracy have no roots in Russian soil. What, then, will fill the ideological vacuum? Let us hope that a Western-type free democracy and economy can before something else does.

NEOCONSERVATISM

In the 1970s, a new ideology emerged in the United States: neoconservatism. Its basic ideas were similar to modern conservatism, but it came from an interesting group of people: disillusioned liberals and leftists. As neoconservative writer Irving Kristol put it, "A neo-conservative is a liberal who's been mugged by reality." Many neoconservatives claimed that they were actually staying true to the modern liberalism of the Franklin D. Roosevelt variety, whereas the Democratic party had moved too far to the left with unrealistic ideas on domestic reforms and a pacifist foreign policy.

Specifically, the neoconservatives reacted against the perceived excesses of the Great Society legislation introduced by Lyndon Johnson in the mid-1960s. This ambitious program aimed to wipe out poverty and discrimination in America. It included food stamps, medical care for the elderly, regional development, urban renewal, prekindergarten education, voting and civil rights for African-Americans, and affirmative action to hire minorities. Some liberals said the Great Society was never given a chance because funds for it were siphoned away by the Vietnam war. But disillusioned liberals said it worked badly, that many of the programs achieved nothing. The cities grew worse; educational standards declined; medical aid became extremely costly; and a class of welfare-dependent poor emerged, people who had little incentive to work. Neoconservatives spoke of negative "unforeseen consequences" of well-intentioned liberal programs. One point especially bothered neoconservatives: Affirmative action seemed to give racial minorities preferential treatment in hiring, sometimes ahead of better qualified whites. This really hit home when affirmative action quotas were applied to academic hiring; liberal, white, male professors sometimes had to taste their own medicine in getting turned down for teaching jobs that went to blacks, Hispanics, and women.

Many neoconservatives were former liberals who had become horrified at the extreme relativism among some scholars.[16] The popular ideas of the 1960s and early 1970s—such as "It's all right if it feels good" and "Well, it just depends on your point of view" and "Who's to say what's right and wrong?"—drove many liberals to neoconservatism. Ironically, some neoconservatives were college professors who had earlier tried to broaden their students' views by stressing the relativity of all viewpoints. Some professors discovered, to their chagrin, that students were becoming vacuous rather than enlightened.

The neoconservatives, however, were not comfortable with older-style conservatives, and vice versa. The former emphasized free-market economics and a refutation of ultraliberal thinking. The older-style conservatives emphasized religious and traditional values.[17] The two strands of conservatism could make common cause during the Reagan years in rolling back liberal programs and viewpoints, but by the late 1980s they angrily split apart, and many neoconservatives assumed middle-of-the-road positions, sometimes within the Democratic party.

COMMUNITARIANISM

In the 1990s a new ideology appeared, chiefly in the United States but also in the British Labour party, stressing the need to revive communities—those institutions *between* the state and the individual. "Communitarianism" has nothing to do with communism and is indeed conservative in many respects. The movement, still a small one, tries to fill the growing gap between left and right. Whereas liberals look to a strong federal government and conservatives to rugged individualism, communitarians worry about the erosion of the basic building blocks of civil society: communities. According to one of its leading lights, George Washington University sociologist Amitai Etzioni, communitarians are "committed to creating a new moral, social, and public order based on restored communities."[18]

No one knew exactly what this meant—what, for example, constitutes a "community"?—and the movement advanced both conservative and liberal ideas. Conservatives might be pleased that communitarians sought to strengthen families and have moral education in schools. Liberals might be pleased that communitarians also sought national service for young people and limits to election campaign funds. Etzioni argues the U.S. system has gone crazy with "rights" while ignoring responsibility and community. People cannot simply do as they wish with drugs and AIDS; communities should be able to control such behavior. Although communitarianism is vague, U.S. political figures started picking up its emphasis on rebuilding communities.

FEMINISM

Springing to new life in the 1960s with a handful of female writers, by the 1970s the women's movement had become an appreciable force in the United States and Western Europe. As a political question, the status of women was not new; it had been debated for centuries. Whereas many thought the question had been set-tled—women had long since ceased to be treated as property, had won the right to vote and hold office, and had moved ahead in education—feminist writers treated these gains as mere beginnings. They pointed out that women were paid less than men for the same work, were passed over for promotion to leading positions, were subjected to psychological and physical abuse from men, were denied bank loans and insurance unless their husbands would cosign, and were in general second-class citizens.

The problem, at heart, was a psychological one, argued feminists. Women and men were forced into "gender roles" that had little to do with biology. Boys were conditioned to be tough, domineering, competitive, and "macho," whereas girls were taught to be meek, submissive, unsure of themselves, and "feminine." It didn't have to be this way, feminists believed. With proper child rearing, males could cultivate a gentler, less aggressive manner and females could learn to be-come assertive and self-confident. Biologically, there were no important differ-ences in mental capacities; the differences that showed up were almost entirely learned behavior, taught by parents and schools of a "patriarchal" society that had long been dominated by men. Why was it taken for granted that boys would grow up to be doctors and girls to be nurses, boys to be lawyers and girls to be secretaries, boys to be builders and girls to be homemakers? Women could do as well as men in most jobs, and men could often become good "househusbands." Gender roles had been learned; they could be unlearned.[19]

Feminists started "consciousness-raising" groups to awaken women around the country to their inferior status. Feminists used the term *male chauvinist pigs* in describing their male enemies. Feminism started having an impact. Many employ-ers gave women a fairer chance, sometimes hiring them over men. Women moved up to higher management positions (although seldom to the corporate top). Work-ing wives became the norm. Sometimes husbands even gave up their jobs to follow the wife's career moves. Commuting marriages became common, and husbands started homemaking and child rearing.

Politically, however, feminists did not achieve all they wished. The Equal Rights Amendment (ERA) to the Constitution failed to win ratification in a suffi-cient number of state legislatures. It would have guaranteed equality of treatment regardless of gender. Antifeminists, some of them conservative women, argued that the ERA would take away women's privileges and protections under the law, would make women eligible for the draft, and would even lead to unisex lavatories. De-spite this setback, women learned that there was one way they could count for a lot politically—by voting. In the 1980 election, for the first time in U.S. history, a sig-nificant "gender gap" appeared between male and female voting: Women were sev-eral percentage points more likely to vote Democratic than were men. Whereas Republicans stressed macho themes of rugged individualism and increased defense spending, Democrats emphasized social welfare measures that helped children and working mothers. Many women were attracted to the peace and antinuclear movements, again to the detriment of the Republicans. Bill Clinton's 1992 victory was based in part on the women's vote.

ENVIRONMENTALISM

At about the same time that feminists were awakening, another movement began to ripple through the advanced industrialized countries: the ecology or environmental movement. Economic development had typically paid little heed to the damage it was inflicting on the environment. Any growth was good growth: "We'll never run out of nature." While the economy grew, mining produced acid runoff that poisoned streams, industries and automobiles polluted the air, chemical wastes made whole communities uninhabitable, and nuclear power raised questions of radioactive leaks and nuclear wastes.

To the credo of "growth" the ecologists responded with "limits." They seem to say, "We can't go on like this forever without producing an environmental catastrophe." Events such as those at Love Canal, Three Mile Island, and Chernobyl seemed to prove the ecologists right. Moreover, the massive burning of fossil fuels and rain forests may be creating a "greenhouse effect," trapping heat inside the earth's atmosphere, thus changing the planet's weather and threatening to raise the level of the oceans by melting the polar icecaps.

The ecologists' demands were only partly satisfied with the founding of the Environmental Protection Agency (EPA) in 1970. Industrial groups, however, found that EPA regulations restricted growth and ate into profits; under President Reagan, the EPA was rendered ineffective and became a scandal.

But government regulation was only part of the environmental credo. Many argued that consumption patterns and lifestyles in the advanced countries should change to conserve the earth's resources, natural beauty, and clean air and water.[20] Americans, only about 6 percent of the world's population, consume close to half the world's manufactured goods and a third of its energy. In addition to being out of balance with the poor nations of the world, this profligate lifestyle was seen to be unnecessary and unhealthy. Ecologists recommended shifting to public transportation and bicycles instead of cars; to whole-grain foods and vegetables instead of meat; and to decentralized, renewable energy sources, such as wind and solar energy, instead of fossil- or nuclear-fueled power plants. The ecology movement helped trigger the American interest in running, biking, camping, natural foods, and relocating to rural areas. Ecologists wanted people to live in balance with nature rather than to destroy it.

Whereas some environmentalists formed a political party, the Citizens party, and ran ecologist Barry Commoner for president in 1980, their main impact was within the two big parties, both of which came to realize they could not ignore the real dangers that an industrialized society poses for the environment. In the 1980s new parties, the Greens (as environmentalists like to call themselves), sprang into life across Western Europe. In Germany and Sweden, bearded and blue-jeaned Greens were elected to parliament, determined to end nuclear power, toxic waste, and the arms race. Although not yet in parliament, French and British Greens grew so fast that the major parties suddenly started getting very interested in ecology. Many young Europeans found the Greens an attractive alternative to the old and stodgy conventional parties.

Is Ideology Finished?

In 1960, Harvard sociologist Daniel Bell advanced the controversial thesis that the great ideological debates that had gone on for a century or more were coming to a close. The failure of tyrannical communism and rise of the welfare state were producing what Bell called the "end of ideology": There simply was not much to debate about. Henceforth political debate would focus on almost technical questions of how to run the welfare state, said Bell, such as whether to include dental care under national health insurance.[21] In 1989, political scientist Francis Fukuyama advanced a more far-reaching thesis that not only had the great ideological debate ended with the victory of capitalist democracy but suggested as well that history itself could be ending.[22] Widely misunderstood, Fukuyama did not mean that time would stand still but rather that the human endpoint propounded by Hegel—free people living in free societies—was now coming into view. Not only had we beaten communism, suggested Fukuyama, there would not likely be any other ideologies to challenge ours. With the end of ideology would come the end of history in the sense of the struggle of great ideas. (Life could get boring, sighed the puckish Fukuyama.)

Is either the Bell or Fukuyama thesis accurate? There are grounds for doubt. First, the collapse of communism in Europe by itself does not disprove Marx's original ideas, although those now propounding them must carefully distance themselves from the Soviet type of socialism.[23] (We use *socialism* here to mean state control of industry, not *welfarism*, which is but a variation on capitalist democracy.) Socialist thought is still alive on some U.S. college campuses.[24] Some still debate the possibility of a benign socialism, whether the Soviet Union was a good or a bad example of socialism, and why it failed. The fact that such debates occur, some on your campus, indicates that ideology is still alive.

Further, there are other ideologies besides socialism. We have mentioned some of them here—feminism and environmentalism, for example—and new and dangerous ideological challenges emerged just as communism collapsed: neofascism, breakaway nationalism, and Islamic fundamentalism. And within free democracy itself there are numerous ideological viewpoints: free market or government intervention, more welfare or less, a secular or religious state, and spreading democracy abroad or avoiding overseas involvement. Fukuyama need not worry about boredom.

Suggested Readings

BRACHER, KARL DIETRICH. *The Age of Ideologies: A History of Political Thought in the Twentieth Century.* New York: St. Martin's, 1984. A critical view of the growth of simplified ideological thinking, especially totalitarianism.

CHICKERING, A. LAWRENCE. *Beyond Left and Right: Breaking the Political Stalemate.* San Francisco, CA: ICS Press, 1994. Argues the old distinctions between left and right are now meaningless; we must now reconstruct a new ideological center.

DIGGINS, JOHN PATRICK. *The Rise and Fall of the American Left.* New York: Norton, 1992. A history of the several waves of U.S. leftism up to today's "academic left."

FUKUYAMA, FRANCIS. *The End of History and the Last Man.* New York: Free Press, 1992. An expansion of the author's 1989 article, replete with Hegelian philosophy.

GREENFELD, LIAH. *Nationalism: Five Roads to Modernity.* Cambridge, MA: Harvard University Press, 1993. Traces and compares the rise of nationalism in Britain, France, Russia, Germany, and the United States.

HAMBY, ALONZO. *Liberalism and Its Challengers,* 2nd ed. New York: Oxford University Press, 1992. An excellent and readable review of American liberalism since World War II, updated to include the Reagan-Bush years.

HOLLANDER, PAUL. *Decline and Discontent: Communism and the West Today.* New Brunswick,
NJ: Transaction, 1992. Intellectuals tend to leftism and will likely continue to do so despite communism's collapse.

HUBERMAN, LEO, and PAUL M. SWEEZY. *Introduction to Socialism.* New York: Monthly Review Press, 1968. Best short introduction available, by two American Marxists.

HUNTER, JAMES DAVISON. *Culture Wars: The Struggle to Define America.* New York: Basic Books, 1992. America is splitting between militant liberal and traditionalist movements.

KELLY, PETRA K. *Thinking Green! Essays on Environmentalism, Feminism, and Nonviolence.* Berkeley, CA: Parallax, 1994. The late German Green leader combines at least three ideologies to present a "green" agenda to save society.

KOHN, HANS. *Political Ideologies in the Twentieth Century,* 3rd ed., rev. New York: Harper & Row, 1966. Masterful study of the great ideological currents by a scholar who lived through them.

KRISTOL, IRVING. *Neoconservatism: The Autobiography of an Idea.* New York: Free Press, 1995. The godfather of neoconservatism traces the evolution of his thinking in a series of essays.

SKIDELSKY, ROBERT. *The World After Communism: A Polemic for Our Times.* London: Macmillan, 1995. An eloquent study of why the free market beat collectivism and what we ought to do next.

Notes

1. See Ed Gillespie and Bob Schellhas, eds., *Contract with America: The Bold Plan by Rep. Newt Gingrich, Rep. Dick Armey and the House Republicans to Change the Nation.* (New York: Times Books/Random House, 1994).

2. Anthony Downs, *An Economic Theory of Democracy* (New York: Harper & Row, 1957), p. 96.

3. See Jerome Huyler, *Locke in America: The Moral Philosophy of the Founding Era* (Lawrence, KS: Kansas University Press, 1995).

4. Isaac Kramnick and Frederick M. Watkins, *The Age of Ideology: Political Thought, 1750 to the Present,* 2nd ed. (Englewood Cliffs, NJ: Prentice Hall, 1979), p. 8. Our discussion owes a great deal to this splendid little book.

5. Edmund Burke, cited in Michael Curtis, ed., *The Great Political Theories* (New York: Avon, 1962), Vol. 2, p. 49.

6. Jeane J. Kirkpatrick, *Dictatorships and Double Standards: Rationalism and Reason in Politics* (New York: Simon & Schuster, 1982).

7. Milton Friedman and Rose Friedman, *Tyranny of the Status Quo* (New York: Harcourt Brace Jovanovich, 1984).

8. See Herbert Kitschelt, *The Transformation of European Social Democracy* (New York: Cambridge University Press, 1994).

9. V. I. Lenin, *Imperialism: The Highest Stage of Capitalism* (New York: International Publishers, 1939).

10. For the classic debate about ideology in the Kremlin, see R. N. Hunt, Samuel Sharp, Richard Lowenthal, and Leopold Labedz, "Ideology and Power—A Symposium," in Abraham Brumberg, ed., *Russia Under Khrushchev: An Anthology* (New York: Praeger, 1962).

11. See Jan F. Triska, ed., *Soviet Communism: Programs and Rules* (San Francisco: Chandler, 1962), pp. 68–129.

12. See John Hutchinson and Anthony D. Smith, eds., *Nationalism* (New York: Oxford University Press, 1995).

13. Denis Mack Smith, *Mazzini* (New Haven, CT: Yale University Press, 1994).

14. See Zeev Sternhell, Mario Sznajder, and Maia Asheri, *The Birth of Fascist Ideology: From Cultural Rebellion to Political Revolution* (Princeton, NJ: Princeton University Press, 1994).

15. See Andrzej Walicki, *Marxism and the Leap to the Kingdom of Freedom: The Rise and Fall of the Communist Utopia.* Stanford, CA: Stanford University Press, 1995.

16. For a blistering critique of academic relativism, see Gertrude Himmelfarb, *On Looking into the Abyss: Untimely Thoughts on Culture and Society* (New York: Knopf, 1994).

17. For an explanation of how Ronald Reagan's conservatism pulled together a variety of groups sometimes at odds with each other, see Jerome L. Himmelstein, *To the Right: The Transformation of American Conservatism* (Berkeley: University of California Press, 1990).

18. Amitai Etzioni, *The Spirit of Community: Rights, Responsibilities, and the Communitarian Agenda* (New York: Crown, 1993).

19. For a look at the ideological infighting within the feminist movement, see Christina Hoff Sommers, *Who Stole Feminism? How Women Have Betrayed Women.* (New York: Simon & Schuster, 1994).

20. See Daniel A. Coleman, *Ecopolitics: Building a Green Society* (New Brunswick, NJ: Rutgers University Press, 1994).

21. Daniel Bell, *The End of Ideology: On the Exhaustion of Political Ideas in the Fifties* (New York: Free Press, 1960).

22. Francis Fukuyama, "The End of History?" *The National Interest* 16 (Summer 1989), 3–18.

23. For a socialist thinker trying to keep socialism alive, see Lawrence Wilde, *Modern European Socialism* (Brookfield, VT: Ashgate, 1994).

24. Some conservative critics claim that U.S. colleges and universities have become the breeding ground for leftist professors. See Roger Kimball, *Tenured Radicals: How Politics Has Corrupted Our Higher Education* (New York: Harper & Row, 1990).

• 7 •

Political Culture

Everyone agrees that the United States and Canada are quite similar in terms of culture. Americans and Canadians read many of the same books and magazines, watch many of the same television shows, and have similar lifestyles. But in terms of *political* culture, Americans and Canadians are somewhat different. Americans are more insistent about their individual rights and limits on government authority than Canadians. Canadians are more law-abiding and willing to let government assume a paternalistic role in guiding the economy and society.[1] Americans sometimes find Canadians a little too obedient; Canadians think Americans are too wild and lawless. The Royal Canadian Mounted Police (RCMP) taps phones and gathers evidence in ways that the Federal Bureau of Investigation wouldn't dare use. Civil liberties groups in the United States would be outraged at the powers of the RCMP, which are accepted as normal by Canadians.

The modern American and Canadian ideas of the proper role of government are, in some ways, divergent. But so are American conceptions of the twentieth century and the eighteenth century. If Thomas Jefferson suddenly found himself in the twentieth century, he would probably be aghast. Instead of a government limited to protecting our frontier and our Bill of Rights, he would be confronted with a monstrous organization that collects our garbage, keeps tabs on our earnings, tells us to wear seat belts, and makes us obtain licenses to sell liquor or own a dog.

The modern Canadian, the modern American, and the American of two hundred years ago have had very different perceptions of what government is and what it should be. What are the forces that work to make their opinions and ideals so strikingly different?

The Environment of Government: Political Culture

Each society imparts its own characteristic set of norms and values to its people, and the people in turn have distinct sets of ideals about how the political system is supposed to work, about what the government may do to them and for them, and about their own claims on the system and their obligations to it. This set of beliefs, symbols, and values about the political system forms the political culture of a nation—and it varies considerably from one nation to another. Simply put, political culture is the psychology of the nation in regard to politics.

The politics of a nation is influenced by many aspects of society: its economy, its religion, its traditions. As Karl Marx pointed out long ago, the way people earn their living has a lot to do with the type of government they have. Industrial societies require far more services—welfare, transportation, urban housing, sanitation facilities—than do agricultural nations, as a glance at the America of the Civil War era and the nation we know now will reveal. When a nation develops a complex industrial system, its culture and political needs change accordingly.

A people's religious beliefs are also reflected in politics. The controversy over abortion is a case in point. Americans generally expect separation of church and state, but the state is here involved in the sanctity of human life, an issue that can hardly be separated from religion and morality. In Roman Catholic Italy, religion is recognized as a concern of the state. The Republic of Ireland narrowly voted to permit divorce in the face of strong church opposition in a nationwide referendum in 1995. An earlier Irish referendum on divorce had failed.

The social structure of a country is also reflected in the political system. The strict divisions of medieval society found their political expression in a hereditary government in which kings, barons, and lords were born into leadership roles. De-

spite a traditional American commitment to democracy the world over, some political scientists argue that perhaps not all societies are able to sustain a democratic government because economic and educational levels of the people and class divisions tend toward authoritarian forms of government. As we discussed in Chapter 4, middle-class values tend to best support democracy.

WHAT IS POLITICAL CULTURE?[2]

As defined by political scientist Sidney Verba, political culture is "the system of empirical beliefs, expressive symbols, and values, which defines the situation in which political action takes place."[3] What are these beliefs, symbols, and values that determine how a people interprets the proper role of government and how that government itself is organized?

A people's perception of the role of government—the proper relationship between ruler and ruled—has a great deal of influence on the political system. In Japan, where the vestiges of a traditional feudal class system still pervade social structure and social relationships, it is often possible to tell who is whose social superior by watching the way acquaintances greet each other when they meet in the street: The person who bows lower is of inferior status.[4] The Japanese have also been traditionally submissive to the authority of those in office, preferring to leave fundamental policy decisions in the hands of their leaders. Americans, who are not influenced by a tradition of strict class divisions, take a far different view of the people's right to participate in government. Although Americans may not be particularly well informed about the issues of the day, they consider it their democratic birthright to have a say in the way the country is governed. Clearly, the way people think of themselves, their leaders, and the relationship between the two has a vital bearing on the nature of a political system.

In America, even people who are hostile to the president will, in most cases, respect the office and the authority. But Latin Americans do not share the same tradition of respect for their heads of government. They have instead been historically more loyal to *caudillos* (charismatic military leaders). Nations that stress the importance of institutions are generally more stable than those that depend on charismatic figures for leadership.

Political Culture and Public Opinion. What is the difference between political culture and public opinion? Obviously, the two overlap, for both look at attitudes toward politics. Political culture aims to tap basic, general feelings toward politics and government. Public opinion, on the other hand, focuses on views about specific leaders and policies. Political culture looks for the underpinnings of legitimacy, the gut attitudes that sustain a political system, whereas public opinion seeks responses to current questions.

The methodologies of political culture and public opinion also overlap: Random samples of the population are asked questions and the responses are correlated with subgroups in the population. The questions, however, will be different. A political culture survey might ask how much you trust government; a public opinion survey might ask how much you like the current administration. The political culture study is more likely to ask the same questions in several countries in order to gain a comparative perspective. Both may want to keep track of responses over time to see, in the case of political culture, if legitimacy is gaining or declining or, in the case of public opinion, how a president's popularity compares with that of predecessors.

Political culture studies are apt to go beyond surveys, however. They might use the methods of anthropology and psychology in the close observation of daily life and in the deep questioning of individuals about their feelings.[5] Public opinion studies rarely go beyond the clipboard with quantified data, whereas political culture studies can use history and literature to gain insights into a particular country. For instance, one noted scholar found the observations of nineteenth-century travelers provided evidence of continuity in American political and social attitudes.[6] Indeed, the brilliant comments of Alexis de Tocqueville, who traveled through the United States in the 1830s, still generally apply a century and a half later.[7] Tocqueville was one of the founders of the political culture approach in political science.

It used to be widely assumed that political culture was nearly permanent or changed only slowly, whereas public opinion was fickle and changed quickly. Recent studies, however, have shown that political culture is rather changeable, too. Periods of stable, efficient government and economic growth solidify feelings of legitimacy; periods of indecisive, chaotic government and economic downturn are reflected in weakening legitimacy. Public opinion, if held long enough, eventually turns into political culture. In the 1960s public opinion on Vietnam showed declining support for the war. Over precisely this same time period, confidence in the U.S. government also declined. Public opinion on a given question was infecting the general political culture, making it more cynical about the political system.

To be sure, a country's political culture changes more slowly than its public opinions, and certain underlying elements of political culture tend to persist for generations, perhaps for centuries. One can easily recognize the America of de Tocqueville in the America of today; basic attitudes haven't changed that much. The French are still inclined to take to the streets of Paris to protest perceived injustice, just as their ancestors did. Italians continue their centuries-old cynicism toward anything governmental. Russians, who have never experienced free democracy, still tend to favor strong leaders and to ignore minority rights. Although not as firm as bedrock, political culture is an underlying layer of attitudes that can support—or fail to support—the rest of the political system. This is one reason why Russian democracy is having difficulty getting established.

THE CIVIC CULTURE

The pioneering study of cross-national differences in political beliefs, symbols, and values was made by Gabriel Almond and Sidney Verba.[8] Interviewing some 5,000 people in five different nations in 1959 and 1960, the authors sought to measure national political attitudes by testing three important variables: what impact the people felt government had on their lives, what obligation they felt they had toward government, and what they expected from government. Almond and Verba discerned three general political cultures: participant, subject, and parochial.

Participant. In a participant political culture people understand that they are citizens and they pay attention to politics. They are proud of their country's political system and are generally willing to discuss it. They believe they can influence politics to some degree and claim they would organize a group to protest something unfair. Accordingly, they show a high degree of *political competence* (knowing how to accomplish something politically) and *political efficacy* (feeling that they have at least a little political power). They say they take pride in voting and believe people should participate in politics. They are active in their communities and often belong to one or more voluntary organizations. They are more likely to trust other people and to recall participating in family discussions as children. A participant political culture is clearly the ideal soil in which to sustain a democracy.

Subject. A notch lower than the participant political culture is the subject political culture. People in this culture still understand that they are citizens and pay attention to politics, but they are involved in a more passive way. They follow political news but are not proud of their country's political system and feel little emotional commitment toward it. They feel uncomfortable in speaking about politics; it is not a good topic for conversation. They feel they can influence politics only to the extent of speaking with a local official. It does not ordinarily occur to them to organize a group. Their sense of political competence and efficacy are lower; some feel powerless. They say they vote, but they vote without enthusiasm. They are less likely to trust other people and to recall voicing their views as children. Democracy has more difficulty sinking roots in a culture where people are used to thinking of themselves as obedient subjects rather than as active participants.

Parochial. At yet another notch lower is the parochial political culture, in which people may not even feel that they are citizens of a nation. They identify with the immediate locality, hence the term *parochial* (of a parish). They take no pride in their country's political system and expect little of it. They pay no attention to politics, have little knowledge of politics, and seldom speak about political matters. They have neither the desire nor the ability to participate in politics. They have no sense of political competence or efficacy and feel powerless in the face of existing institutions. Attempting to grow a democracy in a parochial political culture is very difficult, requiring not only new institutions but also a new sense of citizenship.

Now, as Almond and Verba warn, there is no country that has a purely participant, subject, or parochial political culture. All nations are mixtures in varying degrees of the three types. The United States, they found, was heavily participant with some subject and even parochial attitudes. One of the problems with U.S. political culture, they suggest, is the relatively weak subject component, causing Americans to be not particularly law-abiding. Britain was closer to a happy balance between participatory and subject political cultures: sufficiently participant to be a democracy and sufficiently subject to obey authority. In Germany, the subject culture dominated; people obeyed authority but didn't want to get involved in politics. The same applied to Italy, with a bigger dose of parochial attitudes. Both Germany and Italy at the time of Almond and Verba's studies, only a decade and a half after World War II, illustrated the difficulty of starting a democracy in a relatively weak participant culture. Mexico was a strange mixture in which people made statements that sounded participatory but in practice behaved in a subject and parochial manner. Almond and Verba called Mexico an "aspirational" political culture—where hopes exceed reality.

If you think about it a minute, any country would have to be a mixture of political cultures. If a country were purely parochial—with no one interested in anything political—it would either fall apart or succumb to foreign conquest. Someone has got to participate in politics—at least the king and queen and their court. And someone has got to obey as good subjects—at least the knights and merchants. Without some participation you haven't got a country. The masses of people in the countryside can be parochial with only a few loyal subjects and political participants to guide them. That is the picture of traditional China: Eighty percent of the population toiled as peasants, then a layer of gentry and merchants to run things, and a tiny layer of mandarins and court officials to supervise the empire.[9] Even traditional political systems were not completely parochial.

Today, it would be hard to find parochial political cultures. All corners of the globe have been penetrated by communications, and even very poor and backward people are generally aware of current events. Until recently, for example, the white regime of South Africa imagined that the country's blacks—three-quarters of the population—were still tribal and parochial, with little interest (apart from a few troublemakers) in politics. On the contrary, many black South Africans had long been itching to participate in their nation's politics, and when not allowed to do so, turned to violence. It was, indeed, the white South Africans themselves who, with modern industry, education, transportation, and communication, awakened the previously parochial Africans to the possibility of political participation. Modern times have phased out parochial political cultures.

On the other hand, would a purely participant political culture be possible or even desirable? Probably not. What would happen if everyone were eager to participate in politics? There would be the danger of political turmoil as too many citizens passionately pursue political causes. When that occurs, as during political revolutions, the intense participatory political culture burns itself out after a period of tumult. The sudden growth of feelings of participation accompanies and contributes to the revolutionary upheavals of newly free countries. It is perhaps just as well that few people are truly political animals; most concern themselves with politics only intermittently and devote their chief attention to personal concerns. It is in the mixture of all three attitudes that democracy finds stability: Parochial concerns for family, church, and job give individuals meaning and perspective; subject attitudes give the political system obedience and support; and participant attitudes keep leaders attentive and responsive to the attitudes of people.

PARTICIPATION IN AMERICA

Even in America, relatively few persons actively participate in politics. How, then, can Almond and Verba offer the United States as their model of a "civic culture"? One of their key findings was that for democracy to work, participation need only be "intermittent and potential."[10] In effect, they offer a "sleeping dogs" theory of democratic political culture. Leaders in a democracy know that most of the time most people are not paying close attention to politics. But they also know that if aroused—because of scandal, high unemployment, inflation, or unpopular war—the public can vote them out of office at the next election. Accordingly, leaders usually work to keep the unaroused public quiet. Following the "rule of anticipated reactions," leaders in democracies constantly ask themselves how the public will react to any of their decisions.[11] They are quite happy to have the public *not* react at all; they wish to let sleeping dogs lie.

This theory helps explain an embarrassing fact about U.S. political life, namely, its low voter turnout, the lowest of all the industrialized democracies. Only about half of U.S. voters bother to cast a ballot in presidential elections, even fewer in state and local contests. In Western Europe, voter turnout is usually about three-quarters of the electorate and sometimes tops 90 percent. How, then, can the United States boast of its democracy? Theorists reply that a democratic government culture does not necessarily require heavy voter turnout. Rather, it requires an attitude that, if aroused, the people will participate—vote, contribute time and money, organize groups, and circulate petitions—and that elected officials know this. Democracy in this view is a psychological connection between leaders and led that restrains officials from foolishness. It is the attitudes of the people, and not their actual participation, that makes a democratic government culture viable.

Another of Almond and Verba's key findings was the response to the question of what citizens of five countries would do to influence local government over an unjust ordinance. Far more Americans said they would "try to enlist the aid of others."[12] Americans seem to be natural "group formers" when faced with a political problem, and this trait could be an important foundation of U.S. democracy. In more "subject" countries, this group-forming attitude was weaker.

United States	59 percent
Britain	36 percent
West Germany	21 percent
Italy	9 percent
Mexico	28 percent

Americans also trust their government more than people in other countries. A 1985 survey found that nearly half of the Americans polled said they trusted the U.S. government most of the time.[13] Four out of ten Germans gave this reply about their own government. In Italy, only a third gave the same response, whereas over a quarter said they almost never trusted the government.

The Decay of Political Culture

By the 1990s several American political scientists were expressing concern over what they saw as the decay and decline of U.S. political culture, something that had been underway since the 1960s. In surveys given every two years, two key questions were "How much of the time do you think you can trust the government in Washington to do what is right?" and "Would you say the government is pretty much run by a few big interests looking out for themselves or that it is run for the benefit of all people?" The cynical responses climbed until they outnumbered the trusting responses (Table 7.1). These were the years of the Vietnam war, the Watergate scandal, and inflation—all of which showed Washington in its worst light. Only in 1982 did the trusting responses start to grow again. The growth in cynicism had made America harder to govern. The increase in cynicism is reflected in an unhappy electorate. No nation is blessed with automatic and permanent legitimacy.

One of the key factors in the U.S. case, some claimed, was the decline of the American tendency to form associations, anything from volunteer fire departments to labor unions. In the 1830s, the brilliant French visitor Alexis de Tocqueville noted: "Americans of all ages, all conditions, and all dispositions constantly form associations." Tocqueville was quite amazed at this tendency, for it was (and still is) largely absent in France, and he held it was one of the bases of democracy, a point confirmed much later by the *Civic Culture* study. But several observers claim that lately these grassroots associations are fading. Said former Sen. Bill Bradley (R-NJ), "Like fish floating on the surface of a polluted river, the network of voluntary associations in America seems to be dying." Harvard political scientist Robert Putnam noted that whereas the number of people bowling has increased, league bowling has declined. His eye-catching article, "Bowling Alone," became required reading in the Clinton White House.[14] Putnam had more substantial examples of the decline of associations: union membership, parent-teacher associations, volunteers for the Boy Scouts and Red Cross, even membership in fraternal orders.

Parallel to the "communitarian" movement we discussed in Chapter 6 on ideologies, those who see the decline of voluntary associations fear political and economic repercussions. With only individuals stridently demanding their "rights"

TABLE 7.1   Americans' Trust in Government, 1964–1984

	1964	1966	1968	1970	1972	1974	1976	1978	1980	1982	1984	1986	1988
Trust government all or most of the time	76%	65%	61%	54%	53%	37%	33%	30%	25%	33%	44%	38%	41%
Believe that government is run by a few big interests	29	33	40	50	53	66	66	67	70	61	66	NA	64

Source: National Election Studies, Center for Political Studies, Institute for Social Research, Ann Arbor, MI.

without a corresponding sense of having to contribute something, the demands on government become impossible; there is simply not enough money. Democracy becomes less a matter of concerned citizens meeting face to face to discuss a community problem than passive television viewers being massaged by clever ads and "sound bites." Furthermore, argued Francis Fukuyama (who earlier brought us the "end of history" theory), trust or "spontaneous sociability" underpins economic growth and stability. If you can trust others, you can do more and better business with them. Hence "high trust" economies occur when a web of social institutions exists between families and governments.[15]

The point is that political culture changes. True, it does not change as rapidly as public opinion, but political culture at any given moment is a combination of long-remembered and deeply held attitudes plus reactions to current situations. Since the original Almond and Verba *Civic Culture* study, British political culture has turned untrusting and cynical, West (but not East) German political culture became more trusting and participatory, and American political culture went through a decline in the 1960s and 1970s and a partial recovery in the early 1980s. All these changes are responses to government performance.[16] Political cultures do not fall down from heaven; they are created by government actions and inactions.

ELITE AND MASS CULTURES

The political culture of a country is not uniform and monolithic. One can usually find within it differences between the mainstream culture and subcultures (discussed below) and differences between elite and mass attitudes. Elites—meaning here those people with better education, higher income, and more influence—have rather different political attitudes than the masses. Elites are much more participatory; they are more interested in politics. They are more inclined to vote, to protest injustice, to form groups, and even to run for office. One consistent finding of the *Civic Culture* study has been confirmed over and over again: The more education a person has, the more likely he or she is to participate in politics.

Delegates to the 1996 Democratic convention, for example, illustrate the differences between elites and masses. Half the delegates had some postgraduate education (often law school). Nationwide, only 4 percent of self-identified Democrats had gone to graduate school. Of the convention delegates, over half came from households with annual incomes of $70,000 or more. Nationwide, only 5 percent of Democrats were so favored. In other words, the people representing the Democratic party at the convention were not a representative cross section of the party rank and file. Much the same will be found at any Democratic convention. The Democrats pride themselves on being the party of the common people, but Democrats with more education and money still tend to take the leading positions. There is nothing necessarily wrong with this: Better-educated and better-off people are simply more inclined to political participation. The same is true of the Republican party in the United States, or for that matter, the Japanese Liberal-Democratic party, or the Chinese Communist party.

Why should this be so? Here we return to the words mentioned earlier: *political competence* and *efficacy*. Better-educated people know how to participate in political activity. They have a greater sense of self-confidence when writing letters, speaking at meetings, and organizing groups. They feel that what they do may have at least some small result politically. The uneducated and the poor lack the knowledge and confidence to do these kinds of things. Many of them feel powerless.[17] "What I do doesn't matter, so why bother?" they think. Those at the bottom of the social ladder thus become apathetic.

The differences in participation in politics between elites and masses are one of the great ironies of democracy. In theory and in law, politics is open to all in a democracy. In practice, some participate much more than others. Because the better-educated and better-off people (more education usually leads to higher income) participate in politics to a greater degree, they are in a much stronger position to look out for their interests. It is not surprising that in the 1990s Congress cut welfare spending while delivering tax cuts for better-off people, who can make their voices heard in the political system. There is no quick fix for this imbalance. The right to vote is a mere starting point for political participation; it does not guarantee equal access to decision making. A mass political culture of apathy and indifference toward politics effectively negates the potential of a mass vote. An elite political culture of competence and efficacy amplifies their influence.

POLITICAL SUBCULTURES

Just as there are differences between elites and masses, so also are there differences among ethnic, religious, and regional groups in a country. When the differentiating qualities are strong enough in a particular group, we say that the group forms a *subculture*. Defining subculture is a bit tricky, however. It would probably be a mistake to so label every distinct group in society. Do the Norwegian-Americans of "Lake Wobegon," Minnesota, form a subculture? Their attitudes differ a bit from the mainstream, but their political reactions and orientations are substantially the same as the majority of Americans. We would probably not call them a subculture. But how about African-Americans? They are often poorer and less educated than white Americans. The black vote is overwhelmingly Democratic even during a Republican victory. In one area—attitudes toward the criminal justice system—blacks sharply diverge from whites, as the 1995 murder trial of O. J. Simpson dramatically illustrated. Most blacks, convinced the police and courts are racist and rig evidence, were glad to see Simpson acquitted. Most whites, convinced the police and courts are just and fair, thought the jury (with its black majority) had ignored the evidence. Many whites had naively believed that U.S. society had made great strides since the 1950s in integrating African-Americans; the Simpson trial and the reactions to it showed how great a gap remained. Accordingly, African-Americans probably qualify as a political subculture.

Some subcultures, to be sure, are easy to identify. Groups with a different language and tendencies to break away from the rest of the population surely qualify. Some of the French-speaking people of Quebec, Canada, would still like to withdraw from the federation and become a separate country. The Bengalis of East Pakistan, ethnically and linguistically distinct from the peoples of West Pakistan, did, in fact, secede and found their own country in 1971. The Basques of northern Spain and the Roman Catholics of Northern Ireland are sufficiently different probably to constitute political subcultures. The Scots and Welsh of Britain harbor the resentments of the "Celtic fringe" against the dominant English: They vote heavily Labour, whereas the English vote heavily Conservative. They, too, probably constitute subcultures.

Where subcultures are very distinct, the political system itself may be threatened. The Soviet Union and Yugoslavia ceased to exist because citizens were more loyal to their ethnic groups than to the nation. In India, some Sikhs seek independence for the Punjab, their home province, and resort to arms. Prime Minister Indira Gandhi's Sikh bodyguards assassinated her in 1985 and, in effect, said their subculture was more important than India's. Recalling a term we used earlier, such countries as Lebanon and India are still undergoing a crisis of identification.

Should a nation attempt to integrate its subcultures into the mainstream? Such efforts are bound to be difficult, but if left undone, the subculture in later years may decide it really doesn't belong in that country. After the English defeated the French in Canada, they let the French Canadians keep their language and culture. It was a magnanimous gesture, but it meant that two centuries later Canada faced an angry and defiant Quebec separatist movement. Similarly the Spaniards in Peru who conquered the Incas let the Indians retain their language and culture. But now the Spanish-speaking Peruvians of the cities know little of the Quechua-speaking Peruvians of the mountains. Thirty percent of Peruvians speak no Spanish. Any non-integrated subculture poses at least a problem and at worst a threat to the national political system.

Starting in the 1870s, France deliberately pursued national integration through its centralized school system. Many regions were trapped in backwardness and spoke non-French dialects. The French education ministry sent schoolteachers into the villages almost like missionaries. The teachers followed an absolutely standard curriculum—the education ministry could tell what was being taught across France at any given minute—that was heavy on rote learning and on the glory and unity of France. Gradually, in the phrase of Eugen Weber, they turned "peasants into Frenchmen."[18] After some decades, a much more unified and integrated France emerged, an example of overt political socialization.

The United States has relied largely on voluntary integration to create a mainstream culture in which most Americans feel at home. Immigrants found they had to learn English to get ahead in the New World. The achievement-oriented consumer society tended to standardized tastes and career patterns. The melting pot worked, but not perfectly. Many Americans retain small subculture distinctions—often in the areas of religion and cuisine—but these may not be politically important. Italian-Americans did not rally behind Geraldine Ferraro, the first Italian-American to run for national office as the vice-presidential candidate on the Democratic ticket in 1984. Their failure to do so pointed out how well Italian-Americans had become integrated into the mainstream: They really didn't care that one of their own was at last on the ballot. Asian Americans also integrated rapidly into the U.S. mainstream. Japanese-Americans, only one-quarter of 1 percent of the total U.S. population, hold several of the 535 elected seats on Capitol Hill.

Not all American groups have been so fortunate. Blacks and Hispanics are not yet fully integrated into the American mainstream. They form, arguably, subcultures. Should these subcultures be better integrated into American society? This has been one of the great questions of post–World War II U.S. politics. With the 1954 *Brown* v. *Board of Education of Topeka* decision, the Supreme Court began a major federal government effort to integrate U.S. schools. It encountered massive resistance. In some instances federal judges had to take control of local school systems to enforce integration by busing. Underlying the reasons for integration, as discussed previously, is that an unintegrated group represents a problem, even a danger, for the society. The pro-integrationist Kennedy and Johnson administrations argued that America, in its struggle against communism, could not field a good army and offer an example of freedom and justice to the rest of the world if a considerable fraction of its population was oppressed and poor. Integration was portrayed as a matter of national security.

Should integration be forced in the area of language? Should African-Americans be forced to abandon "black English" in favor of standard English, and should Hispanics be forced to learn English? If they don't, they will be severely

Integration came hard to Little Rock, Arkansas, in 1957. Black students needed a National Guard escort to get past jeering white students at Central High School. The problem was not confined to the South or to the 1950s, however.

handicapped their whole lives, especially in employment prospects. But many blacks and Hispanics, and some native Americans, cling to their language as a statement of ethnic identity and pride. The U.S. Constitution does not specify any national language, nor does it outlaw languages other than English. In some areas of the United States, signs and official documents are in both English and Spanish. In 1986, California voters approved a measure making English the state's official language by a wide margin. People could, of course, continue to speak what they wished, but official documents, such as ballots and other legal matters, would be in English only. Other states passed similar laws, arguing that designating an official language would encourage new immigrants to learn English and hence speed their integration.

Political Socialization

When we think of the socializing process, we remember how we "picked up" such behavior patterns as table manners, correct terms of address, and the rules of personal hygiene. Such behavior is not formally taught; it is mostly absorbed by watching other people who know what they are doing and imitating their actions. Political socialization operates in much the same manner: We watch, listen, and imitate the political attitudes and values of family, friends, and others whom we respect. Learning to pledge allegiance to the flag, to stand up to sing the national anthem, and to acknowledge the authority of political figures, from presidents to police of-

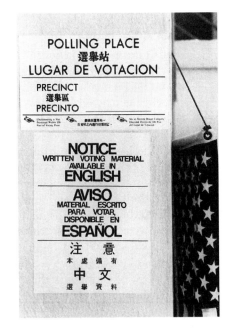

A trilingual sign in California emphasizes the multicultural character of the population of that state. In an effort to promote cultural unity, Californians voted in 1986 to make English the state's only official language.

ficers, are all part of the political learning process. Families, friends, school-teachers, and even television are important teachers. If Catholic children in Northern Ireland or poor children in the urban ghettoes of America are raised to see only the problems and ways of life of their isolated neighbors, with no perspective on how their small group fits into the national whole, they will likely form subcultures apart from the mainstream. If the process of political socialization disintegrates altogether, the entire political culture can break down. Political socialization—the learning of political attitudes and social preference—is crucial to stable government.

THE ROLES OF POLITICAL SOCIALIZATION

Political socialization performs several functions for both the individual and the political system as a whole.

Training the Individual.   Political socialization instills in each person the prevailing values of the political system. It enables him or her to relate to the system—to expect certain treatment from government and to know what it expects: obeying the laws, being involved in local affairs, and voting at election time.

Supporting the Political System.   Political socialization helps to maintain and legitimize the political system and the government in office. It maintains the system by conditioning and educating its members to obey its rules and to fulfill its roles. The system works as it does, and succeeds in governing to the extent that it does, because most people obey the laws and accept different roles—such as judge, police officer, party activist, candidate, and voter—which interact to keep the system going.[19]

Political socialization also plays the important role of training people to recognize those who have the right to exercise official authority, and to accept this right. The mother who brings her son to school on his first day and tells him, "Do as the teacher says," is legitimizing the teacher's authority by training her child to respect the teacher. Politically, we are all so socialized that even though we may be adversely affected by a law we disagree with, enacted by legislators we voted against, and carried out by order of a president we dislike, we nevertheless feel obliged to obey the law. Earlier in this century, thousands of Americans who would have otherwise freely taken an occasional nip refused to let liquor touch their lips solely because it was against the government's prohibition policy (although thousands also broke the law). To some extent, of course, we obey the law because we fear punishment, but in perhaps many more cases, obedience is due to our training to accept government's authority over us.

As discussed in Chapter 1, this sense of obedience is called *legitimacy*. When legitimacy erodes, governments must use more coercion to enforce their writ. One quick test of legitimacy, therefore, is to see how many police are needed. In England, where legitimacy is high, there are relatively few police; in Northern Ireland, however, which forms a subculture within the United Kingdom, legitimacy is low, especially among the Catholic minority, and many police, backed by British army units, are needed. In Poland in the early 1980s, government legitimacy virtually collapsed, and the country was ruled by the army and police.

THE AGENCIES OF SOCIALIZATION

Everything the child encounters is a potential agent of political socialization, but what he or she encounters earliest—the family—is apt to outweigh all the others. Attempts at "overt socialization" by government and schools generally fail if their values are at odds with family orientations. Many Communist countries had this problem: The regime tried to inculcate certain values in a child, but the family conditioned the child to ignore these messages. Where family and government values are generally congruent, as in the United States, the two modes of socialization reinforce one another.

The Family.   Psychologists tell us that long after we've left home, our parents continue to exert a profound influence on us, including our political behavior. An obvious example of this influence is the fact that most people vote as their parents did. More basically, the family forms the psychological makeup of the individual, which in turn determines many of his or her political attitudes. It imparts a set of norms and values, including political aspects, and it transmits beliefs and attitudes such as party loyalty and trust or cynicism about government.

Conditioning and training in the early years have the strongest effect. A study of the shaping of political attitudes found that the most decisive of these attitudes are shaped in the years from ages three to thirteen.[20] The family has almost exclusive control of the child's training in the first three of these years and continues to have the dominant influence during the school years as well. It is natural that the child's parents are the important models because they are the main source for the satisfaction of all basic needs—food and warmth, physical protection, love, and identity. Parents are figures of great power and authority in the child's world, and from them the child accepts many norms, values, and attitudes unconsciously and uncritically.

The psychological set children acquire as a result of family relationships affects their political behavior in adult life in many different ways.[21] In general, people give back to the world as adults what they got from it as children. One extensive study found that American college students with authoritarian personalities had almost invariably been treated roughly as children.[22] But parental overprotection may be just as harmful, causing children to fear leaving the shelter of the family. This fear may later be expressed politically as distrust and dislike of public figures.

As adults, people differ widely in the degree to which they participate in political affairs. Underlying this difference in behavior is a strong difference in beliefs about the effectiveness of their political activity. Those who feel they can influence government policy are, naturally, much more likely to be active. But where does the difference in beliefs originate? The five-nation study by Almond and Verba found an important clue in the style of family decision making.[23] Adults interviewed in the study were asked whether they remembered having had a voice in family decisions when they were children and whether they felt that their actions as adults could influence the government. The answers showed a clear relationship between the remembered family participation and the adult sense of "political efficacy": Those who took part in family decisions were, on the average, more inclined to feel that expression of their political beliefs could influence the government.

Most of the political socialization that takes place in the family is informal—and sometimes it is unconscious. Neither the parent nor the child is actively aware that future political behavior is being shaped when, for example, the father "lays down the law" and refuses to hear any argument, or when the mother thinks aloud that there's no use complaining about the unfair amount of work she has to do around the house without any help because her husband won't pay any attention. And parental attitudes and actions about political matters—for instance, their level of interest in election campaigns or their readiness to accept special favors when they have a slight legal problem (getting a traffic ticket "fixed")—probably are more important in shaping the child's future political behavior than any of the specific ideas about government and politics that the parents consciously try to impart. In contrast is the more deliberate type of socialization that occurs in the schools.

The School.   When a new nation is created, be it by revolution, civil war, or peaceful independence from a colonial power, one of the most important steps the government must take is to teach its citizens that they are a national community. Schools are among the most important agents of socialization in turning scattered groups of people into a nation since they are able to reach large numbers of individuals simultaneously and teach them that they belong to a community—a job for which the family is ill equipped. The developing nations of Africa are currently trying to unify a number of tribes that speak different dialects and that often have histories of conflict with one another. The role of U.S. schools has been profound, as they have been called on to turn immigrants with different political values into one nation. The Communist nations also relied heavily on the schools for systematic inculcation of new political loyalties and concepts. As we saw in 1989, though, this effort was unsuccessful; family and church overrode the attempts of schools to make East Europeans believing Communists.

In nations where the government is well established, the content of the school's political socialization is generally more in harmony with what the family teaches. Then primary schools have a strong effect: They are able to reinforce the students' identification with the community and the nation. In classrooms around the globe, children salute different flags and are taught to feel positive emotion toward their own national symbols. The advocates of broad public schooling have usually stressed its value for teaching the meaning of citizenship and inculcating convictions about one's obligations to the national community.

The amount of schooling a person receives affects political attitudes at a more sophisticated level than the programmed loyalty to the Stars and Stripes or the Union Jack. For example, people with several years of education have a stronger sense of responsibility to their community and feel more able to influence public policy than do less educated citizens. As Table 7.2 shows, even though there may be differences among the political cultures of separate nations, there is a striking correlation between a person's formal education and his or her attitudes toward the political system. Persons with more schooling show a greater awareness of political questions, pay more attention to politics, are more likely to engage in political discussion, and are more inclined to participate in politics.

How much of this is the direct result of what a person learns in class about one's rights and responsibilities, and how much is explained by the fact that longer schooling is associated with higher socioeconomic status? Though this poses an analytical riddle, there is general recognition that education is a force in its own right aside from economic considerations, and consequently, intense battles are often fought over what and how the schools should teach. Black leaders rebelled against the use of textbooks that ignored or slighted the accomplishments of African-Americans, especially those that appeared to do so deliberately. They saw the formal teaching of racial identity to be a vital element of what was needed for African-Americans to progress toward the effective exercise of their political and civil rights.

Peer Groups.   Whereas school lessons are a powerful socializing force, there is also some evidence that they may not have a very lasting effect unless other influences are pushing the individual in the same direction. For example, working-class children in Jamaica who went to school with children of higher social classes tended to take on the political attitudes of those classes, but when they attended school with only working-class peers, their attitudes did not change.[24]

The relative strength of peer-group influence compared with that of school and family appears to be growing. As a result of rapid change and economic specialization in modern society, parents cannot give their children a lot of the knowledge, skills, and perceptions they need in the outside world. Children consequently

TABLE 7.2   Percentage Who Say the Ordinary Man Should Be Active in His Local Community, by Nation and Education

Nation	Overall	Primary Schooling	Some Secondary	Some University
United States	51	35	56	66
United Kingdom	3	37	42	42
West Germany	22	21	32	38
Italy	10	7	17	22
Mexico	26	24	37	38

Source: Gabriel A. Almond and Sidney Verba, *The Civic Culture* (Princeton, NJ: Princeton University Press, 1963), p. 176. Reprinted by permission of Princeton University Press.

spend more time in school and out with their peers and less with their families. The results are that both schools and peer groups are growing more influential than the family, and peer groups seem to have increasingly more to do with the individual's assimilation of what the school presents.

The Mass Media.   The media of mass communications constitute a fourth important socializing force. These media are part of modern industrial civilization. They have no counterpart in primitive societies, nor in classic civilizations of the past, and this is no accident. Modern technology created them, but more to the point, modern society, and particularly its government, depends heavily on them to perform even simple functions. Mass communications constitute a revolution in the way people get information about the world beyond their own daily experience and the way they form their perceptions about it. In the United States, even three-year-olds can recognize the president on television and understand that he is a sort of "boss" of the nation. Senators and members of Congress, who receive much less coverage, are treated with relative indifference, a view the children may hold the rest of their lives.

As with schools, though, the mass media may be unsuccessful if the messages they beam are at odds with what family and religion teach. Even Soviet researchers found that families were much bigger influences on individuals' political views than the all-pervasive Soviet mass media.[25] Iran's mass media, all firmly controlled by the shah, tried to inculcate loyalty to him, but believing Muslims took the word of their local *mullahs* in the mosques and hated the shah. Mass media can't do everything.

The Government.   Government itself is inevitably an agent of political socialization. Virtually everything it does takes into account its citizens' reactions, and many government activities are intended explicitly to explain or display the government to the public.

All the actions of governing affect the people and, consequently, their attitudes, and the information, education, and propaganda supplied by the government are never designed to weaken public support and loyalty. Great spectacles of state, such as the crowning of a British king or queen, have a strengthening effect, so do parades with flags flying and impressive displays of military power. But many other activities of a less formal character and implemented through other agents of socialization, such as the media and the schools, have similar effects. Schools, hospitals, and many office buildings fly flags; and proclamations of kings, presidents, prime ministers, and other dignitaries are announced in tones of respectful awe to young schoolchildren of all nations.

The power of government to control political attitudes is limited, however, because virtually all messages and experiences eventually reach the individual through conversations with primary groups of kin or peers, who interpret the original messages in terms of their own interests and established attitudes. Where alienated groups exist in a society, it is usually the family and the community that have "socialized" their children to dislike the government, in spite of the government's efforts to the contrary.

Suggested Readings

DIAMOND, LARRY, ed. *Political Culture and Democracy in Developing Countries.* Boulder, CO: Lynne Rienner, 1994. Specialists discuss how political culture may encourage or retard the growth of democracy.

ELSHTAIN, JEAN BETHKE. *Democracy on Trial.* New York: Basic Books, 1995. Brilliant argument that obsession with individual rights has undermined Americans' sense of community and civic obligation.

HACKER, ANDREW. *Two Nations: Black and White, Separate, Hostile, Unequal.* New York: Scribner's, 1992. A plea and a warning that racial integration is far from complete in America.

HERO, RODNEY E. *Latinos and the U.S. Political System: Two-Tiered Pluralism.* Philadelphia: Temple University Press, 1992. Author argues that the growing Hispanic community's integration into U.S. politics is largely illusory.

INGLEHART, RONALD. *Culture Shift in Advanced Industrial Society.* Princeton, NJ: Princeton University Press, 1990. A comparative and empirical study charting rise of a "postmaterialist" generation with more open views.

LIPSET, SEYMOUR MARTIN. *American Exceptionalism: A Double-Edged Sword.* New York: Norton, 1996. U.S. political culture really is quite different, argues this master of attitude studies.

MORONE, JAMES A. *The Democratic Wish: Popular Participation and the Limits of American Government.* New York: Basic Books, 1991. Americans' deep fear of governmental power blocks meaningful reforms.

PUTNAM, ROBERT D. *Making Democracy Work: Civic Traditions in Modern Italy.* Princeton, NJ: Princeton University Press, 1993. Impressive findings that Italy's regional governments work or fail depending on attitudes of trust, cooperation, and participation laid down over the centuries.

SCHLESINGER, ARTHUR M., JR. *The Disuniting of America.* New York: Norton, 1992. Noted historian argues against multicultural education as dangerous to an integrated society.

SELIGMAN, ADAM B. *The Idea of Civil Society.* New York: Free Press, 1992. The philosophical basis of tolerant, pluralist democracy and how difficult it is to transplant.

TERKEL, STUDS. *Race: How Blacks and Whites Feel About the American Obsession.* New York: New Press, 1992. Black and white Americans are still separate and afraid of each other.

VELIZ, CLAUDIO. *The New World of the Gothic Fox: Culture and Economy in English and Spanish America.* Berkeley, CA: University of California Press, 1994. The political culture Latin America inherited from Spain explains its backwardness compared to the culture we inherited from England, argues this noted historian.

VERBA, SIDNEY, KAY LEHMAN SCHLOZMAN, and HENRY E. BRADY. *Voice and Equality: Civic Voluntarism in American Politics.* Cambridge, MA: Harvard University Press, 1995. Extensive survey examines why some Americans participate in politics more than others.

Notes

1. For a brilliant comparison of U.S. and Canadian attitudes, see Seymour Martin Lipset, *Continental Divide: The Values and Institutions of the United States and Canada* (New York: Routledge, 1990).

2. For excellent discussions of political culture, see Gabriel A. Almond and Sidney Verba, *The Civic Culture: Political Attitudes and Democracy in Five Nations* (Boston: Little, Brown, 1965); Lucian W. Pye and Sidney Verba, eds., *Political Culture and Political Development* (Princeton, NJ: Princeton University Press, 1965).

3. Pye and Verba, *Political Culture and Political Development,* p. 513.

4. In 1958, 60 percent of the Japanese people who were questioned preferred using status-connoting pronouns to neutral ones such as *I* or *you.* When asked who should control policy-making for national reconstruction, over one-third thought that the job should be in the hands of the preeminent politicians, *not* elected representatives. Warren Tsuneishi, *Japanese Political Style* (New York: Harper & Row, 1966), pp. 16ff.

5. See, for example, Robert N. Bellah et al., *Habits of the Heart: Individualism and Commitment in American Life* (New York: Harper & Row, 1986).

6. Seymour Martin Lipset, *The First New Nation: The United States in Historical and Comparative Perspective* (New York: Anchor Books, 1967), Chap. 3.

7. Alexis de Tocqueville, *Democracy in America* (New York: Washington Square Press, 1964). The original was published in French during 1835–1840.

8. Almond and Verba, *The Civic Culture*. The nations that Almond and Verba studied were Great Britain, the United States, West Germany, Italy, and Mexico.

9. For a brief description of traditional China by a top scholar, see John King Fairbank, *The United States and China*, 4th ed. (Cambridge, MA: Harvard University Press, 1979), Chap. 2.

10. Almond and Verba, *Civic Culture*, p. 347.

11. Carl J. Friedrich, *Constitutional Government and Politics* (New York: Harper & Row, 1937), pp. 16–18.

12. Almond and Verba, *Civic Culture*, p. 148. As noted earlier, the Mexican responses tended to express ideal rather than actual behavior.

13. E. J. Dionne, Jr., "Government Trust: Less in West Europe Than U.S.," *New York Times*, 16 February 1986, p. 20.

14. Robert D. Putnam, "Bowling Alone: America's Declining Social Capital," *Journal of Democracy* 6 (January 1995), 1.

15. Francis Fukuyama, *Trust: The Social Virtues and the Creation of Prosperity* (New York: Free Press, 1995).

16. The authors of the original *Civic Culture* study fully realize the changing nature of political culture and brought out a book that examines the changes in the five countries of the original study. See Gabriel A. Almond and Sidney Verba, eds., *The Civic Culture Revisited* (Boston: Little, Brown, 1980).

17. See Giuseppe Di Palma, *Apathy and Participation: Mass Politics in Western Societies* (New York: Free Press, 1970). Di Palma used data from the *Civic Culture* study to demonstrate that modern society actually creates greater levels of apathy.

18. See Eugen Weber, *Peasants into Frenchmen: The Modernization of Rural France, 1870–1914* (Stanford, CA: Stanford University Press, 1976).

19. One leading sociologist feared that civic education has severely weakened in the present-day United States and this poses dangers for U.S. democracy. See Morris Janowitz, *The Reconstruction of Patriotism: Education for Civic Consciousness* (Chicago: University of Chicago Press, 1983).

20. David Easton and Stephen Hess, "The Child's Political World," *Journal of Political Science* 6 (August 1961), 229–46.

21. For example, political scientist Robert Lane found that tense father-son relationships can result in the grown son's inability to criticize any figure of political authority. See "Fathers and Sons: Foundations of Political Belief," *American Sociological Review* 24 (August 1959), 502–11.

22. T. W. Adorno, Else Frenkel-Brunswick, D. J. Levinson, and R. N Sanford, *The Authoritarian Personality* (New York: Harper & Row, 1950).

23. Almond and Verba, *Civic Culture*, pp. 274–79.

24. Kenneth P. Langton, *Political Socialization* (New York: Oxford University Press, 1969), pp. 126–31.

25. See David Wedgwood Benn, *Persuasion and Communication in the USSR* (New York: Blackwell, 1989).

• 8 •
Public Opinion

Political culture and public opinion are closely linked. They are generally formed through the same influences, and they merge in a way that makes it hard to judge where one leaves off and the other begins. There is a clear connection between the process that shaped the general attitude of Americans toward communism during the late 1940s and early 1950s and the process that shaped American opinion about the right of China's claim to Taiwan today. Yet they are not the same thing. Political culture focuses on more or less permanent values, attitudes, and ideas, which people learn from their society and apply to political questions. Most Americans are indoctrinated with the idea that government power is dangerous and must be controlled. This feeling is built into the permanent value structure of American political culture just as clearly as the conviction that democracy is the only just form of government. Public opinion, whereas it is based on long-term convictions and ideals, relates to people's reactions to specific policies and problems rather than long-term value systems.

Just as public opinion is not synonymous with political culture, it is not to be confused with individual opinion, either. A woman's opinion of her neighbor's religion would not be part of public opinion, but her feeling that adolescents should pray in public schools would. Public opinion refers to political and social issues, not private matters of taste.

Finally, public opinion does not necessary imply a strong, clear, united conviction of the masses. To be sure, there are subjects on which the majority of people are united in their opinion, and when that is the case, public opinion has mighty force indeed. But most often, public opinion involves several small groups of people, each group's views in conflict with those of the other groups, plus a large number who are undecided, plus an even larger number with no interest or opinion at all on the matter. On most subjects, public opinion is an array of diverse ideas and attitudes concerning political and social issues that can change fairly quickly.

The Role of Public Opinion

As a primary input by the people into the political system, does public opinion direct public policy? *Should* it? Both these questions are controversial and difficult to unravel. In a democracy, the average person's offhand answer would probably be "Maybe it doesn't, but it certainly should." But the practical difficulties of realizing control by public opinion are profound. How could pollsters possibly keep tally of what the people think about every issue that comes before legislators and executives? The public doesn't even have an opinion on most issues, and the willingness of its members to make up answers when they don't feel competent to rely on their own knowledge further complicates matters. In 1948 a poll asked respondents what they thought of the "Metallic Metals Act." Fifty-nine percent supported the act, provided that discretion be left to individual states. Sixteen percent thought the act should not be imposed on the American people, and only 30 percent admitted they had no opinion on the matter. In fact, no such act existed nor had any such bill been proposed. Ross Perot's idea of an "electronic town meeting" would likely interest only an attentive minority, who would then have a disproportionate influence on the questions that attracted them.

Aside from the problems of the public's ignorance of many issues of government policy is the problem of morality: Do numbers make right? Most Americans are opposed to raising taxes on gasoline. Does that mean that government should bar this means of taxation at all costs? In spite of public opinion's inadequacies as a guide for policymaking, however, one cannot deny that it plays an important role in governing. Even in totalitarian states, the government knows that public support is vital for stable rule and keeps an ear open for murmurs of dissent.

The role of public opinion in the political system is difficult to define. In a democracy, elections provide a formal means of popular control of government but only a very crude expression of public opinion. An election can register only the verdict of the voters on an official's overall performance; rarely is one issue so important that an election rides on it alone. Of course, if opinion is running strong in one direction, few candidates or legislators will defy it, so in this sense public opinion does provide some control. Few election hopefuls would run on a platform that advocated heavy tax increases or a severe cut in Social Security benefits. But for the most part, candidates, especially in two-party systems such as the British and the American, manage to ride through elections with little commitment to issues.

In many cases, public opinion is created, not followed, by the executive. Why else would some of our government leaders spend as much time as they do addressing the nation in front of TV cameras? When Richard Nixon announced in late 1971 that he would be the first American president to visit the People's Republic of China, he revolutionized public opinion about China (it quickly grew more favorable). Spanish Prime Minister Felipe González, head of a party that opposed Spain joining NATO, changed his mind and supported Spain's affiliation, although public opinion polls showed that most Spaniards didn't want Spain in NATO. González urged support for NATO in a 1986 referendum, and Spaniards swung around to support him. U.S. opinion split evenly on the eve of the Persian Gulf war, but once the war started, Americans massively supported President Bush's policies. Governments can create public opinion.

We won't give up Havel! This sign and a petition drive at Prague's Wenceslaus Square aimed to keep Czech President Vaclav Havel in power in 1992. He resigned later that year rather than preside over the dissolution of his country but returned to office after the split.

If elections provide only a foggy outlet for public opinion, and executives often lead rather than follow the will of the people, the more direct participation of interest groups, be they concerned citizens or lobbyists, often allows opinions to be expressed in crystal-clear terms. In democracies, which provide freedom to express dissent in bold and dramatic form, strategies for bringing grievances to public attention can be very effective in exciting widespread sympathy. The brutality of sheriff's deputies in Selma, Alabama, toward blacks who were protesting the denial of their right to vote was witnessed by television viewers across the nation, and the public reaction was a decisive force in passing the Voting Rights Act of 1965.

The Role of Public Opinion in Nondemocratic States.   Any government is vulnerable to public opinion powerfully mobilized against it. Mahatma Gandhi, by a simple drama of nonviolent protest, used the weapon of public opinion to win independence for India. A gaunt, bespectacled old man in a loincloth, he threatened to starve himself to death if the British did not pull out of India. So powerful was the support he generated that the British decided they could not risk the consequences of ignoring him.

Government by sheer violence and coercion cannot last for any length of time. Even Nazi Germany, with all its brutal apparatus for suppressing dissent, depended on the dream of Germany's world supremacy—not night raids by the Gestapo—to rouse patriotic fervor. The importance of public support to the Hitler regime is attested to by the fact that the government kept careful tabs on how the German public felt about its policies. Documents found after World War II showed that the top Nazi leaders created a monumental network to test the people's reaction to each new policy and propaganda piece and to gather reliable data on the people's morale.[1] Ironically, the regime's enormous power of coercion so intimidated expression that officials were afraid to send in negative reports. The result was that the Nazi government received rose-colored accounts rather than an accurate feedback, so that "public opinion" was never really fathomed.

THE STRUCTURE OF PUBLIC OPINION

Within broad limits, social scientists have been able to discover roughly who thinks what about politics. It is important to bear in mind, however, that no social category is ever 100 percent for or against something. Indeed, 60 or 70 percent is often considered quite high. What we look for are *differences* among social categories, the significance of which can be tested by the rules of statistics. We look for different shades of gray, not for black and white. Once we have found significant differences, we may be able to say something about *salience*, the degree to which categories and issues affect the public opinion of a country. In Scandinavia, for example, social class is salient in structuring party preferences: The working class tends to vote Social Democratic and the middle class votes for the more conservative parties. In Latin Europe, social class is weakly salient, with the working class scattering its vote among parties of the left, right, and center. In Latin Europe, religion and region are typically most salient.

Social Class. Karl Marx described social class as having massive salience. Workers, once they were aware of their situation, would become socialists. More recently, and with qualifications, social scientists have found that social class still matters, even in the relatively classless United States. Over the decades, the American manual worker has tended to vote Democratic; the better-off or professional person has tended to vote Republican.[2] But these are only tendencies, and they are often muddied by other factors. Poor people are often very conservative, whereas affluent people can be liberal or even radical. During hard times, when bread-and-butter issues such as jobs become salient, the American working class tends to rediscover the Democratic party, as it did in 1992. When these issues lose their salience, however, the working class often finds that noneconomic issues gain in importance. Then questions of morality (abortion, prayer in schools) and foreign policy (increasing defense spending) may siphon off a large part of the working class to the Republicans.

Social class can also be hard to measure. There are two general ways of going at the question: objectively and subjectively. An objective determination of social class involves asking a person his or her approximate annual income or judging the quality of the neighborhood. The subjective determination of class involves simply asking the respondent what his or her social class is. Often this diverges from objective social class. A majority of Americans are used to thinking of themselves as middle class, even if they aren't. Sometimes even very wealthy people, thinking of their modest origins, call themselves middle class. The way a person earns a living may matter more than the amount he or she makes. Typically, American farmers are conservative about politics, and miners and steelworkers are not. Different political attitudes grow up around different jobs.

Sometimes social class works in precisely the opposite way envisioned by Marx. The liberalism of some affluent U.S. suburbs stands Marx on his head.[3] Spanish researchers found an *inverse* relationship between social class and preferring the left; that is, better-off persons were more leftist than poorer Spaniards. In the Spanish study, it was education that was most salient: A university education tended to radicalize Spaniards.[4]

Class matters in structuring opinion, but it is seldom a be-all or end-all. Usually social class is important when combined with one or more other factors, such as region or religion. In Britain, class plus region structures much of the vote; in France, it is class plus region plus religiosity (practicing Catholic vs. nonpracticing); in Germany, it is class plus region plus denomination (Catholic or Protestant). As Yale's Joseph LaPalombara put it, the key question might be "Class plus what?"[5]

Education. Educational level is related to social class; that is, children of better-off families usually get more education, and education in turn leads to better-paying positions. Unlike the Spanish case, where university study tended to radicalize, education in the United States seems to have a split impact: It makes people more liberal on noneconomic issues but often more conservative on economic issues. Abundant survey data show that college-educated people are more tolerant, more supportive of civil rights, and more likely to be acquainted with a variety of viewpoints. But when it comes to economic issues, many of these same people are skeptical of efforts to redistribute income in the form of higher taxes on the upper brackets—which happen to be them—and welfare measures for the nonworking. There are, to be sure, some educated people who are consistently liberal on both economic and noneconomic questions, but in the United States the categories sometimes diverge.[6] The same is often true of the American working class: Its members want a bigger share of the national income but are intolerant in the areas of race, lifestyle, and patriotism. When college youths, mostly from middle-class families, protested the Vietnam war, they sometimes ran into the snarls and fists of unionized construction workers, a graphic illustration of the split between economic and noneconomic liberalism.

There is one thing that education does for sure: It increases political participation. College graduates are far more likely to vote, work in campaigns, follow politics, and contact officials than are people with only an elementary education. Those who have completed high school are in an intermediate position. Education, in fact, is the nearly universal gateway to elite status. The elite of most countries are university graduates. (Exceptions are the revolutionary elites in power shortly after their takeover. The successor generation, however, is usually college-educated.) Education seems to contribute in many ways to political participation and then to elite status. Obviously, it increases knowledge, but it also increases self-confidence, speaking and writing ability, and the expectation of individual advancement. Indeed, the mere fact that you are reading this book indicates that you will probably participate in politics more than others and have a better chance of attaining some kind of political influence.

Region.   Every country has a south, goes an old saw, and this is certainly true in politics. What is uncertain, however, is whether a country's south is more conservative or more leftist than its north. France, south of the Loire River, and Spain, south of the Tagus, have for generations tended to go left. The south of Italy, though, is a bastion of conservatism, as is Bavaria in Germany's south. In Great Britain, England is heavily conservative, whereas Scotland and Wales go for Labour. And of course the U.S. South was famous for decades as the "solid South," which went automatically for the Democrats—no longer the case.

A country's outlying regions usually harbor resentment against the capital, creating what are called "center-periphery tensions." Often an outlying region was conquered or forcibly assimilated into the nation and has never been completely happy about it. Regional memories can last for centuries. This is true of the south of France; the U.S. South; the south of Italy, Quebec, and Scotland. Often the region feels economically disadvantaged by the central area. The region may have a different ethnic makeup, as in Catalonia and the Basque country in Spain, Wallonia in Belgium, Quebec in Canada, Slovenia in Yugoslavia, and several parts of India.

Once a region gets set in its politics, the pattern is highly durable. Region plays a big role in the politics of Britain, France, and Germany and even to a certain extent in the United States. The "solid South" has eroded, but the "sunbelt" of southern and western states is generally conservative on both economic and noneconomic issues and jealous of states' rights. The "frostbelt" of northern and eastern states, where industry has declined, tends to be more liberal, especially on questions of economic relief from Washington. In the early 1980s, when President Reagan cut both taxes and welfare expenditures, conservative, southern Democrats, dubbed "boll weevils," supported him, and some liberal, northern Republicans, nicknamed "gypsy moths," opposed him, providing a vivid illustration of the effects of region on U.S. politics.

Religion. Religion is often the most explosive issue in politics and contributes a great deal to the structuring of opinion. In many cases, religion has a greater impact on political viewpoints than does social class. Religion can mean either denomination or religiosity. In Germany, Catholics tend to go to the Christian Democratic Union, whereas Protestants tend to go to the Social Democrats or Free Democrats, although the question of social class is also bound up with this choice. In Germany, it's a question of denomination. In France, where most citizens are at least nominal Catholics, it's a question of religiosity, as many French are indifferent to religion. The more often a French person goes to mass, the more likely he or she is to vote for a conservative party. Few Communist voters are practicing Catholics. In Italy, religion and government are linked through the large Christian Democratic party. One of the biggest divisions in Catholic countries is between clericalists and anticlericalists; the former are for a church role in politics, the latter against. France, Italy, and Spain have long been split over this issue, with the conservative parties more favorable to the Catholic church and the parties of the left hostile to church influence.

Religion plays a considerable role in the United States, too, although here it overlaps with ethnicity. Catholics, especially Polish Catholics, have been the most loyal Democrats of all.[7] In the great immigrations of previous decades, big-city Democratic machines stood ready to welcome and help immigrants from Catholic countries, and in turn these people and their descendants stayed mostly Democratic. For a long time it was believed that no Catholic could be elected president of the United States; John F. Kennedy in 1960 put that view to rest, and now being Catholic probably does no harm to a candidate. Many Catholics and fundamentalist Protestants now have a common cause in fighting abortion.

Of major importance to U.S. politics was the rise of the "religious right" during the 1980s. Many mainstream denominations became more conservative, and rapidly growing fundamentalist groups became highly political.[8] Ministers such as Jerry Falwell mobilized their television flocks against pornography and abortion and for a strong national defense and the Republican party. In 1996, the powerful Christian Coalition, headed by youthful Ralph Reed, was considered the single most conservative force inside the Republican party.

American candidates, especially for the presidency, have always had to be known as churchgoers, but since the rise of fundamentalism many also wish to be known as "born-again" Christians. In 1980, both Ronald Reagan and Jimmy Carter claimed to have been born again in Christ. Former Senator Eugene McCarthy, who tried for the Democratic nomination in 1968, reflected in 1980 that he was the last presidential contender who had been born only once. Baptist Bill Clinton made it clear that he was a good churchgoer. Americans like their leaders to at least appear religious.

Age.   There are two ways of measuring age in terms of political opinions: straight chronologically and generationally. Conventional wisdom sees young people as radical, ready to change the system, with older people more moderate or even conservative. With few responsibilities in youth, young people can indulge their fantasies, but with the burdens of home, job, and children of their own, people become more conservative.

This "life cycle" theory doesn't always work because sometimes whole generations are marked for life by the great events of their young adulthood. Survivors of World Wars I and II, the Great Depression, and the Vietnam war have carried nervous remembrances of these upheavals for decades, coloring their views on war, economics, and politics. Sociologist Karl Mannheim called this phenomenon "political generations."[9] The young Americans of the 1960s and early 1970s who fought in or protested the Vietnam war, although they later became settled and more moderate in their views, continued to be nervous about the use of U.S. troops overseas. Likewise, older people who had personally experienced the Depression of the 1930s were more supportive of federal welfare measures than younger people who had been raised in postwar prosperity. One survey found that in 1992 younger Americans voiced more conservative and pro-Republican views than did older Americans.[10]

Gender.   Even before the women's movement, gender made a difference in politics. Traditionally, and especially in Catholic areas, women were more conservative, more concerned with home, family, and morality. This still applies in Catholic Spain and Italy. But as a society modernizes, men's and women's views become closer. Women leave the home to work, become more aware of social and economic problems, and do not necessarily just take their husbands' political views. In the United States, an interesting "gender gap" appeared in the 1980s as women became several percentage points more liberal and Democratic than men.[11] And this was precisely because women had found the federal government necessary to support the old virtues of home and family. Further, many women disliked the Republican administrations' emphasis on war preparation. In 1992, women were five percentage points more likely to vote for Clinton than were men. It may be that in the modern political world, women will be the natural liberals.

Ethnic Group.   Ethnicity is related to region and religion but sometimes plays a distinct role of its own, especially in the multiethnic United States. America was long touted as a "melting pot" of immigrant groups, but research has revealed the staying power and lively consciousness of ethnic groups for many generations. Democratic presidential aspirant Walter Mondale was described as modest and reticent about himself because he was Norwegian, and Norwegians are socialized in their families never to toot their own horns.

American politics is often described in ethnic terms, with WASPs (white Anglo-Saxon Protestants) and other northern Europeans generally conservative and Republican, and people of southern and eastern European origin, blacks, Hispanics, and Asian-Americans more liberal and Democratic. This simplification sometimes does violence to the complexity of individuals and of politics, but some working politicians still find it a valuable guide. Ethnic politics changes over the decades. After the Civil War, most blacks were Republican, the party of Lincoln. With Franklin D. Roosevelt and the New Deal, most African-Americans became Democrats and stayed that way. In the last century, American Jews were mostly Republican, for the Republicans sharply criticized the anti-Semitic repression of tsarist Russia. The Jewish immigrants of the turn of the century, introduced to U.S. politics by Democratic machines such as New York's Tammany Hall, went Democratic. In the 1970s, many Jews, influenced by neoconservatism (see Chapter 6), swung to the Republicans (but in 1992 swung back to the Democrats). Ethnic politics is not fixed in concrete.

PUBLIC OPINION PATTERNS

What do the people as a whole think about a particular issue? In general, they can be for, against, or undecided. But the factors of uncertainty and changeability are so prominent in many areas that we can't always be confident that the "patterns" tell us a dependable story.

Classic Opinion Curves.   The way that different people feel about a question is often summarized statistically in a curve that shows the distribution of the different opinions sampled along a range from one extreme position to the opposite ex-

A wishing wall was put up in Washington for President Clinton's inauguration. Citizens pinned up notes urging legislation on everything from hunger and child abuse to global warming and nuclear weapons.

treme. A noncontroversial issue—a "home, mother, and apple pie" matter on which there are only a few doubters and dissenters—will show most opinions massed at one extreme, a much smaller number with qualified opinions, or virtually none, at the opposite extreme. For example, if a cross section of America is asked whether more effective measures should be developed to prevent environmental pollution, the answers could be mapped out along a very stable, one-sided curve, sometimes called a "J-curve" for its lopsidedness (Fig. 8.1).

On many issues, however, there is less consensus and little certainty. Here, public opinion may take the form of a "bell-shaped" curve or "unimodal distribution," which shows a relatively few people totally committed to a position at one extreme or the other, with the majority in the moderate area in between. Asked whether the size of the armed forces is too small, too large, or about right, it is unlikely that the majority will answer with either of the extremes. Conflicting factors such as the wish to keep taxes low, fear of a chaotic world, and personal attitudes toward military service in general will cause the "too smalls" to be about equal to the "too larges"; but most people will reply with "about right."

A third characteristic pattern aggregate public opinion can take is that of extreme division, or "bimodal distribution," sometimes called a "U-curve." On a large enough scale, this kind of opinion difference can lead to civil war. For years, there has been a strong divergence between the Protestants and Catholics of Northern Ireland on questions touching majority and minority rights, relations with Britain, and relations with Eire. The result has been violent civil conflict, with few middle-of-the-roaders in Northern Ireland.

Most often, though, opinion distribution does not fall into such well-defined patterns, mainly because most people, most of the time, pay little attention to political and government issues. They have little sustained interest in issues that do not directly touch their lives, and therefore they acquire little information about these issues. Most public surveys, for example, will find that nearly half of those questioned don't know who their representative in Congress is.

Thus on most issues, only a small portion of the total public is attentive

FIGURE 8.1   Classic public opinion curves

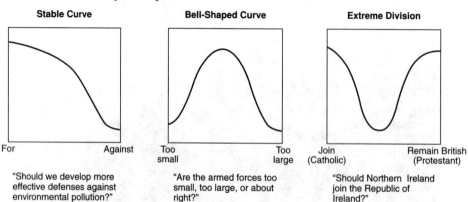

Stable Curve	Bell-Shaped Curve	Extreme Division
For — Against	Too small — Too large	Join (Catholic) — Remain British (Protestant)
"Should we develop more effective defenses against environmental pollution?"	"Are the armed forces too small, too large, or about right?"	"Should Northern Ireland join the Republic of Ireland?"

enough to news reports and editorials to hold a decisive opinion. And in many situations, a general public opinion curve will be a rather dim reflection of the opinion pattern within this "attentive public." With all of the uncertainties, personality quirks, and just plain ignorance involved in public opinion, how are surveys able to reflect an accurate picture of what the people are thinking?

Public Opinion Polls

Any effort to gauge the attitude of the public by means of a representative sample is called a survey or poll. Published polls, particularly in election years, are prominent in today's political landscape. Almost daily we see statistics and percentages on what America thinks of crime, of unemployment, of abortion, of one candidate as opposed to another. The ubiquity of public opinion surveys serves as testament to their usefulness to policymakers and candidates alike. But debate has developed over some of their political side effects. For example, do the polls give undue attention and influence to uncertain opinions? Do journalists create self-fulfilling prophecies by treating the polls as authoritative verdicts, which people read about, then follow? Another area of controversy concerns the role of public opinion surveys. Should they be treated, as some propose, as a truly democratic method of deciding public policies? Even if one feels that all government action in a democracy should take its cue from the people's will, are public opinion polls reliable enough to determine policy? Who uses polls, what purpose do they serve, and can we trust them?

THE HISTORY OF PUBLIC OPINION POLLS

In 1824, the *Harrisburg Pennsylvanian* sent its reporters to the streets to ask passersby whether they intended to vote for John Quincy Adams or Andrew Jackson. The tally was printed on the theory that these "straws in the wind" indicated which way the political wind was blowing. Many other newspapers, using a variety of both careful and haphazard methods, conducted "straw polls" in various elections thereafter. But the popular magazine *Literary Digest* was the first to develop a survey of great prestige. In the early years of this century, it accurately predicted the 1916, 1920, 1924, 1928, and 1932 presidential elections. The guiding principle of the *Literary Digest* technique was to use a huge sample, on the notion that the more people questioned, the more dependable the result. It conducted its survey by mail, drawing close to 10 million addresses from lists of subscribers, car owners, and phone books. All went well until 1936, when 2.4 million people replied that they wanted Franklin D. Roosevelt out of office. The *Literary Digest* predicted the Republican candidate, Alfred M. Landon, as victor with 59.1 percent of the vote. Roosevelt's landslide victory—with over 60 percent of the vote—signaled the demise of both the straw-poll method of sampling and of *Literary Digest* itself.

As it happened, 1936 was also the first year that practitioners of the newly developed techniques of "scientific polling" were on the political scene, branching out from the field of market research. Several newspapers had begun syndication of George H. Gallup's survey results, which, in contrast to *Literary Digest*, forecast Roosevelt's victory. Gallup publicly predicted that the *Digest* poll was riding for a fall, and identified the reason: Its sample was drawn heavily from higher-income people, many of whom were angered by Roosevelt's social and economic policies and who were thus likely to vote Republican. The guiding principle of the new technique used by Gallup was to select a sample as *representative*, rather than as large, as possible.

This scientific sampling method has dominated the field since then, with a very successful record. But even it failed in the 1948 election, when almost every poll predicted that Thomas E. Dewey would defeat Harry S Truman by a landslide. (It looked so certain to one leading pollster that he stopped taking samples in mid-September.) But even science can prove fallible, and Truman won with 49 percent in a four-way contest. The Social Science Research Council found that the sampling methods used were sound, but the key error was in assuming that respondents who said they were undecided would wind up voting in the same ratio as those who had made up their minds.[12] In fact, these voters decided much more heavily in favor of Truman—close to 75 percent. The major polls have further refined their methods since that time and today make special efforts to detect late swings to one candidate or the other. It should be noted, however, that they do not even claim to be able to predict divisions within closer than two to three percentage points. The margin of victory in several presidential elections has been less than 1 percent, so it is clear that even the most accurate polls cannot furnish a confident prediction of the winner in such elections.

POLLING TECHNIQUES

How can a sample of as few as 1,000 people be used to predict the actions of a hundred million? The answer is complex, but it revolves around a technique that can be summarized in a few basic steps.

Asking the Questions.   The goal of a public opinion survey is to get candid replies from a representative sample at a minimum cost. The problem of cost is yet to be overcome, as today's least expensive methods still tend to be the least accurate also. But there are fairly universal guidelines for getting the most candid replies possible and for choosing useful samples.

In finding out what the people think about an issue, the cheapest method is to mail out ballots to a sample and tally the replies, but invariably, the people who are involved enough to make the effort to reply will not be representative of the sample. The same factors that motivate some to respond whereas others don't bother also cause opinion differences, as the *Literary Digest* experience showed. Telephone polling can avoid this problem, but it rarely establishes sufficient rapport to obtain really candid replies. The most dependable method is still the costly face-to-face interview. For reliable results, the interviewers should be carefully selected and trained. But even this method has drawbacks. Because it is costly, it often creates pressure on the pollster to make do with a minimum number of interviews.

The wording of questions to avoid inclining the respondent toward one answer or the other is also an important element in sound polling technique. In 1974, for example, Gallup found that more Americans thought President Nixon should be brought "to trial before the Senate" than be "impeached" for alleged Watergate wrongdoings. The two expressions mean exactly the same, but "impeached" in the public mind carries the connotation of convicted and ousted from office.[13] In 1992, answers to a badly worded question (it had a double negative) suggested that one in five Americans doubted the Nazi Holocaust had really happened. When the question was worded more clearly in 1994 (without the double negative), only 2 percent denied the Holocaust had happened. The pollster must also avoid tones of voice or sympathetic looks that might encourage one response over another—a task that is much harder than it seems. But whereas phrasing and asking opinion questions require some amount of skill, a problem even more difficult is that of selecting the sample.

Selecting the Sample.   In deciding whom to use as the sample, the pollster must make a choice between two major schools of thought. One, the stratified-quota sampling school, tries to include a proportionally representative cross section of the society. Though the method has an undeniable logic, it is very difficult to carry out in practice. It puts a tremendous burden on interviewers, requiring them to pick and choose among respondents to maintain representative ratios in income, gender, race, age, religion, and party preference. The judgments they must make in doing so can easily introduce unintentional errors, as they separate the procedure from a centralized control.

The second major approach is to try for a truly random sample, eliminating all elements of deliberate choice and judgment in deciding which individuals to include. The ideal method to obtain such a sample is to put the name of every potential voter in the country in a data bank and have a computer print out several thousand names at random. This method produces more dependable results than the quota system. For telephone surveys, a computer actually dials the numbers nationwide at random, effectively eliminating human choice. The method most often used is to use one hundred to two hundred regular interviewers whom the polling company has hired from different areas around the country, each of whom interviews fifteen to twenty persons in a designated locality. The result is a total sample that is both random and highly representative. The method is called area sampling. It involves an initial decision of which geographic districts should become sample areas, the classification of these districts into groups according to population characteristics, and random selection of which categories to use and which people to question from each category. The resulting sample is quite close to that which a completely random selection would obtain and is considerably less expensive.

HOW RELIABLE ARE THE POLLS?

The widespread use of public opinion surveys suggests that they have achieved a high degree of public confidence, and this is indeed true. Overall, the opinion research business sells services costing over $200 million a year in the United States alone, and the number of private polls commissioned by candidates in primary and general elections each year is now in the thousands.

A major limitation of polls, however, especially for election forecasting, is the unpredictability of voter turnout. This presents an extremely difficult problem because many respondents who say they intend to vote actually will wind up staying home on election day. These voters and the "I don't knows" are quite likely not to divide up in the same way as those who are very conscientious about voting. Thus, election results may be very different if there is a heavy voter turnout rather than if only a few show up at the booths. The election year pollster must adjust raw findings for this factor, but there is no way to be certain how big the turnout will be and what, if any, will be the effect of last-minute events such as rain storms and foreign-policy announcements.

Public opinion is "volatile," able to change quickly under the impact of events. In 1965, as Lyndon Johnson escalated the war in Vietnam, an aide told him that "we have overwhelming public opinion on our side." Johnson, a crafty political pro who had long read the polls, replied, "Yes, but for a very underwhelming period of time." He was right; majority support for the war in 1965 turned into majority opposition in 1968.[14] Nothing is permanent in public opinion; volatility must be taken into account.

Finally, a survey that is accurate in its overall results cannot assure the same degree of reliability when broken down into finer categories. To get an accurate reading, the sample must be large enough to average out any quirks. But a sample adequate for a national finding will probably not involve a big enough sample from any one category, such as region, income, or religion, to provide the same degree of reliability.

American Opinion

PRESIDENTIAL POPULARITY

One of the oldest and most important items in U.S. public opinion polls measures the popularity of the president at a given moment. In a technical sense, the question asks how the president is handling the job of president, not how much the respondent likes the president. In practice, however, the respondent who likes the president will approve of the president's job performance. President Reagan, for example, was so likable that citizens perceived him as doing a good job even when some of them disagreed with his economic and foreign policies. At any rate, the term *popularity* has stuck to this poll even if the question was designed to measure performance.

Typically, presidents start with high popularity and then decline. During their first year they enjoy a "honeymoon" with the press and the public. The high point of their popularity often comes early in their term of office. After some years, however, problems accumulate: The economy turns sour or foreign policies don't work. This brings a popularity low point. Presidents seldom leave office as popular as they were during their first year.

When a president comes under intense pressure or takes a major action, his popularity enjoys a temporary upturn. Americans rally to a president who faces a difficult decision, and they like decisive responses. Political scientist John Mueller called these "rally events."[15] Subsequent research found that these events on average occur every fourteen months and boost a president's popularity eight percentage points for ten weeks.[16] Some dramatic rally events go higher and last longer. President Carter initially gained nineteen percentage points over the seizure of American hostages in Iran, and the sympathy lasted thirty weeks. Unfortunately for Carter, though, by the time he was up for reelection the next year, the rally in opinion had turned negative, because he was unable to resolve the crisis. Similarly, President Bush enjoyed a fourteen-point boost when Iraq invaded Kuwait and another eighteen-point gain when he began the Persian Gulf war. But by 1992, Bush's approval rating was below 50 percent, owing to the lingering recession.

Some suspect that presidents, especially later in their terms of office, may deliberately try to appear decisive in a dramatic way to boost their sagging popularity. Foreign policy provides the natural arena for such dramatic moves and (as we will consider in the next chapter) the best television coverage. A meeting with foreign leaders, a bold strike against terrorists, or the rescue of American hostages provides a welcome lift in popularity for a president. Notice in Table 8.1 how the highest popularity ratings of Presidents Truman, Kennedy, Nixon, Carter, Reagan, and Bush came with a dramatic foreign policy event. Even a failure, the 1961 Bay of Pigs attempted invasion to overthrow Castro, caused Americans to rally around President Kennedy. When a humiliating situation lasts a long time, however, presidential popularity sinks, as Carter and Reagan both found in dealing with Iran. Similarly, a war that drags on a long time destroys popularity; Truman experienced this in Korea and Johnson in Vietnam. Economic recession is also bad for popularity; four Republican presidents (Eisenhower, Ford, Reagan, and Bush) were rated low during economic downturns.

Presidential popularity based on one situation tends to spill over into other areas of presidential activity. As might be expected, President Reagan's popularity jumped several points in the wake of the successful U.S. takeover of Communist Grenada and the rescue of American students there in the fall of 1983. At that same time, approval of Reagan's economic policies also climbed, although little in the economy had actually changed.

LIBERALS AND CONSERVATIVES

The long stretch of Republican presidents did not necessarily reorient Americans to a conservative ideology. Americans, politically, continued to distribute them-

TABLE 8.1   Highs and Lows of Presidential Popularity

	High	Low	After 5 Years
Truman	87%	23%	37%
event	end of World War II	Korean War	
Eisenhower	79%	49%	60%
event	reelection	recession	
Kennedy	83%	56%	—
event	Bay of Pigs invasion	—	
Johnson	80%	35%	43%
event	election	Vietnam War	
Nixon	68%	24%	27%
event	Vietnam peace	Watergate scandal	
Ford	71%	37%	—
event	takes oath	recession	
Carter	64%	26%	—
event	human rights	Iranian hostage crises	
Reagan	68%	35%	65%
event	Geneva summit	recession	
Bush	86%	33%	—
event	Gulf War	recession	

Source: New York Times, 2 February 1986, 5 March 1991, 20 November 1992. Copyright by The New York Times Company. Reprinted by permission.

selves unimodally, depicted as the familiar bell-shaped curve, with most people at the center (Table 8.2). Such a distribution, social scientists find, is virtually the norm for all industrialized democracies, a fact that probably makes democracy possible.[17] During the Reagan years, the percentage of Americans identifying themselves as conservatives did not increase, and more Americans expressed support for environmental and welfare legislation, typically liberal causes.[18] The percentage who thought the poverty programs of the 1960s—one of Reagan's favorite targets—generally made things better actually increased during the Reagan years. Americans had not repudiated the moderate welfare state. The American people liked Reagan, but they did not become Reaganites.

TABLE 8.2   Americans' Description of Self

Very Liberal	5%
Somewhat Liberal	12
Moderate	48
Somewhat Conservative	24
Very Conservative	8
Don't Know	3

Source: New York Times, February 28, 1984. Copyright © 1984 by The New York Times Company. Reprinted by permission.

How can we explain this seeming inconsistency: eight years of a popular conservative president but little growth in conservatism among the population? Here we return to the difference between economic and noneconomic liberalism discussed earlier in this chapter. Americans are not very clear about what they mean when they say "liberal" or "conservative." Retired people, for example, support Social Security and Medicare—attitudes that might make them economic liberals— but many retired people call themselves conservatives because they oppose the erosion of traditional values. They use "conservative" in the noneconomic sense. College-age people, on the other hand, may disdain the welfare state and celebrate market economics—making them economic conservatives—but they may call themselves liberal in reference to their open-mindedness on social, racial, and lifestyle questions.

This helps explain the Reagan years. President Reagan appealed to both economic and noneconomic conservatives. Some of the economic conservatives who supported him were liberal on other issues such as abortion, foreign policy, and race relations. The so-called "yuppies" were often in this category. Some of the noneconomic conservatives who supported him were liberal on economic policy such as government help for failing industries and for welfare programs. Working-class religious fundamentalists were apt to be in this category. It was Reagan's gift to be able to hold together these two different strands for several years. There had been little overall growth in "conservatism"; rather, Reagan had appealed to the economic conservatism of some and to the noneconomic conservatism of others. Under Bush, this coalition fell apart.

WHO PAYS ATTENTION?

Some decades ago, political scientist Gabriel Almond proposed that there were three American public opinions, not just one:[19]

1. A *general public* that consists of a majority of Americans—people who don't know or care about much beyond their immediate concerns. For example, they show little interest in foreign policy unless the country is in a war or international crisis.

2. An *attentive public* that consists of a minority of Americans—people who are among the better-educated and who follow more abstract political concerns, such as foreign policy. They are the audience the elite plays to; and, in turn, this attentive public passes on views that mobilize the general public.

3. A *policy and opinion elite* that consists of a small number of highly influential people—those who are involved in politics, often professionally. These members of Congress, appointed officials, and top journalists devise foreign and domestic policies and articulate them to the attentive public and to the general public.

Especially regarding foreign affairs, Almond has made a strong case. Survey after survey finds appalling ignorance of world affairs. Some citizens—even college students—may demand strong action against Libya or Iraq but cannot locate these countries on a map. In the case of domestic affairs, the general public has better knowledge and clearer views than they do on foreign policy. They are especially attentive to the state of the economy and react sharply to high inflation or high unemployment—problems no one can escape. Crime and drugs are also widespread concerns, and tough police and courts meet with approval. More abstract economic questions—such as the rate of growth of the money supply—usually arouse less interest because they are not seen as matters of personal concern.

The general public is also fragmented because divergent groups are interested in different questions. Farmers are concerned about produce prices, steel and auto workers about imports, women about wage equality, and minorities about job opportunities. Accordingly, the general public rarely speaks with one voice. A time period in which some groups are satisfied may be a time when others are dissatisfied. Blacks and poor people generally approved of Clinton's welfare programs whereas more affluent whites, who bore the heavier tax burden, didn't approve.

The attentive public, although fewer in number, may have more importance politically because they have ideas which they articulate, demonstrating political competence. Sometimes they are capable of rousing the general public. Opposition to the Vietnam war and to South Africa's policy of apartheid started with small numbers of critics who wrote and spoke of their concerns in churches, newspapers, and classrooms. In the early 1990s, while few people were paying attention, some of the attentive public were raising questions about atrocities in Bosnia and starvation in Somalia. The attentive public can act as "spark plugs" among the apathetic and slow-reacting general public. This is why all regimes treat intellectuals with caution and sometimes with suspicion. For this reason, Communist regimes expended great effort to ferret out a handful of dissident intellectuals. In Washington, administration officials devote much time and energy in trying to win over the attentive public to minimize criticism that might influence the general public and the next election. As we will consider in Chapter 9, relations between the White House and the news media often resemble a cat-and-mouse game. All over the country, the attentive public can offer the general public new ways of looking at issues. And the regime may not like attention drawn to certain issues.

Intensity. The general public's indifference and fragmentation mean that their views are often hard to discern and may have relatively little impact on decision making. A member of Congress is apt to think, "Half the people in my district don't care about gun control. A quarter oppose it, and another quarter support it. So whom do I pay attention to?" Chances are, he or she will pay attention to the group with the most intensely held views. Polls show that most Americans would permit abortion, but few are strongly supportive of abortion. The "pro-life" foes of abortion, although a minority nationwide, feel so intensely about the subject that they can often drown out the greater numbers who are not passionately concerned. Intensely held views of a few can offset large numbers of indifferent people.

Jews make up less than 3 percent of the U.S. population, but among them are such intense supporters of Israel that most elected officials take a pro-Israel stance. Some Jews and many Christians are indifferent or critical about Israel. But these views do not influence politicians because the indifferent views don't count and the critical opinions are held without passion and intensity. Red-hot opinions beat lukewarm ones any day. The same situation occurs with opponents and supporters of gun control. Most Americans favor some form of gun control, but they are mostly lukewarm about the issue. The opponents to gun control are red hot and thus quite influential. The intensity factor means that relatively small groups of citizens can have a great deal of influence.

The disproportionate influence of the attentive public and passionate opinion holders underscores one of the problems of public opinion. Often there is little "public" opinion, just the opinion of scattered and small groups who pay attention to issues and care intensely about them. Should their views be excluded as nonrepresentative of the public, or should they take on added weight as the views of the only people who really care about the issues? Which is the more democratic approach? Most people would be inclined to say democracy means going with the greatest numbers, even if their views are lukewarm. When it comes to a question that deeply concerns them, however, many people do not wish to have a simple head count, arguing that the majority view is ignorant or mistaken and should not be heeded. We will consider some of these questions when we discuss interest groups in Chapter 10.

IS POLLING FAIR?

Polls do not merely monitor public opinion; they also help make it. Critics charge that published or broadcast poll results can distort an election. For example, the news media may give considerable attention to polls that indicate one candidate is leading another by a wide margin. Such publicity, underdog candidates claim, can be devastating to their campaigns. Would-be supporters of the underdog candidate may lose interest. They may even jump on the leader's bandwagon. Even more important, campaign funds may dry up because the candidate behind in the polls looks like a loser. Few political scientists think average voters are likely to change their votes because a poll shows their candidate is losing. But it does seem probable that poor poll showings, especially early in the campaign, can act as a self-fulfilling prophecy of defeat for some candidates. Those who lead in the early polls get more donations, more news coverage, and thus more supporters. Those behind in the early polls are sunk at the start. We will consider the problem of media coverage in the next chapter.

One current controversy is the effect of "exit polls," which question voters just as they leave the balloting area. With the three-hour time difference between the East and West Coasts, exit polls enable television to predict winners in the East while westerners still have hours in which to cast a ballot. Does the early prediction in the East affect the vote in the West? Democrats charged that during the two Reagan landslides many West Coast people were persuaded not to bother to vote because the early East Coast exit polls had already given the contest to Reagan. This development robbed state and local Democratic candidates in the West of votes that might have been theirs if more people had voted. Some urged a delay in broadcasting the results of exit polls, and in 1992 broadcasters voluntarily delayed reporting exit polls. No evidence was found that exit polls influenced the presidential vote, but they might have influenced other contests for the House, the Senate, or the state legislature. Polls, especially when their results are broadcast so quickly, are not neutral in their impact, but no constitutionally legal way has been found to control them.

SHOULD AMERICA BE GOVERNED BY POLLS?

Considering the preceding discussion, it would seem in most cases that America should not be governed by polls. First, public attention varies widely. On many issues, the general public has no knowledge or opinion. In such a situation, the intense concern of a minority might dominate the poll results. Leaders, especially with modern means of communication, can influence public opinion in their direction. This encourages government leaders to try to create the kind of feedback they want to hear.[20] Typically, public opinion follows executive decisions. Public opinion does not usually lead executive decisions.

The wording of the questions and selection of the sample (the people to be polled) can seriously skew results. We must be sure that the survey was done by reliable professionals with standardized questions and a random sample. Polls conducted by partisans of a cause or candidate can seriously mislead and should be ignored. Equally serious is the problem of volatility: the changeable nature of poll results. What the public likes one month it may dislike the next. Decisions made on the basis of a given survey may meet with public displeasure when the consequences of the decision sink in. Accordingly, public officials who are tempted to "go with the polls," who think, "All those voters can't be wrong," may be stepping into a trap that hurts both themselves and their country. The polls, if done well, can provide a useful snapshot of public opinion at a given moment. Poll results are no substitute for a careful analysis of the issues and prudent anticipation of the future.

Suggested Readings

ASHER, HERBERT. *Polling and the Public: What Every Citizen Should Know,* 2nd ed. Washington, DC: CQ Press, 1991. Short, informative introduction to techniques and problems of survey research.

BRACE, PAUL, and BARBARA HINCKLEY. *Follow the Leader: Opinion Polls and the Modern Presidents.* New York: Basic Books, 1992. An integration of many surveys to explain why presidential popularity rises and falls.

CANTRIL, ALBERT H. *The Opinion Connection: Polling, Politics, and the Press.* Washington, DC: CQ Press, 1991. A noted pollster studies how the media use and misuse survey research.

COOK, ELIZABETH ADELL, TED G. JELEN, and CLYDE WILCOX. *Between Two Absolutes: American Public Opinion and the Politics of Abortion.* Boulder, CO: Westview Press, 1992. Attempts to untangle how Americans handle the conflicting pressures of two antithetical viewpoints.

ELAZAR, DANIEL J. *The American Mosaic: The Impact of Space, Time, and Culture on American Politics.* Boulder, CO: Westview Press, 1994. A modern updating and overview of the impact of generation on political views.

GAWISER, SHELDON R., and G. EVANS WITT. *A Journalist's Guide to Public Opinion Polls.* Westport, CT: Praeger, 1994. An easy-to-understand introduction to survey research and how to guard against misinterpreting it.

LANGSTON, THOMAS S. *With Reverence and Contempt: How Americans Think About Their President.* Baltimore, MD: Johns Hopkins University Press, 1995. The problem of and possible cures for how Americans first idolize and then savagely criticize presidents.

NIEMI, RICHARD G., JOHN MUELLER, and TOM W. SMITH. *Trends in Public Opinion: A Compendium*

of Survey Data. Westport, CT: Greenwood, 1989. Splendid boildown of U.S. views over time by three top survey people.

SNIDERMAN, PAUL, and THOMAS PIAZZA. *The Scar of Race.* Cambridge, MA: Harvard University Press, 1993. Race is still important in public opinion, but Americans' views are highly nuanced.

STIMSON, JAMES A. *Public Opinion in America: Moods, Cycles, and Swings.* Boulder, CO: Westview Press, 1991. A sophisticated analysis of how public opinion changes and why.

WORCESTER, ROBERT M., ed. *Political Opinion Polling: An International Review.* New York: St. Martin's, 1983. The history, methods, and problems of polls in ten countries; a rare international comparison.

Notes

1. Aryeh L. Unger, "The Public Opinion Reports of the Nazi Party," *Public Opinion Quarterly* 29 (Winter 1965), 565–82.

2. Seymour Martin Lipset, *Political Man: The Social Bases of Politics,* expanded ed. (Baltimore: Johns Hopkins University Press, 1981), Chap. 7.

3. Everett Carll Ladd, "Liberalism Upside Down: The Inversion of the New Deal Order," *Political Science Quarterly* 91 (Winter 1976–77), 4.

4. Juan J. Linz, "El Electorado Español, un Electorado Europeo," *Opinión* [Madrid], 8 January 1977.

5. Joseph LaPalombara, *Politics Within Nations* (Englewood Cliffs, NJ: Prentice Hall, 1974), pp. 440–44.

6. Seymour Martin Lipset has long emphasized the difference between economic and noneconomic issues in public opinion. See I. L. Horowitz and S. M. Lipset, *Dialogues on American Politics* (New York: Oxford University Press, 1978), pp. 3–6.

7. Andrew M. Greeley, "How Conservative Are American Catholics?" *Political Science Quarterly* 92 (Summer 1977), 2.

8. For an excellent roundup on the impact of religion in U.S. politics, see Charles W. Dunn, ed., *Religion in American Politics* (Washington, DC: CQ Press, 1988).

9. Karl Mannheim, *Essays on the Sociology of Knowledge,* 2nd ed., Paul Kecskemeti, ed. (New York: Oxford University Press, 1952), p. 291.

10. Times Mirror Center for the People and the Press, "The People, the Press, and Politics Campaign '92: The Generations Divide," news release 8 July 1992, pp. 7–12.

11. Adam Clymer, "Polls Suggest Women Support Democrats in '86 Races," *New York Times,* 11 May 1986, p. 22.

12. *The Pre-Election Polls of 1948: Report to the Committee on Analysis of Pre-Election Polls and Forecasts,* Social Science Research Council Bulletin no. 60 (New York, 1949).

13. Michael R. Kagay and Janet Elder, "Numbers Are No Problem for Pollsters. Words Are," *New York Times,* 9 August 1992, p. E5.

14. For a study of how much opinion changed during the Vietnam war among different subgroups, see Hazel Erskine, "The Polls: Is War a Mistake?" *Public Opinion Quarterly* 34 (Spring 1970), 1.

15. John Mueller, *War, Presidents and Public Opinion* (New York: Wiley, 1973).

16. Larry Hugick and Alec M. Gallup, "'Rally Events' and Presidential Approval," paper delivered at meeting of the American Association of Public Opinion Research, Phoenix, 1991.

17. In an interesting 1973 study, West Europeans were asked to place themselves on an ideological scale, one for the most left, ten for the most right. Most of the countries produced neat bell-shaped curves. See Ronald Inglehart and Hans D. Klingemann, "Party Identification, Ideological Preference and the Left-Right Dimen-

sion Among Western Mass Publics," in *Party Identification and Beyond,* ed. Ian Budge et al. (New York: Wiley, 1976).

18. R. W. Apple, Jr., "President Highly Popular in Poll: No Ideological Shift Is Discerned," *New York Times,* 28 January 1986, p. A14.

19. Gabriel A. Almond, *The American People and Foreign Policy* (New York: Praeger, 1960), p. 138. This book was originally published in 1950.

Notice how the three levels of public opinion here correspond to the three types of political culture Almond later discovered in his civic culture study; the parochial, the subject, and the participant cultures (see Chapter 7). Political scientists seem to think in terms of three.

20. See Susan Herbst, *Numbered Voices: How Opinion Polling Has Shaped American Politics* (Chicago: University of Chicago Press, 1993).

· 9 ·

Political Communication and the Media

The mass media have always loomed large in American politics.[1] In the 1780s, the *Federalist Papers* were published in daily newspapers throughout the colonies in an all-out effort to win over the people to the idea of a new constitution. Andrew Jackson's victory in 1828 over John Quincy Adams marked the end of one of the most bitter "media campaigns" in America's history. In it, mudslinging reached its high point (or low point) when Jackson and his wife were accused of moral irregularities, and the press played a key role in the exchange of propaganda. In the early twentieth century, we had a media candidate in Teddy Roosevelt: he tailored his rough-and-ready image to fire the imagination of the people, with great success. And Franklin D. Roosevelt used his famous "fireside chats" on radio, along with hundreds of press conferences, to win support for his policies. In 1992 the announced support of conservative *New York Times* columnist William Safire for Bill Clinton (Safire said he didn't trust Bush on foreign policy) helped Clinton's victory. Today, the mass media are a recognized component of American politics, and modern campaigns depend on television so much that many critics complain that candidates no longer run for office on issues; instead, professional marketing consultants package them and sell them like any product.[2]

Communication in Politics

Political scientists have long recognized the dependence of political power on communications—as any quick comparison of Abraham Lincoln's power with that of Bill Clinton will reveal. Karl W. Deutsch, among the first to study systematically the political uses and implications of modern communications systems, claims the rate of modernization of developing nations and the rise and decline of metropolitan areas around the globe can be measured from patterns and flow of mail, telephone calls, and migration paths of the labor force.[3] The political system and the communication system precisely parallel one another, and it is doubtful that one could exist without the other.

LEVELS OF COMMUNICATION

All political action is a reaction to communication of one kind or another. There are, however, different levels and types of communication. Face-to-face communication is the most basic. It is also the most effective means for altering or reinforcing political opinions because it allows for dialogue where mass media cannot. Listeners in an auditorium can question or challenge the speaker, and he or she can respond directly to the audience to overcome its resistance.

Until the early 1930s, face-to-face communication was the main method of political campaigning and proselytizing. Nominees for office would stump their districts and address small groups of voters, appealing for their support with the help of ward bosses, precinct captains, and political organizers. However, the rise of television and the complexity of modern society have today largely destroyed the tradition of grassroots stumping, except as a means of getting free coverage on newspaper front pages and news programs.

The Mass Media. The great advantage of the mass media over face-to-face communication is that they reach an infinitely larger audience, and therefore yield a greater voter or public opinion return. A speech that gets on television can reach millions of people at once, but a speech given at even the largest rally may be heard by only a few thousand people. If even a small percentage of television viewers respond positively to what the speaker says, that response can become tens of thousands of votes—perhaps enough to swing an election.

But the mass media are essentially a one-way avenue of communication. If a viewer dislikes President Clinton, he or she can turn the channel; if the viewer disagrees with his message, the president can't counter those objections with a custom-made response. Studies of the impact of the mass media on individual thinking and behavior show that mass media can effectively reinforce existing political opinions but can't really convert anyone. Radio and television do have stronger persuasive power than the printed word because they are closer to face-to-face communication, but their impact still depends partly on the influence of chats with friends after the program is over.

The Two-Step Flow of Mass Communications. If most messages bounce off most people without leaving much of an impression, how do the mass media penetrate an audience? Paul Lazarsfeld and Elihu Katz were among the first to perceive a two-step pattern in this process.[4] They found that every community has respected *opinion leaders*—teachers, ministers, community and civic leaders, outstanding businesspersons, and professional leaders—who follow the media carefully. These people take political cues from the mass media and pass them on to their less attentive friends in normal daily contact. In this way, political messages filter down to everyone. The effectiveness of mass media appeals depends on these opinion leaders, and it is they whom successful politicians must reach, influence, and convince. Notice the resemblance here to Almond's distinction between the "general" and "attentive" publics discussed in the last chapter.

Television may have somewhat eroded the role of opinion leaders in the community. The TV newscaster has become an opinion leader on a grand scale. Television not only serves by transmitting direct political messages but also serves indirectly as an instrument of social change by bringing news events into the homes of the people. Most observers agree that the civil rights movement of the 1960s would not have achieved the success it did without television. Racial discrimination in the South was largely unnoticed—perhaps deliberately unnoticed—in the print media and radio. But TV news of fire hoses and police dogs used to attack peaceful marchers turned most Americans in favor of equal black rights. Likewise, the graphic television coverage of the Vietnam war—the world's first television war—turned many people against the war and against President Johnson.

Who Uses the Media? Not everybody watches television, especially TV news coverage. And not everybody reads on subways or buses or listens to the radio while driving to work. The various modern media appeal to different audiences, who can be distinguished by education, income, and age. The better educated individuals are, the more they will use the mass media. College graduates tend to read newspapers, magazines, and books as well as listen to the radio and watch television and motion pictures. But grammar and high school graduates, who use the mass media more for entertainment, generally favor television, radio, and motion pictures more than the print media. Likewise, people in high-income brackets read a lot, whereas low-income groups rely more heavily on television and radio for information and entertainment. Ninety percent of the people in high-income brackets are regular magazine and book readers, but only half of the people in low-income groups are.

Age or maturity also affects the use of the mass media. In general, people between the ages of thirty and fifty pay more attention to the editorial and news content of newspapers and magazines than do teenagers and young adults, who tend to use newspapers for entertainment. Young readers tend to study the sports pages, follow the doings of rock stars, and pay more attention to feature articles than to hard news stories. The eighteen-year-old who keeps up on the news and editorial opinion is the exception.

MODERN MASS MEDIA

Newspapers.   In 1910, the United States had more than 2,600 daily newspapers, and 57 percent of all American cities had two or more competing papers. Today, only 1,550 newspapers remain, and only 33 U.S. cities have two or more separately owned papers. Does this decline in competition mean that the people are being denied access to a healthy variety of political and editorial opinion? The charge that the fabled "free press" is really just a business is backed up by certain facts. Some 75 percent of U.S. newspapers are owned by centrally controlled syndicates or chains, and corporation ownership of most large newspapers gives them a status quo orientation.

But most newspapers do not present the news in an obviously partisan manner. The reasons are both practical and idealistic. Sixty-five to 90 percent of newspaper revenue comes from advertising, and fees from advertisers depend on the newspapers' circulation. Thus, keeping circulation high is the main concern, and the result is usually a middle-of-the-road news policy calculated to not antagonize most people. This often makes newspapers bland.

Journalism itself has a long tradition of objectivity in news reporting (although the editorial page may be another story). The profession's own idealism no doubt influences newspaper people to present the news fairly and honestly. Further, most news printed in U.S. newspapers is from a wire service, and wire services take special pains to be objective and to refrain from editorializing.

How much political impact, then, do U.S. newspapers have? Not as much as they used to. Fewer households take newspapers now than half a century ago, and only 60 percent of adult Americans read a daily paper. The content of newspapers is mostly advertisements (one important reason people read them) and wire-service copy. The editorials of most newspapers carry little weight. There are, of course, some exceptions, and for these we refer to the "elite" media.

The Elite Media.   The *New York Times,* the *Washington Post,* and the *Wall Street Journal* are read by a small fraction of the U.S. population, but they carry by far the most clout. Decision makers in Washington and indeed across the country read them and take both their news stories and their editorials seriously. Leading thinkers fight battles on their "op-ed" pages (opposite the editorial page) or in their letters to the editor. That is why these papers have influence out of all proportion to their circulation. They are what is known as the "elite press." The people who read them are generally wealthier and better educated and have more influence than the reader of a hometown paper. The elite press pursues "investigative reporting," looking for government and partisan wrongdoing, something the average paper usually shuns. The *New York Times* jolted the nation when it published the Pentagon Papers on the Vietnam war in 1971. The dogged pursuit of the 1972 Watergate burglary by the *Washington Post* brought down the Nixon administration in 1974. The editorials of the *Wall Street Journal* influenced economic decisions in the Clinton administration.

The small-circulation magazines of opinion also qualify as the elite press. The conservative *National Review,* the liberal *New Republic,* the leftist *Nation,* and the neoconservative *Commentary* have considerable impact on opinion leaders, the sorts of people who influence others. President Reagan named Jeane Kirkpatrick ambassador to the UN on the strength of an article of hers he had read in *Commentary.* Students are often ignorant of the elite press, but those who themselves aspire to leadership status would be well advised to follow one or more of these journals.

Radio. Like newspapers, radio is not what it used to be. Between the two world wars it zoomed in popularity, and radio news, comments, and political addresses—such as Franklin D. Roosevelt's famous "fireside chats," which served as models for both Jimmy Carter and Ronald Reagan—were quite influential. But with the rise of television in the 1950s, radio became a medium of background music for driving or doing housework. News dwindled into brief hourly spots, much of it "rip and read" from the wire-service printer. Radio now has little political impact, although it too has an elite exception: the radio magazine "All Things Considered" on National Public Radio, full of in-depth explorations of world events, economics, politics, and reasoned opinion. This daily broadcast brought back to radio a portion of better-educated people of all political persuasions.

The Wire Services. Most hard news in newspapers and on radio, and even a good deal of television's news, is not produced in-house but comes from a printer hooked up to the New York offices of the Associated Press (AP). True, the elite press disdains wire-service copy, as it's matter of pride for them to have their own reporters covering the story. But most papers in America are little more than local outlets for the Associated Press. Often editors on small-town papers read just the first two paragraphs, so that they can write a headline, and slap the stories into their papers nearly at random.

The AP is a cooperative, with members paying assessments based on their circulation. They also contribute copies of local stories to the AP, which rewrites them for nationwide transmission. The interesting thing here is that the AP is one of the few wire services not owned, subsidized, controlled, or supervised by a government. It is free of government influence and proud of it. Britain's Reuters gets discreet government subsidies; France's AFP has government supervision, as does Germany's DPA; and China's Xin Hua is wholly a creature of Beijing.

The AP is free, but it has other problems that limit its quality and influence.

First, it moves fast; every minute is a deadline. This means it can give little time to digging. Second, the wire services' definition of news is something from an official source. All wire-service stories are carefully attributed to police, the White House, the State Department or Pentagon, and so on. If it's not official, it's not news. This causes the wire services to miss many explosive situations in the world because they do not like their reporters to talk to opposition people, the average person in the street, or the merchants in the bazaar, who might have a completely different—and sometimes more accurate—perspective than official spokespersons. Most American news media failed to notice the coming of the Iranian revolution for this reason. Often the best news stories are not about a key event or statement but about what people are saying and thinking, which wires don't cover.

The Giant: Television

When most Americans say "the media," they mean television, for television towers over everything else in terms of impact. Most Americans get their political information from television, and most say they believe information obtained from television more than that in newspapers. Television has touched almost everything in American politics and has changed almost everything it has touched. Election campaigns now revolve heavily around the acquisition of TV time; winners are usually those who can raise the most money to hire the best media consultants. Television has become a suspect in the decline of both U.S. election turnout and political parties. Some observers see television as contributing to the more complete trivialization of U.S. politics, which now focus on a "sound bite" of a few seconds (averaging 8.9 seconds in 1988).[5]

TV NEWS

Television, by very definition, favors the visual. Just "talking heads" provide no more news than does radio. (Talking heads do provide something very important, though—a sense of personality and hence credibility, a sort of imitation face-to-face communication.) News producers therefore devote more attention to a news story with "good visuals" than without. As with the wire services, abstract, deeper topics tend to go by with little coverage, whereas dramatic action—if there was a camera crew on hand to catch it—gets played up. Television, like most of the rest of the U.S. news media, ignored the deep hatred that was brewing against the shah of Iran for years but caught the dramatic return of the Ayatollah Khomeini.[6] Television never did explain what the Vietnam war was about, but a brief film clip of a Saigon general shooting a Vietcong assassin in 1968 helped sicken Americans against the war. Just as the wire services are hooked on official sources, television news is hooked on the eye-catching. This makes television inherently a more emotional medium than the others. Television coverage can go straight to the heart, bypassing the brain altogether; that is its great power.[7]

Unfortunately, TV camera crews are expensive to maintain in the field, especially overseas, so they usually arrive where the action is only *after* having been notified by the wire services. Television prefers to know in advance what's going to happen; then it can schedule a camera crew. This makes TV news lopsided with press conferences, speeches, committee hearings, and official statements. Some critics characterize these happenings as "media events," things that would not have occurred without television coverage. A media event is not fake, but it is planned in advance with an eye to catching the attention of TV crews. Not only is this understood by officials, but protest groups, too, stage marches, sit-ins, and mass arrests to get TV exposure for their cause. Chanted protesters at the 1968 Democratic convention in Chicago: "The whole world is watching!" The next time you watch television, count the number of film clips of events that were obviously scheduled in advance as opposed to those that weren't; the former will probably outnumber the latter by a big margin.

Deep analysis is also not television's strong point. An average news story runs one minute; a two- or three-minute story is considered an in-depth report. Walter Cronkite, long dean of TV newspeople, repeatedly emphasized that television news was just a "headline service," meaning that if viewers wanted detail and depth they would have to go elsewhere. Many Americans, of course, don't look deeper and are

Media execution. AP photographer Eddie Adams snapped the summary execution of a captured Vietcong assassin in 1968. Adams later said he was sorry he took the history-making photo, which tended to make the Vietcong look heroic. In truth, the assassin had just murdered the family of one of the assistants to South Vietnam's police chief, who took speedy revenge. Images can mislead.

left with the tardy, the eye-catching, and the media event as their daily diet of information. Thus it is not surprising when polls repeatedly discover that Americans are poorly informed about the great issues of the day.

TELEVISION AND POLITICS

All agree that television has changed politics, and in several ways. Incumbency, especially in the White House, has always brought recognition. Television has enhanced this recognition, but not always to the incumbent's satisfaction. Television news is heavily focused on the president and to a lesser extent on the rest of the executive branch. Congress gets much less coverage, the courts even less. This deepens a long-term American tendency to president-worship. The president—especially with the way television socializes small children—is seen as an omnipotent parental figure, a person who can fix all problems. That in itself should make a current president very happy. But then things go wrong; the president doesn't fix the problems; an ultracritical press implies that presidential policies may be making them worse. The flip side of being treated as all-powerful is catching all the blame. The media, especially television, whips up president-worship and then whips up mass dissatisfaction with the president's performance. This whip-'em-up-and-let-'em-fall factor may have contributed to the rash of one-term presidencies that followed Eisenhower. Expectations, heightened by the media, are very high, and disappointments are correspondingly bitter. Some critics charge that the media are wrecking the U.S. political system with that kind of coverage, making the country unstable and ungovernable.[8]

Nomination by Television.   Television also contributes importantly to the presidential selection process. With all eyes focused on the early presidential primaries—especially New Hampshire—commentators grandly proclaim who is the "real winner" and who is picking up "momentum."[9] The lucky candidate thus designated as front-runner goes into the remaining primaries and the national convention with a bandwagon effect, enhanced recognition, and lots of TV coverage. In the nominating process, television has become a kind of kingmaker. It is no wonder that candidates arrange their schedules and strategies to capture as much TV exposure as possible.

The TV coverage of candidates focuses on their personalities, not on issues. Television, with its sharp closeups and seeming spontaneity, gives viewers what they think is a true glimpse of the candidate's character. Actually, this may not be so; some candidates play the medium like professionals (Ronald Reagan), and others tense up and hide their normal personalities.[10] How a candidate performs on television is a poor index of how he or she will perform in office, but it is the one most American voters use.

While television is playing this major role in nominating and electing candidates, the political party is bypassed. Party organizations and bosses are not very important, as candidates on television go right over their heads to the voters. Since the leading contender or two have already picked up their "momentum" going into the convention, they don't need party professionals to broker a nominating deal. Politics has come out of the proverbial smoke-filled back rooms and into the glare of TV lights, not always for the better. The party and its chiefs used to know a thing or two about politics and were often capable of putting forward tried and tested candidates. With television, a candidate can come from out of nearly nowhere and win the top national office with little political experience. We must be careful, though, in blaming television for the weakening of the parties. American parties, with the exception of a few urban machines, were never as strongly organized as most European parties. Moreover, American parties began declining a long time ago, not just with the advent of television. Other factors, such as special-interest groups, political action committees, and direct-mail solicitation, have also undermined party strength. Television is not the sole culprit.

Television and Apathy. Observers long suspected that television induces passivity and apathy. Harvard political scientist Robert D. Putnam (see his discussion of "bowling alone" on p. 130) believes he's proved "the culprit is television." Systematically reviewing the possible causes of the decline of "civic engagement" in the United States, Putnam finds older people, those born before World War II, are more trusting and more inclined to join groups and participate in politics. The reason: they were raised before the television age. Younger people, raised on televi-

First presidential debates. In the 1960 election campaign, Richard Nixon debated John Kennedy live and nationwide, a TV first. Kennedy's more relaxed performance helped him win.

sion, lack these qualities. Says Putnam: "Each hour spent viewing television is associated with less social trust and less group membership, while each hour reading a newspaper is associated with more."[11]

A related charge is that television has lowered election-day turnouts. There is a close coincidence in time; turnout dropped thirteen percentage points from 1960, when television first established itself as the top means of campaigning, until 1988. Television saturates viewers so far in advance that they lose interest. Perhaps this loss of interest has occurred because the top two candidates usually sound so similar that many voters see little difference. Negative campaigning also disgusts many voters. Charges and countercharges in political spots come so thick and fast that the voter is "cross-pressured" into indecision and apathy.[12] In Western Europe, where paid-for political TV spots are generally prohibited and campaigns are much shorter—usually about a month instead of the year and more in the United States—voter turnout is much higher, sometimes topping 90 percent. Only America does not regulate TV political ads.

One thing U.S. television does for sure: It costs candidates a bundle. Depending on the time of day and locale, a one-minute spot can go for $100,000. The cost factor in itself has transformed American politics. Members of Congress can sometimes get by with little TV advertising, but virtually all senatorial and presidential candidates need it. About half of presidential campaign chests are estimated now to go for television. Political consulting—the right kind of themes, slogans, and speeches presented in the right kind of TV spots—has become a big business. Some critics contend that with enough money, a candidate can, in effect, buy the office through television. In 1992, the winning Clinton campaign raised $71 million to Bush's $62 million. This heightens the importance of special-interest groups and political action committees, which in turn has weakened the role of the parties and perhaps deepened feelings of powerlessness among average voters. In the TV age, chances are that the winning candidate has spent more, most of it on televised spot advertising.

Many Americans are ignoring party labels, either calling themselves "independents," splitting tickets, or voting for the other party. The trend, alarming to some political scientists, is called voter "dealignment," citizens *not* lining up with a party. Lacking party identification, these voters are increasingly open to persuasion via the media, especially television.[13] This development, some suggest, produces great "volatility" as voters, massaged by media professionals, shift this way and that in response to candidates' televised images.

TELEVISION: OWNERSHIP AND CONTROL

The U.S. government exercises the *least* control of communications of any industrialized country. Since the invention of the telegraph, the American government has stood back and let private industry operate communications for profit. In Europe, in contrast, telegraphy was soon taken over by the postal service, as were telephones. The U.S. government—partly because of First Amendment guarantees of free speech and partly because of the U.S. ethos of free enterprise—simply does not like to butt in. For European nations, with traditions of centralized power and government paternalism, national control of electronic communications is as normal as state ownership of the railroads.

The U.S. attitude of nonpaternalism has led to the freest airwaves in the world, but it has also brought some problems. With the rapid growth of radio in the 1920s, the electromagnetic spectrum was soon jammed with stations trying to drown each other out. To bring some order out of the chaos, the Radio Act of 1927 set up a five-member Federal Radio Commission (FRC) appointed by the president to assign frequencies, call letters, and maximum power. Stations had to get licenses and could lose them. Most important, the 1927 act put the government on record for the first time as recognizing that the airwaves were public property and should serve "the public interest, convenience and necessity." The Communications Act of 1934 superseded the FRC and created the Federal Communications Commission (FCC), which monitors broadcasting to this day. The 1934 act recognized the danger of partisanship and now provides for five FCC commissioners appointed by the president and approved by the Senate. The commissioners serve staggered seven-year terms, and no more than three can be members of the same party.

The Wasteland.   In theory, the FCC licenses radio and TV stations to serve "the public interest," but in practice no station has its license revoked. The FCC lays down no rules about program content except for obscenity on the air. Programs can be as trashy or as lofty as the owners want. Most owners, in their appraisals of the viewing audience, emphasize the former. FCC Commissioner Newton Minow decades ago despaired that television was a "vast wasteland," but there was nothing the FCC could do to make programs more cultural, educational, or morally uplifting. Most broadcasting in America is private and profit-oriented. Profits derive from advertising, which depends on audience size. Station owners argue that they automatically serve the public interest in offering the programs most people want. They are also, of course, serving their own interests. If most people want twenty-four hours of rock and roll, that must be the public interest for that area. If most people like violent and sexy detective shows, television must provide them. Thus do self-interest and altruism happily merge.

Critics bemoan this kind of reasoning, pointing out that broadcasters are not merely *following* public tastes but *setting* them by offering only competing junk. About the only outlet for the critics' frustration, though, is public broadcasting. During the 1950s, noncommercial FM and television stations, financed by universities and community donations, began to offer programming at higher cultural and educational levels. The Ford Foundation and Congress came in with more support. In 1967, Congress set up the Corporation for Public Broadcasting (CPB), with National Public Radio (NPR) and the Public Broadcasting Service (PBS) under it. This is as close as the United States has come to establishing a link between government and broadcasting, and it's not very close. Government funding, especially with the budget cuts of recent administrations, accounts for only a minority of NPR's and PBS's finances. Public broadcasting presents all political viewpoints. NPR and PBS are the only exceptions to private ownership and profit orientation in American broadcasting.

The FCC doesn't supervise the content of programs, but it does have a political impact. Section 315 of the 1934 act, known as the "equal-time provision," tells broadcasters that if they give or sell air time to one candidate, they must do the same for others. Station owners, of course, don't like to give away air time. They also fear that public interest programs featuring the candidates of the two big parties will lead to a demand for equal time by minor or frivolous candidates. News broadcasts are exempt from the equal-time rule, so debates between the two leading presidential contenders are conducted by a panel of newspeople to get around the equal-time provision. Broadcasters may also not be too happy about selling air time, for it must go at the lowest rate, which in turn must be offered to the opponents. Broadcasters have repeatedly sought modifications of the equal-time provision.

Another FCC power, more vague than "equal time," is the "fairness doctrine" first published in 1949 by the commission. Recognizing that broadcast editorials are part of the public interest, the fairness doctrine requires broadcasters to offer air time for those with opposing views to respond. Enforcement, though, is left to the broadcasters, and many public-spirited interest groups feel that broadcasters simply try to avoid all controversy so that they won't have to make air time available to anyone. The Reagan-appointed members of the FCC abolished both the equal-time and fairness provisions, arguing that they tended to limit political debate on the airwaves.

THE EUROPEAN EXPERIENCE

The American airwaves are lightly regulated. Could it—or should it—be otherwise? The European experience offers a range of possibilities, all involving greater government control or supervision than the United States has. Television in the Soviet Union was strictly government controlled and was carefully aimed. It was patriotic, upbeat, and positive, calculated to inculcate feelings of loyalty and hard work and to uplift culturally. Instead of the "hands off" American attitude, the Soviet approach was to use television as an instrument of education and guidance. Soviet programming accordingly stressed the glorious but trying events of World War II, factories and workers happily producing more and more goods, and opera and ballet that would be seen only on PBS in the United States. Soviets familiar with American television regarded it as debauchery, an example of capitalism run amok. The concept of giving viewers what they want was alien to them, and Soviet programming had little pop music and light entertainment.[14] Political pronouncements were generally reserved for the party newspaper, *Pravda* (Truth), and its government counterpart, *Izvestia* (News). The Soviets regarded newspapers as more authoritative than television. When, in 1988, Soviet television showed spontaneous coverage of a major party congress that included criticism and accusations of wrongdoing, Soviet viewers were wide-eyed with interest and amazement.

This policy of *glasnost* (openness) contributed a lot to the collapse of the Soviet system. Once truth started coming out, the system could not stand.

French television is also government controlled, although not as heavy-handed as in the ex-Soviet Union. Before he returned to power in 1958, General Charles de Gaulle watched a great deal of television and concluded that it was the perfect way to control a country. As the powerful president of the Fifth Republic, which he created, from 1958 to 1969, de Gaulle did indeed use television as a tool of governance and guidance. In military uniform and with his sonorous voice and superb command of the language, de Gaulle put down two rebellions and won four referendums with his televised calls for loyalty. The government office de Gaulle established, the ORTF, is still at work today, although many French viewers and journalists are aware that it slants the news. The French left protested this rigging of information, but when the Socialists swept to power in 1981 they did not free the ORTF, rather they proceeded to slant things *their* way. The trouble with government-controlled broadcasting, though, is that listeners and viewers will try to go elsewhere. In France, they tune in to radio and television from Luxembourg and Monaco, which are more objective than the French programs. To a certain extent, government control of radio and television is self-defeating, for these media lose credibility. In 1986, a conservative French government "privatized" some of the airwaves by selling the largest of France's three state-owned TV networks, TF1.

The northern European systems are better at putting some distance between the government and broadcasting. The British Broadcasting Corporation (BBC), created in 1927, is run by a board of governors who are nonpartisan but are nonetheless named by the government. The BBC is supported by annual licenses that listeners and viewers must buy; it carries no commercial advertising. During Britain's brief (three-week) campaigns, air time is allocated to the three main parties—Conservative, Labour, and Liberal Democrat—in proportion to their strength in Parliament. Whereas the nonpaternalistic U.S. system lets programming sink to a low level, the BBC system, supervised by cultivated and educated governors, rises high, often too high for the British public; many find it staid and boring. Since 1954, Britain has permitted private, commercial television in the form of the Independent Television Authority, which offers programs more at the mass level. Swedish and German broadcasting are mainly financed by user license fees. They are governed by nonpartisan boards of media people, cultural leaders, and civil servants. The German system has both nationwide and state networks, diffusing control and introducing a certain amount of competition. Advertising is permitted but grouped into several-minute spots throughout the day. Advertisers do not sponsor programs and have nothing to say about content. Paid political advertising is not permitted, but time is allocated to parties during election campaigns for political messages.

The U.S. broadcast media are, paradoxically, free but expensive. They are under virtually no government control, but listeners and viewers pay a price in having programming skewed to earn broadcasters the maximum amount of money. The price is junk programming that does indeed leave America culturally, educationally, and informationally underdeveloped.

Are We Poorly Served?

As may be judged from some of our earlier discussions, the U.S. mass media do not serve Americans very well. First, news coverage is highly selective, overconcentrating on some areas while ignoring others. This is called "structural bias." The president and staff occupy over half the news time given to the federal government. Why is this? The president is inherently more dramatic and eye-catching than the other branches of government. Reporters, editors, and producers are afraid that if they devote more than a little time to Congress and the courts, readers and viewers will become bored. Another reason is that what the president does is visually more exciting than what Congress or the courts do. The president gets in and out of helicopters, greets foreign leaders, travels overseas, or just relaxes at a vacation home; all provide good TV footage. Congress may get some attention when one of its committees faces a tense, controversial, or hostile witness. Then the committee members hurl accusatory questions, the witness stammers back denials, and sometimes shouting erupts. That's good drama; the rest of Congress is pretty dull.[15] And the courts face the biggest obstacle of all: No cameras are allowed in most courtrooms. Accordingly, Americans grow up with the notion that the White House does most of the work and has most of the power, whereas Congress and the courts hardly matter.

One part of the U.S. government is especially undercovered: the civil service, in its myriad departments, agencies, and bureaus.[16] Here is where much of the governance of America takes place. But "faceless bureaucrats" make boring interviewees—some are not allowed to be interviewed—and federal regulations are unintelligible. Still, many of next year's news stories are buried in the federal bureaucracy. What agency using what criteria allowed a nuclear power plant to operate? The media don't pay any attention until a Three Mile Island occurs. What department shoveled out millions in contracts to presidential-campaign contributors? The wrongdoings of federally insured savings and loan associations went on for several years, little noticed by the media. What federal agency decides whether commercial airlines are observing adequate safety standards? The news media don't even try to cover such things; they wait until something goes wrong and then evince shocked surprise. The very stuff of politics is there in the federal agencies, but few pay attention.

On the world scene, too, the news media wait for something to blow up before they cover it. Except for the elite media previously mentioned, there is little background coverage of likely trouble spots. Thus, when war engulfs a disintegrating Yugoslavia or an economy collapses in Latin America, most Americans are surprised. They shouldn't be; even moderate news coverage of these places over the years would have kept Americans informed about the increasing problems. But the U.S. media did not keep reporters in these areas and rarely even sent them on quick visits. Troubled Mexico, with all its implications for the United States, is still largely uncovered. We live in a revolutionary world, but the U.S. media pays little attention until the shooting starts. Providers of "good visuals" rather than analysis and early warning is the way they define their role, and this sets up Americans to become startled and confused.

The biggest problem with the U.S. media is that they do not try to give a coherent, comprehensive picture of what is happening. Operating under tight deadlines, flashing the best action footage, and basing reports heavily on official sources, the media bombard us with many little stories but seldom weave them together into a big story. They give us only pieces of a jigsaw puzzle. Part of this problem is due to the nature of any news medium that comes out daily: Newspapers and television take events one day at a time. Such news is usually incomplete and often misleading. We see people shooting, but we don't know why. The media world is, in Shakespeare's phrase, "full of sound and fury, signifying nothing."

What Can Be Done?   The mass media—except for the elite media—do not provide *meaning*. Some, such as the wire services, deliberately shun analysis and interpretation in their stories; that would be unobjective or editorializing. Reporters are typically unequipped to explain the historical background or longterm consequences of the stories they cover. Reporters are expected to be generalists, to be able to cover everything and anything. All you have to do is write down what the official source says. It is for this reason that editorials and columns of opinion often contain more usable "news" than the straight news stories, for the former set the news into a meaningful context, whereas the latter just leaves the bits and pieces scattered about. Unfortunately, most Americans make do with the bits and pieces as they make decisions on candidates, economic matters, and sending troops abroad.

Can anything be done? Professional newspeople generally agree that the public is ill informed, and some will even admit that their coverage could be wider and deeper. But the limiting factor, they emphasize, is the public itself. Most people don't want to be well informed, especially about things distant or complicated. Audience surveys usually find that people care least about foreign news and most about local news. Newspapers can go broke pushing too much world news; many, in fact, are going the way of the checkout-counter weeklies with the splashy and the trashy. Most people aren't intellectuals and don't like complicated, in-depth analyses. The shooting they care about; the reasons behind it they don't. Do the media have any responsibility, though, in educating the mass public so that citizens can better comprehend our complicated world? Some idealists in the media do feel a responsibility, but they are usually offset by the hardheaded business types, who have the last word. After a while, the idealists become cynical. We cannot expect any major improvements soon. For you, however, the student of political science who is already among the more attentive, the answer is the elite media. Use the mass media for sports coverage.

THE ADVERSARIES: MEDIA AND GOVERNMENT

The role of the press as critic in the healthy functioning of U.S. democracy has long been recognized. Thomas Jefferson wrote in 1787, "Were it left to me to decide [between government without] newspapers and newspapers without government, I should not hesitate a moment to prefer the latter."

Over the centuries, the press has criticized government.[17] In the late 1960s and early 1970s, however, a new adversarial relationship between media and government emerged that is with us today. To be sure, not all the media entered into the fray; most newspapers with their wire-service stories continued to quote official sources. But the elite media and television often adopted hostile stances toward the executive branch.

The Media and Vietnam.   The causes are not hard to see: Vietnam and Watergate. In both episodes the executive branch engaged in considerable lying to the media in order to soothe public opinion. Many media people resented being used in this way and struck back by means of sharp questioning in press conferences and investigative reporting. The presidency of Richard Nixon didn't help matters; he had long feared and hated the press. On losing the governor's race in California in 1962, he slouched off, muttering that the press "won't have Nixon to kick around any more." Before presidential press conferences, Nixon used to calm his nerves by relaxing in a darkened room. He liked to operate in considerable secrecy and then spring his decisions on the public in direct telecasts without any newspeople getting in the way. In turn, the press resented him all the more.

In Saigon, the U.S. military held afternoon press briefings, dubbed the "five o'clock follies," in which the army tried to put its best foot forward with indications of progress in the war. Journalists soon tired of the repetitive, misleading, and irrelevant briefings and took to snooping around themselves. What they found wasn't pretty: a corrupt, inept Saigon regime that was not winning the hearts and minds of its people; a Vietcong able to roam and strike at will; and tactics and morale inadequate to stop them.[18] One young *New York Times* reporter was so critical of the Diem regime that his stories undermined American confidence in Diem and paved the way for Diem's 1963 ouster and murder by his own generals.[19] Such is the influence of the elite media.

Television, too, showed a picture different from what U.S. officials wanted: the bodies of young GIs covered with mud and blood in full color. Because television inherently favors the visual, it beamed gory film clips into America's living rooms. Television also developed, perhaps unwittingly, a devastating style of coverage in which scenes of horror were juxtaposed with calm reassurances of top officials. The contrast silently indicated that the officials were either fools or liars. In 1971, CBS News accused the Defense Department, in a documentary, of spending millions of tax dollars to win public and congressional support. "The Selling of the Pentagon" raised a storm of controversy, with administration accusations of tricky editing that made interviewees look as if they were saying things they weren't. By this time, media and government were in a snarling match.

That same year, another bombshell burst: *The Pentagon Papers* appeared, first in the *New York Times,* then in the *Washington Post.* The papers were a multivolume, top-secret study commissioned by former Secretary of Defense Robert McNamara to document decision making on the Vietnam war.[20] Daniel Ellsberg, a former Pentagon official who had turned against the war, made photocopies and delivered them to the newspapers. In the age of Xerography, there are no more total secrets. The Nixon administration was outraged—although the Papers made the Johnson officials the chief culprits—and ordered their publication halted, the first time the U.S. government ever censored newspapers. The Supreme Court immediately threw out the government's case, and the presses ran again. By this time, there was open warfare between government and the media.

The Media and Watergate.   The next year, 1972, began a process that brought the fall of the Nixon administration and, for at least portions of the media, a new self-image as guardians of public morality. Persons connected to the White House were caught burglarizing and planting telephone "bugs" in the Democratic campaign headquarters in the Watergate office and apartment complex. Dogged investigation by two young *Washington Post* reporters revealed a massive cover-up led by the Oval Office.[21] The more Nixon promised to come clean, the guiltier he looked. Nixon was never impeached. A House special committee voted to recommend impeachment; then Nixon resigned. The House certainly would have voted impeachment and the Senate probably would have convicted. Would the same have happened without media coverage? Ultimately, the legal moves came through the courts and Congress, but the media made sure these branches of government would not ignore or delay their duties. Did the media bring Nixon down? The Nixon people thought so, but then they always loathed the press. Others have argued that the same would have happened without the investigative reporting, but more slowly and with less drama. The point is that media and government are so intertwined that they are part of the same process and hard to separate.[22]

Since Watergate, some branches of the media, namely the elite press and the national television networks, have adopted generally adversarial stances toward the executive branch.[23] Criticism of the occasional changes of course under the Ford and Carter presidencies was immoderate and sometimes unreasonable. Carter, like Nixon, claimed the press was out to get him. The policies of the Bush and Clinton administrations were almost automatically doubted and criticized. The media see "scandal" everywhere in Washington and then descend in a "feeding frenzy" that leaves no reputation untarnished.[24]

Has the press gone too far? Some people are fed up at the high-handedness with which the media impugn all authority. The media seem to think they are always right, the government always wrong. One favorite target of media criticism was the former U.S. commander in Vietnam, retired General William Westmoreland. CBS News produced a documentary that said Westmoreland and his staff deliberately lied about Communist troop strength. Westmoreland sued, and even though he lost, the media world trembled.[25] The threat of libel suits had a "chilling effect" on the news media's efforts to uncover wrongdoing in public life.[26]

What is the proper role of the media in a democracy? That they can and should criticize is clear: this keeps government on its toes. But how much should they criticize? Should they presume wrongdoing and cover-up everywhere?[27] Should many reporters model themselves after Woodward and Bernstein of Watergate fame and try to ferret out scandals at every level of government? The press is largely protected from charges of libel, for "public" persons are presumed to be open to scrutiny. This has left some public figures feeling helpless and bitter at the hands of an all-powerful press and has increased cynical attitudes about politics in general. Public opinion has grown critical of the too critical media. Perhaps the United States can find some happy middle ground.

Suggested Readings

COOK, TIMOTHY E. *Making Laws and Making News: Media Strategies in the U.S. House of Representatives.* Washington, DC: Brookings Institution, 1989. How congresspersons use the press to further their legislative agendas.

DAVIS, RICHARD. *The Press and American Politics: The New Mediator.* White Plains, NY: Longman, 1992. Good overview of the methods and power of the U.S. media.

DIAMOND, EDWIN, and ROBERT A. SILVERMAN. *White House to Your House: Media and Politics in Virtual America.* Cambridge, MA: MIT Press, 1995. Citizen inattention and media manipulation have perverted U.S. politics.

DOVER, E. D. *Presidential Elections in the Television Age.* Westport, CT: Praeger, 1994. Television has made previous ways of analyzing elections obsolete; the author proposes a new way.

ENTMAN, ROBERT M. *Democracy Without Citizens: Media and the Decay of American Politics.* New York: Oxford University Press, 1989. Tough-minded criticism that the U.S. media are making U.S. politics more superficial.

GANS, HERBERT J. *Deciding What's News.* New York: Vintage Books, 1980. Careful empirical study of how editors select and present news stories.

GRABER, DORIS A. *Mass Media and American Politics.* 4th ed. Washington, DC: CQ Press, 1992. Good summation of much research by a noted specialist.

HESS, STEPHEN. *News and Newsmaking.* Washington, DC: Brookings Institution, 1996. Sometimes funny insights on how government and the media use each other.

JAMIESON, KATHLEEN HALL, and KARLYN KOHRS CAMPBELL. *The Interplay of Influence: News, Advertising, Politics, and the Mass Media,* 3rd ed. Belmont, CA: Wadsworth, 1992. How political and commercial interests use the media, by two mass communication specialists.

KELLNER, DOUGLAS. *Television and the Crisis of Democracy.* Boulder, CO: Westview Press, 1990. A critical but historical approach to the rise of television power.

LENART, SILVO. *Shaping Political Attitudes: The Impact of Interpersonal Communication and Mass Media.* Thousand Oaks, CA: Sage, 1994. An updating of the "two-step" communications flow to include the impact of television.

NIMMO, DAN, and JAMES E. COMBS. *The Political Pundits.* Westport, CT: Greenwood, 1992. The rise and role of the great media columnists and opinion molders.

PAGE BENJAMIN I. *Who Deliberates? Mass Media in Modern Society.* Chicago: University of Chicago Press, 1996. The U.S. media have the awesome power to both open and close public debate.

ROSENBLUM, MORT. *Who Stole the News?* New York: Wiley, 1994. A veteran foreign correspondent argues foreign news coverage by U.S. media has declined in quantity and quality.

SCHUDSON, MICHAEL. *The Power of News.* Cambridge, MA: Harvard University Press, 1995. The news media are not as powerful as often assumed, as people interpret reports as they wish.

Notes

1. For a fine historical review, see Thomas C. Leonard, *The Power of the Press: The Birth of American Political Reporting* (New York: Oxford University Press, 1986).

2. See Kathleen Hall Jamieson, *Packaging the Presidency: A History and Criticism of Presidential Campaign Advertising,* 2nd ed. (New York: Oxford University Press, 1992).

3. His basic concepts can be found in Karl Deutsch, *The Nerves of Government; Models of Political Communication and Control* (New York: Free Press, 1966); and *Nationalism and Social Communications: An Inquiry into the Foundation of Nationality* (New York: Wiley, 1953).

4. Paul Lazarsfeld and Elihu Katz, *Personal Influence* (New York: Free Press, 1955); also Elihu Katz, "The Two Step Flow of Communication: An Up-to-Date Report on an Hypothesis," *Public Opinion Quarterly* 21 (1957), 61–78.

5. Daniel C. Hallin, "Sound Bite News: Television Coverage of Elections, 1968–1988," Woodrow Wilson International Center for Scholars, 1991.

6. See William A. Dorman and Mansour

Farhang, *The U.S. Press and the Journalism of Deference* (Berkeley: University of California Press, 1987).

7. Although ignored as a charlatan by most communication scholars, Marshall McLuhan offered valuable insights into the power of television. See his *Laws of Media: The New Science* (Toronto: University of Toronto Press, 1989).

8. See Austin Ranney, *Channels of Power: The Impact of Television on American Politics* (New York: Basic Books, 1983).

9. See Gary R. Orren and Nelson W. Polsby, eds., *Media and Momentum: The New Hampshire Primary and Nomination Politics* (Chatham, NJ: Chatham House, 1987).

10. One researcher argues that only visuals count on television, not words. See Martin Schram, *The Great American Video Game: Presidential Politics in the Television Age* (New York: Morrow, 1987).

11. Robert D. Putnam, "The Strange Disappearance of Civic America," *The American Prospect* 24 (Winter 1996), 34–48.

12. For an excellent summary of the charge that television induces voter apathy, see Curtis B. Gans, "Is TV Turning Off the American Voter?" *New York Times*, 3 July 1988, p. H24.

13. Thomas R. Dye, Robert S. Lichter, and L. Harmon Zeigler, *American Politics in the Media Age*, 4th ed. (Monterey, CA: Brooks/Cole, 1992), Chap. 6.

14. See Ellen Mickiewicz, *Split Signals: Television and Politics in the Soviet Union* (New York: Oxford University Press, 1988).

15. Michael J. Robinson and Kevin R. Appel found that TV network coverage of Congress was heavily negative. See their "Network News Coverage of Congress," *Political Science Quarterly* 94 (Fall 1979), 3.

16. For a look into the world of Washington reporters and why they cover what they do, see Stephen Hess, *The Washington Reporters* (Washington, DC: Brookings Institution, 1981).

17. One history claims that all presidents have disliked the press. John Tebbel and Sarah Miles Watts, *The Press and the Presidency: From George Washington to Ronald Reagan* (New York: Oxford University Press, 1985).

18. The U.S. media were at first not hostile to the war effort in Vietnam. But after several years and as U.S. opinion became more critical, the media, especially television, turned critical. See Daniel C. Hallin, *The Uncensored War: The Media and Vietnam* (New York: Oxford University Press, 1986).

19. See David Halberstam, *The Making of a Quagmire* (New York: Random House, 1965).

20. Neil Sheehan et al., *The Pentagon Papers* (New York: Bantam Books, 1971).

21. Bob Woodward and Carl Bernstein, *All the President's Men* (New York: Simon & Schuster, 1974).

22. See Gladys Engel Lang and Kurt Lang, *The Battle for Public Opinion: The President, the Press, and the Polls During Watergate* (New York: Columbia University Press, 1983).

23. Michael Baruch Grossman and Martha Joynt Kumar found that all administrations since 1960 have passed through successive phases of alliance, competition, and finally detachment in their relationships with newspeople. See their *Portraying the President: The White House and the News Media* (Baltimore: John Hopkins University Press, 1981).

24. The phrases are from two recent books critical of the media: Suzanne Garment, *Scandal: The Crisis of Mistrust in American Politics* (New York: Times Books/Random House, 1991), and Larry J. Sabato, *Feeding Frenzy: How Attack Journalism Has Transformed American Politics* (New York: Free Press, 1991).

25. See Burton Benjamin, *Fair Play: CBS, General Westmoreland, and How a Television Documentary Went Wrong* (New York: Harper & Row, 1988).

26. Lois G. Forer, *A Chilling Effect: The Mounting Threat of Libel and Invasion of Privacy Actions to the First Amendment* (New York: Norton, 1987).

27. Political scientist Thomas E. Patterson, in a study of news reporting on politicians from 1960 to 1990, found it portrayed them increasingly in a negative light. See his *Out of Order* (New York: Random House, 1994).

· 10 ·

Interest Groups

Interest groups are especially numerous, vocal, and visible in the United States, but we have no monopoly on them. They are an element in the political life of every highly organized modern society. Even in countries where social, economic, and political life is dominated by central planning, interest groups exist, though in muted form. Observers detected interest groups even in the Soviet Union under the conservative Brezhnev, quarreling, for example, over whether heavy or light industry will be emphasized in economic plans.[1] And opposing the regime, groups of dissidents sprang up despite the Kremlin's efforts to promote uniformity.

184

What Is an Interest Group?

The term *interest group* covers a wide spectrum of people and issues. In his land-mark work, *The Governmental Process,* David B. Truman defines an interest group as "a shared-attitude group that makes certain claims upon other groups in society" by acting through the institutions of government.[2] Some interest groups are transient, whereas others are more permanently organized. Many are solely interested in influencing the government's public policy, whereas others are only sporadically concerned with political decisions. Some work directly through the executive or administrative agencies, whereas others work through the judicial or legislative sectors, or even through public opinion. But one crucial factor is common to all interest groups: They are all non-publicly accountable organizations which attempt to promote shared private interests by influencing public policy outcomes that affect them.[3]

HOW INTEREST GROUPS DIFFER FROM POLITICAL PARTIES

It may seem that interest groups resemble political parties. But interest group leaders are not elected by the general public, nor are they answerable to the people for their decisions. Both try to influence public policy. But unlike political parties, interest groups lie outside the electoral process and are thus not responsible to the public. The survival of the party depends on the people's support. Private interest groups may try to influence the nomination of candidates who are sympathetic to their cause, but the candidates run under the party banner—not the interest group banner.

Goals.   The goal of the political party is to acquire power though elections. The interest group, however, is concerned with specific programs and issues and is rarely represented in the formal structure of government. The interest group tries to steer political parties and their elected officials toward certain policies rather than enacting those policies itself. Interest groups often try to win the favor of all political parties. Environmentalists want the support of both the Republicans and the Democrats in their fight to minimize ecological damage. But at times they may take a stand in favor of one party if they are convinced that that party will further their objectives with greater vigor. In 1996, for example, environmentalists strongly supported the Democrats.

Nature of Memberships.   Most political parties want broad enough support to win an election, drawing into their ranks different interests. Their membership is much more varied than that of the interest group. Even the conservative Republican party includes people in all income brackets and occupations, and some of its members are more liberal than many Democrats. The Democratic party, on the other hand, seen as the more progressive party of the working class, also counts all walks of life among its supporters.

Interest groups generally have a more selective membership. Members of a labor union are likely to share similar living and working conditions and to have comparable educational and cultural backgrounds. Interest groups for a specific problem or issue, such as ecology or the banning of nuclear weapons, may draw their members from a wider spectrum, but even they tend to have more similarities than members of parties.

Almost Unlimited Number.   The purpose of a party is to nominate and elect its candidates and perpetuate itself in power. For several reasons, including the length of a ballot, the number of political parties must be limited; even in multiparty political systems, all the parties can usually be counted on the fingers of both hands. But interest groups are a different matter. There is no functional limit (such as the length of a ballot) on their proliferation, and some countries seem to offer a particularly fertile environment for their development. The United States has long provided such an environment. As Tocqueville observed in the 1830s, "In no country of the world has the principle of association been more successfully used or applied to a greater multitude of objects than in America." Tocqueville is still accurate. Just open a Washington, DC, phone book to "National . . ." and behold the hundreds of national associations, institutes, leagues, and committees.[4] Much of Washington's prosperity is based on its obvious attraction as a headquarters for interest groups.

INTEREST GROUPS: WHO BELONGS?

In every highly organized technological society, life is maintained by a multitude of different industries. There are differences in the cultural, economic, educational, ethnic, and religious backgrounds of people. These varied categories of people and enterprises represent the raw material of interest groups.

David Truman argued that wherever there are divergent interests, there exists the potential for an interest group. Interest groups play a central role in a democratic government, and we pay considerable attention to the pressure system of organized special interest groups attempting to influence government policies. Because of our highly developed pressure system, the United States is often defined by theorists of Truman's school as a "pluralist democracy," in which a multiplicity of interest groups, all pushing their own claims and viewpoints, creates a balance of opposing interests that prevents any one group from dominating the political system. In this optimistic view, government policy is the outcome of competition among many groups, which represent the varied interests of the people. This is the classic pluralist picture discussed in Chapter 5.

The U.S. system does indeed include many rival pressure groups. But in contrast to David Truman's theory, many observers have noted that the members of these groups tend to be drawn overwhelmingly from the middle and upper classes, and that group activities are dominated by individuals with business-related interests. The mere fact of competition among rival interest groups does not guarantee a democratic system. As E. E. Schattschneider noted, "The flaw in the pluralist heaven is that the heavenly chorus sings with a strong upper-class accent."[5] Many critics of our interest group system would agree that middle- and upper-class interests are disproportionately represented in comparison to the lower classes, which have relatively little voice.

Elite theorists argue that if David Truman's group theory really operated, the poor would begin to organize in groups as soon as they became aware that they were poor and didn't want to be. Yet, with only sporadic exceptions, the poor, who seem to have so much to gain from collective action, have been slow in joining together to promote their common interests. When organizations or aid programs have been developed to tackle the problems of poverty, the ideas, money, and leadership often have come from outside the community. Better-off and better-educated people are much more likely to participate in politics, and this includes organizing and running interest groups. In this area, too, the poor get shortchanged.

Left on their own, the lower classes are more likely to act explosively rather than as organized groups with reasonable approaches. They have a strong sense of grievance which has been demonstrated time after time through history. The storming of the Bastille at the start of the French Revolution is one example of how poverty-nurtured resentments boiled over into violence. In recent U.S. history, the riots in large-city ghettos reflected the anger that race-related poverty produced in many African-Americans.[6] The ghetto riots, while serving to publicize the grievances and anger that exist in certain poor communities, resulted in great destruction that hurt the people living in those communities more than anyone else. They cost their perpetrators a great deal without offering any real challenge to the power and influence of business and industry, labor unions, or other groups that the poor regard as stumbling blocks in the way of their objectives. Not all sectors of society can effectively form and use interest groups.

INTEREST GROUPS AND GOVERNMENT

Interest groups try to influence government. But what if there is no government? To take an extreme example, consider Somalia, where in the early 1990s there was no government. There were, to be sure, plenty of groups: dozens of clans and mafias, each with its own militia engaging in nearly constant fighting. Would we call these "interest groups"? Probably not. Although some interest groups engage in occasional violence, they do so in a context of trying to influence government. In Somalia, there was no government to influence; the groups fought to guard their respective "turfs." Not all clashes of groups automatically qualify as "interest group activity."

Interest groups presuppose an existing government that is worth trying to influence. Government, in fact, virtually calls many interest groups into life, for they are intimately associated with government programs. There are farm lobbies because there are farm programs, education lobbies because there are education programs, and veterans' lobbies because in years past the government chose to go to war.

To take one example, the 1958 National Defense Education Act (NDEA) put millions of dollars into university foreign-area and language programs. A decade later, as enthusiasm for these subjects waned (partly because of the Vietnam war), a vigorous lobby dedicated to "world education" and funded by universities that received NDEA grants tried to persuade Congress to continue the program. Congress had created a program, the program created an interest group, and then the interest group worked on Congress. This is one reason that programs, once set up, are hard to terminate. They develop constituencies with a strong pecuniary interest in continuing the programs. As government has become bigger and sponsored more programs, the number of interest groups has proliferated. By now, virtually every branch and subdivision of the U.S. government has one or more interest groups watching over its shoulder, demanding more grants, a change in regulations, or their own agency. The Departments of Education and Energy were created under these circumstances, and Ronald Reagan vowed to abolish them. He couldn't: The interests associated with them—in part created by them—were too powerful.

Sometimes interest groups participate in government legislation and implementation. In Britain, "interested members" of Parliament are those who openly acknowledge that they represent industries or labor unions. This is not frowned on and is considered quite normal. In Sweden, interest groups are especially large and powerful. Swedish "royal commissions," which initiate most new legislation, are composed of legislators, government officials, and interest group representatives. After a proposal has been drafted, it is circulated for comments to all relevant interest groups. Some Swedish benefits for farmers and workers are administered by their respective farm organizations and labor unions. Some call this "corporatistic," meaning that interest groups are taking on government functions.[7] Top representatives of business, labor, and the cabinet meet regularly in Sweden to decide a great deal of public policy. Critics charge that this too-cozy relationship bypasses parliamentary democracy altogether.

BUREAUCRATS AS AN INTEREST GROUP

Government and interest groups are related in another very important but sometimes overlooked way: The bureaucracy has become one of the biggest and most powerful interest groups of all. Civil servants are not merely the passive implementers of laws; they also have a great deal to say in the making and application of those laws. Much legislation originates in the specialized agencies. Many of the data and witnesses before legislative committees are from the executive departments and agencies.

Needless to say, these bureaucracies develop interests of their own. They see their tasks as terribly important and so naturally think they need a bigger budget and more employees every year. When was the last time a professional civil servant—as opposed to a political appointee—recommended abolishing his or her agency or bureau? Bureaucrats have a lot of knowledge at their fingertips, and knowledge is power. When the Reagan administration came in, it said it would abolish the Department of Energy (DOE). One of the authors of this book asked a friend, an official of the department, why he wasn't worried. "They won't abolish us," he asserted knowingly. "They can't. DOE manufactures nuclear bombs, and the administration needs the DOE budget to disguise how big the nuclear-bomb budget is." He was right; Reagan did not abolish the Department of Energy.

It was earlier proposed that interest groups are offshoots of society and the economy. That is only partly true, for they are also offshoots of government. Government and interest groups, to paraphrase Thomas Hobbes, were born twins. The more government, the more interest groups.

To say that every political system has interest groups doesn't say very much, for interest groups in different systems operate quite differently. One key determinant in the way interest groups operate is the government. Here we can refine our definition of pluralism discussed in Chapter 5. Pluralism is determined not by the mere existence of groups, each trying to influence government, but by the degree to which government permits or encourages the open interplay of groups. Pluralism has a normative component, an "ought" or a "should."

Antipluralism in Europe. The United States and Britain, for example, are considered highly pluralistic, for interest group activity is acceptable and desirable. Many observers consider lobbying the normal functioning of a healthy democracy, with nothing furtive about it.[8] In France, on the other hand, interest group activity, although it does exist, is frowned on and considered a bit dirty. France is heir to centuries of centralized and paternalistic government. The French are used to Paris ministries setting national goals and supervising much of the nation's economic activity. Further, the philosopher Jean-Jacques Rousseau still has a powerful hold on the French mind. Rousseau argued, among other points, that there must be no "partial wills" to muddy and distort the "general will," that which the whole community wants. Rousseau presumed there was such a thing as a general will, something pluralists deny. Accordingly, interest groups are seen as trying to pervert the good of the whole community. The French bureaucratic elites pay little attention to interest groups, considering them "unobjective." French interest groups operate in a more constrained atmosphere than their American or British counterparts.

Communist China takes this a step farther. Open interest group activity is generally taboo. Chinese interests make their case quietly, within the confines of party discussions, and do not lay claim to more than their area of professional interest. Few spontaneous, nongovernment interest groups appear openly to propose major or systemic change. The way groups function is structured by government, which can permit a lot or very little open activity.

Effective Interest Groups

POLITICAL CULTURE

Interest groups are most likely to flourish in democratic societies in which occupational and other contacts put individuals in touch with a wide range of people and where political participation is emphasized. The percentage of people who join organized groups differs greatly from one country to another.

In their study of political cultures, Almond and Verba noted that people in the United States, Great Britain, and Germany were more likely to participate in voluntary associations than were citizens of Italy and Mexico.[9] According to their findings, 57 percent of the respondents in the United States, 47 percent in Great Britain, and 44 percent in Germany were members of groups. In Italy and Mexico, the extent of participation was significantly smaller, amounting to only 30 percent and 24 percent, respectively. Civic participation in every country increased with educational level, and in all except the United States, more men than women were participants. Not all of the groups were political, of course, but some 24 percent of American, 19 percent of British, and 18 percent of German respondents were involved in political associations. By comparison, very few Italian and Mexican respondents participated in politically involved associations. One of the significant findings of the study was that in societies where many join groups, people have a greater sense of political competence and efficacy. It is with concern that political scientists have noted a decline in the U.S. tendency to form groups (see Chapter 7 on political culture).

MONEY: RISE OF THE PACS

Money is probably the single most important factor in interest group success. Indeed, with enough money, interests hardly need a group. Money is especially important for elections, and groups try to secure the victory of candidates known to favor their cause. Most democracies have recognized the danger in too close a connection between interests and candidates, the danger that we will have the "best Congress money can buy."[10] Some, such as Germany and Sweden, provide for almost complete public financing of the major parties in national elections. Spain, which rejoined the democracies only in 1977, subsidizes parties after the election according to how many votes they received and parliamentary seats they won.

The United States has been reluctant to go to public financing of campaigns for several reasons. First, there is the strong emphasis on freedom. The U.S. Supreme Court generally interprets the First Amendment to include dollars as a form of free speech. If a person wants to give money to a candidate, that is a political statement. Second, U.S. campaigns are much longer and more expensive than in other democracies, the result of our weak, decentralized parties and nominating system. In Western Europe, elections can be short and cheap because the parties are already in place with their candidates and platforms. And third, given these two previous conditions, American legislators have not been able to find a formula for public financing that really works in the manner intended. One experiment turned out to have some negative "unforeseen consequences."

We refer to the rise of the political action committees (PACs), the result of 1971 legislation. Congress sharply limited the amount of money that individuals and corporations could contribute directly to candidates in an effort to curb the influence of "big money" in politics. (Currently, individuals may give up to $1,000 directly to a campaign.) But there was no prohibition on individuals and businesses organizing committees and donating money to them that in turn would go to desirable candidates. PACs grew like mushrooms, from 600 in 1974 to over 5,000 now. In 1996, they spent some $500 million on election campaigns. In 1992, the average incumbent congressperson received $261,976 from PACs. Challengers got only $27,621. Although PACs were originally an idea of labor unions, business PACs now greatly outspend labor PACs.[11] Large corporations, many with defense contracts, are heavy PAC contributors. The bulk of contributions go to incumbents, which enables members of Congress to lock themselves into power nearly permanently. Especially favored by PACs are incumbents on committees relevant to the PAC's interests (e.g., farm PACs give to members of the House Agricultural Committee).

Some individuals and PACs contribute to parties and interest groups not directly working for a candidate's election campaign. This "soft money," uncontrolled and unlimited, enables parties and groups to campaign *against* the other side without mentioning their own candidate's name, effectively skirting the intent of federal campaign laws. Soft money thus contributes to the trend toward negative advertising in political campaigns.

Can or should anything be done about interest groups and money? One solution might be to go to a European-type system in which the parties are well organized and campaigns are short and relatively cheap. But that is simply not in the cards for the United States. Another solution might be to limit the amount that any company could give to a PAC and that any PAC could give to a candidate. The Supreme Court rejected such limits in 1985. Public financing of all candidates— presidential nominees who gain at least 5 percent of the national vote are already entitled to federal financing—would be terribly expensive. For the foreseeable future, it will not be possible to break the tie between interest groups and candidates in the United States.

ISSUES: RISE OF SINGLE-ISSUE GROUPS

Perhaps the second greatest factor in the influence of interest groups (after money) is the intensity of the issue involved. The right issue can mobilize millions, give the group cohesion and commitment, and boost donations. There have always been American interest groups pursuing one or another idealistic objective, but during the 1970s the rise of "single-issue" interest groups changed U.S. politics. Typically, interest groups have several things to say about issues, for their interests encompass several programs and departments. Organized labor in the form of the AFL-CIO tries to persuade government on questions of Social Security, medical insurance, education, imports and tariffs, and the way unemployment statistics are calculated. The AFL-CIO has a long-term, across-the-board interest in Washington. The same can be said for many business groups.

But to the single-issue groups only one issue matters, and it matters intensely. Typically, their issues are moral—and therefore hard to compromise—rather than material. The most prominent single-issue group is the right to life or antiabortion movement. In 1973 the Supreme Court ruled that states could not arbitrarily restrict a woman's right to an abortion. Many Roman Catholics and Protestant fundamentalists were shocked, for they believe that human life begins at the moment of conception and that aborting a fetus is therefore murder. "Pro-life" people oppose, for a start, allowing any state or federal medical funds to be used for abortion, and they would like to amend the Constitution to outlaw abortion. They are opposed to the "pro-choice" forces. Abortion rights are linked to the women's movement, and feminists argue that whether or not to have an abortion is a matter for the individual woman to decide and no one else; the right to choose returns to women an element of control over their lives and hence is part of their liberation from second-class status.

The antiabortionists make life miserable for many senators and representatives. They care about nothing else in a representative's record—where he or she stands on taxes, jobs, defense, and so on. They want to know where he or she stands on abortion, and a compromise middle ground—the refuge of many politicians faced with controversial issues—is not good enough. How can you be a "moderate" on abortion? Many elections turn on the abortion issue. Meanwhile, the pro-choice forces organize and grow militant enough to offset the pro-life forces.

Other single-issue causes have appeared, such as prayer in public school and homosexual rights. Taken together, these two and the abortion question are sometimes referred to as the "morality issue." Gun control grew into a major issue, fanned by the assassinations of John and Robert Kennedy and Martin Luther King, Jr. The powerful National Rifle Association (NRA) opposes such groups as Handgun Control. None of these issues makes elected representatives any happier. They like to be judged on a wide range of positions they have taken, not on one narrow issue on which it is hard to compromise.

The abortion battle is being fought on the streets of this nation as well as in the courts. It is a highly emotional issue that activates strongly committed interest groups on both sides.

SIZE AND MEMBERSHIP

Their size and the degree of commitment of their members obviously give groups clout. The biggest and fastest growing U.S. interest group is the American Association of Retired Persons, now claiming 33 million members, many of them educated, forceful, and strongly committed to their cause of preserving and enhancing Social Security and Medicare. When AARP speaks, Congress trembles.[12] Their opposition to cuts in Medicare encouraged President Clinton to veto the Republican measure in 1995.

Size alone, however, is not necessarily the most important element in interest group strength. Money and intensity are often able to offset sheer size. Groups that claim to speak for large numbers are not appreciated if it is known that only a small fraction of the group are committed members. The National Association for the Advancement of Colored People (NAACP) claims to speak for millions of African-Americans, but its actual membership is much smaller. All things being equal, a large group has more clout than a small one—but things are never equal.

The socioeconomic status of members gives groups clout. Better-off, well-educated people with influence in their professions and communities can form groups that get more respect. The socioeconomic status of American Jews boosted the impact of the American-Israel Public Affairs Committee (AIPAC) and other Jewish groups. As Japanese-Americans climbed educationally and professionally, their Japanese American Citizens' League (JACL) started having more of an impact and won apologies for the highly unconstitutional internment of West Coast Japanese in World War II; JACL then worked on getting compensation. Respect leads to clout. This means, paradoxically and unfairly, that disadvantaged groups with the biggest grievances are among the least likely to be listened to.

ACCESS

Money, issue, and size may not count for much unless people in government are willing to listen. To be sure, these ingredients help, but it is often the careful cultivation of relationships with members of Congress and civil servants over the years that makes sure that doors are open. When a group has established a stable and receptive relationship with a branch of government, it is said to enjoy, in the words of Joseph LaPalombara, "structured access."[13] Greek-American members of Congress are, quite naturally, receptive to Greek arguments on questions concerning Turkey and Cyprus.[14] Michigan legislators are likewise disposed to discuss the problems of the automobile industry. Arab-Americans complained bitterly that Jews enjoyed too much access on Capitol Hill and organized their own groups to try to gain such access.

What happens when groups are shut out, have no access? The pluralists tend to think this can't happen in a democracy, but apparently it does. Black and Indian militants argued that no one was listening to them or taking their demands seriously. Only when violence began in urban ghettos and on Indian reservations did Washington begin to listen. When the wealthy and powerful have a great deal of access, the poor and unorganized may have none. The consequences sometimes lead to violence.

Strategies of Interest Groups

APPROACHING THE LAWMAKERS

Although lobbying is not the only strategy of interest groups, it is the one that receives the most attention. Unfortunately, the unscrupulous dealings of a few individuals have given lobbyists an unsavory image with the public.[15] Incidents of blackmail and bribery do occur (as they do in other areas of human endeavor), but such tactics are anathema to the average lobbyist.

Lobbying Techniques.   The approaches and techniques commonly used by lobbyists vary widely according to the types of interest the lobbyists represent and the way in which they conceive of their jobs. In "The Role of the Lobbyist," Samuel C. Patterson identified three types of lobbyists: the "contact man," the "informant," and the "watchdog."[16] The contact man promotes the interests of his group by establishing friendships with legislators to whom he can present his group's case on a person-to-person basis. The informant lobbies in public rather than in private meetings, offering testimony supporting her group's case at legislative hearings and disseminating published materials on the group's behalf. The watchdog keeps close track of what is happening in the legislature so he can alert his group to take action when the time is appropriate.

Criteria for Successful Lobbying.   The success of a lobbyist's approach depends on several factors, one of which is the receptivity of legislators. Surveying lobbyists' evaluations of their various techniques, Lester Milbrath found that those rated most effective by the lobbyists themselves involved direct communication between the lobbyist and the legislature.[17] The highest-rated strategies included not only the personal presentations of viewpoints and "research results" made by the contact-man type of lobbyist to individual legislators but also the lobbyist's testimony at legislative hearings. Rated less effective were the techniques—such as contacts by constituents and close friends, letter and telegram campaigns, public relations campaigns, and publicizing voting records—that involved no personal communication between legislators and lobbyists. The lowest-rated strategies were those of "keeping channels open" between interest groups and legislators. Under this category would fall campaign work, social get-togethers, and financial contributions.

APPROACHING THE ADMINISTRATION

The executive branch of government is also a target for interest group pressure and persuasion. Antipollution groups, for instance, seek support from the Department of the Interior in their efforts to ban automobiles from the national parks. As a general rule, interest groups will approach a department of the government and not the president, who is not readily accessible to such groups and their lobbyists, although perhaps he is aware of the pressures they apply and indirectly involved in deciding how to handle them. Interest groups tend to concentrate their attention on the department that specializes in their own area of interest. Farm groups deal with the Department of Agriculture, public service companies deal with the Federal Power Commission, and so forth. As a rule, each department pays careful heed to the demands and arguments of groups in its area. In fact, at one time or another, many government bureaucracies have been "captured" or "colonized" by powerful pressure groups within their respective spheres of authority.

In dealing with the bureaucracy, interest groups employ about the same tactics they use with legislators, including personal contacts with officials, supplying research and factual materials, public relations and publicity campaigns, and entertaining. However, some kinds of pressuring, such as letter-writing campaigns, are less effective with bureaucrats than with legislators, since jobs in government administration are gained by appointment rather than election, and most are protected by tenure. One special occasion for interest groups to make their influence felt in the bureaucracy is when candidates are up for appointment to top-level government posts, including positions in the president's cabinet. At such times, interest groups may influence the choice of a nominee who is to serve in areas they regard as sensitive to their own interests. In 1981, President Reagan named to head the Environmental Protection Agency a person with long-time professional inter-

Union made. The sign in a union hall reminds a Democratic candidate for the Senate where his support comes from. Many interest groups support candidates in the expectation of future consideration.

est in developing rather than protecting nature. Anne Gorsuch was so pro-industry that her tenure created a scandal, and she was forced to resign in 1983.

APPROACHING THE JUDICIARY

In the United States, interest groups also seek to realize their goals through the judicial process. Every year the state and federal courts hear numerous cases filed or supported by such interest groups as the American Civil Liberties Union, the Sierra Club, and the NAACP. The issue of government-enforced racial segregation is one of many that have been taken to the courts by interest groups. The legal staff of the NAACP, for example, through its chief attorney Thurgood Marshall (later an associate justice of the U.S. Supreme Court), successfully challenged the constitutionality of all state laws requiring racial segregation in public schools. In recent years the U.S. Supreme Court has dealt with several delicate and important social issues brought to it by interest groups, including women's rights, the death penalty, abortion, and school prayer.

Interest groups have generally used two methods to pursue their goals through the judicial process. The first is to initiate suits directly on behalf of a group or class of people whose interests they represent (such suits are commonly referred to as "class actions"). The second method is for the interest group to file a brief as a "friend of the court" (*amicus curiae*) in support of a person whose suit seeks to achieve goals that the interest group is also seeking.

OTHER TACTICS

Government is not the only target of interest group action. Organized interests may often choose to take their case to the public with peaceful—or not so peaceful—appeals.

Appeals to the Public. Even powerful interest groups realize the importance of their public image. For this reason, many interest groups invest considerable sums in public relations programs and publicity campaigns to explain how they contribute to the general welfare and why their programs and policies are good for the country. For example, railroads used television to explain their case for "fair" government policies so they could stay alive and compete with trucking. The "right-to-work" lobby placed many magazine ads attacking unions for preventing nonunion people from getting or keeping jobs.

Even while investing large sums in publicity, some interest groups maintain what is popularly referred to as a "low profile," preferring to promote their objectives without advertising themselves. In such cases, groups may rely on planted news stories that promote their objectives indirectly and behind-the-scenes pressure to prevent the publication of material that they judge to be detrimental to them. The Tobacco Institute, for example, discreetly funds research that casts doubt on findings that smoking is bad for your health. The American Petroleum

Institute seeks no news coverage but lets its officers be quoted as unbiased experts in the field, supposedly above the political fray.

Demonstrations. Whereas certain special interest organizations, such as the American Cancer Society and the Heart Fund, may have access to free advertising space and time, most interest groups do not, and many lack the funds to purchase such publicity. Under these circumstances, a group with limited finances and motivated members may decide to try nonviolent demonstrations as a way of publicizing and promoting their cause. The precedent for such demonstrations in modern times was provided by Mahatma Gandhi, who used this tactic against the British Raj before India gained its independence in 1947. Gandhi, who derived his inspiration for nonviolent protest from an essay on "civil disobedience" by Henry David Thoreau, written in protest against the United States-Mexican War of 1846–1848, also provided a model for the African-American leader Martin Luther King, Jr., who headed the nonviolent civil rights movement during the 1950s and 1960s.

Protesters against nuclear power plants, facing the financial and political resources of power companies, felt that marching, picketing, and sometimes blocking plant entrances through sit-ins was their only option. With news media cover-

Citizens protest plans for a toxic-waste incinerator, claiming it would bring poisonous fumes to nearby towns. In this case, well-organized local citizens beat a well-heeled corporation, which was forced to drop its plans.

age of their protests, they were able to gain adherents, contributors, and sometimes access in Washington. Their powerful opponents, of course, often prevailed, leading some protesters to become frustrated and bitter.

Violent Protest.   A group that loses faith in the efficacy of conventional political channels and modes of action often sees violent protest as its only alternative. Although violent protest occurs more than we would like in this country, it is not a mode of action that interest groups normally use. Rather, it is a reaction that requires a psychological buildup, nurtured by poverty, discrimination, frustration, and a sense of personal or social injustice. An outbreak of violence usually begins spontaneously as a result of an incident that sparks the pent-up anger of a frustrated group, and the momentum of mob behavior escalates the violence. The riots in black ghettos in large cities typify such violence. The more articulate rioters claimed they were simply *opposing* the violence they suffered daily at the hands of police, all levels of government, and an economy that kept them underpaid or unemployed. Did the violent protest work? Perhaps it was no coincidence that the social legislation of the Great Society was passed during this period. The British got out of India and Palestine when outbursts of violence made the areas difficult to govern. The white government of South Africa started offering reforms only when blacks turned to violence. We may not like to admit it, but in certain circumstances, violence works. Americans are certainly no strangers to violence. As black radical H. "Rap" Brown put it, "Violence is as American as cherry pie."

Interest Groups: An Evaluation

Interest groups are an intrinsic part of every modern democracy. Yet how well do they serve the needs of the average citizen?

HOW WELL DO INTEREST GROUPS ARTICULATE IDEAS?

Every question of public policy involves a variety of different, and often conflicting, interests, most of which deserve a hearing in a democracy. Some of these interests are represented in the legislature, but many are not, especially in a two-party system such as that of the United States. Interest groups help represent a wider range of interests in the legislative process.

Many smaller organizations, however, have neither the members nor the money to make an input. Unless they are able to form coalitions, they cannot defend their interests from larger, more powerful groups. The mere fact that interest groups can articulate demands does not mean that the demands will be heeded. Resources are highly unequal among interest groups. Some are rich and powerful and have a lot of influence. Others are ignored.

There is a further problem in a system in which interest groups are accorded a prominent place: What about those individuals who are not organized into groups? Who speaks for them? Many citizens are not members or beneficiaries of interest groups. They vote for elected leaders, but the leaders usually pay more attention to group demands than to the unorganized multitude who elected them. If legislators and executives are attuned to interest groups, who is considering the interests of the whole country? At times, it seems as if no one is. Then we may begin to appreciate Rousseau's emphasis on the "general will" over and above the "particular wills" that make up society.

To try to remedy such defects, the "citizens' lobby," Common Cause, was formed in 1970. Claiming to represent the will of all in promoting good government, Common Cause, funded by voluntary subscriptions, successfully fought for public funding of presidential campaigns, an end to the congressional seniority system, and disclosure of lobbying activities.[18] In a similar vein, Ralph Nader set up several public interest lobbies related to law, nuclear energy, tax reform, and medical care. Although groups such as these have done much good work, they raise an interesting question: Can a society as big and complex as America's possibly be represented as a whole, or is it inherently a mosaic of groups with no common voice?

Interest Groups as a "Safety Valve." In almost every nation there are alienated citizens who feel they have been forgotten or discriminated against by the government. Interest groups often help to stabilize society by providing unhappy citizens with a "safety valve"—a legitimate outlet for their complaints and frustrations. Tenants subjected to the indignities of poor plumbing and roaches may organize to voice their complaints rather than vent their frustrations through violence. Of course, anyone who joins an organized group is largely committed to acting within the system. Truly alienated citizens want radical change, and compromises between interest groups and government may not satisfy them.

Defining Issues and Arenas of Conflict. Individuals with interests in common do not constitute an interest group until they become aware of their shared attitudes, discontents, and problems and are motivated to take action to maintain or improve their position. The women's movement started gathering momentum in the 1960s with books and articles expressing the dissatisfaction of some women with the conditions imposed on them by society. The leaders, ranging from moderates concerned with improving the legal status and employment opportunities of women to extremists who advocated separatism to allow women to "find themselves," gave women a standard by which to measure their own feelings about themselves and the roles assigned to them by society. The movement also made it necessary for government officials and political candidates to develop political stands on the issue.[19] Women's groups organized support not only for such objectives as the ending of job discrimination but also for the accessibility of birth control information, legal abortions, day-care centers, and desegregation of traditionally male restaurants and clubs.

Do such organizations really speak for most of their members, or do they represent the interests of a small but vocal minority within the group? Interest group leaders, like leaders of political parties, often have stronger ideas on issues than their followers. But political party leaders, especially in such nations as the United States, must often compromise on issues in order to appeal to the largest possible majority at election time. Interest group leaders, in contrast, must often take stronger or more extreme stands than many of their members would like in order to retain a favorable bargaining position. Strikes called by union leaders do not always have the full sympathy of the workers, many of whom are more interested in collecting their weekly paychecks than in bargaining for a new contract. And many women who are in favor of equal pay for equal work find the concept of abortion, as presented by many women's leaders, to be an anathema.

INTEREST GROUPS: EDUCATORS OR PROPAGANDISTS?

When important issues of public policy are being considered by Congress, it is customary to permit interested parties to offer testimony at committee hearings to support their stands on the issue. Experts who testify at congressional hearings serve the purpose of presenting important technical, scientific, and statistical information. Hearings may help Congress to pass fairer laws that are more in tune with public needs. But the argument can also be made that the groups that get a hearing in Congress are those with the influence to gain access to the formal government process; grassroots groups often have less access.

In addition to educating the government, interest groups often play a crucial role in developing public awareness and knowledge of issues. Certain groups, such as the Consumers Union, specialize in helping people to use their money more knowledgeably. Others, such as the American Medical Association (AMA) and some insurance organizations, have been sources of advice on such subjects as good health habits, proper nutrition, accident prevention, and planning for financial security. Critics of the interest group system argue that by disseminating information, the groups are acting as propagandists rather than as educators. No interest group is going to publicize information that puts it in an unfavorable light; the information it offers to government and the public is highly selective.

STALEMATING POLITICAL POWER

Interest groups compete with one another, and in the process they may help to limit the power and influence that any group can exercise within Congress or a government agency. However, by dispersing political power, interest groups can also stalemate government action. Certain issues have been aptly characterized as "hot potatoes" because government action in either direction will arouse a loud outcry from one group or another. Typically, such issues are ardently supported and vehemently opposed by competing groups with enough voting power and influence to drive politicians to equivocation. Government may in effect get stuck, trapped between powerful interests and unable to move on important national problems. Italy has been called a "stalemate society" for this reason.

Political scientist Samuel Beer believes that this is what happened in Britain. British interest groups became too strong and too closely connected to government programs. Elections became little more than attempts by the two main parties to promise more and more to all manner of interest groups. Because the groups' demands were inherently in conflict, this led to what Beer calls "the paralysis of public choice."[20] Parties were no longer able to articulate overarching policies for the good of the entire nation; they were too intent on winning over this or that group. Beer's analysis explains why many Britons elected and reelected Margaret Thatcher, for she pointedly ignored the demands of both business and labor groups to do what she believed best for the country. Many Britons thought it was high time somebody said no to the interest groups. Britain is a case in which interest groups may have become too powerful. Ross Perot had much the same criticism of U.S. interest groups, and many Americans agreed with him.

In two-party systems especially, issues tend to be muted by political candidates who try to appeal to as broad a segment of the voting public as possible. The result is a gap between the narrow interest of the individual voter and the general promises of an electoral campaign—a gap that interest groups attempt to fill by pressing for firm political actions on certain issues. But how well do interest groups serve the needs of the average citizen? The small businessperson, the uninformed laborer, and minority groups with limited financial resources tend to get lost in the push and pull of larger interests and government. The successful interest groups, too, tend to be dominated by a vocal minority of well-educated, middle- and upper-class political activists. In some cases interest groups have become so effective that they overshadow parties and paralyze policymaking with their conflicting demands. The precise balance between the good of all and the good of particular groups has not yet been found.

Suggested Readings

BIRNBAUM, JEFFREY H. *The Lobbyists: How Influence Peddlers Got Their Way In Washington.* New York: Random House, 1992. Longtime observer gives details and insights into the work of high-powered lobbyists.

CIGLER, ALLAN J., and BURDETT A. LOOMIS, eds. *Interest Group Politics,* 4th ed. Washington, DC: CQ Press, 1994. Comprehensive, up-to-date, and readable collection on U.S. interest groups.

HREBENAR, RONALD J. *Interest Group Politics in America,* 3rd ed. Armonk, NY: M.E. Sharpe, 1996. Nicely updated overview of the workings and problems of lobbying at the federal level.

JOHNSON, HAYNES, and DAVID S. BRODER. *The System: The American Way of Politics at the Breaking Point.* Boston: Little, Brown, 1996. Interest groups block major change and have become miniature—and negative—political parties.

KEY, V. O., JR. *Politics, Parties, and Pressure Groups.* New York: Crowell, 1958. Classic analysis of diverse groups in American politics.

LOWI, THEODORE. *The End of Liberalism: The Second Republic of the United States,* 2nd ed. New York: Norton, 1979. A critical, insightful, and stimulating analysis of the consequences of pressure group politics in the United States.

MUNDO, PHILIP A. *Interest Groups: Cases and Characteristics.* Chicago: Nelson-Hall, 1992. Excellent overview with case studies of business, labor, and citizen interest groups.

OLSON, MANCUR, JR. *The Logic of Collective Action: Public Goods and the Theory of Groups.* New York: Schocken Books, 1968. Olson creates an original model of the dynamics of group action and comes to some important conclusions.

PETRACCA, MARK P., ed. *The Politics of Interests: Interest Groups Transformed.* Boulder, CO: Westview Press, 1992. Sixteen original essays on the latest empirical findings and theoretical perspectives.

RAUCH, JONATHAN. *Demosclerosis: The Silent Killer of American Government.* New York: Random House, 1994. Interest groups, too many and too efficient, have prevented and blocked effective governance.

SABATO, LARRY J. *PAC Power: Inside the World of Political Action Committees.* New York: Norton, 1985. Perhaps the best book on PACs so far; comprehensive.

SCHULZINGER, ROBERT D. *The Wise Men of Foreign Affairs: The History of the Council on Foreign Relations.* New York: Columbia University Press, 1984. Study of a private group that powerfully influences U.S. foreign policy.

Washington Representatives 1996. New York: Columbia Books, 1996. Latest edition of an annual that lists and identifies the personnel of more than 11,000 Washington lobbying organizations.

Notes

1. See H. Gordon Skilling and Franklyn Griffiths, eds., *Interest Groups in Soviet Politics* (Princeton, NJ: Princeton University Press, 1971).

2. David B. Truman, *The Governmental Process* (New York: Knopf, 1951), p. 37.

3. This general definition is reflected in Arthur Bentley's work, *The Process of Government* (orig. ed., 1908; Evanston, IL: Principia Press, 1949), considered a forerunner of contemporary political science. The book attempts to tie together the common elements of modern interest groups.

4. For a look at the complexity of interest group activity in Washington, see Jeffrey M. Berry, *The Interest Group Society*, 2nd ed. (Glenview, IL: Scott, Foresman, 1989).

5. E.E. Schattschneider, *The Semisovereign People: A Realist's View of Democracy* (New York: Holt, Rinehart & Winston, 1960), p. 29.

6. See Rufus P. Browning et. al., *Protest Is Not Enough: The Struggle of Blacks and Hispanics for Equality in Urban Politics* (Berkeley: University of California Press, 1984).

7. Some authors argue that West European interest groups operate in a generally corporatistic fashion. See Suzanne D. Berger, ed., *Organizing Interests in Western Europe: Pluralism, Corporatism, and the Transformation of Politics* (New York: Cambridge University Press, 1981).

8. For an explanation of British and American concepts of interest, see Stephen Miller, *Special Interest Groups in American Politics* (New Brunswick, NJ: Transaction, 1983).

9. Gabriel Almond and Sidney Verba, *The Civic Culture* (Boston: Little, Brown, 1965). Another survey found that 31 percent of the U.S. population actually belongs to organizations that seek to influence public issues. Robert E. Lane, *Political Life* (New York: Free Press, 1959), p. 204.

10. For an angry look at political contributions, see Philip M. Stern, *The Best Congress Money Can Buy* (New York: Pantheon, 1988).

11. See Theodore J. Eismeier and Philip H. Pollock, *Business, Money, and the Rise of Corporate PACs in American Elections* (Westport, CT: Quorum Books, 1988).

12. For an excellent review of AARP's size, activities, and influence, see John Tierney, "Old Money, New Power," *New York Times Magazine*, 23 October 1988.

13. Joseph LaPalombara, *Interest Groups in Italian Politics* (Princeton, NJ: Princeton University Press, 1963).

14. For studies of the Greek ethnic group, see Paul Y. Watanabe, *Ethnic Groups, Congress, and American Foreign Policy: The Politics of the Turkish Arms Embargo* (Westport, CT: Greenwood, 1984); and Laurence Halley, *Ancient Affections: Ethnic Groups and Foreign Policy* (New York: Praeger, 1985).

15. See, for example, Schattschneider's discussion of the "contagion of conflict" in *Semisovereign People*, Chap. 1.

16. Samuel C. Patterson, "The Role of the Lobbyist: The Case of Oklahoma," *Journal of Politics* 25 (February 1963), 72–92.

17. Lester Milbrath, *The Washington Lobbyists* (Chicago: Rand McNally, 1963).

18. See Andrew S. McFarland, *Common Cause: Lobbying in the Public Interest* (Chatham, NJ: Chatham House, 1984).

19. For an overview of the feminist movement, see Ethel Klein, *Gender Politics: From Consciousness to Mass Politics* (Cambridge, MA: Harvard University Press, 1984).

20. Samuel H. Beer, *Britain Against Itself: The Political Contradictions of Collectivism* (New York: Norton, 1982), pp. 15–19.

· 11 ·

Political Parties and Party Systems

To many Americans, a political party doesn't mean a great deal. The two major U.S. parties often seem to be alike. Both parties share much in the way of basic values, ideologies, and proposals. Elections usually turn on the personality of the candidates rather than party affiliation. Many American political scientists worry that the parties are becoming so weak that they may fail to perform necessary political functions to keep the system running correctly.

This weakness of American parties is curious, for the United States was the first country to develop mass political parties. Mass-based U.S. parties appeared with the presidential election of 1800, decades before parties developed in Europe. The Europeans, however, may have developed political parties more fully. Americans have tended to forget that parties are the great tools of democracy. As E.E. Schattschneider put it, "The rise of political parties is indubitably one of the principal distinguishing marks of modern government. Political parties created democracy; modern democracy is unthinkable save in terms of parties."[1] If American parties are weakening, it may bode ill for the long-term future of American democracy. For what will take their place? Political action committees? Television campaigns? Neither prospect is appealing.

A *political party,* defined by one leading political scientist, is "any group, however loosely organized, seeking to elect governmental office-holders under a given label."[2] Almost all present-day societies, democratic or not, have some sort of political party system to link citizens to government. Occasionally military dictators—such as Franco in Spain, Pinochet in Chile, or generals in Brazil—try to dispense with parties, blaming them for the country's political ills. But this never lasts, for even dictators find that they need parties. Franco regarded all parties with a snarl but set up a "National Movement" that did the same thing parties do. Within two years of Franco's death in 1975, Spain's parties came out into the open to give the country a party system that is not too different from its European neighbors. Similarly, the Brazilian generals tried to set up two obedient and controlled political parties, but when they gave up power in 1985, a genuine party system emerged that resembled the party system they thought they had abolished in their 1964 coup. Pinochet also found that however much he tried to crush Chilean party activity, it persisted underground and reappeared when he left office. Love them or hate them, countries seem unable to do without political parties.

Functions of Parties

In democratic systems parties perform several important functions that help hold the political system together and keep it working. Some of these functions, to be sure, coincide with those of parties in nondemocratic systems, but Communist parties are another species that we will consider separately.

A Bridge Between People and Government. To use a systems phrase, political parties are a major "inputting" device, allowing citizens to get their needs and wishes heard by government. Without parties, individuals would stand alone and ignored by government. By working in or voting for a party, citizens can make an impact on political decisions. At a minimum, parties may at least give people the feeling that they are not utterly powerless, and this belief helps maintain government legitimacy, one reason even dictatorships have a party.

Aggregation of Interests. If interest groups, considered in the last chapter, were the highest form of political organization, government would be terribly chaotic and unstable. One interest group would slug it out with another, trying to sway government officials this way and that. There would be few overarching values, goals, or ideologies that could command nationwide support. Instead, it would be every interest group for itself. (Some worry that the United States already resembles this situation.) Parties help tame and calm interest group conflicts by *aggregating* their separate interests into a larger organization.[3] The interest groups then find that they must moderate their demands, cooperate, and work for the good of the party. In return, they achieve at least some of their goals. Parties—especially large parties—are thus in part coalitions of interest groups. A classic example was the Democratic party that Franklin D. Roosevelt built in the 1930s, which helped get him elected four times. It consisted of unionized workers, farmers, Catholics, Jews, and blacks. Labor unions, for example, working with the Democrats, got labor legislation they could never have obtained on their own. As long as this coalition held together, the Democrats were unbeatable; since then the coalition has badly decayed. President Reagan, as we considered earlier, for a time aggregated economic and noneconomic conservative groups into the Republican party.

Integration into the Political System.   As the aggregation of interest groups goes on, parties pull into the political system groups that had previously been left out. In reaching out for votes, parties usually welcome new groups into their ranks, giving them a say or input into the formation of party platforms. This gives the groups both a pragmatic and a psychological stake in supporting the overall political system. Members of the group feel represented and develop a sense of efficacy in the system and loyalty to the system. The British Labour party and the U.S. Democratic party, for example, enrolled workers with platforms stressing union rights, fair labor practices, welfare benefits, and educational opportunities. Gradually, a potentially radical labor movement learned to play by the democratic rules and support the system.[4] Now, ironically, British and American workers are so successfully integrated into the political systems that many vote Conservative or Republican. In countries where parties were unable to integrate workers into the political system, labor movements turned radical and sometimes revolutionary. In the United States, parties have helped integrate successive waves of immigrants and minorities into American political life.

Political Socialization.   As parties are integrating groups into society, they are also teaching their members how to play the political game. Parties may introduce citizens to candidates or elected officials, giving citizens the feeling that they can make an input, thus deepening their sense of efficacy within the system. In party activities, people learn to speak in public, to conduct meetings, and to compromise, thus deepening their political competence. If nothing else, parties are the training grounds for leaders with talent. In fostering individual leadership skills, parties in democratic countries are also building up among party members a feeling for the legitimacy of the system as a whole. Historically, some European parties attempted to set up distinct political subcultures—complete with party youth groups, soccer leagues, newspapers, women's sections, and so on. The effort was self-defeating, however, for the more these parties socialized their members to participate in politics, the less the members were drawn to the subcultures. The fading remnants of this effort can still be found in Italy in both the renamed Christian Democrats, now the Popular party, and the renamed Communists, now the Democratic Party of the Left. Some American parties even provided social services. New York's Tammany Hall served as a welcome wagon for European immigrants, helping them find jobs and housing, while enrolling them in the Democratic party.

Mobilization of Voters.   The most obvious function of parties is getting people to vote. In campaigning for their candidates, parties are whipping up voter interest and boosting voter turnout on election day. Without party advertising, many citizens would pay no attention to elections. Most political scientists believe there is a causal connection between weak U.S. political parties and low voter turnout. In Sweden, strong and well-organized parties often produce voter turnouts of 90 percent or higher. Some critics object that party electoral propaganda trivializes politics, but even this propaganda has a function. By simplifying and clarifying issues, parties enable voters to choose among complex alternatives.

Organization of Government.   The party's rewards for victory in an election are the government jobs and power it uses to try to shift government policy to its way of thinking. The party with the most seats in the U.S. House or Senate appoints the chamber's leaders and committee chairpersons. The occupant of the White House can appoint some 3,000 people to high-level jobs in the executive departments. This allows the victorious party to put its stamp on the direction governance will take for at least four years. Party control of government in the parliamentary systems of Western Europe (discussed subsequently) is tighter than in the United States because parliamentary systems give simultaneous control of both the legislative and executive branches to the winning party. What a prime minister wants he or she usually gets, and with minimal delay, because party discipline is much stronger. In no system, however, is party control of government complete, for the already established bureaucracies of government have considerable power of their own (see Chapter 16). Parties *attempt* to control government; they don't always succeed.

PARTIES IN DEMOCRACIES

In evaluating party functions, two major factors must be considered: the degree of centralization in the party's organization and the extent to which a party actively participates in government policy.

Centralization.   The control party leadership can exert on its elected members varies widely among democratic systems. At one extreme is Israel, whose highly centralized system of candidate selection calls for each party to draw up a national list of nominees to the parliament, or Knesset. Since Israel's system of elections uses proportional representation, 120 candidates are nominated, but only the names listed at the top of the ballot can be expected to win seats. Party chiefs can place tried and trusted people higher on the list; newcomers, lower. This helps ensure party discipline. Germany also uses party lists, but the country is divided into sixteen states in which state parties have the dominant say. Such a system decentralizes party control. In Britain, the parties select their candidates by a process of bargaining between each party's national headquarters and its local constituency organizations. The national headquarters may suggest a candidate who is not from that district—perfectly legal in Britain—and the local party will look the person over to approve or disapprove the candidate. The local party may also run its own candidate after clearing the nomination with national headquarters. The varying degrees of centralization of these systems gives their parties coherence, discipline, and ideological consistency. When you vote for a party in Israel, Germany, or Britain, you know what it stands for and what it will implement if elected. Once elected, members of these parliaments do not go their separate ways but vote according to party decisions.

Voters have less assurance of party discipline in the United States, where parties have historically been decentralized and weak. State party organizations may have some power, but in most cases, candidates have only themselves to rely on. Candidates for the House and the Senate, in effect, create a new party organization every time they run. Between elections, U.S. parties lie dormant. The Republican National Committee and Democratic National Committee may not have many resources to distribute to candidates. Candidates are expected to raise their own money through contributions from individuals and political action committees (Chapter 10). Candidates then appeal directly to the voters through television and other media. Increasingly, television advertisements fail even to mention the candidate's party affiliation. Candidates are thus in a position to tell their national parties, "I owe you very little. I didn't get much party help to win, and I won't necessarily obey you now that I'm in office." This makes U.S. parties radically decentralized and often incoherent. Elected officials answer to their conscience, to their constituents, and to their PACs, and not to their political parties. Starting with President Reagan and continuing with the Republican Congress elected in 1994, the Republican party became more coherent and cohesive, but only for a while.

Setting Government Policy.   One key to responsible party government is the extent to which the majority party can enact its legislative program. Here, the American party system is exposed to its severest criticism from advocates of strong parties. In parliamentary systems, the majority party must resign when it can no longer muster the votes to carry on its legislative program. In contrast, the problem in the United States is often one of identifying exactly where the majority lies. The platform of the presidential campaign is not binding on the members of the president's party in Congress. What if the party of the president is not the majority party in one or both houses? Furthermore, just what is and who determines the legislative program of a party that may control Congress yet has no central leader like the president? Does Newt Gingrich, Bob Dole, or Richard Armey speak for the national Republican party? Or do the elected minority leaders in each house of Congress have the right to speak for their party members when they are not represented in the White House? These are just some of the problems parliamentary systems don't have.

In the United States, the legislative program is usually initiated centrally, with the president. But it must be acted on by the 535 individual senators and members of Congress, all of whom are ultimately responsible for their own vote, as they are for their own reelection. Is the president, then, to be blamed for failing to fulfill campaign promises, or does the fault lie rather with a party discipline that is too loose? Schattschneider argued that because U.S. national parties are so decentralized, not one of them can agree on a strong national platform, and the result is that the American government is "a punching bag for every special and local interest in the nation."[5] But on the other hand, many of us would prefer our senators and representatives to vote according to their consciences rather than the dictates of a more distant party leadership, as is the style in Europe.

Party Participation in Government.   True, a parliamentary system of government is more conducive to what Schattschneider regards as responsible party government than the American system. Our system, with its rigid set of checks and balances, can make it difficult for parties to bridge the separation of powers in order to enact platforms. But this is not entirely the fault of the American party system. It is inherent in the constitutional separation of powers between the executive and legislative branches. Occasionally, when a powerful president controls both the White House and Congress, party platforms may turn into law, as when Lyndon Johnson got his Great Society program through the Democratic Congress of 1965–1966. No European parliamentary system had ever passed so many sweeping reforms so quickly.

Still, party participation in government is stronger in Western Europe because in parliamentary systems the winning party is the government, or more precisely, its leadership team becomes the cabinet. This system allows for more clear-cut accountability and voter choice than is available in the American system, where the parties are decentralized and stand for many viewpoints. In both systems, parties participate in government by providing jobs for party activists in various departments and agencies. In Britain, about 100 members of the winning party's parliamentary faction take on cabinet and subcabinet positions, compared to the 3,000 Americans who can receive political appointments when a new president takes office.

THE PARTY IN COMMUNIST STATES

Communist systems—that is, countries ruled by Communist parties—have suddenly become rare. In Eastern Europe, Communist parties permitted free elections in 1990 and found themselves out of power. (Some reformed Communist parties, calling themselves Socialist, won elections in these countries, but they now operate in a democratic context.) China, Vietnam, North Korea, and Cuba seemed intent on preserving the classic Communist system of a party-controlled state, but they too may soon change.

The "classic" Communist system founded by Lenin and developed by Stalin in the Soviet Union featured the interlocking of a single party with government and the economy. The Communist party did not rule directly; instead it supervised, monitored, and controlled the personnel of the state and economic structures. Most Soviet officials wore two hats, one as government functionary and another as Communist party member. Every level of government, from local to national, had a corresponding party body that nominated its candidates and set its general lines of policy. At the top of the state structure, for example, was the legislature, the Supreme Soviet. Corresponding to it in the party system, the Central Committee oversaw the nomination of candidates to the Supreme Soviet, set its agenda, and guided its legislative outcomes. Supervising the Central Committee, a Politburo (political bureau) of a dozen or so top party leaders was the real heart of Soviet governance. Guiding the Politburo was the party's general secretary, who could appoint loyal followers to high positions and thus amass great power.

Why did Soviet President Mikhail Gorbachev deliberately undermine this structure? A single party that attempts to control everything important in society develops severe problems over the years. Because it gives members the best jobs, housing, and consumer goods, the party becomes increasingly staffed by opportunists, many of them corrupt. These party *apparatchiks* (people of the apparatus) also become highly conservative. The system favors them, and they have no desire to reform it. With such people supervising it, the Soviet economy ran down and fell farther behind the U.S., West European, and Japanese economies. A Communist party that was to lead the Soviet Union into a radiant future came to be seen as leading the country backwards. Gorbachev seems to have come to the conclusion that to save his country he had to break the Communist party's monopoly on power. Gorbachev failed to understand (as did many Western political scientists) how brittle the system was. Once the Soviet Communist party was discredited and had to face competition, it collapsed.

The Soviet experience suggests that single parties that monopolize power are not workable long-term solutions. Without the invigorating elements of debate, competition, and accountability, Communist-type parties become corrupt, inflexible, and unable to handle the new, complex tasks of a modern world. Study Communist systems while you can; soon there may be none left.

Types of Political Parties

One of the first scholars to formulate a scheme for classifying political parties was French political scientist Maurice Duverger.[6] His relatively simple scheme put all political parties into one of three descriptive categories: mass, cadre, or devotee. The *mass* parties include the Western democratic parties, which vie for members by attempting to cut across class lines and which seek the largest membership possible. European parties, while not as broadly based as the Anglo-American parties, are still mass parties because their membership is open. In contrast, cadre parties, such as the Chinese Communist party and India's Congress party, draw their support from the politically active elite. Generally associated with totalitarian or developing nations, *cadre* parties have centralized organizations and expect the elite group that makes up their membership to be active within the party. Duverger uses the term *devotee* for parties such as the Nazis under Hitler, where the party's formal structure is built around one person. Such a party is now found almost exclusively in Third World developing countries.

Another way to classify parties is on a left-to-right spectrum, according to party ideology (see Chapter 6). Left-wing parties, such as Communists, propose leveling of class differences by nationalizing major industries (i.e., putting them under government control and ownership). Center-left parties, such as the socialist parties of Western Europe, favor expanding the welfare state but usually not nationalizing industry. Centrist parties, such as the German and Italian Liberals, are generally liberal on social questions but conservative (i.e., free market) on economics.[7] Center-right parties, such as the German Christian Democrats, want to rein in (but not dismantle) the welfare state in favor of free enterprise. Right-wing parties, such as the British Conservatives under Thatcher, want to dismantle the welfare state, break the power of the unions, and promote vigorous capitalist growth. Sweden has a rather complete political spectrum (see Fig. 11.1).

THE RISE OF THE "CATCHALL" PARTY

Accompanying the general drift of most democracies to two-plus party systems has been the growth of big, sprawling parties that attempt to appeal to all manner of voters. Before World War II, many European parties were ideologically narrow and tried to win over only certain sectors of the population. Socialist parties were still

FIGURE 11.1 An ideological spectrum: Swedish parties, their number of seats (out of 349), and their percent of the national vote in the 1994–97 Riksdag (parliament).

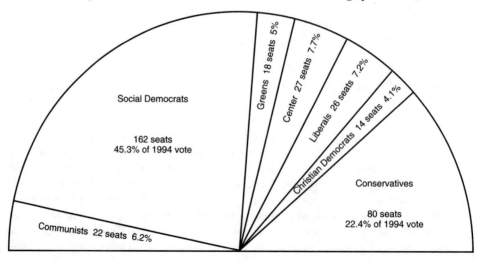

at least partly Marxist and aimed their messages largely at the working class. Centrist and conservative parties aimed at the middle and upper classes, agrarian parties at farmers, Catholic parties at Catholics, and so on. These were called *Weltanschauung* (German for "worldview") parties because they tried not merely to win votes but also to sell their view of the world.

After World War II, Europe changed a lot. As prosperity increased, people began to think that the old ideological narrowness was silly. In most of Western Europe, big, ideologically loose parties that welcomed all voters either absorbed or drove out the *Weltanschauung* parties. The late German political scientist Otto Kirchheimer coined the term *catchall* to describe this new type of party. His model was the German Christian Democratic party, a party that sought to speak for all Germans: businesspersons, workers, farmers, Catholics, Protestants, women, you name it.[8] The term now describes virtually all ruling parties in democratic lands; almost axiomatically, they've got to be catchall parties to win. The British Conservatives, Spanish and French Socialists, and Japanese Liberals (who are actually conservative despite the name) are all catchall parties. And of course the biggest and oldest catchall parties of all are the U.S. Republicans and Democrats.

Whereas most political scientists welcome this move away from narrowness and rigidity, another problem has arisen. Because catchall parties are big and contain many viewpoints, they are plagued by factional quarrels. Struggles between parties have in many cases given way to struggles within parties. Virtually every catchall party has several factions.[9] Scholars counted several factions in the Italian Christian Democrats and Japanese Liberal-Democrats, parties that resemble each other in their near-feudal division of power among the parties' leading personalities. A good deal of American politics also takes place within rather than between the major parties.

CRITERIA FOR PARTY CATEGORIES

Political parties can be classified in several ways, but underlying the categories are usually four broad criteria:

Who Supports the Party?   Broad-based parties such as the Democrats and Republicans combine the political demands of different, and often antagonistic, parts of society. Narrow-interest parties, in contrast, articulate the interests of a single group. Catchall parties that draw from all parts of society stand the best chance of winning control of a stable government because their political appeal is as broad as the community itself. Generally speaking, narrow-interest parties do not have enough support to win power, unallied, through the democratic process. To win control of the government, they must either enter into coalitions or seize power by force.

What Is the Party's Membership Policy?   Political parties are either "open" or "closed" in their membership requirements. The doors of broad-based parties are generally open to anyone who wishes to join, whereas elite parties operate more like an exclusive club. They carefully screen prospective members, and in some cases require them to complete a period of apprenticeship. Such is the case with Communist parties, especially those in power. Catchall parties, naturally, welcome all as members.

How Are Candidates Chosen?   The way in which candidates are chosen varies so widely that meaningful distinctions are difficult. Broad-based parties generally give members the most voice in selecting nominees for office. This doesn't mean that political conventions are totally open, but rather that the party members have some say in who will run on the ticket. Such is the approach of the two big U.S. parties. In Communist parties, candidates are chosen by the party hierarchy. Most democratic parties choose their candidates at party conventions attended by loyal, long-time members, often representing constituency organizations.

What Are the Party's Goals?   The parties we are familiar with are concerned primarily with winning office and control of government. However, third parties such as the Liberal Democratic party in Britain or Barry Commoner's Citizens party in the United States realize the unlikelihood of their gaining legislative control and have different goals. Their main concern is to "send a message" to the big parties. They exist to articulate a specific opinion and to see that this interest is protected by trading their political support for legislative favors. Finally, revolutionary parties, like the Communist party, are concerned with teaching the people a way of life, and they use government power to change existing norms and established institutions. Their goal is to create a utopian society by employing the power of the state to convince its citizens to accept the party's concept of the ideal society.

Inherent in these broad criteria for classifying political parties is the assumption that the parties are aiming for a permanent standing in the political system. The nature of a party's appeal, its membership policy, candidate selection process, and political goals all center on the fact that the parties must hold some measure of support from the people. This support manifests itself in the form of members and money, both of which are vital to the survival of a party.

Recruitment and Financing

Political party leaders and members come and go, but the party itself strives to remain. How do parties recruit new members? Where do their leaders come from? How do they obtain the financial backing necessary to carry on their activities?

RECRUITMENT

The requirements for party membership vary widely. The United States is unique in the Western world in that, strictly speaking, there is no party membership. One may register locally as a Republican or Democrat, but that doesn't mean much. It allows the person to vote in that party's primary but imposes no other obligations, such as paying dues or helping in campaigns. A citizen may, of course, join a local or state party club or committee, which simply makes him or her a member of that group. This is not the case in Western Europe, where one may indeed become a party member. Parties set their own membership requirements and impose their own regulations on members. To join the Conservative party in Britain, one must sign a declaration testifying to support of the party's goals and pay yearly dues amounting to about sixty cents. Many British union members are automatically enrolled in the Labour party, and many European unions divert a part of their dues to the Social Democratic party in their country. Of course, most union members recruited in this manner are not likely to become actively involved in party affairs.

Incentives to Join.   For European union members, joining a labor-type party is often the path of least resistance. But there are other reasons why people choose to identify themselves with a particular party. Political scientist Samuel Eldersveld found nine major reasons, ranging from the involvement of one's friends or relatives in a particular party to more self-generating motives.[10] Among these reasons lies the possibility that a particular candidate or issue may so capture the attention of a person that he or she is motivated to political action and so joins the party. Precinct workers may actively recruit party volunteers. Or a citizen's participation in civic affairs may lead to political dealings with the local government, where one particular party is in office. Ideological commitment can also be a factor in motivating people to identify with a party, though this is true more in Europe than in the United States, where parties are less prone to ideological labels. Finally, people may become active in politics out of ambition for their own personal or professional advancement or for political power itself.

Recruiting Candidates.   Despite Ronald Reagan's jump from Hollywood actor to president, most candidates for public office come up through the party ranks. How large a say does the party hierarchy have in deciding who will become a candidate? Lester G. Seligman's study of recruitment methods in the United States reveals that in "safe" districts, where people consistently vote for the same party, party officials do not play much of a role in candidate selection.[11] Usually, such districts have incumbent officeholders who will probably be returned to power, but when an office falls vacant, party factions are allowed to fight it out among themselves for control of the nomination. In "unsafe" districts, where the minority faces a difficult battle, party officials must go out and draft people to run. Generally, loyal party workers are given the dubious honor of leading the party to certain defeat, and they run out of a sense of obligation to the party. Seligman finds that in competitive areas, party officials do not dominate in choosing candidates. Here, party leaders as well as factions within the party tend to support favored candidates in the primaries, but they are often upset by candidates supported by powerful nonparty interest groups.

Three means of choosing candidates exist outside of direct selection from the ranks by the established party leadership. Some candidates are self-recruited: They enter the primary on their own strength. These may be wealthy persons, who hope to use massive advertising to compensate for their lack of organizational support, or persons who voice points of view that bring them a popular following but not party backing. Candidates may also be recruited by cooptation: A party may ask a "big name" who is not formally identified with it to run as its candidate. This usually happens when the party has no strong candidate of its own and hopes to capitalize on a popular new face. The Republican party's nomination of Eisenhower for president in 1952 is an example of cooptation. Finally, candidates are persuaded to file for office as the agents of groups who hope to win concessions from the established party hierarchy. The Reverend Jesse Jackson's efforts in the 1980s can be seen in this light.

How Representative Are Party Leaders?   How do our political leaders differ from each other? Are they representative of the party members who support them? Kenneth Prewitt studied the process by which eighty-seven San Francisco Bay area communities selected their local leaders.[12] His findings stress the role of social bias in the selection of political officials. Across the board, the city council members were wealthier and better educated than their respective constituencies. Prewitt found that consciously or subconsciously, the American political system tends to favor candidates from the upper socioeconomic classes. Other studies have shown that party leaders in both major parties have more money and education than rank-and-file members.

Political Opinions: Party Leaders and Rank and File.   It is often argued that America's political leaders do not reflect and respond to the needs of their constituents and that party platforms represent vague attempts to dodge rather than satisfy complaints and issues. Curiously enough, much research suggests just the contrary: that political leaders actually hold stronger ideological views than do their followers, and that it is instead the weak and inconsistent ideologies of the party rank and file that prevent the leaders from taking firmer stands on issues.[13]

The leaders of both the Democratic and the Republican parties differ sharply on issues, whereas the broad party memberships often hold almost indistinguishable points of view. Democratic leaders can be counted on—with exceptions, of course—to take a stand that is pro-labor, pro-minority group, and pro-lower-income group in particular issues that arise. Republican leaders in general favor business and agriculture. Their followers, however, are not as likely to apply such broad ideology to specific issues. Instead, their opinions are more likely to have little relation to their party membership. In terms of political opinion, then, party leaders differ from their followers in that they show a greater political sophistication. Their greater involvement in the political system, their education, and their background in general allow them to maintain a more consistent ideology than that of the rank-and-file party members.

Recruitment of Members in Ruling Communist Parties.   In contrast to most Western political parties, ruling Communist parties, of which not many are left, do not actively recruit broad membership to support them at the next election. Instead, they try to limit their rolls to those members who will work most efficiently and actively for the cause. Party members are carefully picked for their intelligence, leadership qualities, and ideological suitability and are admitted to the full privileges of membership only when they have proved their worth and reliability. The result is that party membership is drawn heavily from the educated white-collar professional and technical classes. The Communist party needs skilled members with education, intelligence, and motivation far more than it needs broad numerical support at the polls.

FINANCING THE POLITICAL PARTY

Every organization is faced with the task of raising money to finance its activities, and this includes political parties. Imagine the financial problems involved in conducting a nationwide political campaign in the United States. In 1976, an estimated $540 million was spent on all political campaigns—presidential, congressional, state, and local. Just four years later, in 1980, an estimated $1 *billion* was spent for all political campaigns.[14] In 1996, it was closer to $3 billion. The parties have become desperate to raise money. The Republicans are more successful and outspend the Democrats in most contests.[15] Because we have no formal method for financing political parties, American parties are dependent in great part on voluntary contributions from wealthy donors. Many other countries have official methods for raising financial support.

The Party Membership Fee. In Great Britain, India, Israel, and most continental European nations, political party members, like members of a private club, are required to pay dues in order to keep their membership active. To attract as large a membership as possible, the fee is deliberately kept low. Although effective in this sense, the result is that the dues usually do not come close to covering operating expenses. Thus, parties must turn to external sources, and so the problem of fund-raising, which is so familiar to American parties, is felt on a smaller scale in other nations, too. There are many different solutions. In Germany and India, candidates are expected to contribute what they can to their own campaigns and their party's coffers. This favors wealthy candidates over politicians of only moderate means. Britain strictly limits the amount of money any single candidate can spend on a parliamentary campaign, holding candidates criminally liable for violations of campaign spending laws. Although raising money still presents problems for political parties of these nations, the scale of their dilemma is nowhere near that of the Republicans and the Democrats. Our presidential campaigns, including the primary elections in the spring, require over a year of speeches, appearances, and media exposure for at least one of the contenders. In contrast, European campaigns rarely last more than a couple of weeks to a month, so the expense is proportionally lower.

External Support. Japan, Israel, France, and Italy, like the United States, have laws that restrict or sharply regulate political contributions from industrial corporations, labor unions, and similar economic interest groups. Germany, Spain, Sweden, and Finland use government funds to subsidize political parties in proportion to each party's electoral strength. This system has been criticized for its obvious discrimination against new parties, however. The U.S. Congress in 1974 passed a similar plan (the Presidential Campaign Fund), which allowed taxpayers to authorize the Internal Revenue Service to donate $3 of their income tax payment to the fund; this fund subsidized presidential nominees in proportion to the votes they received, provided they got a minimum of 5 percent of the nationwide vote. About one taxpayer in four authorized the checkoff, not enough even nearly to cover campaign expenses. The Fund was ended by the Republican Congress in 1995. Political action committees (PACs; discussed in Chapter 10) have filled the vacuum with a vengeance. Now U.S. parties rely more and more on PACs, deepening the influence of interest groups.

Party Systems

There is a logical distinction between "parties" and "party systems." *Parties,* as discussed, are organizations aimed at influencing government, usually by winning elections. *Party systems* are the interactions of parties with each other and with the overall political systems. Much of the health of a political system depends on the party system, whether it is stable or unstable, whether it has too many parties, and whether they compete in a "center-seeking" or "center-fleeing" manner. An unstable party system can wreck an otherwise good constitution. Stable, moderate party systems made democracy possible in West Germany after Hitler and in Spain after Franco. In turn, much of the country's party system depends on its *electoral system—* whether it is based on single-member districts or on proportional representation.

CLASSIFYING PARTY SYSTEMS

The One-Party System. The one-party system, generally associated with totalitarian regimes of the left or right, is a twentieth-century phenomenon. The Soviet Union, China, and many of the emerging nations of Africa and Asia are or were one-party states. These are characterized by a single party that controls every level of government and is the only party legally allowed in the country.

The leaders of such parties rationalize that they are still democratic because they represent what the people really want and need. No fair election or honest public opinion poll can substantiate this claim. When allowed, as in East European countries, citizens repudiate the one-party system. Some developing lands, especially in Africa, argue that having several parties would spell chaos, for they would form along tribal lines.

The Dominant-Party System. The American South since the Civil War was until a generation ago the closet facsimile to a one-party system that America had to offer. Eleven states in the American South were traditional Democratic strong-holds: In these states, for many decades, the Republicans were so weak that they didn't even bother to run candidates for office. Likewise, Republicans traditionally controlled much of New England and the midwestern farm belt. It was rare for the Democrats to capture control of major state offices in these areas, and when they did they were rarely reelected. But a crucial factor separates these dominant-party systems, and their counterparts in Mexico and Japan, from true one-party states: Opposition parties in dominant-party systems are free to contest elections.[16] Of course, U.S. regional politics has changed in the last generation. Now every state has competing parties, and the South is nearly solidly Republican.

However, some democratic nations have dominant-party systems at the na-tional level as well. Since winning independence in 1947, India has been governed mostly by the Congress party. Although the Congress party is now in decline, the opposition has generally been too fragmented to win. Similarly, the Liberal-Demo-cratic party of Japan so consistently won that Japan was called a "one-and-a-half party system," with the much smaller Socialists being the half party.[17] In Mexico, the Party of Revolutionary Institutions (PRI) has also totally dominated since 1929, but not completely democratically.[18] The more conservative National Action party (PAN) has threatened civil disobedience if PRI's voting fraud does not cease. Mex-ico is a dominant-party system with a touch of single-party dictatorship.

The Two-Party System. Most familiar to us is the two-party system, found in the United States and Britain. Here two major parties have a fairly equal chance of win-ning. Although third parties, such as that of John Anderson's 1980 presidential at-tempt and Britain's Liberal Democrats, seldom win, they serve to remind the two big parties of voter discontent. Often one or both of the two main parties will then offer policies calculated to win over the discontented. In this way, even small third parties can have an impact.

The Multiparty System. On the other end of the continuum from one-party nations are those with several competing parties. The Swedish party system (as we saw in Figure 11.1) shows how its parties, arrayed on a left-to-right spectrum, re-ceive seats in parliament in proportion to their share of the vote. This system is often criticized as being unstable. Israel and Italy are examples of the shortcomings of having many parties, as each has been unable to keep any government in power for a long time. But whereas it is usually true that the existence of many political parties makes it harder for any one party to win a governing majority, this is not al-ways the case. The Netherlands, Sweden, and Norway generally manage to con-struct stable multiparty coalitions that govern effectively. The number of parties is not the only reason for cabinet instability. Much depends on the political culture, the degree of agreement on basic issues, and the rules for forming and dissolving a cabinet. Scholars have spent considerable effort debating which is better, two-party or multiparty systems. It's hard to say, for both have fallen prey to indecision and immobilism. In the meantime, there has been a drift in both systems toward a middle ground, "two-plus" party systems.

The Two-Plus Party System.   Many democratic countries now have two large parties with one or more relevant smaller parties. Germany has large Christian Democratic and Social Democratic parties, but the Free Democratic and Green parties win enough votes to make them politically important. Austria was long dominated by two big parties, but recently a third party, highly nationalistic, has made major gains.[19] Britain is often referred to as a two-party system, but it has long had third parties of some importance: the Liberal Democrats, the Scottish Nationalists, and Plaid Cymru (the Welsh nationalists). Even Spain, which has a history of multiparty fragmentation, now has a two-plus party system: a large Socialist party, a large center-right Popular party, and a scattering of smaller parties.

To be honest, we should also call the U.S. system two-plus, for it too has long had third parties, some of which were mentioned earlier. In 1912 Teddy Roosevelt stalked out of the Grand Old Party (GOP) with his "Bull Moose Republicans," splitting his party and giving the election to Wilson and the Democrats. In 1948, some southern Democrats ran as "Dixiecrats." In 1968, Governor George Wallace of Alabama won nearly 10 million votes for his implicitly racist American Independent party. The label "two-party" doesn't do justice to the complexity of U.S. politics.

As long as there are at least two parties, we call the system a "competitive party system." Even if there are only two parties, and they are not far apart ideologically (as in the United States), the essence of a competitive party system continues—which is to impede corruption. A single party that locks itself in power, whatever its ideological rationale, inevitably becomes corrupt. Corruption can be kept in check only by the "out" party or parties hammering away at alleged corruption in the administration of the "in" party. The utility of a competitive party system was underscored in 1989 in East Germany, where Communist leaders were revealed to have skimmed millions from foreign-trade deals and stashed them in Swiss banks for personal use. Such antics are generally short-lived in competitive party systems, for the "ins" are soon out.

DEGREE OF COMPETITION

Political scientist Giovanni Sartori, among others, is not completely satisfied with simply counting the number of parties to classify party systems. Also important is the degree and manner in which the parties *compete*. The term *multiparty system* does not differentiate between those systems that are stable and those that are unstable. Sartori's scheme does; it delineates party systems of "moderate pluralism" from those of "polarized pluralism."[20]

In the former, there are usually five parties or fewer, and they compete in a "center-seeking" or centripetal manner; that is, their platforms and promises appeal to middle-of-the-road voters. Left-wing parties curb their radicalism and right-wing parties dampen their conservatism, for both know that the bulk of the voting public is somewhere nearer the center. Thus political life in moderate pluralism tends to be calm and stable, with ideological considerations toned down.

When the number of parties is greater than five or six, Sartori believes, there is the danger of polarized pluralism. Here the parties may compete in a "center-fleeing" or centrifugal manner. Instead of moderating their positions, parties become ideologically extreme and engage in a "politics of outbidding" with their rivals. Many of the parties offer more and more radical solutions, either radical left or radical right. Some of the parties are "antisystem" or revolutionary. Parties that try to stick to the center find themselves attacked from both sides. Such a situation causes political instability, sometimes leading to civil war, as in Spain in the 1930s, or to military takeover, as in Chile in 1973.

"Relevant" Parties. Sartori includes a useful methodological note: Just what do you count as a party? Every group that calls itself a party? Every group that wins a certain percentage of votes or at least one seat in parliament? We should count as "relevant parties," Sartori argues, those which the main parties have to take into account either in campaigning for votes or in forming coalitions. If a party is so small and weak that no major party needs to worry about trying to win over its adherents, it is irrelevant. Likewise, if it is unnecessary in forming a governing coalition, it is irrelevant. Thus British Trotskyists and Irish Communists are ignored by all and don't count as parties, but Sweden's Liberals and Israel's small religious parties, each with only a few percentages of the vote, may be necessary coalition partners and thus count as relevant parties.

Using Sartori's definition of "relevant" parties, would we include various American third-party efforts? Although the Democrats in 1948 denied the importance of the States' Rights party (Dixiecrats) and in 1968 the importance of Wallace's forces, in both elections they took them into account. In 1968, Democratic nominee Hubert Humphrey visited the South and emphasized that the Democratic party was a "very big house" that could accommodate many viewpoints, a lame attempt to make southern voters forget the strong civil rights reforms of the Johnson administration.[21] In 1980, the independent candidacy of John Anderson probably forced President Carter to emphasize foreign and ecological policies he might otherwise have minimized. In 1992, Ross Perot forced Bush and Clinton to pay more attention to the federal budget deficit. In these cases, we could say the United States had relevant third parties. The tiny Communist, Socialist Worker, and Socialist Labor parties no one has to take into account, so under Sartori's definition we should not consider them relevant. The jury is still out on the Libertarian party, an extreme freemarket party that pledges the near dismantling of the federal government.

PARTY SYSTEM AND ELECTORAL SYSTEM

How a given nation gets its party system is often difficult to determine. Much is rooted in its unique historical developments. Some very different countries have similar party systems: Culturally segmented India produced a dominant party system (under the Congress party), as did culturally homogeneous Japan (under the Liberal Democrats). Single-factor explanations will not suffice, but political scientists generally agree on the importance of the electoral system.[22]

Single-member election districts, where a simple plurality wins, tend to produce two-party or two-plus systems. Such is the case in the United States and Britain, based on the original English model. The reason is not hard to understand: Small third parties are grossly underrepresented in such systems and often give up trying. There is a big premium in single-member districts on combining political forces to form the party with a majority or at least a plurality. If one party splits, it often throws the election to the party that hangs together. The factions within a party may not love each other, but they know they've got to stay together to have any political future. This factor goes a long way toward explaining why the two big American parties stay together despite considerable internal differences.

Proportional representation allows and perhaps even encourages parties to split. Proportional systems use multimember districts and assign parliamentary seats in proportion to the percentage of votes in that district. In the Anglo-American single-member districts, the winner takes all. In multimember districts, winners take just their percentage. Accordingly, not such a big premium is placed on holding parties together; a splinter group may decide that it can get one or two people elected without having to compromise with other viewpoints. Israel's proportional representation system helps in this way to produce its many small parties. As we will discuss in Chapter 13, modification of electoral laws can change a country's party system, pushing a country from a multiparty to a two-plus system, as in Germany, or from a multiparty system to a "two-bloc" system, as in France. Interestingly, when France shifted to a proportional system for the 1986 legislative elections, the small, racist National Front won seats for the first time, illustrating how proportional systems encourage minor parties.

THE U.S. PARTY SYSTEM: COULD IT BE DIFFERENT?

There's a great deal of valid criticism of American political parties. Because they are so dependent on affluent donors and PACs, they are open to immoderate special-interest influence. Because they are so weakly organized and so highly decentralized—in effect, every congressional district and state has its own parties, little related to each other—the parties do not cohere at the national level and are rarely able to articulate clear-cut platforms and policy goals. Because there are only two main parties, each usually aiming for the political center, they are not able to offer votes an extensive menu to choose from. Most political scientists agree that U.S. parties, especially in contrast to their West European counterparts, are weak.

Can anything be done about this? Parties and party systems are rooted in their countries' history, society, and institutions. The U.S. Constitution never recognized parties, and the Founding Fathers warned against them. American society is not terribly fragmented; it may not need more than two parties to express the general divisions within the population. And of course the single-member district with a simple plurality win favors a two-party system. Realistically, we can expect no major change in America's two-party system.

But could there be changes in the way the two parties function? Already there may be some move toward party centralization. President Reagan made the Republicans a more thoroughly conservative party with a reasonably clear program.[23] This continued when disciplined House Republicans passed their "Contract With America" in 1995. These policy initiatives have forced the Democrats to get their often incoherent act together. Some of the "reforms" the Democrats had carried out in the 1970s proved to have weakened and divided the party; the reforms themselves had to be reformed.[24] Technology is helping to centralize the parties. Computerized mailing lists are a powerful inducement for state and local party organizations to cooperate with national headquarters. The national party committees can also channel PAC money to loyal candidates. In the long run, this may make the two parties more cohesive and ideologically consistent.

There may be a certain advantage in *not* having strong parties. Strong parties may fall into the hands of oligarchic leaders who control too much and stay on too long, getting the party stuck in rigid and outmoded viewpoints. The U.S. system, by virtue of its very fluidity, may be better able to process demands from a wider range of citizens. The lack of programmatic coherence confers the benefit of flexibility.

Suggested Readings

ALDRICH, JOHN H. *Why Parties? The Origin and Transformation of Political Parties in America.* Chicago: University of Chicago Press, 1995. U.S. parties continually evolve to meet new situations.

EPSTEIN, LEON D. *Political Parties in the American Mold.* Madison: University of Wisconsin Press, 1986. A masterful review by a top scholar of what has been happening to U.S. parties.

KEEFE, WILLIAM J. *Parties, Politics, and Public Policy in America,* 6th ed. Washington, DC: CQ Press, 1991. The multifaceted role of U.S. parties and why the American electorate is not too happy with them.

KLINGEMANN, HANS-DIETER, RICHARD I. HOFFERBERT, and IAN BUDGE. *Parties, Policies, and Democracy.* Boulder, CO: Westview Press, 1994. A deep and important ten-country probe of how parties formulate and initiate polices.

LANE, JAN-ERIK, and SVANTE O. ERSSON. *Politics and Society in Western Europe,* 3d ed. Thousand Oaks, CA: Sage, 1994. An excellent, up-to-date review of European party systems.

LAVER, MICHAEL, and W. BEN HUNT. *Policy and Party Competition.* New York: Routledge, 1992. How parties use policy issues in political competition, with data from twenty-four democracies.

McHALE, VINCENT, ed. *Political Parties of Europe.* Westport, CT: Greenwood, 1983. Encyclopedic handbook detailing all of Europe's parties, including historical ones, by country.

MAIR, PETER, ed. *The West European Party System.* New York: Oxford, 1990. Good choice of both classic and recent discussions of parties in Western Europe.

MAISEL, L. SANDY, ed. *The Parties Respond: Developments in the American Party System.* Boulder, CO: Westview Press, 1990. Top scholars in the area discuss changes in U.S. parties.

MILKIS, SIDNEY M. *The President and the Parties: The Transformation of the American Party System Since the New Deal.* New York: Oxford, 1993. Provocative argument that as the presidency gets stronger, U.S. parties get weaker.

MILLER, WARREN E. *Without Consent: Mass-Elite Linkages in Presidential Politics.* Lexington: University of Kentucky, 1988. A master of party and voting studies uses the election of 1984 to see if parties respond to members.

RANDALL, VICKY, ed., *Political Parties in the Third World.* Ithaca, NY: Russell Sage, 1988. A useful collection of essays showing that even in dictatorships parties still exist and play useful roles.

SORAUF, FRANK J., and PAUL ALLEN BECK. *Party Politics in America,* 7th ed. New York: HarperCollins, 1992. A comprehensive survey of the U.S. party system.

WOLINETZ, STEVEN B., ed. *Parties and Party Sytems in Liberal Democracies.* New York: Routledge, 1989. An excellent overview of change among the parties of Western Europe and North America.

Notes

1. E. E. Schattschneider, *Party Government* (New York: Holt, Rinehart & Winston, 1942), p. 1.

2. Leon D. Epstein, *Political Parties in Western Democracies* (New York: Praeger, 1967), p. 9.

3. For a theoretical explanation of interest group aggregation, see Gabriel A. Almond and G. Bingham Powell, Jr., *Comparative Politics: System, Process, and Policy*, 2nd ed. (Boston: Little, Brown, 1978), Chap. 8.

4. Seymour Martin Lipset stressed the positive function leftist political parties play in integrating the working class into the system. See *Political Man: The Social Bases of Politics* (New York: Anchor Books, 1963), pp. 22–24.

5. Schattschneider, *Party Government*, p. 209.

6. Maurice Duverger, *Political Parties: Their Organization and Activities in the Modern State*, 3rd ed. (London: Methuen, 1964).

7. In Europe, such parties are called "liberal" parties, but this means the classic liberalism discussed in Chapter 6. See Emil J. Kirchner, ed., *Liberal Parties in Western Europe* (New York: Cambridge University Press, 1988).

8. Otto Kirchheimer, "Germany: The Vanishing Opposition," in *Political Oppositions in Western Democracies*, ed. Robert A. Dahl (New Haven, CT: Yale University Press, 1966).

9. Frank P. Belloni, and Dennis C. Beller, eds., *Faction Politics: Political Parties and Factionalism in Comparative Perspective* (Santa Barbara, CA: ABC-Clio, 1978).

10. Samuel J. Eldersveld, *Political Parties: A Behavioral Analysis* (Chicago: Rand McNally, 1964), pp. 118–34.

11. Lester G. Seligman, "Political Recruitment and Party Structure: A Case Study," *American Political Science Review* 55 (March 1961), 77–86.

12. Kenneth Prewitt, *The Recruitment of Political Leaders: A Study of Citizen Politicians* (Indianapolis, IN: Bobbs-Merrill, 1970). See Chapter 5 for a discussion of the elite view of American politics, which Prewitt represents.

13. For a review and summation of elite-mass differences, see Joseph LaPalombara, *Politics Within Nations* (Englewood Cliffs, NJ: Prentice Hall, 1974), pp. 489–94.

14. Herbert E. Alexander, *Financing Politics: Money, Elections, and Political Reform*, 3rd ed. (Washington, DC: CQ Press, 1984), p. 9.

15. Gary C. Jacobson, "Party Organization and Distribution of Campaign Resources: Republicans and Democrats in 1982," *Political Science Quarterly* 100 (Winter 1985–86), 4.

16. See T. J. Pempel, ed., *Uncommon Democracies: The One-Party Dominant Regimes* (Ithaca, NY: Cornell University Press, 1990).

17. See Ronald J. Hrebenar, *The Japanese Party System: From One-Party Rule to Coalition Government* (Boulder, CO: Westview Press, 1987).

18. See Dale Story, *The Mexican Ruling Party: Stability and Authority* (Westport, CT: Praeger, 1986).

19. See Anton Pelinka and Fritz Plasser, eds., *The Austrian Party System* (Boulder, CO: Westview Press, 1989).

20. Giovanni Sartori, *Parties and Party Systems: A Framework for Analysis*, Vol. 1 (New York: Cambridge University Press, 1976), pp. 131–85.

21. For the transformation of the "solid South," see Nicol C. Rae, *Southern Democrats* (New York: Oxford, 1994).

22. See Douglas W. Rae, *The Political Consequences of Electoral Laws* (New Haven, CT: Yale University Press, 1967).

23. See David B. Truman, "Party Reform, Party Atrophy, and Constitutional Change: Some Reflections," *Political Science Quarterly* 99 (Winter 1984–85), 4.

24. For a sharp criticism of what the Democrats did to themselves, see Nelson W. Polsby, *Consequences of Party Reform* (New York: Oxford University Press, 1983).

· 12 ·
Voting

In this chapter we ask three general questions about voting behavior, each followed by a more specific question about voting behavior in the United States. First, we ask why people vote. This leads us immediately to the puzzle of why voting turnout in the United States is so low. Second, we ask how people vote. This brings us to the question of whether party loyalties in the United States are declining or merely shifting. Finally, we ask what wins elections. This takes us to some of the strategies that are applied in U.S. elections.

Why Do People Vote?

In a nation with a strong commitment to democracy and participation, one would expect citizens to show great interest in politics and voting. Curiously, Americans vote considerably less than citizens of other democracies. In the 1992 election, only 55 percent of those eligible to vote in the United States bothered to cast a ballot. And historically, voter turnout in the United States was never very high; it hit a peak of 63 percent in 1960 but by 1988 had declined to 50.16 percent.[1] Election turnout in Sweden, Germany, and Italy sometimes tops 90 percent. Black South Africans in 1994 had not been allowed to vote, yet turnout was 86 percent, perhaps a measure of how much they appreciated the right to cast a democratic ballot.

In nonpresidential elections, U.S. turnout is even worse, perhaps a quarter to a third. Why do Americans have such a poor voting record? Apathy and indecisiveness are partly responsible. Typically, more than half of U.S. nonvoters say they aren't interested in or are dissatisfied with the candidates. Many feel their vote won't make a difference; even more feel that none of the candidates is really good. Another reason is the U.S. party system, in which the two large parties may not offer an interesting or clear-cut choice; both tend to stick to centrist positions. In addition, television saturates voters so long in advance—often with primitive, dirty political spots—that many voters are disgusted with both parties by election day. Fewer than one adult American in twenty is involved enough in politics to attend a political meeting, contribute money, or canvass a neighborhood.[2]

Nonvoting in the United States has inspired a major debate among political scientists concerning both its causes and its meaning. One school views the decline with alarm, arguing that low electoral participation means that many Americans are turning away from the political system, which in turn is losing its legitimacy and authority. If this keeps up, democracy itself could be threatened. Another school is more sanguine, arguing that the decline may mean that Americans are basically satisfied with the system, or at any rate not sufficiently dissatisfied to go to the effort of registering and voting. Indeed, countries with very high voter turnouts may be suffering from a sort of political fever in which partisan politics has become dangerously intense.

In Western Europe, three-quarters or more of the citizens routinely vote; in the United States only half vote. Why the difference? One obvious reason is that in Europe registration is automatic. As soon as one reaches the age of eighteen, one is ready to vote. Local authorities, in effect, do the voters' registering for them. In contrast, America's residency laws and sometimes ponderous registration procedures can present an obstacle to the would-be voter. The citizen, not the government, carries the burden of making sure that any details, such as change of name or residency, are recorded in the official accounts. This requirement may involve the inconvenience of a special visit to the official place of registration several weeks before the election.[3] By the time that campaign excitement has begun to mount, the deadline for registration is long past. Further, elections are held on working days (in much of Europe, voting takes place on Sundays), and the lineup of local, state, and national candidates is often enough to baffle all but those who have memorized the sample ballots. European ballots are simple, usually just a choice of party, and all European countries strictly control and limit TV political advertising; some allow none. America might take a hint.

WHO VOTES?

In his landmark work, *An Economic Theory of Democracy*, Anthony Downs theorized that people will vote if the returns outweigh the costs.[4] That is, if the stakes seem important enough, the citizen will go to the trouble of voting. Thus, the person whose property taxes stand to be raised if a new school bond is passed is much more likely to vote on the issue than his or her neighbor who rents an apartment and will not be hurt by the tax. The cost of political information, both financial and personal, is also influential in determining whether a person will vote. The price of a newspaper, the sacrifice of switching from a favorite TV show to watch the news, and the time involved in attending a political meeting all tend to prevent political information from being distributed equally to everyone because each person places a different value on personal time and political awareness.

The result is that the poor and the uneducated in every society are the least likely to vote. Historically, the typical American nonvoter was a young woman married to a blue-collar worker, with little formal education. Why? Because relatively poor, she had few financial investments and probably felt she had little economic stake in the election outcome. Being poorly educated, the cost of getting political information, in terms of time taken from other interests and chores, was likely to outweigh the benefits she felt she derived from a knowledge of current affairs. Her lack of education also made her part of a tradition in which her gender stayed clear of politics. She was therefore likely to take voting less seriously than men. It should be pointed out that far fewer women fit this pattern than before. More and more, women work outside the home, are educated, and are less likely to defer to male political judgments. Accordingly, women's turnout now resembles men's. Still, the typical voters in almost every democracy are middle-aged, better educated, with white-collar jobs. They are more likely to vote in a national election if they live in a city than if they live in the country. And they are more likely to vote if they identify strongly with a political party than if they call themselves independents.

Within these broad generalizations of characteristics of the typical voter and the typical nonvoter, it is possible to identify several specific factors that are likely to have an influence on whether a person votes or not. Although personality is important, income and education, race, age, gender, and area of residence all act in a predictable manner.

Income and Education. People who enjoy a high income are more likely to vote than those who are less affluent, and people who are well educated are more likely to vote than those who dropped out of high school. Are they in fact the same individuals? Not quite, for a wealthy person who did not finish high school is almost as likely to vote as a wealthy college graduate. Even though certain voters often combine these characteristics (good education makes it easier to earn a good salary), the two influence voting in rather different ways. One is a matter of having a stake in election outcomes, the other a broader question of interest and sophistication.

According to the Survey Research Center, assembly-line workers living in small towns may see little difference between a Bob Dole and a Bill Clinton.[5] They are accustomed to paying taxes, following rules and regulations, and making a living through hard work. They are likely to see little difference in the way they fare under a Democratic administration as opposed to a Republican one and therefore feel that they have little stake in the election's outcome. In contrast, presidents of large corporations feel involved in the election. They see a direct cause-and-effect relationship between who wins the election and their personal fortune, which will be affected by changes in international monetary policy, personal and corporate tax reforms, government policy toward organized labor, interest rates, and a score of other complex fiscal policies. Of course, blue-collar workers may be affected by a change in the administration, but they are less likely to be aware of the stakes.

The difference between upper-class voters and working-class nonvoters is primarily a feeling of *efficacy*. Assembly workers feel that their votes will make little difference. Corporation presidents, on the other hand, believe that their participation is important to the political process and that the difference between one candidate and the next is likely to be significant. Although a change in the party in office is likely to have an impact on blue-collar workers, we can see why corporation presidents feel that the stakes are more important. In their experience, they have seen interest groups and private associations succeed in changing government policy, if only by successfully influencing the local school board to expand a school bus route. In contrast, blue-collar workers are likely to see American political life from the perspective of the "silent majority" subculture. Friends, neighbors, and family have never had any wealth and have never organized to pressure the government successfully.[6]

Many well-educated people have broader interests in elections beyond personal economic stakes. More widely read and more sophisticated than the high school graduate (or dropout), the college-educated person—whether wealthy or not—tends to be more interested, better informed, and more likely to participate in elections.[7] As our discussion in Chapter 7 indicates, schooling helps to provide both a sense of the importance of political participation and a more abstract intellectual curiosity, which makes people more likely to read papers, keep abreast of the news, and feel involved in the political events of their nation and local area.

Race.   Despite federal laws and black organizations, black voting rates are lower than white—about 10 percentage points lower in 1992.[8] The gap may eventually close. Black income and education levels have risen. The 1965 Voting Rights Act overcame many of the barriers placed in the way of black registration, chiefly in the South. Southern black registration rose from 29 percent in 1960 to 63 percent in 1976. In 1984 and 1988, Jesse Jackson campaigned doggedly for the Democratic nomination even though he knew he didn't stand a chance; he did it to encourage blacks to register, and they did. Important in this has been the political consciousness-raising blacks have gone through in the last generation. Many have learned the value of participation and of voting. Some previously racist white politicians got the message and became respectful toward their black constituents. Latinos faced similar problems and also showed low turnouts. Race, accordingly, is still a factor in U.S. election turnout.

Age.   Young people—those under twenty-five—typically feel less politically involved than those who are older; accordingly, they vote less. About half of U.S. citizens eighteen to twenty-five years of age are currently not registered to vote. (This is probably not the case in your political science class, first because you are college students and second because you're at least a little interested in politics.) Nonvoting among the young parallels our discussion of income and voting. Young people, with lower incomes and little property, don't feel economically involved with election outcomes. When they start paying substantial taxes, they become much more interested. Focused on the concerns of youth, many have no time or interest in political questions, which may seem abstract and distant. When jobs become a major issue, however, younger people can quickly take an interest.

In 1971 the Twenty-sixth Amendment lowered the U.S. voting age from twenty-one to eighteen. Interestingly, at almost the same time, most other democracies did the same. The results were similar: The newly enfranchised young people didn't vote as much as their elders, and when they did vote, their preferences weren't much different. Middle-aged and older people are more likely to vote than the young, probably because the middle-aged person is at a peak in earning power and the old person is concerned about Social Security and Medicare. In 1994, those over 70 actually had the highest turnout.[9]

Black voter registration in recent decades has enfranchised a group of citizens who previously had little political clout but who now are courted by candidates of both parties.

Gender.   Traditionally, men were more likely to vote than women in almost every society,[10] largely because women had only comparatively recently won the right to vote. (Switzerland's female population was enfranchised only in 1971.) Since 1920, when female suffrage was granted in the United States, the gap between men's and women's voter turnout has been narrowing steadily. Now the difference in turnout between genders in U.S. elections is negligible.

Area of Residence.   City dwellers are more likely to vote than rural residents. This fact probably reflects the easier accessibility of voting booths in the cities, where a relatively few blocks can make up a voting district with the same population as a rural district of many square miles. In France, unlike Britain and the United States, rural areas traditionally turn out a higher percentage of voters than do cities because in France local politics in small towns is conducted on a much more intimate level than the depersonalized politics of the big city.

People who have lived in the same place for a long time are more likely to vote than are transients or newcomers, for long-time inhabitants of any community feel more involved in their neighborhood affairs and are therefore more likely to participate in groups and activities that will sustain their community.

Voter turnout in the United States is somewhat lighter in the South than in the North and West, even in urban areas. Traditionally lower participation in the South reflected a number of influences, including a lower standard of living for that region of the nation and a traditional lack of strong party competition in the area because of the once unquestioned predominance of the Democratic party. Many of the traditional characteristics of the South and its politics have changed, and now turnout in the South is approaching turnout in other areas of the country. Other nations are also characterized by regional differences in voter participation. In France, the areas south of the Loire River have a lower voter turnout than the northern areas of the country.

Bear in mind: These categories merely explain why some people vote more than others. They do not explain why U.S. voting turnout *overall* is the lowest of the advanced democracies. Indeed U.S. educational levels have been *growing* during the period voting turnout was slumping, and eduction is supposed to make one more participatory.

How Do People Vote?

The reasons that people vote as they do are many and complex. Deep loyalty to a political party, the advice of a friend, fondness for one candidate and distrust of another, and feelings about an issue—each of these can have an overriding effect on a voter's election decision. The influences that determine the way a person will vote can be grouped according to the type of effect they have on the individual voter's political leanings. The result is a pattern of *long-term* and *short-term variables.* For example, many working-class Britons have always been Labourites and will continue to vote Labour for the rest of their years. The same is true of many American

Democrats and Republicans. An affiliation with a political party is a long-term influence: It affects the way a person votes for his or her entire lifetime. In contrast, there are short-term variables, which may cause a person to vote one way or another for one election year but won't influence his or her ballot three or four years later. Margaret Thatcher shrewdly called British elections in 1983 to catch the glow of military victory in the Falklands and again in 1987 during an economic upswing and disarray in Labour's ranks. Her Conservatives won both times.[11] Similarly, in 1976 in the United States, Jimmy Carter benefited from a "morality factor" awakened by the Watergate scandal. In 1992, however, voters deserted President Bush, whose popularly had soared during the 1991 Gulf War, in favor of Bill Clinton and the promise of economic recovery. A particular candidate or a specific issue can have the effect of changing a person's vote for one election without causing any permanent shift in party loyalty.

PARTY IDENTIFICATION

Party identification—party ID, for short—is the tendency many people have to associate themselves mentally with one party over many years. Strong party identifiers habitually vote for that party without question. Weak identifiers can be swayed sometimes to vote for another party. People with no party ID are up for grabs and may shift their votes with every election. Remember, party ID is something that people carry around in their heads; it is not something that parties carry around.

For some people, party ID is strong enough to be compared with a religious affiliation. It is heavily influenced by one's parents and is instilled early in life. By the time they reach fourth grade, something like half of all schoolchildren consider themselves either Democrats or Republicans. And many never change the affiliation they inherited from their parents.

Why does party ID remain a stable element throughout many people's lives? One reason is that what we learn as small children has a way of staying with us. Like a preference for certain foods learned in childhood, a preference for one party is difficult to shake. Another reason is that it is easier to vote along party lines. Party identification provides the easiest means of marking the complicated U.S. ballots. It provides a shortcut for election decision making—a "standing decision." Persons who call themselves Democrats are automatically predisposed toward any Democratic candidate, whether they realize it or not. When asked how they feel about the Republican candidate, they will probably express suspicion of the candidate and his or her views.

Party ID is an important element in electoral stability. People who stick pretty much to one party are like a foundation, allowing politicians to anticipate what people want and to try to deliver it. Weak party ID produces great "volatility" in voting, as citizens, like ships without keels, blow this way and that in the political winds. It is with some concern, then, that political scientists notice a decline in the number of party identifiers in the United States, a topic we shall explore presently.

Party Identification in Europe. Whereas American political parties have some effect on the way most people vote, most European parties are more influential in determining an individual's election choice. Since World War II, Britain has largely been characterized by a consistent split between Labour and Conservative supporters.[12] The "swing" from one major party to another during national elections ranges from only about 1 percent to 5 percent. In voting for representatives to Parliament, over two-thirds of British voters can be counted on to return the same party to Commons.

Great Britain and the United States both have two-party systems. What effect does party identification have in nations with multiparty systems? One study compared party identifiers (as opposed to all voters) in the multiparty system of Norway with those in the American two-party system and found that Norwegian identifiers were significantly more likely to vote along party lines than were American Democrats or Republicans.[13] The smaller political parties of Norway represent more tightly knit points of view. Thus, party identifiers in Norway are more able to express a personal ideology through their vote, unlike Republicans or Democrats in the United States. Not all European systems with several competing parties are characterized by high party identification. A comparative study of French and American voters found that whereas 75 percent of Americans classified themselves as either Republicans or Democrats, less than 45 percent of the French were members of one of their nation's political parties.[14] The French party system, unlike that of Norway, was at that time characterized by many short-lived parties. The authors of the French-American study felt that the confusion caused by these rapid changes was one reason for France's low degree of party identification. Their findings indicate that multiparty systems don't necessarily mean high voter identification with political parties.

Does party identification influence the European voter differently than in the United States? Leon D. Epstein argues that it does.[15] Whereas a relatively high percentage of American voters identifies with a political party, Epstein feels that this party identification means something different in the American, as opposed to the European, setting. Many Americans are registered with a party, but they cannot always be counted on to vote according to their party registration. On the other hand, Europeans, few of whom are party members, are more likely to vote according to their party memberships once they have established such loyalties.

WHO VOTES HOW?

No one can predict with absolute accuracy the voting in a free and fair election, but using the same social categories discussed in Chapter 8 (on public opinion) and earlier in this chapter (on voting turnout), political scientists can arrive at a general description of what kinds of people tend to identify with the various parties.[16] Bear in mind that no social category votes 100 percent for a given party; people are highly individualistic and often go their own way, disregarding group norms. This fact accounts for some poor Republicans and some rich Democrats. If more than half of a given social category supports and votes for one party, there is probably a significant relationship between the social category and the party. If three-quarters identifies with a party, there is a strong relationship. We are making statements here that indicate a *tendency,* not an absolute relationship. Political scientists learn to say things like "Catholics *tend* to vote Democrat," and not "All Catholics are Democrats." Notice in Table 12.1 that 53 percent of Catholics in 1996 voted for Clinton, but 37 percent voted for Dole. Beware of absolute statements.

Once practicing politicians (and sometimes political scientists) detect a tendency in a group to identify with a certain party, they call it a *voting bloc.* The candidates' strategy is then to secure enough blocs to deliver a majority of the electorate, and they tailor their campaign to win over the blocs most likely to vote for them. The concept of voting blocs is an oversimplification, however, for there is no such thing as a solid bloc. Consider, for example, the "working-class vote."

Class Voting. As discussed in Chapter 8, social class is one determinant of party identification and voting behavior. Even in the United States, where class distinctions are blurred, blue-collar workers tend to register and vote Democratic. This tendency is especially strong in families in which the breadwinners are union members. Notice in Table 12.1 how "union households" was one of the few categories that went over 55 percent for Clinton in the 1996 election. In most Euro-

TABLE 12.1　Who Voted How in 1996

	Clinton	Dole	Perot
Overall	49%	41%	8%
Men	43	44	10
Women	54	38	7
Whites	43	46	9
Blacks	84	12	4
College graduate	44	46	8
High school graduate	51	35	13
Less than high school	59	28	11
18–29 years old	53	34	10
30–44 years old	48	41	9
45–59 years old	48	41	9
60 and older	48	44	7
White Protestant	36	53	10
Catholic	53	37	9
Jewish	78	16	3
Union household	59	30	9
Family income			
under $15,000	59	28	11
$15–$30,000	53	36	9
$30–$50,000	48	40	10
over $50,000	44	48	7
over $75,000	41	51	7
over $100,000	38	54	6
East	55	34	9
Midwest	48	41	9
South	46	46	7
West	48	40	8

Copyright © 1996 by *The New York Times.* Reprinted by permission.

pean countries, this tendency is stronger, for unions are often connected to social-democratic or labor parties. This relationship doesn't always work to deliver the vote, however. The gigantic Swedish union, LO, can reliably deliver the labor vote to the Social Democrats in Swedish elections. But in recent British elections only a minority of union members voted Labour.

The middle and upper classes tend to have more conservative political leanings. In 1996, notice that the higher the family income, the greater the tendency to vote for Dole. Better-off Britons and Swedes are also more likely to support their respective conservative parties. Two things muddy class voting. Some working-class people—because they consider themselves middle class, have a family tradition, or have individual convictions—vote for conservative parties. A majority of the U.S. and British working class voted, respectively, Republican in 1988 and Conservative in 1987. Conversely, some middle- and even upper-class people—because they are of working-class origins, have a family tradition, or have individual convictions—vote for parties on the left. Such people are especially important in providing working-class parties with educated leadership. Most of Europe's labor, social democratic, or socialist parties are led by middle-class intellectuals. This two-way crossover—working class identifying with conservatives and middle class identifying with the left—dilutes class voting until it virtually disappears in some elections. In hard economic times, however, class voting can reappear as a major factor, as it did in 1996.

Regional Voting.   Some regions identify strongly with certain parties. Often these are areas that have been conquered and subjugated centuries ago, and the inhabitants still harbor resentments. South of the Loire River, the French tend to vote Socialist. Scotland and Wales vote heavily Labour. And in the United States, the southern states used to be solidly Democratic. By the 1980s, regional loyalties had so shifted that the South is now the strongest area for the Republicans; and the East—which following the Civil War had been a Republican bastion—is now weakest for the Republicans.[17]

Religious Blocs.   Religion can have an even deeper impact than region. In France, for example, devout Catholics vote mostly conservative; nonreligious people vote mostly left.[18] The same applies to Italy, where the Popular party was founded by and is still linked to the Roman Catholic church. The Catholic areas of Germany are more likely to vote Christian Democrat than are the Protestant areas. In the United States, Catholics and Jews tend to vote Democrat, whereas white Protestants tend to vote Republican, tendencies that were borne out in 1996.

Age Groups.   It's not necessarily true that younger people are more radical than their elders. Rather, they tend to catch the tide that is flowing in their youth and stay with it. Young people socialized to politics during the Depression tend to identify with the Democratic party all their lives. By the same token, Republicans hope that the enthusiasm for Reagan among young voters in the 1980s will give them a permanent sense of identification with the Republican party. Age groups react in part to the economic situation. Many young voters felt that Republican policies of growth would lead to jobs, but many retired voters feared Republican cuts in Social Security and Medicare. This leads to retired voters being more liberal than young ones. In 1996, retired voters went heavily to Clinton.

Gender Gap.   It also used to be assumed that women were more traditional and conservative than men, but that tendency has been reversed in the United States. Women voted for Clinton in 1996 by several percentage points more than men. Women have been voting more for the Democrats for some time. They tend to like the Democrats' support for welfare measures and for abortion rights and to dislike the Republicans' opposition to such views.[19]

Racial Minorities.   Blacks are the most loyal Democrats by far; over 80 percent of those who vote generally vote for Democrats. A majority of Hispanic voters also identify with the Democrats, but Asian Americans in 1996 went for Dole. The affinity of racial minorities for the Democrats, however, may cost the party some white votes. Republicans are delighted to portray the Democrats as the party of minorities, feminists, and labor unions—and to portray themselves as the party of everyone else.[20]

Urban Voting.   One of the few laws political science can offer is that big cities vote liberal or left wing. This is explained, partly, by the concentration of the working-class vote in cities—for big cities have big factories. In addition, cities are also centers of education and sophistication, places where intellectuals are often drawn to liberal and leftist causes. Country and suburban dwellers tend to embrace conservative values and vote for conservative parties. England votes overwhelmingly Tory, but not the city of London. Germany's Bavaria is a conservative stronghold, but not the people of Munich. Italy was long dominated by the Christian Democrats, but not Italy's urban population. The mayors of most large American cities are Democrats; even recent Republican gains failed to alter the voting tendencies of U.S. cities.

Electoral Realignment

For some decades political scientists have debated a theory of *critical* or *realigning elections*.[21] Typically people retain their party identification for a long time, sometimes all their lives. But, according to this theory, in several watershed presidential elections, the party loyalties of many voters dissolve, and they establish new, durable party identities. These "critical elections" do not determine how every election will go, but they set the terms of debate and the main topics to be debated. They give one party dominance, although not absolute control. The critical or realigning elections in U.S. history are usually seen as the following:

1800, the emergence of Jefferson's Democratic Republicans
1828, the emergence of Jacksonian populist Democrats
1860, the emergence of Lincoln's Republicans
1896, the emergence of business Republicanism
1932, the emergence of Roosevelt's New Deal Democrats

Between these critical elections, party identifications are stable and most people vote according to them. This is called the "normal vote" or "maintaining elections."[22] Occasionally, enough voters will disregard their party identification to elect the weaker party: Democrat Grover Cleveland in 1884 and 1892, Democrat Woodrow Wilson in 1912 and 1916, and Republican Dwight Eisenhower in 1952 and 1956. These have been called "deviating elections" because the party shift was only temporary; afterward voters went back to their long-term party ID.[23]

A Reagan Realignment?   Republicans anticipated that the Reagan sweeps of 1980 and 1984 marked a realignment in party identification in their favor. Party registration rose for Republicans and declined for Democrats until the parties were about equal in size. Young people, in particular, who are the future of any party, registered and voted Republican. Even more important, Reagan and his intellectual supporters restructured the ideological debate in a conservative direction (see Chapter 6). It was no longer fashionable, as it had been from the election of Franklin D. Roosevelt to the election of Jimmy Carter, to talk about using the powers of government to fix social ills and provide welfare programs. Instead, the political debates concerned how to lower taxes, cut government spending, limit government regulation, reduce the federal deficit, and restore growth through free enterprise. Before Reagan, even Republicans went along with the welfare state, and some of the biggest expansions of welfare programs occurred under Nixon. After Reagan, even the Democrats demanded fiscal responsibility.

But realignments don't come with name tags. It might not be possible to tell if there has been a realignment until some decades later. Furthermore, it may be difficult to spot the precise election in which realignment occurred. Looking at the results of the 1968 election, which brought Nixon to the White House, and carefully dissecting regional trends, Kevin Phillips concluded in 1969 that a Republican majority was emerging.[24] Which, then, was the critical election, 1968 or 1980? If it was 1968, it would mark Carter's election in 1976 as a "deviating election," and, indeed, Carter's victory was largely the result of the Watergate scandal. What was missing from the Nixon years, however, was the ideological conservatism that came with Reagan. We might say that the ingredients for a realignment in favor of the Republicans came with the 1968 election but did not fully coalesce until 1980. What we have then is not a single "critical" election but a time period in which realignment occurred.

If there was a Republican realignment it took some time to reach congressional races. Even during the Reagan landslides, the House of Representatives stayed in Democrat hands, and in 1986 the Senate moved back under Democratic control. In 1994, both houses came under Republican control. Congressional contests, heavily focused on local interests, are relatively insulated from the tides that turn presidential elections. Voters typically look to their representative for services and economic benefits. Often, in these situations, Democrats are better able to deliver than Republicans, who preach (but do not always practice) cutting government programs.

How, then, can we tell if there has been a realignment? If the Republicans regain the presidency, and if they perpetuate their power in Congress, there will be a greater case for a realignment. The economic downturn during a Republican presidency and the Clinton victory in 1992 suggest that the theory of electoral realignment will have to be reexamined. If voters react mostly to current situations and candidates' personalities, the basic supposition of party identification will have to be reconsidered. Perhaps party ID is not as important as it once was. Instead of realignment, we may be seeing dealignment.

ELECTORAL DEALIGNMENT

Since the mid-1960s, the number of voters committed to neither party has increased sharply. In 1948, under 20 percent of U.S. voters called themselves independents. Some polls show more people calling themselves independent than Democrat or Republican.[25] What happened to produce this major change, and what does it mean for American politics?

Studies in the 1950s indicated that people calling themselves independents tended to be least involved in and least informed about politics. This is no longer the case, as many independents are now well informed and politically concerned. Independents tend to be young and college educated. They also came of age during extraordinary times. In 1964 they heard the Democratic candidate for president promise not to send Americans to fight in Vietnam. In 1974 they saw a Republican president resign in shame. Their faith in conventional party politics was considerably shaken; both major parties appeared to be dishonest. This was also the time when the postwar "baby boom" came of age, swelling the numbers of young people who were disillusioned.

Governing the United States had become more difficult. Inflation, unemployment, slow economic growth, and the pressing demands of various groups contribute to dissatisfaction with both parties, which struggled with these problems without much success. Some political scientists noted that this process coincided with three trends: (1) declining voter turnout, (2) declining party loyalty, and (3) declining trust in the government in Washington. Do the three items hang together? Which causes which? Declining political trust is probably the underlying cause, giving rise to the other two.

If things keep on like this, is there a danger for U.S. democracy? There well could be. Presidents are not voted in by a majority of those eligible, only by a majority of those actually voting. With only about half of those eligible voting, presidents often win with only one-quarter or less (if there is a third-party candidate) of the total electorate behind them, hardly a claim for an impressive mandate. Further, the high numbers of independents, when they decide to vote, easily shift their loyalties more on the basis of mood and the candidate's personality than according to issues. This voter volatility makes the country hard to govern, for it deprives elected officials of stability and predictability. Voters become too fickle for any president to please them. Interest groups and media replace parties.[26]

Some researchers doubt there is any significant trend toward electoral dealignment and independent voting. Many voters who call themselves "independent" actually lean to one party or the other, and they vote for that party rather reliably. Instead of the third of the electorate that say they're independent, claim these researchers, only 15 percent are genuine neutrals, and this amounts to only 11 percent who actually cast ballots (because genuine independents tend to be more apathetic about elections). The size of the independent vote is exaggerated and nothing to worry about, they charge. By the time you count the weak identifiers, party ID in the United States is largely unchanged.[27]

What Wins Elections?

In theory, elections are when citizens get to choose and guide their government. In modern elections, however, the element of rational choice is heavily manipulated by the twin factors of personality and the mass media. People vote without clearly realizing what they are voting for or why, and this could become a threat to democracy.

Modern parties showcase their leaders' personalities. Especially in the advanced industrialized world, ideology is seldom emphasized. Ads and TV spots feature the leaders' images, sometimes without even mentioning their parties. The leader is presented as charismatic and decisive but calm and caring. Ronald Reagan was an excellent example of a winning political personality, and leaders in other countries have adopted much the same approach. In the 1988 French election, for example, "Mitterrand's presidential victory was a personal one, that of a popular, paternal incumbent president, elevated . . . to an almost non-partisan status."[28] Mitterrand's ads projected him as *la force tranquille* (the tranquil force) and omitted mention of his Socialist party or any ideology or program.

A good part of a candidate's personality is the degree of optimism he or she exudes, at least in the United States. In ten of the eleven U.S. elections from 1948 to 1988, victory went to the candidate who presented the most upbeat image of America. Pessimistic candidates, who worry about things going wrong, tend to lose. The two University of Pennsylvania psychologists who conducted this study, Harold Zullow and Martin Seligman, in May 1988, gave Bush an optimism rating of 4.6 and Dukakis only 2.1, thus accurately predicting the November results.[29]

The leaders' personalities are sold through the mass media, especially through television, where the candidate's image can be carefully controlled; even physical appearance can be altered. "Photo opportunities" instead of traditional question-and-answer sessions avoid embarrassing probes by journalists. The "photo op" shows seemingly spontaneous candidate activity; words explaining the activity can be added later. The "photo op" itself is largely wordless. The candidates' professional "handlers" worry that their candidates will slip their leashes and start acting like themselves. This can ruin a carefully built-up image. Journalists must be kept distant.[30]

In Britain in 1987 "the political parties tried to use television to build images rather than project arguments," a British network official argued. "The general election of 1987 proved that television very largely *is* the campaign."[31] In France, journalists complained about the *hypermédiatisation* of French politics. The dominance of television is clearly not just an American problem.

The really big medium of modern campaigning is the televised political spot commercial. Here, everything is professionally controlled: set, lighting, music, makeup, narration—a mini-drama more perfect (and often more expensive) than many regular programs. The TV spot, highly developed in America, now occurs in Europe. Labour's Neil Kinnock set new European standards for the rich images of his 1987 TV spots, which were adjudged much better than Prime Minister Margaret Thatcher's (who nonetheless won). The following year, French presidential elections also featured what the French call *le clip politique*. Jean-Paul Gourevitch discerns three types: (1) the "jingle clip," a simple attention-getting device; (2) the "ideological clip," which sets an idea in images; and (3) the "allegorical clip," which portrays the hero-candidate in an epic.[32]

If things keep going like this, what will happen to democratic elections? Increasingly, they will be won by the candidate with the sunniest personality and best media ads. This generally means the candidate with the most money, for the mass media, especially television, are terribly expensive. Candidates, desperate for money, will sell themselves to private interests. Parties will become little more than fund-raising organizations. And notice that this is not just an American problem; it started in the United States but has since spread to Europe.

Incumbent Performance.   Most people do not carefully evaluate issues in a presidential election, but they do accumulate an overall evaluation of the performance of an incumbent president. That is, they feel the president has done a good

Bill Clinton and running mate Al Gore took their show on the road in the 1992 election campaign, crossing parts of the country by bus and stopping for speeches every day, a technique reminiscent of the old "whistle stop" campaigns conducted by rail in earlier decades.

job or a poor one. Especially important are their perceptions concerning the health of the economy and government steps to boost economic growth.[33] The accumulated or package views of voters toward incumbent presidents has been termed "retrospective voting" because it views in retrospect a whole four years of performance in office.[34] When voters think the government in general is doing a good job they reward the incumbent's party: Johnson in 1964, Nixon in 1972, Reagan in 1984, and Bush in 1988. When they think the government in general is doing a poor job they punish the incumbent's party: Humphrey in 1968, Ford in 1976, Carter in 1980, and Bush in 1992.

One indirect measure of voter satisfaction is "consumer confidence" in the economy, a survey of expected prosperity tracked by the Conference Board, which turns out to have foreshadowed the last seven elections. When the consumer confidence index was 99 or above, the incumbent party's candidate won; when 87 or below, the incumbent party's candidate lost. (See Table 12.2.) The finding confirms what many political scientists have long suspected, that modern elections are in large degree referendums on the economy. Since World War II, U.S. economic growth of (a rather robust) 4 percent or higher during the year preceding the presidential election guarantees that the incumbent or his party's candidate will be elected. Less than 4 percent and they're in trouble. The negative growth (i.e., recession) of 1980 doomed Carter. Presidents will do almost anything to avoid a recession during an election year. Small wonder that President Bush complained the media were conveying an unduly pessimistic picture of the economy in the fall of 1992. Some thinkers worry that a too-direct relationship between the economy and elections increases voter volatility and prevents presidents from doing what needs to be done for long-term economic growth. It is as if voters angrily warn presidents: "Give me prosperity, or else!" That kind of voter input, warn some, is a perversion of democracy.

Retrospective voting is colored, naturally, by party identification, issues, and the candidate's personality. A strong Republican is likely to find little good to say about a Democratic administration. For those with weak party identification, plus the many independents, the feeling of overall performance is apt to be the most powerful determinant of voting. Further, if an administration scores well in the minds of such people in retrospect, they may start identifying with that party. Vot-

TABLE 12.2   Relationship of Consumer Confidence and Voting

	Consumer confidence index	Vote for incumbent party's candidate	
1972	112	62%	(Nixon wins)
1976	87	49	(Ford loses)
1980	84	42	(Carter loses)
1984	99	59	(Reagan wins)
1988	117	54	(Bush wins)
1992	53	38	(Bush loses)
1996	106	49	(Clinton wins)

ing behavior is complex. When people say they "like" candidates, what does it mean? Do they like the candidates' party affiliation, their stand on issues, their personal images, or the performance of the economy? Unraveling such puzzles is the crux of campaign strategy.

CANDIDATE STRATEGIES AND VOTER GROUPS

Campaign strategies are geared toward two goals: keeping "one foot on home base" by not alienating the normal party supporters and, at the same time, trying to win over votes from the undecided and from as many of the opposition as possible. There are many forces at play in the ultimate decision of the voter. The political and economic events of an election year—war, depression, treaties—also contribute to both the dimension and the direction of voter reaction. In a year when a major crisis has occurred, voter turnout is likely to be high; in a year when things have gone rather smoothly, voters may be relatively apathetic.

How does the candidate use these variables to plan campaign strategy?[35] In most cases, the campaign is designed to fit the opinions and needs of the constituency. Thus, the candidate must be aware of pockets of party strength and resistance, what city dwellers are thinking versus the opinions of people in the suburbs, what districts contain the lowest rates of participation (and will therefore yield the smallest numbers of votes), and which stands on issues are likely to inflame large groups of people against his or her candidacy. Only when the candidate has some awareness of the direction and intensity of voter opinion will he or she be able to plan an effective campaign. Important in this is a knowledge of "voting blocs."

Voting blocs fall into roughly the same categories as the public opinion blocs discussed in Chapter 8. Class, religion, and geographic characteristics are the most important influences in opinion formation, and these provide general guidelines for predicting voting behavior. Urban and rural voters will oppose each other on a mass-transit bond; blacks and whites may vote differently on a school-busing issue. Election victories are often the result of a major coalition formed by several smaller blocs of voters. On a national scale, the Democrats used to represent a coalition of labor, blacks, Catholics, Jews, and urban voters; the Republicans received their support from a coalition of rural and farm voters, the remaining Protestants, and nonunion workers. By the 1960s, though, these traditional blocs had begun to break up, and neither party has managed to reconstruct them. The breakup of the blocs, it should be noted, coincides with the declining voter turnout and party loyalty discussed earlier.

Increasingly, candidates recognize that "blocs" are not what they used to be, that many Americans do not fit ethnic or religious pigeonholes. Instead, attitudes on free enterprise, welfare, patriotism, civil rights, and other issues cut across the old voting blocs. Trying to make this approach more systematic, an innovative approach for the 1988 and 1996 elections broke the U.S. electorate into several "voter groups" based on their attitudes.[36] The Times Mirror study (named after the sponsoring Los Angeles newspaper group) held that traditional classifications such as "liberal" or "conservative" don't count for much because people are often liberal on some things and conservative on others. Neither does party ID matter much in an era of dealignment and rapid shifts between parties. In contrast to the traditional type of voter survey, exemplified in Table 12.1, the renamed Pew studies argued that clusters of *values* count for more than income, religion, education, region, and so on. "White" or "professional" may not explain very much about how a person votes, but a pro-business "Enterpriser" cluster of values (in Table 12.3) strongly predicts a Republican voter.

The Pew Research approach does offer certain practical advantages to candidates. By knowing what issues appeal to which voters groups, they can target their campaign messages to them. Dole strategists, for example, by knowing that "New Economy Independents" are a good portion of the electorate, attempted to project themes that would win over a considerable portion of them from Clinton. On the other hand, "Partisan Poor," strongly concerned with social welfare, were hard to budge from the Democratic column, so Republicans didn't try.

TABLE 12.3   Voter Groups in 1996

	Clinton	Dole	Perot
The Divided Right/% Voters			
Enterprisers/12% Pro-business, anti-government, worry about economic issues	6	88	3
Moralists/20% Pro-school prayer, anti-abortion, worry about social issues	20	66	7
Libertarians/4% Pro-business and anti-government, but highly tolerant, open to a third party	39	34	12
The Detached Center/% voters			
New Economy Independents/19% Don't like either major party or government but support environment and some welfare	53	14	16
The Embittered/7% Poor and poorly informed; mistrust government, the main parties, and corporations	45	37	11
The "Not So" Left/% Voters			
Seculars/10% Liberal, nonreligious, tolerant, well-educated, heavily Democratic	90	2	2
New Democrats/8% Religious but tolerant, both pro-business and pro-government, lean to the Democrats	86	5	4
New Dealers/8% Older, pro-government, pro-union, socially conservative, worry about foreign competition	74	10	12
Partisan Poor/8% Militantly Democratic, pro-social spending, worry about drug abuse, unemployment, social justice	92	4	3
Total Sample	50	38	6

"Don't Knows," non-voting, and "voted for others" omitted.

Source: Pew Research Center.

Suggested Readings

ALEXANDER, HERBERT E., and REI SHIRATORI, eds. *Comparative Political Finance Among the Democracies.* Boulder, CO: Westview Press, 1994. Examines thirteen countries in this important but overlooked area.

BOWLER, SHAUN, and DAVID M. FARRELL, eds. *Electoral Strategies and Political Marketing.* New York: St. Martin's, 1993. Eleven excellent case studies.

FLANIGAN, WILLIAM H., and NANCY H. ZINGALE. *Political Behavior of the American Electorate,* 8th ed. Washington, DC: CQ Press, 1994. Excellent summary of trends in nonvoting, party dealignment, and declining trust in government.

JAMIESON, KATHLEEN HALL. *Dirty Politics: Deception, Distraction, and Democracy.* New York: Oxford University Press, 1992. Argues that political TV ads lead to vicious campaigning.

LEWIS-BECK, MICHAEL S., and TOM W. RICE. *Forecasting Elections.* Washington, DC: CQ Press, 1992. Explanation of forecasting methods at several levels of U.S. politics.

NEWMAN, JODY, and RICHARD A. SELTZER. *Sex as a Political Variable: Women as Candidates and Voters in U.S. Elections.* Boulder, CO: Lynne Rienner, 1996. A major, data-based study of the multifaceted gender gap.

NIEMI, RICHARD G., and HERBERT F. WEISBERG, eds. *Classics in Voting Behavior.* Washington, DC: CQ Press, 1993. Major articles in the area that political science does best.

PAGE, BENJAMIN I., and ROBERT Y. SHAPIRO. *The Rational Public: Fifty Years of Trends in Americans' Policy Preferences.* Chicago, IL: University of Chicago Press, 1992. Major study that in the aggregate and over time public knows what it wants.

PHILLIPS, KEVIN. *Boiling Point: Republicans, Democrats, and the Decline of Middle-Class Prosperity.* New York: Random House, 1993. Top analyst shows how economic squeeze over two decades has pushed middle class to angry populism.

PIKA, JOSEPH A., and RICHARD WATSON. *The Presidential Contest,* 5th ed. Washington, DC: CQ Press, 1995. Excellent, compact overview of the big race.

POLSBY, NELSON W., and AARON WILDAVSKY. *Presidential Elections: Contemporary Strategies of American Electoral Politics,* 8th ed. New York: Free Press, 1991. An impressive summation by two top political scientists of the many shifts in U.S. presidential politics.

SIMPSON, DICK. *Winning Elections: A Handbook in Modern Participatory Politics.* New York: HarperCollins, 1996. A how-to manual for practitioners.

WATTENBERG, MARTIN P. *The Rise of Candidate-Centered Politics: Presidential Elections of the 1980s.* Cambridge, MA: Harvard University Press, 1992. Parties no longer count for much, and focus on candidates tends to be unstable.

Notes

1. For a sophisticated explanation of declining U.S. voter turnout, see Ruy A. Teixeira, *The Disappearing American Voter* (Washington, DC: Brookings Institution, 1992).

2. Lester W. Milbrath, *Political Participation* (Chicago: Rand McNally, 1965), pp. 16–22.

3. For a statement on the difficulty of registration requirements, see Frances Fox Piven and Richard A. Cloward, *Why Americans Don't Vote* (New York: Pantheon, 1988).

4. Anthony Downs, "The Causes and Effects of Rational Abstention," *An Economic Theory of Democracy* (New York: Harper & Row, 1957), pp. 260–75.

5. Angus Campbell et al., *The American Voter* (New York: Wiley, 1960), Chap. 17.

6. According to Seymour Martin Lipset, both organizing skill and a belief in the effectiveness of organization go hand in hand with higher income. See *Political Man* (Garden City, NY: Doubleday, 1960), pp. 190–203.

7. Raymond E. Wolfinger and Steven Rosenstone found education to be the major factor in voting turnout. See their *Who Votes?* (New Haven, CT: Yale University Press, 1980).

8. Paul R. Abramson, John H. Aldrich, and David W. Rohde, *Change and Continuity in the 1988 Elections* (Washington, DC: CQ Press, 1990), p. 98.

9. See Steven A. Peterson and Albert Somit, *The Political Behavior of Older Americans* (New York: Garland, 1994).

10. See Carol A. Christy, *Sex Differences in Political Participation: Process of Change in Fourteen Nations* (New York: Praeger, 1987).

11. See Austin Ranney, ed., *Britain at the Polls, 1983* (Durham, NC: Duke University Press, 1984), especially Chap. 7.

12. See David Butler and Donald Stokes, *Political Change in Britain*, rev. ed. (New York: St. Martin's, 1976).

13. Angus Campbell and Henry Valen, "Party Identification in Norway and the United States," *Public Opinion Quarterly* 25 (Winter 1961), 505–25.

14. Philip E. Converse and Georges Dupeaux, "Politicization of the Electorate in France and the United States," *Public Opinion Quarterly* 26 (Spring 1962), 1–23.

15. Leon D. Epstein, *Political Parties in Western Democracies* (New York: Praeger, 1967), pp. 78–85.

16. For detailed studies of the 1992 elections, see Paul R. Abramson, John H. Aldrich, and David Rohde, *Change and Continuity in the 1992 Elections* (Washington, DC: CQ Press, 1994) and Herbert F. Weisberg, ed. *Democracy's Feast: Elections in America* (Chatham, NJ: Chatham House, 1995).

17. See Robert H. Swansbrough and David M. Brodsky, eds., *The South's New Politics: Realignment and Dealignment* (Columbia, SC: University of South Carolina Press, 1988).

18. Howard R. Penniman, ed., *France at the Polls: The Presidential Election of 1974* (Washington, DC: American Enterprise Institute, 1975), p. 203.

19. See Carol M. Mueller, ed., *The Politics of the Gender Gap: The Social Construction of Political Influence* (Ithaca, NY: Russell Sage, 1988).

20. For an argument that the Democrats harmed themselves on the race issue, see Thomas Byrne Edsall with Mary D. Edsall, *Chain Reaction: The Impact of Race, Rights, and Taxes on American Politics* (New York: Norton, 1991).

21. The founder of the theory was the great V.O. Key with his article "A Theory of Critical Elections," *Journal of Politics* 17 (February 1955), 3–18. Many others have explored the topic, including Walter Dean Burnham, *Critical Elections and the Mainsprings of American Politics* (New York: Dodd, Mead, 1968); and James L. Sundquist, *Dynamics of the Party System: Alignment and Realignment of Political Parties in the United States*, rev. ed. (Washington, DC: Brookings Institution, 1983).

22. See Angus Campbell et al., "The Concept of the Normal Vote," *Elections and the Political Order* (New York: Wiley, 1966), Chap. 2.

23. Campbell et al., *American Voter*, pp. 531–38.

24. Kevin B. Phillips, *The Emerging Republican Majority* (New Rochelle, NY: Arlington House, 1969).

25. Times Mirror Center for the People and the Press, "The People, the Press and Politics Campaign '92: 'The Generations Divide,'" 8 July 1992, p. 7.

26. For a warning that this trend is underway, see Benjamin Ginsberg and Martin Shefter, *Politics by Other Means: The Declining Importance of Elections in America* (New York: Basic Books, 1990).

27. Bruce E. Keith, David B. Magleby, Candice J. Nelson, Elizabeth Orr, Mark C. Westlye, and Raymond E. Wolfinger, *The Myth of the Independent Voter* (Berkeley, CA: University of California Press, 1992).

28. D. S. Bell and Byron Criddle, "No Majority for the President: The French Legislative Elections of June 1988," *Parliamentary Affairs* [London] 42 (January 1989), 1. Notice how this section uses British political scientists' descriptions of French elections and a French political scientist's description of British elections. Often the best political insights are by foreigners.

29. Daniel Goleman, "For Presidential Candidates, Optimism Appears a Winner," *New York Times*, 8 May 1988, pp. 1, 18.

30. For a devastating portrait of the effects of personality and the media in the 1987 British elections, see Monica Charlot, "Les elections britanniques du 11 juin 1987," *Revue Française de Science Politique* [Paris] 38 (August 1988), 4.

31. Robert Hargreaves, "Election '87: The TV Stopwatch Campaign," *Parliamentary Affairs* [London] 41 (April 1988), 2.

32. Jean-Paul Gourevitch, "Le clip politique," *Revue Française de Science Politique* [Paris] 39 (February 1989), 1.

33. For the link between economics and voting, see Heinz Eulau and Michael S. Lewis-Beck, eds., *Economic Conditions and Electoral Outcomes* (New York: Agathon Press, 1985).

34. See Morris P. Fiorina, *Retrospective Voting in American National Elections* (New Haven, CT: Yale University Press, 1981).

35. For detailed studies in this area, see James A. Thurber and Candice J. Nelson, *Campaigns and Elections American Style* (Boulder, CO: Westview Press, 1995) and Margaret Scammell, *Designer Politics: How Elections are Won* (New York: St. Martin's, 1995).

36. For an explanation of how the study and its categories were devised, see *The New Political Landscape* (Washington, DC: Times Mirror Center for the People and the Press, 1994).

· 13 ·

The Basic Structures of Government

What Is a Political Institution?

The word *institution* is apt to conjure up an image of an impressive building with stately columns, home of a legislature or executive department. True, many institutions are housed in imposing structures—it bolsters their authority—but architecture is not what political institutions are about. *Political institutions*, rather, are established and durable relationships of power and authority.

The U.S. Supreme Court, for example, even if it met in a tent, would be an important institution as long as its decisions were obeyed. As we will consider later, it was not clear what the powers of the Supreme Court were to be when it began, but forceful personalities and important cases slowly gave it power. Like most institutions, the Supreme Court *evolved* into importance.

In Chapter 1 we looked at authority as a fluid thing that requires continual maintenance. A political institution can be looked at as congealed or partly solidified authority. Over time, people have become used to looking to political institutions to solve problems, decide controversies, and set directions. Institutions, because they are composed of many persons and (if they're effective) last many generations, take on lives of their own apart from the people temporarily associated with them. This gives the political system stability; citizens know where they stand.

Institutions are bigger than individual leaders. When President Nixon resigned under a cloud of scandal in 1974, the institution of the presidency was scarcely touched. If there had been a series of such presidents, and if they had refused to resign, the institution itself would have been severely damaged. Sometimes dictators have tried to make themselves into "institutions," but it hasn't worked; no matter how powerful dictators are during their lifetimes, the institutions they have tried to build unravel upon their deaths. Joseph Tito ruled Yugoslavia—sometimes with an iron hand—for thirty-five years. He attempted to ensure that the system he had set up would survive after him, but it was too much based on himself. Eleven years after his death, Yugoslavia split apart in bloody fighting. Dictators seldom build lastingly; they are rarely able to *institutionalize* their personal power.

Powerful inhabitants of an office, however, can sometimes put their personal stamp on the institution. George Washington set standards and precedents that his successors felt compelled to follow even though his actions were not specified in the Constitution. Washington retired after two terms, and until Franklin D. Roosevelt, no president tried to serve longer. Washington had put something into the institution of the presidency that was not codified into law until the Twenty-second Amendment in 1951. In another example, the first chancellor of the Federal Republic of Germany (West Germany), Konrad Adenauer, offered such decisive leadership that the institution of the chancellor has been powerful ever since.

One way to approach the study of institutions is to try to locate the most powerful offices of a political system: Who's got the power? Studying constitutions may help locate power, but sometimes they do not tell the whole story. Reading the U.S. Constitution, for example, you might think the executive and the legislative powers are in equal balance. This is what the Founding Fathers intended, but over the past two centuries power has gravitated into the hands of the president. The French constitution, set up by Charles de Gaulle in 1958, seems to give the presidency near-dictatorial powers. But French legislative elections twice brought a conservative parliament and prime minister to face a Socialist president who was already in office. Before this first occurred in 1986, it was hard to predict how French institutions would handle the problem of the legislative and the executive branches being under the control of different parties. The French constitution was unclear on this point. But now the situation is clearer, and it turns out the French presidency has less power than was previously thought. When the same situation, called "cohabitation," occurred again in 1993, French institutions took it in stride; they had evolved to accommodate a different power relationship. Constitutions are themselves institutions, gradually evolving in practice if not in wording.[1]

Monarchy or Republic

An example of such evolution is the modern constitutional monarchy. Calling a country a monarchy or a republic is to describe its "form of state." A republic is simply a form of state that does not have a monarch. The word *republic* does not imply "good" or "democratic." All but a few countries in the world are republics. Most of the remaining monarchies are figurehead constitutional monarchies such as those of northwestern Europe—Britain, Norway, Sweden, Denmark, Holland, and Belgium. The king of Spain still has an active political role. He restrained the army from accomplishing a coup in 1981, thus becoming a bulwark of Spanish democracy. The traditional, working monarchies still found in the Arab world—Morocco, Saudi Arabia, Jordan, Kuwait—are probably doomed unless they can accomplish the extremely difficult task of turning themselves into limited constitutional monarchies. Failure to do so has in recent decades led to the overthrow of traditional monarchies and their replacement by revolutionary regimes in Egypt, Iraq, Libya, Ethiopia, and Iran.

The constitutional monarchy of Great Britain, with its colorful ceremonies and pageantry, gives the appearance of a traditional monarchy, but the monarch is a figurehead and the real power is in the hands of the Parliament and the prime minister.

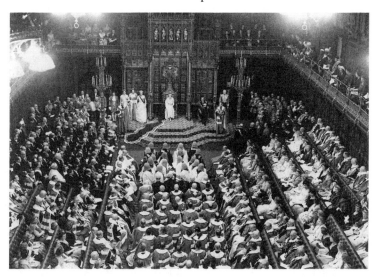

The limited constitutional monarchies of northwestern Europe pose an interesting question. How is it that these countries can combine an old form of state with a modern democracy? Indeed, the countries mentioned are some of the freest and most democratic in the world. The answer seems to be that monarchies perform an integrative function, holding together divergent social groups during the delicate modernization phase. The traditional sectors of society—the clergy, army officers, and great landowners—usually oppose democracy and may be tempted to carry out coups to stop democratization. But these sectors are also monarchist in orientation, and if the king or queen goes along with democratization, the traditional sectors will probably support it also. The monarch thus serves as a bridge between the traditional political system of the Middle Ages and the modern participatory system, easing the way from one to the other.[2]

Consider the histories of countries that retained their kings and queens—gradually limiting the monarchs' powers until they were figureheads. Then consider those countries the deposed their monarchs. Britain temporarily deposed its monarchy in the seventeenth century, but it was soon reestablished. Since then Britain's political evolution has been mostly peaceful and gradual. The French Revolution repudiated monarchy and alienated French conservatives. Since then French politics has been a nasty tug of war between conservative and radical forces, with rare periods of stability. Sweden retained its monarchy and evolved into a modern social welfare state. Germany lost its monarchy after World War I, when the kaiser abdicated and fled to Holland; and after the shaky fourteen years of the Weimar Republic, Hitler took over with his Nazis. It has been suggested that this might not have occurred if Germany had stayed a monarchy with a moderate kaiser (such as Prince Max of Baden) that all sectors of society could trust. Monarchs can confer legitimacy on new democratic institutions. When Juan Carlos of Spain blocked a military coup in 1981, the head of the Spanish Communist party announced his support for monarchy. The king of Spain had thus bridged most sectors of Spanish society, even those that had previously been revolutionary and antimonarchist.

New republics, such as those of the Third World, have to face the multiple crises of nation building (discussed in Chapter 2) without a dominant institution that can confer legitimacy. If their fragile new institutions can survive the first decades, they gradually gain legitimacy. In time, respect for republican institutions may succeed in uniting most elements of the society, as has happened in the United States. As Edmund Burke pointed out two centuries ago, in the world of institutions, old is good, for an institution that has survived and adapted over a long time has also implanted itself into citizens' hearts and minds.

Monarchs are *heads of state*, symbolically representing their nations by receiving foreign ambassadors and giving restrained speeches on patriotic occasions. In republics, their analogues are presidents, some of whom are also little more than figureheads. The republics of Germany, Italy, and Israel, for example, have presidents as heads of state, but they don't do much in the way of practical politics. The *head of government* is the real working executive and, in most systems, is called prime minister (as we shall explore in subsequent chapters).

Unitary or Federal Systems

Another basic institutional choice concerns the territorial structuring of the nation. There are really only two choices: unitary or federal. A unitary system accords its component areas little or no autonomy; most governance radiates from the capital city. The subdivisions—departments in France, provinces in Italy, counties in Sweden—are largely for administrative convenience. Federal systems are composed of units that have considerable political lives of their own: U.S. and Brazilian states, German *Länder*, and Swiss cantons. These units cannot be legally erased or easily altered by the central power.

There is, theoretically, a third alternative: the confederation, a group so loosely formed that the component parts can override the center. Confederations tend to have short lives; they either fall apart or become federations. This was the fate of the United States under the Articles of Confederation. Similarly, the Confederate States of America demonstrate the difficulty of the structure: each state had such independence that they could not jointly coordinate their efforts during the Civil War. Switzerland still calls itself a confederation (Confederatio Helvetia), but it is actually a federal system. Perhaps the European Union (EU) is the only current example of a confederation, with the plans of its headquarters in Brussels sometimes ignored by individual member countries. But it, too, is evolving in the direction of a federation.

UNITARY SYSTEMS

Unitary governments have significant control over local authorities. They usually touch people's daily lives in more ways than a federal government would. For example, in France, elementary school curricula are drawn up by the central ministry in Paris in order to reduce regional differences. Most unitary states have a national police force and control over local police. Generally, there is only one court system, whose judicial officers are appointed by the national government.

Even in a unitary state, the central government cannot run all local affairs.[3] In Great Britain, for example, local governments maintain substantial authority. All the countries and boroughs (cities) elect councils with standing committees for each area of administration. The councils control policing, education, and health and welfare matters. Parliament can always step into local affairs and override these officials; in practice, however, it intervenes only in emergencies because the British people place a high value on local autonomy.

Local nationalism grew in several unitary systems during the 1970s, and for several reasons. Economics was one. Local nationalists usually claim that their region is shortchanged by the central government. The region may have a distinct language or culture that its people want to preserve. Many feel that important political decisions are not under local control, that they are made by distant bureaucrats. Often regions harbor historical resentments at having long ago been conquered and forcibly merged with the larger nation. Several unitary systems grope for solutions to the regional problem.

Devolution in Britain.   The Celtic Scots and Welsh, pushed to the peripheries of Britain centuries ago by the invading Angles and Saxons, retain a lively sense of their differences from England. Many Scots and Welsh resent being ruled by London. The Scots wanted to retain a bigger share of the North Sea oil revenues—"It's Scotland's oil!" was their cry—and the Welsh wanted to make their Cymric language equal to English in schools and on television. During the 1970s, the Scottish and Welsh nationalist parties grew until they won several seats in Parliament. In 1977 Commons passed "devolution" bills that would have given considerable home-rule powers to Scotland and Wales. The devolution plans had to be approved by a referendum by 40 percent of *all* Scots and Welsh eligible to vote, a higher threshold than a simple majority of those voting. Only one-third of Scots and one-fifth of the Welsh voted yes, and the plan failed. Many thought local nationalism was a nice, romantic idea but impractical. In more recent elections the nationalist parties have lost support as both Scotland and Wales have continued their strong pro-Labour orientation. The high point of Scottish and Welsh nationalism seems to have passed, but the problems of these distinct cultures within Britain remain.

Decentralization in France.   France has historically been a more unitary system than Britain. Everything is—or, until recently, was—run from Paris. Both monarchs and republicans pursued centralization with single-minded determination. Most of France's ninety-six *départements* were named after rivers to try to erase the historical memories of the old provinces. It didn't completely work, for France, like Britain, has distinctive regional subcultures: the Celtic Bretons (who fled from Britain centuries ago to escape the Saxons); the southerners of the Midi, whose speech is still flavored with the ancient *langue d'oc;* and the Corsicans, who still speak an Italian dialect.

In 1960, better to coordinate economic development, President de Gaulle decreed twenty-two regions consisting of two to eight *départements* each. These were mere administrative conveniences, however. Starting in 1981, Socialist President François Mitterrand instituted genuine decentralization. Certain economic-planning powers were transferred from Paris to the regions. The Paris-appointed prefects lost some of their powers, especially on economic matters. The hitherto powerless departmental legislatures picked up these powers. Elected regional assemblies took over much economic planning.[4] France thus reversed five centuries of centralization.

Autonomy in Spain.   Spain, too, decentralized its highly centralized system. Here the problem was more urgent, for regional resentments, long buried under the dictatorial rule of Francisco Franco (1939–75), started appearing in a dangerous manner in the 1970s. Spain's regional problems are among the most difficult in Europe. Basques and Catalans, in the north of Spain, speak non-Castilian languages and are intensely proud of their distinctive cultures. In addition, many areas of Spain were granted *fueros* (local rights) in medieval times, which they treasured for centuries. On top of great regional diversity, Spanish centralizers attempted to plant a unitary system on the French model. The result was great resentment that appeared whenever Spain experimented with democracy. Breakaway movements appeared in 1874 and in the 1930s, only to be crushed by the Spanish army, which regards the unity of the country as sacred.

With this background, Spain held its breath in the late 1970s and 1980s as the post-Franco Spanish democracy instituted seventeen regional governments called "autonomies." The big problem was in the Basque country, where a terrorist movement, Euzkadi ta Azkatasuna (ETA), demanded complete Basque independence. To appease regionalist feeling, which also appeared in more moderate forms in Catalonia, Galicia, Andalusia, and other areas, the Madrid government allowed regions to become autonomous, with regional parliaments, some taxation power, language rights, and control over many local matters.[5] Most Spaniards approved of the autonomies.

Pros and Cons of Unitary Systems.   The concentration of authority in unitary states may lead to the feeling among citizens that it is pointless to become active in local affairs, since all power radiates downward from the capital; this feeling can turn into widespread alienation from the government and national political institutions, as in Italy. Furthermore, with national leaders so far removed from community problems—and citizens too disenchanted to make their views known—wise policymaking may prove difficult.

On the other hand, the centralization of power in a unitary state can be a significant advantage in facing the problems of modern society. Clear lines of authority can be useful. In unitary systems, the central government can marshal economic resources and coordinate planning and development; its broad taxation powers make the task of financing social welfare legislation much easier. This may explain why many federal nations have become more centralized in recent years. In the United States, India, and Germany, the federal governments have established national economic policies and have bankrolled social welfare programs.

FEDERAL SYSTEMS

Federalism preserves a considerable degree of local authority while simultaneously allowing the central government enough power to run the country. However, this combination varies a great deal in federal nations.[6] Some countries, such as the ex-Soviet Union and Mexico, became so centralized that some scholars wondered if they were still federal. The crux of a federal system is that the component states have some powers that cannot be easily overridden by the central government. The states are typically represented in an upper house such as the U.S. Senate or German Bundesrat. (Strictly speaking, unitary systems do not need upper houses.) In federal systems, the central government usually has exclusive control over foreign, defense, and monetary policy. The states typically control education, police, and highways. Because the division of these powers is seldom clear or permanent, a federal government rests on a delicate balance between centralized power and local autonomy.

There are several reasons for starting a federal union. The first is to escape the danger of military attack. By combining their resources, a number of small and weak states can defend themselves against a more powerful nation. On the other hand, federations are sometimes formed because member states are interested in aggressive expansion. The pooling of diplomatic and military resources of the states made Bismarck's Germany a major power. Federal unions can serve economic purposes as well, as the United States discovered in creating a continent-wide market without tariff barriers, a feat the EU is trying to duplicate. In some cases, a particular social class within a nation will prefer a federal system in the hopes of gaining economic advantage. Charles Beard saw America's Constitution of 1787 as an attempt by the Founding Fathers to defend their property interests by strengthening the central government.[7] Finally, federalism is often the only way to protect national unity. After the termination of British colonial rule, India set up a federal system that allowed such states as Bengal, Punjab, Marathastan, and Rajastan to maintain their own cultures while joining in the Indian nation. These states were jealous of their identities and would not have entered the federal union without a guarantee of local autonomy.

There are both advantages and disadvantages to making decisions on a local level. One advantage is that citizens are closest to their local government; they may influence officials and can see how a decision is made and what its effects are. Local governments can often experiment with new programs more easily than larger units; the costs of failure are likewise lower. On the other hand, local governments may lack the money to finance programs, and their officials are sometimes poorly trained and occasionally corrupt. Local decision making can lead to duplication of services and poor coordination. When this occurs, the responsibility for straightening out the bureaucratic mess may fall on the state government.

The relationship of the states or provinces to other levels of government varies in different federal systems. Generally, these units have their own governments and handle local problems within the limits of federal law. In Germany, each of the sixteen *Länder* (states) has its own constitution and government.[8] The Landtag (state legislature) can even affect the conduct of foreign policy because it elects members of the Bundesrat (the upper house of the national legislature). The Landtag, of course, legislates on all local matters. States in the Indian federation are given control over certain legislative areas, including education, agriculture, public health, forests, and fisheries.[9] There are also many areas (including marriage and divorce, civil law, and bankruptcy) in which states and the national government share authority. India is unique among federal states because its national government can proclaim a state of emergency, suspend the constitution, and take over the government of any state. Several times "president's rule" has been declared after riots and disorders in various states.

Each of America's fifty states has its own government, which can legislate in any area not delegated to the federal government or to the people. Usually, education, welfare, civil law, property taxes, and licensing of professions are all state functions. However, in the twentieth century, the federal government expanded its activity in the areas of civil law, welfare, and economic regulation. Dependent on federal grants and revenue sharing, the states find themselves having to meet federal standards in many areas. New legislation, for example, threatened to withhold federal highway funds if states did not make twenty-one the legal drinking age.

Originally, the national government in a federal union was expected to handle only the problems the states could not solve themselves. Thus, central governments today regulate the nation's economy, control national defense and foreign policy, and guarantee the civil rights of citizens. All federal governments insist that national law take precedence over state law. Members of the national legislature are usually elected directly by the people, rather than by members of state governments. The national executive is not under the control of the state government officials either.

From its very beginning, the United States has engaged in a long and stormy debate over the proper role of the federal government. Southern attachment to "states' rights" led to a clash with President Lincoln over the issue of slavery, and the nation erupted into civil war. In the 1960s, controversial U.S. Supreme Court decisions prompted a campaign to curb the power of the federal courts. Some political leaders insist that the concentration of power in Washington perverts American federalism and endangers the well-being of the nation. At the same time, local governments and citizens continue to rely on a strong federal government for help in solving complex—and expensive—problems.

Ex-Soviet Federalism.   On paper, the Soviet Union was a highly decentralized federation: Its fifteen "republics" were supposed to have the right to secede. In practice, under the tight control of the Communist party—although usually staffed by local talent (Georgians ran Georgia, Uzbeks ran Uzbekistan, and so on)—they followed Moscow's orders. Few understood that beneath the centralized exterior of the Soviet Union lurked monumental disunion. Even Gorbachev totally underestimated the strength of local nationalism, and when he allowed *glasnost* (media openness) in the late 1980s, many Soviet republics began to clamor for independence, and some—such as the Baltic states of Lithuania, Latvia, and Estonia, which had been brutally annexed by Stalin in 1940—simply proclaimed it. With the collapse of the Soviet Union at the end of 1991, all fifteen republics proclaimed themselves sovereign and independent, and many countries, including the United States, granted each of them diplomatic recognition.

Twelve of the old Soviet republics—all but the three Baltic states—enrolled in the "Commonwealth of Independent States" (CIS), a weak and uncertain entity with headquarters in Minsk, capital of Belarus. The CIS was supposed to have control over nuclear arms, but Ukraine and Kazakhstan were reluctant to relinquish theirs. The CIS was also supposed to promote trade among members. With the ruble rendered worthless, however, this trade shrank. Fighting between two CIS members, Armenia and Azerbaijan, over disputed territory, took thousands of lives; the CIS was unable to settle their quarrel. Some observers suspect the CIS is merely a cover for the eventual take-back of the old Soviet territory by Russia, a point openly advocated by Russian nationalists.

The bulk of the old Soviet Union continued as the Russian Federation, which is composed of many autonomous republics, districts, regions, and even cities, most of which have signed a federation treaty with Moscow. Several areas, home to some of the more than one hundred ethnic groups within Russia, refused to sign and billed themselves as independent. In the Caucasus, Chechnya attempted to break away and was brutally crushed by the Russian army in a long and bloody war.

The tantalizing question with the ex-Soviet Union (as with ex-Yugoslavia and ex-Czechoslovakia) is: Could the former Communist rulers have devised a more genuine federalism that would not have fallen apart? The Communists were the problem; they outlawed all non-Communist political forces, thus blocking the possible formation of crosscutting cleavages (discussed in Chapter 5) that might have held the federation together on a voluntary basis. The Communist regimes imposed what looked like federalism, but when they were ousted, their fake federalism quickly collapsed in the face of newly released local nationalism.

Ex-Yugoslav Federalism.   Yugoslavia, founded only in 1918, was a new and somewhat artificial country whose components were rarely content. It fell apart once before, in World War II. The Communist Partisans who fought the Nazis thought they had the answer: federalism. Under the maverick Communist Tito, Yugoslav federalism went farther than the Soviet variety. Each of Yugoslavia's six republics really did run local affairs and sent equal numbers of representatives to both houses of parliament. Yugoslavia's collective presidency had one member from each republic. This ultra-federal setup, however, did not calm local nationalism; it inflamed it. Each republic wanted its own railroads, steel mills, and control of its economy. Under Tito, the Communist party and security police could hold Yugoslavia together, but after he died in 1980 the republics started going their separate ways.[10] The most advanced republics, Slovenia and Croatia, resented being governed and taxed by heavy-handed, backward Serbia. They declared their independence in 1991, and fighting broke out as ethnic Serbs set up a mini-republic inside Croatia. The bloodshed was much worse after Bosnia, with a Muslim plurality (but not a majority), declared its independence in 1992. Serbian forces brutally practiced "ethnic cleansing" and murdered thousands. The problem was that 3 million ethnic Serbs lived outside of Serbia in areas where Serbs were massacred in World War II. Feeling endangered, Serbs felt entitled to take whatever lands they were living on for an eventual Greater Serbia. Serbia and Montenegro continue as a rump federation calling itself Yugoslavia. The situation calmed after a U.S.-brokered and NATO-enforced peace was agreed to in 1995.

Canadian Federalism.   Canada is another federation with strong centrifugal tendencies. Quebec is not alone in seeking independence; so do some of the western provinces. When the British ousted France from North America in the 1750s, they allowed the French-speaking Québécois to keep their language. Over the next two centuries, the francophones became second-class citizens, poorer than other Canadians and discriminated against because almost all private and government business was conducted in English.

In the 1960s the Parti Québécois (PQ) sprang up, dedicated to Quebec's independence from Canada. To appease them, the federal government in Ottawa in 1969 made Canada bilingual, with French and English having equal rights. This wasn't enough for the PQ, which made French the only official language of Quebec, turning the English-speaking minority into second-class citizens. Trying to hold the federation—which came to look a bit like a confederation as the provinces overruled the center—together, Ottawa and the provincial governments laboriously developed two new federal accords (Meech Lake in 1987 and Charlottetown in 1992) which were then rejected. The stumbling block was a separate status for Quebec as a "distinct society." Quebeckers said it didn't go far enough; many other Canadians said it went too far. In a 1980 referendum, Quebeckers rejected independence 60-40 percent, but in 1995 they (barely) rejected it 50.6-49.4 percent. Quebec separatists, still in control of the province's government, plan on another referendum. A "yes" vote would have disastrous consequences for all of Canada.[11]

Federalism is difficult. The three cases just considered remind us that federalism cannot cure everything. If the components are too different from one another culturally, economically, linguistically, or historically, a federal system may not be able to paper over the cracks. A shared political culture, as in the United States, Australia, and Germany, is a big help. With that as a foundation, the right balance must be found between central and state governments. The United States is still searching for its correct balance.

Linguistic nationalism shows in Quebec, where now all shop signs must be in French. Here a Montreal greengrocer had to paint over his fruit market sign with "marché de fruits" but was allowed to keep "Simcha's" in English as it is an established business name.

THE UNITED STATES: BALKANIZATION OF GOVERNMENT

There are approximately 80,000 local governments in the United States, plus fifty state governments and the national government. These governments often get in each other's way, and the taxpayer is frequently a prime victim. The multiplicity of governments is called, half in jest, "balkanization," after the many little countries that emerged in the Balkans when the Turks were pushed out in the last century. Balkanization in the United States has led to immoderate jurisdictional conflicts over whose rules apply in which situation.

One difficulty is the size of American cities and counties. Since World War II, much of the middle class has moved from cities to suburbs, leaving the cities with a shrinking tax base precisely when poorer people—who cannot pay much in taxes but need many social services—are moving in. If the entire metropolitan area had a single government, the affluent suburbs (many of whose residents earn their livings in the city) could be taxed to share the burden. But suburbs, with their own representatives in state and federal legislatures, block such moves, and the cities become poorer, more blighted, and more desperate. Parts of New York City look as if they've been destroyed in a war. Instead of solving their own problems on a metropolitan basis, the cities tend to go hat in hand to Washington to ask for financial help. As things get worse, more of the middle class and more of industry move out, deepening the problems.

The Growth of Federal Power.   The Founding Fathers would have difficulty recognizing the balance of powers between state and federal governments today. They expected, first, that the amount of actual governing would be small, and second that most of it would be done by the states under their "reserved" powers. For most of the nation's history this was so. States and localities raised their own revenues and spent them on modest programs; federal help was minor. As late as 1932, federal grants were less than 3 percent of state and local revenue.

But things were changing. The passage of the Sixteenth Amendment in 1913 allowed the federal government to tax income. Although little used at first, it meant that Washington had at its disposal an extractive power much stronger than the states'. Soon small federally funded programs for highways, education, and public health appeared. With Franklin D. Roosevelt's New Deal in the 1930s, federal programs increased in number and funding. With Lyndon Johnson's Great Society in the 1960s (Johnson was a great admirer of Roosevelt), federal programs exploded. Now, many billions of dollars flow from Washington to state and local governments. States and localities came to depend on federal grants for a portion of their revenues.

State and local governments often don't like being dependent on Washington, but they need the money. It's easier for the federal government to collect taxes through its progressive income tax (the richer you are, the bigger percentage you pay) than it is for states and cities through their income, sales, and property taxes. The public demand for services has outstripped the financial ability of most states and localities. Theoretically, states and cities could decline federal grants, but no one likes to turn down offers of money, even if there is some red tape involved.

The net impact was a growth of federal power. Because it provided money, it could set standards. The content of school lunches; design and construction of hospitals, highways, and airports; and women's collegiate athletics come under federal supervision. Some have suggested that this development makes the United States less federal than it used to be. Perhaps so, but reversing the process is difficult. Should toxic and nuclear waste disposal be left to state discretion? Is education a purely local concern? Standards and dollar support vary wildly across the fifty states, leaving the U.S. population inadequately educated.

The New Federalism.   The federal grants process is terribly complex, consisting of some five hundred different programs. Firms offer computerized grant-finding services, and states, cities, hospitals, and universities hire people for their "grantsmanship"—their ability to locate and win grants. Further, most of these grants are "categorical," aimed at a specific problem, which takes control and discretion away from state and local authorities. Funds for flood control cannot be used for sewage processing; funds for schoolbooks cannot be used for athletic equipment. State and local officials have complained of being locked into federal programs that don't take local needs into consideration.

Presidents Nixon and Reagan thought they had the answer: Move away from the categorical grants to broader "block grants" and "revenue sharing." Both presidents called their programs the "New Federalism," connoting a return of some power and control to the states. The federal government had become too powerful, they argued, so power should be given back to the states. It didn't quite work that way.

Congress, under President Nixon's leadership, designated $6.9 billion a year to go directly from the federal treasury to the states as revenue sharing, which states could spend as they needed without federal guidelines or supervision. The trouble was that this made states and cities *more* dependent on Washington, not less. Further, because revenue sharing is distributed by formula, it goes to rich cities and poor cities alike. One city may desperately need revenue to keep up police and fire services, whereas another may use it just to improve its parks. Because revenue sharing gives money with virtually no strings attached, it erodes federal control. Revenue sharing isn't "aimed" at problems; it leaves that up to state and local officials, who mostly use the money for general budget (police and fire departments, streets, and schools).

An intermediate ground between categorical grants (too narrow) and revenue sharing (too wide) appeared in 1974 with block grants. These take several related categorical grants, roll them into one, and let state and local officials use them within the general category.[12] President Reagan, for example, reduced dozens of categorical grants into a few block grants and called this the New Federalism. Congressional Republicans in the mid-1990s sought increased block grants as a way to shrink Washington's powers. There is a catch. Whereas the block grants are simpler and have fewer federal strings attached, they also provide less money.[13] In 1978, some 25 percent of state and local government outlays were federal aid. By 1988 federal funding of state and local outlays was down to about 17 percent and has declined since. This decline left many states and municipalities, which had taken on many new tasks, so desperate for funds they had to raise taxes. The question of how much federal money to give and how to give it is a permanent problem of U.S. federalism, for it is one facet of the problem we discussed earlier, that of the proper balance between central and state governments in federal systems.

THE UNITARY-FEDERAL MIXTURE

No country is perfectly unitary, nor is any perfectly federated. Even strongly unitary systems have certain elements of local input and control, and federal systems keep considerable power for the center. The interesting trend of our time is the tugging of unitary systems in a somewhat federal direction while some federal systems move slowly in a more unitary direction. France and Spain are two examples of highly centralized governments moving to quasifederalism. In the United States, the previously limited powers of Washington over the states and cities have grown over the decades. Money led the way: Federal funds meant federal standards and supervision. In so doing, the United States took on some of the characteristics of a unitary system, something Republicans would now like to undo.

It would be premature to say that eventually the two systems will meet in the middle, for both unitary and federal systems carry with them centuries of institutional and cultural baggage. If a unitary system moves too quickly to a sort of federalism, it arouses opposition, such as that of the Spanish army. If a federal system moves too much toward central control, it arouses the anger of the component states. Our task is not simply to classify countries as "unitary" or "federal," but to see how they actually operate in practice. Then we will find all manner of interesting deviations from the model, borrowings, and attempts to modify systems that no longer match a given country's needs.

Electoral Systems

As considered briefly in Chapter 11, electoral systems go a long way to determining the party system, a point made well and early (originally in 1951) by French political scientist Maurice Duverger.[14] In choosing their electoral system, countries are partly determining the number of parties, the ease of forming a stable government, and the degree of citizen interest in politics.

SINGLE-MEMBER DISTRICTS

The simplest electoral system is the Anglo-American *single-member district,* wherein one member of Parliament or one member of Congress is chosen to represent the entire district by winning a plurality (not necessarily a majority) of the votes. The system is sometimes called "single-member districts with plurality win" or "first past the post." This system puts pressure on interest groups and political factions to coalesce into two big parties. If there were, say, four parties who received 25, 25, 24, and 26 percent of the vote for their candidates, respectively, the last party would win the election. Under these circumstances, at least two of the losing parties recognize it is to their advantage to combine forces for the next election. The other two parties would also be forced to combine. In South Korea in 1987, for example, two liberal candidates split the opposition vote and handed the election to the conservative incumbent. If Kim Dae Jung and Kim Young Sam had joined forces, they would have won a majority of the vote. Countries with single-member districts and elections decided by a plurality of the vote tend to have two-party systems, such as the United States and Britain.

Third parties can and do exist in such systems, but without much hope of winning. They continue as protest groups or as pressure groups on the big parties. The British Liberal Democrats win nearly one vote in five, but because they are dispersed rather evenly throughout the country they rarely win more than a score of seats. Single-member systems are unkind to third parties.

Advantages of Single-Member Districts. Single-member districts do have certain advantages. The two parties they tend to produce usually stick to the center of the political spectrum, for this is where the votes are. This tendency inhibits the growth of extremism. If, for one election, leaders out of touch with mainstream views should capture control of the party, the party will likely lose. After the election the party will probably soon dump the extremists. This is what happened with the Republicans under the conservative Goldwater in 1964, the Democrats under the liberal McGovern in 1972, and the British Labourites under left-wing Michael Foot in 1983. As was mentioned in Chapter 8, public opinion in most democracies arrays itself as a bell-shaped curve. Parties that depart too far from the center penalize themselves.

A further advantage of such systems is that they generally give a parliamentary majority to one party, and therefore coalitions are rarely necessary. Victories are magnified in single-member systems. A relatively small "swing" of votes from one party to another can translate into many parliamentary seats, perhaps enough to form a parliamentary majority and a new government. This result gives the majority party a clear and stable mandate to govern until the next election. The United States, with its constitutionally mandated separation of powers, muddies the advantage of this system by frequently giving the White House to one party and the Congress to another.

Disadvantages of Single-Member Districts. Single-member districts create a somewhat artificial majority in the parliamentary body, which makes governing easier. In so doing, however, such systems do not fairly or accurately reflect actual public opinion or voting strength. In each district the winner takes all. The losing party, even if it received 49 percent of the vote, gets no representation. This is particularly unfair to third parties, especially if their supporters are not sufficiently concentrated to form a plurality in a few districts, as is the fate of the British Liberal Democrats.

Single-member districts teach parties a sort of golden rule about sticking to the political center. This can make politics safe but dull. The two big parties, in trying to win over the many votes in the middle, often end up sounding rather alike. The resulting voter boredom helps explain the low voter turnout in U.S. elections, discussed in the last chapter. The European multiparty systems have much higher voter turnouts, partly because voters can choose from a more interesting menu of parties.

The French Variation.   France also uses single-member districts, but with a difference: two rounds. Any candidate in parliamentary elections, held every five years, can enter the first round; in most districts half a dozen do. If they gain an outright *majority* (over 50 percent, not the same as the simple plurality in the Anglo-American system), they are elected on the first round, but this is usually not the case. In most districts, they have to go to a second round a week later. This time only candidates with at least 12.5 percent can run, and simple plurality suffices to win. By previous agreement between parties, however, some candidates withdraw and urge their supporters to vote for the candidate closest to them ideologically. On the right side of the French political spectrum, for example, the center-right Republicans will have agreed with the conservative Gaullists that the weaker candidate will drop out on the second round. To run both on the second round would split the conservative vote and give the election to the Socialists. On the left side of the spectrum, Socialists make the same deal with Communists: the weaker vote-getter (in most districts, the Communist) drops out and throws his or her support to the Socialist candidate. For presidential elections, held every seven years, the runoff comes two weeks later, with only the top two candidates running; they make the same sort of deal with the parties who have dropped out.

The French system—"single-member districts with runoffs"—permits many parties to exist and to run in the first round. Then the system narrows the choice in the second round and forces politicians to make the same choices as in the Anglo-American system; that is, it forces parties to combine. The first round of the French system is the functional equivalent of American primary elections. If the French were to drop the first round and go straight to the second round, they would encourage the formation of just two big parties, as in the United States and Britain. Some French thinkers argue, however, that French history, society, and ideologies are more complex and thus need more than two parties to represent them.[15] Some East European countries adopted the French-style single-member districts with runoff.

PROPORTIONAL REPRESENTATION

Proportional representation (PR) systems overcome the disadvantages of single-member systems but bring in problems of their own. These systems are based on multimember districts; that is, each district sends several representatives to parliament, not just one as in single-member systems. In the small countries of the Netherlands and Israel, the entire country is one big district. In Sweden the district is a county, in Spain a province. If the district is entitled to ten seats, each party offers voters a *party list* of ten candidates. Each voter picks one list, and the party gets seats in proportion to the votes it receives. If the party won 60 percent of the votes in a ten-member district, it would send the first six names on its party list to parliament. A party with 20 percent would send its first two names.

Mathematical problems immediately appear. Rarely does the vote divide itself as neatly as 60 percent, equal, in our example, to six seats. In a more typical situation, one party might win 42 percent of eleven seats. Would the party get 4.62 seats? How do you send a fraction of a person to parliament? There are a couple of ways to handle this. The most common is the d'Hondt system, which uses a mathematical formula to divide the seats; it tends to overrepresent the larger parties at the expense of smaller ones.[16] Sweden also uses a mathematical formula plus an interesting provision for nationwide seats. Its 28 districts elect only 310 of the Riksdag's 349 seats. Naturally, mathematical discrepancies appear, so the remaining 39 seats are parceled out to rectify any variances from the parties' national percentages.

To minimize the problem of splinter, nuisance, or extremist parties, some PR systems require parties to win a certain percentage of the vote in order to obtain any seats at all. These are called "threshold clauses." Germany and Poland require a party to get at least 5 percent of the vote nationwide; Sweden and Italy require 4 percent.

Advantages of Proportional Representation.   The chief advantage of PR is that the country's legislature accurately reflects the main currents of public opinion and party strength. Parties are not quite so dominated by the need to capture the middle of the electoral spectrum as is the tendency in Anglo-American systems. Parties can thus articulate their ideologies and principles more clearly because they aren't trying to please everybody. If a small part of the population—as low as 2 percent in Israel—really believes in something, they can run as a party and win a seat or two. They are not forced to amalgamate into bigger parties and dilute their views, as would happen in a "first past the post" system.

Disadvantages of Proportional Representation.   However, PR systems tend to encourage party splintering, or more accurately, where political views are splintered it permits small groups to organize as parties and win seats in parliament. This tendency, however, is waning, and two-plus party systems have emerged even in PR systems. Sweden and Spain have one or two large parties plus a few smaller ones. Their political systems are not terribly splintered. Israel, on the other hand, is plagued by splinter parties; as many as fifteen parties are elected to the Knesset. If the chief party falls short of half the seats in PR systems it must form a coalition with other parties. These coalitions are often unstable and unable to decide important issues. Some Israelis protest their country's PR system and urge reforms that would reduce the number of parties. It's not true that multiparty systems are always unstable. Where one party is big enough to govern alone, the system is quite stable. Nonetheless, the Anglo-American systems confer an almost automatic majority and thus stability.

Germany: A Hybrid.   One interesting system combines the best of both worlds. Germans elect their lower house, the Bundestag, on the basis of both single-member districts and proportional representation. On a split ballot, a German votes for both an individual to represent his or her district and a party to represent his or her *Land* (state) in proportion to the votes received. Overall strength in the Bundestag is set by the second vote, the one for parties, so seats are always proportional to votes. Half of the seats, though, are reserved for the 328 winners of the district contests. The net effect of Germany's split representation system has been to produce a two-plus party system (discussed in Chapter 11) and great governing stability. The German system is a modification of the PR system that was designed after World War II to prevent a repetition of the weak and unstable Weimar system, which had proportional representation that treated the country as one big district. In the 1990s, Russia, Italy, New Zealand, and Japan adopted German-style hybrid systems that combine single-member districts with PR for their parliamentary elections. Its electoral system has become one of Germany's best export products.

CHOOSING INSTITUTIONS

Political institutions are, in large measure, artificial creations. Most of them, of course, have evolved over time, but at key points in a nation's history, people have had the opportunity to choose their institutions. This brings an element of creativity into politics. Institutions neither fall from heaven nor rise from earth. They are crafted by a handful of people who can do a good job or a poor one. They are guided both by past experience and by reason. Often they are taking a leap in the dark. The Founding Fathers had little in the way of precedent when they constructed a presidential federal republic. Modified by time, usage, amendments, statutes, and court decisions, their handiwork has endured. The drafters of Germany's Weimar constitution in 1919 were less fortunate. On paper, the Weimar constitution looked like a perfect democracy, but some of the institutional choices were poor: no monarch, a weak president, a PR electoral system that treated the entire country as one district and encouraged splinter parties and cabinet instability, and a provision for emergency powers that could be misused. One wishes we could have warned them of their fateful choices.

When political science was young, it focused heavily on constitutions, as if selecting the right institutions could confer moderation and stability on a political system. Well, often the right choices can help. We may wonder if political science, in trying to imitate the natural sciences, has strayed too far from its origins. There was something noble and challenging about trying to devise workable, durable constitutions. In a tumultuous world, there can be few higher tasks than the development of effective political institutions.

Suggested Readings

ANTON, THOMAS J. *American Federalism and Public Policy: How the System Works.* Philadelphia: Temple University Press, 1989. A brilliant synthesis of the literature that argues that U.S. federalism is a permanently evolving system.

DUCHACEK, IVO D. *Comparative Federalism: The Territorial Dimension of Politics,* rev. ed. Lanham, MD: University Press of America, 1987.

Thorough cross-national overview of how states are organized geographically.

LIJPHART, AREND. *Electoral Systems and Party Systems: A Study of Twenty-Seven Democracies, 1945–1990.* New York: Oxford University Press, 1994. A leading scholar describes and analyzes 70 electoral systems and their consequences.

OSBORNE, DAVID. *Laboratories of Democracy.* Boston: Harvard Business School Press, 1988. American federalism, by giving governors room to maneuver, encourages imaginative solutions to many problems.

PADDISON, RONAN. *The Fragmented State: The Political Geography of Power.* New York: St. Martin's, 1983. Compares and contrasts unitary and federal solutions in a number of countries.

REDISH, MARTIN H. *The Constitution as Political Structure.* New York: Oxford, 1995. Argues that the Framers built "gridlock" into the U.S. Constitution to preserve liberties.

REEVE, ANDREW, and ALAN WARE. *Electoral Systems: A Comparative and Theoretical Introduction.* New York: Routledge, 1991. A good survey of various theories and comparisons chiefly focused on Britain.

RIVLIN, ALICE M. *Reviving the American Dream: The Economy, the States and the Federal Government.* Washington, DC: Brookings Institution, 1992. A Democrat (and Clinton official) recommends a massive devolution of functions from Washington to the states.

SARTORI, GIOVANNI. *Comparative Constitutional Engineering: An Inquiry into Structures, Incentives and Outcomes.* New York: New York University Press, 1994. A top scholar reviews electoral systems and presidential versus parliamentary systems.

SIEGAN, BERNARD H. *Drafting a Constitution for a Nation or Republic Emerging into Freedom,* 2nd ed. Fairfax, VA: George Mason University Press, 1994. An expert who has consulted on many new constitutions explains what he thinks a good constitution should and should not include.

WALKER, DAVID B. *The Rebirth of Federalism: Slouching toward Washington.* Chatham, NJ: Chatham House, 1995. A critic of centralization looks to devolving more responsibilities to states and localities.

WILLIAMSON, RICHARD S. *Reagan's Federalism: His Efforts to Decentralize Government.* Lanham, MD: University Press of America, 1990. A pro-Reagan review that minimizes the difficulties of shifting financial burdens to the states.

Notes

1. For a classic essay on this subject, see Karl Llewellyn, "The Constitution as an Institution," *Columbia Law Review* 34 (January 1934), 1.

2. This point is well made in Seymour Martin Lipset, *Political Man: The Social Bases of Politics,* expanded ed. (Baltimore: Johns Hopkins University Press, 1981), pp. 65–66.

3. See Edward C. Page and Michael J. Goldsmith, eds., *Central and Local Government Relations: A Comparative Analysis of West European Unitary States* (Ithaca, NY: Russell Sage, 1987).

4. For an excellent summary of what French decentralization has brought, see Lynne L. Bernier, "Political Consequences of Change in the French Intergovernmental System" (paper delivered at the American Political Science Association, Atlanta, 31 August 1989).

5. See Audrey Brassloff, "Spain: The State of the Autonomies," in Murray Forsyth, ed., *Federalism and Nationalism* (Leicester, England: Leicester University Press, 1989), pp. 24–50.

6. The best comparative studies are Arthur W. Macmahon, ed., *Federalism: Mature and Emergent* (Garden City, NY: Doubleday, 1955); Valerie Earle, ed., *Federalism: Infinite Variety in Theory and Practice* (Itasca, IL: Peacock, 1968); and William H. Riker, *Federalism: Origin, Operation, Significance* (Boston: Little, Brown, 1964).

7. See Charles A. Beard, *An Economic Interpretation of the Constitution* (New York: Macmillan, 1935). A criticism of Beard's thesis is A. C. McLaughlin, *A Constitutional History of the United States* (New York: Appleton-Century, 1935).

8. See Arthur B. Gunlicks, *Local Government in the German Federal System* (Durham, NC: Duke University Press, 1986).

9. See M. V. Pylee, *India's Constitution,* 3rd rev. ed. (New York: Asia House, 1980); and Richard L. Park and Bruce Bueno de Mesquita, *India's Political System,* 2nd ed. (Englewood Cliffs, NJ: Prentice Hall, 1979).

10. See Sabrina Ramet, *Nationalism and Federalism in Yugoslavia, 1962–1991,* 2nd ed. (Bloomington, IN: Indiana University Press, 1992).

11. Canadian political scientist Robert A. Young, assuming the 1995 Quebec referendum would pass, wrote a sober assessment of what would (and still may) happen. See his *The Secession of Quebec and the Future of Canada* (Montreal: McGill-Queen's University Press, 1995). For prescriptions to help Canada save itself, see Gordon Gibson, *Thirty Million Musketeers: One Canada, for All Canadians* (Toronto, Porter Books, 1995).

12. See Paul E. Peterson, *The Price of Federalism* (Washington, DC: Brookings Institution, 1995).

13.   See Richard P. Nathan and Fred C. Doolittle, *Reagan and the States* (Princeton, NJ: Princeton University Press, 1987).

14.   Duverger's linkage of the electoral system and party system holds up remarkably well. Maurice Duverger, *Political Parties,* 3rd ed. (London: Methuen, 1964), pp. 206–55.

15.   See Philip E. Converse and Roy Pierce, *Political Representation in France* (Cambridge, MA: Harvard University Press, 1986).

16.   For the mathematically inclined, the d'Hondt and other systems are explained in Douglas Rae, *The Political Consequences of Electoral Laws,* rev. ed. (New Haven, CT: Yale University Press, 1971), Chap. 2.

· 14 ·
Legislatures

Political institutions, it is theorized, become more specialized, complex, and differentiated as they become more modern. Primitive hunting bands may have nothing more than a single leader who decides everything. Tribes may add councils of elders to debate major problems and adjudicate disputes. The Athenian assembly combined legislative, executive, and judicial roles. The Romans developed a senate, but it, too, combined several roles, and its powers declined as Rome went from republic to empire. In the Middle Ages, the prevailing feudal system was a balance among a monarch, nobles, and leading churchmen, and it is in feudalism that we first get a glimpse of the "balance of power." Pledged the nobles of Aragon (in northeast Spain) to a new king, "We, who are as good as you, swear to you, who are no better than we, to accept you as our king and sovereign lord provided you observe all our statutes and laws; and if not, no."[1]

Ambitious monarchs, who were often at war, desperately needed revenues. Some of them started calling assemblies of notables to levy taxes. In return for their "power of the purse," some of these assemblies were allowed a modest input into royal policies. Such were the beginnings of the British Parliament, which is divided into two houses (Lords for peers and church leaders and Commons for knights and burghers), and the Swedish Riksdag, which originally had four chambers (for nobles, clerics, burghers, and farmers). The French Estates General, with three houses (for nobles, clerics, and commoners), got off to a weak start and was soon forgotten as French monarchs gathered more and more personal power in what became known as absolutism.

In Britain, Sweden, and some other European countries, though, legislatures slowly grew in power and were able to resist the absolutist demands of monarchs. In Britain in the sixteenth century, Henry VIII, who broke with Rome because he wanted a divorce, developed a partnership with Parliament because he needed its support in passing laws to get England out of the Catholic church and the church out of England. By the seventeenth century, Parliament considered itself coequal with the monarch and even supreme in the area of taxes. The English Civil War was a quarrel between royalists and parliamentarians over who had top power. In 1649 Parliament decided the issue by executing Charles I.

Mother of Parliaments. Westminster, on the banks of the Thames River in London, represents the slow, gradual march to democracy over many centuries.

John Locke, the English philosopher who lived through this momentous period, extolled the power of the "legislative" as the most basic and important.[2] During the Age of Enlightenment in the eighteenth century, political theorists such as Montesquieu and Jefferson declared that liberty could be secured only if government were divided into two distinct branches, the legislative and the executive, each having the ability to check and balance the other. Modern governments are generally still divided into these two branches. Theoretically, at least, the legislature enacts laws (rule initiation) that allocate values for society and the executive branch enforces the statutes (rule application) passed by the legislature. (A coequal judicial branch is rare; it is chiefly a U.S. invention.) But these responsibilities often overlap, and the separation of powers is rarely clear-cut.

Presidential and Parliamentary

Presidential democracies most clearly show the separation of power between the executive and legislative branches. The chief hallmark of these systems is that the president is not just a figurehead but also a functioning *head of government*. He or she is elected more or less directly by the people (in the United States, of course, the quaint Electoral College mediates between the people and the actual election), is invested with considerable powers, and cannot be easily ousted by the legislative body. In parliamentary systems, the *head of state* (figurehead monarch or weak president) is an office distinct from the head of government (prime minister, premier, or chancellor). In this system, the prime minister is the important figure.

Notice (see Figure 14.1) that in parliamentary systems voters elect only a legislature; they cannot split their tickets between the legislature and executive. The legislature then elects an executive from its own ranks. If the electoral system is based on proportional representation (see Chapter 13), chances are there will be several parties in parliament. If no one party has a majority of the seats, two or more parties will have to form a coalition. Whether one party or several, a majority of parliament must support the cabinet. Usually a monarch (as in Britain and Spain) or weak president (as in Germany or Israel) "asks"—there's no real choice in the matter—the head of the largest party to "form a government." In most countries, the words *cabinet* and *government* are used interchangeably. The prime minister, after consulting with the parties likely to support him or her, names a team of ministers for the cabinet who are themselves members of the parliament.[3] These ministers then guide the various ministries or departments of government that form the executive branch. The prime minister and cabinet are "responsible" (in the original sense of the word, "answerable") to the parliament. (Prior to democratization in the nineteenth century, ministers were responsible only to the monarch.)

Presidents in presidential systems are not responsible to legislatures. The close connection between the legislative and executive is broken. Presidents are elected on their own and choose cabinet ministers or department secretaries from *outside* the ranks of the legislative body. In the United States, of course, top execu-

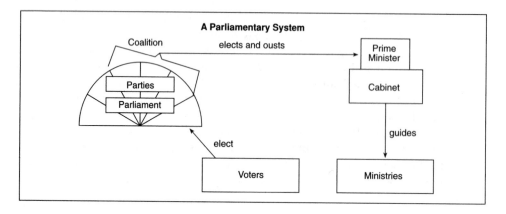

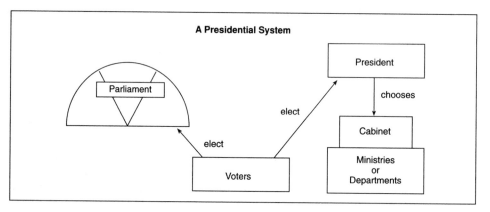

FIGURE 14.1   Parliamentary versus Presidential Systems

tive and judicial officers must be approved by the Senate. The two branches of government cannot control, dissolve, or oust the other, as can happen in parliamentary systems. This gives presidential systems great stability. The president may be unpopular and face a hostile Congress, but he or she can still govern with existing constitutional and statutory powers already in hand.

ADVANTAGES OF PARLIAMENTARY SYSTEMS

The United States takes great pride in its separation of powers, the famous "checks and balances" that the Founding Fathers insisted on. Under this system, no branch of government should accumulate too much power. Having just won independence from George III and his feared executive dictatorship, they set one branch of government as a check against the power of another. It was an extremely clever arrangement, and it has admirably preserved America from tyranny. But it is a terribly slow and cumbersome arrangement, an "invitation to struggle" between the executive and legislative branches.[4] Rarely does either branch get everything it wants. The two branches can effectively stymie each other. Congress can fail to pass something the president wants, and the president can veto something Congress wants. Some scholars think such an executive-legislative *deadlock* is virtually the norm for the U.S. presidential system.[5]

Important legislative matters, such as tax reform, can get stuck for years between the two branches of government. The president cannot dissolve Congress and hold new elections, which are set by the calendar. Congress cannot oust a president except by the impeachment procedure. Only one president, Andrew Johnson in 1868, has ever been impeached, and he was not convicted by the Senate. Richard Nixon resigned before the House of Representatives could vote to impeach him. The repeated showdowns of the sort between the Clinton administration and the Republican-dominated Congress are quite common in U.S. history.

West Europeans consider the American system inefficient and unintelligible, and actually they are equipped with more modern systems that evolved after the U.S. Constitution was devised. Their parliamentary systems have a *fusion of power* that does not set the branches against each other. In fact, it's sometimes hard to distinguish between legislative and executive branches, for the top executives are themselves usually members of parliament. In the British, German, Japanese, and Dutch systems, the prime ministers must be elected to parliament, just like an ordinary legislator, before he or she can become head of government. As leaders of the biggest parties, they are formally called on (by the monarch or figurehead president) to form a government. The individuals forming this government or cabinet then transfer from the parliament to the executive departments in order to run them. They must report back nearly continuously to the parliament. At any time, about a hundred British MPs (members of Parliament) also serve at various levels in the executive ministries and departments. Thus legislators are also executives. The cabinet, in effect, is a committee of parliament sent over to supervise the administration of the executive branches of government.

When Britain's parliament is in session, the cabinet members are present and must answer questions from their fellow members of parliament. Britain's House of Commons holds a Question Hour every afternoon at the beginning of the session. The members of the two main parties sit facing each other across an aisle on, respectively, the "government benches" and "opposition benches." The front bench of the former is reserved for cabinet ministers, the front bench of the latter for the opposition's "shadow cabinet," who are the MPs who would become ministers if their party should win the next election; MPs without any executive responsibilities sit behind the cabinets and are called "backbenchers." Most questions to the prime minister and his or her cabinet come from the opposition benches—first written questions and then oral follow-ups. The questions elicit government answers on policy. The answers are criticized, and the opposition generally tries to embarrass the government with an eye to winning the next election. Most parliamentary systems have analogues to the British Question Hour. In the U.S. system, with its separation of powers, committees of the Senate or House can summon cabinet members and other officials of the executive branch to committee hearings. But appearing before a committee is not the same as a grilling before the entire legislative body. The president, of course, as equal to and separate from Congress, cannot be called to testify.

There are several advantages to a parliamentary system. The executive-legislative deadlock, which happens frequently in the American system, cannot occur because both the executive and legislative branches are governed by the same party. If the British Conservatives win a majority of the seats in the House of Commons, the leaders of the party are automatically the country's executives. When the Conservative cabinet drafts a new law, it is sent to the House of Commons to be passed. There is rarely any difficulty or much delay in getting the law passed because the Conservative MPs almost invariably obey the wishes of the party's leaders. If, by some strange circumstance, members of the governing party should disagree with their own leaders in the cabinet, they can withdraw their support and vote "no confidence" in the government. The government then "falls" and must be replaced by a new leadership team that commands the support of a majority of the House of Commons. If a new election gives the opposition party the numerical edge in parliament, the cabinet resigns and is replaced by the leaders of the newly victorious party, formerly known as the "shadow cabinet." Either way, there cannot be a long disagreement between executive and legislative branches; they are fused into one.

The prime minister and cabinet can be speedily ousted in parliamentary systems. Any important vote in parliament can be designated a vote of confidence. If the prime minister loses, he or she takes it as a signal of lack of parliamentary support and resigns. There is no agony of impending impeachment of the sort that paralyzed Washington for more than a year under President Nixon. A new prime minister can be voted in immediately. If the government makes a major policy blunder, parliament can get rid of the cabinet without waiting for its term to expire. When many Americans became unhappy with President Carter's policies, there was nothing the system could do to remove him from the White House earlier than January 1981. Many Americans felt they were stuck with an unpopular president; parliamentary systems don't get stuck with unpopular prime ministers.

PROBLEMS OF PARLIAMENTARY SYSTEMS

Parliamentary systems have other difficulties, however. First, because members of parliament generally obey their party leaders, votes in parliament can be closely predicted. The parties supporting the government will vote for a bill the cabinet has drafted. Parties opposing the government will vote against it. Floor speeches and corridor persuasion have no impact; the legislators vote the way their party instructs. Members of a parliament in such systems have lost their independence, and their parliaments have become little more than rubber stamps for the cabinet. The passage of legislation is more rational, speedy, and efficient, to be sure; but the legislature in such systems can no longer "talk back" to the executive or make independent inputs. This makes European parliaments rather dull and less important than Capitol Hill in Washington, where legislators often oppose the president, even when of their own party. Many European legislators are jealous of the spunky independence and separate resources that American representatives and senators enjoy.

Second, depending on the party system and electoral system, parliamentary democracies often have many parties, with no single party controlling a majority of seats in parliament. This means the largest party must form a *coalition* with smaller parties in order to command more than half the seats.[6] Typically, the head of the largest party is prime minister, and the head of the second largest party is foreign minister. Other cabinet positions, or portfolios, are assigned by bargaining. Italy and Israel are often examples of coalition governments, and they illustrate what can go wrong: the coalition partners frequently quarrel over policy. Eventually one or more parties withdraw from the coalition, bringing it below the required majority in parliament. The government then "falls" for lack of parliamentary support, with or without a formal vote of no confidence. This leads to instability, frequent cabinet changes, and loss of executive authority. Italy, for example, has had some fifty governments since the end of World War II.

This is not as bad as it sounds—remember, the "government" simply means "cabinet"—and Italian cabinets are usually put back together again after bargaining among the same coalition partners. The trouble is that prime ministers must concentrate on not letting the coalition fall apart, and thus they hesitate to launch new policies that might alienate one of the member parties. The Italian problem is not one of too much change but of too little: the same parties putting together the same coalitions and getting stuck over the same issues. Poland had a similar problem. *Immobilism*, the inability to decide major questions, is the danger of multiparty parliamentary systems. Notice how this parallels the problem of deadlock in presidential systems.

Not all parliamentary systems, to be sure, suffer from immobilism. Britain, Germany, New Zealand, and Spain have cohesive and effective cabinets because they have to share little or no power in coalition governments. The largest parties in these countries are big enough to govern either alone or with only a little help from like-minded parties. The German coalition has fallen only once, in 1982, when the small Free Democratic party abandoned the Social Democrats and went to the Christian Democrats to form a new coalition. The fall of a cabinet because of defection is equally rare in Britain: since World War II it happened only once, when the small Scottish Nationalist party withdrew its support from the minority Labour government in 1979. In general, the more parties in a coalition, the less stable it tends to be.

The Roles of the Legislature

The main purpose of legislative bodies, in theory, is to formulate the laws that govern society. In practice, the degree to which the legislature acts as law initiator varies among political systems and is generally believed to be in decline. Ideally, legislatures initiate laws, propose constitutional amendments, ratify treaties, control tax revenues, and act as a check on the other branches of government.[7]

LAWMAKING

The chief job of democratic legislatures is supposed to be that of rule initiation: making the laws that govern society. How does a bill become law? The first step is to draft and introduce the proposed bill. In the German Bundestag, individual legislators may not introduce bills on their own but must join a *Fraktion* (a group of fifteen members) to propose legislation. In most democratic legislatures, any member may introduce a bill. Without the support of a larger group, however, it may not get very far. Rule initiation, though, often originates in the executive branch, with an agency drafting a proposal and finding a sympathetic legislator to introduce the bill in Congress. When senators or representatives want to propose a bill of their own, their staffs usually do the actual writing, with the Office of the Legislative Council checking to ensure proper wording. In parliamentary governments, the executive branch may introduce legislation directly, since cabinet members hold seats in the legislature. The Swiss save time by introducing all bills in both houses simultaneously, and whereas this is not always the case in the United States, here, too, high-priority bills are usually introduced in both houses at the same time.

Formal introduction of a bill in the U.S. Congress begins when the proposal is registered with the clerk of the House or Senate and referred to the appropriate committee. Most bills are tabled, or laid aside, by the committee after brief consideration, never to be heard of again. However, when the committee thinks a bill has merit, it is sent to a subcommittee for further investigation. Public hearings, which can last for months if a controversial measure is up for discussion, may be held on very important bills. When staff investigations or public hearings are concluded, the bill is then reviewed by the full committee. At this point, the committee may modify certain sections of the bill before voting for or against its passage. If the bill is approved, it goes to the House Rules Committee or Senate majority leader and is then placed on the calendar of the appropriate house for floor consideration.[8]

Once on the floor, the bill is again debated, amended, and revised before it is voted on by the House or Senate. If a majority of each house carries the bill, the Senate and the House then create a conference committee, where differences between the two versions are ironed out. The agreed-on bill then goes back to the House and Senate for a routine revote, where it rarely encounters any controversy. The legislation is then signed by the heads of both houses and sent to the president for action. If the president signs the bill, it becomes law. If not, Congress needs a hard-to-achieve two-thirds majority to override the veto. If the president neither signs the bill nor vetoes it, it automatically becomes law in ten days—if the Congress is still in session. But if Congress adjourns before the ten days have elapsed, the bill does not become law. This latter approach is known as the "pocket veto."

Although legislatures *pass* laws, few of them *originate* laws—which is why we must take their "rule-making function" with a grain of salt. In a highly technical age, much legislation actually originates in government departments and agencies, comes to the attention of cabinet officers, and is sent on to the legislature, which may alter it somewhat. In highly developed parliamentary systems, where one party controls both the executive and legislature (as in Britain and New Zealand), the cabinet gets what it wants. Committee work and parliamentary debate don't count for much because party discipline makes sure that members of the ruling parties will nearly automatically vote the way their party leaders instruct them to vote. Votes in such legislatures are highly predictable along party lines; some observers say such parliaments have become rubber stamps for the executive. The U.S. Congress, with its weak and decentralized party system, represents at least a partial rejection of this development. Party discipline is weak, and members sometimes buck their own party. But even in the United States, notice how much of the legislative agenda is determined by items sent over from the White House: economic initiatives, use of troops overseas, expanding or cutting domestic programs, and setting new criteria for pollution or auto safety. Even the budget, the original "power of the purse" that gave legislatures their importance, is now an annual congressional *reaction* to the budget produced by the White House budget office. Accordingly, "lawmaking" is not the only nor perhaps even the most important thing that legislatures do.

Constituency Work.   Legislators spend a prodigious amount of time helping constituents.[9] Some have staffs in their districts and capitol offices to answer letters, make sure people get their Social Security checks, and generally show that the members of Congress really care. Often the "lawmaker" is so busy with constituency casework—which is important in getting reelected—that he or she pays little attention to making laws. In effect, elected representatives have partly transformed themselves into *ombudsmen,* specialists who intervene with government on behalf of people with complaints. Is there anything wrong with this? Is it not a perfectly valid and necessary role for legislators to play? It is, but at the same time something gets lost: the wider view that a representative of the people should have in helping guide the country. A legislator immersed in constituency work has no time for or interest in bigger questions, so the initiative goes more and more to the executive branch. What then will become of democracy?

Constituency service is one main way elected representatives keep getting reelected. Incumbents are in a position to do favors. They frequently visit their home districts to listen to local problems and arrange for government help, something an out-of-office challenger cannot do. Thus legislators in systems as different as those of the United States and South Korea can lock themselves into power.[10]

Supervision and Criticism of Government.   The potentially more important role of modern legislatures is keeping a sharp and critical eye on the executive branch. Even if they don't originate much legislation, legislatures can powerfully affect the work of government by monitoring government activity to make sure it is in the nation's interest, uncorrupt, and effective. The Bush administration, for example, found it had to modify its policies on Eastern Europe, environmental pollution, judicial appointments, and strategic weapons, all because Congress had raised difficult and sometimes embarrassing questions, even though it had passed little legislation on these matters.

In Britain, the Question Hour allows members of Parliament to grill ministers, sometimes with devastating results. Even if the British cabinet knows that it is almost immune to a vote of no confidence—because it controls the largest party in Commons—its members must be very careful in answering these questions. If they give a bad, unconvincing answer to a difficult question, or, even worse, if they try to cover up by lying, it can cost the ruling party dearly in the next election. In the 1963 Profumo affair, a Tory minister was caught lying (about his affair with a call girl) in Parliament; Labour charged the government with laxity on national security and with covering up for one of its "old boys." Labour won the 1964 election in large part because of the Profumo scandal.

In Israel in 1983, the Begin government had partly to pull out of Lebanon because of criticism in the Knesset that the campaign was lasting too long, costing too many lives, and not producing a stable solution. In 1987, congressional investigations of White House dealings with Iran and Nicaraguan contras shook the Reagan administration. Keeping the government on its toes is one of the best things a legislature can do, even if it doesn't pass any laws.

Education.   One of the less noticed functions of legislatures is their ability to inform and instruct the citizenry on the affairs of government; they are not merely passive inputting devices, taking mass demands and channeling them into government. Legislatures also create mass demands by calling public attention to problems.[11] In the mid-1960s, Senator J. William Fulbright (D–Arkansas), chair of the Senate Foreign Relations Committee, educated many Americans about the Vietnam war by televising his committee's hearings, in which a series of experts and government officials variously defended and criticized U.S. policy. In Britain and in countries based on its "Westminster model," such as Australia and India, much parliamentary debate is carried in the press nationwide.

Representation.   One of the chief functions of legislatures is to represent people. Although nowhere is there a close match between the characteristics of legislators and those of the people they represent, nonetheless most legislators in most democracies feel they must consider the interest of all their constituents. Even in the U.S. South, now that African-Americans are voting in considerable numbers, members of Congress generally take care not to offend them. A large part of representation is psychological; people like to *feel* they're represented. When they don't feel represented, they become resentful of government power, and the government loses legitimacy. "No taxation without representation," chanted the American colonials. One may wonder if some members of parliament representing the thirteen colonies might not have headed off the Declaration of Independence. The laws of South Africa, until recently passed by a white-dominated legislature, evoked little support and much disobedience from the black majority of that country.

The foregoing are some of the roles performed by legislatures. Note that only one of them is lawmaking, and that is usually just a follow-up on ideas initiated by bureaucrats and executives. Still, if legislatures fulfill the other roles mentioned, they're doing a lot.

The Structure of Parliaments

BICAMERAL OR UNICAMERAL

Some two-thirds of the legislative bodies in the world have two chambers, an upper house (the U.S. Senate, the British House of Lords, or the German Bundesrat) plus a lower house (the U.S. House of Representatives, the British House of Commons, or the German Bundestag). These are called *bicameral* (two chambers) legislatures. Despite its name, the upper house usually has less and sometimes much less power than the lower house; only the two houses of the U.S. Congress are coequal. A smaller number of parliaments are *unicameral* (one chamber), such as China's National Peoples Congress, Sweden's Riksdag, and Israel's Knesset. Yugoslavia once experimented with a five-chambered parliament. South Africa had a curious and short-lived three-chambered parliament with one house each for whites, mixed-race peoples, and East Indians. The majority black population was unrepresented in the national parliament of South Africa. (Since 1994, South Africa has had a bicameral parliament with a black majority.)

The reason for two chambers is clear in federal systems (see Chapter 13). The upper house represents the component parts of the federal system, and the lower house represents districts based on population. This was the great compromise solution incorporated in the U.S. Constitution: The Senate represented the states and the House the people. A federal system axiomatically requires an upper chamber. Germany's Bundesrat, for example, represents the sixteen *Länder* and is coequal to the lower house on constitutional questions. On other issues, however, it can be overridden.

The utility of an upper house in unitary systems, however, is unclear. Britain's House of Lords (its members or "peers" are chosen by either heredity or by lifetime appointment) is mostly an elderly debating society that sometimes catches errors in laws passed too quickly and obediently by the House of Commons. Otherwise the Commons overrides any objection from the House of Lords with a simple majority vote. This is also true of the French Senat, an indirectly elected body that largely expresses farming interests. The New Zealanders, Danes, and Swedes—all with unitary systems—came to the conclusion that their upper houses served no purpose and abolished them in recent decades.

THE COMMITTEE SYSTEM

Virtually every legislature has a number of standing or permanent committees, and may from time to time create special ad hoc committees to study urgent matters. The British House of Commons has five standing committees plus several new specialized committees. These committees are less important than their U.S. counterparts, for the fusion of powers of the British system means that Parliament is not supposed to review carefully, criticize, or reject bills the cabinet has submitted. Operating within the framework of the separation of powers, it is in the U.S. Congress

The Finnish parliament is unicameral—no upper chamber—and consists of 200 seats arrayed in a semicircle, the standard layout for parliaments. Also standard are the buttons on each member's desk to register his or her vote, which is then electronically tabulated and displayed instantly.

that the committee system has been most fully developed.[12] The House of Representatives has twenty-seven standing committees—the Senate, twenty-one—and they often make the news. We often hear of the more prestigious of these committees, such as the House Ways and Means and Foreign Affairs, and we know that a good committee assignment is a boon to the career of a new member of Congress.

What purposes do these committees serve? Their major function, of course, is to screen the thousands on thousands of bills that are introduced at every session and pick out the few that merit serious study and consideration. Second, legislatures are so large that bills cannot be drafted by the entire membership; to work out an agreement on the precise wording and scope of legislation, proposals must be referred to relatively small groups of lawmakers who will iron out differences and submit polished bills for the consideration of the whole membership. It should not be surprising, therefore, that the bulk of legislative work is not performed on the floor of the House or Senate but is done in committee and subcommittee rooms.

Further, each committee usually has several specialized subcommittees; the two houses have a total of about 250 subcommittees. Changes in the 1970s weakened what were considered to be the tyrannical powers of committee chairpersons by making it easier to establish subcommittees. It worked; committees and their chairpersons are not what they used to be. But now, critics charge, subcommittees and *their* chairpersons have decentralized and fragmented power too much, weakening Congress as an institution. A cure for one problem produced new problems, the story of many political reforms.

A Senate subcommittee hearing chaired by Senator Joseph Biden (D–Delaware) hears testimony from experts and interest groups on the situation of East European minorities. Much legislative work is done in such committees, often with little notice from the press or public.

These same reforms of the 1970s broke the power of appointment of the senior House and Senate leaders of both parties. Committee chairs and membership were generally assigned on the basis of seniority. Now, when the parties caucus at the beginning of a session in each house, members vote for committee chairpersons by secret ballot, effectively breaking the seniority system. Party committees in each house make committee assignments and usually try to take members' interests and expertise into account. Capitol Hill is now more open and democratic than it used to be, but interestingly, this has not enhanced its power vis-à-vis the executive branch.[13]

Standing Committees.   In Great Britain and France, standing committees are not as specialized and lack the political influence of their American counterparts. The standing committees in the British Parliament are designed to be flexible and broad and have traditionally played a less critical role than the American committees. They work out the details of a bill after the House of Commons has approved it, rather than sitting in judgment on the bill before it reaches the Commons floor. However, the age of specialization has been felt in Britain too, and parliamentary reforms have increased the degree of committee specialization. Education, overseas aid and development, race relations, science and technology, nationalized industries, and Scottish affairs all rate permanent committees in Commons. The counterpart in the French National Assembly is the commission—again not as compartmentalized as the American committee. In studying a bill, the commission assigns only one member—called the *rapporteur*—to the task, rather than working collectively as in the United States and Britain. In the United States, specialization is the name of the game. The larger committees, such as the Senate Foreign Relations Committee, may have a dozen subcommittees.[14]

Standing committees in Congress are balanced so that they will represent both political parties and the states or geographic regions with the greatest interest in the committee's area of specialization. For example, Nebraska has someone on the Agricultural Committee, and New York is usually represented on the Education and Labor Committee. Each standing committee is bipartisan, made up of Democrats and Republicans in direct proportion to each party's representation in that house of Congress. If the House is 60 percent Republican, the House Ways and Means Committee will be, too. Italy adds an interesting power to its standing committees, which also reflect proportional representation of the whole chamber. Italian committees, meeting *in sede deliberante,* can actually pass legislation without bringing it to the full house. This can speed up much routine legislation. Given Italy's disciplined parties, the vote in committee duplicates the vote of the whole chamber, so nothing is lost but delay.

The Decline of Legislatures

By the late nineteenth century, observers began to notice that parliaments were not working the way they were supposed to.[15] Contrary to Locke's expectations, legislatures seemed to be losing power to the executive. Most political scientists would agree that the trend has continued and perhaps worsened.[16] Some, however, such as Jean Blondel, hold that the original Lockean expectations were too high to begin with and that parliaments provide useful checks on the executive even though they do not originate much legislation.[17]

Structural Disadvantages.   There are many reasons why legislatures do not fulfill the Lockean ideal. In parliamentary systems, party discipline is strong, and legislators obey party whips. Members of the legislative body are rarely moved by speeches or debates to vote against their party. If they do, they can lose their party's endorsement and be dropped from the party list at the next election. In effect, they are fired from parliament. Gilbert and Sullivan summed it up in the words of a successful British politician in *H. M. S. Pinafore:* "I always voted at my party's call and never thought of thinking for myself at all." In European parliaments we can usually predict within a vote or two how the issue will be decided: most often in favor of the government because the government (or cabinet) commands a majority of seats. In such systems, there's not a great deal for an individual member of parliament to do. No special excitement is evident in the press and public about parliamentary affairs. Only when coalitions break up or when members of one party defect to another (a rare occurrence) do things get unpredictable and therefore interesting. The European parliaments really are more rational and efficient than the U.S. Congress, but they are also less powerful and less interesting. Efficiency has led to atrophy.

The U.S. Capitol Hill has no such problem with efficiency. Its near feudal dispersion of power with weak party discipline and its tendency to deadlock with the executive have made it most inefficient. Yet it is precisely these impediments that keep Congress lively and important. In few other countries can the national legislature as a whole "talk back" to the executive and even override a presidential veto. In parliamentary systems, the opposition parties criticize the government party, but the government party does not criticize its own cabinet in power. Nevertheless, even in the United States power has drifted to the executive. The president speaks with one voice, Congress with many. Congress is fragmented into committees and subcommittees—with chairpersons vying for media attention—and this delays and often prevents agreement. Congress expects and even demands presidential leadership and usually gives presidents most of what they want after some controversy and debate. Even the Republican-controlled Congress had to bend in the direction of Clinton's wishes.

One case illustrates Congress's dependency on the president's power. Despairing of ever being able to cut the huge spending budget, Congress attempted to hand the power to an appointed congressional official in the 1985 Gramm-Rudman Act. The Supreme Court, more aware of the constitutional issues than most members of Congress, immediately threw out this provision in the law. Congress then attempted to hand the power to cut the budget to the White House with the 1996 "line-item" veto, a major (and possibly unconstitutional) shift in power from the legislative to the executive. It was almost as if Congress were saying, "We give up; we're too divided. So here, Mr. President, you take over our constitutional duties." The astonishing thing about the U.S. Congress, the last Mohican of independent legislatures, is that it *wants* to surrender power to the executive.

Lack of Expertise. Few legislators are experts on technical, military, economic, or social problems. Of the 535 senators and representatives in the 105th Congress, nearly half are lawyers. European nations have fewer lawyers in their parliaments and more schoolteachers, journalists, and full-time party people. But hardly any technical experts are elected to legislatures, and few legislators are professionally equipped to deal with such technical matters as nuclear power, medical care, international currency fluctuations, and environmental pollution. Accordingly, legislators must rely chiefly on experts sent over from the executive departments. Much legislation originates with these specialists, and they are often called as witnesses to committee hearings. The ensuing legislation usually grants these executive specialists considerable discretion in applying the law.

Most parliaments have little or nothing in the way of independent research support; their data come either from the government or from private interest groups. Only the U.S. Congress—again, based on the idea of separation of powers—can generate its own data. The General Accounting Office (GAO), Congressional Research Service (CRS), and Congressional Budget Office (CBO) are all part of the legislative branch. They attempt to provide independent evaluations and data to lessen Congress's dependence on the executive.[18] No other legislature in the world has a fraction of this research capability. Still, it remains to be seen if the research agencies of Congress can counterbalance the massive information advantage of the executive branch.

Some hope computers can help legislators overcome this information gap. At first computers were used in legislators' offices simply as advanced typewriters, to speed up the handling of constituent letters. More recently, though, computer networks have been set up to put at the legislators' fingertips all types of government and private data.[19] Theoretically, this step could make parliamentarians almost as knowledgeable as bureaucrats. The catch is that the legislator still needs the time and interest to review reams of data. In most cases, legislative assistants who specialize in certain areas are the ones who make use of computerized data bases; they then pass on their findings to the elected member.

Psychological Disadvantages.   The citizenry of any country is more impressed with its presidents or prime ministers than with its parliament. There may be a deep human need to respond to a single leading personality. A president can have charisma, but whoever heard of a charismatic legislature? American children are socialized to revere the president but to disdain members of Congress. As was mentioned in Chapter 12, even in parliamentary systems voters now respond to the personalities of the candidates for prime minister. Television, by giving a great deal more air time to chief executives than to any other political figure, heightens this tendency. People come to see their president or prime minister as a parental figure, calmly guiding the country toward safety while the silly parliamentarians squabble among themselves. School textbooks in the United States often depict the president as a sort of "daddy." This leads to what some political scientists fear is "president worship."

The Absentee Problem.   If you visit a legislature in session you might be disappointed, for usually the chamber is nearly empty. Most of the time, most members don't have to be present, and they aren't. They have a lot of other things to do: helping and visiting constituents, giving speeches to interest groups, and sitting on committees. Why bother listening to speeches in the chamber? They're not going to change anyone's mind, and everyone pretty much knows their content in advance. The speeches are not for other legislators; they're for the mass media.

Absent most of the time, the member is really needed only to vote, and sometimes not even then. British party whips can get a high turnout for an important vote. In Sweden, an electronic system summons members from all over the Riksdag after the speeches are over. They press their *ja* or *nej* button according to their parties' wishes, glance up at the electronic tabulation (which was never in doubt), and then leave. The Riksdag chamber has been full for only five to ten minutes.

Most systems have ways of recording members' votes without their presence. When the French National Assembly votes, a few members of each party move down the rows of absent fellow party members' desks and flick their voting switches to a *pour* or *contre* position, as the party has specified. The press then reports that the measure passed by a vote of around 300 to 200, but that account is deceptive, as typically only three dozen members were present for the vote.[20] Theoretically, the French system could function with just one member present from each party.

The U.S. House and Senate require members to be present to vote, but even if absent they can arrange to have their votes "paired against" that of another absent legislator with the opposite viewpoint. The yes vote cancels out the no vote, so the passage of the measure is unaffected, and the member can still claim to have voted for or against something.

What is the impact of legislative absenteeism? It may indicate that the legislator is busy doing other important things of the sort discussed earlier. It may also indicate just plain laziness. But it surely means that legislators no longer regard legislating as their chief function. By their absence they admit that they are not important, at least not in the way originally seen for legislators. Is there any way to fix the problem? Only by weakening party discipline and party-line voting so that no one could predict how a floor vote would go. If bills were up for grabs, some excitement and tension would return to floor debate, and members would have an interest and incentive to show up and participate. The trade-off would be that the passage of legislation would be more chaotic and unpredictable.

Lack of Turnover. In most democratic parliaments, members tend to become career, lifetime legislators. Once elected, they usually get reelected until retirement. This means it's difficult for fresh, young blood with new ideas to enter parliament, and on average parliamentarians are rather old, in their fifties. In the U.S. House, most representatives run for reelection, and almost all win. Incumbency brings terrific advantages: name recognition, favors done for constituents, media coverage, and plentiful campaign funds from PACs and other interest groups. Unless the representative has gotten involved in some scandal, he or she is almost automatically reelected. Challengers are so discouraged that several dozen House incumbents run unopposed. In many other contests opposition is only token. Why waste time and money in a hopeless race?

What happens to democracy when an elected representative is not often ousted until death or retirement? It loses some of its ability to innovate and respond to new currents in public opinion. It gets stodgy. The Founding Fathers made the House term deliberately short, just two years, to let popular views wash freely into the chamber. Alexander Hamilton described the frequent elections to the House in this way: "Here, sir, the people govern. Here they act by their immediate representatives." He might have a hard time believing that usually almost all representatives who wish to run win reelection and that turnover is actually higher in the Senate, a chamber that was designed to be insulated from mass passions. All this has raised the question of limits on congressional terms.[21] Elections in the 1990s, however, have brought a major influx of new faces—partly due to the retirements of incumbents—so that now the average Representative has served less than ten years. With turnover like that, mandatory limits seem unnecessary.

The parliamentary systems have similar problems. Few legislators are replaced by elections and most consider their membership in parliament a career. If the system is proportional representation (discussed in Chapter 13), the more senior party people are higher up on the election list, ensuring their election. Young newcomers may be entered at the bottom of their party lists with scant chance of winning. However, PR systems do have the advantage of letting new, small parties into parliament with fresh faces and new ideas. In the 1980s, the Greens (as ecology parties like to be called) entered several West European parliaments, forcing the big, established parties to pay attention to environmental problems.

The Dilemma of Parliaments

The showdown between Russian President Boris Yeltsin and the Russian legislature, the Supreme Soviet, in 1993 illustrates the dilemma of parliaments. To get things done, power must be concentrated, as in the hands of a powerful executive. To keep things democratic, however, power must be dispersed, that is, kept divided between an executive and a legislature. Russia urgently needed vast reforms—the entire economy had to be redone, for example—and Yeltsin claimed to be the leader to carry them out. The Supreme Soviet, on the other hand, disputed and blocked Yeltsin. Personalities and economic interests were part of the problem. Yeltsin, a long-time Communist official, was a newcomer to the idea of democracy; it was circumstances that pushed him in a democratic direction. He preferred one-man rule, and many believed he harbored dictatorial tendencies. The Supreme Soviet was not so pure, either; it was elected when the Communists were still in power and was composed partly of ex-Communists. Some of them represented, or were themselves, bosses of industries that would disappear with economic reforms, thus ending their privileged lifestyle. For the first time Russia was experiencing the sort of executive-legislative deadlock well known in the United States, a problem that continued even after a new parliament, the State Duma, was elected in 1993.

How this problem is solved will determine much of the future course of democracy in Russia. One man may take over and "get things done," but it may not be democratic. An obstreperous parliament, stacked with special interests, may preserve pluralism and block dictatorship, but at the price of accomplishing little. The new Duma elected in late 1995 made matters worse, as power in it shifted to anti-reformers led by a revived Communist party, producing a French-style "cohabitation" (see next chapter) until Russian presidential elections were held in 1996. Although the two branches stymied each other, it is precisely this struggle between them—making sure that neither gains too much power—that helps build democracy. We cannot offer the Russians much in the way of specific advice on how to achieve executive-legislative balance. The Russians have no tradition of democracy, parliaments, or limited government, and their problems are far larger and more desperate than outs. We can assure them, however, that executive-legislative problems can be solved and offer ourselves as a modest and ungainly example.

Suggested Readings

COPELAND, GARY W., and SAMUEL C. PATTERSON, eds. *Parliaments in the Modern World: Changing Institutions.* Ann Arbor, MI: University of Michigan Press, 1994. Six valuable case stud-ies of how European parliaments have adapted over time.

CRABB, CECIL V., JR., and PAT M. HOLT. *Invitation to Struggle: Congress, the President, and Foreign*

Policy, 4th ed. Washington, DC: CQ Press, 1991. Details how Congress tries, but does not always succeed, in making a policy impact.

DODD, LAWRENCE C., and BRUCE I. OPPENHEIMER, eds. *Congress Reconsidered,* 5th ed. Washington, DC: CQ Press, 1993. Excellent collection of essays by knowledgeable specialists.

FIORINA, MORRIS P., and DAVID W. ROHDE, eds. *Home Style and Washington Work: Studies of Congressional Politics.* Ann Arbor: University of Michigan Press, 1989. Excellent collection of essays exploring legislators' roles.

FRANKLIN, DANIEL P. *Making Ends Meet: Congressional Budgeting in the Age of Deficits.* Washington, DC: CQ Press, 1992. An in-depth case study of passing the 1991 budget.

HARRIS, FRED R. *In Defense of Congress.* New York: St. Martin's, 1995. A former U.S. senator considers the many media criticisms of Congress and ably refutes them.

———. *Deadlock or Decision: The U.S. Senate and the Rise of National Politics.* New York: Oxford University Press 1993. There is a tradeoff between the Senate's efficiency and its democracy, between responsibility and responsiveness.

LIJPART, AREND, ed. *Parliamentary versus Presidential Government.* New York: Oxford University Press, 1992. Major essays, both historical and current, comparing and contrasting the two systems.

MEZEY, MICHAEL L. *Congress, the President, and Public Policy.* Boulder, CO: Westview Press, 1989. Argues that stalemate is built into the U.S. system and is difficult to reform.

PETERS, RONALD M., ed. *The Speaker: Leadership in the U.S. House of Representatives.* Washington, DC: CQ Press, 1994. Interesting collection on the roles and functions of the House leader, including essays by three former Speakers.

PETERSON, MARK A. *Legislating Together: The White House and Capitol Hill from Eisenhower to Reagan.* Cambridge, MA: Harvard University Press, 1990. Congress does have a major input into legislating, argues this empirically based study.

SULEIMAN, EZRA N., ed. *Parliaments and Parliamentarians in Democratic Politics.* New York: Holmes & Meier, 1986. Seven countries show different and changing powers of parliaments and relations with executives.

SUNDQUIST, JAMES L. *Constitutional Reform and Effective Government.* Washington, DC: Brookings Institution, 1986. A long-term specialist on Congress casts a thorough but skeptical eye at reforming the U.S. system.

THURBER, JAMES A., and ROGER H. DAVIDSON, eds. *Remaking Congress: Change and Stability in the 1990s.* Washington, DC: CQ Press, 1995. Charts the upheaval of the 1994 Congressional elections, which brought a Republican-dominated Congress.

Notes

1. Cited in William C. Atkinson, *A History of Spain and Portugal* (Baltimore: Penguin, 1960), p. 80.

2. John Locke, *Second Treatise on Civil Government* (1690), Chap. 11.

3. For critical comparisons and contrasts of the two systems, see the special conference issue of *Political Science Quarterly,* "Presidential and Parliamentary Democracies: Which Work Best?" 109 (Special Issue 1994), 3.

4. This well-known phrase is from Edward S. Corwin, *The President: Office and Powers, 1787–1948* (New York: New York University Press, 1948), p. 208.

5. See James MacGregor Burns, *The Deadlock of Democracy: Four-Party Politics in America,* rev. ed. (Englewood Cliffs, NJ: Spectrum, 1963).

6. For the complexities of coalition formation, see Michael Laver and Norman Schofield, *Multiparty Government: The Politics of Coalition in*

Europe (New York: Oxford University Press, 1990).

7. See K. C. Wheare, *Legislatures* (New York: Oxford University Press, 1963).

8. For an insider's view of the functioning of Congress, see Robert Cwiklik, *House Rules: A Freshman Congressman's Initiation to the Backslapping, Backpedaling, and Backstabbing Ways of Washington* (New York: Villard, 1992).

9. For a comparison of members of the U.S. House of Representatives and British House of Commons and how they both serve the voters, see Bruce Cain, John Ferejohn, and Morris Fiorina, *The Personal Vote: Constituency Service and Electoral Independence* (Cambridge, MA: Harvard University Press, 1987).

10. For an interesting look at the "home style" of South Korean rural legislators and why they keep getting reelected, see Chan Wook Park, "Constituency Representation in Korea: Its

Sources and Consequences," *Legislative Studies Quarterly* 13 (May 1988), 2.

11. For Congress's ability to trigger national debate on foreign-policy issues, see James M. Lindsay, *Congress and the Politics of U.S. Foreign Policy* (Baltimore, MD: Johns Hopkins University Press, 1994).

12. Woodrow Wilson's study points out the power and distinctiveness of the U.S. committee system. See *Congressional Government: A Study in American Politics* (Baltimore: Johns Hopkins University Press, 1981).

13. See Steven S. Smith and Christopher J. Deering, *Committees in Congress*, 2nd ed. (Washington, DC: CQ Press, 1990).

14. For a thorough overview of congressional committees, see Barbara Hinckley, *Stability and Change in Congress*, 3rd ed. (New York: Harper & Row, 1983), Chap. 6.

15. Lord Bryce, *The American Commonwealth* (London: Macmillan, 1888), I, 165–232; and A. B. Lowell, *Governments and Parties in Continental Europe* (Cambridge, MA: Harvard University Press, 1896). Bryce made explicit his worry

about the "decline of legislatures" in his *Modern Democracies* (London: Macmillan, 1921), I, 367–77.

16. See Gerhard Loewenberg, ed., *Modern Parliaments: Change or Decline?* (Chicago: Aldine-Atherton, 1971).

17. Jean Blondel, *Comparative Legislatures* (Englewood Cliffs, NJ: Prentice Hall, 1973).

18. See William H. Robinson and Clay H. Wellborn, eds., *Knowledge, Power and the Congress* (Washington, DC: CQ Press, 1991).

19. For more on how the U.S. Congress has adopted television and computers, see Stephen Frantzich, *Political Parties in the Technological Age* (New York: Longman, 1989).

20. For a worried discussion of absenteeism in the French National Assembly, see Henri Paillard, "L'absentéisme chronique au parlement," *Figaro* [Paris], 5 and 8 July 1989.

21. See George F. Will, *Restoration: Congress, Term Limits and the Recovery of Deliberative Democracy* (New York: Free Press, 1992).

· 15 ·
Executives

There have been executives a lot longer than there have been legislatures. Tribal chiefs, kings and queens, and emperors appeared with the dawn of civilization, and most of the time they didn't have legislatures to worry about. Parliaments are a relatively new invention. Even today, powerful executives somehow seem more natural to us than divided and contentious parliaments. Executives have a built-in psychological advantage over legislatures.

Indeed, the word *government* in much of the world means the executive branch. There is some confusion between Americans and Europeans over what the term means. In Europe, *government* basically equals *cabinet*. The "Major government" is just another way of saying Prime Minister Major's cabinet plus some additional subcabinet assistants. In the United States (and nowhere else), this is called the *administration*. What Americans call the *government*, meaning all the bureaus and bureaucrats, is known in Europe as the *state*.

Presidents and Prime Ministers

As discussed in Chapter 14, there is a considerable difference between parliamentary and presidential systems.[1] A parliament indirectly elects a chief executive from one of its own numbers, usually called a prime (originally meaning "first") minister but also known as a premier in France or a chancellor in Germany. (As considered in Chapter 13, some of these systems also have a weak president to symbolize the nation, but he or she has few political powers.) The parliament can also oust a prime minister and the cabinet by a vote of no confidence, although this happens rarely now. Still, the prime minister is responsible (meaning answerable) to parliament. If the prime minister represents a party with a majority of seats, he or she is rather secure in office and can get a legislative program passed quickly and with little backtalk. Margaret Thatcher of Britain, for example, with a sizable and disciplined majority in the Commons, at times wielded powers that might make an American president jealous.

If no party has a majority, however, a government is formed by a coalition of parties, each of whom gets one or more ministries to run. The head of the largest party is usually prime minister, and the head of the second largest is usually foreign minister, the second most important position. Sometimes the coalition partners quarrel over policy and threaten to split up. This weakens the hand of the prime minister, as he or she knows that any major policy shift could lead to new quarrels. This situation can lead to immobilism in parliamentary systems, as is often the case in Italy, where a five-party coalition came apart an average of once a year. Accordingly, it's not quite right to say that prime ministers are "weaker" than presidents; it depends on whether prime ministers have a stable majority in parliament.

A presidential system bypasses this problem by having a strong president not dependent on or responsible to a parliament but elected on his or her own for a fixed term. Parliament—for example, the U.S. Congress—may not like the president's policies and may vote down presidential proposals, but parliament may not vote out the president. The president and the parliament stand side by side, sometimes glaring at each other, knowing there is nothing they can do to get rid of one another. It is sometimes said that presidents are "stronger" than prime ministers, and in terms of being able to run the executive branch for a fixed term, they are. But they may not be able to get vital new legislation or budgeting out of their legislatures. This has been called the "deadlock of democracy," the curse of the U.S. political system, as discussed in Chapter 14. Notice, however, the close parallel of parliamentary immobilism to presidential-congressional deadlock. Neither system can guarantee cooperation between legislative and executive. Indeed, any system that could would be a dictatorship.

"Forming a Government" in Britain.   Great Britain is the classic of parliamentary systems, one in which we still see its historical roots. The monarch, currently Queen Elizabeth II, initiates a new government (in the European sense) by formally inviting the leader of the largest party in the House of Commons to become prime minister and form a government. As such, the prime minister appoints the two dozen ministers (executive department heads), the parliamentary secretaries, the legal officers, the ministers without portfolio, and the parliamentary whips. They are all members of the prime minister's party and are usually chosen to represent most significant groups within the party. The cabinet is charged with the formulation of government policy. Theoretically, the prime minister is *primus inter pares* (first among equals) and must carry out decisions reached by the whole cabinet even when personally opposed. But like an American president, the prime minister can dismiss a cabinet member at any time, and those who oppose his or her decisions are expected to resign. Conceivably, a cabinet that is strongly united against the prime minister could force a change in government policy or even the prime minister's resignation. But this happens rarely, and hasn't occurred since Neville Chamberlain was ousted from party leadership in 1940.

"Constructive No Confidence" in Germany.   The chancellor of Germany is even stronger than the British prime minister. The chancellor, too, is majority leader in the lower house (Bundestag). But cabinet appointments are not subject to legislative confirmation, and once in the office the chancellor doesn't necessarily have to resign just because the Bundestag has voted "no confidence" in his or her government. The German constitution requires the Bundestag to vote in a replacement cabinet as part of ousting the old one. This is called "constructive no confidence," and it has contributed a lot to the stability of Germany's governments. It's much harder to replace a cabinet than just oust it; as a result, constructive no confidence has succeeded only once, in 1982, when the small Free Democratic party defected from the Social Democrat–led coalition to the opposition Christian Democrats. A prime minister supported by constructive no confidence is a more powerful figure than one without it, as one might see in a comparison of the average tenures of Italian and German cabinets (several months as compared to several years).

"Cohabitation" in France.   President Charles de Gaulle of France (1958–1969) designed a hybrid system that has both a working president and a prime minister. The president is elected directly by the people for seven years, and a parliament is elected for five years. If both are of the same party, there is no problem. The president names a like-minded premier, who then serves as the link between president and parliament. In 1986 and again in 1993, though, an interesting thing happened. A Socialist president, François Mitterrand, with two years left in his term, faced a newly elected parliament dominated by conservatives. The constitution gave no guidance in such a case. Mitterrand solved the problem by naming opposition Gaullists as premiers and letting them dismantle many Socialist measures. Mitterrand reserved for himself the high ground of foreign policy. The French, tongue-in-cheek, called the arrangement "cohabitation," a couple living together without benefit of wedlock. It actually worked, and the French didn't much mind. France was thus handling the problem of deadlock that is almost the norm in the United States. The 1993 Russian constitution incorporated a French-style system with both president and premier, and it quickly led to executive-legislative deadlock.

The "Presidentialization" of Prime Ministers. Observers have noticed a tendency for parliamentary systems to "presidentialize" themselves. Prime ministers, with stable majorities supporting them in parliament, gradually start acting like presidents, like powerful chiefs only dimly accountable to legislators. Many prime ministers know they won't be ousted in a vote of no confidence. The only thing they have to worry about is the next election, just like a president.

In 1996 Israelis elected a parliament and a prime minister *separately and directly* for the first time, possibly the first time any country has done so. A directly elected prime minister partially turns Israel's system from purely parliamentary toward presidentialism. The crux of a presidential system is the separate and direct election of a chief executive instead of one elected by a majority of parliament. The Israeli government, in the past often dependent on fickle parties to form a coalition cabinet, may now enjoy more stability, although the Knesset can still vote out the prime minister on a motion of confidence. The prime minister, in return, can dissolve the Knesset, that is, send it home for new elections. It remains to be seen if the Knesset, often fractionalized into ten or more parties, will defer to the prime minister, who now enjoys the psychological advantage of being the "people's choice."

Increasingly, elections in parliamentary systems resemble presidential elections. Technically, there is no "candidate for prime minister" in parliamentary elections. Voters vote for a party or a member of parliament, not for a prime minister. But everybody knows that the next prime minister will be the head of the largest party, so indirectly they are electing a prime minister. For these reasons, virtually all West European elections feature posters and televised spots of the party chiefs as if they were running for president. As in U.S. elections, personality increasingly matters more than policy, party, or ideology.

How Long a Term?

Presidents have fixed terms, ranging from four years for U.S. presidents to seven for French presidents.[2] A U.S. president may be reelected once, a French president theoretically without limit. What is the right length for a presidential term? Many U.S. critics, on both sides of the political fence, say four years is too short. Presidents are so worried about getting reelected that much of their first term is wasted in cautious image building. They are afraid to be themselves and to try significantly new policies. Only in his second term can a president "be oneself," according to this view.

To fix the problem, if indeed it is one, some have proposed adopting a single six-year term for the U.S. president. Once elected, the president would feel free to do what needs to be done, even if it's unpopular, because he or she wouldn't have to worry about reelection. Six years would be long enough to put major policies into place.

Before we tinker with the Constitution, we ought to think this proposal through. Many in France wonder whether the seven years of their system isn't too long. If the French president gains too much power and grows aloof and distant, there is nothing the French can do except wait until the long term is up. During this time scandals may tarnish the administration, and the president's policies may fail. Citizens' frustration mounts. This is what happened during the presidency of Valéry Giscard d'Estaing (1974–1981). His successor had the same problem but was saved by the funny "cohabitation" just discussed. Mitterrand cleverly arranged to let his rival, Jacques Chirac, whom he appointed premier, take the blame for France's economic problems while Mitterrand stood above the fray as a dignified, symbolic president with curtailed powers. By the time Chirac ran against Mitterrand for the presidency in 1988, Chirac was unpopular and Mitterrand was rather well liked. Mitterrand won reelection for another seven years, during which time citizens got exceedingly tired of him. Chirac won the presidency in 1995 but quickly became unpopular. There was nothing French voters could do but wait until 2002.

Another problem: Is it really desirable to let the president "be oneself"? The threat of losing reelection keeps presidents on their toes; they don't want to awaken mass disapproval. This is Friedrich's "rule of anticipated reactions" discussed earlier. Take that constraint away and the president may resort to imprudent and dangerous policies. With a single, six-year term, a president might say, "I don't have to worry about reelection, so what the heck?" The president of Mexico is elected (not precisely democratically) for a single six-year term, and some have made serious errors in office, errors that brought Mexico to the brink of bankruptcy. Maybe they should have been worried about reelection. It is best to err on the side of caution in instituting a major change.

The Terms of Prime Ministers. In parliamentary systems, prime ministers have no limits on their tenure in office, providing their party wins elections. As noted, increasingly their winning depends on the personality of their leader, almost as if they were presidential candidates. Britain's Margaret Thatcher, elected for a third time in 1987, said merrily she "might just go on and on, into the next century." By 1990, however, her mounting political problems persuaded her to resign after a total of eleven and a half years in office. Furthermore, most prime ministers have the power to "dissolve" parliament (send it home for new elections) earlier than the end of the parliamentary term. Prime ministers thus can call elections when they believe they'll do best at the polls. A good economy, sunny weather, and high ratings often persuade prime ministers to call elections a year or two early. Powers such as these might make an American president jealous.

On the other hand, prime ministers can get ousted quickly if they lose the support of a majority of parliament. When British Labour Prime Minister James Callaghan lost the support of just eleven Scottish Nationalist MPs in 1979, he slipped below a majority in Commons and was replaced virtually overnight by Tory chief Thatcher. Some Italian premiers have held office only briefly as their coalitions disintegrated. Japanese prime ministers, the playthings of powerful faction chiefs within the ruling Liberal-Democratic party, average only two and a half years in office. Prime Minister Uno, implicated in one of Japan's frequent scandals, lasted only two months in 1989. Theoretically, prime ministers can serve a long time; in practice their tenure depends on political conditions such as elections, coalition breakups, and scandals. Parliamentary systems practice a kind of easy-come, easy-go with their prime ministers, something an American president would definitely not like. Presidents in presidential systems are partially insulated from the ups and downs of politics.

A U.S. president, of course, can be impeached, but this is a lengthy and uncertain procedure that has been attempted only twice. Andrew Johnson was impeached by the House in 1868 but saved from conviction in the Senate by only one vote. Richard Nixon was about to be impeached by the House but resigned just before the vote. He was the only president ever to resign. When faced with a problem character as chief executive, parliamentary systems have a big advantage over the U.S. system. A simple vote of no confidence in parliament and the rascal is out. This helps explain why, even though there are lots of scandals in parliamentary systems, few become as big and damaging as Watergate: it's much easier to get rid of the chief. Watergate paralyzed the American system for a year and would have been a lot worse if Nixon had stayed on to fight impeachment.

The Roles of the Executive

Richard E. Neustadt, a leading authority on the American presidency, has written that "from outside or below, a President is 'many men' or one man wearing many 'hats,' or playing many roles . . . the President himself plays every 'role,' wears every 'hat' at once."[3] Not only the U.S. president, but most modern chief executives wear more than one hat. The unique powers of the presidency, however, put the occupants of the White House in an uncommonly strong position. They are elected independently of the legislature and, as such, are the direct choice of the nation as well as of their party. In addition, they have several exclusive roles: official chief of state, head of government, party leader, commander in chief of the armed forces, chief diplomat, chief executive, and chief legislator. These powers reinforce each other to make the presidency the most respected office in the nation. Great responsibility also comes with these broad powers. And in the last analysis, there is no one to whom presidents can pass the blame for mismanaged affairs. As the sign on Harry Truman's desk so aptly put it, "The buck stops here." Since 1789, the powers of the president have grown enormously, as have those of the chief executives of all other nations.

Chief of State. Presidents are the surrogates and spokespersons for the American people. They are the visible symbol of the nation and must perform numerous ceremonies usually saved for monarchs and figurehead presidents in other nations. Whereas the vice-president or the president's spouse is sometimes sent to dedicate major public works projects or christen boats, tradition still demands that the president greet visiting dignitaries, entertain the diplomatic corps, and represent the country at important international conferences.

Head of Government. Every head of government—president, prime minister, or chancellor—is responsible for making and carrying out decisions. He or she must also supervise the bureaucratic machinery at the national level, which makes the responsibilities of the job staggering. The president is responsible for fourteen major departments of government, more than 100 executive bureaus, 500 administrative offices, and 600 divisions employing 2.8 million civil servants. One American worker in fifty is a federal employee (compared to one in 2,000 in Washington's day), and the president is—at least in theory—each federal worker's boss. To aid the president in this enormous task, the Executive Office of the President, now employing some 1,700 full-time workers, was formed in 1939 to conduct the day-to-day supervisory functions of running the bureaucracy.

Party Chief. Although presidents are chosen directly by the people, they are still leaders of their political party, as are the British, French, and German heads of government. The chief executive is expected to take the lead in raising campaign funds and in endorsing and campaigning on behalf of his or her party's candidates for local, state, and national office. More important, he or she is expected to play a major role in formulating the party's legislative program. The president is not as powerful a party leader as the prime minister in a parliamentary government because of the lack of centralization and discipline in the American party system.

Commander in Chief. The U.S. Constitution specifies—and the Supreme Court has upheld—the right of presidents to deploy the country's armed forces as they see fit. Congress has long been exasperated with this power and has tried, never successfully, to curb it. Congress fears that the president's power as commander in chief infringes on its power to declare war. In the late 1930s, Congress passed a series of Neutrality Acts designed to keep the country out of the coming war, but President Roosevelt managed to circumvent them. In 1973 Congress, which was too much timid to move when the Vietnam war was at its height, passed (over President Nixon's veto) the War Powers Act, which is supposed to limit the president's use of troops in overseas combat to ninety days unless Congress approves an extension. This law did not prevent President Reagan from sending U.S. troops into Lebanon, Grenada, or Central America; Bush from sending troops to Panama and the Persian Gulf; or Clinton from sending troops to Bosnia.

Chief Diplomat. Likewise, presidents can do almost anything they want in diplomacy without congressional approval. This holds for most prime ministers as well. Chief executives can grant diplomatic recognition to foreign countries, negotiate trade deals, and conclude "executive agreements" that are almost like treaties. Treaties themselves, those most important international contracts, must be ratified by the countries' legislatures. In the United States, that means a two-thirds assent from the Senate. The Supreme Court has upheld presidential preeminence in foreign relations,[4] and Congress has gone along with it.

Dispenser of Appointments. Since the introduction of the merit system into the U.S. Civil Service at the turn of the century, the power of patronage has been considerably diminished. However, all federal judges and legal officers are appointed by the president, as are top diplomats and upper-echelon management personnel in the federal departments, agencies, offices, bureaus, and divisions. All in all, a new president has some 3,000 jobs to dispense. One of the key ways a president can enforce party discipline within the congressional ranks is through influence in patronage appointments. Although the power of patronage is not as important as it once was, it carries enough weight so that few legislators willingly incur the wrath of the party leadership.

To a large extent, the success of a president's program is determined by the kind of people appointed to office, for those appointees can bring either creative leadership or routine administration to their jobs. In making appointments, a president considers a candidate's experience, talent, and temperament to manage the responsibilities of office. The decision is also influenced by how many votes an appointee will bring to the administration, the political debts he or she must pay, and the responsibility to call on prominent political and national leaders to serve the office of the president.

Chief Legislator. The president is not only responsible for executing the laws passed by Congress but also has—as has already been discussed—considerable lawmaking powers. Congress gives the chief executive broad discretionary powers in interpreting and implementing law. In many cases, Congress passes very general legislation and leaves it up to the president to fill in the details. Finally, the president initiates legislation. The State of the Union message and national budget spell out the general direction of the administration for the coming year and suggest programs and laws the president believes are in the best and most urgent interests of the nation.[5]

AN IMPERIAL PRESIDENCY?

"The accumulation of all powers, legislative, executive, and judiciary, in the same hands," James Madison wrote in *The Federalist,* no. 47, "may justly be pronounced the very definition of tyranny." The Founding Fathers held that power must be balanced internally to prevent one person or group from seizing all political control. Checks and balances, John Adams declared, are as effective as "setting a thief to catch a thief," and he was confident that interbranch jealousies would ensure that each branch would confine the other to the political limits set down in the Constitution. In recent years, many political scientists have voiced the fear that the breadth of responsibility required to run a modern nation has caused the office of the presidency to become too powerful. How valid are these fears? Certainly, the relationship between Congress and the president has changed profoundly in the last century.

Samuel P. Huntington noted some startling statistics. From 1882 to 1909, Congress was responsible for shaping more than half (55 percent) of all significant pieces of legislation; between 1910 and 1932, the figure dropped to 46 percent; and from 1933 to 1940, Congress was primarily responsible for initiating a mere 8 percent of all major laws. "Since 1933," Huntington wrote, "the initiative in formulating legislation, in assigning legislative priorities, in arousing support for legislation, and in determining the final content of legislation enacted has clearly shifted to the executive branch."[6] This situation has significantly altered the traditional separation of powers between the legislative and executive branches and has produced a variety of studies both decrying the fall of Congress and defending the increased legislative responsibilities of the presidency.

The imbalance is even more extreme in European parliaments, where practically no legislation is introduced on members' initiative. It should be remembered that on a world scale, the U.S. Congress is the most independent and lively legislature. This is the positive side to the weakness of U.S. parties and built-in conflict between the legislative and executive branches. It is Congress's very lack of discipline that gives it the autonomy many European parliamentarians envy. The price the U.S. system pays is slowness. With the fusion of powers of the parliamentary system, legislation moves quickly. With the separation of powers between the White House and Capitol Hill, legislation can take a long time, although the president usually prevails in the end.

As the Vietnam war was winding down and Watergate was boiling up, a noted historian produced a book that captured the worried feeling of the time—*The Imperial Presidency*, by Arthur Schlesinger, Jr.[7] Lyndon Johnson had taken the country into a major war without a declaration of war from Congress. Richard Nixon had expanded that war into Laos and Cambodia, again without a declaration of war. Nixon also "impounded" appropriations made by Congress; he simply refused to spend funds in certain areas, in effect exercising an item veto after bills had been signed into law. Was the president overstepping constitutional bounds? Were we on our way to an imperial presidency, going the way of ancient Rome, from republic to rule by the Caesars? Many thought so.

Congress attempted to reassert some of its authority, passing the War Powers Act in 1973 and moving toward impeachment of Nixon the following year. It looked like the beginning of a new era, with Congress and the president once again in balance. But this didn't really happen, for the U.S. system *needs* a strong president to function properly.

When Jimmy Carter took office in 1977, he attempted to deimperialize the presidency, but this effort simply led to an ineffective White House. Carter, catching the spirit of the time, ran against Washington in 1976. He billed himself as the average American who was not part of the establishment. Symbolically, on his inauguration day he and his family walked down Pennsylvania Avenue instead of riding in the presidential limousine. As an outsider, though, Carter was ignorant of the ways of Washington and quickly alienated a Congress that was dominated by his own party. His important legislation stalled on Capitol Hill and was often diluted by amendments, especially his crucial energy proposals. By the 1980 election, much of the American electorate—and perhaps even some people in Congress—wished for a more forceful and experienced chief executive.

Congress's reassertion of independent authority in the 1970s proved brief, for with the arrival of Ronald Reagan in the White House in 1981, the president once again had a fair degree of command over Capitol Hill.[8] But this, too, did not work for long. In late 1986 it was revealed that officials of the president's National Security Council totally bypassed Congress in selling arms to Iran and using the money to fund contras attempting to overthrow the Nicaraguan government. Even President Reagan's supporters in Congress turned angry and subjected his appointees to pointed questions in committee hearings. Once again, a Congress disappointed with alleged executive misuse of power was trying to assert a check over an executive branch it had repeatedly invested with enormous powers.

Presidential Character

Can you tell in advance what a president is going to be like? One political scientist thinks you can, at least in general terms. James David Barber in 1969 virtually predicted how Richard Nixon would handle a major crisis. A political scientist who can predict anything deserves our attention. Barber focuses on something he calls "presidential character" and claims you can get a fair idea of it from a psychological study of the individual's earlier life and how he or she reacted to problems.[9] For example, virtually all presidents had been in college politics (often student body president), and how they handled their campaigns and student offices then was pretty much how they would handle them as president. Character is laid down early, by college years, and stays consistent, Barber argues.[10]

Barber looks at two key variables: (1) how much a person likes political office and (2) how much energy he or she puts into it. The first variable is divided into two types. A person who really likes the job, relishes the power and perquisites, Barber calls "positive." A person who doesn't especially enjoy the job but is ambitious and driven to achieve it, Barber calls "negative." The second variable is also divided into two types. A person with a lot of energy for the job is called "active"; one with little energy is called "passive." This gives Barber a fourfold table and allows him, based on studies of both their earlier and presidential careers, to place presidents into each square:

	Active	*Passive*
Positive	Roosevelt Kennedy Bush	Taft Harding Reagan
Negative	Johnson Nixon	Coolidge Eisenhower

Presidents with an active-positive character enjoy being president and put a lot of energy into their tenure. They are flexible, have a sense of humor, and are willing to learn and change in office. The passive-positive characters, on the other hand, like being president but do not energetically throw themselves into it. They prefer to delegate matters to subordinates. They are friendly and want to be liked. Passive-negative characters are hard to find in the presidency; they are politicians who have been drafted for the job, don't particularly relish it, and don't have much energy for it. Active-negative characters are the real "meanies" in office. They've got plenty of energy, but they don't really enjoy power in a relaxed, happy way. The office is a heavy burden on them, and they take political opposition personally, as if numerous foes are "out to get them." It was no accident, Barber argues, that America's most troubled postwar presidencies came with—and because of—the active-negative characters of Johnson and Nixon, who tended to get themselves into deeper and deeper trouble.

Many objected that just four classifications is much too simple, that people are a lot more complicated. Moreover, few presidents have not actively sought the position—they have to work very hard to win it. How can a "passive" person advance so high? By the same token, how can a person who does not relish the office want to assume it? Barber argues that people can be driven to achieve the presidency and then discover that they are not especially happy in the office.

Barber, long before the Watergate break-in and investigation ever occurred, predicted that Nixon would behave in a devious fashion, would dig in his heels and refuse to confess, and would make things worse for himself. This is precisely how Nixon behaved under the pressure of Watergate. He became overtense and ruined his own presidency. Chronically insecure, Nixon felt he had to ensure the election, even though he was certain to win in 1972. Barber urges political scientists and journalists to look into the lifelong character of presidential candidates in order to discern such general patterns. This will give us a much better idea of the person we are electing than following the silly charges candidates hurl at each other during campaigns.

There is a problem with this method, however: how many investigators have the ability and time to do a really exhaustive study of each major candidate? "Character" is a tricky area, open to many interpretations. Suppose half a dozen journalists, political scientists, and psychologists each do a study of candidates and finish with six different analyses? Whom do we believe? We might trust Barber for a good, impartial study, but can we trust others who claim to have insight into a candidate's character? There is a potential for hiding personal likes and dislikes under the heading of "presidential character" studies.

One way to weed out potentially dangerous characters, suggests Barber, is to have each party's leading politicians caucus and select three or four candidates who would then run in nationwide primaries.[11] Practicing politicians—senators, representatives, and governors—know the candidates well enough to screen out problem personalities. In effect, each party would practice "peer review." Legally, however, this would be hard to enforce. Even harder would be getting the problem personalities to go along with the decision. They are usually clever manipulators who would say they were excluded for political reasons. They would raise their own money and campaign for the nomination without their peers' blessings.

EXECUTIVE LEADERSHIP: HANDS ON OR HANDS OFF?

Back to back, America was treated to two distinctly different leadership styles.[12] President Carter (1977–1981) was a hands-on, detail person; he tried to supervise nearly all parts of his administration. Gifted with great intelligence and energy, he put in long hours and memorized prodigious amounts of material. President Clinton had a similar style. Critics, including management experts, say this is the wrong approach, that chief executives only scatter and exhaust themselves if they try to run everything.

President Reagan (1981–1989) was the opposite; he supervised little, preferring to leave the workings of his administration in the hands of trusted subordinates. He took afternoon naps and frequent vacations. Critics say Reagan paid no attention to crucial matters, letting things slide until they turned into serious problems. The Iran-contra fiasco showed what can happen when subordinates are given only general directions and are allowed to go off on their own. The National Security Council staff thought it was doing what the president wanted when it illegally sold arms to Iran and illegally transferred the profits to the Nicaraguan contras.

President Bush moved into the office so energetically that some feared he would become a Carter-type of detail executive, busy trying to make everything run just the way he wanted it. This impression, however, may have simply resulted from the contrast with Reagan's hands-off approach, which made anyone look energetic. Bush tended to make decisions—especially in foreign policy—with a handful of close, trusted advisers. He would then present the policy to the nation and to Congress as a fait accompli.

Can there be a happy middle ground between hands on and hands off? Some say President Eisenhower (1953–1961) achieved it without letting it show. He superficially appeared to be an early version of Reagan, a hands-off type of president who was too busy golfing to look closely into the affairs of state. The press used to make fun of Eisenhower's relaxed style. Princeton political scientist Fred Greenstein, however, carefully analyzed Eisenhower's schedule and calendar and concluded that he was actually a very active and busy president who made important and complex decisions.[13] He just didn't want to show it, preferring to let others take the credit (and sometimes the blame). Greenstein called Eisenhower's style the "hidden-hand presidency." (Notice how Greenstein's findings at least partially refute those of Barber, who saw Eisenhower as a passive character.)

Instead of appearing to be a grandstanding leader, Eisenhower quietly manipulated things to go his way. It fooled most observers at the time, but it was an effective style. In 1954, for example, faced with the question of whether to commit U.S. forces to help the French in the Indochina war, Eisenhower called top senators to the White House. He knew they would be cautious, for the United States had just ended the unpopular Korean War. The senators did not favor sending U.S.

forces, and Eisenhower went along with their view. Actually, he never wanted to send troops, but he made it look as if the senators had decided the issue.[14]

President Franklin D. Roosevelt (1933–1945) used a style that some call deliberate chaos. Setting up numerous agencies and advisers, some of them working at cross-purposes, Roosevelt would let them clash until they either hashed things out or submitted the question to him for a decision. The really important decisions would rise to the top; the others would be settled without him. This, too, was a kind of middle ground between hands on and hands off. The Clinton White House borrowed this spontaneous and creative approach, but Clinton participated personally in many policy deliberations in a more hands-on manner.

Disabled Presidents

Presidential systems have another problem that parliamentary systems do not. If a prime minister becomes disabled or insane in office, he or she can be replaced overnight. Presidential systems don't know quite what to do with a seriously ill chief executive. The U.S. Constitution says that a president unable "to discharge the powers and duties" of office should be replaced by the vice-president, but it never explained how inability would be determined. As a result, several presidents have stayed in office even though seriously infirm.[15] In France, President Mitterrand was slowly dying of cancer for most of his two terms (fourteen years) in office, but his physicians went public with it only after his death in 1996.

Woodrow Wilson (1913–1921) had suffered strokes even before he went to the Versailles Peace Conference in 1918. His poor health may have weakened his diplomatic bargaining power there. He collapsed while touring the United States, trying to drum up support for the Versailles Treaty and the attached League of Nations Covenant. After that, his wife ran things, saying she was just conveying the president's wishes. In 1944, when he was elected for a fourth term, Franklin Roosevelt was suffering from heart failure and hypertension. Near death's door, he went to the historic Yalta Conference in early 1945; perhaps that is why he conceded too much to Stalin. Kennedy had Addison's disease, a failure of the adrenal glands, and had been on steroids for years. Could this have affected his judgment and willingness to take risks?

Why didn't White House physicians speak out? They instinctively protected the president, partly because the doctor-patient relationship is privileged and partly because they genuinely liked the president and did not want to see him lose power. Their personal motivation is impeccable, but they may have done their country a real disservice by keeping a sick president in power when he should have stepped aside.

The Twenty-fifth Amendment, ratified in 1967, tried to define presidential inability, but it too has not solved the problem. In 1981 President Reagan was severely wounded in an assassination attempt; he lost half his blood and was in surgery more than two hours. A lung infection and fever kept him bedridden the following week. Yet at no time was the Twenty-fifth Amendment invoked to let Vice-President

Close miss. President Reagan came close to death in the 1981 assassination attempt. The ability of a young, unbalanced man to purchase a gun, get close to the president, and fire off six shots demonstrated how vulnerable the chief executive is.

Bush take over, even temporarily. Presidential advisers James Baker and Edwin Meese decided not to alarm the public.[16] Again, the tendency is to close ranks around an ill president, even if that is not what the Constitution specifies or the public interest requires.

If a President Becomes Insane.   Even more difficult, what can be done if a president suffers a nervous breakdown or mental disability in office? It may have happened in the 1960s. Richard Goodwin, who worked closely with Lyndon Johnson (1963–1969) as a presidential assistant, argues that Johnson took on the appearance of clinical paranoia under the pressure of Vietnam.[17] *Paranoia* does not mean simply "fear"; it denotes unreasonable suspicion of others. In private, Johnson often thundered that "those Kennedy people" were "out to get him." Goodwin suspects that Johnson was always a bit paranoid but hid it and used its energizing effect to climb politically. He always got his way and had a fierce reputation for revenge if he thought someone had crossed him. Once in the Oval Office, Johnson snapped under the strain of Vietnam, a war he didn't want but didn't know how to avoid.

But how can you tell if something like this is an illness, the temporary effects of difficult decisions, or just the president's normal (if overbearing) personality? Who should be in a position to declare the president psychologically disabled? There was then and is now nothing to be done about a president who gets a "little funny" in office; you just have to wait until the term is up.

Goodwin's claims remind us of a classic work by Harold Lasswell of Yale, who introduced concepts from Freudian psychology into political science.[18] Lasswell suspected that politicians start out mentally unbalanced, that they have unusual needs for power and dominance, which is why they go into politics. Normal people find politics uninteresting. If Lasswell is even approximately right, many executives should be removed from office, and only people who don't want the job should be elected. This is the kind of analysis that cannot be applied in practice; it is fascinating but useless.

It was Plato who first wrote that even sane people who become too powerful in high office go crazy. They've got to, for they can trust no one. They imagine, probably accurately, that they have many enemies, and they amass more and more power to crush these real and imaginary foes. It's an insightful description of Hitler and Stalin. According to Plato, tyrants must go insane in office; there's no such thing as a sane tyrant. The problem is not personal psychology but the nature of a political office that has grown too powerful. The solution, if Plato is right (and we think he is), is to limit power and have mechanisms to remove officeholders who abuse it. In the U.S. system, the threats of electoral defeat and impeachment tend to keep the presidency and its occupants healthy.

Cabinets

Virtually all chief executives are assisted by cabinets. A cabinet member heads one of the major executive divisions of government called a *department* in the United States and a *ministry* in most of the rest of the world. The former is headed by a *secretary* and the latter by a *minister.* Cabinets range in size from a compact fourteen in the United States to twenty or more in Europe.

The United States enlarges its cabinet only slowly and with much discussion, for it takes an act of Congress, and the provision for its own budget, to do so. For most of its history, the United States had fewer than ten departments. Health and Human Services, Housing and Urban Development, Transportation, Energy, Education, and Veterans Affairs were added only since the 1960s. In Western Europe, chief executives can add, delete, combine, and rename ministries at will; their parliaments routinely regard this as an executive right. In the 1980s, for example, most West European governments added an environment ministry as this issue took on greater importance. The U.S. Environmental Protection Agency stayed at the subcabinet level, and environmental responsibilities were divided between it and several departments.

What's the right size for a cabinet? It depends on how the system is set up and on what citizens expect of it. The United States has been dedicated to keeping government small and letting the marketplace make decisions. When this led to imbalances—for example, bankrupt farmers, unemployed workers, and business collapses—the U.S. system added the Departments of Agriculture, Labor, and Commerce. The Department of Energy was added after the "energy shocks" of the 1970s. Slowly, U.S. cabinets have been creeping up to West European size.

Who Serves in a Cabinet?   There is another difference between parliamentary and presidential systems. In parliamentary systems like Britain and Germany, ministers are drawn from parliament and keep their parliamentary seats.[19] They are both legislators and executives. Usually they have had years of political experience in winning elections and serving on parliamentary committees. The chair of Germany's Bundestag defense committee, for example, could be a good choice to become defense minister. In a presidential system like that of the United States or Brazil, secretaries or ministers are generally not working politicians but businesspersons, lawyers, and academics. They may have some background in their department's subject area, but few have won elective office. President Clinton named three members of Congress to his cabinet, a trend that started with President Bush, who named four. If the trend grows, U.S. cabinets will look more like European cabinets, with knowledgeable politicians shifting from the legislative side to the executive.

Which is better, a cabinet member who's a working politician or one from outside government? The elected member of a West European parliament who becomes a minister may have a great deal of both political and subject-area knowledge. Further, he or she knows all the relevant members of parliament personally and has worked closely with them. The minister and parliament do not view each other with suspicion, as enemies. The ministers are, of course, open to hefty criticism in parliament, but it is usually from the opposition benches; their own party members support them.

Outsiders appointed to the cabinet, the traditional U.S. style, may bring with them fresh perspectives, but they may also be politically naive, given to brash statements and unrealistic programs. These may get them in trouble with Congress, where members of their own party do not necessarily support them. Their lack of political experience in the nation's capital leads to another problem.

The Rise of Noncabinet Advisers.   In the United States especially, the cabinet counts for less and less. A cabinet meeting has little utility and takes place rarely. Few Americans can name three or more cabinet members. What has happened? Why has the chief executive body fallen into neglect? Part of the problem was just mentioned: the fact that few cabinet secretaries are well-known political figures. And their jobs are rather routine: get more money from Congress to spend on their department's programs. Cabinet secretaries are in charge of administering established programs with established budgets, "vice-presidents in charge of spending," as Coolidge's vice-president Charles G. Dawes called them. As such, they are not apt to be consulted on much. They are largely administrators, not generators of ideas.

A more basic problem is what has happened to government in modern times: It moves fast and combines several subject areas. The president typically wants people who can produce new ideas and a quick estimate of what's happening close at hand. Thus Washington, and to a lesser extent other capitals, have seen the rise of noncabinet advisers who are often more important than cabinet secretaries. These people make up the Executive Office of the President (EOP), and most of them do not have to be confirmed by Congress or answer to Congress, unlike secretaries. Most answer only to the president and are located either in the White House; the adjacent, ornate Executive Office Building; or the New Executive Office Building across Pennsylvania Avenue from the White House. The EOP keeps getting bigger.

In recent years, for example, great attention has focused on the "White House chief of staff," an office mentioned nowhere in the Constitution or in statutes. The chief of staff, however, is the president's gatekeeper, possibly the president's brains. No one, not even a cabinet secretary, gets in to see the president without approval by the chief of staff, and most of the president's activities and agenda are determined by this person. Information flows to the president as the chief of staff deems necessary. Invariably, the White House chief of staff is a long-term and close associate of the president who knows—or thinks he knows—exactly what the president wishes. President Bush picked a New Hampshire governor, John Sununu, as his powerful chief of staff. A person of strong opinions, Sununu was jettisoned when he became a political liability.

In foreign affairs, a "national security adviser" holds sway. In 1947 Congress provided for a National Security Council (NSC), consisting of the president, the secretaries of State and Defense, and a few others. They were to meet to coordinate foreign policies. There was no mention of a staff for the NSC, but over the years a large and powerful staff has grown up, supervised by a national security adviser. The NSC staff gets all the relevant State, Defense, and CIA cables and reports and structures them into policy alternatives for the president. In some cases, the national security adviser, who is close at hand and can preserve secrecy better, has become more important than the secretary of State or Defense. Secretary of State George Shultz, for example, angrily told the Senate that his department had not been informed about the Iran-contra plan, a scheme that was hatched and carried out by the NSC staff.[20]

There are other White House offices that wield more power than departments. The Office of Management and Budget (OMB) commands compliance from all departments because it decides whose budgets will be cut the most. This office often knows as much about specific programs as the departments who run them and is better able to initiate new policies because it can see the whole picture of government activity. Those who control the budget control policy. (This is also the case with the British Treasury Ministry, but it is a full-fledged ministry.) The chair of President Clinton's new National Economic Council is the architect of economic policy, more so than the secretary of Treasury, Commerce, or Labor.

There is no plot here. There is a gradual drift of power away from official departments and into the hands of the chief executive's personal staff. It is a tendency in many governments. The culprit is the complexity of modern government and the speed with which decisions have to be made. A chief executive has to surround himself or herself with advisors and assistants, who become powerful, secretive, and unaccountable before Congress.[21]

The Danger of Expecting Too Much

In both presidential and parliamentary systems, attention focuses on the chief executive. Presidents or prime ministers are expected to deliver economic growth with low unemployment and low inflation. They are expected to keep taxes low but government benefits high. They are held responsible for anything that goes wrong but told to adopt a hands-off management approach and delegate matters to subordinates. The more problems and pressure, the more they have to delegate.

How can they do it all? How can they run a government, economy, subordinates, and policies? They can't, and increasingly they don't. Instead, the clever ones project a mood of calm, progress, and good feeling, and this makes most citizens happy. President Reagan was a master at this tactic.[22] The precise details of governance matter little; they are in the hands of appointed advisers and career civil servants, and few citizens care about them. What matters is getting reelected. For this, personality counts for more than policy, symbols more than performance.

Worldwide, power has been flowing to the executive, and legislatures have been in decline. The U.S. Congress has put up some good rear-guard actions, but it, too, has been generally in a slow retreat. Some observers have argued that this can't be helped, that a number of factors make this shift of power inevitable. If this is true, what can we do to safeguard democracy? Democracies still have a trump card, and some say it is enough: electoral punishment. As long as the chief executive, whether president or prime minister, has to face the electorate at periodic intervals, democracy will be preserved. The "rule of anticipated reactions," of which we spoke in Chapter 5, will keep them on their toes. Perhaps the concept of checks and balances was a great idea of the eighteenth century that doesn't fit the twentieth. Maybe we will just have to learn to live with executive dominance.

Even if we admit that, however, there is another problem. Within the executive, power has been flowing to the unelected civil servants, the bureaucrats. What can protect us from them? For further discussion of this question, let us turn to the next chapter.

Suggested Readings

BARBER, JAMES DAVID. *Politics by Humans: Research on American Leadership.* Durham, NC: Duke University Press, 1988. Essays by a top scholar on how presidential psychology interacts with leadership ability and the mass media.

CAMPBELL, COLIN, and BERT A. ROCKMAN, eds. *The Clinton Presidency: First Appraisals.* Chatham, NJ: Chatham House, 1996. A good early review of the bold plans and frustrated hopes of the Clinton administration.

DUFFY, MICHAEL, and DAN GOODGAME. *Marching in Place: The Status Quo Presidency of George Bush.* New York: Simon & Schuster, 1992. Two journalists argue that Bush had neither energy nor goals.

EASTLAND, TERRY. *Energy in the Executive: The Case for a Strong Presidency.* New York: Free Press, 1992. Don't worry about concentrated power; the president needs more of it.

HOFF, JOAN. *Nixon Reconsidered.* New York: Basic Books, 1994. A positive evaluation of Nixon focusing on his domestic accomplishments.

JONES, CHARLES O. *The Presidency in a Separated System.* Washington, DC: Brookings Institution, 1994. A top scholar analyzes recent U.S. legislative-executive relationships and concludes the system doesn't work badly.

KERNELL, SAMUEL. *Going Public: New Strategies of Presidential Leadership,* 2nd ed. Washington, DC: CQ Press, 1992. The dangers of presidents bypassing Congress by using the mass media.

LINZ, JUAN J., and ARTURO VALENZUELA, eds. *The Failure of Presidential Democracy.* Baltimore, MD: Johns Hopkins University Press, 1994. Focusing on Latin America, essays demonstrate presidential systems tend toward instability.

LOWI, THEODORE J. *The Personal President: Power Invested, Promise Unfulfilled.* Ithaca, NY: Cornell University Press, 1985. A worried look at the growth of presidential power and public expectations that the president cannot meet.

MCDONALD, FORREST. *The American Presidency: An*

Intellectual History. Lawrence, KS: University Press of Kansas, 1994. A distinguished historian masterfully traces the growth of presidential power.

NELSON, MICHAEL, ed. *The Presidency and the Political System,* 4th ed. Washington, DC: CQ Press, 1994. Good anthology of articles by academics and journalists; readable.

NEUSTADT, RICHARD E. *Presidential Power and the Modern Presidents: The Politics of Leadership from Roosevelt to Reagan.* New York: Free Press, 1991. Top scholar examines what makes presidents effective.

NICHOLS, DAVID K. *The Myth of the Modern Presi-*

dency. University Park, PA: Pennsylvania State University Press, 1994. Asks just what is the "modern" presidency and when did it arrive.

SHUGART, MATTHEW SOBERG, and JOHN M. CAREY. *Presidents and Assemblies: Constitutional Design and Electoral Dynamics.* New York: Cambridge University Press, 1992. Which are better, presidential or parliamentary systems? Methodologically sophisticated.

WALCOTT, CHARLES E. *Governing the White House: From Hoover Through LBJ.* Lawrence, KS: University Press of Kansas, 1995. A look at the hows and whys of staffing the Executive Office.

Notes

1. For a fuller discussion, see Sergio Fabbrini, "Presidents, Parliaments, & Good Government," *Journal of Democracy* 6 (July 1995), 3.

2. For a good general discussion of executive terms, see Henry Bienen and Nicolas van de Walle, *Of Time and Power: Leadership Duration in the Modern World* (Stanford, CA: Stanford University Press, 1991).

3. Richard E. Neustadt, *Presidential Power* (New York: New American Library, 1964), p. viii.

4. The landmark case is considered to be *U.S. v. Curtiss-Wright* (1936). For the Supreme Court decision, see Alpheus T. Mason and Donald G. Stephenson, *American Constitutional Law: Introductory Essays and Selected Cases,* 10th ed. (Englewood Cliffs, NJ: Prentice Hall, 1992).

5. The president leads chiefly by his power to persuade, an old thesis nicely confirmed by Craig Allen Smith and Kathy B. Smith, *The White House Speaks: Presidential Leadership as Persuasion* (Greenwood, CT: Praeger, 1994).

6. Samuel P. Huntington, "Congressional Responses to the Twentieth Century," in *The Congress and America's Future,* ed. American Assembly (Englewood Cliffs, NJ: Prentice Hall, 1965), pp. 23–24.

7. Arthur Schlesinger, Jr., *The Imperial Presidency* (Boston: Houghton Mifflin, 1973).

8. For a review of the Reagan presidency, especially his relations with Congress, see *Congress and the Nation,* Vol. 7, 1985–1988 (Washington, DC: CQ Press, 1989).

9. James D. Barber, *The Presidential Character: Predicting Performance in the White House,* 4th ed. (Englewood Cliffs, NJ: Prentice Hall, 1992).

10. A recent biography of Clinton confirms Barber's thesis by finding he has been the same since youth. See David Maraniss, *First in His Class: A Biography of Bill Clinton* (New York: Simon & Schuster, 1995).

11. James D. Barber, "Pick Candidates by Peer Review," *New York Times,* 10 April 1988, p. E31.

12. See Colin Campbell, *Managing the Presidency: Carter, Reagan, and the Search for Executive Harmony* (Pittsburgh: University of Pittsburgh Press, 1986).

13. Fred Greenstein, *The Hidden Hand Presidency: Eisenhower as Leader* (New York: Basic Books, 1982).

14. For an overview of how Eisenhower organized his office for foreign affairs, see Philip G. Henderson, *Managing the Presidency: The Eisenhower Legacy—From Kennedy to Reagan* (Boulder, CO: Westview Press, 1988).

15. See Robert E. Gilbert, *The Mortal Presidency: Illness and Anguish in the White House* (New York: Basic Books, 1992) and Jerrold Post and Robert Robins, *When Illness Strikes the Leader* (New Haven, CT: Yale University Press, 1993).

16. Herbert L. Abrams, *"The President Has Been Shot": Confusion, Disability, and the 25th Amendment in the Aftermath of the Attempted Assassination of Ronald Reagan* (New York: Norton, 1992).

17. Richard N. Goodwin, *Remembering America: A Voice from the Sixties* (Boston: Little, Brown, 1988), pp. 392–416.

18. Harold Lasswell, *Politics: Who Gets What, When, How* (New York: World, 1958; originally published 1936).

19. See Michael Laver and Kenneth Shepsle, eds. *Making and Breaking Governments: Cabinets and Legislatures in Parliamentary Democracies.* (New York: Cambridge University Press, 1996).

20. For an argument that Reagan should have been impeached for letting Iran-contra happen,

see Ann Wroe, *Lives, Lies and the Iran-Contra Affair* (New York: St. Martin's, 1991).

21. See Mark J. Rozell, *Executive Privilege: The Dilemma of Secrecy and Democratic Accountability* (Baltimore, MD: Johns Hopkins University Press, 1994).

22. See Jane Mayer and Doyle McManus, *Landslide: The Unmaking of the President, 1984–1988.* (Boston: Houghton Mifflin, 1988).

· 16 ·

Administration and Bureaucracy

What Is Bureaucracy?

When the term *bureaucracy* is mentioned to the average citizen, he or she thinks of the red tape that must be cut to obtain a service or information. Actually the term refers to any large-scale organization of appointed officials whose primary function is to implement the policies of the decision makers. Ideally, a bureaucracy is a rational system or organized structure designed to permit the efficient and effective execution of public policy. To do so, a bureaucracy operates in accordance with a fixed set of rules and procedures. It has a clearly recognized chain of command (or hierarchy of authority) through which responsibility flows from the top down. The job of the bureaucracy is to apply policy guidelines to particular situations. It is a method of organization that enables government to operate with some uniformity—and, therefore, predictability—and in a manner that is rational and subject to internal supervision and control.

Another definition of bureaucracy—the nicer term is *civil service*—is that it is the *permanent* government. Much of what we have studied until now might be called the "temporary government" of elected officials who come and go. The career civil servants stay, often spending their whole working lives with one government agency. They may take orders from the elected officials, but they also must follow the law and do things "by the book." They usually know a lot more about their specified areas than the new political appointee who has been placed above them. There is often friction between elected officials and career bureaucrats. The former sometimes want to redo the system with bold, new ideas; the bureaucrats, who have seen bold, new ideas come and go, move with caution.[1] A bureaucracy, once set up, is inherently conservative, and trying to move it is one of the hardest tasks of politicians.

Bureaucracy is by no means confined to government. At a time when most Western governments were little more than loose confederations of feudal powers, the Roman Catholic church had an impressive and influential administrative system. Through a chain of command, authority flowed from the pope down to parish priest. Until the advent of strong monarchies, this organizational pattern was the envy and model of secular rulers. Armies are also characterized by their rigid bureaucratic structures, which are based on the military chain of command. Bureaucracy is equally pervasive in most civilian institutions, including schools, hospitals, large corporations, and so on. Corporations such as Exxon and General Motors have clearly defined chains of command, and they organize their necessary functions into specialized departments and offices.

THE U.S. FEDERAL BUREAUCRACY

Fewer than 15 percent of the civil servants in the United States are federal. Of our 22 million civil servants, some 15 million are employed by local governments, 4 million by state governments, and only 2.8 million (not counting military personnel) by the federal government. Remember, most government services—schools, police, and fire protection—are provided by local governments.

The Cabinet Departments. In the United States, the fourteen cabinet departments—employing between 85 and 90 percent of all federal civil servants—share a common anatomy, even thought they differ in size and scope of operations. Each is headed by a secretary who is appointed by the president (with the consent of the Senate) and serves at the president's pleasure. The undersecretaries and assistant secretaries are also political appointees. This differs from, for example, the British system, where officials up through the equivalent of our undersecretaries are members of the permanent civil service.

The basic function of the cabinet departments is to carry out legislative and executive policies; for example, the Department of Agriculture is charged with enforcing congressionally mandated farm-price supports. This is no simple matter, however, for the departments must determine how to interpret the intent of Congress. Very often, when a controversial issue is involved, the only way Congress can muster even the barest majority to pass the legislation is by couching it in the most general and politically nonoffensive terms. Thus, the legislation that a department must enforce often sets only broad guidelines for action, and the bureaucracy has latitude to establish specific working policy that suits its own interests or those of the chief executive.

The cabinet departments are subdivided into bureaus that are headed by career civil servants rather than political appointees. For example, the Bureau of Labor Statistics is part of the Department of Labor, and the Bureau of the Census is part of the Department of Commerce. Here the day-to-day work of the departments is carried out, and bureau chiefs have a great deal of discretionary authority, even though they must work within the framework of statutory law and executive policy. In addition, the cabinet departments maintain local offices in each state, and, ideally, uniform policies prevail at all departmental levels.

Federal Agencies. Some independent agencies of the federal government, like the departments, are accountable to the president. Each is headed by a single administrator whom the president appoints and can remove. Sometimes created in response to a particular lobby, the agency performs a single, highly complex function that may be more political than administrative. For example, the U.S. Information Agency (USIA) is frankly ideological; its function is to portray the United States in a favorable light to win foreign support for American policies. At the other end of the spectrum is the National Aeronautics and Space Administration (NASA), which was organized to coordinate America's explorations into space.

Federal Corporations. Government-owned corporations are combinations of government agencies and private business enterprises which serve vital needs that private enterprise cannot meet. Although corporation heads are appointed by the president and, in many cases, confirmed by the Senate, they exercise a good deal of autonomous power. They can, for example, use their own judgment to handle and reinvest the funds that the legislature has appropriated. The U.S. Postal Service, the Tennessee Valley Authority (TVA), the St. Lawrence Seaway Development Corporation, and the Export-Import Bank are a few of the more important federal corporations. The TVA and St. Lawrence Corporation undertook massive public works construction that few private corporations could have financed. Similarly, no private corporation would be willing to risk the post office's deficits. Federal corporations operate under the basic guidelines set down by Congress, and since few of them are profitable, they depend on annual legislative appropriations. They are therefore liable to congressional criticism of their organizational structure and policies.

Independent Regulatory Agencies. These agencies are charged with economic regulation of private businesses that directly affect the public welfare. They have quasi-judicial and quasi-legislative authority that derives from Congress. For example, Congress has given the Nuclear Regulatory Commission (NRC) the power to shut down nuclear power plants it deems unsafe. Such decisions are enforceable in the courts and are not often overturned by the judiciary.

These agencies have been the target of a great deal of criticism. Ralph Nader and others charge that they are overly influenced by the very industries they should be controlling. Many commissioners are drawn from the ranks of private industry and, critics say, are more concerned with preserving certain vested interests than with protecting the public. The Federal Power Commission, for example, is often under attack by those who feel it is staffed solely by representatives of industry rather than of consumer interests. There is a measure of truth in this criticism, but it must be acknowledged that agency employees need a technical understanding of the industries they regulate if they are to do their jobs. There can be little doubt that the responsiveness of the various agencies has increased since critics have brought agency deficiencies to the attention of the public.

BUREAUCRACIES IN OTHER NATIONS

As formidable as our federal bureaucracy may seem to us, government bureaucracies in some other countries are even more pervasive in both scope and authority.[2]

Communist Countries. The Soviet Union was one of the most bureaucratic nations in the modern world, and that was one of the causes of its collapse. Tied to the Communist party, it was corrupt, inefficient, and unreformable. Although according to Communist dogma, a dictatorship of the proletariat had no need for a Western-style bureaucracy, immediately after the Russian Revolution the Soviets instituted bureaucratic management in their developing industrial society.

Upper-echelon Soviet bureaucrats formed a privileged elite; their salaries and lifestyles were far superior to those of the average citizen. Special shops, a house in the country, and Western clothes were regular features of the high-level bureaucrat's life.[3] To rise in the hierarchy, one had to be a party member, for party loyalty was all-important. The members of the bureaucracy were drawn from the university graduates, who in return for their free education had to work in a state agency for three years following graduation. After that period, many of them chose to remain.

Each department was headed by a minister, who was a member of the Council of Ministers (roughly equivalent to a Western cabinet). This council—the highest executive authority in the government—was made up of high-ranking party members, some of whom were also members of the Politburo (the innermost ruling authority of the party). Not only did the ministers control their departments, but, wherever possible, loyal party members were placed strategically in subordinate positions in an effort to make sure that policy was carried out to party specifications. This made the Soviet bureaucracy extremely conservative, an obstacle

President Gorbachev was unable to overcome. Still guarding their perks, Russian bureaucrats often sabotaged Yeltsin's reforms.

France.   Many European countries pattern their bureaucracies on the French model.[4] Most of Europe shares traditions of Roman (code) law and centralized rule. After the French Revolution destroyed the monarchy, Napoleon restored central control of the bureaucracy and, by making it more rational and effective, increased its power. Napoleon, with the *intendants* of Richelieu as his model, created the prefects to carry out government policy at the local level.

Since then, merit and technical expertise have been the primary considerations in the appointment of French bureaucrats. Most top civil servants are graduates of one of the "Great Schools," such as the Ecole Polytechnique, an engineering school, or, since World War II, the Ecole Nationale d'Administration, which was specifically created to train government officials. The severe instability of the Third (1871–1940) and Fourth (1947–1958) Republics increased the bureaucracy's power because it had to take on the responsibilities of initiating and enforcing policy if the day-to-day business of government was to proceed at all. In many cases, permanent civil servants, called *directeurs* (roughly equivalent to American bureau chiefs), had to operate independently. The Fifth Republic brought greater stability and stronger ministerial control, and the bureaucracy has become more consistent in the day-to-day administration of French government.

The American concept of decentralization has only recently come to France; the French viewed local levels of government primarily as administrative conveniences. The French national government still centrally controls the country's bureaucratic network. From the American viewpoint, this centralization was often carried to an extreme. For example, at any given moment in the school day, all schoolchildren in a particular grade throughout France were likely to be engaged in the same activity. Local conditions, problems, or initiatives were secondary considerations in bureaucratic decisions. The Socialists, who swept to power in 1981, however, began the decentralization of France. A 1982 law reduced the powers of the prefects, and elected councils in the ninety-six *départements* and twenty-two regions got policy and taxation powers in education and economic development. Decentralization reversed five centuries of centralized French administration.

Germany.   Prussia and its ruling class, the *Junkers,* put their stamp on German administration. Obedient, efficient, hard-working—these are the qualities the aristocratic *Junkers* cultivated. They were also a state nobility, dependent on Berlin, and controlling all its higher civil service positions. Frederick the Great of Prussia, who ruled from 1740 to 1786, had a passion for effective administration and established universities to train bureaucrats. When Germany united in 1871, under Prussia's leadership, Prussian administrative styles permeated the new nation. Democracy counted for little among German administrators; loyalty to the emperor was more important. One of the reasons the short-lived Weimar Republic (1919–1933) failed, it is believed, was because the civil servant class had little but contempt for democracy. With the Third Reich, they eagerly flocked to Hitler.

The current German government has a strongly federal structure that limits

Bonn's administrative powers.[5] Theoretically, it is responsible for controlling foreign affairs, collecting taxes, defense, transportation, the postal service, some social insurance programs, and intelligence activities. But in practice, the federal government controls only one domestic program—unemployment insurance. It also operates jointly with the *Land* governments to collect taxes; all other domestic programs are administered by the *Länder*, under federal guidelines. If we followed this system in the United States, the state governments rather than the Department of Labor and the Justice Department would be charged with enforcing the Taft-Hartley Act. Today's German civil servants are committed to democracy. Trained in law—throughout Europe law is at the undergraduate level—at various universities (there is no equivalent of the French Great Schools), Bonn bureaucrats tend to bring with them the mentality of Roman law, that is, law neatly organized into fixed codes rather than the more flexible U.S. and British common law, "judge-made" law. Used throughout Europe, Roman law (mostly the updated Napoleonic Code version) gives civil servants a somewhat rigid, by-the-book mentality.

Great Britain.   Britain, unlike France, has strong traditions of local self-government and dispersion of authority. This pattern of administration, which is also common to the United States, relates to the Anglo-American experience with representative government, which encouraged legislative control of administrative authorities. During the nineteenth century, the growth of British government at the local level also encouraged the dispersion of administrative authority; it was not until the twentieth century that the central government began to participate in local affairs.

Curiously, Great Britain was rather late in developing a modern bureaucracy. Until the Northcote-Trevelyan Report calling for major reform was issued in 1854, the bureaucracy was rife with corruption and nepotism. Positions in the bureaucracy (for instance, military commissions) were openly bought and sold. By 1870, however, a merit civil service based on competitive examinations had been established.

British ministers are accountable to Parliament for the conduct of their departments and, along with their cabinet colleagues, make departmental policy. However, real bureaucratic power is in the hands of the "permanent secretary" (a career administrator) and the career deputy secretaries, undersecretaries, and assistant secretaries who serve at lower ranks. Thus, even though the British and American bureaucracies share the same tradition of decentralized administrative authority, control over the bureaucracy is tighter in Britain than in America.[6] British bureaucrats feel that their primary loyalty belongs to their departments rather than to a political party or leader; and so they faithfully carry out the ministry's policies and seldom initiate policy on their own.

CHARACTERISTICS OF BUREAUCRACIES

Bureaucrats have often been pictured as plodding counters of paper clips who spend their time passing the buck and figuring out how much their pensions will amount to. As is the case with most caricatures, this one contains some germs of truth. The first scholar to make a systematic analysis of bureaucracy and bureaucrats was the German sociologist Max Weber (1864–1920). His classic studies provide the starting point for a current examination of bureaucracy.

Weber's Characteristics of Bureaucracies. Weber's analysis was based on the German bureaucratic model, but his principles can be applied worldwide. Weber's criteria for defining bureaucracy were:[7]

1. Administrative offices are organized hierarchically.

2. Each office has its own area of competence.

3. Civil servants are appointed, not elected, on the basis of technical qualifications as determined by diplomas or examinations.

4. Civil servants receive fixed salaries according to rank.

5. The job is a career and the sole, or at least primary, employment of the civil servant.

6. The official does not own his or her office.

7. The official is subject to control and discipline.

8. Promotion is based on superiors' judgment.

Weber felt he was studying something relatively new. Some of the preceding characteristics could be found in classic China, but not all. Like the nation-state, bureaucracies started in Western Europe around the sixteenth century but were reaching their full powers—which Weber distrusted—only in the twentieth century.

Goodnow and Wilson. At the turn of the century, Frank J. Goodnow and Woodrow Wilson made significant studies of the American bureaucratic system.[8] Bureaucracy in the United States, they noted, must work within the framework of our democratic society. But how can professional civil servants, who are not directly accountable to the electorate, be reconciled with the goals of democracy? Wilson and Goodnow set up the theoretical base that allowed turn-of-the-century political scientists to accept the ideals of democracy together with the efficiency of a professional civil service. They made a distinction between political (policy-making) and administrative (enforcement) officials. To ensure that our democratic system is always run by elected officials, Goodnow concluded that the political officials must always control the administrative officials. This subordination must be clearly defined on an individual and agency level. Administrators, then, never initiate policy; they merely follow the policy guidelines laid down for them by the political leaders.

Political scientists today feel that these distinctions are not applicable to modern government. Administrative officials, they note, when given only the broadest policy guidelines by Congress and the president, do make policy decisions. Many of these decisions are made on the basis of the administrators' expertise in their fields, which because of our highly specialized government, political leaders do not always have.

The overlapping of administrative and political functions, therefore, is a result of the demands of modern government and not of the desire for power of professional civil servants. It is clear that the United States of the 1990s can no longer look to Weber or to Goodnow and Wilson for an analysis of modern bureaucracy. We must go further.

Beyond Weber.   Weber's bureaucracy served a highly stratified, authoritarian society—one in which the average citizen did not "talk back" to bureaucrats. Late twentieth-century America is a far different place, and private citizens and legislators do not hesitate to criticize bureaucrats or call them before investigating committees to explain their actions. These investigations, however, can be carried to extremes, as the excesses of Senator Joseph McCarthy in the 1950s illustrate. McCarthy's almost fanatical crusade against communism eliminated from public service such people as an entire generation of experts on China. Bureaucrats in sensitive political posts try to keep themselves attuned to prevailing public and congressional opinion.[9] They do not—indeed, they cannot—function solely on the basis of precedent and paper rules and procedures.

Further, anyone who has had to deal with a bureaucracy can testify to the fact that it is not as impersonal, predictable, and precise as the Weberian ideal would have it. Bureaucrats are psychological beings and seldom act in the sterile manner implied by Weber. In a bureaucracy, as in other organizations, improvisation, informality, and entrepreneurship in the decision-making process are common.

Additionally, some political scientists have noted the tendency for bureaucratic agencies to become interest groups themselves. Far from being neutral and passive administrators, bureaucrats are active participants in the formation of laws and policies. Elected and appointed executives are often entirely dependent on the data and ideas that career civil servants provide. Leaders, in effect, become followers. Civil servants frequently lobby legislators to get the programs they want. The danger here, some feel, is government of the bureaucrats, by the bureaucrats, and for the bureaucrats. It is startling to realize that no government, East or West, democratic or dictatorial, civilian or military, has managed fully to control its bureaucracy.

Role of Bureaucracy in Modern Governments

GENERAL FUNCTIONS

The functions of modern government bureaucracies include administering, servicing, regulating, licensing, information-gathering, and "housekeeping" chores. All government bureaucracies perform at least two of these basic functions, with some bureaus specializing and some carrying out multiple functions.[10]

Administration. The primary function of most government bureaus can be defined, simply, as the execution and enforcement of the laws enacted by the legislature and the policies promulgated by the executive. For example, the United States has a policy of channeling federal funds to the states to defray the cost of various welfare programs. The Department of Health and Human Services administers this policy by deciding how much federal money each state is entitled to and seeing to it that the money is used for its intended purpose. Britain provides free medical care to citizens. Its National Health Service administers this policy by overseeing medical training, assigning patients to doctors, running the hospitals, and so on. Administration, therefore, is the implementation of public policy, and because it involves policy decisions, it also entails rule making. In conjunction with their administrative duties, departments often initiate campaigns to publicize their work and to educate the public about a program's benefits and purposes. In many countries there are also continuous programs of education in such areas as traffic safety, fire prevention, and conservation of natural resources.

Patterns of administration vary from country to country. In China, for example, the party serves as a watchdog over the bureaucratic network. Virtually all Chinese officials in decision-making positions are party members, and all offices have party people in them. What the party calls its control function keeps Chinese bureaucrats on their toes. If their unit doesn't run right or if they are egregiously crooked (and many are), they can be fired, demoted, or transferred to a remote area. This threat tends to make them extremely cautious and to go by the book. Indeed, lack of innovation is a hallmark of the Chinese system. The Chinese bureaucracy is huge, partly because it also supervises much of the economy. Party control is probably indispensable for such a system. Note that the West does not have a comparable mechanism for supervising and checking its bureaucracies.

In Britain, executives and administrators oversee the day-to-day operations of their departments, and higher administrative officials help draft proposed legislation as well as help their ministers answer questions from members of Parliament. Since Britain, like France, has a partially nationalized economy, such basic services as steel plants, coal mines, railroads, and telegraph and telephone lines are run by government-controlled corporations, which make policy decisions normally reserved to the private sector in the United States.

Services. Many government agencies are created to serve the general public or specific groups. The U.S. Weather Bureau is, perhaps, the best example of a service agency. Although those of us who have been caught without an umbrella when the Weather Bureau promised no rain may not think much of the service, it is nevertheless vital to farmers and the fishing industry. The U.S. Department of Agriculture conducts research in pest control, land management, and livestock improvement; dispenses surplus food to the poor; and provides information about nutrition to the general public. In Britain, most health care is dispensed by the government. In Sweden and Germany, the government runs extensive job-finding services. And in China, the government provides free education at all levels for those who qualify.

The Internal Revenue Service office in Andover, Massachusetts, is one of nine regional centers. It processes about $41 billion in taxes a year.

Regulation.   The regulatory functions of government are also designed to safeguard the general public's welfare. In the United States, the Securities and Exchange Commission (SEC), for example, protects investors by establishing guidelines for the registration of new issues as well as the buying and selling of stocks and bonds. Britain has had legislation on the books since 1819 regulating working conditions in factories, and similar legislation exists in most industrialized countries. This legislation is enforced by particular agencies. The U.S. Department of Labor, for example, oversees elections in unions to make sure that they are conducted fairly. The election of a reform candidate to the scandal-ridden United Mine Workers Union shows how successful the Department of Labor's regulating powers can be. In Germany, the enforcement of federal law by the *Land* governments is supervised by the Bundesrat (the upper house of the national legislature), and federal administrative courts are empowered to compel *Land* governments to enforce national law. In all instances, the regulation powers are backed by the potential of force. In the United States, for example, regulatory agencies can issue "cease and desist" orders. Although offenders may challenge these orders in court, most voluntarily choose to comply.

Licensing.   Licensing is closely related to regulation. It enables governments to impose minimum standards and qualifications in certain areas. For example, if you want a license to drive a car, practice medicine or law, sell real estate, teach in the public schools, or work as a barber, you must meet certain government standards. In the United States and other federal countries, these standards are usually set by the individual states. In countries such as France or Great Britain, the national government sets the standards and administers the tests. Even in the United States, however, some licenses are issued by the federal government. For example, an FCC license is needed to operate a radio or television station.

Information Gathering.   Information is needed for two major purposes: to determine whether a law has been violated and to make policy decisions that are rational and based on factual evidence. For example, if a U.S. citizen complains that his or her civil rights have been violated, an investigation—usually by the Civil Rights Division of the Justice Department—has to be made before any action can be taken. The Environmental Protection Agency must know the exact state of air and water pollution before it can issue orders concerning violations. Similar investigations are conducted by all modern states. The French government made an extensive study of the nation's energy needs before plunging into a massive nuclear energy program.

Some agencies act only when there has been a complaint. Others, like the Food and Drug Administration (FDA), are constantly making investigations on their own initiative. The FDA does not allow a drug to go on the market—regardless of whether a complaint has been made—until it is satisfied that the product is safe and effective. Sometimes the problem of invasion of privacy arises when organizations, such as the Federal Bureau of Investigation (FBI), investigate the activities of alleged subversives and question their friends, neighbors, and family members. The line between investigation necessary to protect the public interest and invasion of privacy is a fine one, and it is often difficult to tell where one leaves off and the other begins.

The Trouble with Bureaucracy

The world does not love bureaucracy. The very word has a pejorative connotation. In France and Italy, hatred of the clerk or official on the other side of the counter or desk has become part of the political culture. The United States, with its long-standing theories of minimal government and individual self-reliance, is pleased to hear every major candidate—from both parties—denounce the bureaucracy. One of the funniest experiences is to ride a commuter train or bus into Washington, DC, and overhear career civil servants complain about "those damn bureaucrats." The paradox of the modern state is that whereas bureaucratic administration is a necessity, it is also often an impediment to the fulfillment of national goals.

Incoming U.S. administrations, particularly Republican, usually vow to bring business-type efficiency to public administration. They rarely make a dent in the problem and sometimes make things worse. "Efficiency" is much harder to apply in public affairs than in private industry. A businessperson can calculate profits and productivity; a civil servant doesn't make any profits and productivity, too, is hard to measure. Government offices are sometimes overstaffed, but it is difficult to pick out which workers should be gotten rid of.

At its worst, bureaucracy can show signs of "Eichmannism," named after the Nazi official who organized the death trains for Europe's Jews and later calmly assured his Israeli judges that he was just doing his job. Nazi bureaucracy connotes treating people like things, a problem not limited to Germany. On the humorous side, bureaucracy can start to resemble Parkinson's Law: Work expands to fill the staff time available for it.[11] Parkinson never called himself a humorist, and many who have worked in featherbedded, purposeless, paper-shuffling agencies agree that Parkinson's Law is accurate.

Bureaucracy and corruption are intertwined. Whenever there are rules to be carried out by public officials, there is a constant temptation to bend them for friends and benefactors.[12] The more regulations, the more bureaucrats, and the more corruption becomes possible. Only a few countries with a strong ethos of public service—New Zealand and Denmark, for example—have been able to maintain uncorrupt public administration into the modern age. Most countries in the world are corrupt, some a little and some egregiously. Throughout the Third World, to be a public official means to take money on the side.[13] Perhaps the most serious problem with bureaucracy, alluded to previously, occurs when it becomes interlocked with and sometimes replaces other branches of government.

THE BUREAUCRACY: ADMINISTRATOR OR POLICYMAKER?

The early theorists of bureaucracy (Weber, Goodnow, and Wilson) assumed that professional bureaucrats would never make public policy but merely execute the will of elected officials. And, indeed, nonpartisan administration was the original motivation behind the development of a merit civil service. However, as Guy S. Claire warned many years ago, most Western nations have developed—however unwittingly—"administocracies" (defined as an aristocracy of administrators) whose personnel are not publicly accountable but who nevertheless make policy.[14] Whereas a return to the nineteenth-century spoils system is neither possible nor desirable, the question of whether a democracy can afford to allow nonelected and nonresponsible administrators make decisions that will affect the lives of the people must be considered. First it is necessary to define the specific ways in which bureaucracies affect policymaking.

Adjudication.   Many regulatory agencies maintain administrative courts that operate much like regular courts and whose edicts and awards are enforceable in the regular courts. Most states, for example, have administrative tribunals that grant workers' compensation awards. All parties to such an action are entitled to legal counsel and may offer evidence. The FDA can order a drug off the market, and the SEC can ban trading in a particular stock. Two major questions have been raised in this connection. Some maintain that these tribunals' cease-and-desist orders, edicts, and so on should be made by the regular courts: If a cosmetic is harmful, should not the courts—and not the FDA—make this decision? Proponents of the administrative courts answer this objection by pointing out that the courts, by their own admission, often lack the expertise to judge highly technical matters. The second question is raised by those who doubt the wisdom of giving so much power to the administrators. These critics feel that even though the law has empowered an agency or department to "regulate in the public interest, convenience, or necessity," the creation of administrative courts means that Congress has given administrators a blank check.

Discretionary Implementation. When a legislature enacts a law, the bureaucracy must enforce it, and when statute law is specific, this is a relatively simple matter. However, this is not usually the case. For example, the U.S. Congress passed a law requiring that toxic dump sites be cleaned up. The law enabled the Environmental Protection Agency (EPA) to do whatever necessary to achieve this goal. The EPA made certain decisions, because every dump cannot be cleaned up at once, and each one entails different ecological, economic, and political problems. Deciding how to go about achieving the general goal became the responsibility of the EPA. When agencies are granted the prerogative of deciding how to implement a law or policy, they are in effect being permitted to make law for society.[15] Defenders of discretionary implementation point out, however, that no code of law can anticipate all circumstances that might arise and that administrators must therefore have some leeway. Furthermore, administrators can always be overruled by public or legislative pressure or by executive edict.

Rule Making. The rule-making authority of regulatory agencies is related to discretionary implementation. For example, higher rates for telephone use must be approved by the Public Service Commission (PSC).[16]

One of the best examples of bureaucratic rule making was the fight to force cigarette manufacturers to place health hazard warnings on their cigarette packages and to include them in advertisements. For several years, the Federal Trade Commission (FTC) and the Public Health Service had been urging such practices. Congress had been reluctant to go along, however, primarily because of pressure from the tobacco industry. In 1965 the Advisory Committee on Smoking and Health and the surgeon general (the nation's chief public health officer) concluded that heavy cigarette smoking increased the likelihood of contracting lung cancer and shortened one's life span considerably. The report disturbed the public, and public pressure on Congress increased. Since 1966 cigarette manufacturers have been required to print warnings on all packs.

Meanwhile, the tobacco industry tried, unsuccessfully, to discredit the surgeon general's report, and organizations such as the American Cancer Society were agitating for still firmer antitobacco legislation. In 1967 the FCC entered the crusade. Citing the fairness doctrine, it ordered all radio and television stations accepting cigarette commercials to make free time available for antismoking commercials. Soon the American Cancer Society was producing one-minute anti-smoking announcements.

In 1969 the FCC banned cigarette advertising on radio and television. And in 1971 President Nixon signed an FTC-sponsored bill requiring cigarette companies to print health warnings on all advertising copy as well as on every pack of cigarettes. Political scientist A. Lee Fritschler reached the following conclusion:

The initiation and continuation of the cigarette controversy were possible because of both the political power and delegated authority possessed by bureaucratic agencies. Had the decision on cigarettes and health been left to Congress alone, it is safe to assume that the manufacturers would have triumphed, and no health warnings of any kind would have been required. The cigarette-labeling controversy is a clear example of agencies' power to influence and even formulate public policy.[17]

Here was a vivid case of federal agencies openly lobbying for a particular policy and getting it.

Advisory Roles.   The growing complexity of modern life has caused legislatures and executives to rely more and more heavily on the technical expertise of bureaucrats. Congress may decide that unsafe mines should be shut down, but only mining experts can determine exactly what conditions make a mine unsafe. Many laws require administrative interpretation. For example, Congress may outlaw deceptive advertising, but the determination of what *is* deceptive is made by the FTC. Bureaucrats do not usually have to convince legislators to take their advice; the lawmakers are often only too happy to have the technical assistance of specialists. This is yet another way in which bureaucrats influence the formulation of public policy.

Conflicts can arise, however. For example, Kennedy's Secretary of Defense Robert McNamara, a political appointee, was intent on cutting costs where possible. He ran into a wall of opposition from military leaders, who claimed that they alone knew the technical side of security needs. McNamara's relationship with the military high command was frequently stormy. Similarly, in 1948, President Truman was under intense pressure by State Department experts not to recognize Israel when it became an independent state. Both McNamara and Truman realized that some decisions are, by their very nature, political and that only a politically responsible official ought to make them.

The bureaucracy's role of adviser is not peculiar to the United States; rather, it is an inevitable feature of the modern industrial state. In France, for example, laws and presidential decrees are drawn up and promulgated with the active assistance of the bureaucracy (particularly the Council of State), and career executives thus have the opportunity to shape policy. Bureaucrats play a large role in the framing of legislation in Germany. Since federal bureaucrats do not have to supervise field or branch offices, they can devote their energies to policy matters. In fact, they are often successful in convincing their political superiors to accept their way of thinking on issues.[18]

WHAT TO DO WITH BUREAUCRACY?

Bureaucracy in the twentieth century has become big, powerful, rigid, unresponsive, and intrusive. Some contend it has taken on a life of its own, divorced from the needs of the citizens and governments that first gave it birth. Can anything be done about this?[19] As Joseph LaPalombara has observed, most of the ideas offered to cure bureaucracy entail adding more bureaucrats.[20] Here are some suggested remedies:

Ombudsmen. The ombudsman is Sweden's contribution to the art of governance. Established by the 1809 Swedish constitution, the *Justitieombudsman* (literally, agent of justice) is named and paid by the parliament, not the executive. This is important, for no government agency can be its own ombudsman; that must come from outside. An official who says, "Bring all complaints to me. I'm my own ombudsman," doesn't understand the concept. Absolute independence is necessary for an ombudsman to work effectively. The ombudsman is a legislative-branch lawyer who intervenes on behalf of citizens treated wrongly by the bureaucracy. The ombudsman has subpoena power, and a reprimand to errant officials is usually enough to set things right. Denmark, Norway, Britain, and New Zealand have set up similar institutions.

Some have suggested the ombudsman concept for the United States. In a sense, we already have it: the member of Congress, whose constituency work is much like that of the ombudsman. It might further be argued that since the United States is already overrun with lawyers, no citizen has far to go to find one. Poor people can often obtain free legal assistance. Where the ombudsman idea works is in countries with a tradition of respect for law and a political and moral climate in which a simple reprimand is enough. The American context is not precisely as law-abiding, and an ombudsman might have difficulty working effectively.

Legislative Checks. Whereas an ombudsman system might be difficult to implement in the United States, we have some other mechanisms to oversee the bureaucracy. The U.S. Congress has the General Accounting Office (GAO), Congressional Research Service (CRS), and Congressional Budget Office (CBO). The GAO looks to see that federal funds are spent correctly and effectively; the CRS tries to give Congress the expertise needed to check on the executive-branch specialists; and the CBO, established only in 1974, consolidates Congress's budget-making functions to reply to the White House's powerful Office of Management and Budget. In effect, what the United States has done is set up competing bureaucracies—one executive, the other legislative. This does not save money or reduce the number of bureaucrats; it is simply an effort to keep the executive side tied to the national purpose as represented on Capitol Hill.

Cutting. Americans dream of some golden yesteryear in which there were no bureaucrats on their backs. Politicians often promise to cut the bureaucracy, but they rarely succeed. Cutting bureaucrats means cutting programs, and most citizens soon find their favorite programs getting the ax. They meant to cut other people's wasteful programs, not the necessary and prudent expenditures they benefit from. Once a welfare state has been built, it is terribly difficult to dismantle because so many people have a stake in its bounties. In the 1980s, the Reagan administration tried a different tack: keep the programs on the books but fail to fund or staff them adequately.[21] Many federal offices, especially those providing services the president and his supporters disliked, found themselves operating with reduce budgets and employees, unable to carry out their legislated mandates. At a time of massive federal budget deficits, Congress found it difficult to restore these cuts. In highly public areas such as education and environmental pollution, however, irate citizens and their interest groups demanded attention, and President Reagan had to back down partially. He did not, for example, abolish the Department of Education as he had promised during the 1980 campaign. Plans by Congressional Republicans to "save" Medicare (by cutting it) produced a similar outcry in the mid-1990s. The meat-ax approach to bureaucracy is tempting but hard to carry out in practice.

Decentralization.   For highly centralized systems, as in France and Italy, decentralization offers some improvement. Decisions can be made closer to home, in consultation with the people they will affect. Decentralization can solve some problems but create others. It brings bureaucratic decision making closer to the local level, but this can *increase* corruption and inefficiency. Without Paris or Rome looking over their shoulders, who knows what those bureaucrats in the provinces will do? For most of its history, the United States has had a decentralized education system. The result has been a great deal of freedom and local control but also extreme unevenness of quality and blatant racial segregation. Many Americans wish they could go back to strict local control, but they don't want to do without federal dollars. True decentralization means that localities have to raise their own taxes, something they dislike doing.

Decentralization may entail widely varying standards and problems of coordination. With Germany's strongly decentralized federal system, it took years to get the different *Länder* to agree on a program and standards to clear up the seriously polluted Rhine River. Each state saw its environmental responsibilities differently and didn't want its authority eroded.

Further, decentralization does not mean reducing the number of bureaucrats, just placing them at different levels. As such, it may actually seem to put more bureaucrats on the people's backs, not fewer.

Politicize the Bureaucracy.   Most governments are proud that they have moved to a nonpolitical, neutral, professional bureaucracy. In the United States, we disdain the corrupt "spoils system" of the last century in which political bosses would place their people in choice jobs. But maybe we've gone too far with the career, neutral, detached bureaucrat. Perhaps it's time to reinject a certain amount of political control into the system. Political appointees bring fresh approaches, innovative plans, and a mandate from the people and elected officials for improvement. Bureaucrats live by routine and hate to rock the boat; they are not capable of changing their own system. Only outsiders, appointed from other walks of life for a few years, can do that.

The old U.S. urban machines, such as that of the late Mayor Daley in Chicago, were decried for their corruption, but they were generally responsive to citizens' needs and often worked better than the reform administrations that succeeded them. A new American president has some 3,000 appointive positions to fill, a very high number compared with the numbers in other countries. Some say this is too many, that we should use career civil servants to fill more of these slots. But it is this appointive power that gives a president what little leverage he or she has over the U.S. bureaucracy.[22] Decrease it and the civil service will be less responsive.

The negative side to political appointments is the corruption that often comes with them. Because the political appointees are often from the very branches of industry their bureaus are supposed to be monitoring, they tend to see things the industry's way, to overlook irregularities, and sometimes to dispense favors to friends and party contributors. Bear in mind that almost all cases of corruption in U.S. government offices are wrongdoings of political appointees, not career civil servants. Career civil servants in the Federal Home Loan Bank Board in the 1980s, for example, tried early to signal irregularities with Lincoln Savings and Loan in California. Their politically appointed bosses and five senators, recipients of $1.3 million in campaign donations by Lincoln's owner, overrode the civil servants and delayed action against the firm. The Iran-contra fiasco occurred precisely because the White House insisted on bypassing State and Defense Department bureaucrats, who could have told them that the plan was illegal and unworkable. Political guidance of bureaucracy, yes; bypassing bureaucracy, no.

BUREAUCRACY AND SOCIETY

For all our dislike of bureaucracy, we must remember that it was not visited on us from an alien planet. It was set up, funded, and given its duties by our representatives. They did this for particular reasons, and although agencies sometimes take on lives of their own, the initial reasons still apply. Do you think a lot of red tape is involved in getting a driver's license? Imagine a society where drivers weren't required to be licensed. Do you think bureaucrats interfere too much with private industry? What would happen if we rolled back our standards on foodstuffs, drugs, and product safety? Do equal-opportunity bureaucrats harm a white person's chances to get into law school or secure a good job by ensuring preference to minority candidates? It wasn't bureaucrats who set up these laws; it was Congress. Congress, to be sure, was vague and sloppy, leaving administrators too much leeway in drawing up guidelines and then dropping the whole thing on the courts.[23] But the bureaucrats themselves have only the smallest part of the blame.

　　We live in a complex society. We may try from time to time to make it simpler, to do away with what appear to be burdensome regulations and officious bureaucrats. But when we do, we discover anew that the regulations and civil servants were put there for a purpose. Whereas we may—indeed must—attempt to improve our rules and the agencies that implement them, we are unlikely to eliminate them unless we are prepared to return to a simpler age, a time without nuclear power, automobiles, telecommunications, or employment security. Until then, we are stuck with our unlovely bureaucrats, for in the final analysis, they are us.

Suggested Readings

CARTER, STEPHEN L. *The Confirmation Mess: Cleaning up the Federal Appointments Process.* New York: Basic Books, 1994. A Yale law professor offers criteria for qualifying and disqualifying federal appointees.

CROZIER, MICHEL. *The Bureaucratic Phenomenon.* Chicago: University of Chicago Press, 1964. A leading French sociologist takes a jaundiced look at bureaucracy, especially French bureaucracy.

Downs, George W., and Patrick D. Larkey. *The Search for Government Efficiency: From Hubris to Helplessness.* New York: Random House, 1986. Argues that government is not so inefficient and that it is possible to improve it.

Fry, Brian R. *Mastering Public Administration: From Max Weber to Dwight Waldo.* Chatham, NJ: Chatham House, 1989. Excellent summation of the leading theorists.

Garand, James C. *Are Bureaucrats Different? A Study of Political Attitudes and Political Behavior.* Armonk, NY: Sharpe, 1993. An empirical comparison of the attitudes of bureaucrats and the general public.

Gruber, Judith E. *Controlling Bureaucracies: Dilemmas in Democratic Governance.* Berkeley, CA: University of California Press, 1987. Theories and case studies of how a democracy might control its bureaucracies.

Harris, Richard A., and Stanley M. Milkis. *The Politics of Regulatory Change: A Tale of Two Agencies.* New York: Oxford University Press, 1989. A critical look at the Reagan administration's effort to use agencies to skirt the law.

Howard, Philip K. *The Death of Common Sense: How Law Is Suffocating America.* New York: Random House, 1994. Too many laws, mindlessly enforced by too many bureaucrats!

Knott, Jack H., and Gary J. Miller. *Reforming Bureaucracy: The Politics of Institutional Choice.* Englewood Cliffs, NJ: Prentice Hall, 1987. An excellent overview of bureaucracy with emphasis on how to reform it.

Ripley, Randall A., and Grace A. Franklin. *Congress, the Bureaucracy, and Public Policy,* 5th ed. Belmont, CA: Wadsworth, 1991. Solid study of how congressional-bureaucratic interactions tend to preserve the status quo.

Suleiman, Ezra N., ed. *Bureaucrats and Policy Making.* New York: Holmes & Meier, 1984. Collection of essays on how civil servants get their way in several countries.

Weber, Max. *Theory of Social and Economic Organization.* Glencoe, IL: Free Press, 1958. One of the earliest and perhaps most influential studies of public administration.

Wildavsky, Aaron. *The New Politics of the Budgetary Process,* 2nd ed. New York: Harper/Collins, 1992. A specialist in the budget process examines how it operates.

Wilson, James Q. *Bureaucracy: What Government Agencies Do and Why They Do It.* New York: Basic Books, 1990. A top scholar takes a critical but nuanced and supportive look at U.S. bureaucracies.

Yates, Douglas. *Bureaucratic Democracy: The Search for Democracy and Efficiency in American Government.* Cambridge, MA: Harvard University Press, 1987. Searching look at how democracy can survive in a bureaucratic era.

Notes

1. For a study of how career civil servants at the Environmental Protection Agency clashed with their politically appointed chiefs, see Brian J. Cook, *Bureaucratic Politics and Regulatory Reform: The EPA and Emissions Trading* (Westport, CT: Greenwood, 1988).

2. For a broader, theoretical view of bureaucracies, see B. Guy Peters, *The Politics of Bureaucracy: A Comparative Perspective,* 3rd ed. (New York: Longman, 1989).

3. See Michael Voslensky, *Nomenklatura: The Soviet Ruling Class* (Garden City, NY: Doubleday, 1984).

4. See F. F. Ridley and J. Blondel, *Public Administration in France,* 2nd ed. (London: Routledge & Kegan Paul, 1969).

5. See K. Konig, et al., eds., *Public Administration in the Federal Republic of Germany* (Hingham, MA: Kluwer Academic, 1983).

6. For a good account of the British bureaucracy, see Gavin Drewry and Tony Butcher, *The Civil Service Today* (London: Blackwell, 1988).

7. This is a paraphrase of Weber's criteria. See Robert K. Merton et al., eds., *Reader in Bureaucracy* (Glencoe, IL: Free Press, 1952), pp. 21–22.

8. Frank J. Goodnow, *Politics and Administration* (New York: Macmillan, 1900); and Woodrow Wilson, "The Study of Administration," *Political Science Quarterly* 2 (June 1887), 197–222.

9. Dan B. Wood and Richard W. Waterman found that bureaucracies are not isolated but quite responsive to the prevailing political climate. See their *Bureaucratic Dynamics: The Role of Bureaucracy in a Democracy* (Boulder, CO: Westview Press, 1994).

10. The following section is based on Charles E. Lindblom, *The Policy-Making Process,* 3rd ed. (Englewood Cliffs, NJ: Prentice Hall, 1992); Harold Seidman, *Politics, Position, and Power: The Dynamics of Federal Organization,* 4th ed. (New York: Oxford University Press, 1986); and Peter Woll, *American Bureaucracy,* 2nd ed. (New York: Norton, 1977).

11. C. Northcote Parkinson, *Parkinson's Law* (Boston: Houghton Mifflin, 1957).

12. See James C. Scott, *Comparative Political Corruption* (Englewood Cliffs, NJ: Prentice Hall, 1972).

13. For a survey of Third World bureaucracy, see Krishna K. Tummala, ed., *Administrative Systems Abroad,* rev. ed. (Lanham, MD: University Press of America, 1984).

14. Guy S. Claire, *Administocracy* (New York: Cromwell-Collier, 1934).

15. See Gary C. Bryner, *Bureaucratic Discretion: Law and Policy in Federal Regulatory Agencies* (New York: Pergamon, 1987).

16. See Cornelius M. Kerwin, *Rulemaking: How Government Agencies Write Law and Make Policy* (Washington, DC: CQ Press, 1994).

17. A. Lee Fritschler, *Smoking and Politics: Policymaking and the Federal Bureaucracy,* 5th ed. (Englewood Cliffs, NJ: Prentice Hall, 1995), p. 142.

18. See Joel D. Aberback, Robert D. Putnam, and Bert A. Rockman, *Bureaucrats and Politicians in Western Democracies* (Cambridge, MA: Harvard University Press, 1981).

19. For a study on possible ways to control the U.S. Civil Service, see Douglas Yates, *Bureaucratic Democracy: The Search for Democracy and Efficiency in American Government* (Cambridge, MA: Harvard University Press, 1982).

20. Joseph LaPalombara, *Politics Within Nations* (Englewood Cliffs, NJ: Prentice Hall, 1974), p. 279. Our discussion owes much to LaPalombara's splendid Chap. 8, "Bureaucratic Pathologies and Prescriptions."

21. For a study of the effects of the Reagan cuts, see Irene S. Rubin, *Shrinking the Federal Government: The Effects of Cutbacks on Five Federal Agencies* (New York: Longman, 1985).

22. See G. Calvin Mackenzie, ed., *The In-and-Outers: Presidential Appointees and the Transient Government in Washington* (Baltimore: Johns Hopkins University Press, 1987).

23. See Gary C. Bryner, "Congress, Courts, and Agencies: Equal Employment and the Limits of Policy Implementation," *Political Science Quarterly* 96 (Fall 1981), 3.

• 17 •

Legal Systems and the Courts

The yearning for "equal justice under law" is one of humankind's oldest aspirations. Justice Oliver Wendell Holmes once remarked, "My freedom to swing my arm stops where the other man's nose begins." Because humans are social beings, their freedom of action must have its limits if the freedom of all is to be preserved. But who decides what these limits are? Without a legal system, force alone would settle disputes. Even in primitive societies, two parties who disagree often look to an objective third party to provide a solution. Modern nations depend on laws to regulate human relations, and courts help to maintain order by enforcing these laws.

However, courts and laws may favor certain groups over others. In recent decades, the United States has become concerned with ensuring equal treatment under law for men and women of all races, religions, and economic means. Both lawmakers and courts play important roles in establishing this equality.

For example, federal laws have eliminated lynching, which was fairly common in the southern states at the turn of the century and in which 85 percent of the victims were black. Similarly, racial segregation gradually gave way to the persistent and patient legal work that ended in the Supreme Court's landmark ruling in *Brown* v. *Board of Education of Topeka* (1954). This decision, the first of many to establish the principle that racial segregation is a violation of the U.S. Constitution, produced a revolution in American race relations. Some violence did take place, and the battle is by no means over. But to appreciate the importance of law to the civil rights movement, compare the position of the American black to that of the South African black. In South Africa, the whole legal system until recently supported segregation, leaving violence the only avenue of change.

The law does more than resolve private conflicts among individuals and social groups, granting rights and privileges and imposing duties and responsibilities. Law is also an expression of society's goals and aspirations. The passage of child labor laws, for instance, expressed society's determination to eliminate a practice it had come to regard as a social evil. Changes in the law—in regard to the legality of labor unions, for example—indicated changes in the thinking of the people as a whole with respect to specific questions. Although the law is often slow to catch up with changing mores, it usually does catch up with them in democratic societies because the legislators, who represent the people who elect them, change the laws to suit the voters' new goals and desires. Some wish to use law to bring about social change, however. Critics suggest that Americans place too much of a burden on the law and endanger its status by expecting it to resolve all social and political problems.

The Nature of Law

WHAT IS LAW?

For our purposes, law may be defined as "that which must be obeyed and followed by citizens, subject to sanctions or legal consequences."[1] Terms such as *higher law* or *natural law* have appeared in political and social philosophy since the beginning of recorded civilization. In the Western tradition, the concept of a "higher law" grew out of a mingling of Stoic philosophy and the Judeo-Christian tradition. Higher law was attributed to God or the Creator and was thus higher than laws made by humans. Our own system depends on the idea that people are "endowed by their Creator" with the rights to life, liberty, and the pursuit of happiness and the right to own property and enjoy the fruits of one's labor—rights that no just government can take away. Many argue that this so-called higher law takes precedence over the laws enacted by humans, and some justify their defiance of society's laws by citing the higher law of nature. Mahatma Gandhi in India and Martin Luther King, Jr., in the United States claimed that their actions, which were violations of existing human-made laws, were morally correct because they conformed to the higher edicts of natural law. However, to focus our discussion, we will restrict ourselves to the definition of law given at the beginning of this paragraph.

TYPES OF LAW

Our complex society requires many types of law. There are five major branches of law.

Criminal Law. In these days when fear of crime is a persistent feature of our lives, it is the workings of the criminal law system that we hear, read, and think most about. Modern criminal law is largely statutory (or code) law and covers a specific category of wrongs committed against persons or institutions. Acts defined as criminal are considered social evils and are threats to the entire community because they disturb the public order or threaten the public welfare. Consequently, the state rather than the aggrieved party is always the prosecutor (plaintiff). Offenses are usually divided into three categories. *Petty offenses,* such as traffic violations, are normally punished by a fine. Offenses that are somewhat more serious but not major (e.g., gambling and prostitution) are known as *misdemeanors* and are characteristically punishable by larger fines or short jail sentences. Major crimes, called *felonies* (e.g., rape, murder, robbery, and extortion), are punished by imprisonment. In the United States, some criminal offenses (such as kidnapping and interstate car theft) are federal in nature; others (murder, rape, and mugging) are mainly state concerns; and a few (bank robbery and drug traffic, for instance) violate both state and federal criminal laws.

Civil Law. Many legislative acts (statutes) govern civil rather than criminal matters. Marriage and divorce, custody of children and inheritance, and bankruptcy and the conduct of business are civil concerns. Not every contingency is covered by a statute, however, and in the English-speaking countries, statutory law is supplemented by common law (judge-made law based on precedent) and equity law. Civil law is distinguished from criminal law in that it provides redress for private individuals or corporations who feel they have been injured. Because a breach of civil obligation is not regarded as endangering the peace or welfare of the community, private individuals conduct most civil litigation.

Unfortunately, both common law and statutory law have one major drawback: They can provide redress (usually a monetary award) only after an injury has been done; they cannot prevent it. Equity (or chancery) law was developed in England to remedy this defect. Arising as an appeal to the "king's conscience," it traditionally dealt with property matters (e.g., estates, inheritances, and real estate). Only one feature of it, the injunctive process, is still used widely. An injunction is a court order requiring the person or persons to whom it is directed to do or not to do a particular thing. Equity law can therefore provide a preventive mechanism.

Constitutional Law. Written constitutions are usually general documents that describe the organs of government, their powers, and individual guarantees of freedom. General legislation and court interpretation must fill in the details. An important role of the courts, under a constitutional system of government such as ours, with the recognized authority of judicial review, is to make sure that statutory laws and their administrative interpretations do not violate the spirit or meaning of the constitution. Constitutional law in the United States comprises mainly the judicial decisions which interpret the various sections of the Constitution.

In the United States, with its tradition of judicial review, the ultimate responsibility of interpreting the Constitution rests with the U.S. Supreme Court. The Supreme Court's interpretations of the Constitution change with time. The cliché "The Constitution is what the Supreme Court says it is" is not unfounded. In 1896, for example, the Court ruled, in *Plessy* v. *Ferguson,* that state laws requiring racial segregation in public transportation did not necessarily violate the Fourteenth Amendment, which provides for equal protection under the laws, as long as the transportation facilities for whites and blacks were physically equal. Fifty-eight years later the court reversed itself and ruled that separate public education facilities for whites and blacks are *inherently* unequal, even if physically alike. The Constitution didn't change, but society's conception of individual rights did. Constitutional law (indeed, law itself) is not static, but a living, growing institution.

Administrative Law.   A relatively recent development, administrative law includes the regulatory orders enacted by appropriate government agencies. Administrative law develops when regulatory agencies interpret the statutes that Congress has enacted. For example, a federal statute prohibits "unfair or deceptive acts" in commerce. But what business practices are "unfair or deceptive"? The Federal Trade Commission must decide. As the agencies interpret the meaning of Congress's laws, they begin to build up a body of regulations and case law that guides the commission in its future decisions. Administrative rulings may be appealed to the federal courts. The federal government now codifies administrative regulations, and a fairly substantial body of administrative law has grown up in the past half century.

International Law.   International law consists of international treaties and conventions and long-established customs recognized by most nations. It is a very special body of law because it cannot be enforced in the same way as national law. Treaties and agreements among nations may be signed, but their effectiveness depends mainly on voluntary compliance; reciprocal benefit; and threat, coercion, or deprivation. More important, neither domestic nor international courts are always able to ensure that judicial decisions will be executed. Matters are further complicated by the fact that not all states subscribe to existing rules of law. For example, whereas the United States and Russia comply with the limited Nuclear Test Ban Treaty, which they and several other nations signed in 1963, neither France nor China is a party to the treaty and each continues nuclear testing in the atmosphere. Hence, New Zealand can do no more than protest the radioactive effects of French tests. To be sure, there is an International Court of Justice at The Hague, but it hears only those cases that states bring to it voluntarily. Thus, the system can work only when the individual nations respect the rules. For example, when the court ruled against the United States in 1985 for aiding the Nicaraguan contras in their war against the Managua regime, the United States just ignored the verdict and there was nothing to be done. International law is a legal system in that it has built up a fairly uniform body of law over the centuries, but it lacks the cohesion and enforceability we are accustomed to in domestic law.

Legal Systems

Legal systems consist of two major elements used to govern society: a recognized body of law and an enforcement apparatus. In primitive cultures the system is oral and consists of the mores, traditions, and beliefs that govern behavior. In modern society, legal systems are largely codified, that is, embodied in written laws. Committing the systems to writing makes them more precise in intent and, thus, usually more uniform in application.

Legal codification began in ancient times and has been a major feature in the development of civilization. The Ten Commandments and the Code of Hammurabi—still influential—are among the earliest examples of law codes. However, the supreme legal code of the ancient world was Roman law. Its details, covering all aspects of social life, were based on the idea that "right reason" should govern humanity's affairs. They were so universal, flexible, and logical that they are still in use in much of the world today.[2] Roman law was incorporated by the Catholic church in its canon law, and in the East by the Byzantine Emperor Justinian. The celebrated Code of Justinian (*Corpus Juris Civilis*), based on Roman law and dating from approximately A.D. 533, is the foundation that Europe's modern legal systems (with the important exception of Britain's) were built on. After a long intermediate period during which the more primitive Germanic and Salic systems were used, Roman law was revived in the twelfth century, partly because of the work being done in medieval universities by legal scholars. Modern European law, then, is mostly an amalgamation of Roman, feudal, and ecclesiastical law.

THE ENGLISH COMMON LAW

Development. The English common law, originally based on the customary usage of the Angles and Saxons who settled Britain, developed after the Norman Conquest in 1066 and during the reign of Henry I (1100–1135).[3] At this time, feudal lords and the church dispensed justice. Henry began the practice of tightening royal control over the administration of justice. In this way, he made it more uniform and less subject to the whims of the barons. It was Henry II (1154–1189), however, who did the important work of legal reform. New legal remedies (such as trial by jury), new modes of litigation, and new forms of action were created. The principles of the grand jury were also developed at this time. Itinerant royal judges began traveling throughout the kingdom, and the feudal and ecclesiastical courts thus lost influence. Over time, the itinerant judges came to use similar principles to decide similar cases in different parts of the kingdom, and there emerged a judge-made body of law which was "common" to all of England. Eventually, the new system led to a regular system of royal courts.

By the opening of the thirteenth century, this entire structure of royal justice rested on the shoulders of the humble justice of the peace (JP). A local citizen appointed by the Crown, the JP was supposed to take custody of prisoners until the monarch's judges arrived to try them. As time passed, JPs began to take on limited judicial functions. For example, they had authority to try minor infractions of law and supervise local police functions; later they were allowed to perform civil marriage ceremonies. The traveling royal justices, the common law courts, and the JPs laid the foundation for the development of English common law.

Features. In administering justice, the judges and courts were forced to improvise. Most of the early judges had a clerical education and were familiar with Roman law as interpreted by the church. Accordingly, when royal law proved inadequate to the case at hand, the judges applied Roman and canon law provisions. If these were not applicable, they relied on their own common sense and judgment as well as the common practices of the English people. Over the centuries, a substantial body of common law developed—an amalgam of Roman law, church law, and local English customs.[4]

Common law has three distinctive features. First, it is *case* law; that is, it is based on individual legal decisions rather than on a comprehensive code of statutes. Second, common law was made by *judicial decision* (it is "judge-made" law), and thus has great flexibility. Judges can easily reinterpret or modify previous rulings and principles to fit new social and economic circumstances and institutions. Third, common law relies heavily on *stare decisis,* or precedent. Because no two cases are exactly alike, a judge can pick on the smallest point of difference to justify a ruling that breaks precedent. In this way, common law remains relevant to changing social needs. With the rise of Parliament as a dominant institution in seventeenth-century England, statute law supplemented (and in some cases supplanted) specific provisions of the common law. Today, when the two conflict, statute law always takes precedence.

Significance. Despite the fact that common law has declined somewhat in importance, its influence is still considerable. It has remained important in the legal systems of England, the United States, Canada, Australia, New Zealand, and a number of former British colonies.[5] In many instances, statute law is formal enactment, with minor modifications, of existing common law provisions. A pervasive effect of the common law is that it shaped the development of English society and politics and gave distinctive habits of thought to all English-speaking societies.

CODE (ROMAN) LAW

Development. The legal systems of continental Europe (France, in particular) developed very differently from that of England. Feudalism was stronger in

France than anywhere else, and until the thirteenth century the feudal lords were virtually independent of royal control. Unifying the country was a long, drawn-out process, with the local lords resisting the central government. The process was finally completed under Louis XIII's reign (1610–1643), mainly due to his brilliant adviser, Cardinal Richelieu. Roman law, meanwhile, was enjoying a revival because of the work of legal scholars and changing conditions in Europe. Central governments were asserting themselves throughout Europe, and commerce was reviving on a large scale. It was becoming obvious that some form of centralized justice would be needed for this new age. French jurists, in particular, saw the value of Roman law. It was universal and written. If this law could work so well for the ancient world, why not introduce it into France? Many of its principles, in fact, were already known because of the Roman Catholic church's canon law. The task that remained was codification.

Codifying the law was Napoleon's lasting contribution to the rationalization of justice for France and, eventually, for most of Europe. The Code Napoleon (1804) was the first modern codification of European law. Feudal laws were bypassed, and the emancipation of civil law from religious influence—begun during the French Revolution—was maintained. Although it preserved many of the gains of the revolution, such as the elimination of torture and arbitrary arrest and imprisonment, as well as the guarantee of civil liberty and civil equality, it also reflected Napoleon's authoritarian views. These views are seen in the provisions concerning family life: The father's authority was firmly established, and the status of women was depressed. Nevertheless, the code was a great step forward, and Napoleon's invasions of Belgium, Spain, Italy, and Germany brought the code to these countries; their legal systems are still based on it. It is also in use in Louisiana, and European colonists carried it to Asia and Africa later in the nineteenth century. The centralization of French life even to this day is a reflection of its basic philosophy.

Features.   Today, most of the Western world lives under some form of Roman law as interpreted by the Code Napoleon.[6] Most code law is detailed, precise (more so than the written laws in the common law countries), comprehensive, and understandable by laypersons. Judges are not expected to "make" law, merely to apply it. Precedent carries less weight. Another feature of Roman law is that the judiciary is not independent of the executive (as it is in the Anglo-American system). Therefore, its powers of judicial review are quite limited—either shared with the legislative branch or assigned to a special national court. In Italy, for example, only the *Corte Costituzionale* can rule on the constitutionality of legislation, and the regular supreme court must assume that laws are constitutional unless this court rules otherwise.

COMMON FEATURES OF BOTH LEGAL SYSTEMS

The differences between the common law and the Roman system are self-evident. The former is general and largely judge-made, and it relies on precedent and custom. The latter is specific and is largely the product of legislation. It is interesting to note that both systems developed to serve the needs of modernizing and centralizing monarchs—Henry I and II in England and Louis XIII and Napoleon in France.

The differences between these two systems should not obscure their similarities; in fact, they are becoming more and more alike. As the volume of statute law increases in the English-speaking nations, the importance and relevance of common law decreases. More and more, the details of legislative enactment are being outlined by administrative agencies, whose regulations are now an integral part of the legal system. In both systems, the law is relatively uniform in its application, universal in its scope, and amenable to change.

The Courts, the Bench, and the Bar

As legal systems developed, so did judicial systems, for it is these systems that handle the day-to-day administration of the law. The organization of a judicial system is always hierarchical, which means that the courts are ranked in a specific order. The different courts have specific jurisdiction; that is, they generally hear different kinds of cases and have authority in specific geographical areas.

THE U.S. COURT SYSTEM

Our court system is unique, consisting of fifty-one judicial structures: the national system, comprising the federal courts, and fifty state systems. A confusing element is that the federal system overlaps that of the states. The federal courts hear many cases in which the issue is one of state laws but the parties to the litigation are citizens of different states, the so-called "diversity jurisdiction." Also, of course, they hear cases involving the application of federal laws. Conversely, issues of federal law (constitutional or statutory) may arise in the course of a litigation in state court. In that situation, as discussed below, the Supreme Court of the United States has jurisdiction to review the state court's judgment insofar as it turns on a determination of the federal question.

The National Court Structure.   The federal district court is at the base of the national court system.[7] Congress has divided the nation into ninety-four federal court districts employing over 500 judges. The district court is a trial court and hears a wide variety of civil suits arising under federal law, as well as criminal cases involving federal infractions. It also exercises the "diversity" jurisdiction previously noted. In many criminal cases, in which the accused is charged with violating state law as well as federal law, the defendants are turned over to state criminal courts for trial. Bank robbery, kidnapping, and auto theft are examples of offenses that often have interstate ramifications and hence may violate both state and federal laws.

Federal district court decisions can be appealed to a U.S. court of appeals.

There are thirteen courts of appeals presided over by 132 judges. Besides hearing appeals from the district courts within its circuit, a court of appeals may also review the rulings of administrative tribunals and commissions, such as the Federal Trade Commission, the Federal Aviation Administration, and the Food and Drug Administration. Each court of appeals consists of three or more judges, depending on need, and arguments are heard by panels of three judges. For the most part, these courts do not question the facts of the case but consider only whether or not the law has been misinterpreted or misapplied. The court of appeals bases its majority-vote verdict on the appeal primarily on the briefs submitted by the attorneys for both parties to the dispute; oral arguments are quite limited.

At the pinnacle of the federal court system stands the Supreme Court, consisting of one chief justice and eight associate justices.[8] Its jurisdiction is almost entirely appellate. The nation's highest court, unlike a court of appeals, is not obliged to hear every case presented to it, and it accepts for a review only a small fraction of the petitions for review that it receives. The Court will generally not agree to hear a case unless it involves a substantial constitutional question, a treaty, or some significant point of federal law. Here we see the importance of precedent, because the Court's ruling will establish a basis for future decisions. In addition to hearing cases arising in the lower federal courts, the Court will review cases that come from the state supreme courts if a substantial federal question, constitutional or statutory, is presented. For example, if a state supreme court declares a federal statute unconstitutional, it is almost certain that the Court will hear the case.

The State Court System. Each of the fifty states maintains and operates it own court system. Perhaps 90 percent of the nation's legal business is handled in the state courts.[9] Most of the cases that come before them are civil in nature. Generally, state trial courts operate at the county level, although a number of sparsely populated rural counties may be combined into a single court district. These courts have original jurisdiction in all civil and criminal cases and can hear appeals from local JP courts and magistrate's courts.

At the local level, JP courts in rural counties try minor matters and criminal infractions. In urban areas, magistrate's or police courts have jurisdiction over minor traffic cases, violations of city ordinances, and misdemeanors such as public drunkenness. For the most part, these local courts operate without juries because serious cases are handled by the state courts. Most of the penalties they impose are fines or short jail terms.

JUDGES

Federal Judges. Federal judges are nominated for the federal bench by the president and are appointed with the advice and consent of the Senate. Federal judges hold their positions during "good behavior," which generally means that they serve for life unless impeached and convicted for criminal behavior. The purpose of a "lifetime" appointment is to free the judges from executive and other political pressure.

Federal judges are invariably lawyers. Some undoubtedly owe their appointments to political favors, but they usually knowledgeable in the law. The attorney general will draw up a list of eligible candidates; as vacancies occur, the president selects a few names from that list. Before the names are made public, it has been the practice for the president to consult with the American Bar Association (ABA), which rates the judges. Although presidents are not obliged to take the ABA's advice, they are usually influenced by it. At the same time, the FBI inquires into the candidates' past and present activities. The Senate must approve all federal judges, which sometimes generates controversy. Appointees of Nixon and Reagan, charged by Senate Democrats as marginally qualified, withdrew from consideration. In 1986, the vice-president broke a Senate tie to confirm the appointment of a controversial individual as a federal judge.

Some presidents—Eisenhower, for example—have argued that the federal judiciary should be nonpartisan, or at the very least bipartisan. Eisenhower appointed some Democrats to the federal bench (including Supreme Court Justice William J. Brennan) and made an effort to achieve a balance between judicial liberals and judicial conservatives. Most presidents, however, appoint judges of their own political party who share their judicial philosophy. President Johnson, for example, appointed Thurgood Marshall—a liberal who believed that the Court should take an active role in promoting social justice—to the Supreme Court. President Nixon, in contrast, appointed four justices whose general political philosophy was conservative and who believed that the Warren Court of the 1950s and 1960s went too far in protecting the rights of the individual, to the detriment of society as a whole. President Reagan followed the Nixon example with the appointment of a conservative who happened to be a woman, Sandra Day O'Connor, the first female on the Court.

State Judges.   State judges are popularly elected or appointed, for terms ranging up to fourteen years. Both parties often nominate the same slate of judges, so that the judicial elections have become largely nonpartisan affairs; only rarely do party fights for a judicial office take place. In a 1986 referendum, Californians ousted their state chief justice, Rose Bird, who had been totally opposed to the death penalty. California justices are appointed but later have to be confirmed by voters.

COMPARING COURTS

What role should judges play? Should they act as umpires, passively watching the legal drama, confining their responsibility simply to ruling on disputed points of procedure? Or should they actively direct the course of the trial, question witnesses, elicit evidence, and comment on the proceedings as they unfold? The idea of judges playing such a role would undoubtedly seem strange—if not harmful—to those of us who have been raised within the common law framework. Yet in code law countries, judges play just such an active role, and this is one of the crucial differences between the common law and code law systems.

The Anglo-American Adversary and Accusatorial Process. English and American courts are passive institutions in that they do not look for injustices to correct, and they do not apprehend or search out lawbreakers. Instead, they wait until a law is challenged or broken by someone, and the case then works its way up the court system.

The Anglo-American system of justice operates on a set of principles that together make up the adversary and accusatorial process. In the adversary process, two sides (plaintiff and defendant) are vying for a favorable decision from an impartial court. The operating principles are as follows: First, the courts will not accept a case that does not involve a real conflict of interest; in other words, the plaintiff must demonstrate how, and in what ways, the defendant has caused damage. Second, once a case has been accepted for trial, the presiding judge acts as an umpire. Both parties present their evidence, call and cross-examine witnesses, and try to refute each other's arguments. The judge rules on the evidence and testimony to be admitted, sees that proper legal procedures are followed, and rules on disputed points of procedure. After both sides have presented their cases, the judge rules on the basis of the facts and the relevant law. If a jury is hearing the case, the judge will instruct the members concerning the weight of the evidence (those factors that they may or may not consider). The judge makes an appropriate decision after the jury gives its verdict on the factual issues.

In criminal cases, the police investigate and report to the public prosecutor, who must decide whether prosecution is warranted. The actual trial proceeds much like a civil one: The government is the plaintiff, the accused the defendant, and the court controls the proceedings. Unless a jury has been waived, the jury determines the ultimate issue of guilt under instructions from the judge concerning the governing law.

Many decisions of the Warren Court led to increased protection of the rights of the accused in situations in which the investigating police officers were alleged to have invaded constitutional rights in gathering evidence. Some people felt the Warren Court's decisions threatened the rights of law-abiding citizens by making it easier for criminals to avoid conviction. With the conservative appointments of Nixon and Reagan, the Burger Court and the Rehnquist Court refined and modified some of these decisions to give more power to law officers.

THE BRITISH COURT SYSTEM

The court system in operation in Britain today was established by the Judicature Act of 1873. For the most part, the system continues common law traditions and is divided into civil and criminal branches.

Selection and Tenure of Judges. All British judges are appointed by the monarch on the advice of the prime minister, whose choices are based on recommendations of the lord chancellor, who presides over the House of Lords and is usually a cabinet member. To encourage independence, British judges are given lifetime tenure. By tradition, the English bench is supposed to be above party politics and is not supposed to make policy—a tradition bolstered by the fact that there is no judicial review of the constitutionality of legislation in Britain. Judicial review would be difficult in Britain because there is no written constitution. English courts, moreover, are less disposed to review administrative decisions to determine whether they are consistent with statutory grants of authority. The British judiciary is therefore weaker in relation to both the legislative and executive branches than in the United States.

Lawyer's Role. Although the United States and Britain share a common legal heritage, there are important differences between their systems. One of the biggest distinctions is that in Britain the Crown hires lawyers to prosecute crimes. There are no professional prosecutors to parallel the district attorneys in the American system. Another difference is in the ordering of the legal profession. American lawyers, once they have passed the bar exam, may take on any type of legal work, in or out of the courtroom. British *solicitors* handle all legal matters except representing clients in court. That is reserved to a small number of lawyers called *barristers* who are specialists in courtroom procedure.

THE EUROPEAN COURT SYSTEM

Based heavily on the French system, European courts, unlike the English courts, are not divided into separate criminal and civil divisions. Instead, most European countries maintain separate systems of regular and administrative courts.[10] European judges sit as a panel to rule on points of law and procedure, but at the conclusion of the trial they retire *with* a jury to consider the verdict and the sentence. Obviously, there is great pressure on the lay jurors to go along with the superior— or at least professional—knowledge and wisdom of the judges. In some systems, such as the German, a judge either sits alone or with two "lay judges."

Role of Judges in Adjudication: The Inquisitorial Process. In code law countries—that is, throughout most of Europe—judges play a more active role than in common law countries. The prosecutor (French *procureur*, German *Staatsanwalt*) is an official who forwards evidence to an investigating judge (*juge d'instruction, Ermittlungsrichter*), a representative of the justice ministry who conducts a thorough inquiry (*enquête*), gathering evidence and interrogating those involved. There is no parallel to the investigating judge in the Anglo-American system. The French (or German) judge first makes a preliminary determination of guilt *before* sending the case to trial, something that is quite out of bounds under the common law.

The major differences between Anglo-American and European criminal procedures are that (1) the decision to indict is made not by a district attorney but by a judge, and (2) the weight of evidence is not controlled by the adversaries (plaintiff and defendant) but by the court, which can take the initiative in acquiring needed evidence.

Another major point of difference in the two systems is that in the Anglo-American system the accused is presumed innocent until proven guilty; in Europe the assumptions are nearly reversed. In an American or English court, the burden of proof is on the prosecution, and the defendant need not say one word in his or her defense; the prosecutor must prove guilt "beyond a reasonable doubt." In code law countries, the accused bears the burden of having to prove that the investigating judge is wrong.

Lawyer's Role.   Unlike a British or American trial lawyer, the European *avocat* (*Rechtsanwalt*) does not question witnesses (the court does that). Instead, he or she tries to show logical or factual mistakes in the opposition's argument or case, attempting to sway the sympathy of the lay jury as in the summation argument of an American trial lawyer. For the most part, the role of the European lawyer is not as vital or creative as that of the English or American, for the court takes the initiative in discovering the facts of the case.

LAW IN THE EX–SOVIET UNION

The Legal System.   Although now largely of historical interest, the Soviet legal structure partly carried over into the post-Communist Russian legal system, virtually all of whose personnel were trained under the Communists. Now Russian law is rapidly adding "bourgeois" concepts of property law and civil rights. In 1991 a Constitutional Court with 15 justices was established, the first independent tribunal in Russian history. By 1993, it was ruling on the constitutionality of the moves made by President Yeltsin and by the Supreme Soviet. In time, this court, chaired by young law Ph.D. Valery Zorkin, an admirer of the U.S. Supreme Court, may become a major force for stability and democracy.

The basic concepts of Soviet law and the workings of the Soviet judicial process were quite different from those of the Western democracies, even though they were similar in strictly criminal—as opposed to political—matters.[11] Soviet law started with Marx's idea that law exists to serve the ruling class. Capitalists naturally have bourgeois laws designed to protect private property. Proletarians, who were supposed to be in power in the Soviet Union, had socialist law to protect state property, the property of all society. Much Soviet law was concerned with state property, and those who stole or diverted it could be executed by firing squad. Almost nothing was said of private property, which scarcely existed. Another part of Soviet law dealt with sedition and subversion, areas of extremely minor importance in the West. Soviet citizens could receive harsh sentences to Siberia for "antistate activities" or "slandering the Soviet state," areas in which U.S. citizens would be protected by the First Amendment.

Cases with no political overtones were generally handled fairly under Soviet law. Prosecutors with the powers of European investigating judges gathered evidence and brought cases to court but sometimes took into account mitigating social factors and asked for lighter sentences. Defense attorneys were permitted, but they merely advised their clients on points of the law and did not challenge the prosecutor's evidence. There were no jury trials. Courts were organized federally and hierarchically up to the Supreme Court of the USSR. So far as is known, all judges in the Soviet Union were party members.

Some politically sensitive cases never came to trial, for the Soviets wanted to avoid bad publicity around the world. Obedient Soviet psychiatrists used to diagnose dissidents as "sluggish schizophrenic" and put them in prisonlike hospitals with no trial. Nobel Prize-winning writer Alexander Solzhenitsyn was simply bundled onto a plane for West Germany in 1974 with no trial. Likewise, dissident physicist Andrei Sakharov was banished to a remote city in 1980 to get him away from Western reporters. The Committee on State Security (KGB) was so powerful, it sometimes acted independently of Soviet courts.

The Role of the Courts

In the United States, we look to the courts to strike down laws that violate the terms of the Constitution, and we expect the justices to leave their personal feelings and beliefs out of their interpretations. Judicial review is more highly developed in the United States than in any other country, and Americans expect more of their courts than do other peoples.

However, this function is not completely absent from the courts in other Western democracies. In Switzerland, for example, when cases from the cantonal (state) courts come before the Federal Tribunal (their supreme court), the tribunal determines whether a cantonal law violates the federal constitution. However, the tribunal does not pass on the constitutionality of laws passed by the Swiss parliament. The German Constitutional Court reviews statutes to make sure they conform to the Basic Law, as the German constitution is called.[12] The court, located in Karlsruhe, was included in the Basic Law partly on American insistence after World War II; it was a new concept for Europe. The Karlsruhe court consists of sixteen judges, eight elected by each house of parliament, who serve for nonrenewable twelve-year terms. The court decides cases between states, protects civil liberties, and outlaws dangerous political parties. Its decisions have been important. In the 1950s it found that both neo-Nazi and Communist parties wanted to overthrow the constitutional order and declared them illegal. It found that a 1974 abortion bill was in conflict with the strong right-to-life provisions of the Basic Law. Because the Constitutional Court operates with the more rigid Roman law, its decisions do not have the impact of U.S. Supreme Court decisions, which under the common law are literally the law of the land.

U.S. SUPREME COURT

The U.S. Supreme Court's power to review the constitutionality of federal legislative enactments is not mentioned specifically in the Constitution, and throughout much of our history the doctrine that the Supreme Court has this prerogative has been vehemently challenged.

The doctrine was first considered and debated at the Constitutional Convention of 1787. Delegates to that convention suggested that when in doubt, legislators might call on the judges for an opinion on a proposed law's constitutionality. James Madison stated that a "law violating a constitution established by the people themselves would be considered by the judges as null and void." However, this position was challenged by those who believed that such a power would give the Court a double check and compromise its neutrality. Others felt it would violate the principle of separation of powers. Elbridge Gerry stated that it would make "statesmen of judges," a prophetic remark. At the close of the convention, judicial review had not been explicitly provided for. However, Alexander Hamilton supported the idea, and in *The Federalist* no. 78, which was written to promote ratification of the Constitution, he specifically stated that only the courts could limit legislative authority. John Marshall (chief justice of the Supreme Court from 1801 to 1835) agreed with this position; in fact, he went on record in favor of it nearly fifteen years before the landmark decision *Marbury* v. *Madison* (1803). Therefore, his assertion of the doctrine of judicial review in that case should have come as no surprise.

The doctrine has never been universally popular, however. Strong-willed presidents have tried to resist the authority of the Court. Thomas Jefferson, Andrew Jackson, Abraham Lincoln, and Franklin D. Roosevelt all differed sharply with equally strong-willed judges.

***Marbury* v. *Madison*.**   The background to *Marbury* v. *Madison* is as follows.[13] President John Adams, a Federalist, had appointed William Marbury, a Washington, DC, justice of the peace shortly before leaving office. For some unknown reason, however, Secretary of State John Marshall had neglected to deliver the commission to Marbury. Marshall's successor, the Republican[14] James Madison, refused to deliver the commission. Marbury brought suit in original jurisdiction before the Supreme Court, asking the Court to issue a writ of *mandamus* commanding Madison to deliver the commission. This presented the Court with something of a dilemma. If Chief Justice Marshall and the Supreme Court issued the writ, and Madison refused to deliver the commission, the prestige and authority of the Court would be dealt a severe blow. If, however, Marshall refused to issue the writ, he would in effect call into question the legitimacy of the hasty judicial appointments given to Federalists in the final days of the Adams administration. Marshall's solution was nothing short of brilliant, for it not only criticized Madison and Jefferson but also established explicitly the principle of judicial review. On the one hand, Marshall ruled that Marbury was entitled to his commission and that Madison should have given it to him. On the other hand, however, he stated that the Supreme Court had no authority to issue a writ of *mandamus* in a case brought to it in original jurisdiction and that because Section 13 of the Judiciary Act of 1789 implied otherwise, that part of the act was unconstitutional. The decision infuriated President Jefferson, for he understood all too well how cleverly Marshall had escaped the trap and asserted the authority of the Court into the bargain. He realized that the precedent for judicial review had been laid and called it "both elitist and undemocratic."

From 1803 to 1857, the Supreme Court did not invalidate any act of Congress.

In the latter year, it threw out the Missouri Compromise of 1820, which had barred slavery in the old Northwest Territory. This touched off a political storm that was to make Abraham Lincoln president. In the twentieth century, the doctrine has been used extensively. The court itself, however, has always been divided on how it should be used. Judicial "activists," led by Hugo Black,[15] William O. Douglas, and Earl Warren, have argued that the Supreme Court must be vigilant in its protection of the Bill of Rights' guarantees. Advocates of judicial "restraint," such as Oliver Wendell Holmes, Felix Frankfurter, and Warren Burger, have argued that only Congress should make public policy and that unless a legislative act clearly violates the Constitution, the law should stand. The Warren Court (1953–1969), named after its chief justice, was markedly activist, issuing decisions in the areas of racial segregation, reapportionment, and rights of the accused that had substantial impacts on U.S. society. The Burger Court that followed was more cautious, reflecting the fact that seven of its members were appointed by conservative Republicans.

THE SUPREME COURT'S POLITICAL ROLE

In this country, the Supreme Court's rulings have often become political issues. This is not true in other countries, simply because their courts do not have the authority and independence that our courts have. When the Supreme Court of Franklin Roosevelt's day ruled that many New Deal laws were unconstitutional, Roosevelt referred to the justices contemptuously as "nine tired old men." Richard Nixon, in the 1968 campaign, charged that the Warren Court's liberal decisions had added to the crime problem and, by implication, had endangered the safety of society. It should be obvious by now that the justices do play important political roles. Moreover, the appointment of just one new justice can make an enormous difference. Suppose the Court frequently splits its decisions five to four. A new justice who sides frequently with the minority obviously turns it into a majority. Therefore, it is important to know whether, and to what extent, judges let their personal beliefs interfere with their decisions. Are their ideological views incompatible with the idea of the Court as an "impartial dispenser of justice"?[16]

THE VIEWS OF JUDGES

However conscientiously judges may try to keep their personal beliefs out of decisions, their own outlook and background no doubt play some part in their work. Most Supreme Court justices are and have been white, Protestant, male, and from upper- or upper-middle-class families, most of whom can trace their origins to the British Isles. Those critics who claim that the judicial system is too conservative state that the judges cannot possibly identify with the needs of the poor or racially oppressed. But others argue that selecting judges from lower-class and minority groups will not ensure fairness; it will merely replace one set of prejudices with another.

There are other, more concrete factors that affect a judge's rulings. Southern jurists have been, traditionally, more conservative on racial matters. However, there are exceptions. One of the strongest champions of civil rights was Alabama's Hugo L. Black, who had been a member of the Ku Klux Klan during his youth. Similarly, eastern judges are expected to be more responsive to the needs of large industry than judges from farm states. Occupational background may also affect decision making; for example, former corporation lawyers may be more sympathetic than others to the problems of business. Some justices, like Louis D. Brandeis (one of five Jewish justices) and Thurgood Marshall (the first black justice), were active in reform and civil rights causes and brought their liberalism to the bench. Others who have served on state courts believe that the states' rights should be strengthened.

The two most important influences on voting, however, seem to be political party affiliation and the justice's conception of the judicial role in the American system of government. Although we should be wary of generalizations, studies indicate that Democratic justices are much more likely to support liberal stands than are Republican justices.[17] Democrats tend to be judicial activists and to see the Supreme Court as a defender of oppressed minorities and economic groups. They are more likely to distrust state power and to favor an increase in federal authority, while also seeking to protect individual rights under the Fourteenth Amendment against state authority. Republicans, on the other hand, usually favor judicial restraint, are more likely to uphold state authority within the federal system of government, and are less likely to accept the Bill of Rights as a blanket guarantee. There are, of course, exceptions to this pattern. When President Eisenhower appointed California Governor Earl Warren in 1953, he thought he was picking a good Republican with a "middle-of-the-road philosophy" as chief justice. Later Eisenhower called the choice "the biggest damned-fool mistake I ever made."[18]

Supreme Court justices are undoubtedly influenced by changing public attitudes. However, many justices see the Court's role as standing firm on certain constitutional principles, despite fluctuations in public opinion. Justice Jackson put it this way: "One's right to life, liberty and property, to free speech, a free press, freedom of worship and assembly, and other fundamental rights may not be submitted to vote; they depend upon the outcome of no election."

In the 1936 election, after the Court had struck down several important laws designed to alleviate the Depression, President Roosevelt was given the greatest mandate in the nation's history. In the following year, he submitted legislation that would have had the effect of expanding the Supreme Court to fifteen members and would have allowed every sitting justice over the age of seventy to retire at a sizable pension. The plan failed because the people felt that Roosevelt was going too far in attacking the constitutional principle of an independent judiciary, but it did force the Court to look beyond its own narrow world and accept the fact that change could not be postponed indefinitely. Most legal scholars believe that the election of 1936 and the controversy over "court packing" led directly to the Court's becoming more restrained in dealing with New Deal legislation.[19] As one jokester put it, "A switch in time saves nine."

Still another influence on a Supreme Court justice is colleagues' opinions. Both Chief Justices John Marshall (1801–1835) and Earl Warren (1953–1969) were able to convert some of their colleagues to their judicial philosophies by the force of their personalities as well as their judicial reasoning. In short, many factors—not all of them knowable—influence a given decision. Perhaps one factor overshadows all others, the fact that Supreme Court justices are appointed for life. They are in- dependent and relatively immune to congressional, White House, and private-in- terest pressures. This factor may change them, and in unpredictable ways. Liberals may turn into conservatives, activists into restrainers, and vice versa. The serious- ness of their position and the knowledge that their votes may alter the structure of America makes justices think deeply and sometimes change viewpoints. In the Supreme Court, as well as in many other places, the office in considerable part makes its occupant.

POLITICAL IMPACT OF THE COURT

Our legal system—in theory and practice—poses a basic conflict. On the one hand, justices are expected to be impartial; on the other hand, the importance of the Court gives them considerable political power. In the twentieth century, this power is increasing. Earl Warren's Court was as active as it was controversial, and in three key areas—civil rights, criminal rights, and legislative reapportionment—it sub- stantially rewrote constitutional law.[20] In the opinion of some, as ninety-six south- ern members of Congress put it, the Court overturned "the established law of the land" and implemented its "personal political and social philosophy."

Civil Rights.   The Supreme Court's decision in *Brown* v. *Board of Education of Topeka* (1954) led to crucial changes in American race relations. In a unanimous ruling, the Court accepted the sociological argument of Thurgood Marshall (then attorney for the NAACP) that segregated public school facilities were "inherently unequal" because they stigmatized black children and thus deprived them of the Fourteenth Amendment's guarantee of equal protection of the law. One year later, in *Brown II* (1955), the process of desegregation in the public schools was ordered to proceed "with all deliberate speed." Southern whites vowed massive resistance.

America's blacks, encouraged by this legal support, attempted to gain equal treatment in other areas. By 1963, passive resistance had given way to massive con- frontation. In *Lombard* v. *Louisiana* (1963), the Warren Court supported by impli- cation the sit-in tactic, ruling that blacks who had refused to leave a segregated lunch counter could not be prosecuted where it appeared that the state was in- volved in unequal treatment of the races, relying on the command of the Four- teenth Amendment that no state may deny any person the equal protection of the laws. The sit-in had become a major weapon in the civil rights struggle. In 1964 Congress followed the Court's lead when it passed the Civil Rights Act, which barred segregation in public accommodations such as hotels, motels, restaurants, and theaters.

Criminal Justice.   The Warren Court's rulings in the area of criminal justice and procedural rights in state criminal cases were even more disturbing to many Americans. An important case in this area was *Mapp* v. *Ohio* (1961), in which the

Court ruled that except in exigent circumstances, evidence seized by police without a warrant was inadmissible in a state court. In 1963, in *Gideon* v. *Wainwright*, the Court held that unless they waive the right, indigent defendants charged with misdemeanors or felonies must be provided with legal counsel. In *Escobedo* v. *Illinois* (1964), in a five-to-four decision, it ruled that a suspect could not be denied the right to have a lawyer during police questioning and that any confessions so obtained could not be used in court. One of the Court's most controversial rulings came in 1966 in the case of *Miranda* v. *Arizona*. The majority (five to four) ruled that as soon as a suspect is detained by the police, he or she must be told of the right to remain silent and to have a lawyer present during police questioning. Once again the Court had upset local criminal procedures, and once again its ruling was unpopular.

Legislative Reapportionment.   Equally controversial was the Supreme Court's "one man, one vote" ruling. Until 1962, state legislative districts had been gerrymandered notoriously, and yet the Supreme Court had consistently maintained that only the states and Congress had the right to draw electoral boundaries. This meant that in many states rural districts were grossly overrepresented and cities underrepresented. In a series of decisions in 1962 and 1964, the Warren Court found that unequal representation denied citizens their Fourteenth Amendment (equal protection) rights. The Court ordered that state legislatures apply the principle of "one man, one vote" in redrawing electoral lines.

Much of this angered people who felt they had been hurt: segregationists who didn't like to share schools or other accommodations with blacks, police who felt hampered in dealing with suspects, and rural people who wanted a more-than-equal vote. There were billboards shouting "Impeach Earl Warren," and Nixon in 1968 ran as much against the Supreme Court as against Hubert Humphrey. The Warren Court overthrew Jim Crow laws, rewrote the rules for criminal procedure, and redrew legislative maps. With the possible exception of the Marshall Court, it was the most active, ground-breaking Court in U.S. history.

The Post-Warren Courts.   The Burger Court (1969–1986) and the current Rehnquist Court were sometimes characterized as conservative, an effort to roll back some of the decisions of the Warren Court. Actually, their decisions were not so clear-cut. Overall, there was a conservative drift, but an unpredictable one.[21] The Burger Court in the 1978 *Bakke* case found that reserving quotas for black applicants to medical school violated equal protection for whites.[22] The next year, however, in *Weber*, it found that quotas to help black workers attain skilled positions were constitutional. In criminal law, the Burger Court issued some hard-line decisions. In 1984 it added a "good faith exception" to the *Mapp* rule, which excluded wrongfully seized evidence. If the police, with a warrant to look for a particular piece of evidence, stumble on another, it may be used as evidence. This modified but did not overturn *Mapp*. In 1976, the Burger Court found that capital punishment was not necessarily "cruel and unusual" if the rules for applying it were fair.

The Rehnquist Court both pleased and alarmed conservatives. In 1988, in a move that stunned the Reagan administration, the Court upheld the constitutionality of independent federal prosecutors, something the White House said inter-fered with the powers of the executive branch. The 1989 *Webster* decision gave state legislatures the power to limit abortions. This was seen as a victory for pro-life forces, but in some states it energized pro-choice forces to block such laws. The Court also ruled that burning the American flag could not be outlawed; it is a form of free speech. This ruling brought a mass outcry and a new federal statute out-lawing flag burning (which, if the Court is consistent, will probably be declared un-constitutional). In sum, the post-Warren Courts modified rather than repudiated the Warren Court.

One of the problems with evaluating the thrust of Court decisions is the def-inition of *conservative.* The term may be applied to the substance of decisions, such as giving minorities special treatment, or it may be applied to the maintenance of existing institutions. Often the two coincide, as when the Court says states can pass laws limiting abortion. That would be both conservative concerning substance and conservative concerning the powers of states. But sometimes the two can diverge, as when the Rehnquist Court unanimously overturned a $200,000 libel award for the Reverend Jerry Falwell. Some might call that a "liberal" ruling, but it really just upholds the First Amendment right to a free press. What the mass media and pub-lic opinion call "conservative" may be irrelevant to the Court, which is intent only on preserving constitutionality. "Liberal" and "conservative" are simplified labels used by the mass media and the other branches of government; they are not used by the Supreme Court.

LIMITATIONS ON THE COURT

Despite the fact that the Court's decisions made basic changes in American society, the Court cannot just rewrite the law. Institutional as well as noninstitutional checks on its authority do exist. For one thing, the Court hears only a handful of the cases brought before it. Once the Court has ruled, moreover, Congress can pro-pose—and the states may enact—constitutional amendments to reverse Court rul-ings. The Sixteenth Amendment, for instance, reversed a Supreme Court ruling that said that the federal income tax was unconstitutional. Congress can also rede-fine the authority of the Supreme Court, removing whole areas of litigation from the Court's appellate jurisdiction. In addition, the Court must rely on the chief ex-ecutive to enforce its rulings, and the president can always refuse. In the famous words of Andrew Jackson, "John Marshall has made his decision, now let him en-force it." If Eisenhower had not sent federal troops to Little Rock in 1958, its school would not have been desegregated despite the Court's 1954 ruling. Moreover, lower federal courts have been known to ignore or evade Supreme Court rulings with which they disagree. Finally, no law and no court order can be enforced well, or for long, unless it has substantial popular support. The Supreme Court cannot afford to get too far ahead or too far behind public opinion. The Court's leftward swing in 1937 and the Rehnquist Court's rightward swing illustrate the importance of public opinion.[23]

The federal courts are thus an integral part of the policy-making apparatus of government—not just mechanical interpreters of law. They are involved in the political process in three distinct ways. First, judges are selected on the basis of their political party affiliation and judicial philosophy. Second, judicial decisions in such areas as civil rights and economic matters are influenced by politics. Groups whose welfare depends on the court's decisions will try to influence the court to adopt their point of view; and groups that do not succeed with the president or Congress hope that they will have better luck with the courts. Finally, Supreme Court decisions *technically* bind only those parties in the case decided by the Court. By extension, however, such rulings set precedents for similar cases, but the lower courts must decide how and in what ways previous rulings affect the cases that they are considering.

Suggested Readings

ABRAHAM, HENRY J. *The Judicial Process: An Introductory Analysis of the Courts of the United States, England, and France,* 6th ed. New York: Oxford University Press, 1993. Introduction to the U.S. judicial process from a comparative perspective.

ABRAMSON, JEFFREY. *We the Jury: The Jury System and the Ideal of Democracy.* New York: Basic Books, 1994. Worries the U.S. jury system is changing its function from deliberation to representation.

BAUM, LAWRENCE. *The Supreme Court,* 5th ed. Washington, DC: CQ Press, 1994. Excellent introduction that includes recent trends.

BORK, ROBERT H. *The Tempting of America: The Political Seduction of the Law.* New York: Free Press, 1990. Conservative scholar who almost made it to the high bench argues that it has been seriously misused.

CARP, ROBERT A., and RONALD STIDHAM. *Judicial Process in America,* 3rd ed. Washington, DC: CQ Press, 1995. Excellent overview that emphasizes how courts make public policy.

DWORKIN, RONALD. *Freedom's Law: The Moral Reading of the American Constitution.* Cambridge, MA: Harvard University Press, 1996. Collection of insightful essays by a top legal scholar.

EPSTEIN, LEE, and THOMAS G. WALKER. *Constitutional Law for a Changing America,* 2nd ed. Washington, DC: CQ Press, 1994. Cases and commentary calculated to intrigue a new student.

FLOWERS, RONALD B. *That Godless Court?: Supreme Court Decisions on Church-State Relationships.* Louisville, KY: Westminster/John Knox, 1994. Calm, balanced review of the Court's evolving positions on questions of religion.

GROSSFELD, BERNHARD. *The Strength and Weakness of Comparative Law.* New York: Oxford University Press, 1990. Originally an argument aimed at German lawyers to start comparing, lesson is for all.

HALL, KERMIT L., and JAMES W. ELY, eds. *The Oxford Companion to the Supreme Court of the United States.* New York: Oxford University Press, 1992. An important reference work covering just about everything related to the Supreme Court.

MASON, ALPHEUS T., and DONALD G. STEPHENSON, JR. *American Constitutional Law: Introductory Essays and Selected Cases.* 10th ed. Englewood Cliffs, NJ: Prentice Hall, 1992. Excellent compilation covering all major decisions.

OLSON, WALTER K. *The Litigation Explosion: What Happened When America Unleashed the Lawsuit.* New York: Dutton, 1991. Too many lawsuits are degrading the law.

PELTASON, J. W. *Understanding the Constitution,* 13th ed. San Diego, CA: Harcourt Brace Jovanovich, 1991. Latest update of a classic.

REHNQUIST, WILLIAM H. *The Supreme Court: How It Was, How It Is.* New York: Morrow, 1987. The chief justice gives an interesting insider's look at how the Supreme Court functions.

TUSHNET, MARK. *Red, White and Blue: A Critical Analysis of Constitutional Law.* Cambridge, MA: Harvard University Press, 1988. Argues that our system of law, based on judicial review, is inconsistent and contradictory.

WELLINGTON, HARRY H. *Interpreting the Constitution: The Supreme Court and the Process of Adjudication.* New Haven, CT: Yale University Press, 1991. A common law approach that interpreting is the crux of judicial opinions.

Notes

1. *Black's Law Dictionary,* 6th ed. (St. Paul, MN: West, 1993).

2. See W. W. Buckland and A. D. McNair, *Roman Law and Common Law* (New York: Oxford University Press, 1936); and B. Schwartz, ed., *The Code Napoleon and the Common Law World* (New York: New York University Press, 1956).

3. Good histories are T. F. T. Pluckett, *A Concise History of the Common Law,* 2nd ed. (New York: Lawyers' Cooperative, 1936); and Oliver Wendell Holmes, Jr., *The Common Law* (Boston: Little, Brown, 1881).

4. See Melvin Aron Eisenberg, *The Nature of the Common Law* (Cambridge, MA: Harvard University Press, 1988).

5. For an interesting look at how lawyers act in several common law countries, see Richard L. Abel and Philip Lewis, eds., *Lawyers in Society: The Common Law World* (Berkeley, CA: University of California Press, 1988).

6. Schwartz, *Code Napoleon and the Common Law World.*

7. See Robert A. Carp and Ronald Stidham, *The Judicial Process in America,* 3rd ed. (Washington, DC: CQ Press, 1995).

8. For an overview of the U.S. Supreme Court, see Bernard Schwartz, *Decision: How the Supreme Court Decides Cases* (New York: Oxford University Press, 1996).

9. See G. Alan Tarr and Mary Cornelia Aldis Porter, *State Supreme Courts in State and Nation* (New Haven, CT: Yale University Press, 1988).

10. See René David, *French Law: Its Structure, Sources, and Methodology,* trans. Michael Kindred (Baton Rouge: Louisiana State University Press, 1972).

11. See John N. Hazard and William E. Butler, *The Soviet Legal System: The Law in the 1980's* (Dobbs Ferry, NY: Oceana Publications, 1984).

12. Donald P. Kommers, *The Constitutional Jurisprudence of the Federal Republic of Germany* (Durham, NC: Duke University Press, 1990).

13. See Christopher Wolfe, *The Rise of Modern Judicial Review: From Judicial Interpretation to Judge-Made Law,* rev. ed (Lanham, MD: Rowman Littlefield, 1994); and John Arthur, *Words That Bind: Judicial Review and the Grounds of Modern Constitutional Theory* (Boulder, CO: Westview Press, 1995).

14. The Republican party of 1803 was not the Republican party of today, which dates only from 1860. The former, roughly equivalent to the English Whigs of that time, was more liberal than the Federalist party.

15. Black was an activist on Bill of Rights issues, not across the board.

16. For a discussion of the political roles of the courts—especially the Supreme Court—see Glendon Schubert, *Judicial Policy-Making* (New York: Scott, Foresman, 1974); Donald L. Horowitz, *Courts and Social Policy* (Washington, DC: Brookings Institution, 1977); and Robert H. Birkby, *The Court and Public Policy* (Washington, DC: CQ Press, 1983).

17. For an unscholarly—and perhaps conjectural—look at the political viewpoints of Supreme Court justices, especially the shift from the Warren to the Burger Court, see Bob Woodward and Scott Armstrong, *The Brethren: Inside the Supreme Court* (New York: Simon & Schuster, 1979).

18. Quoted in *The Supreme Court: Justice and the Law,* 3rd ed. (Washington, DC: CQ Press, 1983), p. 163.

19. C. H. Pritchett, *The Roosevelt Court* (New York: Macmillan, 1948); and E. V. Rostow, *The Sovereign Prerogative* (New Haven, CT: Yale University Press, 1962).

20. For good accounts of the Warren Court's decisions, see Archibald Cox, *The Warren Court* (Cambridge, MA: Harvard University Press, 1968); and Bernard Schwartz, *Inside the Warren Court* (Garden City, NY: Doubleday, 1983).

21. For comparisons and contrasts between the Warren and Burger Courts, see Ronald Kahn, *The Supreme Court and Constitutional Theory, 1953–1993* (Lawrence, KS: University Press of Kansas, 1994).

22. See D. F. B. Tucker, *The Rehnquist Court and Civil Rights* (Brookfield, VT: Ashgate, 1995); and Peter Irons, *Brennan vs. Rehnquist: The Battle for the Constitution* (New York: Knopf, 1994).

23. For an argument that political factors play a major role in abrupt shifts on the Supreme Court, see Lee Epstein and Joseph F. Kobylka, *The Supreme Court and Legal Change: Abortion and the Death Penalty* (Chapel Hill, NC: University of North Carolina Press, 1992).

· 18 ·
Public Policy

Everything we have discussed so far serves as a prelude for our consideration of public policy. We have looked at the various inputs into politics and how they are processed by the institutions of government. Now we are at last going to focus on the output of the machine: policy. For a long time, political scientists scarcely bothered to look at what came out of the system; they were interested only in the *process*. The actual content of policies was without great meaning. With the cries of the 1960s for "relevance," however, political scientists began to look more closely at the actual content of policies, and soon a new subfield, "public policy" or "policy analysis," was born. By now, most political science departments consider policy analysis a worthwhile branch of the discipline.

What Is Policy?

Political scientist Thomas R. Dye, noting that whole books have been written in an effort to define the word *policy*, offers his own concise definition: "Public policy is whatever governments choose to do or not to do."[1] This is good, but it raises some questions. Does government always "choose" to do what it does? Many policies come into being as the result of incremental change in bureaucratic practice. In most cases, no one sits down and figures out what should be done; the policy just grows as administrators react to events. Perhaps Dye's definition would be improved if we were to drop the word *choose* and just say that policy is whatever government *does*.

This definition, however, is at variance with common use of the term to indicate *intentions*, not what the policy actually does. In 1995, Congressional Republicans urged cuts in Medicare spending as part of a budget-balancing policy. Their Democrat critics charged this would eventually mean the end of the popular (but very expensive) program of medical insurance for the elderly. The Republicans emphasized that it was their intention to save Medicare from bankruptcy by trimming it. Who was right? Should we ignore stated intentions? Aren't intentions a component of policy as well as actual performance? Perhaps we could define policy as what government is *trying* to do.

Should we consider *results* in defining the word *policy?* If a given economic policy is intended to produce prosperity but instead produces a recession, would we say that the government's policy is recession? Some policy analysts separate results from policy and call them "policy impact." But can a policy be divorced from its impact? Isn't the net result the true definition of what government is doing? Perhaps we could define policy as a relationship between what government is trying to do and what actually happens. Good policymaking would include the recognition that policies need to be continually modified to take account of new problems, some of which may have been created by the previous policies. This process of continual modification and adjustment can be seen in U.S. economic policy over the last three decades.

Economic Policy

Economics undergirds everything else in public policy. Virtually all policy choices have economic ramifications, and these are often sufficient to make or break the policy. A policy designed to protect the environment that cause a slowing down of industry and loss of jobs is probably not going to last very long. An energy policy aimed at squeezing fuel from oil shale or tar sands and delivering a barrel of petroleum at three times the cost of Saudi crude can continue only if the government is willing to subsidize it for, say, national security reasons.

With a growing economy, a country can afford to play around with new welfare measures, as the United States did in the booming 1960s. With a stagnant economy, an administration has to cut back on welfare expenditures and devise policies to spur the economy into greater production. Whatever the issue— environment, energy, welfare, you name it—the policy will be connected to the economy. Some of the worst policy choices are made when decision makers forget this elementary point. Accordingly, economic policy takes priority, and it over- shadows all other policies. Every political scientist should be to some degree an economist.[2]

GOVERNMENT AND THE ECONOMY

Nowadays, no one, not even a good conservative, expects the government to keep its hands off the economy. Everyone expects the government to induce economic prosperity, and if it doesn't, voters will punish the administration at the next elec- tion, as happened in 1992.[3] Earlier in the century this was not the case. Many Eu- ropean governments, as well as Washington, followed the "classic liberal" doctrines discussed in Chapter 6 and pretty much kept their hands off the economy. With the outbreak of the Great Depression in 1929, however, the hands-off policies tended to make things worse, and people began to demand government intervention.

A book by the English economist John Maynard Keynes helped chart the way.[4] Keynes argued that the free market by itself may reach a balance of supply and demand only with unacceptably high unemployment. The solution, he sug- gested, was for government to increase "aggregate demand" by spending on pub- lic works and welfare. Some say the "Keynesian revolution" brought us out of the Depression. Others say Franklin D. Roosevelt's New Deal never fully applied Keynesianism; only the massive defense spending of World War II did that. Still others doubt that the New Deal achieved anything lasting except inflation. After World War II, government leaders all over the world, even those who disliked Keynes's theory, turned to Keynesian methods to correct their economies. As vice- president during the 1950s, Richard Nixon denounced Keynesian economics as a Democratic trick. In the White House in the 1970s, however, Nixon announced that he was "now a Keynesian" and could "fine-tune the economy." (He didn't.)

What are some of our leading economic problems and government responses to them? Consider the approximate sequence of events the United States has gone through since the 1960s, and notice how the problems reoccur.

Inflation.   Until 1965, the U.S. inflation rate was low, but as President John- son escalated the Vietnam war in that year, it kicked up. War spending pumped some $140 billion (now worth more than four times that, after adjusting for infla- tion) into the U.S. economy but not a corresponding amount of goods and services to buy with it. Too many dollars chased too few goods, the classic description of de- mand-pull inflation. The inflation engendered by the Vietnam war took on a life of its own and lasted into the 1980s. Johnson thought he could win in Vietnam quickly and cheaply, before the war had had much economic impact. He failed. Many economists say that he could have avoided the worst of the inflation if he had been willing to raise taxes at the start of the war.

Tax Hike.   President Johnson was reluctant to ask for a tax increase to pay for the Vietnam war for two reasons. First, he had just gotten a tax cut through Congress in 1964; it would have been embarrassing to reverse course the following year. Second, he did not want to admit to the country that he had gotten it into a long and costly war. By the time Johnson and Congress had changed their minds and introduced a 10 percent tax surcharge in 1968, it was too late; inflation had taken firm hold. The moral is that if you must go to war, you should be sure to increase taxes simultaneously; if you don't there will be the devil to pay with inflation.

Balance of Payments.   Starting in the late 1950s, the United States spent more abroad than it sold. With the war-induced prosperity of the 1960s, America sucked in growing imports without exporting enough to cover them. American industries invested heavily overseas, and American tourists spent freely. A gigantic balance-of-payments deficit grew. The too-high value of the dollar in relation to foreign currencies meant it was cheaper to buy foreign goods but harder to sell ours in foreign markets. Japanese products, especially, took a large share of the U.S. market. American dollars flooded the world; they were too plentiful.

Gold Standard.   In an effort to stem this outflow in 1971, President Nixon cut the link between the dollar and gold, letting the dollar "float" to a lower level in relation to other currencies. In effect, he devalued the dollar by about one-fifth. The dollar went back up, however, and U.S. trade and payments deficits soared even higher.

Wage-Price Freeze.   At the same time, Nixon froze wages and prices to try to knock out the inflationary psychology that had taken hold. The 1971 wage-price freeze was popular at first, but then some people began to complain that there was no corresponding freeze on profits, so that businesses were benefiting unduly. A bigger problem with wage-price freezes, however, is that when they are removed, pent-up inflationary pressures push inflation higher than ever. Many economists think Nixon's eighteen-month freeze just set the stage for even greater inflation. Some (mostly liberal) economists supported the idea of wage and price controls—called "incomes policy"—but now, few economists of any stripe want to try them again.

Oil Shocks.   International oil deals, like most international trade arrangements, are made with U.S. dollars. The dollar's loss in value meant that the oil exporters were getting less and less for their black gold. The price of oil in the 1960s was ridiculously low. As a result of the 1973 Mideast war, the members of the Organization of Petroleum Exporting Countries (OPEC) were able to do what they had been itching to do: quadruple oil prices. In 1979, in response to the revolutionary turmoil in Iran, they increased prices again. World oil prices soared from $2.50 to $34 a barrel. The impact on economies around the world was devastating.

Stagflation.   During the 1970s a new word appeared—*stagflation*—to describe a new phenomenon, inflation with stagnant economic growth. Previously, economists had seen a connection between economic growth and inflation; as one went

The oil shortages of the 1970s made this country aware of our dependence on imported oil and the threat of ever-increasing prices.

up, so did the other. In the 1970s, this connection was broken. Inflation hit double-digit levels (10 percent or higher), but the economy shrank and joblessness increased. Since 1973, the average American family has had a stagnant standard of living. The biggest single culprit is believed to be the massive increase in oil prices that affected every corner of the economy, from agriculture and transportation to manufacturing and construction. The United States was especially hard hit, for Americans had gotten used to cheap energy and had based their industry and lifestyle on it. The manyfold increase in petroleum prices produced inflation everywhere while simultaneously depressing the economy.

Interest Rates. President Jimmy Carter attempted to stimulate the economy, but this made inflation worse than ever; in 1980 it was 13.5 percent and probably cost him reelection. The members of the independent Federal Reserve Board, who are appointed by the president for four years but cannot be fired, took it upon themselves to stem inflation by means of "monetary policy," control of the growth of the U.S. money supply. The board (also known as "the Fed") can force banks to raise or lower their interest rates on loans. High interest rates mean slower economic growth and a dampening of inflation. Economist Paul A. Volcker, appointed by Carter in 1979 and reappointed by Reagan in 1983, brought interest rates to record levels; at one point they were over 20 percent. It was painful medicine. Inflation did cool, but at the cost of the greatest rate of unemployment (over 10 percent) since the Depression. Americans became aware of how important the Fed is in our economic life and began to wonder if Reaganomics wasn't less important than Volckernomics.

Tax Cut. Again trying to stimulate the economy, President Reagan turned to an approach called "supply-side economics," which focuses on investment and production rather than on consumer demand, as Keynesian policy does. The inspiration of supply-siders was the Kennedy idea that lowering tax rates stimulates economic growth and ultimately generates more tax revenue. Too-high taxes discourage effort and investment. Congress bought the idea and cut income taxes 25 percent over three years. Actually, this scarcely offset the "bracket creep" that American taxpayers had suffered as a result of inflation; their purchasing power had stayed the same, but they found themselves in ever-higher tax brackets. The Reagan tax cut did stimulate the economy, but it also helped produce another problem.[5]

Budget Deficits. President Reagan presented Congress with budgets that featured both tax cuts and major increases in defense spending. He figured this would force Congress to cut domestic and welfare spending drastically. But Congress didn't cut that much, and the U.S. federal budget reached record deficits—at one point approaching $300 billion. By issuing Treasury bills, the federal government borrowed the money, and this "crowded out" commercial borrowing and raised interest rates.[6] Because interest rates were high, foreigners found the United States a good place to invest, so in effect much of the U.S. budget deficit was covered by foreign investment. The Reagan and Bush deficits acted like a gigantic vacuum cleaner that swept in both goods and capital from around the world.

Trade Deficits. America for several years consumed about 4 percent more than it produced and imported about twice as much as it exported. The result is a gigantic foreign trade deficit that makes the United States the world's greatest debtor nation. This in turn leads to the buying up of American assets by foreigners. Americans tend to blame foreigners for this, but the fault and the cure are at home. Budget deficits lead to trade deficits. The cure is simple but painful: cut the federal budget deficit, either by cutting spending or raising taxes. If left unfixed, the deficits mean a slow foreign takeover of the U.S. economy. It's not so much that foreigners are buying America as that we are selling it.

Budget Balancing. Clinton brought the federal deficit down to $171 billion by 1995, but Congressional Republicans demanded it be brought down faster, reaching a balance between income and expenditures by 2002. Every year's deficit is added to the national debt—the sum total owed by the federal government, which by then was $4.7 trillion—which is covered by additional government borrowing, provided Congress agrees to raise the debt ceiling. In a 1995 showdown with the White House, the Republicans under House Speaker Newt Gingrich (R-GA) refused to raise the debt limit, thus temporarily making the federal government broke and unable to pay its workers, who were sent home. The public was disgusted with both sides, and they compromised. The cuts involved in balancing the budget, however, were fairly drastic. Their chief target: entitlements.

Who's Entitled to What?

The federal budget is divided into two general categories, discretionary and mandatory. The former can be raised or lowered from year to year. Congress, for example, may decide to increase defense and cut highway spending. Mandatory spending cannot be so easily changed; it's what the federal budget is stuck with from previous statutory commitments. Mandatory spending in turn is divided into interest payments on the national debt (14 percent of the budget in 1993) and "entitlements" (47 percent in 1993); together they made up more than 60 percent of the federal budget. Interest payments are totally untouchable; if they were cut, future offerings of bonds and treasury notes would lack credibility and customers. And entitlements are extremely difficult to cut because people are used to them and expect them as a right. They are payments to which one is automatically entitled by law: turn sixty-five and you get Social Security and Medicare; earn an income below specified level and you get Food Stamps, Aid to Families with Dependent Children, and Medicaid. There is no annual cap on entitlement spending; it grows as more people are entitled. And grow it did; with the Great Society programs started under Johnson and greatly expanded under Nixon, entitlement spending doubled from 23 to 45 percent of the budget from 1963 to 1983. In 1990, about half of American families received some form of entitlement, averaging $10,000 per recipient family. For such reasons it is called "uncontrollable" spending.

Only a small fraction of entitlements is traditional "welfare" spending; most entitlements go to the middle class. Here are the programs and their costs that in 1993 went mostly to families earning more than $20,000 a year:

Social Security	$302 billion
Medicare	143 billion
Federal civilian retirement	39 billion
Unemployment	35 billion
Military retirement	26 billion
Veterans	17 billion
Farm price supports	16 billion

And here are the programs that went mostly to families earning less than $20,000 and hence might be termed welfare for the poor:

Medicaid	$76 billion
Food Stamps	25 billion
Supplemental Security Income	21 billion
Welfare and family support	16 billion

In sum, programs aimed chiefly at the nonpoor cost more than four times as much as programs aimed at the poor. With political realism in mind, of the first category, largely for the middle class, what can be cut? Some people argue that if we eliminated "welfare" spending we could balance the budget. Such cuts still might not be enough, and they would inflict terrible hardship on society's most vulnerable members. How did this welfare policy come about?

In the mid-1960s, President Lyndon B. Johnson launched his War on Poverty, aimed at creating a Great Society by eliminating poverty. Johnson, who had long been Senate majority leader, got Congress to deliver almost everything he wanted. Then the Vietnam war, amid rising costs and acrimony, seemed to cut down the War on Poverty in its infancy. There wasn't enough money for the growing programs, and Johnson became increasingly discredited. Many of the Great Society programs were substantially dismantled or left to die quietly on the vine. Some say the Great Society was never given a chance. The conservative conventional wisdom of the late 1970s and early 1980s held that the undertaking was inherently impossible, a waste of money that often did more harm than good.[7] Some specialists in that area, however, say the Great Society programs generally did succeed and markedly lowered the incidence of poverty in the United States. Conservatives have exaggerated the inefficiency and misuses that accompany any welfare program and have understated the very real accomplishments.[8]

WHAT IS POVERTY?

But what is "poverty" in the United States? What's "poor" here might be defined as comfortable elsewhere. Trying to define poverty could be as tricky as trying to define policy. The U.S. Department of Labor came up with a formula in 1955 that has been used ever since, although it is obviously not a complete definition. They found that families spend about one-third of their incomes on food. The department therefore set the "poverty line" at three times an economy food budget, usually for nonfarm families of four. Using this definition, the percentage of Americans below the poverty line fell from 17.3 percent in 1965, when Johnson's War on Poverty started, to 11.7 percent in 1973, according to the Census Bureau. With the economic recession and budget tightening that started under Carter and expanded under Reagan, however, by 1983 the poverty rate was back up to 15.2 percent, the highest in eighteen years. (In 1992, it was still 14.5 percent.) The black and hispanic rates were much higher throughout the whole period. Over one-fifth of America's children are below the poverty line.[9]

Conservatives and defenders of the Reagan-Bush program hastened to point out that the figures did not tell the whole story, for the Labor Department's definition of poverty does not include *noncash* benefits transferred to the poor by government programs—food stamps, for example. Taking this factor into account raises some poor families above the poverty line, according to one economist.[10] The poor, in other words, now have a certain cushion.

Further, before we conclude that the War on Poverty was either a success or

Poverty in the United States. A homeless man—one of a growing
number of poor—camps out under a bridge in New York City.

a failure, we must look at the poverty rate in longer perspective. In 1950, some 30
percent of the U.S. population was classified as below the poverty line. Since then,
the rate has dropped almost steadily, with one of the fastest decreases occurring between 1960 and 1965, *before* the War on Poverty programs were enacted. What explains this? The U.S. economy expanded from 1950 to 1965, especially during the
early 1960s. Jobs were plentiful. It's hard to tell if the further drop in the poverty
rate from 1965 to 1973 was the result of government programs or of an economy
fueled by Vietnam war spending.

By the same token, when the poverty rate began to go up again in the mid-
1970s, cutbacks in antipoverty spending were only partly to blame; also responsible
were the recessions caused by oil prices and high interest rates. Some thinkers
blame the increase of poverty and homelessness on the transfer of much manufacturing to low-wage countries overseas, making many working-class Americans
unemployed and pushing them down into the lower class.[11] With the disappearance of modestly paying factory jobs they faced either low-paid service jobs ("flip-
ping hamburgers") or unemployment and welfare. Antipoverty programs cannot
offset massive unemployment caused by long-term trends in the U.S. economy.[12]
To repeat: most public policy questions are based on the economy.

THE COSTS OF WELFARE

Food Stamps.   Begun as a modest trial program under Kennedy in 1961, the
Food Stamp program was made nationwide under Johnson in 1964. From a few

million dollars a year, it rose by 1995 to $27.5 billion a year. Over 10 percent of all U.S. households benefited, getting an average of less than $1,000 a year. One did not dine royally on food stamps; cost per meal per person was figured at about half a dollar. One-third of families headed by women received food stamps.

The Carter administration simplified the program in 1977 by eliminating the provision that recipients *buy* the stamps at a discount with their own money.[13] This policy had meant that the absolutely destitute, people with no money at all, could get no food stamps. Congress changed the law to eliminate the cash payment, and the number of recipients expanded. Reagan, citing an apocryphal story of a young man who used food stamps to buy vodka, tightened eligibility requirements in an effort to eliminate fraud and misuse. The trouble was that some genuinely poor families were also bumped from the program, and hunger in America reappeared. Callous remarks by a White House official that he saw no proof of hunger flew in the face of widespread reports of a big increase in the number of homeless people eating at soup kitchens.

What should be done? The Food Stamp program has become bigger than expected, but outright fraud and waste have not been major factors. Recipients selling food stamps at 50¢ on the dollar to buy liquor and drugs probably account for only a few percent of the program. There are poor people in America. Should they be helped? Outright cash grants, considered for a time by Carter as a replacement for food stamps, could easily be used for nonessentials, such as liquor. Direct delivery of surplus commodities, as was done on a small scale in the 1950s and episodically in the 1980s to get rid of government cheese stocks (the result of price supports for dairy farmers), was clumsy and spotty. One alternative to food stamps might be to borrow a tactic applied in many countries: subsidizing basic foodstuffs, such as bread and milk. However, subsidizing food basics, because it would benefit the nonpoor as well, would not necessarily cost less than food stamps. The Food Stamp program will probably continue with little change, for there is no clear, acceptable alternative.[14]

Aid to Families with Dependent Children (AFDC). The original "welfare" program set up by the 1935 Social Security Act, Aid to Dependent Children (ADC, as it was then known) provided federal matching funds for state programs. For years, most states had either no ADC programs or only small programs. Starting in the 1960s, though, participation and costs grew to around $25 billion (partly state, partly federal) by 1993, going to 5 million families, most of them headed by single mothers. The average monthly family benefit was $373. The program was renamed AFDC in 1967, when Congress mandated work training for all adult recipients and gave dollar incentives. Day-care centers were to be provided. In practice, most of this aid went to single mothers for whom child care was unavailable. State efforts to make sure no man was around the house—if one was, the aid would be stopped—led to early-morning snooping. Conservatives pointed to AFDC as underwriting immorality and "welfare dependency"; it was the favorite target of those who liked to speak of the "welfare mess." Because many of the 14.5 million recipients were nonwhite, the issue became connected with the struggle for racial equality. Attacks against "welfare mothers" were sometimes veiled racism.

What can be done? Undoubtedly, some welfare dependency—that is, getting stuck on welfare with no incentive to get off—was created. AFDC may also have encouraged a casual attitude toward bringing fatherless children into the world. But can we make it illegal for poor people to have babies? Should there be mandatory sterilization or abortion? Once a child is born, can we let it starve? Recognizing these problems, in 1973 Congress started WIC (Women, Infants and Children) to improve the diet and give medical checkups to poor pregnant and nursing mothers and their children. The results have been good, but WIC receives less than $5 billion a year and reaches only half of those eligible. In 1995, Congressional Republicans tried to turn AFDC over to the states with support from federal block grants. President Clinton, claiming the shift would unduly harm the truly needy, vetoed the measure.

At least two factors induced exponential growth in medical assistance: greater numbers of people becoming eligible and soaring medical costs. Medicare is especially expensive, for everyone is automatically eligible on reaching age sixty-five, even rich people. The proportion of older people in American society is increasing steadily, and the elderly are by far the biggest consumers of medical care.[15]

Hospitals and doctors, once they are assured of payment, have no incentive to economize. When in doubt, they put the patient in the hospital—often at $1,000 a day—and order batteries of expensive tests with the latest multi-million-dollar machines.[16] Some hospitals expanded into medical palaces, and some physicians got rich from Medicare and Medicaid. (Ironically, the powerful American Medical Association had for years lobbied against such "socialized medicine.") By 1995, medical costs consumed an amazing 15 percent of the U.S. gross domestic product, in part as a result of Medicare and Medicaid, which paid a good part of the nation's medical bills. Other countries paid less and had healthier populations.

Washington tried various ways of tightening up. Recipients were required to contribute more of the total payment to hold down overuse. Hospitals and doctors were monitored on costs and on how long they kept patients hospitalized. Hospices—nursing homes for the terminally ill—were made allowable under Medicare, as such care is cheaper than hospital care. Competitive bidding was begun in some states, and patients were assigned only to low-bid hospitals. Fees for each type of disorder were established, and overruns were not reimbursed. Recipients were encouraged to enter managed-care organizations. Every time the government tightens medical assistance, however, patients, doctors, and hospitals complain bitterly, and they form a powerful lobby. Some hospitals turn away poor patients.

HOOKED ON ENTITLEMENTS

As with the weather, everybody complains about the "welfare mess" but no one has succeeded in cleaning it up. Critics speak of "welfare dependency" in referring to successive generations of one family that are either unable or unwilling to get jobs. But in a larger sense, the United States as a whole has become entitlements-dependent, for it is impossible to repeal or seriously cut most programs. Congressional Republicans suffered a drop in popularity when they proposed cutting Medicare; older Americans had come to regard it as something sacred.

What can be done? Several proposals have been advanced. New Jersey initiated a law that capped benefits to single welfare mothers even if they had another child. This was based on the theory that some young women deliberately have babies in order to collect benefits; the New Jersey experiment could not prove this was the case. The 1996 welfare reform bill turned much of it over to the states and imposed time limits and a requirement to work. "Workfare" had been talked about for decades and was implemented in the early 1990s by Wisconsin Governor Tommy Thompson. It showed some success but wasn't cheap; job training, child care, and state subsidies to create jobs added up to a bigger bill, at least initially, than standard welfare. In the longer run, it was hoped, the plan would get people off welfare and keep them off. Denying benefits to immigrants, both legal and illegal, was proposed in California, but identifying such people might be difficult. Social Security numbers, widely misused, would require elaborate crosschecking. Both civil libertarians and right-wing militias would oppose universal ID cards. There are no easy solutions.

Medicare and Medicaid.   These are the two giants of entitlements; if the budget is to be balanced, they too will have to absorb some of the cuts. Medicare and Medicaid, both enacted in 1965, serve different purposes. Medicare is a federally funded program for elderly people; Medicaid combines federal and state funds for poor people. Both grew so rapidly even supporters had to admit that benefits had to be limited and eligibility requirements tightened. In the 1990s, the two programs cost over $200 billion a year and were growing at an unsustainable rate of 10 percent a year.

President Clinton arrived in Washington promising to revamp the nation's medical insurance programs. But a massive study chaired by his wife worked at cross-purposes: a new plan was to include all Americans—some 37 million, mostly people working for themselves or in small firms, had no insurance—but it was also to hold down soaring costs. Congress rejected the complex and expensive proposals out of hand. In 1995, Congressional Republicans proposed cuts in Medicare, ostensibly to "save" it, and suffered a drop in popularity; it seemed to be withdrawing a right older Americans had come to depend on. Whatever is proposed in medical care will face hefty and usually overwhelming resistance.

Oregon at this same time experimented with its Medicaid system by trying to do the most good for the least money. Medical-care providers drew up a list of what Oregon would pay for care for its poor and uninsured, starting with the most effective and least costly procedures, such as appendectomies. Proceeding down the list, procedures were ranked as less effective and costlier. When it was estimated that Oregon's Medicaid funds would run out, they drew a line and paid for no procedures below it. Alcoholics, for example, would not get liver transplants. Although controversial, the Oregon plan underscored an unhappy axiom in medical insurance: you can't cover everyone for everything; the money is simply not there. The plan also illustrated the utility of states, those "laboratories of democracy," trying new and creative approaches from which other states could learn. This then brings us to the next question.

Whose Programs, Federal or State?   The Republican takeover of Congress in 1995 raised anew the old question, discussed in Chapter 13, of which level of government should administer and finance programs, the federal government in Washington or the various state governments. The "New Federalism" of Nixon and Reagan devolved administrative discretion in certain areas to the states in the form of "block grants," federal funds to help states run programs according to local needs rather than the dictates of Washington. The Congressional Republicans in the mid-1990s took up the approach with renewed zeal. On the face of it, devolution sounds like a great idea. Why should Washington try to micromanage a one-size-fits-all program when there are major variations among the states? In addition, many states have interesting new ideas, such as the Oregon Medicaid plan above.

With thirty of the fifty U.S. governors Republicans, the mid-1990s seemed like the right time for major new block grants. Democrats have generally disliked block grants, fearing they are the beginning of the end for many worthwhile programs. Many see devolution as nothing but "burden shifting," passing the bill from the federal to the state level. Most states require balanced budgets and no one, least of all Republican governors, wants to raise taxes. On the contrary, they like to cut taxes. This leaves the states with very tight budgets. What would happen during a recession, when the demand for welfare benefits swells? The states would find themselves required to cover more people, but with reduce tax revenues. The simplest solution would be to cut benefits, even eliminate whole programs. And would the federal government step back in with supplementary block grants? That might push the federal budget back into deficit. There are no simple fixes for the entitlements problem.

Welfare and Ideology

The debate about welfare or entitlements is passionately ideological: conservatives almost uniformly hate it, and liberals generally defend it (although some admit it must be reformed).[17] The policy analyst must cast ideology aside and gather factual answers to questions such as these:

Is the program we're talking about welfare or entitlement? The two categories overlap, but the essence of a welfare program is that it's "means tested," meaning recipients must demonstrate that they're poor according to certain criteria (typically, how much income and how many children). If the program is a pure entitlement, such as Social Security or Medicare, can it realistically be cut without incurring the electoral wrath of its recipients?

Does a given welfare program have negative consequences? Here is the great conservative attack: welfare programs offer incentives for unemployment, illegitimacy, and drug use. Welfare, in other words, makes things worse. Can this be proved or disproved? New York City, with its extensive welfare programs, has a high incidence of poverty. But so does Mississippi, with its weak and underfunded welfare programs. Would a massive, nationwide ending of all welfare programs—the dream of some conservatives—force the indolent to work? This raises the next question.

Is poverty an unfortunate circumstance or a character defect? Are people poor because they can't find work or because they don't want to work? In other words, are the poor really different from you and me? Do they embody a "culture of poverty" that instills a "radical improvidence," an indifference to providing for their families and futures? If poverty is a character defect, as most conservatives maintain, then there is little that can be done. If it is the product of unfortunate circumstances, as most liberals maintain, then programs that change those circumstances might get people out of poverty.

How much poverty is simply a lack of good jobs? Do the jobs available to poor people pay enough for them to raise their families? In most of America, people line up around the block for jobs paying $7 an hour, even though a single mother earning that would fall below the poverty line. Factory jobs are hard to find because many have been moved overseas, to low-wage countries. Those who would drastically cut welfare should demonstrate there are sufficient jobs with adequate pay. But are poor people generally qualified for decent-paying jobs, or do they lack the skills?

Can we train people out of poverty? Job training and retraining have long been part of poverty-fighting programs.[18] But do they work? Some who have completed job training boast improved skills, but there are still few jobs for them. Can we take people with poor reading and math abilities and in a few months make them into skilled technicians? The deeper, underlying problem is the lack of proper education in grade schools, which creates an illiterate and innumerate workforce. But is the lack of proper education in America the fault of schools and teachers or families and attitudes? Liberals like to blame schools, conservatives families. Either way, how do you fix the U.S. education system?

What is the international context of domestic poverty? Referred to above, how much poverty is due to the export of American jobs to low-wage countries? Considering what Santa brought you last Christmas, how many of these gifts were made in Mexico, Indonesia, or Taiwan? While possibly lowering the cost of such items to consumers, overseas manufacturing has closed thousands of American factories. Is then American poverty in some degree the natural result of an open world economy in which many countries have much lower labor costs? Should we close our borders to such commerce in order to boost domestic employment? If we did, many Americans would live a little less well—their shirts, rechargeable flashlights, and VCRs would cost more, so they would buy fewer of them—but other Americans would exit poverty through new factory jobs. Our trading partners across the Pacific and in Mexico would get very angry and retaliate by keeping out U.S. products, so other U.S. factories would close. On balance, then, would trade protectionism be worth it?

These are some of the questions we must ask. Simple ideological approaches, either liberal or conservative, often deal with consequences rather than causes. Where ideology reigns, reason has difficulty making its voice heard.

Cut the Federal government, say most citizens, but not a program that helps me, such as aid to flood victims coordinated by the Federal Emergency Management Agency (FEMA), here set up for one-stop disaster relief.

Conclusion: How Big Should Government Be?

We have only touched briefly on a few of the more prominent areas of public policy. We could add energy, the environment, education, defense, criminal justice, and much more. But we would keep coming back to one question: Should government intervention in these areas expand? Just how big do we want government to get?[19]

The American answer is to keep government small and to suspect and criticize expansion of government power. But we also recognize that we need government intervention in the economy, energy planning, environmental protection, and so on. We have trouble making up our minds how much government we want. Americans want various forms of government intervention, but scarcely is the ink on new laws dry before we begin to criticize government bungling. Fearing cuts in her Medicare, one elderly American lady told an interviewer, "Don't let the government get its hands on Medicare!" The Europeans generally do not suffer from this kind of split personality; they mostly accept that government has a major role to play and try to live with this fact.[20]

This reluctance to expand government's role may redound to America's long-term advantage. Government programs tend to expand, bureaucracy is inherently inefficient, and ending an established program is all but impossible. Government programs become so sprawling and complex that officials don't even *know* what is in operation, much less how to control it. As political scientist Ira Sharkansky put it, "All modern states are welfare states, and all welfare states are incoherent."[21] Accordingly, it is probably wise to act with caution in expanding government programs.

Suggested Readings

BARTLETT, DONALD L., and JAMES B. STEELE. *America: What Went Wrong?* Kansas City, MO: Andrews & McMeel, 1992. Two top journalists find that government has been aiding the rich and powerful at the expense of everyone else.

BLANKENHORN, DAVID. *Fatherless America.* New York: Basic Books, 1995. The absence of fathers is the cause of much of America's poverty and crime.

GALBRAITH, JOHN KENNETH. *A Journey Through Economic Time: A Firsthand View.* Boston: Houghton Mifflin, 1994. Top economist leads laypeople on a rich but clear discussion of what went wrong.

GANS, HERBERT J. *The War Against the Poor: The Underclass and Anti-Poverty Policy.* New York: Basic Books, 1995. A top sociologist makes a liberal counterattack on such views as Charles Murray's, below.

KAUS, MICKEY. *The End of Equality.* New York: Basic Books, 1992. A liberal proposes replacing welfare with massive public works jobs.

KRUGMAN, PAUL. *Peddling Prosperity.* New York:

Norton, 1994. A rising star economist scathingly critiques popular and simplified economic nostrums.

MARMOR, THEODORE R., JERRY L. MASHAW, and PHILIP HARVEY. *America's Misunderstood Welfare State: Persistent Myths, Enduring Realities.* New York: Basic Books, 1992. Cuts through a lot of gloomy misinformation to put welfare into perspective.

MEAD, LAWRENCE M. *The New Politics of Poverty: The Non-Working Poor in America.* New York: Basic Books, 1992. U.S. poverty is different than in the past and needs "workfare" to get people out of poverty.

MURRAY, CHARLES. *Losing Ground.* 10th anniversary ed. New York: Basic Books, 1995. Reissue of the classic conservative view that welfare programs make things worse.

SOWELL, THOMAS. *The Vision of the Anointed: Self-Congratulation as a Basis for Social Policy.* New York: Basic Books, 1995. Conservative black economist and columnist incisively criticizes the liberal elite who presume to speak for the poor.

Notes

1. Thomas R. Dye, *Understanding Public Policy,* 7th ed. (Englewood Cliffs, NJ: Prentice Hall, 1992), p. 2.

2. For a critical overview of recent U.S. economic history, see Hobart Rowen, *Self-Inflicted Wounds: From LBJ's Guns and Butter to Reagan's Voodoo Economics* (New York: Times Books/Random House, 1994).

3. See Douglas A. Hibbs, Jr., *The American Political Economy: Macroeconomics and Electoral Politics in the United States* (Cambridge, MA: Harvard University Press, 1987).

4. John Maynard Keynes, *The General Theory*

of Employment, Interest, and Money* (New York: Harcourt, Brace, 1936).

5. For a pro-Reagan argument that Reaganomics worked, see Robert L. Bartley, *The Seven Fat Years: And How To Do It Again* (New York: Free Press, 1992).

6. David P. Calleo, *The Bankrupting of America: How the Federal Budget Is Impoverishing the Nation* (New York: Morrow, 1992).

7. The leading attack on the Great Society programs is Charles Murray, *Losing Ground: American Social Policy, 1950–1980* (New York: Basic Books, 1984).

8. See Sar A. Levitan, *Programs in Aid of the Poor,* 6th ed. (Baltimore: Johns Hopkins University Press, 1990).

9. For an overview of child poverty, see Frank J. Macchiarola and Alan Gartner, eds., *Caring for America's Children* (New York: Academy of Political Science, 1989).

10. Martin C. Anderson, *Welfare: The Political Economy of Welfare Reform in the United States* (Stanford, CA: Hoover Institution Press, 1978).

11. For an excellent discussion of the drying up of jobs for black workers, see William Julius Wilson, *The Truly Disadvantaged: The Inner City, the Underclass, and Public Policy* (Chicago: University of Chicago Press, 1987).

12. For data on how the poverty rate follows the ups and downs of unemployment, see David T. Ellwood, *Poor Support: Poverty in the American Family* (New York: Basic Books, 1988).

13. For a critical view of the efforts and mistakes of the Carter administration's efforts at welfare reform see Laurence E. Lynn, Jr., and David deF. Whitman, *The President as Policymaker: Jimmy Carter and Welfare Reform* (Philadelphia: Temple University Press, 1981).

14. For a brief overview of food stamps, see Barbara A. Claffey and Thomas A. Stucker, "The Food Stamp Program," in *Food Policy and Farm Programs,* eds. Don F. Hadwiger and Ross B. Talbot (New York: Academy of Political Science, 1982).

15. For the problems of paying for America's medical care, see Joseph A. Califano, Jr., *Radical Surgery: What's Next for America's Health Care* (New York: Times Books/Random House, 1994).

16. See Rosemary Stevens, *In Sickness and in Wealth: American Hospitals in the Twentieth Century* (New York: Basic Books, 1989).

17. Many welfare programs don't work, a liberal scholar admits, but he finds that marriage is one of the best measures against poverty. Reason: it keeps two incomes under one roof. See Christopher Jencks, *The Homeless* (Cambridge, MA: Harvard University Press, 1994).

18. Clinton's liberal labor secretary urges job retraining for higher skills. See Robert Reich, *The Work of Nations: Preparing Ourselves for 21st Century Capitalism* (New York: Knopf, 1991).

19. For a critical history of the expansion of U.S. government, see Robert Higgs, *Crisis and Leviathan: Critical Episodes in the Growth of American Government* (New York: Oxford University Press, 1987).

20. For a comparative perspective, see Francis G. Castles, *Families of Nations: Patterns of Public Policy in Western Democracies* (Brookfield, VT: Ashgate, 1993).

21. Ira Sharkansky, *Wither the State? Politics and Public Enterprise in Three Countries* (Chatham, NC: Chatham House, 1979), p. 7.

· 19 ·
Violence and Revolution

Many political science texts talk about systems and stability; some even depict political systems as well-oiled machines that never break down. Pick up a newspaper, on the other hand, and you will find it filled with stories of violence and revolution. Some years ago, political scientists began criticizing the seemingly status-quo orientation of much of their discipline and began to direct their attention to breakdown and upheaval.[1] The systems approach, it was argued, is incomplete if it cannot account for the violent and often bloody changes that are wracking the world.

Sometimes scholars overlooked the tension and violence in their own backyards. With the black riots of 1965–1968, academics suddenly rediscovered violence in America.[2] From viewing violence as abnormal, many came to suggest, along with black militant H. Rap Brown, that "violence is as American as cherry pie." By the same token, Europeans were shocked to learn, as the nationalities of ex-Yugoslavia slaughtered each other by the thousands in the early 1990s, that they too were not immune from violence.

System Breakdown

Political systems can and do break down.[3] Indeed most countries in the world today have suffered or are suffering system breakdown, marked by major riots, civil wars, revolutionary movements, military coups, and authoritarian governments of varying degrees of harshness. Dictatorships are rarely the work of small bands of conspirators alone; they are the result of system collapse, which permits small but well-organized groups—usually the military—to take over. This is why it does little good to denounce a cruel military regime. It is true enough that some regimes commit acts of great evil; military regimes in Argentina, Chile, and Guatemala killed thousands on the slightest suspicion of leftism. But how is it that these military regimes came to power? Why does system breakdown recur repeatedly in such countries? These are the deeper questions that must be asked if we are to begin to understand these horror stories.

Underlying breakdown is the erosion of legitimacy. Legitimacy is the feeling among citizens that the regime's rule is rightful, that it should be generally obeyed. Where legitimacy is high, governments need few police officers; where it is low, they need many. In England, for example, people are mostly law-abiding; police are few in number and most carry no firearms. In Northern Ireland, on the other hand, terrorists until recently killed with bombs and bullets, for a large minority of the population saw the government as illegitimate. Here the police are armed and British troops patrolled with automatic weapons and armored cars. The civil war in Northern Ireland has cost over 3,200 lives.

One prominent reason for an erosion of legitimacy is the regime's loss of effectiveness in running the country. Uncontrollable inflation, blatant corruption, massive unemployment, or defeat in a war demonstrate that the government is ineffective.

VIOLENCE AS SYMPTOM

Violence—riots, mass strikes, terrorist bombings, and political assassinations—by itself does not indicate that revolution is nigh. Indeed, the most common response to serious domestic unrest is not revolution at all but military takeover. Violence can instead be seen as symptomatic of the erosion of the government's effectiveness and legitimacy. Perhaps nothing major will come of the unrest; perhaps new leadership will calm and encourage the nation and begin to deal with the problems that caused the unrest, as Franklin D. Roosevelt did in the 1930s. But if the government is clumsy, if it tries to simply crush and silence discontent, it can make

things worse. In 1932, the "Bonus Army" of World War I veterans seeking early payment of veterans' benefits to tide them through the mass unemployment of the
Depression was dispersed by army troops under General MacArthur. Public revul-
sion at the veterans' rough treatment helped turn the country decisively against
President Herbert Hoover in that fall's election.

Domestic violence is both deplorable and informative. It tells that not all is
going well, that there are certain groups that, out of desperation or conviction, are
willing to break the law in order to bring change. A government's first impulse
when faced with domestic unrest is to crush it and blame a handful of "radicals and
troublemakers." To be sure, there may well be instigators deliberately trying to pro-
voke incidents, but the fact that people are willing to get involved should telegraph
a message to the authorities that something is wrong. At the Democratic national
convention in 1968, Chicago police went wild in attacking those who had come to
protest the Vietnam war—as well as many who just happened to be in the wrong
place at the wrong time. The convention ignored the protesters and nominated
President Johnson's vice-president, Hubert Humphrey, who lost, largely because of
his equivocal position on the war. The riot showed that the Democratic party had
drifted out of touch with important elements of its constituency, which only four
years earlier had voted for Johnson because he said he'd keep the country out of
war. The Democrats should have been listening to instead of ignoring the protesters.

As much as we may deplore violence, we have to admit that in some cases it
serves its purpose. The United States as a whole and Congress in particular paid little attention to the plight of inner-city blacks until a series of riots ripped U.S. cities
in the late 1960s. The death and destruction were terrible, but there seemed to be
no other way to get the media's, the public's, and the government's attention. The
rioting in this case "worked"; that is, it brought a major—if not very successful—effort to improve America's decaying cities. When America "forgot" about its inner
cities during the Reagan-Bush era, new rioting served as a powerful reminder.

The white minority government of South Africa used to announce with pride
the capture or killing of black guerrillas. The South African security forces were
proficient, but the fact that thousands of young black South Africans were willing
to take up arms against the whites-only regime told the Pretoria government something. The ruling National party had told its supporters for decades that blacks (75
percent of the country's population) would simply keep their place (on 13 percent
of the land). Until recently, the South African government engaged in no dialogue
with blacks; it expected them merely to obey.[4] However, the growing violence in
South Africa persuaded the government to begin a dialogue leading to the political enfranchisement of the black majority and a government elected by all citizens.

TYPES OF VIOLENCE

Not all violence is the same. Various thinkers have categorized violence in several
ways. One of the best is that of political scientist Fred R. von der Mehden, who sees
five general types of violence.[5]

Primordial.   Primordial violence grows out of conflicts among the basic communities—ethnic, national, or religious—into which people are born. Fighting between Armenians and Azerbaijanis in the ex–Soviet Union, Serbs and Muslims in ex-Yugoslavia, the multigroup war in Lebanon, and clan conflicts in Somalia are examples of primordial violence. It is not necessarily confined to the developing areas of the world, though, for such antagonisms appear in Quebec, the Basque country of Spain, and Northern Ireland, where there is something akin to a tribal feud between Protestants and Catholics.

Separatist.   Separatist violence, which is sometimes an outgrowth of primordial conflict, aims at independence for the group in question. The Ibos tried to break away from Nigeria with their new state of Biafra in the late 1960s, but they were defeated in a long and costly war. The Bengalis, on the other hand, did succeed in breaking away from Pakistan with their new state of Bangladesh in 1971. Croatia and Slovenia fought successfully to separate from Yugoslavia in 1991. Elsewhere in Europe, the Basques, Bretons, and Corsicans have given rise to separatist movements.

Revolutionary.   Revolutionary violence is aimed at overthrowing or replacing an existing regime. The Sandinistas' ouster of Somoza in Nicaragua in 1979, the fall of the shah of Iran that same year, and the independence of the former Portuguese colonies of Angola and Mozambique in 1975 are examples of successful revolutionary violence. Until recently, Central America and southern Africa were scenes of continuing revolutionary violence. Von der Mehden includes under this category "counterrevolutionary" violence, the efforts of more conservative groups to counteract revolutionary attempts—for instance, the efforts of Salvadoran rightists. The attempts to crush liberalizing movements in Hungary in 1956, Czechoslovakia in 1968, and Poland in 1970 and 1980 would also come under this heading, with the ironic twist that here the Communists became the counterrevolutionary, conservative force. The distinctive form of terror of our day, the car bomb, would probably come under the rubric of revolutionary violence.

Coups.   Coups are usually counterrevolutionary in intent, aimed at heading off a feared revolutionary takeover. Coups are almost always military, although the military usually has connections with and support from key civilian groups, as in the Brazilian coup of 1964. Most coups don't involve much violence, at least initially. Army tanks surround the presidential palace, forcing the president's resignation and usually exile, and a general takes over as president. Some coups are virtually bloodless. When the military still senses leftist opposition, though, it sometimes goes insane with legalized murder. The Chilean military killed approximately 10,000 people following the 1973 coup.[6] Some 15,000 Argentines "disappeared" following the military takeover of 1976. The military rulers of little Guatemala murdered some 100,000 of their fellow citizens in the 1970s and 1980s on suspicion of opposing the regime. In Latin America, the counterrevolutionary terror that follows some coups is far bloodier than anything the revolutionaries have done. Once a country has had one coup, chances are it will have another.

Some countries get stuck in "praetorianism"—named after the Praetorian Guard in ancient Rome—and take decades to return to civilian rule.[7] In part, coups occur because the conventional institutions of government—parties, parliaments, and executives—are terribly weak, leaving the military with the choice of either taking over or facing growing chaos.

Issues.   Some violence doesn't fit into any of these categories. Violence oriented to particular issues is a catchall category and generally less deadly than the other kinds. The protests against the Vietnam war, the student strikes at American and French universities in the late 1960s, the sometimes violent protests at nuclear power plants or missile sites, and the anger that grows around some economic problems are examples of issue-oriented violence. Amid worsening unemployment and rapidly rising prices, lower-class Brazilians sometimes invade and loot supermarkets. French farmers stopped and burned trucks of Spanish produce, which they perceived as undercutting their livelihood. In 1976, black students in South Africa's Soweto township protested against having to learn Afrikaans in school; police shot down several hundred of them. There may be a fine line between issue-oriented violence and revolutionary violence, for if the issue is serious enough and the police repression brutal enough, protests over an issue can turn into a revolutionary tide.

All these categories—and others one might think of—are apt to be arbitrary.[8] Some situations fit more than one category. Some start in one category and escalate into another. No country, even a highly developed one, is totally immune to some kind of violence, however.

CHANGE AS A CAUSE OF VIOLENCE

Many writers have found the underlying cause of domestic unrest in the changes a given society may be going through. Purely traditional societies with long-established patterns of authority and simple but workable economies are relatively untroubled by violence. People live as their ancestors lived and do not expect much. Likewise, modern, advanced societies with rational types of authority and productive economies have relatively minor types of violence. It is at the in-between stage, when modernization is stirring and upsetting traditional societies, that violence is most likely.[9] The modernizing societies have left one world, that of traditional stability, but have not yet arrived at the new world of modern stability. Everything is changing in such societies—the economy, religious attitudes, lifestyle, and the political system—leaving people worried, confused, and ripe for violent actions.

Economic change can be the most unsettling. The curious thing about economic change is that improvement can be as dangerous as impoverishment. The great French social scientist Alexis de Tocqueville observed in the last century that "though the reign of Louis XVI was the most prosperous period of the monarchy, this very prosperity hastened the outbreak of the Revolution of 1789."[10] Why should this be? There are several reasons. When people are permanently poor and beaten down, they have no hope for the future; they are miserable but quiet. When things improve, they start imagining a better future; their aspirations are awakened. No longer content with their lot, they want improvement fast, faster than even a growing economy can deliver. Worse, during times of prosperity, some people get richer faster than others, arousing jealousy. Certain groups feel bypassed by the economic changes and turn especially bitter; the Marxists call this "class antagonisms." Revolutionary feeling, however, typically does not arise among the poor but among what Crane Brinton called the "not unprosperous people who feel restraint, cramp, annoyance" at a government that impedes their right to even faster progress.[11]

Rising Expectations.   One way of looking at what economic growth does to a society is to represent it graphically. In Figure 19.1, the solid line represents actual economic change in a modernizing society—generally upward. The broken line represents people's expectations. In a still-traditional society—at the graph's left— both actual performance and expectations are low. As growth takes hold, however, expectations start rising faster than actual improvement. Then may come a situation that produces a downturn in the economy—bad harvests, a drop in the price of the leading export commodity, or too much foreign indebtedness—and expectations are frustrated. A big gap suddenly opens between what people want and what they can get.[12] In the words of Daniel Lerner, the "want:get ratio" becomes unhinged, producing a "revolution of rising frustrations."[13]

   This is an extremely delicate time in the life of a nation. Rebellion and revolution can break out. The underlying problem, as Ted Robert Gurr has empha-

FIGURE 19.1   The Expectations Curve

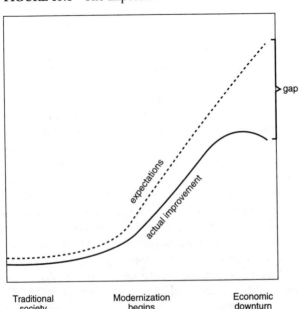

sized, is not poverty itself but "relative deprivation."[14] The very poor seldom revolt; they're too busy feeding their families. But once people have a full belly they start looking around and notice that some people are living much better than they. This sense of relative deprivation may spur them to anger, violence, and occasionally revolution. Gurr's findings, it is interesting to note, are consonant with those of Tocqueville and Brinton: Revolutions come when things are generally getting better, not when they're getting worse.

Other economic change can spur unrest. Anthropologist Eric R. Wolf has argued that the shift from simple subsistence farming to cash crops dependent on markets, landlords, and bankers impoverishes many peasants and turns them from quietude to revolution. It was precisely the economic modernization of agriculture in Mexico, Russia, China, Vietnam, Algeria, and Cuba that paved the way for successful peasant-based revolutions in those countries, according to Wolf.[15] Economic change is, to be sure, not the only pressure on a modernizing society. The political system may be out of date as well, based on inherited position with no opportunity for mass participation. As the economy improves, educational levels rise. People become more aware of abstract ideas such as "freedom" and "democracy." Especially among intellectuals, the educated elite, there is growing fury at the despotism that rules the land. Peasants may hate the system for squeezing them economically, but the urban intellectuals will hate it for suppressing rights and freedoms. It is the confluence of these two forces, argues Huntington—the "numbers" of the peasants and the "brains" of the intellectuals—that makes revolutions.[16]

Revolutions

A revolution is a quick, dramatic system change. Change here means throwing out the old system along with its elites. A small or moderate change that essentially leaves the system intact may be reform, but it is not revolution. Some regimes, to quiet mass discontent, claim they are going through a revolution, but the changes may be largely cosmetic. One test of whether a real revolution has occurred is to see if it has swept out old elites. If they are still in power, there has been no revolution. In a radical revolution, the new elite gets rid of the old one by guillotine, firing squad, and exile. Revolution is not necessarily bloody, however. In 1989, most of the East European countries underwent a dramatic system change without bloodshed. (Romania was the bloody exception.)

Frustration is one thing; revolution is something else. People may be unhappy over one thing or another—peasants over crop prices, intellectuals over lack of freedom, businesspeople over corruption, and so on. But if there is no organization to focus their discontents, probably not much will happen. Unrest and discontent by themselves will not bring down a regime; for that to happen, organization is absolutely essential. In a study of Brazilian political attitudes, Peter McDonough and Antonio Lopez Pina found "a substantial amount of unchanneled dissatisfaction with the authoritarian regime," but it was "free-floating" resentment not especially directed against the military-run government. They suggest that "in the absence of organizational alternatives, resistance is most likely to take the form of apathy and indifference."[17]

The previous factors we have considered may point to violence—rioting and strikes—but without organization they will not produce a revolution. Who provides the organization? For this we turn to the role of intellectuals.

Intellectuals and Revolution. Intellectuals are nearly everywhere discontent with the existing state of affairs because they are highly educated and acquainted with a wide variety of ideas, some of them utopian. Preachers, teachers, lawyers, journalists, and others who deal with ideas often have a professional stake in criticizing the system. If everything were fine, there wouldn't be much to talk or write about. Intellectuals, although often among the better-off, are seldom wealthy. They may resent people who are richer but not as smart—businesspeople and government officials.

Such factors predispose some intellectuals—but by no means all or even a majority—to develop what James Billington called a "revolutionary faith" that the current system can be replaced with something much better.[18] According to Billington, revolution begins, first and foremost, with this "fire in the minds of men." Common folk, ordinary workers and peasants, are seldom interested in the intellectuals' abstract ideologies (see Chapter 6); they want improved material conditions. It is the intellectuals' idealistic convictions, however, that provide revolutionary movements with the cement that holds them together, the goals they aim for, and a leadership stratum.

It is an interesting fact that most twentieth-century revolutionary movements have been founded and led by educated people. Lenin, son of a provincial education official, was a brilliant and highly educated man. Mao Zedong helped found the Chinese Communist party while he was a library assistant at the Beijing National University. Fidel Castro and most of his original guerrilla fighters were law-school graduates. One of them, however—the famous Che Guevara, who was killed in 1967 while trying to foment revolution in Bolivia—was a medical doctor. The leader of Peru's Shining Path guerrillas was a university professor. The leaders of Iran's revolution against the shah were either religious or academically trained intellectuals.

REVOLUTIONARY POLITICAL WARFARE

Many people speak of "guerrilla warfare," but this is a misnomer and a redundancy, for *guerrilla* is simply Spanish for "little war." It is not the use of ambush and punji stakes that should interest us but the accompanying political action. The two, when combined, equal revolutionary political warfare, which Bernard Fall described as the struggle "to establish a competitive system of control over the population." Fall, an expert on Vietnam who died when he stepped on a land mine there in 1967, emphasized *administration* as the crux of revolutionary warfare. "When a country is being subverted it is not being outfought; it is being outadministered. Subversion is literally administration with a minus sign in front."[19]

In studies Fall conducted, both under the French in North Vietnam during the early 1950s and under the Americans in South Vietnam during the early 1960s, he discovered that the Communists were collecting taxes throughout most of the country under the very noses of the regimes they were overthrowing. The occupying power, whether French or American, deceived itself through its ability to drive through a village in an armored convoy; this does not indicate administrative control, which may be in the hands of the insurgents. The emphasis on military hardware is a big mistake, argued Fall, for it detracts from the human element.

The Vietnamese insurgents were able to outadminister the regime for several reasons. In the first place, they were able to identify closely with the population, something the French and Americans could never do. Indeed, the fact that the anti-Communist side in both Vietnam wars was connected with white foreigners gave the kiss of death to the effort. There was no political package the French or Americans might assemble that could be sold to the locals. Even the Saigon rulers had trouble identifying their own countrymen. The Diem and subsequent Saigon governments were run by Central and North Vietnamese Catholics who were at a considerable psychological distance from the largely Buddhist South Vietnamese. The Saigon officials were urban dwellers who disdained assignments in the provinces and working with the peasants. This was precisely the Communists' strong point.

Terror, to be sure, plays a role in revolutionary political warfare. The Vietcong murdered many Saigon officials and government-appointed village headmen. The villagers were not uniformly horrified at such terror, however, because it was selective and targeted at people who were outsiders anyway. To many peasants, the Vietcong executions seemed like extralegal punishment for collaborators. When the Americans made whole villages disappear, that was terror. There's nothing selective about napalm.

While the insurgent is patiently building a network to supplant the regime, the occupier or government is impatiently trying to substitute firepower for legitimacy. The killing of civilians produces more sympathizers and recruits for the guerrillas. The government's overreliance on firepower erodes its tenuous moral claims to leadership of the nation. Fall urged that

> what America should want to prove in Vietnam is that the Free World is "better," *not* that it can kill people more efficiently. If we would induce 100,000 Viet Cong to surrender to our side because our offers of social reform are better than those of the other side's, *that* would be victory. Hence, even a total military or technological defeat of the Viet Cong is going to be a partial defeat of our own purposes—a defeat of ourselves, by ourselves, as it were.[20]

Some critics wonder if the American people and leadership ever understood what we were up against in Vietnam. We fought a military war while our opponents fought a political war, and in the end the political mattered more than the military. Said one American officer as he surveyed the smoking ruins of a village, "Unfortunately, we had to destroy the village in order to save it." Some observers, perhaps misapplying the Vietnam analogy, warned the United States against intervention in Haiti and Bosnia.[21]

STAGES OF REVOLUTION

In a little book published in 1938 that became a classic, Harvard historian Crane Brinton developed a theory that all revolutions pass through similar stages, rather like a human body passing through the stages of an illness.[22] In the English revolution of the 1640s, the American Revolution of 1776, the French Revolution of 1789, and the Russian Revolution of 1917, Brinton found the following rough uniformities.

The Old Regime Decays.   Administration breaks down and taxes rise. People no longer believe in the government; in fact, the government doesn't believe in itself. The intellectuals transfer their allegiance from the regime to a proposed idealized system. All this is happening while the economy is generally on the upgrade, but this provokes discontent and jealousy.

The First Stage of Revolution.   Committees, networks, cells, or conspiracies form, dedicated to overthrowing the old regime. People refuse to pay taxes. A political impasse arises that cannot be solved because the lines are too deeply drawn. When the government calls out troops, the move backfires because the troops desert and the people are further enraged. The initial seizure of power is easy, for the old regime has just about put itself out of business. Popular exultation breaks out.

At First, the Moderates Take Over.   People who opposed the old regime but were still connected with it by dint of background or training assume command. They initiate moderate, middle-of-the-road reforms. These changes are not enough for the extremists among the revolutionaries; they accuse the moderates of being cowardly and of trying to compromise with the forces of the old regime. The moderates are "nice guys" and are not ruthless enough to crush the radicals.

The Extremists Take Over.   More ruthless and better organized than the moderates, knowing exactly what they want, the extremists oust the moderates and drive the revolution to a frenzied high point. Everything old is thrown out. People are required to be "good" according to the canons of the new, idealistic society the extremists try to instigate. "Bad" people are punished in a reign of terror. Even revolutionary comrades who are deemed to have strayed from the true path are executed: "The revolution devours its children." The entire society appears to go mad in what Brinton likened to a high fever during an illness.

A *"Thermidor"* Ends the Reign of Terror.   Eventually the society can take no more. People come to a breaking point, at which they long to settle down, get the economy working again, and enjoy some personal security and pleasure. They've had enough of revolution. Even the extremists get tired of it. Then comes a "Thermidor"—so named after the French revolutionary month during which the extremist Robespierre was himself guillotined—which Brinton described as a convalescence after a fever. Often a dictator, who ends up resembling the tyrants of the old regime, takes over to restore order, and most people don't mind.

IRAN AS A CASE STUDY

Although written two generations ago, Brinton's *Anatomy of Revolution* can be applied to our day. The Iranian revolution unrolled as if its participants had read Brinton's script.[23] The Iranian economy boomed, especially following the quadrupling of oil prices in 1973–1974, but economic growth was uneven. Some people became very rich very fast, provoking jealousy. Corruption and inflation soared. Most educated Iranians came to oppose the shah's regime; students especially hated the shah for his repression of freedoms. Networks of conspirators formed, rallying around the figure of exiled Ayatollah Khomeini and using mosques as their meeting places. By 1978 there was extensive rioting, and the use of troops to quell the rioting simply enraged more Iranians. Troops began to desert. Always disdainful of democracy and mass participation in politics, the shah had relied on his dreaded SAVAK secret police, but even they could no longer contain the revolution. In January 1979, the shah left and Khomeini returned to Iran.

Before he left, the shah named a moderate revolutionary, Bakhtiar, to head the government. But the very fact of being chosen by the shah ruined Bakhtiar, and the newly returned Ayatollah, who instantly became the de facto power in Iran, replaced him with Bazargan, another moderate, but one never connected with the shah. Bazargan's government didn't count for much, though, because real power resided with Khomeini's Revolutionary Council. In November 1979, radical Islamic students, angered over the shah's admission into the United States, seized the U.S.

Fundamentalist revolutionaries demonstrated in Tehran against the United States and President Carter.

Embassy and began the famous "hostage crisis" that lasted over a year. Bazargan, realizing he was powerless, resigned.

The Iranian Muslim extremists, totally devoted to Khomeini, took over and a bloodbath ensued. Firing squads worked overtime to eliminate suspected "bad" people, including fellow revolutionaries who had deviated. Tens of thousands of young Iranians, promised instant admission to heaven, threw their lives away in repelling Iraqi invaders. Strict Islamic standards of morality were enforced—no alcohol or drugs, veils for women, and suppression of non-Islamic religions. After the elderly Khomeini died in 1989, the Iranian revolution calmed and stabilized.[24] No revolution lasts forever; all must establish some kind of normalcy sooner or later. The final element of an Iranian Thermidor would be the reestablishment of diplomatic relations with the United States.

After the Revolution

The big problem with revolutions is not that they change things so much but, ironically, that they end up changing things so little. Revolutions show a persistent tendency to overthrow one form of tyranny only to replace it with another. In little more than a decade, the French kings had been replaced by Napoleon, who crowned himself emperor and supervised a police state far more thorough than anything the kings had had at their disposal. The partial despotism of the tsars was replaced by the perfect despotism of Stalin. Life was freer and economic growth faster at the turn of the century under the inefficient tsarist system than it has been at any time in Russia since. Fidel Castro threw out the crooked Batista regime, and Cuban freedom and economic growth declined abruptly.

What good are revolutions? One is tempted to despair with Simon Bolivar, the liberator of South America, who said, "He who aids a revolution plows the sea." In general, revolutions end badly. (As soon as you can accept that statement, you have become to some degree a conservative.)

But what about the United States? Don't we call our 1776–1781 struggle with Britain the Revolutionary War? One way to handle this question is to say that it wasn't really a revolution, for it was not an effort to remake American society. Indeed, some of its greatest leaders were wealthy and prominent figures in colonial society. They wanted simply to get rid of British rule, not overturn society as a whole. The American struggle was more a war of independence than a revolution. Extremists never seized control, and there was no reign of terror. Some 100,000 Tories, colonials who remained pro-British, simply got up and left, many to the lands the Crown gave them in New Brunswick and Nova Scotia in Canada.

The late, great Hannah Arendt, on the other hand, thought the American struggle was indeed a revolution, perhaps the only complete revolution that has ever been carried out, for it alone ended with a new foundation of liberty instead of the tyranny of other revolutions.[25] According to Arendt, the fortunate thing for the American revolutionaries is that they did not have to wrestle with the difficult "social question" that obsessed the French revolutionaries. America was prosperous and wealth was distributed rather equally. The American struggle didn't become sidetracked by the poverty problem, so it could focus on establishing a just and durable constitution with balanced powers and political freedom. It was the genius—or, in part, luck—of the American Revolution that it was a purely *political* and not a social matter. America needed no guillotine, for there was no aristocratic class to behead. It needed no demagogues of the Robespierre stripe because there was no rabble to arouse. The French Revolution, deeply involved in these social matters, became a bloody mess and ended in dictatorship. In Arendt's terms, it wasn't a really successful revolution because it didn't end with the constituting of liberty, as the American Revolution did.

In France, the French Revolution is still controversial two centuries after it occurred. Few celebrate it uncritically, and many French conservatives hate it. Most French people are proud of its original idealistic impulses—liberty, equality, fraternity—but many admit that it went wrong, that it turned to bloodshed and dictatorship. The big question here is whether this was an accident—the Revolution fell into the hands of extremists and fanatics—or whether there was something built into the revolutionary process that made breakdown inevitable.[26] Most serious scholars now argue for the inevitability thesis.

In Russia, this question is asked about the 1917 Bolshevik Revolution. Lenin, an intelligent and sophisticated man, died in 1924. Had he lived, would communism have taken a more humane and less brutal path? Stalin, in the view of some diehard socialists, was the culprit who betrayed the revolution by turning it into his personal dictatorship. Historian Roy Medvedev wrote a scathing attack on Stalin and urged bringing the Communist party back to "Leninism," meaning a relatively democratic system. Updating his book, however, Medvedev came to the conclusion that the entire system is at fault, not just one man.[27] This is a far more sweeping indictment, for it rejects Lenin as well. Most Russians are now willing to admit that Lenin was wrong from the start.

THE WANING OF REVOLUTION

Since World War II, the globe has experienced a tide of revolutions, but now the tide is receding. Revolution, popular in the 1960s, developed a bad reputation in the 1970s. By the 1980s, many radical countries were trying to back out of their revolutionary systems. There were no positive examples of a revolution that had worked out well. The Soviet Union and China, earlier the model for many revolutionaries, admitted they were in economic difficulty and tried to change to a more open market system. Several East European lands simply walked away from communism. Then communism collapsed in the Soviet Union itself. In Africa, the revolutionary Communist lands of Angola, Mozambique, and Ethiopia liberalized their systems and begged for aid from the capitalist West.

The worst horror was in Southeast Asia. In the late 1970s, the Khmer Rouge (Red Cambodia) murdered between 1 and 2 million of their fellow citizens. The nonfiction movie about this bloodbath, *The Killing Fields,* shocked the world. Vietnam, united by the Communists in 1975 after its fierce war with the United States, turned itself into one of the poorest countries in the world. Tens of thousands of Vietnamese "boat people" risked the open sea and Thai pirates to leave their starving land. Sadly, few countries wanted them. In 1995, Vietnam and the United States established diplomatic relations, and the Vietnamese economy turned to the world market. In Cuba, Fidel Castro continues to proclaim his regime revolutionary, although the Cuban people have long since tired of the shortages and restrictions. In Nicaragua, a free election in 1990 voted out the revolutionary Sandinistas who still sought a socialist system, and replaced them with a democratic coalition.

There are few major revolutionary movements struggling to overthrow regimes they alleged kept their lands in poverty and injustice. In Peru, the *Sendero Luminso* (Shining Path), made up of radical students, wages guerrilla warfare even though its leader has been captured.[28] They follow the revolutionary teachings of Mao Zedong that had been abandoned in China. In the Philippines, the Communist-led New Peoples Army, growing out of the terrible poverty of a society dominated by rich plantation owners, controls considerable areas of the countryside and routinely ambushes army patrols.[29] These movements are motivated by great passion and a burning sense of injustice.

Notice the difference between countries where revolution has triumphed and where it is still being fought. The former is characterized by disillusionment and bitterness; many people would like to get rid of the revolutionary regime. The latter movements are still idealistic and convinced they will bring a better social system after their triumph. Revolutions are based on the belief that by seizing state power, a truly committed regime can redo society, making it just, fair, and prosperous. This feeling grows in societies that are unjust and miserable. But after seizing power, the revolutionary regime discovers it's a lot harder to make an economy work than they thought. For some years, sometimes decades, they blame capitalist holdouts and imperialist saboteurs. To control these alleged plotters, they give themselves draconian police powers to virtually stamp out private industry and criticism.

But things don't get better; they get worse. Farmers won't plant unless they get a good price for their crops. Workers won't work without something to buy. Reluctant to admit they are mistaken after having killed so many people, the revolutionary regime locks itself into power through police controls. After some time of hardship and poor growth, a new generation may come to power and admit that the system needs to loosen up. Embarrassment may be a factor here. Comparing themselves with capitalist neighbors, the revolutionary country sees itself falling behind. The Chinese could note with regret that on China's rim—in Singapore, Hong Kong, and Taiwan—Chinese were prosperous, but not in China. Under Deng Xiaoping, China turned (incompletely) to capitalist industry and foreign investment. The great revolution had failed.

It takes large-scale revolutionary experiences to demonstrate that revolutions end badly. The revolutionary promise is golden; the revolutionary results are mud. If you don't see it, you don't believe it. With several revolutionary experiences to ponder, many would-be revolutionaries turned away from revolution. This helps explain why the 1980s was a conservative decade: It could look back and survey the results of the 1960s. By the 1990s, hardly anyone wants a revolution.

"Albanians are revolutionary heroes" is the message of this mural facing Tirana's main square. It tries to foster the feeling that Albanian history is a steady march to communism.

Western Europe was an influential example in the 1980s. France in 1981 elected a Socialist government that promised to redo society. Without asking where the money was going to come from, the government of President François Mitterrand hired thousands of new state employees; raised wages, benefits, and vacation time; and nationalized many industries and banks. Quickly, Socialist policy led to inflation and chaos, and Mitterrand backed away from it and pursued centrist policies, focusing on the market rather than the state. The French people liked that direction and reelected Mitterrand. The intellectual debate that accompanied the change was probably more important. French intellectuals had for most of a century been addicted to Marxism, socialism, and revolution. With Mitterrand, they got a little taste of how it goes wrong. In a wave, French intellectuals abandoned leftist positions and rediscovered the market, free enterprise, and capitalistic growth. French intellectuals are influential beyond France, so their conversion had a ripple effect in the Third World and in the rest of Europe. The many African students in Paris, for example, in the 1980s picked up very different attitudes than they had in earlier decades. (The murderous Pol Pot of the Khmer Rouge, for example, picked up his lunatic Marxism as a student in Paris in the 1950s.)

The crux of revolutionary thinking is the feeling that it is possible to remake society. Without that, few would bother to make revolutions. With the discovery that remaking society leads to terrible difficulties and poor results, the revolutionary dream dies. Does this mean that we will not see another major wave of revolutions? Not necessarily. There is plenty of injustice in the world, and this brings rage. Rage, as Hannah Arendt pointed out, leads to revolution.[30]

What can be done to head off revolutions? The answer is simple but difficult to carry out: reforms to end the injustices that revolutions feed on. Land reform in Peru and the Philippines and free elections in Persian Gulf lands could dampen or even end revolutionary movements in these countries. But landowners are not about to give up their holdings, and they are politically powerful. The rulers around the Persian Gulf fear the loss of their wealth and power if they democratize. In practice, reforms are hard to apply because there is strong resistance from the conservative class in power that has much to lose.

In South Vietnam, for example, the United States repeatedly urged the Saigon regime to carry out sweeping land reform to win the peasants away from the Communist guerrillas. But landowners, many of whom collected exorbitant rents from tenant farmers, wouldn't let land-reform bills pass. If they had given up their land, they might have saved their country; instead, they lost both. The message is to institute reforms before revolutionary feeling is implanted, to head off the problem before it becomes dangerous.

ANTI-COMMUNIST REVOLUTIONS

One of the more interesting phenomena of our day has been the revolution *against* communism. Communist regimes long claimed for themselves the title "revolutionary" and denounced as "reactionary" anyone against them. But if, as we argued, revolution means a sweeping system change, especially the ouster of the ruling elite, people who overthrow Communist regimes are also revolutionaries.

The impulse to revolution in Communist systems is the same as in other systems: injustice and poverty. Promised a socialist paradise for generations, workers became tired of the failure to deliver. Actually, Soviets generally enjoyed rising living standards, but their expectations, fanned by the party propaganda line, rose faster. A really explosive element was jealousy. Soviets were aware that the privileged party elite enjoyed special apartments, food shops, medical care, and vacation cottages. They were also aware that much of the consumer economy ran on the basis of corruption. Desirable products never made it to the store shelf; they were sold through the back door for big profits. The same feelings that smoldered in non-Communist countries smoldered in Communist countries.

As in earlier revolutions, the most dangerous time in the life of a Communist regime was when it tried to reform itself. Reform in Communist countries was as difficult as in non-Communist countries, for Communist elites also had a lot to lose in terms of power and privilege. In their system, the Communist party elite became the conservatives who didn't want things to change and were in a position to block reforms. When things got so bad that reform had to come, it was too late. Things were bad in the Soviet Union under Brezhnev, but mass unrest didn't burst out until Gorbachev instituted major reforms. By admitting that things were wrong, he gave the green light to restive workers and nationalities to demand more than any

The secret police headquarters in Moscow was, until 1991, presided over by this statue of the KGB's founder, Felix Dzerdzinsky. Three months after this photo was taken, a mob tore down the statue.

had dared mention a few years earlier. By asking for support and patience, Gorbachev also showed he was running scared, a further incitement to revolution. By letting in more Western media, he showed the Soviets how well Americans and West Europeans lived. Soon the pressure for massive change became explosive.

Halfway reform does not suffice and often makes things worse. The Communist regimes of Eastern Europe tried to calm their angry people by promising reform and bringing in fresh, new leadership. But most East European citizens were not fooled; they recognized that the reforms would basically leave defective systems intact and that the new leaders were simply younger party members who were intent on keeping the Communist party in power. In Czechoslovakia in 1989, for example, the rapidly growing Civic Forum movement hooted down a new cabinet that the frightened Communist regime presented. The "new" cabinet, still dominated by Communists, looked pretty much like the old one. After massive street protest, Civic Forum obtained a cabinet of non-Communists, some of whom had been in jail only two weeks earlier. This was what Czech President Vaclav Havel called the "velvet revolution." When an unpopular regime begins by offering "reforms," it may end by putting itself out of business.

Faced with this prospect, some regimes attempt to crush mass demands with military force. An example is the bloody 1989 crackdown in China. Hundreds of protesting students were gunned down in Beijing's Tiananmen Square because an elderly party elite feared what they called a "counterrevolutionary revolt."[31] Deng Xiaoping had attempted halfway reform only to find that it would not stay halfway.

Halfway reform of a corrupt dictatorship is impossible because as soon as you let people criticize it, they demand to replace it. Give them a free-speech inch and they want a democratic mile. That, of course, would mean ouster of the Communist elite, which then fights tenaciously for its power and privileges. But by digging in their heels and refusing to institute major reform, the party elite just builds up a head of steam for a later and greater explosion. They can crush political opponents, but they can't produce the economic growth necessary to feed and house their people, who just get angrier. Ironically, Communist countries in the late twentieth century indeed led the way to revolution.

Suggested Readings

ANDRAIN, CHARLES F., and DAVID E. APTER. *Political Protest and Social Change: Analyzing Politics.* New York: New York University, 1995. Two top thinkers demonstrate the role of values and religion in fomenting civil unrest.

CHALIAND, GÉRARD. *Revolution in the Third World: Currents and Conflicts in Asia, Africa, and Latin America,* rev. ed. New York: Penguin, 1989. French specialist on the subject surveys thirty revolutions.

COLBURN, FORREST D. *The Vogue of Revolution in Poor Countries.* Princeton, NJ: Princeton University Press, 1994. A brief but interesting review and comparison of twenty-two post-World War II revolutions.

DEFONZO, JAMES. *Revolutions and Revolutionary Movements.* Boulder, CO: Westview Press, 1991. The historical and social factors that make revolutions.

DIAMOND, LARRY, and MARC F. PLATTNER, eds. *Nationalism, Ethnic Conflict, and Democracy.* Baltimore, MD: Johns Hopkins University Press, 1994. Collection on the causes and cures of some of the more dangerous tendencies of our day.

GILBERT, DENNIS. *Sandinistas: The Party and the Revolution.* New York: Blackwell, 1988. Thorough study of the ideology and organization of Nicaragua's revolutionary regime.

GOLDSTONE, JACK A., TED ROBERT GURR, and FARROKH MOSHIRI, eds. *Revolutions in the Late Twentieth Century.* Boulder, CO: Westview Press, 1991. A close look at eleven current situations with a theoretical framework for understanding revolutions.

GREENE, THOMAS H. *Comparative Revolutionary Movements: Search for Theory and Justice,* 3rd ed. Englewood Cliffs, NJ: Prentice Hall, 1990. Interesting attempt to build an analytic framework, using comparative cases.

SCHAMA, SIMON. *Citizens: A Chronicle of the French Revolution.* New York: Knopf, 1989. A critical, conservative, but scholarly analysis of how the French Revolution went insane.

SEDERBERG, PETER C. *Fires Within: Political Violence and Revolutionary Change.* New York: HarperCollins, 1994. Good roundup of revolutionary theory and examples.

TARAZONA-SEVILLANO, GABRIELA. *Sendero Luminoso and the Threat of Narcoterrorism.* Westport, CT: Praeger, 1990. Uncovers the link between Peru's revolutionaries and the drug trade.

WOOD, GORDON S. *The Radicalism of the American Revolution.* New York: Knopf, 1992. Argues that in terms of sweeping change, it was indeed a revolution.

Notes

1. One of the first and best efforts to integrate systems theory with revolution is that of Chalmers Johnson, *Revolutionary Change* (Boston: Little, Brown, 1966).

2. President Johnson appointed a commission to study the riots, and its reports contributed to further scholarly inquiry. See *Report of the National Advisory Commission on Civil Disor-*

ders (New York: Bantam, 1968); and Hugh Davis Graham and Ted Robert Gurr, eds., *Violence in America: Historical and Comparative Perspectives* (New York: New American Library, 1969).

3. For a magisterial study of system breakdown, see Juan J. Linz and Alfred Stepan, eds., *The Breakdown of Democratic Regimes* (Baltimore: Johns Hopkins University Press, 1978).

4. For the pressures South Africa was under, see John D. Brewer, ed., *Can South Africa Survive? Five Minutes to Midnight* (New York: St. Martin's, 1989).

5. This discussion draws on Fred R. von der Mehden, *Comparative Political Violence* (Englewood Cliffs, NJ: Prentice Hall, 1973), Chap. 1.

6. See Pamela Constable and Arturo Valenzuela, *A Nation of Enemies: Chile Under Pinochet* (New York: Norton, 1991).

7. For a thorough discussion of praetorianism, see Eric A. Nordlinger, *Soldiers in Politics: Military Coups and Governments* (Englewood Cliffs, NJ: Prentice Hall, 1977).

8. Some writers include a category called "anomic violence," representing spontaneous and unorganized rampages, such as the looting of shops during a power blackout or frustrations vented by slum dwellers against police.

9. Samuel P. Huntington, *Political Order in Changing Societies* (New Haven, CT: Yale University Press, 1968), especially pp. 32–71.

10. Alexis de Tocqueville, *The Old Regime and the French Revolution* (Garden City, NY: Doubleday Anchor, 1955), p. 169.

11. Crane Brinton, *The Anatomy of Revolution*, rev. ed. (New York: Vintage Books, 1965), p. 250.

12. This figure was inspired by F. LaMond Tullis, *Politics and Social Change in Third World Countries* (New York: Wiley, 1973), Chap. 12.

13. Daniel Lerner, "Toward a Communication Theory of Modernization," in *Communications and Political Development*, ed. Lucian Pye (Princeton, NJ: Princeton University Press, 1963), pp. 330–33.

14. Ted Robert Gurr, *Why Men Rebel* (Princeton, NJ: Princeton University Press, 1970).

15. Eric R. Wolf, *Peasant Wars of the Twentieth Century* (New York: Harper & Row, 1969). Another work that stresses the peasant as the basis for revolution is James C. Scott, *The Moral Economy of the Peasant: Rebellion and Subsistence in Southeast Asia* (New Haven, CT: Yale University Press, 1976).

16. Huntington, *Political Order in Changing Societies*, p. 241.

17. Peter McDonough and Antonio Lopez Pina, "Authoritarian Brazil and Democratic Spain: Toward a Theory of Political Legitimacy" (paper presented at the Latin American Studies Association, Pittsburgh, 1979), pp. 57–58.

18. James H. Billington, *Fire in the Minds of Men: Origins of the Revolutionary Faith* (New York: Basic Books, 1980).

19. Bernard B. Fall, "The Theory and Practice of Insurgency and Counterinsurgency," *Last Reflections on a War* (Garden City, NY: Doubleday, 1967), p. 220. The article first appeared in the *Naval War College Review*, April 1965, and was a transcription of a talk Fall gave at the Naval War College on 10 December 1964.

20. Fall, "This Isn't Munich, It's Spain," *Last Reflections on a War*, p. 234. The original appeared in *Ramparts*, December 1965.

21. See, for example, Adam Garfinkle, "Into the Shooting Gallery," *The National Interest* 42 (Winter 1995/96), 117–20.

22. Brinton, *Anatomy of Revolution*.

23. For a review of the Iranian revolution, see Richard W. Cottam, *Iran and the United States: A Cold-War Case Study* (Pittsburgh: University of Pittsburgh Press, 1988).

24. Shireen T. Hunter, *Iran after Khomeini* (Westport, CT: Praeger, 1992).

25. Hannah Arendt, *On Revolution* (New York: Viking Press, 1963), especially Chap. 4, "Foundation I: Constitutio Libertatis."

26. Even two centuries later, in 1989, picking an official historian to explain the French Revolution was a political act. The French government, wanting to celebrate the Revolution as a unifying symbol, avoided both radical and conservative scholars to settle on moderate François Furet, an ex-Marxist who had come to the conservative conclusion that the Revolution had to "skid out of control" (*dérapage*). See François Furet, *Interpreting the French Revolution* (New York: Cambridge University Press, 1981).

27. Roy Medvedev, *Let History Judge: The Origins and Consequences of Stalinism*, rev. ed. (New York: Columbia University Press, 1989).

28. Simon Strong, *Shining Path* (New York: HarperCollins, 1993).

29. See Gregg R. Jones, *Red Revolution: Inside the Philippine Guerrilla Movement* (Boulder, CO: Westview Press, 1989).

30. Arendt, *On Revolution*, pp. 61–110.

31. For a reconstruction of the Chinese Politburo's decision to crush the democracy movement, see Nicholas D. Kristoff, "How the Hardliners Won," *New York Times Magazine*, 12 November 1989.

· 20 ·
International Relations

Politics Without Sovereignty

International politics is quite a bit different from the domestic politics we have been studying. Domestic politics generally occurs *within* a sovereign entity—what we call a state or nation—whereas international politics occurs *among* such entities. Sovereignty, as considered in Chapter 1, means being boss on your own turf, the last legal word within a country. The concept grew up in the sixteenth century, when absolutist monarchs were strengthening their positions and sought legal justification for it.[1] Sovereignty is the dominant force within a country. Criminals, rebels, and breakaway elements are, in theory, controlled or crushed by the sovereign, who now, of course, is no longer a king or queen but the national government. Sovereignty also means that foreign powers have no business intruding into your country's affairs; their reach—again in theory—stops at your borders.

So much for theory. In practice, nothing is so clear-cut. Just because a nation is legally sovereign does not necessarily mean it really controls its own turf. Witness poor Lebanon in the 1980s: its territory occupied by outside forces (Syria, Israel, and several Arab or Islamic organizations), its weak government propped up by friendly forces (the United States, France, and Italy), unable to stop the violence among its several politico-religious private armies. At the same time, there was much more peace and order among the sovereign states of Europe who formed the Common Market. They had agreed to settle their economic differences by negotiating and politicking at the European Union headquarters in Brussels.

Further, the idea that sovereignty precludes outside intervention doesn't hold up. Small, poor countries are routinely dominated and influenced by large, rich countries. Afghanistan could scarcely be said to be sovereign under Soviet occupation, nor could the small countries of Central America under the watchful eye of the United States. Some Canadians claimed U.S. economic and cultural penetration was so great that they had lost some of their sovereignty. What meaning had sovereignty in Bosnia?

Still, the term *sovereignty* has some utility. Where established, national sovereignty does indeed bring internal peace, and most countries can claim to have done this. By and large, countries still do what they want. When France resumed nuclear testing in the South Pacific in 1995 there was nothing Australia and New Zealand could do to stop it, although they protested strongly. That was sovereignty in action.

Within a sovereign entity there is—or at least there is supposed to be—law. If you have a grievance against someone, you don't take the law into your own hands. You take the person to court. In international relations, nearly the opposite applies: Taking the law into your own hands—by the threat or use of military force—is quite normal. Often there is no other recourse.

This important difference between domestic and international politics sometimes exasperates skilled practitioners of one when they enter the realm of the other. President Johnson was a master of domestic politics; whatever he wanted from Congress he got. But he couldn't make skinny little Ho Chi Minh back down, for Ho was boss on *his* own turf. What worked domestically for Johnson—deals, threats, persuasion—flopped internationally. Some have suggested that it was Nixon's use of the "dirty tricks" of international politics in domestic politics that brought about the Watergate scandal and his downfall. Nixon was indeed a clever statesman; he simultaneously improved ties with the Soviet Union and China. But his deviousness and penchant for secrecy served him ill in dealing with a delicate domestic problem. International politics is not just domestic politics on a grander scale. Without a world sovereignty to establish rules and authority, international politics is wilder and more complex.

POWER AND NATIONAL INTEREST

Lacking the sovereignty that prevails in most domestic situations, international relations depend a lot on power. The late, great Hans Morgenthau held that power is the basic element of international politics and that idealists ignore it at their peril.[2] Without sufficient power, a country cannot survive, let alone prevail, in a tumultuous world. One should bear in mind that power is not the same as force. Force is the specific application of military might; power is a country's more general ability to get its way. Power includes military, economic, political, and psychological factors.[3] Power is tricky to calculate. Whole departments of the CIA spend millions trying to figure out how much power various countries have. Some elements of power—such as a country's geography, natural resources, population, and economy—are tangible or calculable. Some of the most important factors, however—such as a country's military capability, the quality of its political system, and its psychological determination—cannot be learned until it is involved in a war. The war then provides—at a terrible price—the answer about which side had more power.

In this situation, countries generally pursue their "national interest," what is good for the nation as a whole in world affairs. This makes international politics inherently selfish; nations rarely behave like saints. Countries may practice generosity and altruism, but often with an eye to enhancing their international power and prestige. The world did little to staunch the horrible bloodletting in Rwanda in 1994; perhaps half a million were butchered, far more than in Bosnia. Rwanda was out of the way and had no strategic or economic value. Only France sent some peacekeeping forces, because France wishes to portray itself as the dominant and protecting power of Central Africa, where it has strong economic ties.

National interests may be divided into vital versus secondary, temporary versus permanent, specific versus general, and complementary versus conflicting. A vital interest is one that potentially threatens the life of your nation, such as Soviet missiles in Cuba. When a country perceives a threat to its vital interests, it often goes to war. A secondary interest is usually more distant and less urgent. The United States, for example, has an interest in an open world oil supply, with no nation restricting or distorting it. Nations are more inclined to negotiate and compromise over their secondary interests, although military action may become necessary, as against Iraq in 1991. Notice how many nations saw their national interests as complementary during this war. Many Arab countries sided with the West in the Gulf War. Complementary interests are what make alliances. When interests conflict, as in Russian support for the Serbs, countries pull apart. A temporary interest is one of fixed duration, as in U.S. support for Iraq during its 1980s war with Iran. U.S. diplomacy had trouble understanding that as soon as the war was over, their complementary interests receded. A permanent interest lasts over centuries, as in the U.S. interest in keeping hostile powers out of the Western hemisphere. A specific interest focuses on a single problem, such as Japanese trade barriers to U.S. goods. A general interest might be universal respect for human rights.

Two countries, even allies, seldom have identical national interests. The best one can hope for is that their interests will be complementary. The United States and Albania, for instance, may have a common interest in opposing Serbian "ethnic cleansing," but the U.S. interest is a general, temporary, and secondary one concerning human rights and regional stability. The Albanian interest is a specific, permanent, and possibly vital one of forming a Greater Albania that would include Serbian-held Kosovo with its Albanian majority. Our interests may run parallel for a time, but we must never mistake Albanian interests for U.S. interests.

It's sometimes hard to anticipate how another country will define its national interest. They see things through different eyes. Hungary in the 1990s is very cooperative with the West and eager to join NATO. In 1994, however, when the U.S. and France proposed air strikes to curb Serbian artillery atrocities in Bosnia, Hungary stopped the U.S. use of its territory for AWACS flights. An American looking at this refusal is puzzled: "But don't they want to be on our team?" A Hungarian looking at the refusal says, "We'll have to live with the Serbs for centuries; that border is a vital, permanent interest for us. Some 400,000 ethnic Hungarians live under Serbian control in Voivodina as virtual hostages. The Americans offer no guarantees of protection, but they expect us to join them in an act of war. Sorry, not a good deal." (The AWACS flights were quickly restored as the crisis passed.)

The diplomat's work is in finding and developing complementary interests so that two or more countries can work together. (Better diplomatic spadework would have signaled in advance the difference between Hungarian and U.S. interests in 1994.) Often countries have some interests that are complementary and others that are conflicting, as when NATO members cooperate to block the Soviet threat but clash over who will lead the alliance. The French-U.S. relationship can be described in this way. Where interests totally conflict, of course, there can be no cooperation. Here it is the diplomat's duty to say so and find ways to minimize the damage. Do not despair in this situation; national interests can shift and today's adversary may be tomorrow's ally.

Defining the national interest in any given situation may be difficult. Intelligent, well-informed people may come up with totally opposite definitions of the national interest. Hawks in the 1960s, for example, claimed a Communist victory in Southeast Asia would destabilize the United States' defense, economic, and political interests. Others claimed Vietnam was a distant swamp of no importance to us. In the 1990s, Americans quarreled over whether Bosnia was a U.S. national interest or a foolish attempt to stop people who were intent on fighting each other. How can you tell when a genuine national interest is at stake?

Feasibility is linked to national interest; power is the connecting link. An infeasible strategy—where your power is insufficient to carry out your designs—is inherently a bad strategy. If the type of power is wrong for the setting (for example, helicopters and artillery to counter Vietnamese or Afghan nationalism; air power to stop a three-sided civil war), you are undertaking an infeasible strategy.

Why War?

Much has been written on why there is war. Most thinkers agree that war has many causes, not just one. Very broadly, though, theories on the cause of war are divided into two general camps, the micro and the macro—the little, close-up picture that focuses on individuals, as opposed to the big, panoramic picture that focuses on whole nations and their interactions.[4]

MICRO THEORIES

Micro theories are rooted largely in biology and psychology. They might attempt to explain war as the result of genetic human aggressiveness. Millions of years of evolution have made people fighters—to obtain food, defend their families, and guard their territory. In this, humans are no different from many animals.[5] Most anthropologists angrily refute such biological determinism, arguing that primitive peoples exhibit a wide variety of behavior—some are aggressive and some aren't—that can be explained only by culture. Writers with a psychological orientation explore the personalities of leaders, what made them this way, and how they obtained their hold over the masses, with an ability to bring them to war.[6]

Biological and psychological theories offer some insights but fall far short of explaining wars. If humans are naturally aggressive, why aren't nations at war all the time? How is it that countries can fight a long series of wars—the Russian-Turkish struggle around the Black Sea or the Arab-Israeli wars—under different leaders who surely must have been psychologically distinct? Biological and psychological approaches may offer insights into some of the *underlying* causes of war but not the immediate causes. There is a certain human aggressiveness, but under what circumstances does it come out? For this we turn to macro theories.

MACRO THEORIES

Macro theories are rooted largely in history and political science. They concentrate chiefly on the power and ambitions of states. States, not individuals, are the key actors. Where they can, states expand, as in the Germans' medieval push to the east, the Americans' "manifest destiny," the growth of the British empire, and the Soviets' takeover of Eastern Europe and Afghanistan. Only countervailing power may stop the drive to expand. One country, fearing the growth of a neighbor, will strengthen its defenses or form alliances to offset the neighbor's power. Much international behavior can be explained by the aphorisms *Si vis pacem para bellum* ("If you want peace, prepare for war") and "The enemy of my enemy is my friend." Political leaders have an almost automatic feel for national interest and power and move to enhance them.[7] Does the pursuit of power lead to war or peace? Again, there are two broad theories.

Balance of Power.   The oldest and most commonly held theory is that peace results when several states, improving their national power and forming alliances, balance one another. Would-be expansionists are blocked. According to balance-of-power theorists, the great periods of relative peace—between the Peace of Westphalia in 1648 and the wars that grew out of the French Revolution (1792–1814), and again from 1815 to the start of World War I in 1914—have been times when the European powers balanced each other. When the balances broke down, there was war.

Hierarchy of Power.   Sophisticated analysts have questioned the balance-of-power theory. First, because calculations of power are so problematic, it is impossible to know when power balances. Second, the periods of peace, some writers note, occurred when power was out of balance, when states were ranked hierarchically in terms of power. Then every nation knew where it stood. It is in times of transition, when the power hierarchy is blurred, that countries are tempted to go to war. After a big war with a definitive outcome, there is peace because then relative power is clearly known.[8] If this theory is correct, then trying to achieve an accurate balance of power is precisely the wrong thing to do; it will lead to war because the participating states will think they have a good chance of victory.

MISPERCEPTION

Weaving micro and macro approaches together, some thinkers have focused on "image" or "perception" as the key to war.[9] Both psychological and power approaches have something to contribute, but they are incomplete. It's not the real situation (which is hard to know) but what leaders perceive it to be that makes them decide for war or peace. They often misperceive, seeing hostility and development of superior weaponry in another country, which sees itself as acting defensively and as just trying to catch up in weaponry. John F. Kennedy portrayed the Soviets as enjoying a "missile gap" over us; he greatly increased U.S. missile-manufacturing efforts. It turned out that the Soviets were actually behind us, and they perceived the American effort as a threat that they had to match. The misperceptions led to the 1962 Cuban missile crisis, the closest we have come to World War III. President Reagan saw Soviet strength as greater than ours and extremely dangerous; he sped up development of new missiles to offset it. The Soviets saw this as an aggressive move and countered it with new weapons of their own. Both sides were trapped in their own insecurities. As Henry Kissinger brilliantly put it, "Absolute security for one power means absolute insecurity for all others."[10]

In misperception or image theory, the psychological and real worlds bounce against each other in the minds of political leaders. They think they are acting defensively, but their picture of the situation may be distorted. In our time, it is interesting to note, no country ever calls its actions anything but defensive. The Americans in Vietnam saw themselves as defending the free world; the Serbs in Bosnia saw themselves as defending their people. In its own eyes, a nation is never aggressive. A country, under the guidance of its leaders, its ideology, and its mass media, may work itself into such a state of fear that even its most aggressive moves are rationalized as defensive.[11] Even Hitler and the Germans in World War II saw themselves as defending Germany against hostile powers.

KEEPING PEACE

Whatever its causes, what can be done to prevent or at least limit war? Many proposals have been advanced; none has really worked.

World Government.   The real culprit, many thinkers claim, is the old doctrine of sovereignty. The solution is to have states give up at least some of their sovereignty—the ability to decide to go to war—to an international confederation that would prevent war much as an individual country keeps the peace within its borders. But that's exactly the rub: What country would give up its sovereignty? Would the United States place its future in the hands of over 180 members of the UN General Assembly who might vote to share its wealth with poor countries? Did Serbia heed a UN call to give Bosnia its independence? Without the teeth of sovereignty, the United Nations, or any organization like it, becomes a debating society, perhaps useful as a place for diplomatic contact, but little more.

Collective Security.   The United Nations' predecessor, the League of Nations, tried to implement an idea that had been around for some time: collective security. Members of the League (which did not include the United States) pledged to join immediately in economic and military action against any aggressor state. If Japan, for example, invaded China, every other power would break trade relations and send forces to defend China. Aggressors, faced with the forces of the rest of the world, would not practice aggression. It was a great idea on paper, but it didn't work in practice. When Japan took Manchuria from China in 1931, the league merely sent a commission to study the situation. Japan claimed the Chinese started it (a lie), and the other powers saw no point in getting involved in a distant conflict where none of their interests was involved. Aggression went unpunished because the League had no mechanism to make the other countries respond. The same happened when Italy invaded Ethiopia in 1935. Japan, Italy, and Germany withdrew from the league to practice aggression on a larger scale, and the league collapsed with World War II.

Functionalism.   Another idea related to world organizations is to have countries cooperate first in specialized or "functional" areas so that they will see that they can accomplish more by cooperation than by conflict. Gradually they will work up to a stable peace as a result of being increasingly able to trust each other. Functional cooperation will produce a "spillover" effect. Dozens of UN-related agencies now promote international cooperation in disease control, food production, weather forecasting, civil aviation, and nuclear energy.[12] Even hostile countries are sometimes able to sit down to solve a mutual problem in these and other specialized areas. But there is no spillover; they remain hostile. Sometimes the functional organization becomes a scene of conflict, as when the Third Word Bloc expelled Israel and South Africa from the UN Educational, Scientific, and Cultural Organization (UNESCO) and the United States quit UNESCO over alleged Soviet dominance. The functionalist approach has brought some help in world problems but has not touched the biggest problem, war.

Third-Party Assistance.   One way to settle a dispute is to have a third party not involved in the conflict shuttle between the contending parties to try to find a middle ground. The third party may simply carry messages back and forth, as the UN's Ralph Bunche did between Arabs and Israelis in 1949. Or the third party may provide suggestions, as President Carter did with Begin and Sadat at Camp David in 1978 and Richard Holbrooke did at Dayton in 1995. Third parties can help calm a tense situation, but the contenders have to *want* to find a solution. If not, third-party assistance is futile.

Diplomacy.   The oldest approach to preserving peace is through diplomatic contact, with envoys sent from one head of state to another. A good diplomat knows all of the foregoing power factors and the interests of the countries involved and has some suggestions for reaching a compromise that leaves both parties at least partly satisfied. This is crucial: There must be a willingness to compromise. This is often very difficult, however, because countries define their vital, nonnegotiable interests grandly and are unwilling to cut them down to compromisable size. If successful, diplomats draw up treaties—contracts between countries—which must be ratified and, one hopes, observed. If one country feels a treaty harms it, there is nothing to stop it from violating the bargain. Countries enter into and observe treaties because it suits them. Some observers say the United States and Soviet Union, both relative newcomers to the world of great-power politics, were unskilled at diplomacy, too unwilling to compromise. The climate of mistrust between them was one of the hallmarks of the Cold War.

Peacekeeping.   Related to diplomacy is the idea of using third-party military forces to support a cease-fire, truce, or other agreement to end hostilities. Such forces, wearing the blue berets of the UN, helped calm and stabilize truce lines between Israel and its Arab neighbors and between Greeks and Turks on Cyprus. Such forces cannot "enforce peace" by stopping a conflict that is still in progress. The only way to do that would be to take sides in the war, and that would be the opposite of peacekeeping. It was therefore inherently unrealistic to expect UNPROFOR (the UN Protective Force) to separate and calm the warring parties in Bosnia. The IFOR (Implementation Force) that took over from UNPROFOR was different and far more successful, because it came after the three sides—Bosnia, Croatia, and Serbia—agreed to a U.S.–brokered peace in Dayton. IFOR was also equipped and instructed to fight and win if attacked; these robust "rules of engagement" no doubt dissuaded some rambunctious elements, something UNPROFOR was unable to do. Some propose the IFOR model for future peacekeeping, but it must be borne in mind that such actions work only if a peace agreement has been reached beforehand.

The Cold War

Starting around 1946, the Cold War was a period of armed tension and profound mistrust between the Soviet Union and the United States. Each perceived the other side as a hostile enemy. The Cold War started shortly after and as a direct consequence of World War II. Stalin's Red Army had fought the Nazis back through Eastern Europe, and Stalin was not about to give up what his country had lost some 20 million lives for. Stalin turned Eastern Europe into a protective barrier for the Soviet Union by setting up obedient Communist governments in each land and stationing Soviet troops in Central Europe. This state of affairs lasted until the Berlin Wall fell in 1989.

The West, led by the United States, viewed Stalin's action with great alarm. Stalin looked like another Hitler, a dictator bent on world conquest, and the United States took steps to stop it. In the spring of 1947, Washington came up with three connected policies that formed the basis of U.S. foreign policy for decades.[13]

Truman Doctrine.   President Harry S Truman asked a joint session of Congress for military aid to prevent the Communist takeover of Greece and Turkey, then under Soviet pressure. The United States should come to the aid of "free peoples" anywhere in the world. This was a repudiation of traditional American attitudes of isolationism and, some say, contained the seeds of a globalism that eventually wrecked itself in Vietnam.

Marshall Plan.   At Harvard's commencement that year, Secretary of State George C. Marshall proposed a multi–billion-dollar U.S. aid package to lift up war-torn Europe and prevent its takeover either by local Communists or by the Red Army. The aid started flowing in 1948 and did put Western Europe back on its feet.

Containment.   At this time a State Department official, George F. Kennan, was drafting an influential memo that was soon published in the journal *Foreign Affairs* under the byline "X" (to conceal his identity). Republished many times since, "The Sources of Soviet Conduct" spelled out the Kremlin's expansionistic tendencies and called for a "policy of firm and vigilant containment" of them. Wherever the Soviets tried to expand, we would stop them.

The Berlin Airlift (1948–1949), the formation of the North Atlantic Treaty Organization (1949), and the Korean War (1950–1953) deepened the Cold War and the U.S. containment policy. The two major U.S. parties competed over which of them could best stop communism. A "red scare," fostered by the accusations of Senator Joseph McCarthy (Republican, Wisconsin), persuaded many public figures to appear tough and hawkish; no one wished to be accused of being "soft on communism."

At the height of the Cold War, the world seemed divided into two camps, one led by Washington, the other by Moscow, with very little in between. The condition was called *bipolarity.* Some see a bipolar system as essentially stable and comforting: You know where you stand. Others argue that it was a dangerous system, for it induced a "zero-sum" mentality (whatever I win, you lose), which pushed the superpowers into dangerous positions in the Third World. Every place on earth seemed to be strategic and worth fighting for. The United States, for example, intervened in Iran, Guatemala, Indonesia, Lebanon, the Congo (now Zaire), the Dominican Republic, and elsewhere on the suspicion that if we did not secure these areas, the Soviets would. What is called the "contingency argument" was often heard: If we don't take it, someone else will. In this way, Cold War fears drove both superpowers to extreme and ill-advised interventions, the Americans in Vietnam and the Soviets in Afghanistan.

DETERRENCE

At no time did the superpowers—the only two countries with global warmaking powers, the United States and the Soviet Union—fight each other directly. Both were afraid of *escalation,* the natural tendency for a conflict to become more and more intense. If U.S. and Soviet forces started even a little battle somewhere, say, over Berlin, it would probably grow, engaging conventional forces all over Europe. Then one or both sides would use small tactical nuclear weapons. The other side would strike back with bigger nuclear weapons, and soon the superpowers would be raining nuclear missiles on each other's homeland. The fear of such escalation is the basis for *deterrence;* both sides are so afraid of the results that they deter each other from starting a major war.

The crux of deterrence is not just having enough nuclear warheads and missiles to deliver them but also making sure that enough of them could survive a *first strike* by the other side. Then you can hit back in a *second strike.* If you have credible second-strike capability, the other superpower will not attack you, for it knows that it will be horribly mutilated in retaliation. Deterrence is based on both sides understanding that they will suffer mutual assured destruction.

Did deterrence work? Sure, say its proponents; there was no nuclear war.[14] Skeptics wonder, though, what could happen in times of great stress, when mistrust is especially high and fingers are very close to nuclear triggers.[15] Supporters argue that the deterrence system had "crisis stability," the ability to withstand even a major U.S.-Soviet confrontation. They point to the Cuban missile crisis of 1962 as a close call. We learned decades later that there were indeed Soviet nuclear warheads in Cuba and that local commanders would likely have used them if attacked. Kennedy's choice of a naval blockade allowed Khrushchev to back down without direct conflict. The missile crisis had a sobering effect on both superpowers, which soon began arms control talks to slow down and control the arms race. Perhaps the high point of arms control was the 1987 Intermediate-range Nuclear Forces (INF) treaty by which the Soviets eliminated 1,835 missiles with 3,000 warheads and the

United States 850 missiles with one warhead each. Triumphantly, President Reagan left office as a man of peace. The fall of the Berlin Wall in late 1989 and the breakup of the Soviet Union in late 1991 ended the Cold War.

SOVIET "OVERSTRETCH"

We now realize that Soviet President Mikhail Gorbachev was willing to relinquish Eastern Europe and give up nuclear warheads because the Soviet economy was in terrible shape. He had to call off the Cold War because he was broke. The socialist economic system was defective and every decade fell farther behind the West's, especially in the crucial high-tech sectors. Soviet defense spending ate perhaps a quarter of the economy. The Soviets' far-flung empire cost billions in subsidies for Eastern Europe, Cuba, Vietnam, and several African countries. The Soviet Union was going through what Yale historian Paul Kennedy called "imperial over-stretch."[16] The crux of Kennedy's argument is economic, especially relative economic growth. Strong powers are constantly tempted to expand. They have the money and work force, and other areas seem ripe for domination. Their empires expand until they overexpand; then they decay. Gradually their economic base weakens, and their empires grow increasingly expensive to maintain and defend. Other powers, whose economies have not been drained by imperial expenses, grow faster and become richer and more powerful.

In this way, Kennedy tries to account for the rise and fall of empires. The Hapsburg and British empires afford him some excellent examples. The Hapsburg dynasty of the sixteenth century united Spain, the Netherlands, and Austria and had shiploads of gold and silver pouring in from the New World. The wars it fought were only partly wars of religion—Catholic versus Protestant, in which the Hapsburgs were the leading Catholic power. They were also a Hapsburg attempt to dominate Europe. The Hapsburgs overstreched themselves and went into bankruptcy and decline. Spain especially was economically ruined and stayed backward for centuries.

Britain, the world's first industrial country, used its sea power to construct an incredible empire, with holdings on every continent. But Britain's economic growth did not keep up with its imperial expenses. By the late nineteenth century, several powers, including Germany and the United States, had become economically more powerful. The two world wars finished off the British Empire.

The controversy over Kennedy's book had to do with the application of his theory to the United States. The theory explained Soviet collapse beautifully—a military empire that Russia's decaying economy could no longer afford—but is it applicable to the United States? Conservative critics strongly rejected the book's suggestion that the United States was in any sort of decline.[17] Still, America's resources were thin; we were no longer the economic kings of the world as in the 1940s and 1950s. Although in not nearly as much economic difficulty as the Soviet Union, the United States grew tired of subsidizing the security of more vigorous trading partners, such as Germany and Japan.

International Systems

With the 1990s, many observers believed the world moved beyond the Cold War bipolar system. Moscow gave up the East European nations and no longer posed any invasion threat to Western Europe. Russia itself, with a badly deteriorating economy, looked to the West for technology and investments.

At the same time, Western Europe was moving closer to unity in the European Union (EU). All barriers among the fifteen members disappeared, producing a single economy, if not yet a single political entity. Across the Pacific, Japan had become a giant in the world economy. Along the rim of Asia, the "four tigers" of South Korea, Taiwan, Hong Kong, and Singapore also enjoyed great economic growth.

The United States, as considered in Chapter 18, had some economic problems. Massive trade deficits followed massive budget deficits, making us the world's biggest debtor. Foreign firms bought up American real estate, factories, and farms. The United States simply did not have the economic dominance it once had. It could no longer call the tune and get compliance from allies in Europe and Asia.

Added together, some observers feel these changes amounted to a new "international system." International systems, like the systems discussed in Chapter 1, have many components (countries or groups of countries) that interact with each other. These systems change over time, with the rise of new powers, new technologies, and new alliances.[18] Looking back more than a century, scholars believe there have been at least four international systems, each operating with different numbers of major players and with a different logic.[19]

The Nineteenth-Century Balance of Power System. As considered earlier, relative peace prevailed after the fall of Napoleon and the agreement among the major European powers not to try for supremacy. Instead, they agreed to carve up the globe into great empires. This agreement got weaker and weaker after the rise of two new major players, unified Germany in 1871 and rapidly modernizing Japan after the Meiji Restoration of 1868. Balance of power requires flexible, shifting alliances. By the start of the twentieth century, Europe was arrayed into two rigid, hostile blocs. The start of World War I in 1914 did not necessarily prove that balance of power does not work; it showed that the balance had already broken down earlier.

The Interwar System. In World Wars I and II, the European powers destroyed themselves. Between the two wars, Britain and France, drained by the first conflict, refrained from trying to balance Germany's resurgent power under Hitler. The Axis dictatorships—Germany, Italy, and Japan—sensing weakness, moved to take what they could. The interwar system was inherently unstable, what E. H. Carr called "the twenty years' crisis."[20] After World War II, the European powers were so weak that they had to give up their empires, and they became dominated and in some cases occupied by two new giant empires, the United States and the Soviet Union.

The Bipolar Cold War System. As discussed earlier, after World War II, the world seemed to be generally divided between the two superpowers into what

Stalin called *sotslager* and *kaplager,* the socialist camp and the capitalist camp, what we called Communism and the Free World. Most of the small and medium-sized powers found themselves in one alliance or the other, and few tried to break out. The bipolar system decayed, however. The superpowers' arms race grew increasingly expensive and drained both economically. Third World nationalism burned both the Americans (in Vietnam) and the Soviets (in Afghanistan). The Soviet bloc split; China moved out of it in the 1960s. The Warsaw Pact ended in 1991 as the countries of Eastern Europe and the ex-Soviet Union showed how much they disliked Soviet domination.

The Multipolar Economics Race.   A postbipolar system is just emerging; no one can be sure how it will work or if it will last.[21] Its main features seem to be the breakup of the old bipolar blocs into several blocs, what is called *multipolarity.* There are at least two additions to the superpowers, the European Union and a Japanese-led Pacific Rim. East Europeans don't obey Russia, and West Europeans and Japanese no longer automatically accept American leadership. Instead of military confrontation, economic growth becomes an obsession as countries strive to hold down unemployment, develop a trade advantage, and move ahead technologically. Fear of falling behind motivates all the players.

The good news about such a system, if it indeed develops, is that the chances of major war are much reduced. The world relaxes as Russian and U.S. troops and nuclear weapons pull out of Europe. The zero-sum mentality and struggle for Third World clients recedes: what good are they? The two powers reach important arms control agreements and reduce the warheads they have aimed at each other.

The bad news about such a system—already visible—is the murderous quality of the economic competition. Some players are more efficient than others. They develop huge trade and capital surpluses and start buying up the weaker players. There is a constant temptation to turn protectionist, to keep out foreign products and limit foreign business takeovers. Nasty accusations of trade protectionism already flow both ways across the Atlantic and the Pacific. What will happen cannot be foreseen. Much depends on the abilities of politicians to keep the blocs open to foreign trade. Should they close, trade wars could disrupt the global economy and plunge the world into a new Great Depression. We are sobered to remember that economic closure contributed to the coming of World War II.

Foreign Policy: Involved or Isolated?

The end of the Cold War reawoke an old question that had been asleep during the long period of tension with the Soviet Union: should the United States defend its interests on the near or far side of the oceans?[22] For most of America's history, it was assumed that we should generally stay on our own shores, that little overseas really concerned us. For the most part, Americans are natural-born isolationists. With Pearl Harbor in 1941, however, isolationism was rejected in favor of massive involvement in world affairs, first in winning World War II and then in waging the

Cold War. Isolationism was not an option. Suddenly, as the Berlin Wall opened in 1989 and the Soviet Union dissolved in 1991, it became an option.

Under the budgetary squeeze discussed in Chapter 18, the size of U.S. armed forces shrank to half or less what it had been during the Cold War. There was no clear mission for them. Presidents Bush and Clinton both articulated idealistic new uses for U.S. forces overseas. Bush sent peacekeeping forces into chaotic Somalia, where the government had collapsed and people were starving as local warlords robbed everything. The mission, a partial success in getting food to the hungry, continued under Clinton, but a shootout in the streets of Mogadishu with the warriors of an ambitious strongman left eighteen U.S. soldiers dead. The body of an American helicopter pilot being dragged through the streets was shown on television. Americans quickly lost their idealism, and Clinton withdrew U.S. forces.

In 1993, with Haiti in the hands of a brutal dictatorship and desperate Haitians fleeing in rickety boats to Florida, President Clinton was faced with a decision on using U.S. forces. Much of the country, including the White House and Congress, hesitated. The image of endless guerrilla warfare in tropical jungles, with us since Vietnam, was not far under the surface. Senator Robert Dole (R-KS) was totally against U.S. military intervention. The arrogance of Haiti's dictator and arrival of thousands of Haitians in Florida finally forced Clinton to intervene. Although many Americans were skeptical, the 1994 intervention went well. In almost textbook fashion, U.S. forces first disarmed and then deposed the dictatorship with scarcely a shot fired.

At this same time, massacres in Bosnia horrified American TV viewers, but few wanted any direct U.S. intervention. Many swore it would turn into another Vietnam; besides, it was none of our business. Finally, in 1995 the U.S. mediated a peace agreement among the warring parties in Dayton, Ohio, and then contributed 20,000 U.S. troops to a 60,000-troop NATO peacekeeping force. Clinton made the decision even though U.S. public opinion was two to one against sending troops, and Congress nearly blocked the move. Again, the operation went well, and the United States showed it could and would take a leadership role in the world.

The question remained, however: should the United States send forces overseas? Even when no direct U.S. national interests were involved? If the United States turns its back on horror and aggression overseas, the emerging international system will resemble the unstable and chaotic interwar system, a system in which the democracies held back from involvement until they were plunged into World War II. U.S. foreign policy tends to swing between extremes of interventionism and isolationism. Can we find a stable and moderate middle ground?

Beyond Sovereignty?

The end of the Cold War and of the most violent century in history brought into question the basic point of international politics, sovereignty—namely, is sovereignty slipping? Increasingly, the world community is acting in ways that infringe on the internal workings of sovereign states. For some decades the International

Monetary Fund has been able to tell countries that wanted loans to turn from inflationary economic policies. The recipients of such advice often fumed that the IMF was infringing on their sovereignty, but if they wanted the loan, they took the advice. With the end of the Cold War, now even former Communist countries are going along with this sort of infringement on their sovereignty.

After a broad, U.S.-led coalition booted Iraq out of Kuwait in 1991, UN inspectors combed through Iraq looking for the capacity to build weapons of mass destruction (nuclear, chemical, and bacteriological). The Baghdad dictatorship screamed that Iraq's sovereignty was being infringed upon. Indeed it was, and most of the world was glad of it. Should the international community stand back while a tyrant develops the power to annihilate neighboring countries? By the same token, should the civilized world stand by while Somali warlords and bandits steal from the starving? Should the rest of Europe act as if Balkan massacres were none of its concern?

The world seems to be changing, willing to move beyond sovereignty and toward some kind of order. The trouble is, no one knows what kind of order. President Bush used the term *new world order* in building a coalition against Iraq, but he dropped the expression just as debate on it was starting. What to do in the face of the disorder unleashed by the dissolution of Soviet power? Paradoxically, the world was more orderly during the Cold War, because the two superpowers controlled and restrained their respective allies and spheres of influence.

Few wanted the United States to play world cop, but most understood that if there was to be leadership, only America could provide it. Could *supranational* (above-national) entities be getting ready to take on some of the security responsibilities previously associated with individual nations' right of self-defense? If so, which entities?

United Nations.   This organization comes quickly to mind, and indeed the UN has been functioning far better after the Cold War than during it. But it still has problems. As permanent members of the Security Council, Russia and China have the power to veto anything they don't like. Russia, for example, was reluctant to do anything against Serbia, long regarded as a Slavic little brother. The UN has sent many peacekeepers to observe truces, as in the Middle East and Balkans, but these few and lightly armed forces from small countries were in no position to enforce peace. The bloodthirsty Khmer Rouge in Cambodia repeatedly kidnapped UN peacekeepers, knowing they would do nothing. Without enforcement powers and fragmented into blocs, the UN remained largely a "talking shop."

North Atlantic Treaty Organization.   This is arguably the best defensive alliance ever devised. Since 1949 it coordinated Western Europe and North America to act as a single defender under unified command in the event of Soviet attack. But now its very reason for being has ceased to exist. Why not use NATO for something else? But the North Atlantic Treaty is extremely specific—that an attack on one member in Europe or North America be treated as an attack on all—and it has no validity anywhere else, not in the Middle East, the Balkans, or Africa. Anywhere else is called "out of area." NATO members can, to be sure, cooperate out of area, but it's on a purely voluntary basis, as they did in Bosnia with IFOR. What worked in Bosnia may not work elsewhere. Accordingly, NATO would not be a reliable force for keeping peace. Another, much broader European entity, the OSCE, has been suggested for such a purpose.

Organization on Security and Cooperation in Europe. This grouping grew out of the 1975 Helsinki Final Act that guaranteed borders and human rights in Europe. It helped to stabilize and eventually end the Cold War. Afterward, all European states, including the republics of the former Soviet Union and Yugoslavia, joined the OSCE, bringing total membership to fifty-two. The OSCE, however, has no enforcement provisions or NATO-style command structure. It could take on such functions, but all or most members would have to agree. The ideal blend, some observers think, would be to combine the command structure of NATO with the broad membership of OSCE. This would still, however, cover only Europe.

There is no security structure that seriously covers Europe, let alone the entire world. Should there be one, or should the civilized world put together a series of ad hoc arrangements as the spirit moves it? Either way, the United States will have to take a leading role. If we don't lead, no one else will. But should the United States intervene overseas to stop horrors that do not directly affect U.S. national interests? Do we have, in Stanley Hoffmann's words, "duties beyond borders"?[23] The answers to such questions are the great challenge to your generation. You have the privilege of coming of age precisely as the world is undergoing system change. By your political participation and choices, you can help influence the direction of change.

Suggested Readings

BARBER, BENJAMIN R. *Jihad vs. McWorld.* New York: Random House, 1995. Is the world falling apart through primitive particularism or consolidating through American commercialism?

BROWN, SEYOM. *International Relations in a Changing Global System: Toward a Theory of World Polity.* Boulder, CO: Westview Press, 1992. A hopeful view of a more orderly world.

DOUGHERTY, JAMES E., and ROBERT L. PFALTZGRAFF, JR. *Contending Theories of International Relations: A Comprehensive Survey,* 3rd ed. New York: HarperCollins, 1990. Complete, balanced, indispensable.

GABRIEL, JÜRG MARTIN. *Worldviews and Theories of International Relations.* New York: St. Martin's, 1994. Interesting interweaving of ideology and IR theory.

HUNTINGTON, SAMUEL P. "The Clash of Civilizations?" *Foreign Affairs* 72 (Summer 1993), 3. Controversial theory of culture clashes.

IKENBERRY, G. JOHN, ed. *American Foreign Policy: Theoretical Essays,* 2nd ed. New York: HarperCollins, 1996. Good anthology of the many ways to analyze U.S. foreign policy.

JACKSON, ROBERT H., and ALAN JAMES, eds. *States in a Changing World: A Contemporary Analysis.* New York: Oxford University Press, 1993. National interests and power have changed after the Cold War.

KENNEDY, PAUL. *Preparing for the Twenty-First Century.* New York: Random House, 1993. Top historian urges us to get ready for a new world system.

KISSINGER, HENRY. *Diplomacy.* New York: Simon &

Schuster, 1994. Scholar-statesman sums up a lifetime of thinking.

LUKACS, JOHN. *The End of the Twentieth Century and the End of the Modern Age.* New York: Ticknor & Fields, 1993. This century was bad; the coming may be worse.

NIJMAN, JAN. *The Geopolitics of Power and Conflict: Superpowers in the International System, 1945–1992.* New York: Belhaven/Halsted, 1994. Advanced, complex theory of the Cold War.

Notes

1. Jean Bodin is credited with developing the concept, Thomas Hobbes with amplifying it in the next century.

2. Morgenthau, in fact, defined *all* politics as a "struggle for power." See *Politics Among Nations,* 6th ed. (New York: Knopf, 1985), p. 31.

3. See John G. Stoessinger, *The Might of Nations,* 9th ed. (New York: McGraw-Hill, 1990).

4. The terms *micro* and *macro* are drawn from the lucid discussions of James E. Dougherty and Robert L. Pfaltzgraff, Jr., *Contending Theories of International Relations: A Comprehensive Survey,* 3rd ed. (New York: HarperCollins, 1990).

5. Konrad Lorenz, *On Aggression* (New York: Bantam, 1967).

6. John G. Stoessinger has adopted a mostly psychological viewpoint in his readable *Why Nations Go to War,* 6th ed. (New York: St. Martin's, 1992).

7. Morgenthau claimed that when we understand a nation's power and national interests, we in effect "look over the shoulder" of political leaders as they write their dispatches. *Politics Among Nations,* p. 5.

8. A. F. K. Organski developed this theory in his *World Politics* (New York: Knopf, 1958). More recently, Geoffrey Blainey has rendered it in highly readable form in *The Causes of War,* 3rd ed. (New York: Free Press, 1988).

9. Robert Jervis, *Perception and Misperception in International Politics* (Princeton, NJ: Princeton University Press, 1976).

10. Henry Kissinger, *The Necessity for Choice: Prospects of American Foreign Policy* (New York: Harper & Row, 1961), p. 148.

11. For a social psychologist's review of the kind of thinking that leads up to war, see Ralph K. White, *Nobody Wanted War: Misperception in Vietnam and Other Wars* (Garden City, NY: Doubleday, 1968).

12. See Douglas Williams, *The Specialized Agencies and the United Nations: The System in Crisis* (New York: St. Martin's, 1987).

13. For an excellent overview of U.S. Cold War policy, see Thomas G. Paterson, *Meeting the Communist Threat: Truman to Reagan* (New York: Oxford University Press, 1988).

14. See George H. Quester, *The Future of Nuclear Deterrence* (Lexington, MA: Lexington Books, 1986).

15. See Richard Ned Lebow, *Nuclear Crisis Management: A Dangerous Illusion* (Ithaca, NY: Cornell University Press, 1987).

16. Paul Kennedy, *The Rise and Fall of the Great Powers: Economic Change and Military Conflict from 1500 to 2000* (New York: Random House, 1987).

17. Perhaps the best critique came from Samuel P. Huntington, "The U.S.—Decline or Renewal?" *Foreign Affairs* 67 (Winter 1988/89), 2.

18. The classic work on international systems is Morton A. Kaplan, *System and Process in International Politics* (New York: Wiley, 1957).

19. For a fuller discussion of these systems see Michael G. Roskin and Nicholas O. Berry, *IR: The New World of International Relations,* 3rd ed. (Upper Saddle River, NJ: Prentice Hall, 1997), Chap. 1.

20. Edward Hallett Carr, *The Twenty Years' Crisis, 1919–1939: An Introduction to the Study of International Relations* (New York: Harper & Row, 1964).

21. See Michael J. Hogan, ed. *The End of the Cold War: Its Meaning and Implications* (New York: Cambridge University Press, 1992).

22. Nicholas John Spykman, *America's Strategy in World Politics: The United States and the Balance of Power* (New York: Harcourt, Brace, 1942), pp. 5, 7.

23. Stanley Hoffmann, *Duties Beyond Borders: On the Limits and Possibilities of Ethical International Politics* (Syracuse, NY: Syracuse University Press, 1981).

Index

Sabato, Larry, 183, 202
Safire, William, 166
Sakharov, Andrei, 335
Sampling, survey, 155
Sartori, Giovanni, 218–19, 222, 261
Scales v. *United States*, 56
Scammell, Margaret, 242
Schama, Simon, 378
Schattschneider, E. E., 66, 79, 187, 202, 204, 222
Schellhas, Bob, 121
Schlesinger, Arthur, 141, 291, 301
Schlozman, Kay, 141
Schofield, Norman, 281
Schools, 138–39
Schram, Martin, 183
Schubert, Glendon, 343
Schudson, Michael, 182
Schulzinger, Robert, 202
Schumpeter, Joseph, 66, 79
Schwartz, Bernard, 343
Schwartz, Michael, 96
Science, 12–14
Scott, James, 321, 379
Sederberg, Peter, 378
Sedition, 55–57
Seidman, Harold, 320
Seligman, Adam, 141
Seligman, Lester, 222
Seligson, Mitchell, 79
Seltzer, Richard, 241
Separatist violence, 364
Serbs, 42, 92
Seroka, Jim, 42
Shaka, 27
Shapiro, Ian, 24
Shapiro, Robert, 241
Sharlet, Robert, 59
Sharkansky, Ira, 360
Sharp, Samuel, 122
Sheehan, Neil, 25, 183
Shefter, Martin, 242
Shepsle, Kenneth, 301
Shiratori, Rei, 241
Shugart, Matthew, 301
Siegan, Bernard, 261
Sigleman, Lee, 23
Simmel, Georg, 97
Simpson, Dick, 241
Simpson, O. J., 132
Single-member districts, 220, 256–58
Sisk, Timothy, 96
Skidelski, Robert, 121
Skilling, H. Gordon, 202
Slovakia, 29
Slovenia, 29
Smith, Adam, 99, 101–2
Smith, Anthony, 42
Smith, Craig, 301
Smith, Denis, 122
Smith, Kathy, 301
Smith, Steven, 282
Smith, Tom, 163
Smolla, Rodney, 59
Sniderman, Paul, 163
Snyder, Louis, 43
So, Alvin, 42

Social class, 105, 147, 226, 231–32
Social democrats, 107–9
Socialism, 35–36, 105–7
Socialization, political, 135–40, 205–6
Social Security, 350
Solzhenitsyn, Alexander, 335
Somalia, 9, 393
Somit, Albert, 241
Sommers, Christina, 122
Sorauf, Frank, 221
South Africa, 27, 30, 42, 128, 198
violence in, 363
Sovereignty, 4–5, 7, 380–82, 393–94
Soviet Union, 16, 29
collapse of, 77, 115–16
constitution, 47, 57–58
Sowell, Thomas, 359
Spain, 4, 27, 75, 115, 133, 204
Spiro, Herbert, 59
Spitzer, Robert, 59
Spykman, Nicholas, 396
Stagflation, 347
Stalemate society, 200–201
Stalin, 11, 16, 57–58, 70, 72, 73
States, 26–37
Statism, 35, 36
Staufer, Samuel, 96
Steele, James, 359
Stepan, Alfred, 379
Stephens, Evelyne, 79
Stephens, John, 79
Stephenson, Donald, 301
Stern, Philip, 202
Sternhell, Zeev, 122
Stevens, Rosemary, 360
Stidham, Ronald, 342, 343
Stimson, James, 163
Stoessinger, John, 386
Stokes, Donald, 97, 242
Story, Dale, 222
Stucker, Thomas, 360
Subcultures, 132–35
Subsystems, 39
Suleiman, Ezra, 96, 281, 320
Sundquist, James, 242, 281
Sunstein, Cass, 60
Supreme Court, 46–47, 196, 335–42
Burger Court, 340
Rehnquist Court, 340–41, 342
Warren Court, 337–40
Surveys, 153–62
techniques, 154–55
Swansbrough, Robert, 242
Sweden, 4, 35, 36, 101, 108, 232
electoral system, 258, 259
legislature, 264
Switzerland, 92
Symbols, 4, 40–41, 88
Systems theory, 20–23, 77, 391–92
Sznajder, Mario, 122

Tarazona-Sevillano, Gabriela, 378
Tarr, G. Alan, 343
Taxes, 32, 108, 109, 347, 349

Tebbel, John, 183
Teixeira, Ruy, 241
Television, 170–76, 236–37
Terkel, Studs, 141
Term limits, 279
Territory, 29–30
Terrorism, 2
Thatcher, Margaret, 32, 104
Theories, 17–23
Thermidor, 370
Third-party assistance, 387
Thoreau, Henry, 68, 79, 197
Thurber, James, 242, 281
Tierney, John, 202
Tilly, Charles, 43
Titoism, 111
Tocqueville, Alexis de, 126, 130, 142, 186, 365, 379
Totalitarianism, 39, 70–74
right-wing, 74
Tribe, Laurence, 59
Triska, Jan, 122
Truman, David, 97, 185, 186, 202, 222
Truman, Harry, 154
Doctrine, 388
Tsuneishi, Warren, 141
Tucker, D. F. B., 343
Tullis, F. LaMond, 379
Tummala, Krishna, 321
Tushnet, Mark, 342
TVA, 305
Twenty-fifth Amendment, 295
Two-step flow, 167

Unger, Aryeh, 163
Unicameral parliaments, 273
Unions, trade, 88, 191, 195
Unitary systems, 39, 247–49
United Nations, 386, 387, 394
Universal Declaration on Human Rights, 53
UNPROFOR, 387
Urban-rural differences, 228, 233
USIA, 305

Valen, Henry, 83, 96, 242
Valenzuela, Arturo, 300, 379
van de Walle, Nicolas, 301
Vanhanen, Tatu, 79
Vargas, Getulio, 115
Veliz, Claudio, 141
Verba, Sydney, 24, 96, 126–29, 138, 141, 142, 202
Veto, 270, 277
Vietnam war, 22, 368–69
mass media and, 180–81
Violence, 198, 361–67
types of, 363–65
Volatility, opinion, 156
von Beyme, Klaus, 43
von der Mehden, Fred, 363, 379
Voslensky, Michael, 320
Voting, 31–32, 129, 223–42
blocs, 239–40
registration, 224
turnout, 224–26
Voting Rights Act, 146